# The Republic of Letters

*The Correspondence between Thomas Jefferson and James Madison 1776–1826*

EDITED BY

*James Morton Smith*

VOLUME ONE

*1776–1790*

W · W · Norton & Company · New York · London

Copyright © 1995 by James Morton Smith. *All rights reserved.* Printed in the United States of America.

THE TEXT OF THIS BOOK *is composed in Galliard with Janson Alternate and Avanta. The display type is set in Garamond and Naomi Script. Composition and manufacturing by The Haddon Craftsmen. Book design by Marjorie J. Flock.*

Library of Congress Cataloging-in-Publication Data

Jefferson, Thomas, 1743–1826.
    The republic of letters: the correspondence between Thomas Jefferson and James Madison, 1776–1826.
        p.    cm.
    Includes bibliographical references (v.3, p.    ) and index.
    Contents: v.1. 1776–1790 — v.2. 1790–1804 — v.3. 1804–1836
    1. Jefferson, Thomas, 1743–1826 — Correspondence.  2. Madison, James, 1751–1836 — Correspondence.  3. Presidents — United States — Correspondence.  I. Madison, James, 1751–1836.  II. Smith, James Morton.  III. Title.
E332.88.M33   1995
973.4′092′2 – dc20                                      94-22924

ISBN 0-393-03691-X
(for the set of three volumes)

W. W. Norton & Company, Inc.
500 Fifth Avenue, New York, N.Y. 10110
www.wwnorton.com

W. W. Norton & Company Ltd.
Castle House, 75/76 Wells Street, London W1T 3QT

4 5 6 7 8 9 0

*To*
*Scott David and Carolyn Ann Thompson,*
*the "busy bees,"*
*who, as John Adams observed to Thomas Jefferson*
*about Grandchildren,*
*have "been cheering to have . . . hovering about Us,"*
*and to the memory of my brother,*
*Vergil Earl Smith, Jr.*

# CONTENTS

### VOLUME ONE
### 1776–1790

|   |   |
|---|---|
| Preface | xi |
| Abbreviations | xix |
| Introduction: An Intimate Friendship | 1 |

*Photographs appear following page 10*

1. Parallel Lives: Jefferson, Madison, and the Revolutionary Crisis, 1773–1775 — 37
2. Getting Acquainted: Jefferson, Madison, and the Virginia House of Delegates, 1776 — 48
3. The Beginnings of Friendship: Governor Jefferson and Councillor Madison, 1779 — 57
4. "A Most Melancholy Crisis," 1780–1781 — 124
5. Wartime Cooperation: The Congressman and the Governor, 1781 — 171
6. From Friendship to Partnership, 1782–1783 — 204
7. From War to Peace, 1783 — 228
8. "The Justlings of States": The Partners Change Places, 1783–1784 — 270
9. "The Dark Side of Our Commercial Affairs": The Minister to France and the Virginia Legislator, 1784–1785 — 325
10. State and National Reforms: The Virginia Legislator and the Minister to France, 1785–1786 — 393
11. Miracle in Philadelphia, 1787 — 435

| | |
|---|---:|
| 12. The Constitution and the Movement for a Bill of Rights, 1788–1789 | 518 |
| 13. "The Great Rights of Mankind": The Adoption of the Bill of Rights, 1789 | 590 |
| 14. The Congressman and the Secretary of State, 1790 | 638 |

VOLUME TWO
## 1790–1804

| | |
|---|---:|
| Abbreviations | ix |
| 15. The Battle with Hamilton, 1790–1791 | 662 |
| 16. Party Conflicts, 1791–1792 | 708 |
| 17. The French Connection and American Neutrality, 1793 | 744 |
| 18. "Pinching British Commerce," 1793–1794 | 821 |
| 19. Dolley, Domesticity, and the Whiskey Rebellion, 1794–1795 | 847 |
| 20. The Jay Treaty, 1795–1796 | 881 |
| 21. The Election of 1796 | 940 |
| 22. The Vice President and the Farmer: The Partners Trade Places Again, 1797 | 966 |
| 23. Crisis in Freedom: The XYZ Affair and the Alien and Sedition Acts, 1798 | 995 |
| 24. The Kentucky and Virginia Resolutions and American Civil Liberties, 1798–1799 | 1063 |
| 25. The Resolutions Renewed, 1799 | 1108 |
| 26. The Election of 1800 and the Crisis of Succession | 1137 |
| 27. The Revolution of 1800 | 1164 |
| 28. An Interlude of Peace, 1801–1802 | 1206 |
| 29. "This Affair of Louisiana," 1803 | 1253 |
| 30. "The Empire for Liberty," 1803–1804 | 1287 |

VOLUME THREE
## 1804–1836

| | |
|---|---:|
| Abbreviations | ix |
| 31. Foreign-Policy Priorities, 1804–1805 | 1352 |

## Contents

32. The Perils of Neutrality, 1805–1806 — *1404*
33. A Conspiracy at Home and a Bad Treaty Abroad, 1806–1807 — *1442*
34. Embargo: The Rights of Neutrals and "the Wrongs of the Belligerents," 1807–1808 — *1503*
35. The End of the Embargo, 1808–1809 — *1548*
36. Madison Takes Over, 1809 — *1561*
37. The Macon Bills, 1810: "Better Than Nothing" — *1614*
38. The Politics of Neutrality, 1811 — *1650*
39. War or Submission: 1812 — *1674*
40. The War of 1812: A Few Victories but More Defeats, 1812–1813 — *1708*
41. The Critical Year: 1814 — *1729*
42. Mr. Madison's War Ends: 1815 — *1753*
43. A Joint Retirement Project: The Origins of the University of Virginia, 1816–1817 — *1771*
44. Founding the University of Virginia, 1818–1819 — *1791*
45. Liberty and Learning, 1820–1822 — *1817*
46. Reminiscing about the Revolution and the Republic, 1823 — *1842*
47. Recruiting a Faculty, 1824 — *1883*
48. The University Opens, 1825 — *1915*
49. Jefferson's Last Year, 1826 — *1952*
50. "Take Care of Me When Dead": Madison's Final Years, 1826–1836 — *1972*

Bibliographical Essay — *2003*
Index — *2019*

# PREFACE

When I retired as director emeritus of the Henry Francis du Pont Winterthur Museum and Gardens in 1984, I told my colleagues on the staff and the board of trustees that it was seldom that a man my age had an opportunity to go straight again. But after shaking off the shackles of administrative responsibility, I headed straight for the Morris Library and a research carrel at the University of Delaware, where I have since had the privilege of sharing each of my work days with Messrs. Jefferson and Madison.

I first became fascinated with the correspondence between the two men over forty-five years ago, while I was a graduate student, studying their combined efforts against the Alien and Sedition Acts. Two years later, in 1950, Adrienne Koch published her enlightening book, *Jefferson and Madison: The Great Collaboration.* Several years after that, while working with Lester J. Cappon on his edition of *The Adams-Jefferson Letters,* I decided to begin collecting and transcribing the letters that Jefferson and Madison had exchanged.

Julian P. Boyd, then editor of *The Papers of Thomas Jefferson,* took a friendly interest in the project, helping me to obtain an initial planning and research grant from the Thomas Jefferson Memorial Foundation in Charlottesville, Virginia. At the Princeton University office of *The Papers of Thomas Jefferson* project, Boyd and his colleagues opened their files so that I could compile a list of the 1,250 letters that Jefferson and Madison had exchanged. With the assistance of Patricia Curtis Blatt at the Institute of Early American History and Culture in Williamsburg, I then began transcribing the letters, working for the most part from microfilm copies of the originals in the Library of Congress and other depositories.

When I first began this project in 1960, I thought of it almost exclusively as an editorial undertaking—a classic example of an extended correspondence in the golden age of letter writing, when Jefferson and Madison were America's leading contributors to what Jefferson called "the republic of letters." But once I got into the correspondence, I became more and more fascinated by the friendship between the two men and the way in which it first developed and then flourished as a partnership. All of the biographers of both men agree that they became friends with "extraordinary rapidity," as Irving Brant observes. But no one, I discovered, explains how or why they became friends.

My first task, then, was to concentrate on the year 1779 when Jefferson succeeded Patrick Henry as governor and inherited James Madison and seven other members of the Virginia Executive Council to constitute the Governor-in-Council, which conducted the business of managing the American Revolution in the Old Dominion. Chapter 3, which does not include any letters between Jefferson and Madison, is designed to show how the daily meetings of the governor and council around the table in the council chamber of the Virginia capitol made it possible for Jefferson to view Madison as his most valued councillor, even more so than his oldest friend, Lieutenant Governor John Page, whom he had known since their college days at William and Mary. It took only fourteen weeks of collaboration for the friendship to jell.

After I presented my conclusions to the members of the Williamsburg Seminar in Early American History in 1985, several participants suggested that I add an introductory section on the way in which Jefferson and Madison first became acquainted in 1776. The first two chapters contain no correspondence between the friends; they do show how the two men came to similar conclusions about the necessity for the American Revolution. The final chapter demonstrates how Madison, in the years following Jefferson's death, tried to protect his friend's reputation—and, as it turned out, his own—from the states' rights politicians, who twisted his words to their own ends during the nullification crisis.

In my original planning years ago, I viewed this work as a "reader's edition," the first time that the complete correspondence between Jefferson and Madison would have been brought together for study, contemplation, and pleasure. I, therefore, decided to keep annotations to a minimum and leave the scholarly paraphernalia to the *Jefferson Papers* at Princeton University and the *Madison Papers,* then at the University of Chicago and now at the University of Virginia. At that time, Boyd's *Jefferson* volumes were appearing at the rate of two a year, and the *Madison* volumes, once they were inaugurated in 1962, got off to a fast start.

But just as my work on this project was slowed by administrative duties, the pace of publication for the Jefferson and Madison papers also slackened over the years. I, therefore, decided to increase the annotation of the letters and expand the introduction to each chronologically arranged chapter so that readers whose recall may have become obscured by a historical haze, as mine became while I was an administrator, would not have to resort too often to the *Dictionary of American Biography,* the *Encyclopedia of American History,* or specialized monographs in order to track down individuals or events mentioned by Jefferson and Madison.

The present edition is designed to fill the gap between growing public

# Preface

interest in Jefferson and Madison stimulated by the bicentennial of the Constitution and the Bill of Rights—including the astounding international interest in the movement for American independence exhibited by the Tiananmen Square movement in China and the revival of democratic movements in Eastern Europe following the collapse of the Iron Curtain—and the rapidly expanding world of scholarship that has broadened our knowledge of the new nation created by the American Revolution. I hope that these volumes, with the denser documentation than that which I first envisioned, will be of interest to the general reader, the scholar, and the student alike both in the United States and in other countries where Jefferson's Declaration of Independence and Madison's Constitution have become, as Jefferson phrased it in his last public message, "the signal of arousing men to burst the chains under which monkish ignorance and superstition had persuaded them to bind themselves, and to assume the blessings and security of self-government. That form which we have substituted, restores the free right to the unbounded exercise of reason and freedom of opinion. All eyes are opened, or opening, to the rights of man."

Jefferson believed that "the letters of a person, especially of one whose business has been transacted by letters, form the only full and genuine journal of his life," and can be viewed as an autobiography. Madison agreed "that the biography of an author must be a history of his writings. So must that of one whose whole life has in a manner been a public life, be gathered from his . . . manuscript papers on public subjects, including letters to as well as from him." In a sense, then, the correspondence between the two men almost amounts to a dual biography, and I have viewed my editorial role as that of a facilitator whose introductory chapters are designed to follow Madison's principle of writing "a historical review of the Biographical period," setting the stage for the exchange of letters by placing the characters, concepts, and events being discussed in a wider historical context. Then I step aside while the two men engage in their elegant dialogue and friendly banter, intervening occasionally to annotate an obscure reference or to cite sources that analyze the topic referred to.

Even with the fuller annotation, however, I have kept in mind Julian Boyd's disclaimer in the first volume of *The Papers of Thomas Jefferson*, one that applies equally to Madison's writings: "However tempting it is to any editor of Jefferson's papers to explore the multitudinous bypaths that his letters invariably point to; to attempt to assay the historical significance of each document in relation to its context; to identify or explain all persons, events, and places; to separate fact from rumor; to explain obsolete, technical, and regional terms; to trace literary quotations to their sources; or to furnish references to pertinent literature, &c.—such a procedure would prolong the editorial task indefinitely, if not postpone its completion altogether. . . . The policy decided upon with respect to annotation is that of providing a certain minimum basis for identification essential to the understanding of each document." Boyd did not always take his own advice, but I have treasured it and have tried to follow it throughout this work.

I have treasured even more the editorial enterprises headed first by Julian Boyd, then Charles Cullen, and now John Catanzariti for *The Papers of Thomas Jefferson,* and William T. Hutchinson and William M. E. Rachal, then Robert A. Rutland, and now J. C. A. Stagg for *The Papers of James Madison.* They and their colleagues on the editorial staffs of these projects have put every investigator in their debt by their enormous erudition and industry. I am also immensely indebted to Dumas Malone for his six-volume study of Jefferson and to Irving Brant for his six-volume biography of Madison. I have relied on their work throughout. This is also true of two first-rate shorter biographies of Jefferson—Merrill D. Peterson, *Thomas Jefferson and the New Nation,* and Noble E. Cunningham, Jr., *In Pursuit of Reason: The Life of Thomas Jefferson*—and two excellent shorter studies of Madison—Ralph Ketcham, *James Madison: A Biography,* and Robert A. Rutland, *James Madison: The Founding Father.*

Many years ago, at the inception of this project, I received a fellowship from the John Simon Guggenheim Foundation and began my work in Williamsburg, thanks to the interest of Lester J. Cappon, Lawrence W. Towner, and Carlisle H. Humelsine. Later assistance came from a sabbatical leave granted by Cornell University, which also made humanities research funds available periodically, thanks in large part to Frederick G. Marcham. I also had research assistance while serving as director of the State Historical Society of Wisconsin, but my administrative duties at Winterthur Museum made it necessary to postpone further work on the project until I retired in 1984.

I have treated my years of retirement as an extended sabbatical leave, one that has given me the privilege of holding academic appointments as senior fellow at two institutions designated by the National Endowment for the Humanities as Centers for Advanced Research: the Institute of Early American History and Culture in Williamsburg, Virginia, in 1984–1985, and the Henry E. Huntington Library in San Marino, California, in 1985–1986. I am especially appreciative of the assistance of Thad W. Tate, Philip Morgan, Michael McGiffert, and the members of the Williamsburg seminar for helping me get the project under way in the colonial town where Jefferson and Madison first became acquainted. On the other side of the United States, at the Huntington Library, I wish to thank Robert Middlekauff, Martin Ridge, and Paul Zall for their interest and assistance. Thanks are also due to Dr. Robert I. Boyd and Dr. Stephen Petit at the other Huntington—the Memorial Hospital in Pasadena—for seeing me through a mysterious malady that laid me low while I was at the Huntington Library.

For assistance along the way, I also gratefully acknowledge my indebtedness to John Agresto, Lance Banning, Roberto Celli, Richard Ekman, Wendell Garrett, Michael T. Gilmore, Neil Harris, William Homer, Daniel Jordan, Edwin L. Kantor, Stanley N. Katz, J. A. Leo LeMay, John A. Munroe,

David Peeler, Merrill D. Peterson, George Roeder, Judy Rondinaro, James F. Shilling, John Sweeney, Neville Thompson, and Alfred F. Young. I am particularly indebted to the staff members of *The Papers of James Madison* at the University of Virginia—Robert A. Rutland; his successor, J. C. A. Stagg; and the unsung heroes of their editorial department: Jeanne Cross, David Mattern, Susan Hackett, and Mary Perdue—for the help they gave while I was double-checking my transcriptions and for calling to my attention items that I might otherwise have missed. In a similar way, I have been assisted by John Catanzariti, Eugene R. Sheridan, and staff members of *The Papers of Thomas Jefferson* at Princeton University. The staff of the Morris Library at the University of Delaware have been uniformly helpful. For every summer of the last decade, I have also utilized the Hawthorne-Longfellow Library at Bowdoin College as well as the Skidompha Library in Damariscotta, Maine. And on several occasions, I have used the Jefferson and Madison papers in the Manuscript Division of the Library of Congress whenever I could not read a portion of either man's handwriting on the microfilm edition of his works.

Finally, I wish to acknowledge the assistance of James L. Mairs, Carol Flechner, Marjorie J. Flock, Tabitha L. Griffin, and Cecil G. Lyon at W. W. Norton & Company for their careful work in getting this book through the press. Ms. Flechner in particular is an editor's editor, and I take pleasure in mentioning my gratitude to her for her good humor, her dedication to excellence, and her meticulous attention to detail.

The preparation of this work was made possible in part by a grant for 1986–1988 from the Division of Research Programs of the National Endowment for the Humanities, an independent federal agency. I completed the task during a magical month as a scholar-in-residence at the Bellagio Study Center of the Rockefeller Foundation on Lake Como, a perfect way to wind up the project near Milan, Jefferson's easternmost penetration of Europe while he was serving as American minister to France. The Bellagio Center is truly a "republic of letters" in the Jeffersonian sense since the resident scholars "form a great fraternity spreading over the whole earth" and "communicating to all parts of the world whatever useful is discovered in any one of them." To my fellow residents, a marvelous mix of scholars from many nations and many disciplines—poets, composers, lyricists, historians, sociologists, physicians, psychiatrists, painters, scientists, and statesmen—go my thanks for an immensely stimulating, companionable, and productive tenure.

Throughout the preparation of this work, I have been fortunate to have the cooperation of the editorial staffs of *The Papers of James Madison,* on whose editorial board I serve, and *The Papers of Thomas Jefferson*. Since these monumental projects give the location of each document, I have omitted that information in most instances. But, like the editors of these projects, I have made every effort to present the reader with a faithful transcription of the original letter, using the recipient's copy whenever possible. In the letters by the two men, I have followed their grammar, punctuation, capitalization, and spelling, without the use of *"sic"* (Jefferson frequently misspelled *received* ["recieved"] and *knowledge* ["knolege"]). That includes my adoption of Madison's spelling of *Montpellier*, which somehow got shortened to "Montpelier" after his death. Words written in a cipher have been printed in italics as decoded in the *Jefferson Papers* or the *Madison Papers*.

The only exceptions to printing the letters literally are as follows. For some reason known only to himself, Jefferson invariably began the first word in every sentence with a lowercase letter, but in this edition, each of his sentences begins with a capital letter. He also used the lowercase in spelling *Mr.* or *Mrs.*, but I have capitalized these throughout. I have put the place where a letter was written and the date it was written at the head of the letter, no matter where Jefferson or Madison located it. I have also standardized all date lines, abbreviating the name of the month in which each letter was written and spelling out the place name even though the author may have abbreviated it. Whenever either of the correspondents has failed to give the date when and/or the place where a letter was written, I have tried to supply that information in brackets. The complimentary close appears as part of the last paragraph of the body of the letter even if it was written as a separate paragraph in the manuscript.

A dash that ends a sentence has been replaced with a period, and other extraneous dashes have been eliminated. I have also provided a replacement for the thorn and have substituted "and" for the ampersand, unless it appears as part of the name of a business firm. Bracketed punctuation has been supplied occasionally for ease of reading. Similarly, some ambiguous contractions and abbreviations have occasionally been expanded, but otherwise I have retained all other abbreviations exactly as written in order to give the reader a feel for the pressures that kept these men virtually chained to the writing desk each day—"under the whip and spur," as Jefferson wrote in retirement, "from morning to night."

By keeping a chronological chart of the location of the men at any given time, I have been able to indicate where the letter originated. As for the date that I have assigned to undated letters, since Jefferson nearly always noted the date of receipt on the letters, Madison's undated letters can be dated fairly precisely; moreover, the index to the microfilm edition of the *Presidential Papers of James Madison* gives the best educated guess for most of his undated correspondence. For Jefferson's undated letters, his Epistolary Ledger usually supplies the necessary date. But for an example of one of his few mistakes in properly noting the place and date of receiving one of his correspondent's letters—an error that has misled his and Madison's biographers—see Chapter 26, where I report that it was Madison who handed Jefferson, visiting overnight at Montpellier, the letter that informed him that he had been elected president of the United States in 1800.

My dedication indicates my indebtedness to our lively grandchildren, the "busy bees" who have uniformly—and blessedly—interrupted progress on this book from time to time in both Maryland and Maine. To their mother, our daughter Melissa, and to our son Jimmy, a horticulturist who accompanied us as research associate on our trip to England to retrace Jefferson's visits to country gardens, go my continuing thanks and admiration for their interest and support. Finally, to my wife Kassie, who nursed me through the illness in California and has been a partner, for almost as long as Madison and Jefferson were friends, in all our enterprises, be they scholarly, family, administrative, or otherwise, I am once again pleased to acknowledge that she is now, as she has been from the beginning and, I hope, ever shall be, the power behind the drone. Together, they constitute what Jefferson called "a family which has blessed me by their affection."

Before leaving Mr. Jefferson and Mr. Madison, whose daily company I have been privileged to share for the past ten years, I want to say hail but not farewell. I owe them an immense debt of gratitude for their amiability, brilliance, and character. Their letters speak for themselves, and I hope that the readers of the correspondence, which spans fifty-years of friendship, will find it, as Julian P. Boyd did, "the most extended, the most elevated, the most significant exchange of letters between any two men in the whole sweep of American history." At the end of this project to collect their correspondence for the first time in order to document their intimate friendship, I could not agree more.

JAMES MORTON SMITH

*Bellagio (Como)*
*Elkton, Maryland*

# ABBREVIATIONS

**AHA** American Historical Association.
***AHR*** *American Historical Review.*
**Amer. Phil. Soc.** American Philosophical Society.
***ASP*** Walter Lowrie and Matthew St. Clair Clarke, eds., *American State Papers: Documents, Legislative and Executive,* 38 vols. (Washington, 1832-61): **FR** (Foreign Relations); ***M*** (Miscellaneous).
**Brant** Irving Brant, *The Life of James Madison,* 6 vols. (Indianapolis, 1941-61): I, *James Madison: The Virginia Revolutionist* (1941); II, *James Madison: The Nationalist* (1948); III, *James Madison: Father of the Constitution* (1950); IV, *James Madison: Secretary of State* (1953); V, *James Madison: The President* (1956); VI, *James Madison: Commander in Chief* (1961).
**Cappon** Lester J. Cappon, ed., *The Adams-Jefferson Letters: The Complete Correspondence between Thomas Jefferson and Abigail and John Adams,* 2 vols. (Chapel Hill, 1959).
**Fitzpatrick** John C. Fitzpatrick, ed., *The Writings of George Washington . . . , 1745-1799,* 39 vols. (Washington, 1931-44).
**Ford** Paul Leicester Ford, ed., *The Writings of Thomas Jefferson,* 10 vols. (New York, 1892-99).
**Hamilton, *Writings of Monroe*** Stanislaus Murray Hamilton, ed., *The Writings of James Monroe . . . ,* 7 vols. (New York, 1898-1903).
**Hening** William Waller Hening, ed., *The Statutes at Large; Being a Collection of All the Laws of Virginia, from the First Session of the Legislature, in the Year 1619,* 13 vols. (Richmond and Philadelphia, 1819-23).
**Hunt** Gaillard Hunt, ed., *The Writings of James Madison,* 9 vols. (New York, 1900-10).
***JAH*** *Journal of American History.*
***JER*** *Journal of the Early Republic.*
**JM** James Madison.
***J. So. Hist.*** *Journal of Southern History.*
**Ketcham** Ralph Ketcham, *James Madison: A Biography* (New York, 1971).
**L. and B.** A. A. Lipscomb and A. E. Bergh, eds., *The Writings of Thomas Jefferson,* 20 vols. (New York, 1903).
**Malone** Dumas Malone, *Jefferson and His Time,* 6 vols. (Boston, 1948-81): I, *Jefferson the Virginian* (1948); II, *Jefferson and the Rights of Man* (1951); III, *Jefferson and the Ordeal of Liberty* (1962); IV, *Jefferson the President: First Term, 1801-1805* (1970); V, *Jefferson the President: Second Term, 1805-1809* (1974): VI, *The Sage of Monticello* (1981).
***MVHR*** *Mississippi Valley Historical Review.*
**Peterson** Merrill D. Peterson, *Thomas Jefferson and the New Nation: A Biography* (New York, 1970).
***PJM*** William T. Hutchinson, William M. E. Rachal, Robert A. Rutland, J. C. A. Stagg, *et al.,* eds., *The Papers of James Madison,* 22 vols. to date (Chicago and Charlottesville, 1962-93): **(SS ser.)** is Secretary of State series; **(Pres. ser.)** is Presidential series.
***PMHB*** *Pennsylvania Magazine of History and Biography.*
***PTJ*** Julian P. Boyd, Charles Cullen, John Catanzariti, *et al.,* eds., *The Papers of Thomas Jefferson,* 28 vols. to date (Princeton, 1950-92).
**Richardson** James D. Richardson, ed., *A Compilation of the Messages and Papers of the Presidents, 1789-1897,* 10 vols. (Washington, 1907).
**Syrett** Harold C. Syrett and Jacob E. Cooke, eds., *The Papers of Alexander Hamilton,* 26 vols. (New York, 1961-79).
**TJ** Thomas Jefferson.
***VMHB*** *Virginia Magazine of History and Biography.*
***WMQ*** *William and Mary Quarterly.*

# The Republic of Letters

# INTRODUCTION:
# AN INTIMATE FRIENDSHIP

POETS AND PRESIDENTS are not noted as historical commentators. But John F. Kennedy and Robert Frost, who read his poem "The Gift Outright" at President Kennedy's inauguration, have offered fascinating insights on Thomas Jefferson and James Madison. At a state dinner honoring the Nobel laureates of the Americas, Kennedy observed that the distinguished guests were "the most extraordinary collection of talents that has ever been gathered together at the White House, with the possible exception of when Thomas Jefferson dined alone."

A few years earlier, Frost had been reading *The Federalist* to discover in those papers the dream of the Founding Fathers. "And lately," he concluded, "I've decided that the best dreamer of it was Madison. . . . I think I know . . . what Madison's dream was. It was a dream of a new land to fulfill with people in self-control." It may also have been Frost's influence that led Kennedy to label Madison as "our most under-rated president."

Long before Kennedy's comment, another New England president had given his measured judgment of Madison at the conclusion of the War of 1812. Writing to Jefferson, who was the third president, "Honest" John Adams, the second one, had this to say about the fourth president: "Notwithstanding a thousand Faults and blunders," Madison's administration "has acquired more glory, and established more Union, than all his three predecessors, Washington Adams and Jefferson, put together."

As extraordinary as were Jefferson and Madison, even more unusual was their fifty-year friendship, one that began in Williamsburg, Virginia, in the fall of 1776 and ended only with the death of Jefferson on the fiftieth anniversary of the Declaration of Independence in 1826. On the relationship between the two friends, John Quincy Adams observed that "Mr. Madison was the intimate, confidential, and devoted friend of Mr. Jefferson, and the mutual influence of these two mighty minds upon each other is a phenomenon, like the invisible and mysterious movements of the magnet in the physical world, and in which the sagacity of the future historian may discover the solution of much of our national history not otherwise easily accountable."

The greatest creations of these two mighty minds—the historic documents that have produced much of our national history—were the Declaration of Independence, written by Jefferson, and the federal Constitution, shaped by Madison. In terms of historical consequences, there is probably no more powerful statement written by an American than Jefferson's "all men are created equal" unless it is Madison's "We the people." Like John Adams, they seemed "sent into life at a time when the greatest lawgivers of antiquity would have wished to live. How few of the human race have ever enjoyed an opportunity of making an election of government—more than of air, soil, or climate—for themselves or their children. When, before the present epoch, had three millions of people full power and a fair opportunity to form and establish the wisest and happiest government that human wisdom can contrive?"

Jefferson's and Madison's places in history are based on the experiment in representative government introduced by the American Revolution—"a period glorious for our country," Madison observed late in life, "and, more than any other preceding one, likely to improve the condition of man." Both men had read Francis Bacon's essay "Of Honour and Reputation," which outlined categories of fame and honor, headed by "founders of states and commonwealths" such as Romulus, Cyrus, Ottoman, and Julius Caesar, followed immediately by men who gave constitutions and principles to the commonwealth such as Solon, Justinian, and Lycurgus. In his *Federalist* Number 38, Madison hailed the formation of the Constitution for creating "as fair a chance for immortality, as Lycurgus gave to that of Sparta."[1]

Their claim to fame, Jefferson believed, rested ultimately with "the tribunal of posterity." At the end of his life, in the last letter he wrote, Jefferson made this point in a comment celebrating the fiftieth anniversary of the Declaration of Independence: "May it be to the world, what I believe it will be, (to some parts sooner, to others later, but finally to all,) the signal of arousing men to burst the chains under which monkish ignorance and superstition had persuaded them to bind themselves, and to assume the blessings and security of self-government."

And after Jefferson and John Adams died on the Fourth of July 1826, Madison recalled the Revolutionary era as "a source of peculiar gratification to those who had any great part in the great event," knowing that he and the few remaining members of the founding generation had earned "a place in the galaxy of faithful citizens who did their best for their country when it needed their services."

When Jefferson wrote the inscription for the obelisk at Monticello that

---

1. For an imaginative analysis of "Fame and the Founding Fathers," see Douglass Adair's appraisal in his *Fame and the Founding Fathers: Essays by Douglass Adair,* ed. H. Trevor Colbourn (New York, 1974), pp. 3-26.

serves as his gravestone, he listed himself as "Author of the Declaration of American Independence, of the Statute of Virginia for Religious Freedom, and Father of the University of Virginia." Had Madison written with similar simplicity an epitaph for his obelisk at Montpellier, he could have listed himself as "Father of the Constitution of the United States and the Federal Bill of Rights, Author of the Memorial and Remonstrance for Religious Freedom, and Co-founder of the University of Virginia."

"Author" and "Father" are terms applicable to both men, although the words were used only by Jefferson. If it is clear that Jefferson chose to be remembered as an author, it is equally true that Madison deserves to be remembered in the same way. Both men were active contributors of what Jefferson called "the republic of letters." Both understood that their fame would be based on what they wrote, be it formal public papers or personal, private letters. They were historical-minded and knew that they were building in the New World a republican system of representative government unlike anything in recorded history—"the world's best hope," as Jefferson proclaimed in his first inaugural address. They, therefore, carefully preserved their voluminous correspondence, building archives that will finally yield, when completely published in the twenty-first century, at least fifty substantial volumes for Madison and perhaps eighty-five for Jefferson.[2] Among the most valuable of these thousands of letters are those exchanged by the author of the Declaration of Independence and the father of the Constitution, a correspondence that Julian P. Boyd has characterized as "the most extended, the most elevated, the most significant exchange of letters between any two men in the whole sweep of American history."

Jefferson and Madison were products of the eighteenth century, the golden age of letter writing in England and America. If Horace Walpole and William Cowper were the leading practitioners of what Logan Pearsall Smith calls "atticism"—simplicity, elegance, and effortless ease[3]—it can be argued that Jefferson and Madison stand supreme on the American scene. Eleanor Berman has called Jefferson "one of the world's greatest letter-writers," and Robert Dawidoff has observed that "Jefferson's real rival is not Emerson, it is not even Hamilton. It is Madison , whose standing as the favorite founder among the intellectual classes has deservedly grown. Madison and Jefferson understood each other as allies." They shared a "vision of the American future, the pastoral of the American democratic republic," with Jefferson supplying "the imaginative grounds of faith in the republic" and Madison, who had a better "grasp of what is difficult and unyielding in the world," working out in the Constitutional Convention "his tough-minded arrangements for a republican future." "The care with which Jefferson invested both the ordinary and the

---

2. See in *JAH* 74 (1988): 1333, Joyce Appleby's estimate of the year 2050 for the completion of the Princeton edition of *PTJ*.

3. William Henry Irving, *The Providence of Wit in English Letter Writers* (Durham, N.C., 1955), p. 360, cites Smith.

superior person with a role in a free and enlightened future," Dawidoff concluded, "is his companion piece to Madison's harder-headed political thinking. They should not be separated."[4]

Neither Jefferson nor Madison ever reduced his thought to a systematic presentation. Madison's essays in *The Federalist* are the best single index to his mind, just as Jefferson's *Notes on the State of Virginia* is the best introduction to his views. Both men also wrote a wide variety of government reports, addresses to Congress, and related documents. And both took stabs at autobiography, Jefferson beginning a fairly extensive memoir in 1821 at the age of seventy-seven and Madison writing a much briefer outline of his life in 1831 at the age of eighty. But each was reticent to write about himself, Jefferson confessing midway through his text that "I am already tired of writing about myself" and Madison trailing off after a solid beginning and concluding by citing source material for the biographer and historian.[5]

Both men realized that their literary legacy lay in their letters. "It has been remarked," Madison wrote late in life, "that the biography of an author must be a history of his writings. So must that of one whose whole life has in a manner been a public life, be gathered from his . . . manuscript papers on public subjects, including letters to as well as from him." Jefferson agreed. "The letters of a person," he observed, "especially of one whose business has been transacted by letters, form the only full and genuine journal of his life."

Historians and biographers have long recognized the significance of letters as sources of historical and personal illumination. Charles Francis Adams, the grandson of John and Abigail Adams, concluded that "our history is for the most part wrapped up in the forms of office. The great men of the Revolution, in the eyes of posterity, are many of them like heroes of a mythological age." But to get at the human story behind the historic event, to penetrate the façade that masks the inner self, to obtain "an exact transcript of the feelings" of the participants during "times of no ordinary trial," Adams continued, one needs to read private letters meant only for the eyes of the recipient. And he observed that "we look for the workings of the heart, when those of the head alone are presented to us. . . . The solitary meditation, the confidential whisper to a friend, never meant to reach the ear of the multitude, the secret wishes, not blazoned forth to catch applause, the fluctuations between fear and hope that most betray the springs of action—these are the guides to

---

4. Eleanor Davidson Berman, *Thomas Jefferson among the Arts* (New York, 1947), p. 198; Robert Dawidoff, "Man of Letters," in Merrill D. Peterson, *Jefferson: A Reference Biography* (New York, 1986), p. 197. Dawidoff, James M. Cox, and Louis C. Schaedler present strong arguments for restoring Jefferson and Madison to the history of American letters, which tends to skip from Jonathan Edwards to Ralph Waldo Emerson, after taking a short bow in the direction of Benjamin Franklin. See James M. Cox, "Jefferson's *Autobiography:* Recovering Literature's Lost Ground," *Southern Review* 14 (1978): 635, and Louis C. Schaedler, "James Madison, Literary Craftsman," *WMQ* 3 (1946): 515-33.

5. The fullest discussion of Jefferson's "Autobiography" is in Cox, 633-52. The best analysis of Madison's is in Douglass Adair, "James Madison's Autobiography," *WMQ* 2 (1945): 191-209.

character, which most frequently vanish with the moment that called them forth, and leave nothing to posterity but those coarser elements for judgment that are found in elaborated results."

Historian Carl Becker once observed that "the record of events, of what men have done, is relatively rich and informing. But a record of the state of mind that conditioned those events, a record that might enable us to analyze the complex of instincts and emotions that lie behind the avowed purpose and the formulated principles of action—such a record is largely wanting. What one requires for such investigation are the more personal writings—memoirs, and, above all, letters—in which individuals consciously or unconsciously reveal the hidden springs of conduct."[6] In the nineteenth century, letters were viewed as "magic scrolls," according to Nathaniel Hawthorne, "if read in the right spirit. The roll of the drum and the fanfare of the trumpets is latent in some of them; and in others, the echo of the oratory that resounded in the old halls of the Continental Congress, at Philadelphia; or the words may come to us as with the living utterance of one of those illustrious men, speaking face to face, in friendly communion."[7]

It is the spirit of friendly communion that makes the correspondence between Jefferson and Madison so revealing. Between 1780 and 1826, they exchanged nearly 1,250 letters, running the gamut from short notes—"Will you come and sit an hour before dinner to-day?" Jefferson scribbled to his friend when they were in Philadelphia in 1791, "also take soup with me tomorrow"—to Madison's remarkable seventeen-page letter on the results of the Constitutional Convention.

Whether dashed off quickly or composed with care and polished, the letters between Madison and Jefferson constitute a correspondence of Americans that seems to confirm the insight of playwright and novelist James Agee on the significance of literate life:

Letters are in every word and phrase immediate to and revealing of, in precision and complex detail, the sender and receiver and the whole world and context each is of: as distinct in their own way, and as valuable, as would be a faultless record of the dreams of many individuals. The two main facts about any letter are: the immediacy, and the flawlessness, of its revelations. In the true sense that any dream is a faultless work of art, so is any letter; and the defended and conscious letter is as revealing as the undefended.[8]

Whether every letter written by Jefferson or Madison to the other was "a faultless work of art" may be debated. But their correspondence reveals, in

---

6. Charles Francis Adams, quoted in L. H. Butterfield, Marc Friedlaender, and Mary-Jo Kline, eds., *The Book of Abigail and John: Selected Letters of the Adams Family* (Cambridge, 1975), pp. 9–10, and Carl Becker, quoted in M. Lincoln Schuster, *The Treasury of the World's Great Letters* (New York, 1940), p. xl.

7. Nathaniel Hawthorne, "A Book of Autographs," cited in *PTJ*, I, pp. xxv–xxvi.

8. Robert Fitzgerald, ed., *The Collected Short Prose of James Agee* (Boston, 1968), pp. 134–35.

precision and complex detail, what Jefferson called "freshness of fact." Since neither Jefferson nor Madison kept a diary, their innermost thoughts went directly into their letters. Both viewed their "epistolary intercourse," as Samuel Johnson called it, as private conversation. Both had read Francis Bacon's essay "Of Friendship," which argued that "this communicating of a man's self to his friend worketh two contrary effects, for it redoubleth joys, and cutteth griefs in halfs." They agreed with John Locke that "the writing of letters has so much to do in all the occurrences of human life, that no Gentleman can avoid shewing himself in this kind of writing." A private letter, like a private conversation, allowed more open, less inhibited expression of one's true views, and the lifelong correspondence between the two friends illustrates how highly they valued the opportunity for a free and frank exchange of views. Like the English novelist Samuel Richardson, each man viewed familiar letter writing as the "cement of friendship . . . friendship avowed under hand and seal." Or, as one of Richardson's characters observed, letter writing was friendship "more pure . . . and less broken in upon, than personal conversation can be amongst the most pure, because of the deliberation it allows, from the very preparation to, and action of[,] writing."[9] In their first decade of correspondence, they perfected the familiar letter as intimate conversation, reporting, interpreting, and re-creating in friendly fashion the social, cultural, and political world each knew. At critical junctures, they utilized a secret cipher in order to preserve the privacy of their written conversation and to thwart any snooper tempted to tamper with their mail.

Whenever the two friends were together, they relied on verbal communications instead of letters. As Jefferson once observed, "A short conference saves a long letter." On another occasion, he invited Madison to Monticello, "where a great deal can be said to you which could not be confided to paper."[10] Madison also occasionally reserved some comments for "verbal communication,"[11] when he could "say more than I cou'd well put on paper."[12] But when they were not together, they resumed their correspondence, and posterity has been the richer. That includes "all us F.B.I. types," as Russell Baker once observed, "who like to read other people's mail."[13] For it seems clear that Jefferson and Madison, like Washington and Adams, meant their letters to be read as a part of the history that they helped create.

Both men wrote words that identified them with the origins of the new nation, which first required bullets to validate the Declaration and, later, ballots to ratify the Constitution. Neither author ever regretted his role in helping create the world's first popular government, and neither ever became alien-

9. Quoted in Andrew Burstein, "Jefferson, Letter-Writing and Self-Expression," a paper read at the 1993 conference of the Society for the History of the Early American Republic.

10. TJ to JM, Sept. 1, 1807, below. TJ to JM, Apr. 4, 1800, below.

11. JM to TJ, Feb. 5, 1797, below.

12. JM to TJ, Aug. 16, 1809, below.

13. Russell Baker, "A Letter to Groucho Marx," in *The Historian As Detective: Essays on Evidence,* ed. Robin W. Winks (New York, 1969), p. 537.

ated from the American people, whose actions confirmed their reading of the American mind. As authors, they were the two sides of early American thought, each setting forth, with a different emphasis, the eighteenth-century version of the wisdom of the ages transformed by the radicalism of the Revolution into a completely republican American synthesis. Their correspondence vividly illustrates the point made by Howard Anderson and Irvin Ehrenpreis that the eighteenth-century letter "belongs to a human relationship in a way that is rarely seen in either earlier or more recent periods. Just as the writer's purity of style must act to reveal his character, so the 'substantive' nature of the letter must constitute a link between the correspondents."[14]

There was more than a link between these correspondents. There was an irresistable, even magnetic, attraction, as John Quincy Adams suggested, that pulled the two together into a harmonious relationship, one that easily withstood the stresses and strains that occasionally surfaced between them. Jefferson valued above all else amiability—"good humor," as he called it—in a friend, rating it above integrity, industry, and science. "The preference of the first to the second quality," he explained, "may not at first be acquiesced in; but certainly we had all rather associate with a good-humoured, light-principled man, than with an ill-tempered rigorist in morality."[15]

Unlike John Adams, who reveled in aggressive argument whether he was furiously scribbling notes in his diaries, dashing off denunciatory marginalia in his books, or writing pugnacious letters to his friends, Jefferson always had a certain reserve that avoided confrontation, preferring to take things by "the smooth handle," a quality that was reciprocated by Madison. When Madison, after reading Adams's letters to Congress in the 1780s, portrayed the New Englander as vain and pompous, Jefferson conceded that Adams could be vain and irritable, but he stressed Adams's profound views and keen judgment before adding that "he is so amiable, that I pronounce you will love him if ever you become acquainted with him."

In the republic of friendship built by their correspondence, the two men carried on an elevated, enlightened, and rational exchange of information, relieved occasionally by gossipy news of the neighborhood, be it Philadelphia, Paris, Richmond, or Albemarle and Orange counties in Virginia. Each remained rooted in his "obscure corner of the world," as Madison observed, thirsting for local news while staying abreast of state, national, and international developments. Their gossip was more than "mere insignificance and chatter." The word *gossip,* as Elizabeth Drew has noted, has an older meaning, "with its suggestion of close intimacy and friendliness that linked the exchangers of letters. But it is true," she added, "that the inspired scribbler . . . can always inspire the commonplace with uncommon flavor, and transform trivialities, by some original grace or sympathy or humor or affection."[16]

14. Howard Anderson and Irvin Ehrenpreis, *The Familiar Letter in the Eighteenth Century* (Lawrence, Kans., 1966), p. 277.
15. Cited in John M. Dorsey, ed., *The Jefferson-Dunglison Letters* (Charlottesville, 1960), p. 100.
16. Elizabeth Drew, *The Literature of Gossip: Nine English Letterwriters* (New York, 1964), p. 15.

In Paris, cut off from home, Jefferson hungered for such gossip and lamented that "I can persuade nobody to believe that the small facts which they see daily passing under their eyes are precious to me at this distance; much more interesting to the heart than events of higher rank." But he did persuade Madison, who sent a steady stream of reports about events of lesser rank: prices current on tobacco, wheat, corn, and pork; promotions to the Virginia congressional delegation; demotions from the Executive Council in Virginia because of the "triennial purge" that removed some councillors in order to promote others to that body—"the graveyard of useful talents," according to Madison; the depth of snowfalls; recent deaths; and news of "a destructive insect which goes under the name of the Hessian fly."

Jefferson devoured such gossip, and his replies, as Joyce Appleby has noted, "reveal the intense conviviality of a solitary person."[17] Jefferson knew that Madison also hungered for the same sort of gossip, and he often passed along his budget of such news, even while he was president. "I presume," Jefferson wrote to Madison while Jefferson was summering at Monticello in 1806, "that you will have heard of the death of Frank Walker, and that he died drunk in his carriage unknown to the driver. It was discovered only when the carriage stopped at the next house."[18]

Although Jefferson held good humor in high regard, he did not have much of a sense of humor himself. But occasional glimpses peep through in his letters to Madison. When Benedict Arnold headed a British invasion of Virginia in 1781 and holed up temporarily in Portsmouth, Governor Jefferson observed with tongue in cheek that "we have no reason to believe they came here to Sleep." During his presidency, when British warships were ordered out of American waters, a landing party from one of His Majesty's ships came ashore to fill their water kegs, and irate Americans smashed the kegs and drove the British off. When the British minister in Washington demanded reparations for the kegs, Jefferson told Madison that it reminded him of the story of "one who having broke his cane over the head of the other, demanded paiment for his cane." And in 1825, when he was eighty-two years old, Jefferson complained facetiously that he had "one foot in the grave, and the other uplifted to follow it."

Madison, by contrast, had developed a taste for ribald jokes as a young man at Princeton, and he continued to tell "the most racy anecdotes" into his eighties.[19] Edward Coles, Madison's private secretary during his presidency, thought that "few men possessed so rich a flow of language, or so great a fund of amusing anecdotes, which were made the more interesting from their being well-timed and well-told."[20] George Tucker, professor of moral philosophy at

---

17. Appleby, 1333.
18. TJ to JM, May 11, 1806, below.
19. Douglass Adair, "James Madison," in Adair, *Fame and the Founding Fathers*, p. 130; Brant, VI, p. 509.
20. Merrill D. Peterson, *James Madison: A Biography in His Own Words* (New York, 1974), p. 251.

the University of Virginia who knew him well, agreed that Madison's "large fund of anecdote which he told very well, made him one of the most companionable men in existence."[21] His lifelong neighbor and eulogist James Barbour, a powerful figure in both Virginia and national politics in the early nineteenth century, singled out Madison's "playful Attic wit" as a key feature of his gentle charm but noted that it was "always without a sting," "the rose without the thorn."[22]

As the youngest member of Congress in 1781, Madison attended the celebration of the ratification of the Articles of Confederation, the new nation's first constitution. According to the *Journals of the Continental Congress,* the celebrants met in Independence Hall and ate from "a keg of biscuit, in the room of cake." When he later read these minutes, he added an asterisk, then wrote an impish footnote—"Does it mean in the cake room?"—one of the few humorous quips in the voluminous records of the Continental Congress. Later, while secretary of state, he hosted the visit of Sidi Suliman Mellimelli, ambassador from Tunis, who came to protest the seizure of a Tunisian vessel during the Barbary wars. When the diplomat requested concubines for his entourage of eleven, they were furnished at State Department expense. One suspects that Madison relished charging the cost to "appropriations to foreign intercourse."[23] And late in life, after noting that he was the last survivor of the Revolutionary leaders, he quipped: "Having outlived so many of my contemporaries, I ought not to forget that I may be thought to have outlived myself."[24] But he seldom introduced his anecdotes into his letters to Jefferson, so the correspondence between the two friends seems to float on an air of agreeableness and amiability, with only an occasional flash of wit or irony to relieve its graceful prose.

Despite their talent for epistolary camaraderie, the correspondence between these Virginia gentlemen, these closest of friends, is characterized by a grave formality, a dignified reserve, a mannered elegance, with little display of affection except for the friendly salutary close. Near the end of his life, in one of the last letters he wrote, Jefferson confided to a granddaughter whom he dearly loved that it was "easier to write ten letters of business than one of the intangible affections of the mind."[25] As a young man, Madison had reached a similar conclusion. "Friendship like all Truth delights in plainness and simplicity and It is the Counterfeit alone that needs Ornament and ostentation." Writing to his best friend in college, he confessed that "I have not the face to

---

21. Quoted in Drew R. McCoy, *The Last of the Fathers: James Madison and the Republican Legacy* (New York, 1989), p. 29.

22. *Ibid.,* p. 22.

23. Brant, IV, p. 306.

24. JM to Jared Sparks, June 1, 1831, in Hunt, IX, p. 460. See also "CC" Proctor, ed., "After-Dinner Anecdotes of James Madison: Excerpts from Jared Sparks' Journal for 1829–1831," *VMHB* 60 (1952): 255–65.

25. TJ to Ellen W. Coolidge, June 5, 1826, quoted in *Jefferson Himself: The Personal Narrative of a Many-sided American,* ed. Bernard Mayo (Charlottesville, 1942), p. 343.

perform ceremony in person and I equally detest it on paper though as Tully says It cannot blush."[26]

Plainness, simplicity, and sincerity are the most noticeable qualities of the letters exchanged by the two friends. Unlike the second half of the Adams-Jefferson letters, which Lester Cappon labeled "their philosophical correspondence,"[27] the letters between Jefferson and Madison are, for the most part, specific and matter-of-fact, written by men of affairs busily engaged in the daily tasks of politics and diplomacy. Fortunately, both men had the gift, honed to a fine edge by reading and reflection, of articulating their thoughts with clarity, broad civility, compelling vigor, and unrelenting rigor.

For that reason, the letters between Jefferson and Madison are the best way, as Adrienne Koch suggested forty years ago, to study the "interplay of ideas between the two greatest philosopher statesmen of the American Enlightenment."[28] Since each had unlimited confidence in the other, they wrote without reserve, their friendship quickly growing into a working partnership. "In the constant exchange of ideas and services between them," Merrill Peterson concluded, "the account balanced. Men who were enough alike to work together, yet sufficiently different to complement each other, their alliance was remarkably beneficial."[29]

The lifelong collaboration was based on friendship, which Jefferson, then in retirement, compared to wine—"raw when new, ripened with age, the true old man's milk and restorative cordial." But in this case, the raw stage, if it ever existed, quickly disappeared. Indeed, as a younger man, Jefferson had observed that "friendship is precious, not only in the shade, but in the sunshine of life; and thanks to a benevolent arrangement of things, the greater part of life is sunshine." Almost from the beginning, both men cordially signed their letters "your friend," with the shy Madison taking the lead.

Although it is difficult, as James Boswell wrote, to "tell the precise moment when friendship is formed," we know that it flowered between the two men in Williamsburg in 1779, when Governor Jefferson inherited Madison and seven other men from Patrick Henry's Executive Council as his advisers. Jefferson remembered Madison from their meeting in 1776, when Madison was "a new member and young; which circumstances, concurring with his extreme modesty, prevented his venturing himself in debate before his removal to the Council of State in November 1777."

But Jefferson dated their friendship from 1779, as did Madison: "With the exception of an intercourse in a session of the Virginia Legislature in 1776, rendered slight by the disparity between us, I did not become acquainted with Mr. Jefferson till 1779, when being a member of the Executive Council, and he the Governor, an intimacy took place."

26. In *PJM*, I, p. 83.
27. Cappon, I, p. xlix.
28. Adrienne Koch, *Jefferson and Madison: The Great Collaboration* (New York, 1950), p. vii.
29. Peterson, p. 266.

*John Adams's replica of the life portrait of Jefferson
(age forty-three) painted in London by Mather Brown in 1786.*

Courtesy of Charles Francis Adams, Dover, Massachusetts.

*The life portrait of Jefferson (age forty-eight) painted in Philadelphia by Charles Willson Peale in 1791.*

Courtesy of Independence National Historical Park.

*The life portrait of Madison (age forty-one) painted in
Philadelphia by Charles Willson Peale in 1791.*

Courtesy of the Thomas Gilcrease Museum, Tulsa, Oklahoma.

*The life portrait of Jefferson (age fifty-seven) painted
in Philadelphia by Rembrandt Peale in 1800.*

Copyright by the White House Historical Association. Photograph by National Geographic Society.

*The life portrait of Madison (age fifty-four) painted in Washington by Gilbert Stuart in 1804.*

Courtesy of Colonial Williamsburg Foundation.

*The life portrait of Madison (age sixty-five) painted in Washington by Joseph Wood in 1816.*

Courtesy of the Virginia Historical Society.

*The life portrait of Dolley Madison (age forty-eight) painted in Washington by Joseph Wood in 1816.*

Courtesy of the Virginia Historical Society.

*The life portrait of Jefferson (age seventy-eight) painted at Monticello by Thomas Sully in 1821.*

Courtesy of the American Philosophical Society.

*The life portrait of Madison (age eighty-three) painted at Montpellier by Asher B. Durand in 1832–1833.*

Courtesy of the New-York Historical Society.

*Monticello.*

*Courtesy of the Thomas Jefferson Memorial Foundation. Robert C. Lautman photograph.*

*Poplar Forest.*

*Courtesy of Jefferson's Poplar Forest.*

approve. even these will be a great addition to the energy of your government. at all events I hope you will not be discouraged from other trials, if the present one should fail of it's full effect. — I have thus told you freely what I like & dislike: merely as a matter of curiosity, for I know your own judgment has been formed on all these points after having heard every thing which could be urged on them. I own I am not a friend to a very energetic government. it is always oppressive. the late rebellion in Massachusets has given more alarm than I think it should have done. calculate that one rebellion in 13 states in the course of 11 years, is but one for each state in a century & a half. no country should be so long without one. nor will any degree of power in the hands of government prevent insurrections. France, with all it's despotism, and two or three hundred thousand men always in arms has had three insurrections in the three years I have been here in every one of which greater numbers were engaged than in Massachusets & a great deal more blood was spilt. in Turkey, where Montesquieu supposes more despotic, insurrections are the events of every day. in England, where the hand of power is lighter than here, but heavier than with us they happen every half dozen years. compare again the ferocious depredations of their insurgents with the order, the moderation & the almost self-extinguishment of ours. — after all, it is my principle

*Jefferson to Madison, December 20, 1787.*

that the will of the majority should always prevail. if they approve the proposed Convention in all it's parts, I shall concur in it chearfully, in hopes that they will amend it whenever they shall find it work wrong. I think our governments will remain virtuous for many centuries; as long as they are chiefly agricultural; and this will be as long as there shall be vacant lands in any part of America. when they get piled upon one another in large cities, as in Europe, they will become corrupt, as in Europe. above all things I hope the education of the common people will be attended to; convinced that on their good sense we may rely with the most security for the preservation of a due degree of liberty. I have tired you by this time with my disquisitions & will therefore only add assurances of the sincerity of those sentiments of esteem & attachment with which I am Dear Sir your affectionate friend & servant

Th: Jefferson

P.S. the instability of our laws is really an immense evil. I think it would be well to provide in our constitutions that there shall always be a twelvemonth between the ingrossing a bill & passing it: that it should then be offered to it's passage without changing a word: and that if circumstances should be thought to require a speedier passage, it should take two thirds of both houses instead of a bare majority.

*Courtesy of the Library of Congress.*

should be so inaccurately defined by experience. ‖

Supposing a bill of rights to be proper, the articles which ought to compose it, admit of much discussion. I am inclined to think that absolute restrictions in cases that are doubtful, or where emergencies may overrule them, ought to be avoided. The restrictions however strongly marked on paper will never be regarded when opposed to the decided sense of the public; and will after repeated violations in extraordinary cases, they will lose even their ordinary efficacy. Should a Rebellion or insurrection alarm the people as well as the Government, and a suspension of the Hab. corps. be dictated by the alarm, no written prohibitions on earth would prevent the measure. Should an army in time of peace be gradually established in our neighbourhood by Brit:n or Spain, declarations on paper would have as little effect in preventing a standing force for the public safety. The best security agst. these evils is to remove the pretext for them. With regard to Monopolies they are justly classed among the greatest nuisances in Government. But is it clear that as encouragements to literary works and ingenious discoveries, they are not too valuable to be wholly renounced? would it not suffice to reserve in all cases a right to the public to abolish the privilege at a price to be specified in the grant of it? Is there not also infinitely less danger of their abuse in our Governments, than in most others? Monopolies are

*Madison to Jefferson, October 17, 1788.*

are sacrifices of the many to the few. Where the power is in the few it is natural for them to sacrifice the many to their own partialities and corruptions. Where the power, as with us, is in the many not in the few, the danger can not be very great that the few will be thus favored. It is much more to be dreaded that the few will be unnecessarily sacrificed to the many.]

X I inclose a paper containing the late proceedings in Kentucky. I wish the ensuing Convention may take no step injurious to the character of the district, and favorable to the views of those who wish ill to the U. States. One of my late letters communicated some circumstances which will not fail to occur on perusing the objects of the proposed Convention in next month. Perhaps however there may be less connection between the two cases than at first one is ready to conjecture. I am D'r Sir with the sincerest esteem & affec'n

Yours
Js. Madison Jr

*Courtesy of the Library of Congress.*

*Montpellier.*

*Courtesy of the National Trust for Historic Preservation.*

## INTRODUCTION: AN INTIMATE FRIENDSHIP

Jefferson's oldest friend, Lieutenant Governor John Page, a classmate at the College of William and Mary, was also on the council, but Madison quickly became Jefferson's closest friend. It was the quality "of his [Madison's] luminous and discriminating mind," his immense knowledge and "extensive information," "the powers and polish of his pen," and his sound judgment that most impressed Jefferson.[30] By contrast, Jefferson thought that "our friend Mr. Page, from the benevolent and unsuspicious cast of his mind, is the most unsafe recommender we can possibly follow. He never sees but the good qualities of a man, [and] those through the largest magnifiers."[31]

Jefferson and Madison made a good team throughout life, partners in what Adrienne Koch called "The Great Collaboration." Sir Augustus Foster, the British minister to the United States during Jefferson's and Madison's presidencies, thought "Mr. Jefferson more of a statesman and man of the world than Mr. Madison, . . . yet the latter was better informed, and, moreover, a social, jovial, and good-humoured companion, full of anecdote, sometimes rather of a loose description, but oftener of a political and historical interest."[32] In 1824, an itinerant bookseller who visited Monticello and Montpellier reached much the same conclusion: "Mr. Madison," he observed, ". . . is very sociable, rather jocose, quite sprightly, and active. . . . [He] appears less studied, brilliant and frank but more natural, candid and profound than Mr. Jefferson . . . [, who] has more imagination and passion, quicker and richer conceptions. Mr. Madison has a sound judgment, tranquil temper and logical mind."[33]

In 1825, Count Carlo Vidua from Turin, Italy, visited the Virginia patriarchs, "the two most famous statesmen still living in America." He observed that Jefferson "is almost as tall as I am, still retains his reddish disorderly hair, and has a youthful look and the figure and manners which would be lively in any country, but more remarkable in America where manners are so cold." Although he noted that "Jefferson is eight years older than Madison," he thought the younger partner looked older: "His bearing is very aristocratic, and without assuming the air of importance and dignity befitting one of his station, he displays an indescribable gentleness and charm, which I thought impossible to find in an American. I have heard very few people speak with such precision and, above all, with such fairness." "In general," he concluded, "Madison's reflections seemed to me the most profound, the most weighty, denoting a great mind and a good heart." He quickly conceded that "Americans generally celebrate Jefferson as the first man" in their country, "the living patriarch of the American Republic." He agreed that "Jefferson's intellect

30. TJ, "Autobiography," in *Thomas Jefferson: Writings,* ed. Merrill D. Peterson (New York, 1984), p. 37.
31. Quoted in Noble E. Cunningham, Jr., *The Process of Government under Jefferson* (Princeton, 1978), p. 185.
32. Richard Beale Davis, ed., *Jeffersonian America: Notes on the United States of America . . . 1805-6-7 and 11-12, by Sir Augustus John Foster* (San Marino, Calif., 1954), pp. 139-47.
33. Samuel Whitcomb, "Journal of Samuel Whitcomb," June 1, 1824, cited in Ketcham, p. 630.

seemed to me the most brilliant," but he concluded that "Madison's [was] the most profound."³⁴

Dr. Robley Dunglison, professor of medicine at the University of Virginia who became doctor to both men, admired the intellectual powers of both, but he thought that "Mr. Jefferson had more imagination, Mr. Madison excelled perhaps in judgment."³⁵ In assessing their great collaboration, John Quincy Adams elaborated on these same qualities, observing that "the influence of Mr. Jefferson over the mind of Mr. Madison was composed of all that genius, talent, experience, splendid public services, exalted reputation, added to congenial tempers, undivided friendship, and habitual sympathies of interest and of feeling could inspire. Among the numerous blessings which it was the rare good fortune of Mr. Jefferson's life to enjoy was that of the uninterrupted, disinterested, and efficient friendship of Madison. But," he concluded, "it was the friendship of a mind not inferior in capacity, and tempered with a calmer sensibility and a cooler judgment than his own."³⁶

Jefferson was the more speculative, inventive, and theoretical, gifted at coining generalizations and powerful metaphors and writing felicitous prose. Madison was tougher-minded, more analytical, the more persistent student of politics, the harder-headed thinker of the art of the possible. Benjamin Henry Latrobe, the brilliant architect who knew both men well, summarized his views neatly when he said that "Mr. Jefferson is a man out of a book. Mr. Madison is more a man of the world." Jefferson was the eternal optimist, thinking always in terms of human happiness. Madison was the occasional pessimist, constantly aware of the power of human selfishness. In balancing the elements of liberty and power in a republican system, Jefferson, the author of the Declaration of Independence, tended to emphasize the first, fearing governmental power as a threat to liberty, while Madison, the father of the Constitution, tended to stress the second, viewing the new and more powerful government under the Constitution as a protector of liberty.³⁷

Jefferson was generally more extreme than Madison in his views of men and issues, occasionally giving way to impulsive outbursts. Noted for his philosophical intellectuality, he nonetheless tended to reduce men and issues to questions of conflicting opposites. In the Declaration of Independence, he contrasted freedom with tyranny. In Europe, he viewed society as divided

---

34. Elizabeth Cometti and Valeria Gennaro-Lerda, "The Presidential Tour of Carlo Vidua, with Letters on Virginia," *VMHB* 77 (1969): 396–400.

35. Dorsey, p. 78.

36. John Quincy Adams, *The Lives of James Madison and James Monroe* (Buffalo, 1850), pp. 66–68, 86–92; cited in *The Selected Writings of John and John Quincy Adams,* ed. Adrienne Koch and William Peden (New York, 1946), pp. 384–85.

37. See Benjamin Henry Latrobe to John Lenthall, May 2, 1805, cited in William Seale, *The President's House: A History,* 2 vols. (Washington, 1986), I, p. 120. JM wrote that the main purpose of the federal Constitution was to defend "liberty against power, and power against licentiousness, and . . . [to keep] every portion of power within its proper limits"; see Saul K. Padover, ed., *The Forging of American Federalism: Selected Writings of James Madison* (New York, 1953), p. 16.

## INTRODUCTION: AN INTIMATE FRIENDSHIP    13

between "sheep and wolves," where social conflicts were decided by "hammer and anvil." And his famous letter to Maria Cosway was a dialogue between "the head and the heart."

In domestic politics, he contrasted Republicans with Federalists, honest men with "monocrats," farmers with merchants, France with England. As Winthrop Jordan has suggested, "It is virtually impossible . . . to imagine Jefferson as author of the Federalist No. 10; Madison's stress on a multiplicity of factions was entirely foreign to him. Jefferson was at his best on occasions calling for the vigor of simple dichotomy, as in 1776 when he contrasted the virtues of a free people with the crimes of a tyrannical King."[38]

On more than one occasion, Dumas Malone, the distinguished biographer of the "Sage of Monticello," referred to Jefferson's "verbal violence" and to "the rhetorical excess in which Jefferson could indulge."[39] And Madison himself, writing after the death of his friend, said that allowance ought to be made for Jefferson's habit, "as in others of great genius, of expressing in strong and round terms, impressions of the moment."[40]

The friendship initiated in Williamsburg in 1779 matured as a result of the continuous flow of correspondence between 1780 and 1790, when the two men were, as Madison wrote, "for the most part separated by different walks in public and private life, till the present Government [under the Constitution] brought us together."[41] Watching from his post in Paris the phenomenal rise of Madison's reputation in the Virginia assembly, the Confederation congress, the Constitutional Convention, and the new national government, where he almost single-handedly pushed through the adoption of the Bill of Rights, Jefferson became convinced by 1790 that Madison was "the greatest man in the world" and persuaded the editor of the *Encyclopédie méthodique,* successor to Denis Diderot's work in Paris, to publish a biographical sketch of his friend.

In his "Autobiography," Jefferson wrote that Madison as a young man had quickly "acquired a habit of self-possession which . . . rendered him the first of every assembly afterwards of which he became a member. Never wandering from his subject into vain declamation, but pursuing it closely in language pure, classical, and copious, soothing always the feelings of his adversaries by civilities and softness of expression, he rose to the eminent station which he held in the great National convention of 1787, and in that of Virginia which followed, he sustained the new constitution in all its parts, bearing off the palm against the logic of George Mason, and the fervid declamation of Mr. Henry."[42]

---

38. Winthrop D. Jordan, *White over Black: American Attitudes toward the Negro, 1550–1812* (Chapel Hill, N.C., 1968; rpt. New York, 1977), pp. 476–77.
39. Malone, VI, pp. 65–66. For other references to TJ's "verbal extravagance," see *ibid.,* pp. 100, 127.
40. JM to Nicholas P. Trist, May 15, 1832, in Hunt, IX, p. 479
41. JM to Samuel Harrison Smith, Nov. 4, 1826, in Hunt, IX, p. 259.
42. TJ, "Autobiography," in Peterson, *Thomas Jefferson: Writings,* p. 37.

Since the two friends shared assumptions, attitudes, and acquaintances, they could count on instant recognition of allusions often so brief as to amount to a subtle form of encoded shorthand.[43] They also shared another, unlikely bond. Both bordered on being hypochondriacs. Jefferson suffered from intense migraines and Madison from cholera morbus, an acute gastrointestinal disorder, that dogged him throughout his life. As a young man, Madison also feared that he might have epilepsy: "My sensations for many months past have intimated to me not to expect a long and healthy life."[44] According to an article in *Smithsonian* magazine, "Many prominent researchers are now convinced that some headaches, especially the notorious migraines, arise from an upset in the brain's delicate chemistry and could be distant cousins to the 'nerve storms' of epilepsy."[45] If it is true that hypochondriacs feel the need to "share melancholy confidences in the security of a clearly defined relationship," then Jefferson and Madison had an unusually strong bond of recognition, one that threaded through their correspondence for years. When Madison, for example, emerged as the leader of the Republican party (often called "Madison's party") in the early 1790s, Jefferson, writing from Monticello after retiring from Washington's cabinet, suggested that his friend run for the presidency in 1796. Madison's instant refusal was a shorthand reference to what he considered to be his affliction: there were "reasons of *every* kind, and some of them, of the most *insuperable* as well as *obvious* kind" that shut his mind "against the admission of any idea such as you seem to glance at."[46]

Another powerful bond between the two friends was their love of books and the life of the mind. Jefferson once wrote, "I cannot live without books"; neither could Madison. Early in their friendship, they collaborated in compiling a list of books for the use of the Confederation Congress—the first proposal for a Library of Congress—with Madison, then a Virginia congressman, taking the lead and Jefferson, in the nation's capital preparing for his assignment to the peace commission in France, helping list titles for acquisition.[47]

A year later, after his appointment to France to join Benjamin Franklin and John Adams on foreign commercial negotiations, Jefferson offered to purchase for his friend "such books as may be 'either old and curious or new

---

43. For a superior analysis of the familiar letter in eighteenth-century English literature, see Bruce Redford, *The Converse of the Pen: Acts of Intimacy in the Eighteenth-Century Familiar Letter* (Chicago, 1986); I am indebted to Michael T. Gilmore of Brandeis University for this reference. There is no parallel study for American letters.

44. JM to William Bradford, Nov. 9, 1772, in *PJM,* I, p. 15. See Brant, I, pp. 105–8, on the possibility of JM's having epileptoid hysteria.

45. Edwin Kiester, Jr., "Doctors Close In on the Mechanisms behind Headache," *Smithsonian* 18 (1987): 176. See also Jane E. Brody, "Scientists Report Migraine Is No Longer Headache of Old," *International Herald-Tribune* (Rome) (Oct. 12, 1988), on "the new view of migraine as a biological disease of the central nervous system."

46. JM to TJ, Mar. 23, 1795, below. For the need to "share melanchoy confidences," see Allan Ingram, *Boswell's Creative Gloom: A Study of Imagery and Melancholy in the Writings of James Boswell* (London, 1982), pp. 103–4.

47. For the failure of this effort, see ch. 6, below; also see Fulmer Mood, "The Continental Congress and the Plan for a Library of Congress in 1782–1783," *PMHB* 72 (1948): 3–24.

and useful.'" Together they poured over book catalogues, and Madison requested books on ancient and modern federal republics, the law of nations, and the history of America and the New World, "to which I will add such of the Greek and Roman authors where they can be got very cheap."[48] Jefferson's first letter from Paris contained a shipment of 45 books, which included 37 volumes of the *Encyclopédie méthodique,* Madison's first choice for books needed by Congress when he and Jefferson had listed their choices two years earlier.[49] Jefferson thereafter mailed a steady stream of books to Madison, including one massive shipment of 207 volumes in 1785.

But their greatest collaboration involving books came during the War of 1812, when the British torched the President's House and the Capitol, including the Library of Congress. Jefferson promptly offered his personal library of of "9, or 10,000 vols." as a replacement, and a delighted President Madison predicted that the Library Committee of Congress "will report favorably on your proposition to supply the loss of books.... It will prove a gain to them, if they have the wisdom to replace it by such a Collection as yours."[50] It seems fitting and proper that the Library of Congress today bears the names of the two friends who loved books, the main structure being designated the Thomas Jefferson Building and the newest the James Madison Annex.

Paradoxically, the Virginia friends, two "of the greatest theoreticians on the subject of human liberty,"[51] were also bound together by the ownership of slaves. Until the last twenty-five years, historians usually portrayed the Founding Fathers as being authentically committed to antislavery, even though Jefferson, Madison, Washington, and others owned slaves. George Washington, they pointed out, freed his slaves in his final will and testament, and the Revolutionary principles of liberty and equality announced in the Declaration of Independence put the peculiar institution on the road to extinction. Jefferson, the great champion of the inalienable rights of man, was thus the patron saint of antislavery thought.[52]

But this image of the Founding Fathers has been radically altered in the past quarter of a century by Robert McColley, Winthrop D. Jordan, Staughton Lynd, William Cohen, Donald L. Robinson, David Brion Davis, John T. Noonan, Jr., and John Chester Miller,[53] revisionists whom Professor Davis

---

48. JM to TJ, Apr. 27, 1785, below.

49. TJ to JM, Nov. 11, 1784, below.

50. See TJ to JM, Sept. 24, 1814, below, and JM to TJ, Oct. 10, 1814, below.

51. Kurt Vonnegut uses this phrase about TJ in *Breakfast of Champions* (New York, 1973), p. 34, cited in Stanley Katz, "Thomas Jefferson and the Right of Property in Revolutionary America," *Journal of Law and Economics* 19 (1976): 467.

52. I am indebted to William W. Freehling for this observation; see his article, "The Founding Fathers and Slavery," *AHR* 77 (1972): 81–93.

53. Robert McColley, *Slavery and Jeffersonian Virginia* (Urbana, Ill., 1964); Jordan (see n. 38, above); Staughton Lynd, *Class Conflict, Slavery, and the United States Constitution* (Indianapolis, 1968); William Cohen, "Thomas Jefferson and the Problem of Slavery," *JAH* 56 (1969): 503–26; Donald L. Robinson, *Slavery in the Structure of American Politics, 1765–1820* (New York, 1971); David Brion Davis, *The Problem of Slavery in the Age of Revolution, 1770–1823* (Ithaca, N.Y., 1975);

has called "debunkers—or more properly, the disillusionists."⁵⁴ In his pioneering study *Slavery and Jeffersonian Virginia,* McColley argues that "the years of slavery's supposed decline were in fact the years of its greatest expansion . . . a social and economic institution of such power that it sustained and extended an economic system whose demands went far to determine the domestic and foreign policy of the 'agrarian' party in our early history." In his brilliant book *White over Black,* Jordan analyzes Jefferson's deep-seated anti-Negro views and ambivalent feelings about his ownership of slaves violating his natural-rights philosophy. Although he credits Jefferson with "heartfelt hatred of slavery"—indeed, stresses his authentic commitment to antislavery—he concludes that Jefferson was intellectually paralyzed by racial prejudice. And in his distinguished study, Davis goes further, denying that Jefferson was an authentic opponent of slavery: "When the chips were down, as in the Missouri crisis, he threw his weight behind slavery's expansion."⁵⁵

Only William W. Freehling has ventured to revise the revisionists, cautioning that "the trouble with the new condemnatory view is not so much that it is a one-sided judgment of the Founding Fathers as that it distorts the process by which American slavery was abolished. The new charge that the Founding Fathers did next to nothing about bondage," he argues, "is as misleading as the older notion that they almost did everything." By viewing the abolitionist impulse as a long-term process from 1776 to 1860, he places Jefferson, Madison, and the Founding Fathers "back into the creeping American antislavery process," one that proceeded "slowly in part because of what Jefferson and his contemporaries did not do, inexorably in part because of what they did. The impact of the Founding Fathers on slavery, like the extent to which the American Revolution was revolutionary, must be seen in the long run not in terms of what changed in the late eighteenth century but in terms of how the Revolutionary experience changed the whole of American antebellum history."⁵⁶

No one denies that Jefferson's democratic ideals and Madison's republican faith were important to the antislavery cause. In principle, both men

---

John T. Noonan, Jr., *Persons and Masks of the Law: Cardozo, Holmes, Jefferson, and Wythe As Makers of the Masks* (New York, 1976); and John Chester Miller, *The Wolf by the Ears: Thomas Jefferson and Slavery* (New York, 1977).

54. D. B. Davis, p. 168.

55. McColley, pp. 3-4; Jordan, pp. 429-35; and D. B. Davis, p. 184.

56. Freehling, 82. More recently, Freehling has elaborated his appraisal of "the persistent 'antislavery'(?) tradition" that Jefferson epitomized, substituting for the questionable word "antislavery(?)" the concept of "Conditional Termination" of slavery, the condition being the removal of freed slaves from America, a proposal that he labels the "noxiously anti-republican side of 'Jeffersonian republicanism.'" Both Jefferson and Madison believed that their republican legacy "could, should, and would eventually lead blacks to be removed from republican America," using "the massive proceeds from federal land sales to free and colonize blacks." See Freehling's brilliant discussion "Conditional Termination in the Early Republic" in his *The Road to Disunion: Secessionists at Bay, 1776-1854* (New York, 1990), pp. 121-43, 583.

consistently condemned the peculiar institution throughout their extended public careers and their long years in retirement, dreaming of its ultimate extinction. In practice, they remained slaveholders throughout their long lives, with Jefferson manumitting only five slaves by his will in 1826 and Madison none in 1836.[57] Their antislavery conception of republicanism, a noble dream that they shared, was undermined by the fatal flaw of slave ownership, the tragic underside of that dream, for the rise of liberty and equality in America was accompanied by the rise of slavery.[58]

Throughout their lives, Jefferson and Madison were inextricably bound to slavery. Convinced of its immorality, hopeful of its eradication, depressed by its intractability, they were dependent throughout their lives on its perpetuation, both men destined to participate in a system that they abhorred, their early antislavery precepts ironically discounted by the practice of human bondage, their deeds at odds with their democratic dreams. Throughout their public careers, they believed that slavery was an evil so incongruous in a nation conceived in liberty and dedicated to the proposition that all men are created equal that it must some day be ended. Yet both lived on the profits generated by the labor of slaves; and when the profits dropped to deficits, their indebtedness prevented the emancipation of most of the slaves whom they had hoped to free.

As young men, both Jefferson and Madison took antislavery stands. Shortly after his election to the House of Burgesses in 1769, the twenty-six-year-old Jefferson persuaded Richard Bland, "one of the oldest, ablest, and most respected members," to propose "certain moderate extensions of the protection of the laws" to slaves, a move that led to the denunciation of Bland "as an enemy of his country." Because of his relative youth, Jefferson noted, he "was was spared in the debate."[59]

Between 1774 and 1784, Jefferson made several attacks on slavery and the slave trade, terms about which there was then "widespread confusion," as David B. Davis has pointed out. "Both American and British abolitionists," he observes, "assumed that an end to slave imports would lead automatically to the amelioration and gradual abolition of slavery."[60] In his *Summary View* (1774), Jefferson accused the British Crown of saddling slavery on the colonies and of refusing to allow the colonies to restrict or prohibit the slave trade, arguing that "the abolition of domestic slavery is the great object of desire in those colonies where it was unhappily introduced in their infant state."[61] In the Declaration of Independence, he wrote that "all men are created equal"

---

57. McCoy, pp. 317-22.
58. For a fascinating appraisal of this topic, see Edmund S. Morgan, "Slavery and Freedom: The American Paradox," *JAH* 59 (1972): 5-29.
59. David Brion Davis, *Was Thomas Jefferson an Authentic Enemy of Slavery?* (Oxford, 1970), p. 7.
60. D. B. Davis, *The Problem of Slavery in the Age of Revolution*, p. 129.
61. TJ, *A Summary View of the Rights of British America*, in *PTJ*, I, p. 130.

and are entitled to "Life, Liberty, and the pursuit of Happiness." By substituting "pursuit of happiness" for "property," which had been used by George Mason in the Virginia Declaration of Rights, he excluded by implication property in slaves from the rights of man and strengthened the case for including blacks among all men, who "are created equal." But he omitted any reference to abolition, concentrating instead on condemning George III for "[waging] cruel war against human nature itself, violating its most sacred rights of life and liberty in the persons of a distant people," establishing an "execrable commerce" and carrying black Africans into that "assemblage of horrors," "slavery in another hemisphere." After vehement objections by the South Carolina and Georgia delegations, however, Congress struck out this protest against the king and slavery.

Jefferson's draft of a Constitution for Virginia in 1776 included a clause prohibiting any future importation of slaves. In 1778, he supported—indeed, claimed responsibility for drafting—the Virginia bill abolishing the foreign slave trade, "leaving to future efforts . . . [the] final extinction" of slavery. But in his revision of the laws of Virginia, there were neither provisions to ameliorate the conditions of slaves nor any proposals to experiment with gradual emancipation.[62] In 1783, however, his draft of a new constitution for Virginia proposed gradual emancipation, providing for the freedom of all children born of slaves after 1800. And the next year, in the Land Ordinance of 1784, he urged Congress to exclude slaves from the western territories after the year 1800, a measure that failed, as he told Madison, by "an individual vote only. Ten states were present. The 4. Eastern states, [and] N. York, Pennsva. were for the clause. Jersey would have been for it, but there were but two members, one of whom was sick in his chambers." "Thus we see," Jefferson wrote two years later, "the fate of millions unborn hanging on the tongue of one man, and heaven was silent in that awful moment. But it is to be hoped it will not always be silent and that the friends to the rights of human nature will in the end prevail."[63]

Like Jefferson, Madison knew that slavery and liberty were antithetical and hoped for the gradual disappearance of the institution. While serving in the Continental Congress in 1780, he opposed a Virginia bill offering slaves as a recruiting bounty. "Would it not be as well to liberate and make soldiers at once of the blacks themselves as to make them instruments for enlisting White soldiers? It wd. certainly be more consonant to the principles of liberty which ought never to be lost sight of in a contest for liberty," he argued.[64] As his first term in Congress drew to an end in 1783, he concluded that his slave Billey, who had accompanied him to Philadelphia, had developed views on freedom that made him "too thoroughly tainted to be a fit companion for fellow slaves in Virginia." In Pennsylvania, Billey could become an indentured servant and

---

62. TJ, "Autobiography," in Ford, I, pp. 51–52. See also Noonan, pp. 29–64.
63. TJ to JM, Apr. 25, 1784, below, and TJ to Jean Nicolas Démeuniev, June 22, 1786, in *PTJ*, X, p. 58.
64. JM to Joseph Jones, Nov. 28, 1780, in *PJM*, II, p. 209.

attain freedom after seven years. Madison could not "think of punishing him . . . merely for coveting that liberty for which we have paid the price of so much blood, and have proclaimed so often to be right, and worthy the pursuit, of every human being."[65]

Back home again in Virginia after almost four years in Philadelphia, Madison turned to the study of law in order "to provide a decent and independent subsistence" since he hoped "to depend as little as possible on the labor of slaves."[66] In 1785, he helped defeat a bill abolishing the right of an owner to manumit individual slaves, but he failed in his effort to push through Jefferson's bill for gradual abolition of slavery.[67] According to an English observer, Madison "has had the humanity and the *courage* (for such a proposition requires no small share of courage), to propose a general emancipation of slaves."[68] Looking back thirty-five years later, Jefferson wrote in his "Autobiography" that "the public mind would not yet bear the proposition, nor will it bear it even at this day. Yet the day is not distant when it must bear and adopt it, or worse will follow."[69]

Jefferson's strongest stand against slavery was set forth in his *Notes on the State of Virginia,* which he began in 1781 while serving as governor of Virginia but did not publish until 1785 while American minister to France. He forcefully denounced "the whole commerce between master and slave" as "a perpetual exercise of the most boisterous passions, the most unremitting despotism on the one part, and degrading submission on the other." "Can the liberties of a nation be thought secure," he asked in the same paragraph, "when we have removed their only firm basis, a conviction in the minds of the people that these liberties are of the gift of God? That they are not to be violated but with his wrath? Indeed I tremble for my country when I reflect that God is just: that his justice cannot sleep for ever. . . . The Almighty has no attribute which can take side with us in such a contest." Jefferson concluded on an optimistic note, however, claiming that the Revolution had inaugurated a change that prepared the way, he hoped, "under the auspices of heaven, for a total emancipation," one that would be made "with the consent of the masters, rather than by their extirpation."[70]

For a man of Jefferson's convictions, Winthrop Jordan has written, "entanglement in Negro slavery was genuinely tragic."[71] Once he had cleared off his debts, he vowed in France, he planned to try "some plan of making their

---

65. JM to James Madison, Sr., Sept. 8, 1783, *ibid.,* VII, p. 304.
66. JM to Edmund Randolph, July 26, 1785, *ibid.*
67. See JM to Ambrose Madison, Dec. 15, 1785, in *PJM,* VIII, pp. 442-44; *PTJ,* II, pp. 470-73; Brant, II, pp. 360-61; and Jordan, pp. 552-53.
68. George Grieve, quoted in *Travels in North America in the Years 1780, 1781 and 1782 by the Marquis de Chastellux,* ed. Howard C. Rice, Jr., 2 vols. (Chapel Hill, 1963), II, p. 653.
69. TJ, "Autobiography," in Ford, I, p. 68.
70. William Peden, ed., *Notes on the State of Virginia, by Thomas Jefferson* (Chapel Hill, 1955; rpt. New York, 1982), pp. 162-63.
71. Jordan, pp. 430-31.

situation happier, determined to content myself," he added with a pre-Freudian slip of the pen, "with a small portion of their liberty labour."[72] But Jefferson never cleared off his debts.

Nor were Jefferson's antislavery views his only observations on Negroes in *Notes on the State of Virginia,* for he coupled his proposal for gradual abolition with one for the deportation and colonization of emancipated blacks. Jefferson believed that racial prejudice was a fixed fact of life in the United States. "Deep rooted prejudices entertained by the whites," he wrote, and "ten thousand recollections, by the blacks, of the injuries they have sustained" made it impossible for Negroes ever to be incorporated into white society on equal terms.[73] The reason for that, he thought, was "the real distinction which nature has made." Negroes were different physically, mentally, and temperamentally. They were, he suggested, inferior to whites, although he conceded that "it will be right to make great allowances for the difference of condition, of education, of conversation, of the sphere in which they move." But after making such allowances, he failed to find "that a black had uttered a thought above the level of plain narration"; nor had he seen a black with "even an elementary trait of painting or sculpture."[74]

Whether inferior or not, Jefferson later wrote, there was no justification for enslaving Negroes. "Whatever be their degree of talent it is no measure of their rights. Because Sir Isaac Newton was superior to others in understanding, he was not therefore lord of the person or property of others."[75] Slavery was a "blot in our country," a "great political and moral evil," but he hoped that "the minds of our citizens may be ripening for a complete emancipation of human nature."[76]

When emancipation came, however, Jefferson thought that the blacks "should be colonized to such a place as the circumstances of the time should render most proper," where they would become a "free and independant people." To replace them as laborers, vessels should be sent "at the same time to other parts of the world for an equal number of white inhabitants; to induce whom to migrate hither, proper encouragements were to be proposed. It will probably be asked," he wrote, anticipating the obvious question, "Why not retain and incorporate the blacks into the state, and thus save the expence of supplying, by importation of white settlers, the vacancies they will leave?"

Racial prejudice was his answer—white prejudice against blacks and black prejudice against whites. The two races could never live in harmony together, even if both were free, because one was inferior and that inferiority would

---

72. TJ to Francis Eppes, July 30, 1787, quoted *ibid.,* p. 432.
73. Peden, pp. 138–39.
74. *Ibid.,* pp. 139–40.
75. TJ to Henri Gregoire, Feb. 25, 1809, cited in Jordan, p. 454.
76. Peden, p. 87.

spread to the white race in case of miscegenation. Separation of the races by colonizing the blacks in Africa or Haiti would remove the temptation of miscegenation and preserve the experiment in republican government for those who had inaugurated it—the white citizens of the nation. Jefferson, therefore, consistently linked emancipation with colonization, removing the black population beyond "the mixture of colour."[77]

Aware that his bald statements seemed to condemn blacks to an inferior place based on biology, Jefferson, in his concluding remarks, had sober second thoughts on Negroes and slavery, denying any intention to "degrade a whole race of men from the rank in the scale of beings which their Creator may perhaps have given them." What he had at first reported as proof, he now set forth as a tentative hypothesis—not necessarily a factual analysis, but a theory, advanced "as a suspicion only, that the blacks, whether originally a distinct race, or made distinct by time and circumstances, are inferior to the whites in the endowments both of body and mind."[78]

Such an opinion, he acknowledged, "must be hazarded with great diffidence. To justify a general conclusion, requires many observations," especially when one is examining "a faculty, not a substance . . . where it eludes the research of all the senses."[79] Nonetheless, Winthrop Jordan writes, Jefferson's judgment "on the matter, with all its confused tentativeness, stood as the strongest suggestion of inferiority expressed by any native American" until that time.[80] At the same time, however, Jordan observes that Jefferson also "left to Americans something else which may in the long run have been of greater importance—his prejudice for freedom and his larger equalitarian faith."[81] And John Chester Miller, whose book *The Wolf by the Ears: Thomas Jefferson and Slavery* is the most extensive study of the subject, concludes that "the significance of the *Notes on Virginia* is not that Jefferson presented a brief for black inferiority but that he demanded the extinction of slavery. . . . The institution of slavery was not set above the principles proclaimed in 1776."[82]

Unlike Jefferson, Madison seems never to have said that blacks as a race were inferior to whites. His analysis of their degraded condition suggested instead that it stemmed from the "repugnance of the whites" to blacks, whether slave or free, a view "founded on prejudices, themselves founded on physical distinctions, which are not likely soon, if ever, to be eradicated." It

77. *Ibid.*, p. 138; TJ to William Short, Jan. 18, 1826, cited in Jordan, p. 467.
78. Peden, pp. 142–43.
79. *Ibid.*, p. 143.
80. Jordan, p. 455.
81. *Ibid.*, p. 481.
82. John C. Miller, "Slavery," in Peterson, *Thomas Jefferson: A Reference Biography,* p. 426. For a stimulating assessment of why a slaveholder should be the nation's most eloquent champion of equality, see Douglas L. Wilson, "Thomas Jefferson and the Character Issue," *Atlantic* 270 (Nov. 1992): 57–74.

was the ineradicable nature of white prejudice, not black inferiority, that swayed Madison to Jefferson's proposal to transport blacks back to Africa. Emancipation, which he favored, had to be accompanied by removal of the blacks because "the objections to a thorough incorporation of the two people are, with most of the whites, insuperable; and are admitted by all of them to be very powerful. If the blacks, strongly marked as they are by physical and lasting peculiarities, be retained amid the whites, under the degrading privation of equal rights, political or social, they must be always dissatisfied with their condition, as a change only from one to another species of oppression; always secretly confederated against the ruling and privileged class; and always uncontrolled by some of the most cogent motives to moral and respectable conduct. . . . Nor is it fair, in estimating the danger of collisions with the whites, to charge it wholly on the side of the blacks. There would be reciprocal antipathies doubling the danger."[83]

In 1789, Madison wrote that if emancipation were to be "eligible as well to the Society as to the Slaves, a compleat incorporation of the latter into the former should result from manumission." In theory, the freed slaves were rightly entitled to full incorporation, or integration, into the republic. In practice, however, this was "rendered impossible" not from any fault of the blacks, but "by the prejudices of the Whites, prejudices which proceeding principally from the difference of colour must be considered as permanent and insuperable."

For that reason, Madison early on coupled emancipation with the creation of "some proper external receptable" for slaves "restored to freedom." If such an asylum could be found in Africa, he wrote, it might make possible a general emancipation, for it would probably "prove a great encouragement to manumission in the Southern" states. In short, it might "afford the best hope yet presented of putting an end to the slavery in which not less than 600,000 unhappy negroes are now involved."[84]

Madison, therefore, joined and later became president of the American Colonization Society, which proposed to establish a colony in Africa for American blacks who were already free or who might be emancipated. The society should be given "encouragement from all who regard slavery as an evil, who wish to see it diminished and abolished by peaceable and just means, and who have themselves no better mode to propose." To make "the great mass of blacks" eligible for participation, he proposed that the federal government, once empowered by an appropriate amendment to the Constitution, establish a fund by selling off western land to pay the enormous cost of a program of general emancipation and relocation.[85]

---

83. JM to Robert J. Evans, June 15, 1819, cited in McCoy, p. 279. McCoy's excellent book is the first systematic study of Madison's views on slavery.

84. JM, "Memorandum on an African Colony for Freed Slaves," ca. Oct. 20, 1789, in *PJM*, XII, pp. 437–38; cited in McCoy, pp. 283–84.

85. JM to Robert J. Evans, June 15, 1819, cited *ibid.*, pp. 276–81.

At almost the same time that he published his *Notes on the State of Virginia* in 1785, Jefferson retreated from participation in the antislavery movement to the sidelines, leaving the younger generation to work for the gradual abolition of the "hideous evil" of slavery. "Not a man on earth" desired emancipation more than he did, nor was anyone more prepared to make any sacrifice to "relieve us from this heavy reproach in any practicable way," he wrote, but the public mind would not yet "bear the proposition." Only when the slaves's groans "shall have involved heaven itself in darkness" would a god of justice "awaken to their distress." Fortunately, he added much too optimistically, "nearly the whole of the young men" in Virginia were joining the antislavery cause "as fast as they come into public life."[86]

One of those younger men was James Madison, who was busily engaged in pushing Jefferson's revision of the laws of Virginia through the state legislature. Although Jefferson later claimed that on the floor of the House of Delegates he and the committee of revisers had drafted an amendment for gradual emancipation and colonization, it was never submitted to the legislature, nor has a copy of the draft survived. Madison did notify George Washington that a petition on general manumission had been submitted; and although it had "an avowed patronage of its principle by sundry respectable members," it was rejected without dissent. Indeed, "a motion was made to throw it under the table, which was treated with as much indignation on one side as the petition itself was on the other." Moreover, there were several petitions "against any step towards freeing the Slaves, and even praying for the repeal of the law [of 1782] which licenses particular manumissions."[87]

The federal Constitution, which was drafted in part by Madison, valued the Union more than abolition, not only recognizing slavery, but prohibiting the federal government from interfering with the foreign slave trade for twenty years. Nonetheless, Madison was opposed to any mention of slavery, contending at the Philadelphia convention that although the property rights of slaveholders should be protected, it would be "wrong to admit" in the specific language of the Constitution "the idea that there can be property in men." Throughout his long life, his biographer Drew McCoy has written, Madison "never wavered for a moment in utterly condemning the institution," finding it incompatible with a democratic form of government.[88]

Two years after drafting the Bill of Rights, Madison outlined his thoughts on instances that demonstrate "the danger of oppression to the minority from unjust combinations of the majority," citing "the case of Black slaves in Modern times." As the early leader of the Republican party, organized to protest publicly against what he condemned as aristocratic tendencies of the Federal-

---

86. *PTJ*, X, pp. 61–63.
87. JM to George Washington, Nov. 11, 1785, in *PJM*, VIII, pp. 403–4. For the petitions against freeing slaves, see Fredrika Teute Schmidt and Barbara Ripel Wilhelm, "Early Proslavery Petitions in Virginia," *WMQ* 30 (1973): 133–46.
88. . McCoy, p. 260.

ists, he noted privately that "in proportion as slavery prevails in a State, the Government, however democratic in name, must be aristocratic in fact." This meant that "the Southern States of America" were "aristocracies," where slavery illustrated "the danger of oppression to the minority from unjust combinations of the majority" because power was concentrated "much more into the hands of [people of] property, than in the Northern States."[89]

But Madison omitted these passages from his newspaper essays, knowing that his views would furnish the Federalists with arguments too true to be denied. Neither in public nor in private, however, did he deny that slaves were human beings whose natural rights should be restored in a republican system. When—not if—cleansed of the stain of slavery, America's republican example would become an even brighter beacon of hope for the rest of the world, for emancipation would remove the ground for "the taunts to which this misfortune exposes us in Europe."[90] Throughout his life, he continued to hope "that the time will come when the dreadful calamity" of slavery would end, "thus giving to our Country the full enjoyment of the blessings of liberty and to the world the full benefit of its great example."[91]

After the Missouri Compromise admitted Missouri as a slave state but banned slavery north of the line 36°30′, both Jefferson and Madison subscribed to the theory of "diffusion," although Madison's support was more tentative than Jefferson's. Madison's advocacy of diffusing slaves throughout the West, a view he had not held before 1808, turned upon the constitutional provision that allowed, but did not require, Congress to abolish the slave trade twenty years after ratification of the federal charter. In his presidential message to Congress on December 2, 1806, Jefferson enthusiastically urged the implementation of this provision, congratulating his fellow citizens and their representatives "on the approach of the period when you may interpose your authority constitutionally" to bar Americans throughout the Union "from all further participation in those violations of human rights which have been so long continued on the unoffending inhabitants of Africa, and which the morality, the reputation, and the best interests of our country have long been eager to proscribe."[92] In 1807, Congress followed Jefferson's recommendation, prohibiting the slave trade after January 1, 1808, a law that William Freehling has called "one of the most important acts an American Congress ever passed."[93]

Once the importation of slaves was prohibited, the growth of this institution was limited to the natural increase of slaves already living in the United

---

89. See JM's notes for essays in the *National Gazette*, 1791–1792, in *PJM*, XIV, pp. 160–64. McCoy, pp. 234–36, has a discerning discussion of JM's views.
90. JM to the marquis de Lafayette, Nov. 1826, cited in McCoy, p. 264.
91. JM to R. R. Gurley, Dec. 28, 1831, cited *ibid.*, p. 265.
92. Richardson, I, p. 396.
93. Freehling, "The Founding Fathers and Slavery," 88.

States. That changed things considerably, as Madison pointed out. When the Confederation Congress had barred slavery from the Northwest Territory in 1787, "the importation of slaves was rapidly going on, and the only mode of checking [the increase of their numbers] was by narrowing the space open to them," a move that Madison supported. With importation shut off after 1808, Madison thought that diffusing slaves among the "greater masses of free people" in the West would not add to the number of slaves, but would reduce racial tensions, encourage more humane treatment of the dispersed slaves, and ease fears about the consequences of emancipation. In general, he thought that the treatment of slaves was most humane when they were held in small numbers and harshest when they were held in large numbers. By reducing the density of the slave population relative to the number of whites, as had been the case in post-Revolutionary Pennsylvania, New Jersey, and New York, where slavery had been abolished, the movement towards "a general emancipation" would be greatly "accelerated."[94] He, therefore, concluded that "an uncontrouled dispersion of the slaves now in the United States was not only best for the nation, but most favourable for the slaves, also both as to their prospects of emancipation, and as to their condition in the meantime."[95]

Although Jefferson and Madison did not discuss the "diffusionist theory" in their exchange of letters, they must have reviewed it extensively when they were together at Monticello or Montpellier, for their views were remarkably similar on that subject. "All know that permitting the slaves of the South to spread into the West," Jefferson told the marquis de Lafayette, "will not add one being to that unfortunate condition, that it will increase the happiness of those existing, and by spreading them over a larger surface, will dilute the evil every where, and facilitate the means of getting finally rid of it, an event more anxiously wished by those on whom it presses than by the noisy pretenders to exclusive humanity."[96]

Writing his "Autobiography" in the same year that he wrote to Lafayette, Jefferson said that "nothing is more certainly written in the book of fate than that these people are to be free" and, he added, that they were to leave the United States. Five years later, during the final year of his life, he revived and revised his plan for gradual abolition, shifting the responsibility from the states to the United States, after the Constitution had been amended to authorize the payment of the costs of emancipation and transportation of the slaves to a new land (Jefferson now preferred Haiti to Liberia) for colonization. Like Madison, he thought that part of the costs could be covered by the sale of western lands. By now, a confirmed states' righter on most issues, he nonetheless concluded that constitutional issues raised by his proposal could be easily resolved. "A liberal construction, justified by the object, may go far," he

94. McCoy, pp. 268–69.
95. JM to James Monroe, Feb. 23, 1820, cited *ibid.*, p. 272.
96. JM to the marquis de Lafayette, Dec. 26, 1820, cited *ibid.*, pp. 269–70. See Miller's chapter on TJ's views, "The Diffusion of Slavery," in *The Wolf by the Ears*, pp. 234–42.

wrote, "and an amendment of the Constitution, the whole length necessary" to dispose of such questions.[97]

If Jefferson and Madison are judged by their words rather than their acts, they may rightfully be accorded a place in the antislavery movement. Jefferson's contribution was to tie emancipation to the Declaration of Independence. For Madison, too, the transforming effects of the Revolution condemned slavery to ultimate extinction, and he never stopped "acknowledging, without limitation or hesitation, all the evils with which it has been charged," views that impressed the British abolitionist Harriet Martineau when she visited him in the last year of his life.[98]

Despite their principled antislavery views, however, both Jefferson and Madison accommodated themselves to the practice of slavery, knowing that their republican dream was tragically flawed by the existence of slavery in a system founded on liberty and equality. Jefferson had called the Missouri crisis "a Firebell in the Night" tolling the "knell of the Union" unless the "momentous question" of slavery was resolved. "I regret that I am now to die in the belief that the useless sacrifice of themselves by the generation of 1776, to acquire self government and happiness in their country, is to be thrown away by the unwise and unworthy passions of their sons, and that my only consolation is to be, that I live not to weep over it."[99]

The ambiguous antislavery posture of Jefferson and Madison grew out of the Revolutionary tradition that combined their radical ideal of human liberty with their conservative institution of Negro slavery, an incompatible mix containing the seeds of a tragic catastrophe, one that was to plunge the heroic creation of the Founding Fathers into the greatest crisis in American history a quarter of a century after Madison's death in 1836.[100]

Throughout their long and intimate friendship, Jefferson and Madison maintained a high regard for the independent judgment of the other. Even in retirement, when they were working together to found the University of Virginia, "it was beautiful to witness the deference that was paid by Mr. Jefferson and Mr. Madison to each other's opinions," acording to Dr. Robley Dungli-

---

97. Miller, *The Wolf by the Ears,* pp. 266–72.

98. For Martineau's visit, see McCoy, pp. 1–6, 261.

99. TJ to John Holmes, Apr. 22, 1820, in Ford, X, p. 158.

100. For a careful analysis of JM's role in accommodating the Constitution to slavery as it existed in 1787, see Paul Finkelman, "Slavery and the Constitutional Convention: Making a Covenant with Death," in *Beyond Confederation: Origins of the Constitution and America National Identity,* ed. Richard Beeman, Stephen Botein, and Edward C. Carter II (Chapel Hill, 1987), pp. 188–225. For an analysis of TJ's ambiguous antislavery stance, see Charles L. Griswold, Jr., "Rights and Wrongs: Jefferson, Slavery, and Philosophical Quandaries," in *A Culture of Rights: The Bill of Rights in Philosophy, Politics, and Law, 1791 and 1991*, ed. Michael J. Lacey and Knud Haakonssen (New York, 1991), pp. 144–214, and essays by Lucia C. Stanton, Paul Finkelman and Scot A. French and Edward L. Ayer, in *Jeffersonian Legacies,* ed. Peter S. Onuf (Charlottesville, 1993), pp. 147–221, 418–56.

son, professor of medicine at the university. "When, as secretary, and as chairman of the faculty, I had to consult one of them," he recalled, "it was a common interrogatory—what did the other say of the matter? If possible, Mr. Madison gave indications of a greater intensity of this feeling; and seemed to think, that everything emanating from his ancient associate must be corret."[101]

But the generally harmonious relationship between Jefferson and Madison was occasionally ruffled by muffled notes of discord. Their dialogue on the Constitution reflected their differing views of human nature and the equation between liberty and authority, with Madison, rooted in Congress, stressing a realistic assessment of politics and government, and Jefferson, uprooted in Paris, taking a more philosophical and idealistic view.

In the early years of their friendship, both were advocates of a stronger national government, just as both favored a stronger state executive to check and balance the power of the Virginia House of Delegates, "an elective despotism," as Jefferson called it in his *Notes on the State of Virginia*. As a member of Congress, Madison had perceived the infirmities of the Confederation at close range, while Jefferson, in France, saw them from an international perspective: "All respect for our government is annihilated on this side of the water, from an idea of its want of tone and energy."[102] The Americans, he lamented, were "the lowest and most obscure of the whole diplomatic tribe."

When Jefferson saw the roster of delegates to the convention in Philadelphia, he called the gathering "an assembly of demigods." But when he first read the radically new Constitution, he was temporarily stunned, having expected "three or four new articles to be added to the good, old, and venerable fabric," the Articles of Confederation, "which should have been preserved even as a religious relique." Indeed, he thought the convention had sent up "a kite to keep the hen yard in order."[103]

But while Jefferson at first thought that too much power had been granted the new government, Madison feared that not enough had been assigned. He especially regretted the failure to include the power of Congress to veto state laws. In a remarkable letter to Jefferson, written only a month after the Philadelphia convention had adjourned, he outlined his tough-minded view that the countervailing forces of self-interest and ambition, not public virtue, were the sources of political stability.

Madison linked his defense of the national negative with his innovative theory of the extended republic, the key to the creation of a free and expansive nation designed to protect "individuals against encroachments on their rights." The chief advantage of a large republic over a small one, he empha-

---

101. Robley Dunglison, *The Autobiographical Ana of Robley Dunglison, M. D.*, ed. Samuel X. Radbill, *Transactions* (American Philosophical Society) n.s. 53, p. 8 (1963): 34.
102. Peterson, pp. 300, 302.
103. TJ to John Adams, Nov. 13, 1787, in Cappon, I, p. 212, and Peterson, p. 359.

sized, was the fact that it encompassed a greater number of "various and unavoidable" interests, classes, groups, parties, and factions, based on differing "political, religious and other opinions," who were scattered over a more extensive geographical sphere of government so that "no common interest or passion will be likely to unite a majority of the whole number in an unjust pursuit" such as encroachment on individual liberties or private rights. "In a large Society," Madison explained to his friend in Paris, "the people are broken into so many interests and parties, that a common sentiment is less likely to be felt, and the requisite concept less likely to be formed, by a majority of the whole." In creating a free and representative republic, he argued, divide and conquer, "the reprobated axiom of tyranny, is under certain qualifications, the only policy, by which a republic can be administered on just principles."[104]

Had Jefferson responded to the philosophical part of Madison's letter, he would have been hard put to square it with his view of human nature and public virtue. But he avoided the possibility of a basic philosophical disagreement by skipping over Madison's discussion of a federal negative on state laws, which he had already rejected because the patch did not match the hole. Instead, he concentrated on the absence of a bill of rights, a challenge that Madison quickly accepted. A reservation of rights, he argued, was unnecessary and improper in a constitution of limited and specified powers; the government had no authority in the area of individual rights. Any attempt to define such rights also ran the risk of omitting rights unnamed. Moreover, parchment guarantees too often were not worth the parchment they were written on. Finally, the argument for such guarantees was based on the flawed idea that government was the enemy, instead of the guarantor, of liberty. The Declaration of Independence, after reciting the trinity of life, liberty, and the pursuit of happiness, made the point: "To secure these rights, governments are instituted among men." "In our Governments," Madison declared, "the real power lies in the majority of the community, and the invasion of private rights is chiefly to be apprehended, not from acts of Government contrary to the sense of its constituents, but from acts in which the Government is the mere instrument of the major number of the constituents."

After his first reaction to the Constitution, Jefferson quickly became friendlier to it, even without a bill of rights, ultimately calling it "the wisest ever yet presented to man."[105] He favored its adoption, therefore, calling for ratification by the nine required states, thus establishing the new government, but suggesting that the other four hold out until a bill of rights was enacted. Such guarantees, Jefferson insisted, are "what the people are entitled to against every government on earth, general or particular, and what no just government should refuse, or rest on inferences."

Madison was irritated with Jefferson's critique of the Constitution not

---

104. JM to TJ, Oct. 24, 1787, below.
105. TJ to David Humphreys, Mar. 18, 1789, in *PTJ,* XIV, p. 678.

because of the intellectual exchange between the two on a bill of rights, but because Antifederalists in Virginia and North Carolina, in their efforts to block ratification, used Jefferson's letters written to others. Patrick Henry, who had long been an opponent of both Madison and Jefferson in combating the Virginia Statute for Religious Freedom, cited "this illustrious citizen [who] advises you to reject this government till it be amended." Henry's effort failed in Virginia because Madison cited Jefferson's growing support for the Constitution, but in North Carolina Jefferson's letters were a factor in the defeat of ratification at the first convention.

Although Madison avoided a confrontation with Jefferson, he wrote a sharp reply to a mutual friend in Paris who was also critical of the Constitution, knowing that his views would be quickly relayed to Jefferson:

> Had you been a member of that assembly [the Constitutional Convention], and been impressed with the truths that our situation discloses, you would have concurred in the necessity which was felt by the other members. In your closet in Paris and with the evils resulting from too much Government all over Europe fully in your view, it is natural for you to run into criticisms dictated by an extreme on that side. Perhaps in your situation I should think and feel as you do. In mine I am sure you would think and feel as I do.[106]

In one instance, Madison seemed almost Jeffersonian in trying to avoid a frontal clash with his philosophical friend in France, not referring to his authorship of some of the *Federalist* papers until they were published in book form, even though he had sent Washington copies of the individual essays from the beginning. In his letter about his desire for a national negative of state laws, Madison had sketched his interest-centered scheme for extending the sphere of republican government, an idea that he elaborated in his famous *Federalist* Number 10. But Jefferson had not responded to that presentation of the core of Madison's political system.

Several months later, in *Federalist* Number 49, Madison revealed to the public an important area of disagreement with Jefferson, who had never liked the Virginia Constitution of 1776 because it had not been submitted to the people for ratification. Madison, who had been in the Virginia legislature that promulgated the Constitution of 1776, agreed that *acquiescence* was not the proper basis for the fundamental law of the commonwealth. But he disagreed with a provision in the substitute constitution outlined by Jefferson as the new basis of state government that he had appended to his *Notes on the State of Virginia*. After praising his friend for his efforts on behalf of popular government, Madison attacked Jefferson's proposal for periodic constitutional revision through conventions elected by the people after endorsement by two branches of government. Madison thought that periodic appeals to the people for constant remodeling of government would too often excite "the public passions" and thus "deprive the government of that veneration which time

---

106. JM to Philip Mazzei, Oct. 8, 1788, in *PJM,* XI, pp. 278–79.

bestows on everything, and without which perhaps the wisest and freest government would not possess the requisite stability." Agreeing that frequent appeals to the reason of man might work in "a nation of philosophers"—a distinct jab at Jefferson and his fellow philosophes in Paris—he realistically added that "a nation of philosophers is as little to be expected as the philosophical race of kings wished for by Plato." Madison, who was in the midst of a bitterly contested controversy about *establishing* a new government and fending off Antifederalist attempts to call a second federal convention to replace the work of the first, was clearly in no mood to favor frequent revisions of the fundamental law.[107]

The same issue came up two years later in a purely theoretical discussion between Jefferson and Madison. While watching the beginnings of the French Revolution in 1789, Jefferson wrote a fascinating letter to Madison about the sovereignty of the living generation, arguing " *'that the earth belongs in usufruct to the living'*: that the dead have neither powers nor rights over it." According to Jefferson's actuarial calculations, the life of a generation during its majority spanned nineteen years. Applying these two propositions, he concluded that "no society can make a perpetual constitution, or even a perpetual law. The earth belongs always to the living generation.... The constitution and the laws of their predecessors [are] extinguished ... in their natural course with those who gave them being.... Every constitution then, and every law, naturally expires at the end of 19 years. If it be enforced longer, it is an act of force, and not of right."

Although formulated as a theoretical proposition in France, Jefferson hoped that Madison, recently elected to the first federal Congress under the new Constitution, could make it a preamble to early legislation and thus "exclude at the threshold of our new government the contagious and ruinous errors of this quarter of the globe, which have armed despots with means, not sanctioned by nature, for binding in chains their fellow men."

Madison flatly, though politely and softly, rejected the proposal. He thought the presentation a brilliant philosophical disquisition, although he doubted that it was "in *all* respects compatible with the course of human affairs." As he had done in *The Federalist* Number 49, he suggested that public passions would generate constitutional controversies, conflict, and disorder, creating an interregnum every nineteen years. Even if it were true that the earth in a state of nature belonged to the living generation, "the *improvements* made by the dead form a charge against the living who take the benefit of them."

Moreover, the implementation of the generational theory would not only be impractical, it would be impossible since generations do not spring up instantly in self-contained units every nineteen years. Unlike Jefferson's static

---

107. See Merrill D. Peterson's *Jefferson and Madison and the Making of Constitutions* (Charlottesville, 1987) for a brief but brilliant analysis.

INTRODUCTION: AN INTIMATE FRIENDSHIP                                    31

model, the generations changed constantly—even daily and hourly—as new members joined society and old members were subtracted from it, with the laws, the lands, and the constitution descending from the dead to the living, who gave their tacit assent to these obligations.

After demolishing Jefferson's theory with stubborn realities, Madison tried to smooth things over by assuring him that the response was not meant to challenge the bolder truths contained in the "great plan"—it was a beautiful theory. But, he added from the new national capital in New York City, it would be some time before such truths, "seen thro' the medium of Philosophy, become visible to the naked eye of the ordinary Politician."[108]

But Madison was no ordinary politician or ordinary friend. When he and Jefferson were reunited in 1790, one in Congress, the other in the cabinet, they soon joined in opposition to the Hamiltonian measures of the Federalist administration. Jefferson, like Madison, became a practical politician, opposing Hamilton's plan for creating a national bank. Both men agreed on the need for a strict interpretation of the Constitution, Madison publicly in Congress and Jefferson privately in his memoranda to President Washington. From that time, they cooperated as leaders of the emerging "republican interest," which became the Republican, or Democratic-Republican, party. Although they were in broad general agreement on political principles, Madison was more moderate than the doctrinaire Jefferson, the closer student of constitutional nuances and more open to interpretation of the 6,000 words in the Constitution.

While Jefferson was still in France, Madison had kicked off the first debate in Congress on constitutional construction when he wrote a provision to the legislation that created the State Department (which Jefferson was soon to head). This provision authorized the president to remove the secretary of state. The Constitution vested in the president the power to appoint executive officers with the advice and consent of the Senate, but it made no mention of the removal power. Should the Senate be consulted on removals? Stressing the rights and the responsibilities of the chief executive, Madison said no and argued for presidential power. Thus, almost from the beginning, an unwritten constitution based on interpretation has grown up beside the written document.

Indeed, Madison was always more flexible in his constitutional views than Jefferson. Although he, like Jefferson, had opposed the constitutionality of the Bank of the United States in 1791, he advocated the reestablishment of a second national bank in 1815 after the nearly disastrous difficulty of financing the War of 1812 without one, and he signed the bill rechartering the bank in 1816. When the Federalists clamped down on political opposition with the Alien and Sedition Acts in 1798, Madison's protest—the Virginia resolutions—counseled "interposition," while Jefferson's used the fatal word "nul-

108. See TJ to JM, Sept. 6, 1789, below, and JM to TJ, Feb. 4, 1790, below.

lification," although he did not use it then or later in the way that Calhoun and the nullifiers did.

The sharpest disagreement between Jefferson and Madison in the 1790s came when Jefferson, in retirement at Monticello, read about Madison's proposal in 1796 to survey the national post road from Maine to Georgia, the commencement of an extensive work of establishing post roads for an expanding postal service. Jefferson viewed the development with alarm, arguing that "the power to *establish* post roads" merely involved the designation of roads already in existence, not the construction of new ones.

"If the term be equivocal, (and I really do not think it so) which is the safest construction?" he asked. Since America's roads were "the best in the world except those of France and England," he denied that "the state of our population, the extent of our internal commerce, [or] the want of sea and river navigation" required federal expenditures on them. Moreover, he did not think "our means adequate to it." Finally, such federal outlays would open the door to corruption—"a source of boundless patronage to the executive, jobbing to members of Congress and their friends, and a bottomless abyss of public money"—and a standing invitation to further spending. Congress would move from the post-office surplus, which Madison had proposed to tap for $5,000, to other sources of revenue, creating "a scene of eternal scramble among the members who can get the most money wasted in their state, and they will always get most who are meanest." If federal funding were necessary, Jefferson thought that a constitutional "amendment, securing still due measure and proportion among us," was necessary, one that gave Congress "some means of information" about the need for the post roads as well as a report based on visual inspection of the site.[109]

Madison was not swayed by Jefferson's alarm. His proposition, he assured his friend, did not involve "any dangerous consequences. It is limited to the choice of roads where that is presented, and to the opening [of] them, in other cases, so far only as may be necessary for the transportation of the mail. This I think," he concluded matter-of-factly, is "fairly within the object of the Constn. [Constitution]."[110]

It was not until both patriarchs had retired from the presidency that they had their sharpest disagreement since their spirited exchange about the sovereignty of the living generation. Both had long been alarmed by Chief Justice John Marshall's expansive and nationalistic rulings on the Supreme Court, with Jefferson veering off in the direction of states' rights politics and the "principles of '98" of the Old Republicans, and Madison, for all of his alarm about Marshall's obiter dicta, holding fast to the position he had staked out in *The Federalist* in 1787–1788. Jefferson denied the authority of the Supreme Court to decide constitutional controversies between the states and the

109. TJ to JM, Mar. 6, 1796, below. For TJ's changing views on the constitutionality of internal improvements, see Joseph H. Harrison, Jr., "*Sic et non:* Thomas Jefferson and Internal Improvement," *JER* 7 (1987): 335–49.
110. JM to TJ, Apr. 4, 1796, below.

Union, just as he had earlier rejected the supremacy of the Court to decide constitutional questions for the other branches of the federal government. "The judiciary of the United States," he wrote in 1820, "is the subtle corps of sappers and miners constantly working under ground to undermine the foundations of our confederated fabric. They are construing our Constitution from a general and special government to a general and supreme one alone. This will lay all things at their feet." Although he at first kept his criticism confined to personal letters, he finally yielded to pressure from the Old Republican clique and publicly endorsed John Taylor's attack on the Marshall Court for upholding the constitutionality of the second Bank of the United States, which Madison had established in 1816. Taylor's denial of the Court's power, Jefferson declared, was "the true political faith, to which every catholic republican should stedfastly hold."[111]

Judicial independence seemed to the ancient author of the Declaration of Independence an anomaly in a democratic system: "Independence can be trusted nowhere but in the people in mass." The Supreme Court did not have the power to decide issues arising in the federal system; the Constitution was "a compact of many independent powers, every single one of which claims an equal right to understand it, and to require its observance. However strong the cord of compact may be," Jefferson warned ominously, "there is a point of tension at which it will break."[112] The ultimate arbiter was not the Supreme Court but the people, acting in their supreme capacity in conventions. Since the Constitution had been established by the people of two-thirds of the states, acting in specially elected ratification conventions, a similar majority acting in a similar capacity could decide controverted questions: "Let them decide to which they mean to give an authority claimed by two of their organs."[113]

More protective of the constitutional fabric that he had helped create and more knowledgeable about the political process by which it was ratified, Madison thought that the reference of "every point of disagreement to the people in Conventions would be a process too tardy, too troublesome, and too expensive; besides its tendency to lessen a salutary veneration for an Instrument so often calling for such explanatory interpositions." If the ultimate arbiter were the states, he observed, the Constitution and the laws of the United States would surely be interpreted differently in different states and would thus destroy "that equality and uniformity of rights and duties which form the essence of the Compact." Moreover, conflicting decisions between the state and nation would ultimately have to be settled by force. "The end must be a trial of

---

111. For TJ's criticism of Marshall, see TJ to Thomas Ritchie, Dec. 25, 1820, in Ford, X, p. 170; for his endorsement of Taylor's book, see TJ to Spencer Roane, June 27, 1821, *ibid.*, pp. 189-90. There is a good brief discussion in Malone, VI, pp. 354-58. For a controversial revisionist argument, see David E. Engdahl, "John Marshall's 'Jeffersonian' Concept of Judicial Review," *Duke Law Journal* 42 (1992): 279-339

112. Peterson, pp. 994-95.

113. See TJ to William Johnson, June 12, 1823, enclosed in TJ to JM, June 13, 1823, below.

strength between the [federal] Posse headed by the Marshal and the [state] Posse headed by the Sheriff."[114]

But Madison had always believed that the Constitution itself resolved the question of where the ultimate authority lay to decide disputes about state and federal authority. "Believing as I do," he told Jefferson, "that the General Convention regarded a provision within the Constitution for deciding in a peaceable and regular mode all cases arising in the course of its operation, as essential to an adequate System of Gov$^t$: that it intended the Authority vested in the Judicial Department as a final resort in relation to the States, for cases resulting to it in the exercise of its functions, . . . and that this intention is expressed by the articles declaring that the federal Constitution and laws shall be the supreme law of the land, and that the Judicial Power of the U. S. shall extend to all cases arising under them: . . . thus believing[,] I have never yielded my original opinion indicated in the "Federalist" N$^o$ 39 to the ingenious reasonings of Col: [John] Taylor ag$^{st}$ this construction of the Constitution."[115]

Then to soften his disagreement with Jefferson, Madison agreed that the tendency of the Marshall Court, both by its decisions as well as by its "extrajudicial reasonings and dicta . . . to enlarge the general authority in derogation of the local, and to amplify its own jurisdiction," was not what he and the Founders had expected. "But," he quickly added, "the abuse of a trust does not disprove its existence. And if no remedy for the abuse be practicable under the forms of the Constitution, I should prefer a resort to the Nation for an amendment of the Tribunal itself, to continued appeals from its controverted decisions to that Ultimate Arbiter."

However, it was clear that Madison thought no such amendment was necessary. To make that point, he enclosed for Jefferson's perusal two letters that he had written to Spencer Roane, chief justice of the Virginia Court of Appeals, who had blasted Marshall's opinions in a series of newspaper articles signed "Algernon Sidney." Acknowledging that "the Gordian Knot of the Constitution seems to lie in the problem of collision between the federal and State powers, especially as eventually exercised by their respective Tribunals," he told the Virginia judge that he had "always thought . . . that on the abstract question whether the federal or the State decisions ought to prevail, the sounder policy would yield to the claims of the former." If the power to settle federal-state disagreements were vested in the states individually, the Constitution would have a different meaning in every state, and "the State Gov$^{ts}$ would not stand all in the same relation to the General Gov$^t$, . . . and the vital principle of equality, which cements their Union [would] thus gradually be deprived of its virtue."[116] If this trust was "vested in the Gov$^t$ represent-

114. JM to TJ, June 27, 1823, below.
115. *Ibid.*
116. JM to Spencer Roane, June 29, 1821, enclosed in JM to TJ, June 27, 1823, below.

ing the whole," however, no such adverse consequences would result. Madison hoped that state and federal judicial opinions would vary less and less on judicial subjects "and thereby mutually contribute to the clearer and firmer establishment of the true boundaries of power, on which must depend the success and permanency of the federal republic, the best Guardian, as we believe, of the liberty, the safety, and the happiness of men."[117]

Towards the end of his life, Jefferson moved closer to the vehement states' rights advocates.[118] But Madison, in one case, exercised his notable powers of persuasion to prevent Jefferson from making his views public. Worried about President John Quincy Adams's proposals to fund internal improvements, Jefferson dashed off a "solemn Declaration and Protest of the commonwealth of Virginia on the principles of the constitution of the U.S. of America and of the violations of them." Although Adams's program resembled proposals that Jefferson had made in his second term, the Sage of Monticello now accused the federal government of "usurpations of the powers retained" by the states. "The federal branch has assumed in some cases and claimed in others, a right of enlarging it's own powers by constructions, inferences, and indefinite deductions, from those directly given." For example, "they claim . . . and have commenced the exercise of a right to construct roads, open canals, and effect other internal improvements within the territories and jurisdictions exclusively belonging to the several states," a right that he denied and that he thought Virginia should deny. Indeed, Virginia should not accept "submission to a government of unlimited powers," although that state's attachment to the Union would bar resistance until it was the last resort. If a majority of the states agreed with Adams's program, "we will be patient and suffer much, under the confidence that time, ere it be too late, will prove to them also the bitter consequences in which this usurpation will involve us all." Once again, he proposed an amendment to add the "power of making roads and canals" to those "directly given to the federal branch," provided that this amendment was "sufficiently guarded against abuses, compromises, and corrupt practices, not only of possible, but of probable occurrence."

Until remedial measures were taken, however, Virginians should submit to federal "usurpations," recognizing temporarily and under protest "the assumption of this power rather than it's acceptance from the free will of their constituents, and [thus] to preserve peace in the meanwhile." Finally, Jefferson suggested that the Virginia legislature enact legislation legitimating the federal laws on internal improvements by requiring Virginia citizens to obey such laws "as if the said acts were . . . past by the legislature of this commonwealth."[119]

---

117. *Ibid.*
118. See the excellent summary in Robert E. Shalhope, "Thomas Jefferson's Republicanism and Antebellum Southern Thought," *J. So. Hist.* 42 (1976): 529–56.
119. TJ to JM, Dec. 24, 1825, below.

Madison promptly persuaded Jefferson to suppress his solemn protest, using tactful arguments related to practical politics as much as to constitutional construction. Madison preferred legislative instructions to Virginia's representatives in Congress to Jefferson's "stronger course." To make his point, Madison sent his friend a copy of his recent letter to Thomas Ritchie, editor of the *Richmond Enquirer*, about "the license of construction applied to the Constitution of the U. States." Neither in his letter to Ritchie nor in his reply to Jefferson did he call the federal enactments "usurpations." Instead, he used such words as "aberrations" and "abuses." He observed that "all power in human hands is liable to be abused," although the danger of abuse in a republican form of government is less than in any other, offering "a greater security to the minority against the hasty formation of oppressive majorities." If there were abuses, such as "the apparent call of a majority of the States and of the people for national Roads and Canals," how should they best be opposed? "The appeal," Madison counseled, "can only be made to the recollections, the reason, and the conciliatory spirit of the Majority of the people ag$^{st}$ their own errors; with a persevering hope of success, and an eventual acquiescence in disappointment unless indeed oppression should reach an extremity overruling all other considerations."[120]

Madison did not think that advocates of internal improvements had appealed to unlimited power. "In general," he reported, "the advocates of the Road and Canal powers, have rested the claim on deductions from some one or more of the enumerated powers." If there had been abuses, they did not amount to usurpations. Instead of declaring federal enactments null and void, Madison suggested an appeal to public opinion, "either by protest or other equivalent modes." If that failed, he proposed that the losing minority acquiesce "in disappointment" in the majority decision.[121]

It was the last disagreement between the two great friends, and Jefferson willingly suppressed his solemn protest as premature. Within six months, Jefferson died, leaving Madison to "take care of me when dead." For another decade, Madison opposed the vehement states' righters and the nullifiers who appealed to Jefferson's writings and to his own. And his final advice to his fellow citizens, as it had been to Jefferson in modified form, was "that the Union of the States be cherished and perpetuated."

120. JM to Thomas Ritchie, Dec. 18, 1825, enclosed in JM to TJ, Dec. 28, 1825, below.
121. *Ibid.*

# 1

# PARALLEL LIVES: JEFFERSON, MADISON, AND THE REVOLUTIONARY CRISIS, 1773–1775

THOMAS JEFFERSON AND JAMES MADISON first met in Williamsburg, Virginia, in October 1776. Jefferson, a veteran legislator at thirty-three, had written the Declaration of Independence that summer, then resigned from the Continental Congress, and hurried home to share in "new modeling our governments." Madison, a freshman legislator at twenty-five, had shaped the religious-liberty guarantee in the Virginia Declaration of Rights in early June before voting for the Virginia Constitution on June 29, 1776, the first of the new state governments established during the American Revolution.

When the two men met in the Virginia General Assembly in the fall, Jefferson was "one of the most learned men of the age," Madison later recalled, "a walking Library" whose "relish for Books never forsook him."[1] Indeed, Jefferson was a prodigy with whom "the Genius of Philosophy ever walked hand in hand." Madison was impressed by the remarkable range of Jefferson's readings in a variety of languages—French, Italian, and Spanish as well as "the Anglo-Saxon, as a root of the English, and an element in legal philosophy. The law itself he studied to the bottom, and in its greatest breadth, of which proofs were given at the Bar which he attended for a number of years, and occasionally throughout his career. For all the fine arts, he had a more than common taste; and in that of architecture, which he studied in both its useful, and its ornamental characters, he made himself an adept; as the variety of orders and stiles, executed according to his plan founded on the Grecian and Roman models and under his superintendance, in the Buildings of the University [of Virginia] fully exemplify."

1. JM to Samuel Harrison Smith, Nov. 4, 1826, in Hunt, IX, pp. 256–61.

Madison added that their acquaintance in 1776 was "rendered slight by the disparity between us," and Jefferson agreed that Madison, "a new member and young," was extremely modest and never ventured himself in debate. But three years later, Governor Jefferson, after working with Madison on the state's Executive Council, was captivated by the young man's "luminous and discriminating mind," his immense knowledge and extensive information, and "the powers and polish of his pen," qualities that "rendered him the first of every assembly afterwards of which he became a member."[2] And by 1790, after learning of Madison's leading role in the Constitutional Convention and in the first federal Congress, where he pushed through the Bill of Rights, Jefferson thought Madison "the greatest man in the world."[3]

Nor did Jefferson ever change his mind about his friend. Writing in 1812, he reported that "I have known him [intimately] from 1779 . . . and from three and thirty years' trial, I can say conscientiously that I do not know in the world a man of purer integrity, more dispassionate, disinterested and devoted to republicanism; nor could I, in the whole scope of America and Europe, point out an abler head."[4]

As a politician, Madison blossomed early and matured quickly. In 1773, fresh out of the College of New Jersey in Princeton at the age of twenty-two, he had stated flatly that "I do not meddle with Politicks" and described himself as "very sedate and philosophic" about living in Orange County, Virginia, his "Obscure Corner" of America.[5] His customary enjoyments were "Solitude and Contemplation," which allowed time for literary, historical, legal, and philosophical reading.

At Princeton, where he had graduated in 1771 and then stayed on for graduate work in 1772, he and his classmates Philip Freneau and H. H. Brackenridge had been captivated by belles lettres and poetry, wit and criticism, and romance and plays.[6] By 1773, he was back home in Orange County, tutoring his brothers and sisters, occasionally studying law, and shifting his reading from literary topics to the study of government, a field that he found "more substantial more durable more profitable" and, he added with growing maturity (he was now twenty-three), more appropriate for "a Riper Age."[7] To William Bradford in Philadelphia, his closest friend at Princeton, he observed that "the principles and modes of government are too important to be disregarded by an inquisitive mind." Attracted by William Penn's ideas on religious freedom, he asked Bradford to send him a sketch of the origin and principles of

---

2. TJ, "Autobiography," in *Thomas Jefferson: Writings,* ed. Merrill D. Peterson (New York, 1984), pp. 36-37.

3. Benjaman Rush, *The Autobiography of Benjamin Rush: His Travels through Life together with his Commonplace Book for 1789-1813,* ed. George W. Corner (Princeton, 1948), p. 181.

4. TJ to Thomas C. Flourney, Oct. 1, 1812, in L. and B., XIII, pp. 190-91.

5. JM to William Bradford, Sept. 25, June 10, and Apr. 28, 1773, in *PJM,* I, pp. 97, 89, 84.

6. *Ibid.,* pp. 75, 100-17.

7. JM to William Bradford, Jan. 24, 1774, *ibid.,* pp. 105-6.

the Pennsylvania Constitution, "particularly the extent of your religious Toleration."[8] He was especially interested in two questions: "Is an Ecclesiastical Establishment absolutely necessary to support civil society in a supream Government? And how far is it hurtful to a dependant State?"[9]

News of the Boston Tea Party jolted Madison from his philosophic concerns, converting him from a political nonparticipant into a political activist. Early in 1774, he began to pay careful attention to the growing controversy between the American colonies and Great Britain. He lauded Boston for dumping taxed tea into the harbor and Philadelphia for rejecting a shipment and threatening the ship's captain with a coat of tar and feathers. These were "heroic proceedings" against parliamentary taxation, he told Bradford, noting that "Political contests are necessary sometimes as well as military to afford exercise and practise and to instruct in the art of defending Liberty and property. I verily believe the frequent Assaults that have been made on America Boston especially Will in the end prove of real advantage."[10] After learning that Parliament had retaliated against Boston by closing that city's harbor to all commerce, he wrote that Virginians warmly supported the Bostonians. "The Natives are very unanimous and resolute, are making resolves in almost every County," he told his friend in Philadelphia, "and I believe are willing to fall in with the Other Colonies in any expedient measure, even if that should be the universal prohibition of Trade."[11]

Madison's interest in colonial rights focused most sharply on freedom of religion. Worried about "the State and Liberty of my Country," he requested information on how freedom of religion worked in the City of Brotherly Love. "If the Church of England had been the established and general Religion in all the Northern Colonies," he observed, "and uninterrupted tranquility had prevailed throughout the Continent, It is clear to me that slavery and Subjection might and would have been gradually insinuated among us." Citing the imprisonment of five or six dissenting preachers in neighboring Culpeper County for publishing their religious sentiments, he denounced "that diabolical Hell conceived principle of persecution [that] rages among some and to their eternal Infamy the Clergy can furnish their Quota of Imps for such business. This vexes me most of any thing whatever."[12] Late in life, he reviewed his efforts on behalf of dissenters and proudly proclaimed that "he spared no exertion to save them from imprisonment, and to promote their release from it."[13] Indeed, he was so exasperated with persecutions in Virginia that he had "neither patience to hear talk or think of any thing relative to this

---

8. JM to William Bradford, Dec. 1, 1773, *ibid.*, pp. 100–1.
9. *Ibid.*, p. 101.
10. JM to William Bradford, Jan. 24, 1774, *ibid.*, p. 105.
11. JM to William Bradford, July 1, 1774, *ibid.*, p. 115.
12. JM to William Bradford, Jan. 24, 1774, *ibid.*, p. 105.
13. *Ibid.*, p. 107.

matter, for I have scolded abused and ridiculed so long about it, to so little purpose that I am without common patience. So I leave you," he told Bradford, "to pity me and pray for Liberty of Conscience to revive among us."[14]

Contrasting the City of Brotherly Love with the Old Dominion, Madison told Bradford that "I want again to breathe your free air. I expect it will mend my Constitution and confirm my principles." Three months later, Madison congratulated his friend on "dwelling in a Land where those inestimable privileges are fully enjoyed and [the] public has long felt the good effects of their religious as well as Civil Liberty." Elaborating on this point, Madison observed that the "liberal catholic and equitable way of thinking as to the rights of Conscience, which is one of the Characteristics of a free people and so strongly marks the People of your province is but little known among the zealous adherents to our Hierarchy."[15] He was convinced that "religious bondage shackles and debilitates the mind and unfits it for every noble enterprize every expanded project."[16]

By the middle of 1774, Madison had rejected the idea of parliamentary authority over colonial America, viewing his stance as "political orthodoxy" in Virginia.[17] Noting the call for a continental congress to meet in Philadelphia later in the year, he reported that Virginia "has appointed seven delegates to represent it on this grand occasion, most of them glowing patriots and men of Learning and penetration," "real friends of American Freedom."[18] He favored immediate defense preparations rather than reliance on "the generosity and Justice of the crown," although he conceded that continuation or cessation of defensive measures should depend on the success of a petition presented to George III.

"Delay on our part," he wrote, "emboldens our adversaries and improves their schemes; whilst it abates the ardor of the Americans inspired with recent Injuries and affords opportunity to our secret enemies to disseminate discord and disunion." But he counted on the Congress to resolve this issue with "wisdom and judgment," and vowed that "all private opinions" must support united action against parliamentary encroachments on American liberty.[19]

Jefferson had reached a similar conclusion about parliamentary authority by means of a more systematic appraisal of the constitutional relationship between Great Britain and the American colonies. But the stimuli were the same—the Boston Tea Party and Parliament's retaliatory acts designed to coerce Massachusetts into compliance with the tea tax. News of the closing of Boston as a port reached Williamsburg while the legislature was meeting, and

14. *Ibid.*, p. 106.
15. JM to William Bradford, Apr. 1, 1774, *ibid.*, p. 112.
16. *Ibid.*, pp. 112–13.
17. JM to William Bradford, July 1, 1774, *ibid.*, p. 115.
18. JM to William Braford, Aug. 23, 1774, *ibid.*, p. 121.
19. *Ibid.*

Jefferson drafted a resolution "for appointing the 1st day of June, on which the port bill was to commence, for a day of fasting, humiliation, and prayer, to implore Heaven to avert from us the events of civil war, to inspire us with firmness in support of our rights, and to turn the hearts of the King and Parliament to moderation and justice."[20]

After Governor Dunmore dissolved the assembly for its effrontery, the members met informally at the Raleigh Tavern and declared that an attack on one colony should be viewed as an attack on all, "a most dangerous attempt to destroy the constitutional liberty and rights of all North America." Denouncing Parliament's coercive acts as an attempt to reduce "the inhabitants of British America to slavery, by subjecting them to the payment of taxes, imposed without the consent of the people and their representatives," the members called for a meeting of a continental congress. On the fast day, Jefferson recalled,[21] "the people met generally, with anxiety and alarm in their countenance, and the effect of the day, through the whole colony, was like a shock of electricity, arousing every man, and placing him erect and solidly on his center."

Although illness prevented Jefferson from attending the Virginia convention in 1774, he drafted for the Virginia delegates to the first Continental Congress a set of instructions that was published anonymously in Williamsburg by his friends as *A Summary View of the Rights of British America* and immediately reprinted in Philadelphia and London. Jefferson suggested that "an humble and dutiful address" be presented to King George III reviewing the "unwarrantable incroachments and usurpations" on rights "which god and the laws have given equally and independently to all." Relying on natural rights, he argued that "the British parliament has no right to exercise authority over us" and then reviewed parliamentary invasions of American rights, from the Revenue Act of 1764 to the Boston Port Act of 1774, concluding that these oppressive measures "too plainly prove a deliberate, systematical plan of reducing us to slavery," constituting a "connected chain of parliamentary usurpation."

Jefferson called on the king, as the only mediator among the several parts of the British Empire, to recommend the revocation of these acts by Parliament. It was the responsibility of the king, who held "the executive powers of the laws of these states, . . . to prevent the passage of laws by any one legislature of the empire which might bear injuriously on the rights and interests of another." Not only had the king failed in this duty, but he had also used his executive powers arbitrarily in British America, dissolving assemblies, delaying laws by neither confirming nor disallowing them, refusing assent to other laws for "trifling reasons, and sometimes for no conceivable reason at all," endeavoring to take from the people the right of representation, rendering more

---

20. TJ, "Autobiography," in Peterson, *TJ: Writings,* p. 8.
21. *Ibid.,* p. 9.

difficult the acquisition of land, sending armed troops to enforce arbitrary measures, and making military power superior to civil authority.[22]

Although the long list of charges against the king anticipated the indictment in the Declaration of Independence, it was designed not to reject, but to reform, him: "Open your breast Sire, to liberal and expanded thought. Let not the name of George the third be a blot in the page of history.... Only aim to do your duty, and mankind will give you credit where you fail. No longer persevere in sacrificing the rights of one part of the empire to the inordinate desires of another: but deal out to all equal and impartial right. Let no act be passed by any one legislature which may infringe on the rights and liberties of another," Jefferson concluded. "This, Sire, is the advice of your great American council, on the observance of which may perhaps depend your felicity and future fame, and the preservation of that harmony which alone can continue both to Great Britain and America the reciprocal advantages of their connection."

Jefferson's *Summary View* moved the constitutional debate between Great Britain and America to a new level and set the stage for action by the first Continental Congress, which met in Philadelphia in September 1774. Madison and Jefferson learned about the steps taken by the Congress by reading the *Virginia Gazette* in November. The delegates had declared the Coercive Acts unconstitutional and void, urged all Americans to support their countrymen in Massachusetts, recommended the establishment of an independent government in Massachusetts to replace the one suspended by Parliament, established the Continental Association to enforce economic sanctions against Great Britain, and stressed the need for the people to arm in defense of their rights. The association also forbade importation of merchandise from the British Isles and West Indies until the repeal of objectionable parliamentary acts. The boycott was to be enforced by local committees chosen in every county, city, and town in America and was the chief means "to be taken for the preservation of the liberties of America."[23]

"The proceedings of the Congress," Madison told Bradford, "are universally approved of in this Province and I am persuaded will be faithfully adhered to. A spirit of Liberty and Patriotism animates all degrees and denominations of men. Many publickly declare themselves ready to join the Bostonians as soon as violence is offered them or resistance thought expedient. In many counties independent companies are forming and voluntarily subjecting themselves to military discipline that they may be expert and prepared against a time of Need. I hope it will be a general thing throughout this province. Such firm and provident steps will either intimidate our enemies or enable us to defy them."[24]

22. TJ, *A Summary View of the Rights of British America*, in *PTJ*, I, pp. 121-35.
23. For an excellent account, see Robert Middlekauf, *The Glorious Cause: The American Revolution, 1763-1789* (New York, 1982), pp. 231-50.
24. JM to William Bradford, Nov. 26, 1774, in *PJM*, I, p. 129.

The association's ban on imports from Britain took effect on December 1, 1774, and Madison was elected an organizing member of the Orange County Committee of Safety to enforce it.[25] "We are very busy at present," he told Bradford, "in raising men and procuring the necessaries for defending ourselves and our fr[i]ends in case of a sudden Invasion. The extensiveness of the Demands of the Congress and the pride of the British Nation together with the wickedness of the present Ministry, seem, in the Judgment of our Politicians to require a preparation for extreme events."[26]

By the end of the year, royal government in Virginia had begun to crumble. So effective was the boycott of British trade that the king's authority was "entirely disregarded, if not overthrown," Governor Dunmore lamented. "There is not a Justice of the Peace in Virginia," he reported, "that acts, except as a Committeeman." Moreover, military companies were being organized in every county "for the avowed purpose of protecting the committees,"[27] which exposed violators of the boycott to public disapproval. The most effective enforcement procedure was requiring signatures of compliance, Madison wrote, "that being the method used among us to distinguish friends from foes and to oblige the Common people to a more strict observance of it." Indeed, support was almost unanimous, he concluded, with Quakers being the only people who refused to sign. But Madison thought them "too honest or simple to have any sinister or secret Views."[28]

At its session in Williamsburg in March 1775, the provincial convention resolved "that a well regulated Militia, composed of Gentlemen and Yeomen is the natural strength, and only security, of a free government," and Jefferson drafted a plan for embodying, arming, and disciplining a militia for the purpose of "putting this colony into an immediate posture of defence."[29] Madison had already predicted that "there will by the Spring, I expect, be some thousands of well trained High Spirited men ready to meet danger whenever it appears, who are influenced by no mercenary Principles, bearing their own expences and having the prospect of no recompense but the honour and safety of their Country."[30] After learning that George III had recommended to Parliament the suppression of colonial opposition, Patrick Henry concluded that "the war is actually begun" and announced his choice: "Give me liberty, or give me death."[31]

Shortly after the Virginia convention had adjourned, Governor Dunmore

25. *PJM*, p. 146.
26. JM to William Bradford, Jan. 20, 1775, *ibid.*, p. 135.
27. Irving Brant, *The Fourth President: A Life of James Madison* (Indianapolis, 1970), p. 24.
28. *Ibid.* For suppression of political dissent in Orange County and elsewhere in Virginia, see Middlekauf, pp. 250-60.
29. *PTJ*, I, pp. 160-61.
30. JM to William Bradford, Jan. 20, 1775, in *PJM*, I, p. 135.
31. Richard Beeman, *Patrick Henry: A Biography* (New York, 1974), is a concise biography. For a longer one, see Robert Douthat Meade, *Patrick Henry*, 2 vols. (Philadelphia, 1957 and 1969).

seized the colony's supply of gunpowder in the Williamsburg magazine, transferred it to a British warship in the James River, and retreated behind the walls surrounding the Governor's Palace. Acting under the authority of the Hanover County Committee of Safety, Captain Patrick Henry and the local militia marched to Williamsburg to redress the insult, persuading the king's receiver general to give them £330 from royal funds to replace the confiscated powder. Madison and the Orange County committee applauded Captain Henry and the gentlemen independents of Hanover for their "seasonable and spirited proceedings in procuring a compensation for the powder fraudulently taken from the country magazine, by command of Lord Dunmore."[32]

By that time, news of the armed encounter at Lexington and Concord had reached Virginia, and Madison added the opinion of the Orange County committee that "the blow struck in the Massachusetts government is a hostile attack on this and every other colony, and a sufficient warrant to use violence and reprisal, in all cases where it may be expedient for our security and welfare."[33] In a personal letter, Madison endorsed Henry's action, observing that it "gained him great honor in the most spirited parts of the Country." Madison aligned himself with this more radical group and was critical of those who feared "a Civil war in this Colony"; he censored the latter for "a pusilanimity little comporting with the professions or the name of Virginian."[34]

The shots exchanged "between the king's troops and our brethren of Boston," Jefferson wrote, "has cut off our last hopes of reconciliation, and a phrenzy of revenge seems to have seized all ranks of people. It is a lamentable circumstance that the only mediatory power acknowledged by both parties [the king], instead of leading to a reconciliation [of] his divided people, should pursue the incendiary purpose of still blowing up the flames as we find him constantly doing in every speech and public declaration."[35] Nonetheless, Lord North forced through Parliament a conciliatory proposition under which the British government would forbear taxing the colonies if each assembly would agree to make a grant for the civil government and common defense, with the funds to be "disposable by Parliament." Governor Dunmore then called the assembly into session to consider North's proposal, but he fled to a British warship in the York River before that body adjourned.

Jefferson wrote the reply to North's proposition, vowing "that next to the possession of liberty, we should consider such Reconciliation the greatest of human blessings," for it would bring "to a good end our unhappy disputes with the Mother Country." After careful deliberations, however, the Virginia representatives rejected North's plan because "it only changes the form of

32. May 9, 1775, in *PJM*, I, pp. 144-47.
33. In his *History of the Life and Times of James Madison*, 3 vols. (Boston, 1859-68), I, p. 95, William Cabell Rives reproduces the address from a copy in JM's handwriting. The editors of the *PJM* follow the text in the *Williamsburg Virginia Gazette* (Purdie) (May 19, 1775), I, pp. 146-47.
34. JM to William Bradford, May 9, 1775, in *PJM*, I, pp. 144-45.
35. TJ to William Small, May 7, 1775, in *PTJ*, I, p. 165.

oppression, without lightening the burthen." According to Jefferson, the British Parliament had no right to meddle with civil government in the colonies, which had been instituted "for us, not for them." "We cannot conceive that any other legislature had a right to prescribe either the number or pecuniary appointments of our offices." In order to receive a perpetual exemption, the colonies would have to agree to a perpetual tax at the disposition of Parliament alone, whereas, "we alone are the judges of the condition, circumstances, and situation of our people." Nor did the conciliatory proposal repeal other oppressive acts, long complained of by all the colonies. Moreover, the offer seemed not to be made in good faith "because at the very time of requiring from us grants of money they are making disposition to invade us with large armaments by Sea and land which," Jefferson concluded dryly, "is a stile of asking gifts not reconcilable to our freedom." Finally, Virginia was now bound into a union with all the colonies in the Continental Congress and could not depart from the common cause by taking action distinct and apart from "our sister colonies."[36]

From Orange County, Madison followed the meeting of the House of Burgesses with intense interest. Critical of Lord Dunmore's flight to a warship, he wrote that "we defy his power as much as we detest his villany," citing "the Union Virtue and Love of Liberty at present prevailing thro'out the Colonies." In Virginia, he noted great unanimity and military ardor; "the progress we make in discipline and hostile preparations is as great as the Zeal with which these things were undertaken." He especially praised the riflemen of the frontier counties, who could hit "the bigness of a man's face at the distance of 100 yards." He had also become an expert himself, noting that he seldom missed from that distance.[37]

The second Continental Congress met a month after Lexington and Concord, and Jefferson joined the delegates on June 21, 1775, replacing Peyton Randolph, who had been called from Philadelphia to preside over the Virginia convention. Jefferson's "reputation for literature, science, and a happy talent of composition" had preceded him, according to John Adams, who admired Jefferson's "peculiar felicity of expression."[38] When the news of the battle of Bunker Hill reached Philadelphia, Jefferson wrote a friend that "the war is now heartily entered into without a prospect of accomodation, but thro' the effectual interposition of arms." He reported that the Congress had sent George Washington to take command "as Generalissimo of all the Provincial troops in North-America," and he hoped optimistically that a vigorous campaign would "dispose our enemies to treaty."[39]

While the fighting went on, so did negotiations on imperial issues. Since

---

36. See TJ, "Virginia Resolutions on Lord North's Conciliatory Proposal," June 10, 1775, *ibid.*, pp. 170–74.
37. JM to William Bradford, June 19, 1775, in *PJM*, I, pp. 152–53.
38. Peterson, p. 80.
39. TJ to Francis Eppes, June 26, 1775, in *PTJ*, I, pp. 174–75.

Jefferson had written the Virginia response to Lord North's proposal, he was also assigned that task by Congress. He modeled his argument at the continental level on his earlier reply, stating that colonial assemblies had the sole and exclusive privilege of giving and granting their own money and of deciding on the purposes for which taxes would be applied. Parliament's "pretended power of taxation" was both unreasonable and insidious, "unreasonable, because, if we declare we accede to it, we declare without reservation, we will purchase the favour of Parliament, not knowing at the same time at what price they will please to estimate their favor: It is insidious, because, individual colonies, having bid and bidden again, till they find the avidity of the seller too great for all their powers to satisfy; are then to return into opposition, divided from their sister colonies whom the minister will have previously detached by a grant of easier terms, or by artful procrastination of a definitive answer." Parliament seemed to suggest that nothing was at stake except the mode, not the purpose nor the right, of levying taxes. But this actually would "lull into fatal security; our well-affected fellow subjects on the other side the water, till time should be given for the operation of those arms, which a British Minister pronounced would instantaneously reduce the 'cowardly' sons of America to unreserved submission." In the face of such a challenge and of the continuation of indiscriminate and oppressive legislation over the colonies, it was clear to Congress that "nothing but our own exertions may defeat the ministerial sentence of death or abject submission."[40]

Jefferson also joined the congressional committee appointed to justify to the American people, the British authorities, and the "opinion of Mankind" the necessity of armed resistance. Working with John Dickinson of Pennsylvania and Delaware, he expressed hope for the restoration of harmony but justified the taking up of arms as a cruel necessity forced by tyrannical authority that declared Americans "to be Rebels and Traitors" and unleashed troops "to spread destruction and devastation." "Our Forefathers," he continued, "Inhabitants of ... Great-Britain, left their Native Land to seek on these Shores a Residence for civil and religious Freedom." But Parliament had recently adopted a series of innovations that amounted to "the pernicious Project" of subjugating the colonies.

As he had done in his *Summary View,* Jefferson presented a long indictment of parliamentary measures taken in the period between 1764 and 1775. Reduced to a choice between unconditional submission to tyranny or resistance by force, the colonists chose the latter. "Our cause is just. Our union is perfect. Our internal Resources are great, and, if necessary, foreign Assistance is undoubtedly attainable." Armed resistance was employed "for the preservation of our Liberties; being with one Mind resolved to die Freemen rather than to live Slaves." At the same time, the declaration rejected separation from Great Britain, asking instead for the restoration of harmony and the reuniting

---

40. TJ, "Congress's Resolution on Lord North's Proposal," July 31, 1775, *ibid.,* pp. 230–33.

of the empire on terms consistent with "the Freedom that is our birthright."[41]

Madison was impressed by this spirited address, attributing it and an address to the citizens of Great Britain "to a few illustrious writers" in Congress. "Is it discernible," he asked Bradford in Philadelphia, where the Continental Congress was meeting, "who are the original Authors of them?" Since the proceedings of Congress were secret, he was not to know that Jefferson had collaborated on the first and that Richard Henry Lee of Virginia had written the other document. But he was sure that the unknown authors deserved "every encomium that can be bestowed on them," praising them for an eloquence that could vie "with the most applauded Oration of Tully himself."[42] He was especially intrigued by "the confident assertion of the Congress that foreign Assistance if necessary was *undoubtedly* attainable.' " Indeed, he hoped that some secret overtures had already been made, conceding that if they had been, they were almost certainly "wrapped up in impenetrable secrecy as yet."[43]

Madison was also concerned about the scarcity of ammunition, a concern that must have reached new heights when he was appointed colonel of the Orange County militia on October 2, 1775, by the Virginia Committee of Safety for the Colony. "Can you tell me," he wrote his friend in Philadelphia, "how they are supplied in New England and what steps are taking to procure a sufficiency for the time to come."[44]

When the second Continental Congress adjourned briefly in August 1775, Jefferson dashed back to Virginia, where, on September 26, the Virginia Committee of Safety appointed him lieutenant and commander in chief of the Albemarle County militia, the highest military officer in the county. But neither Jefferson nor Madison was to serve in the armed forces during the American Revolution. Instead, both entered into a succession of public offices, where the life and careers of each became inextricably intertwined with the other's for the next fifty years.

---

41. TJ, "Declaration of the Causes and Necessity for Taking Up Arms," July 6, 1775, *ibid.*, pp. 187–219. See also Julian P. Boyd, "The Disputed Authorship of the Declaration of the Causes and Necessity for Taking Up Arms," *PMHB* 74 (1950): 51–73.
42. JM to William Bradford, July 28, 1775, in *PJM*, I, pp. 159–61.
43. *Ibid.*
44. *Ibid.*; for JM's commission, see *ibid.*, p. 163.

# 2

# GETTING ACQUAINTED: JEFFERSON, MADISON, AND THE VIRGINIA HOUSE OF DELEGATES, 1776

ROYAL GOVERNMENT in Virginia ended unofficially on June 8, 1775, when Lord Dunmore abandoned the Governor's Palace in Williamsburg and took refuge on the British man-of-war *Fowey* in the York River. By the end of year, he informed London that the legal government of the province "is entirely disregarded, if not overthrown." At the county level, local committees of safety enforced the Continental Association, he wrote, and publicized all violators of "what they are now hardy enough to call the laws of Congress."[1]

When the Continental Congress learned that Dunmore had placed Norfolk under martial law, Jefferson and the Virginia delegates supported Congress's recommendation that the Virginia convention "call a full and free representation of the people, establish such form of government as in their judgment will best produce the happiness of the people, and most effectually secure peace and good order in the colony, during the continuance of the present dispute between Great Britain and these colonies." In the county elections held in April 1776, the Albemarle voters again chose Jefferson, even though he was also a member of Congress, but they also selected an alternate to represent them until he returned. The freeholders of Orange County picked Madison as one of their "most fit and able men" to serve in the Virginia convention, and he took his seat in Williamsburg on May 8, 1776.

It was Madison's first visit to the colonial capital. He found the small town even more crowded than it usually was when the legislature met. Virginia

---

1. For the quotation, see Irving Brant, *The Fourth President: A Life of James Madison* (Indianapolis, 1970), p. 24. The best discussion of Virginia's revolt against the Crown's government is by John E. Selby, *The Revolution in Virginia, 1775–1783* (Williamsburg, 1988); his chapter "The Collapse of Royal Government," pp. 41–54, is excellent.

minutemen and Continental troops commanded by General Charles Lee, recently appointed by Washington to head the newly created Southern Department, guarded the town, with officers and soldiers quartered in or near the College of William and Mary.[2] At the other end of the Duke of Gloucester Street, the convention delegates gathered at the colonial capitol, some of them wearing hunting shirts, which had become the uniform for the Virginia resistance forces, and carrying tomahawks in their belts. According to a foreign observer, legislators often wore "the same clothes in which one goes hunting or tends his tobacco fields. . . . There are displayed boots, trousers, stockings, and Indian leggings; great coats, ordinary coats and short jackets, according to each man's caprice or comfort, and all equally honorable."[3]

On May 15, Madison and the members of the Virginia convention voted unanimously to instruct Jefferson and their other delegates in the Continental Congress to declare the United Colonies "free and independent States, absolved from all allegience to, or dependence on, the Crown or Parliament of Great Britain."[4]

Jefferson resumed his seat in Congress on May 14, 1776. The next day, he and his congressional colleagues called on the colonies to establish independent governments, a motion that John Adams called "a machine to fabricate independence." On June 7, Richard Henry Lee, acting on the Virginia instructions of May 15, introduced a congressional resolution declaring that the United Colonies "are, and of right ought to be, free and independent states." Four days later, Congress appointed a committee of five—Jefferson, Adams, Benjamin Franklin, Robert R. Livingston, and Roger Sherman—to draft the Declaration of Independence.

Jefferson was the committee's choice to prepare the Declaration. John Adams recalled persuading him to do it: "Reason first—You are a Virginian, and a Virginian ought to appear at the head of this business. Reason second—I am obnoxious, suspected, and unpopular. Reason third—You can write ten times better than I can."[5] Jefferson wrote clear, readable, and polished prose that reached beyond constitutional and ideological issues to the mass of the people, and his Declaration translated a political and legalistic document into a classic statement of human liberty. Designed to justify to the opinion of mankind America's separation from Great Britain and the assumption of a

---

2. Selby, pp. 89–94; John R. Alden, *General Charles Lee: Traitor or Patriot* (Baton Rouge, 1951), pp. 112–19.

3. Selby, p. 42, mentions hunting shirts and tomahawks in the 1775 assembly. The foreign observer was Johann David Schoepf, a surgeon to the Hessians in the British army who reported on his visit to the Virginia assembly in Richmond at the end of the Revolution; see his *Travels in the Confederation, 1783–1784,* ed. Alfred J. Morison, 2 vols. (Philadelphia, 1911), II, pp. 55–56.

4. In a missing letter of about May 15, JM informed William Bradford "of the declaration of Independency" made by the convention; see the entry from Bradford's Memorandum Book, May 28, 1776, in *PJM,* I, p. 180.

5. John Adams, "Autobiography," in *The Works of John Adams . . . ,* ed. Charles Francis Adams, 10 vols. (Boston, 1850–56), II, pp. 514–15.

separate and equal place among the powers of the earth, the Declaration set forth the political ideology of the new nation: just governments are founded on equal and inalienable rights, "deriving their just powers from the consent of the governed. That whenever any form of Government becomes destructive of these ends, it is the Right of the People to alter or to abolish it, and to institute new Government, laying its foundation on such principles and organizing its powers in such form, as to them shall seem most likely to effect their Safety and Happiness."[6]

As he had done in the *Summary View of the Rights of British America* in 1774 and in the *Declaration of the Causes and Necessity of Taking Up Arms* in 1775, Jefferson listed a series of indictments against the king for injuries and usurpations of the rights of Americans, demonstrating that George III was a tyrant unfit to be the ruler of a free people. If the people had a right to overthrow a tyrannical government, they also had a right to institute a new one to secure their inalienable rights of life, liberty, and the pursuit of happiness. Acting by the authority of the people of the colonies, Congress, therefore, absolved the Americans of allegiance to the British Crown and dissolved all political connection with Great Britain, solemnly declaring "that these United colonies are and of right ought to be free and independent states."[7]

In Virginia, Madison was appointed on May 16 to a committee formed "to prepare a Declaration of Rights, and such a plan of government as will be most likely to maintain peace and good order in this colony, and secure substantial and equal liberty to the people." The Virginia Declaration was written by George Mason, but Madison played a major role in shaping the guarantee of religious freedom, replacing Mason's words "that all Men should enjoy the fullest Toleration in the Exercise of Religion" with the more liberal phrasing "all men are equally entitled to the free exercise of religion, according to the dictates of conscience."[8] Indeed, Madison also attempted the total disestablishment of the state church, offering an amendment that linked freedom of conscience with a statement that "no man or class of men ought, on account of religion to be invested with peculiar emoluments or privileges." Although the amendment was rejected, young Madison was pleased that the convention had accepted his first proposal "with a view, more particularly to substitute for the idea, expressed by the term 'toleration,' an absolute and equal right in all, to the exercise of religion according to the dictates of conscience."[9] George Bancroft, the great historian of the nineteenth century, hailed Madison's guarantee as "the first achievement of the wisest civilian in Virginia."[10]

6. TJ, "The Declaration of Independence," in *PTJ*, I, p. 429.
7. TJ, "Notes on Proceedings in the Continental Congress," *ibid.*, pp. 315–19.
8. *PJM*, I, p. 175.
9. *Ibid.*, pp. 174, 177.
10. George Bancroft, *History of the United States*, 6 vols. (New York, 1883–85), IV, pp. 416–17; cited by Ketcham, p. 73.

In Philadelphia, Jefferson's thoughts also turned to Virginia, and he proposed that the congressional delegation should return home for a short time to assist in building a new form of government. On May 16, he wrote to Thomas Nelson, who had been a colleague in the Continental Congress in 1775, observing that constitution making "is a work of the most interesting nature and such as every individual would wish to have his voice in. In truth it is the whole object of the present controversy; for should a bad government be instituted for us in future it had been as well to have accepted at first the bad one offered to us from beyond the water without the risk and expence of contest."[11]

Although Jefferson was not called home, he gave a draft of his proposed state constitution to Richard Henry Lee and George Wythe, who were returning to Williamsburg. Wythe, his former law teacher, reported that he had shown Jefferson's bill for "new modelling the form of government" to "those who had the chief hand in forming" the constitution and that "two or three parts of this were, with little alteration, inserted in that."[12] These parts include the Preamble, which presented the list of charges against the king in a slightly different order from the indictment in the Declaration of Independence.[13] As Madison later wrote, "The Preamble is known to have been furnished by Thomas Jefferson."[14] The convention also reopened its discussion of the text of the Constitution, adding parts of Jefferson's draft dealing with land forfeiture, the structure and tenure of the judiciary, and state boundaries, which staked out Virginia's expansive claims to western territories and barred purchases of land from Indians unless authorized by the General Assembly on behalf of the public.[15] Thus amended, the Virginia Constitution of 1776 was adopted unanimously, with Madison joining in the final vote. The convention then made the temporary transition to a one-house legislature, elected Patrick Henry governor along with an eight-member Executive Council, called for the election of a senate, began to pass laws for the commonwealth, and finally adjourned on July 5 until October.

After Congress had adopted the Declaration of Independence, Jefferson was doubly anxious to return to Virginia and resume his seat in the convention-turned-legislature. His wife Martha was not well, and he wished to be with her and their family. When the Virginia convention reelected him to another term in Congress, therefore, he resigned, pleading "the situation of

---

11. TJ to Thomas Nelson, May 16, 1776, in *PTJ*, I, p. 292.
12. George Wythe to TJ, July 27, 1776, *ibid.*, pp. 476–77. On Wythe, see Joyce Blackburn, *George Wythe of Williamsburg* (New York, 1975), and Alonzo Thomas Dill, *George Wythe: Teacher of Liberty* (Williamsburg, 1979).
13. *PTJ*, I, pp. 332, 377–79.
14. *PJM*, I, p. 178.
15. For the Virginia Constitution as adopted on June 29, 1776, see *PTJ*, I, pp. 377–85. For a brilliant analysis of the Virginia Constitution, see Merrill D. Peterson, *Jefferson and Madison and the Making of Constitutions* (Charlottesville, 1987).

my domestic affairs."[16] Accordingly, he retired from Congress in September and spent a month at Monticello with his family before moving them in October to Williamsburg.

When Jefferson, the veteran Virginia legislator since 1769, returned from Congress, he knew most of the leaders in the House: Edmund Pendleton, the Speaker; Benjamin Harrison, a former colleague in Congress; and George Mason, author of the Virginia Declaration of Rights and of the state Constitution of 1776, whom Jefferson labeled his "most steadfast, able and zealous" supporter in implementing the principles of the American Revolution. And he later recalled the aid of two other men: George Wythe, a fellow delegate in Congress who returned to the assembly in 1777, and the delegate from Orange, James Madison, "a new member and young."[17]

Madison agreed that he "was a stranger to Mr. Jefferson till the year 1776, when he took his seat in the first Legislature under the constitution of Virginia then newly formed; being at that time myself a member of that Body, and for the first time a member of any public Body. The acquaintance then made," he added, "was very slight; the distance between our ages being considerable, and other distances much more so."[18] Jefferson was thirty-three, married to the lovely Martha Wayles Skelton, and the father of two golden daughters. Madison was twenty-five and already a confirmed bachelor. The social distance between the two men can be gauged by their living accommodations in the pleasant town of Williamsburg, the capital of Virginia. While the distinguished delegate from Albemarle County lived with his family in one of the city's nicest houses—George Wythe's handsome home near the Governor's Palace—no one knows where the bachelor member from Orange County lodged in 1776.[19]

Even before they met in October, Jefferson and Madison knew each other by reputation. While he was still in Philadelphia, Jefferson had referred to "Mr. Madison (of the College)," a professor at William and Mary, thus distinguishing him from his cousin in Orange County.[20] And Madison had voted for Jefferson's Preamble and amendments to the Virginia Constitution in June 1776. But the two legislators first got acquainted while serving on several

16. TJ to Edmund Pendleton, June 30, 1776, in *PTJ*, I, p. 408. On Aug. 11, Jefferson wrote that every letter from his wife "brings me such an account of the state of her health, that it is with great pain that I can stay here"; see TJ to John Page, July 30, 1776, *ibid.*, p. 483.

17. TJ, "Autobiography," in *Thomas Jefferson: Writings*, ed. Merrill D. Peterson (New York, 1984), pp. 36–37.

18. JM to Margaret Bayard Smith, Sept. 1830, in Hunt, IX, p. 404.

19. For a contemporary description of Williamsburg as a "pleasant town," see Nicholas Cresswell, *The Journal of Nicholas Cresswell, 1774–1777* (New York, 1924), p. 206; quoted in Jane Carson, *We Were There: Descriptions of Williamsburg, 1699–1859* (Williamsburg, 1965), p. 31. Wythe was in Philadelphia serving as Virginia delegate to the Continental Congress. See also Willie Graham, "Renovating the Wythe House," *Colonial Williamsburg Journal* 16 (1993): 68–71.

20. TJ to Francis Eppes, Aug. 9, 1776, in *PTJ*, I, p. 487, and TJ to Edmund Pendleton, Aug. 13, 1776, *ibid.*, p. 494.

committees in the fall, including the Committee on Religion, the Committee to Draft a Bill Abolishing Some Special Privileges of the Anglican Church, and the Committee of Privileges and Elections. There and in the later sessions, Jefferson developed a high regard for Madison's skill in drafting committee reports and resolutions.[21]

What sort of men were Jefferson and Madison when they first met in 1776? Jefferson was a recognized leader of Revolutionary America. Shortly after he resumed his seat in the Virginia legislature, Congress elected him as a commissioner to join Benjamin Franklin and Silas Deane in France to negotiate a treaty of alliance. But Jefferson preferred to remain at home, "where much was to be done, of the most permanent interest, in new modeling our government."[22] Seizing this opportunity, he quickly became, as Julian P. Boyd notes, "a veritable legislative drafting bureau."[23] Always a serious reader, he was an omniverous researcher, a believer in the Baconian axiom that "knowledge is power." A Whiggish student of English law and history, he was widely read in classical philosophy, literary classics, natural science, and religion.[24]

But he was also fond of detail and given to orderly arrangement of useful knowledge, whether it was meteorological notations or political observations. An activist who disliked idleness, he could, as James Parton long ago observed, "calculate an eclipse, survey an estate, tie an artery, plan an edifice, try a cause, break a horse, dance a minuet, and play a violin." But it was his "diligence, ability, and integrity" that won the praise of the Virginia House of Delegates for his service in Congress when he returned home in 1776.[25]

Madison was eight years younger and considerably less experienced than Jefferson, but they had a lot in common. Madison's appetite for books, whetted by his graduate work at Princeton and his self-imposed discipline at home, marked him as a serious student of English history, law, and government as well as religion. His friend Edmund Randolph, who met him at the Virginia convention in May 1776, later wrote that Madison was too shy to enter debate but kept up a running commentary that made colleagues "wish to sit daily within the reach of his conversation . . . [where] he delivered himself without affectation upon Grecian, Roman, and English history from a well-digested fund, a sure presage of eminence." He had not yet delved much into natural science, but he read widely in the literary classics and contemporary literature and poetry. Randolph recalled that Madison was a mature classical scholar as a young man: "As a student of belles lettres, his fancy animated his judgment,

---

21. *PJM,* I, pp. 186-87.
22. TJ, "Autobiography," p. 42.
23. Julian P. Boyd, in *PTJ,* II, p. 306.
24. See H. Trevor Colbourn's chapter "Thomas Jefferson and the Rights of Expatriated Man," in his *The Lamp of Experience: Whig History and the Intellectual Origins of the American Revolution* (Chapel Hill, 1965), pp. 158-84.
25. Resolution of Oct. 12, 1776, in *Journal of the House of Delegates, 1776* (Richmond, 1828), p. 9.

and his judgment, without damping his fancy, excluded by the soundness of criticism every propensity to tinsel and glitter. It still glowed, but it glowed without glare."[26] In short, Madison and Jefferson shared an abiding interest in ideas and the life of the mind.

They also shared ideas about liberty and order in Revolutionary America, each having arrived at his basic position prior to their initial meeting. Both were intensely republican, devoted to individual rights and religious freedom, and hostile to the privileges of aristocracy. As Madison wrote late in life, he was "under very early and strong impressions in favor of liberty both Civil and Religious," and he cited his youthful opposition to the persecution of dissenters in Orange and Culpeper counties.[27] Jefferson's views on life, liberty, and the pursuit of happiness were set forth in the Declaration of Independence that created the new nation. Although the connection with Great Britain was broken, the people retained their rights. "For the nation was not dissolved, was not annihilated," according to Jefferson; "its will, therefore, remained in full vigor: and on the establishing of the new organs, first of a convention, and afterwards a more complicated legislature, the old acts of national will continued in force, until the nation should, by its new organs, declare its will changed."[28]

There was much to change, and Jefferson's reputation for hard work—"the laboring oar," he called it—marked him as a leader in the effort to establish a code of law "with a single eye to reason, and the good of those for whose government it was framed." Less than a week after the legislature met in October 1776, the House gave him two important assignments: drafting a bill for the abolition of the law of entail and coordinating the general revision of the laws of the new state. The first was reported in two days and was passed by the legislature in two weeks, replacing feudal land tenure with freehold or fee simple tenure, a measure that Jefferson considered essential to a "well-ordered republic" and "indicative of the strength and general pulse of reformation." The bill authorizing the general revision of the laws also passed promptly, and the House made Jefferson chairman of the revision committee, which included George Mason, George Wythe, Edmund Pendleton, and Thomas Ludwell Lee.[29]

For more than two years, the committee of revisers worked on their task, bringing "so much of the Common Law as it was thought necessary to alter, all the British statues from *Magna Charta* to the present day, and all the laws of Virginia from the establishment of our [colonial] legislature . . . which we thought should be retained, within a compass of one hundred and twenty-six bills." The revised legislation was not enacted as a unified code, however, but

26. Edmund Randolph, *History of Virginia*, ed. Arthur H. Shaffer (Charlottesville, 1970), pp. 234–35.
27. *PJM*, I, p. 107.
28. Peterson, p. 157.
29. TJ, "Autobiography," pp. 32, 37.

was taken up by the assembly on a piecemeal basis over a number of years, the major action occurring in 1785, while Jefferson was serving as ambassador to France. By that time, Madison, who had supported the reform efforts in 1776, had gained legislative experience and leadership qualities that allowed him to steer most of the new laws through the assembly.[30]

It was on the Committee on Religion that Madison and Jefferson cooperated most closely in the fall of 1776. Both men favored the disestablishment of the Anglican Church in the Old Dominion. Dissenting sects had hailed Madison's clause on freedom of conscience in the Virginia Declaration of Rights "as the rising sun of religious liberty" and proposed that "all church establishments might be pulled down, and every tax upon conscience and private judgement abolished."[31] Petitions against what Jefferson called the "spiritual tyranny" of the established church flooded the legislature, the one from Hanover County observing that "every argument for civil liberty gains additional strength when applied to liberty in the concerns of religion." The dissenters concluded by saying that "they ask no ecclesiastical establishments for themselves, neither can they approve of them when granted to others."[32]

Jefferson later claimed that these petitions "brought on the severest contest in which I have ever been engaged. Our greatest opponents were Mr. [Edmund] Pendleton [the Speaker] and Robert Carter Nicholas [the treasurer], honest men, but zealous churchmen." The debates in the Committee on Religion became "desperate contests," pitting Jefferson, Madison, and those supporting disestablishment against Pendleton, Nicholas, and those defending the status quo. After more than a month of debate, the churchmen rallied to halt the movement for disestablishment, leading to the discharge of the committee and the referral of the issues to the Committee of the Whole House. For another ten days, the contest continued until a compromise set of resolutions became the basis for legislation. Jefferson, Madison, and those favoring disestablishment insisted on the repeal of any English statutes "which renders criminal the maintaining [of] any opinions in matters of religion, forbearing to repair to church, or exercising of any mode of worship whatsoever, or which prescribes punishments for the same." They also advocated exemption of dissenters from all taxes and compulsory contributions for the established church or their own churches, noting that any legislation making provision for the support of clergy "ought to be repealed."[33]

But, as Jefferson noted, "our opponents carried . . . a declaration that religious assemblies ought to be regulated, and that provision ought to be made for continuing the succession of the clergy, and superintending their conduct." Jefferson and Madison were appointed to a committee of seventeen

30. *Ibid.*, p. 40.
31. Petition from Prince Edward County, Oct. 11, 1776, in *Journal of the House of Delegates, 1776*, p. 7.
32. Oct. 24, 1776, *ibid.*, pp. 24–25.
33. *Ibid.*, p. 63.

to draft legislation based on the compromise resolutions, but so were Treasurer Nicholas and other church supporters. In December 1776, the legislature repealed parliamentary legislation oppressive to dissenters and exempted them from paying taxes to support the church. But Pendleton and friends of the establishment avoided repeal of tax levies on members of the church for the support of clergy, although they agreed to a year's suspension of parish levies.

Thus, the legislation left a major issue concerning freedom of religion unresolved, specifically withholding a decision on the question of "whether a general assessment should not be established by laws, on every one, to the support of the pastor of his choice, or whether all should be left to voluntary contributions."[34] Almost a decade elapsed before the issue of separation of church and state was resolved by Jefferson's Bill for Establishing Religious Freedom, which Madison pushed to enactment while Jefferson was in France.

34. TJ, "Autobiography," p. 35.

# 3

# THE BEGINNINGS OF FRIENDSHIP: GOVERNOR JEFFERSON AND COUNCILLOR MADISON, 1779

"I DID NOT BECOME ACQUAINTED with Mr. Jefferson till 1779," Madison recalled late in life, "when being a member of the Executive Council, and he the Governor, an intimacy took place." It was in Williamsburg that their "friendship was formed, which was for life, and which was never interrupted in the slightest degree for a single moment."[1] Jefferson's recollections coincided, for he wrote that he had known Madison "intimately . . . from 1779."[2] Although they had worked together on committees in 1776, their relationship, according to Madison, was "rendered slight by the disparities between us."

Nonetheless, Madison had made a favorable impression on Jefferson and other members of the legislature in 1776. After the voters of Orange County defeated Madison's bid for reelection in 1777—he blamed his loss, the only one in his long political career, on his refusal to treat the voters to free whiskey—the legislature elected him a member of the Council of State in November, with Jefferson joining the majority in voting for "James Madison the younger, of Orange, Esq."[3] Throughout 1778 and 1779, Madison served as one of eight members of the executive cabinet advising the commonwealth's first governor, Patrick Henry. Although Madison later branded the Executive Council "a grave of useful talents,"[4] it was the council that allowed him to

---

1. JM to Samuel Harrison Smith, Nov. 4, 1826, in *Letters and Other Writings of James Madison*, (ed. William C. Rives and Philip R. Fendall), 4 vols. (Philadelphia, 1865), III, pp. 531–35; JM to Margaret Bayard Smith, Sept. 1830, in Hunt, IX, pp. 404–5.
2. TJ to Thomas C. Flournoy, Oct. 1, 1812, in L. and B., XIII, pp. 190–91.
3. TJ served as a member of the House committee that sat with the Senate committee to examine the joint ballot of both houses; see Brant, I, pp. 314–15.
4. JM to TJ, Mar. 16, 1784, below.

become better acquainted with Jefferson, who succeeded Henry as governor in 1779.

While Jefferson was serving in the Virginia assembly and Madison in the Executive Council, the war for American independence was being fought on battlefields to the north, in the halls of Congress, and in diplomatic maneuvers abroad. By the summer of 1776, the British army, which had evacuated Boston in the spring, invaded New York to drive a wedge between New England and the southern states, pushing General George Washington's troops from New York through New Jersey into Pennsylvania before the Americans, in a surprise offensive, crossed the ice-choked Delaware River and won stunning victories at Trenton and Princeton.

When General Sir William Howe moved his troops from New York to Philadelphia in the summer of 1777, Washington tried to block the redcoat occupation of the "rebel capital" but failed. Shortly thereafter, he led his battered and tattered troops into winter quarters at Valley Forge. On January 14, 1778, Madison's first day as a member of Virginia's Executive Council, Governor Henry submitted a congressional report that quoted Washington as saying the American army must either *"Starve Dissolve or Disperse"* unless it received supplies immediately.[5]

But just as Washington's victories at Trenton and Princeton had raised American spirits in 1776, the capture of Burgoyne's army at Saratoga revived them once again in the fall and winter of 1777-1778. More importantly, that victory led directly to the announcement of the Franco-American alliance, a diplomatic achievement that brought an open break between France and Great Britain. "The coup de grace is given to British glory," wailed a despairing American Loyalist on hearing the news of the Revolutionary Alliance: "Its Sun is set. Alass, how fallen, my friend how short sighted is human wisdom, how weak is human power at best! The roar of the british lion will no more be heard; the french cock may now crow and strut undisturbed. America that lately were humble supplicants to Great Britain for aid against a few french troops and indian savages disturbing her frontier settlements, have dared to renounce her authority, set her power at defiance, reduced her commerce, defeated her armies, sunk her natural credit, nay invaded her coasts, established her independency in spite of all efforts, and tell it not in Gath, allied itself to her natural, professed, and most dangerous enemy."[6]

The entry of France as a wartime ally of the United States and the loss of Burgoyne's army created a crisis for Great Britain in 1778. General William Howe resigned as British commander in chief in America and was replaced by Sir Henry Clinton. Strategic planning for 1779 called for the evacuation of Philadelphia and an attempt to "unravel the thread of rebellion from the

---

5. H. R. McIlwaine, ed., *The Official Letters of the Governors of the State of Virginia: The Letters of Patrick Henry* (Richmond, 1926), p. 226.

6. Samuel Curwen to Isaac Smith, quoted in Samuel Curwen, *The Journal of Samuel Curwen, Loyalist,* ed. Andrew Oliver, 2 vols. (Cambridge, Mass., 1972), I, p. 434.

southward," utilizing military assistance from Loyalist legions along the coast and Indian allies on the frontier.[7] Georgia fell quickly to the British, and by May redcoats had raided Charleston. At the same time, a British detachment sailed into Chesapeake Bay and for two weeks moved in the Hampton Roads area without meeting resistance, seizing Norfolk and Portsmouth, plundering several towns, destroying military and naval supplies, and capturing or sinking 130 vessels before embarking again for New York.[8] "The whole trade of the Chesapeake is at an end," reported the British commander, "and consequently the sinews of rebellion destroyed." "It is a melancholy fact," wrote a Virginian after the British hit-and-run invasion, "that there were not arms enough to put in the hands of the few militia who were called down . . . [and of ] those which were to be had, a great number were not fit for use." And another observed, "Never was a country in a more shabby situation."[9]

On June 1, 1779, during this period of adversity, the General Assembly elected Thomas Jefferson governor of Virginia "to exercise the executive powers of Government," "with the advice of a Council of State." Neither the governor nor the council had any significant constitutional authority except when they worked together. As St. George Tucker, professor of law at the College of William and Mary, wrote in his edition of Blackstone's *Commentaries on the Laws of England:* "The council of state seems to possess whatever power to deliberate, that may remain with the governor. The governor can constitutionally perform no one official act without their advice." Thus, the state's executive power rested with the governor and eight councillors or, as Madison once observed, with "eight governors and a councilor."[10]

The social distance between Jefferson and Madison was still considerable, however, since Mr. and Mrs. Jefferson and their two daughters lived in the magnificent Governor's Palace on the Duke of Gloucester Street in Williamsburg, halfway between the Capitol and the College of William and Mary. But the bachelor councillor no longer lived in anonymity in one of the taverns or rooming houses in town. Instead, he had a room at the President's House at the college, where he was the guest of his cousin, also a bachelor—the Reverend James Madison.[11]

In addition to Madison, with whom he had worked as a legislator in 1776, the new governor's associates on the council included John Page of Gloucester County, his oldest friend from college days at William and Mary; Joseph

7. See Paul H. Smith, *Loyalists and Redcoats: A Study in British Revolutionary Policy* (Chapel Hill, 1964).

8. Christopher Ward, *The War of the Revolution,* 2 vols. (New York, 1952), II, p. 867.

9. Peterson, pp. 168, 170; St. George Tucker to Theodorick Bland, Jr., June 6, 1779, in Theodorick Bland, Jr., *The Bland Papers, Being a Selection from the Manuscripts of Theodorick Bland, Jr., of Prince George County, Virginia,* ed. Charles Campbell, 2 vols. (Petersburg, Va., 1840–43), II, p. 11.

10. Brant, I, pp. 316–17.

11. Parke Rouse, Jr., *A House for a President: 250 Years on the Campus of William and Mary* (Richmond, 1983), pp. 88–89.

Prentis and Benjamin Waller of Williamsburg; Dudley Digges and David Jameson of York County; Bolling Stark of Dinwiddie County; and Thomas Walker of Albemarle County, a friend and neighbor from the Charlottesville area. Since the council, like the governor, was on call year round, the majority were from Williamsburg and nearby counties, with Stark, Walker, and Madison coming from the western part of the state. Both Jefferson and Madison had served in the 1776 House of Delegates with Page, Digges, Prentis, and Stark. Madison had also served with the other councillors—Jameson, Walker, and Waller—under Governor Patrick Henry.

Although Jefferson knew Page and Walker much better than he did Madison, the governor and the councillor from Orange forged a warm working relationship with "extraordinary rapidity," laying the foundation for the most important collaboration between two of the greatest statesmen in American history.[12] Their friendship flowered in two seven-week bursts of intensive work, when they and the other council members met daily at ten o'clock in the council chamber on the second floor of the Virginia Capitol at the end of the Duke of Gloucester Street. There they reviewed public-policy issues and decided what actions to take in conducting the Revolutionary War in Virginia. No longer the shy and inhibited novice, Madison, now twenty-eight, had one year's experience as a legislator and another year and a half's service as councillor to Governor Henry. As administrators, he and his colleagues on the council had more executive experience than Jefferson, who promised that he would rely on the wise counsels of those appointed by the assembly "for my aid in those duties."[13]

Unfortunately, the minutes of the meetings of the Governor-in-Council for 1779—the period when Jefferson and Madison first worked closely together—were destroyed by the British during a raid led by the turncoat general Benedict Arnold in 1781. Thus, there is no official journal that records how the council worked while Madison was a member or that lists all the letters written by Governor Jefferson "in Council."

Despite the destruction of the official records, however, two monumental editorial projects have pulled together all the extant letters written by Jefferson during his two terms as governor, making it possible to determine which were written by the Governor-in-Council when both Jefferson and Madison were in attendance.[14] Moreover, a study of the official records of the Governor-in-Council during the three terms (1776-1779) of Patrick Henry, the first governor of Virginia as a state and Jefferson's immediate predecessor, has made it possible to determine the kinds of issues the first governor and council acted upon, thus setting precedents to be followed by Governor Jefferson and the Council of State. A comparison of Governor Jefferson's letters published in

12. Brant, I, p. 354, uses the phrase quoted but did not examine the issues that came before the Governor-in-Council while TJ and JM were in attendance.
13. TJ to the General Assembly, June 2, 1779, in *PTJ*, II, p. 278.
14. H. R. McIlwaine, ed., *The Official Letters of the Governors of the State of Virginia: The Letters of Thomas Jefferson* (Richmond, 1928), and *PTJ*, II-III.

# The Beginnings of Friendship, 1779

the McIlwaine and Boyd editions demonstrates that the new governor and the carryover members of the council adhered to those precedents.

For example, Governor Henry, writing on behalf of the "minds and will of the Executive Power of the State of Virginia," requested aid from Bernardo de Gálvez, Spanish governor of Louisiana, on January 14, 1778, the day Madison joined the council. Noting that he had succeeded Henry as governor, Jefferson mentioned this letter when he wrote to Gálvez on November 8, 1779, seeking a loan for Virginia. Although he made no reference to the Executive Council, clearly Jefferson followed the procedures established under the Virginia Constitution of 1776 and discussed his letter with the council before submitting it to them for approval.[15]

Together, Jefferson, Madison, and the Executive Council quickly learned the hardships and frustrations of wartime government. Before dispatching letters to implement the decisions of the Governor-in-Council, the governor laid them before the council for advice and approval. Jefferson, therefore, used the collective "we" more often than "I" in his official letters and papers.

Although these letters are not correspondence between Jefferson and Madison, they were jointly approved by the Governor-in-Council when the two statesmen were together and are the first indications in writing of the close cooperation between them. Indeed, in one instance, the text of a letter signed by Jefferson is in Madison's handwriting.[16] By examining the letters from the Governor-in-Council when Jefferson and Madison were in attendance, one can see the kinds of questions engaging their attention and can begin to understand why the two developed the cordial working relationship that led them to date their friendship from this period.[17]

Wartime issues crowded the Governor-in-Council's daily calendar in 1779: paper money, taxation, and the issuance of financial warrants; military and naval affairs, including the recruiting, training, equipping, provisioning, and stationing of troops and seamen; erection of fortifications, barracks, military hospitals, and gun factories; supervision of Indian affairs and the defense

---

15. See McIlwaine, *The Letters of Patrick Henry*, I, pp. 227-29. For TJ to Bernardo de Gálvez, Nov. 8, 1779, see below.

16. The letter of TJ, "in Council," to Thomas Whiting, June 26, 1779, and its enclosed memorandum, below, "are in JM's hand rather than that of Archibald Blair, the clerk of the Council of State"; see *PJM*, I, p. 299.

17. The first period of collaboration between Governor Jefferson and Councillor Madison ran from June 1, 1779, through mid-July 1779, when JM left Williamsburg for Orange County; see Brant, I, pp. 340-41. The second period ran from Oct. 25, 1779, when Madison advertised in the *Virginia Gazette* for his horse, which had strayed or been stolen (the first evidence that he had returned to Williamsburg), through Dec. 16, 1779, when he accepted his election by the Virginia assembly to Congress.

McIlwaine and Boyd identify 107 letters written by TJ during the two seven-week periods when TJ and JM were in attendance and list 48 as having been written "in Council." But a close analysis reveals that only 6 of the letters were written by the governor as personal letters, the remaining 101 having been written "in Council," whether they were so labeled or not. Between June 1, 1779, and July 24, 1779, there were 41 letters; there were 60 between Oct. 25, 1779, and Dec. 16, 1779. I have selected 48, 23 from the first period and 25 from the second, for this chapter to indicate the range of problems dealt with by Jefferson, Madison, and the Executive Council.

of the frontier; apprehension of accused traitors and disposition of forfeited property; suppression of domestic insurrections, Indian uprisings, counterfeiting, and speculation in war commodities; maintenance of fair prices; regulation of trade to protect articles needed by the army and navy; guarding of British prisoners of war captured at Saratoga, who were quartered near Charlottesville, and exchange of such prisoners. Jefferson, Madison, and the Executive Council were in constant communication with the assembly in the promulgation and execution of the laws of the commonwealth, with the state Board of War and the Board of Trade on military and commercial matters, with General Washington and Continental officers on the raising of troops, and with the president of the Continental Congress on financial requisitions, troop allocations, and peace negotiations.

Early in 1779, Spain offered to mediate the war at a peace conference to be held in Madrid, if both sides agreed to an immediate suspension of hostilities. Before the United States could enter into any negotiations, however, Congress had to agree upon American peace objectives such as national boundaries, commercial arrangements, fishing rights, navigation of the Mississippi River, and territorial claims. While Congress debated these issues over a six-month period, newspapers reported congressional divisions along sectional and party lines, with New England holding out for fishing rights and cessions of Canadian territory, and the middle and southern states insisting on navigation of the Mississippi. Only three days after Jefferson moved into the Governor's Palace in Williamsburg, a neighbor wrote to a North Carolina congressman complaining that "it is currently said that the Independence of the thirteen united States had been offered Congress by G. Britain, and that peace on these [terms] has been rejected by them, they demanding Canada and Nova Scotia."[18]

In a letter to Congressman William Fleming written four days later, Governor Jefferson, Madison, and the Executive Council were also critical of Congress's failure to agree on peace proposals, citing that action—or inaction—as the reason that the French minister plenipotentiary to the United States, Conrad Alexandre Gérard, had decided, in disgust, to return to France.[19] Although Congress had unanimously ratified the Franco-American treaties of alliance and commerce on May 4, 1778,[20] the Virginia assembly and the Governor-in-Council made a conciliatory effort to spike rumors of disunion, reassuring the French minister of the high value they set on the treaties by ratifying, confirming, and declaring them binding on the Old Dominion.[21]

---

18. Henry Tazewell to Thomas Burke, June 4, 1779, cited in William C. Stinchcombe, *The American Revolution and the French Alliance* (Syracuse, 1969), p. 71. No such offer was made by Great Britain, nor was a peace conference held in Madrid.

19. See TJ, JM, and the Executive Council to William Fleming, June 8, 1779, below.

20. Edmund Cody Burnett, *The Continental Congress* (New York, 1941), pp. 331–33.

21. TJ, JM, and the Executive Council to Conrad Alexandre Gérard, June 8, 1779, below. See also Brant, I, pp. 352–53.

While he was a member of the House of Delegates, Jefferson had supported plans for a campaign against the British and Indians north of the Ohio River in order to protect the new Virginia counties in Kentucky. In a brilliant series of forced marches, Colonel George Rogers Clark, who held his commission from Virginia, conquered Kaskaskia and Cahokia in the Illinois country and captured at Vincennes British superintendent of Indian warfare Lieutenant Governor Henry Hamilton of Detroit. Clark then dispatched his prize captives to Williamsburg as prisoners of war. Hamilton's reputation as "the Famous Hair Buyer General"—Clark's term[22]—had preceded him, and the assembly voted Rogers an "elegant sword" for his distinguished victory. When Hamilton and the other captives arrived in Williamsburg, Jefferson, Madison, and the Executive Council not only confined them in jail, but also put them in irons, publishing the Order-in-Council on June 16, 1779.[23]

The Governor-in-Council's treatment of these prisoners, who had surrendered by capitulation, as war criminals created a bitter controversy that lasted for well over a year. The harsh treatment of "Hair Buyer" Hamilton stood in sharp contrast to the mild treatment of other British prisoners in American hands, particularly the army that Burgoyne had surrendered at Saratoga, which was now quartered near Charlottesville. Jefferson had entertained some of them as officers and gentlemen at Monticello. The prisoners, the Governor-in-Council wrote, had "been treated with moderation and humanity" as prisoners of war. But the council contrasted this humane treatment with that dealt out to American prisoners in British hands, charging that the treatment of American prisoners had "been so rigorous, and cruel" that a "very great proportion of the whole . . . have perished miserably, from that cause only." Others had been kept in "common miserable jails, built for the confinement of Malefactors" or in prison ships "infected with malignant disorders," where death carried off "from five to ten a day." Jefferson, Madison, and the Executive Council argued, therefore, that Hamilton and others guilty "of inciting the Indians to perpetrate their accustomed cruelties on the citizens of these states" were "fit subjects to begin on with the work of retaliation."[24]

When General William Phillips, senior officer among the Saratoga prisoners stationed in Jefferson's home county of Albemarle, wrote to intercede on Hamilton's behalf, the Governor-in-Council defended its action "on the general principle of National retaliation" and reviewed "British Cruelty to American prisoners" from 1775 to 1779.[25] The Governor-in-Council had already

---

22. George Rogers Clark to Patrick Henry, Feb. 3, 1779, in George Rogers Clark, *George Rogers Clark Papers, 1771–1781,* ed. James A. James, Illinois State Historical Library Collections 8 (Springfield, 1912), p. 97.

23. See TJ, JM, and the Executive Council's Order of June 16, 1779, below.

24. TJ, JM, and the Executive Council to William Phillips, July 22, 1779, below.

25. *Ibid.* Francis Abell, in *Prisoners of War in Britain, 1756 to 1815* (London, 1914), states that "the American prisoners conveyed to England during the war of Independence seem to have been regarded quite as unworthy of proper treatment." Recent scholarship agrees that "whether by

written to General Washington about Hamilton, and they now forwarded General Phillips's letter to him, asking that he "authoritatively decide" the issue.[26] Washington had originally endorsed the action by the Governor-in-Council on the principle of just retaliation. But consultation with his general staff on the usage of war led him to conclude that Hamilton's capitulation precluded "any uncommon severity," although "he may unquestionably without any breach of public faith or the least shadow of imputation, be confined to a Room."[27] Washington's decision led to the removal of Hamilton's shackles and the offer of parole, which Hamilton refused as too confining. But eventually he signed a parole, was exchanged for an American officer, and returned to England in 1781.[28]

In their early discussions, the governor and the Executive Council expressed hope that recent measures had put state "finances into a better way and [would] enable us to cooperate with our sister states in reducing the enormous sums of money in circulation"; they cited new revenues from the sale of western lands, the sale of confiscated British and Loyalist property, and new taxes in kind instead of cash.[29] "Every other remedy"—especially printing more money—"is nonsensical quackery," they wrote.[30] In a private letter written later in the month, however, Jefferson complained that currency depreciation was running so far ahead of taxation that the latter "is become of no account, for it is foreseen that notwithstanding it's increased amount there will still be a greater deficiency than ever." Financial disaster could be avoided only by an early peace—a forlorn hope—"or a plentiful loan of hard money."[31]

In 1778, the General Assembly had empowered the Governor-in-Council to seek loans of gold and silver, and Governor Henry, Madison, and the Executive Council had appointed Philip Mazzei, Jefferson's neighbor, as agent to his native Tuscany to borrow £1 million sterling, with Madison taking the lead in pushing the mission.[32] Similarly, Jefferson, Madison, and the council

---

policy or by neglect, the conditions under which American prisoners were confined were wretched and lethal"; see Charles Royster, *A Revolutionary People at War: The Continental Army and American Character, 1775–1783* (Chapel Hill, 1979; rpt. New York, 1981), pp. 377–78.

26. See TJ, JM, and the Executive Council to George Washington, June 19, 1779, and July 17, 1779, below.

27. George Washington to TJ, Aug. 6–10, 1779, in Fitzpatrick, XVI, pp. 68–69.

28. After a year in the Williamsburg jail, Hamilton was transferred to Chesterfield on Aug. 1, 1780, where he wrote that his confinement was very tolerable. On Oct. 10, he was paroled to British headquarters in New York before returning to England; see John D. Barnhart, *Henry Hamilton and George Rogers Clark in the American Revolution, with the Unpublished Journal of Lieut. Gov. Henry Hamilton* (Crawfordsville, Ind., 1951).

29. On June 16, 1779, the assembly levied a tax on specific items such as one bushel of wheat or its equivalent value in other grains, hemp, or tobacco for every able-bodied man and every woman slave over sixteen years of age; see *Journal of the House of Delegates, 1779* (Richmond, 1827), p. 70, and Hening, X, p. 79.

30. TJ, JM, and the Executive Council to William Fleming, June 8, 1779, below.

31. TJ to Richard Henry Lee, June 17, 1779, in *PTJ*, II, p. 298.

32. Brant, I, pp. 343–52.

appointed Peter Penet of Nantes, France, to obtain a loan of £100,000 sterling.[33] And in a letter to Don Bernardo de Gálvez, governor of Louisiana, they also sought a loan from Spain.[34] But none of these efforts was successful.

A week after appointing Penet as a loan agent, Governor Jefferson, working with Madison and the council, launched an even more ambitious project, contracting with Peter Penet, Wendel and Company of France to build an armament factory and foundry near Richmond to produce muskets, carbines, pistols, cannons, swords, bayonets, powder, and bullets, and to construct a canal around the falls of the James River in order to transport the cannon and other arms to military bases. Jefferson and the council thought the contract very important since the blockading British navy made importation of arms "insecure and distressing." The domestic manufacture of arms and other implements of war, they concluded, "is as necessary as to make our bread within ourselves."[35] Unfortunately, this project failed, but cannon and military supplies were manufactured on a more modest scale at state foundries in Westham and Fredericksburg. Jefferson, Madison, and the Executive Council gave these public manufactories priority, authorizing the purchase of slaves to carry on the operations.[36]

The British raid on Portsmouth and Norfolk highlighted the shortage of firearms in Virginia. Accordingly, the Governor-in-Council authorized an inventory of all military supplies in Virginia.[37] In reporting on "the low State of our Magazines," Jefferson, Madison, and the council estimated that there were not more than 3,000 stand of usable muskets in the state. In addition to arms furnished to the Virginia troops in the Continental army, the state had recently lent a stand of 1,000 arms to South Carolina for the "common defence." With rumors of another invasion circulating, the Governor-in-Council, acting under Lieutenant Governor John Page in Jefferson's absence, took advantage of an unusual opportunity when a shipment of arms intended for Continental use "seemed to be guided by the hand of providence into one of our harbours." They retained 5,000 muskets for Virginia's use, arguing that "they were for the common defence too, and we were part of the Body to be defended." When Congress and the Continental Board of War complained, Jefferson, Madison, and the Executive Council upheld the justice of the action, noting that the Virginia Board of War had authenticated the free gift of 5,664 muskets and 580 rifles by Virginia to Continental forces and could, by

---

33. See TJ, JM, and the Executive Council to Peter Penet, July 15, 1779, below. For Penet's efforts to arrange a loan of 800,000 livres, see Peter Penet to Governor-in-Council, May 20, 1780, in *PTJ*, II, pp. 383–85.

34. See TJ, JM, and the Executive Council to the Board of Trade, Nov. 6, 1779, and TJ, JM, and the Executive Council to Bernardo de Gálvez, Nov. 8, 1779, below.

35. See TJ, JM, and the Executive Council to Benjamin Harrison, Oct. 30, 1779, below. The contract is printed in McIlwaine, *Official Letters . . . of Thomas Jefferson*, pp. 23–28.

36. TJ, JM, and the Executive Council to the Board of Trade, Dec. 10, 1779, below.

37. See TJ, JM, and the Executive Council to Charles de Klauman, June 12, 1779, below. For de Klauman's report of July 17, 1779, see *PTJ*, III, p. 254.

additional research, establish a right to 10,000 stand of arms. But rather than justify the action as "one of the Articles of Debt in our Account of Arms against the continent," they rested Virginia's case on the "sacred cause" of "establishing our rights" on a continental basis. "Necessity alone dictated the measure," they declared; "no sentiment of disrespect to congress entered into the transaction."[38]

The more usual way of acquiring military supplies was to have them shipped from France, if the ships could avoid the British navy. That happened so seldom that the arrival of three shiploads of arms, ordnance, and military implements, purchased by one of Virginia's commercial agents, Jacques Le Maire, led Jefferson, Madison, and the Executive Council to recommend him for the brevet commission of lieutenant colonel.[39]

Through the fall of 1779, invasion from the sea was a constant worry for Virginia. Jefferson, Madison, and the council agreed that Virginia's "only practicable defence was naval," and they noted that the assembly had authorized the construction of two frigates and two large galleys in 1776. Unfortunately, the vessels were so unseaworthy that Jefferson and his colleagues concluded that "we should be gainers were we to burn our whole navy" and build anew. In fact, one of the galleys sank off the North Carolina coast, and the other one on that station was offered to North Carolina "at such fair estimation as may be agreed on." Deploring the unpreparedness of "our miserable navy," the Governor-in-Council pleaded for Congress to send naval help to the Chesapeake Bay.[40]

The Virginia Board of War agreed on the need for naval protection and warned Jefferson, Madison, and the Executive Council in November that British forces would probably launch an offensive against the state shortly. "Not only the exposed position of this Country, and its particular situations so favorable to the plans of predatory warfare, lead them to this opinion," the board wrote, "but they are Strengthened in it, by the unsuccessful Attempt on the Savannah [to drive the British out of Georgia], and the departure of the french fleet from the American Coasts, whereby our enemies being left masters of the American Seas, may commence operations here, freed from the apprehensions of a superior maritime power."[41]

As the war in the South threatened to move into the Carolinas and Virginia, Jefferson, Madison, and the Executive Council ordered the expulsion of British subjects as alien enemies[42] and endorsed the removal of the state capital from Williamsburg, within easy reach of invading forces by the James or York

---

38. See TJ, JM, and the Executive Council to Samuel Huntington, Dec. 16, 1779, below. TJ was not in Williamsburg when the muskets were seized, so Lieutenant Governor Page headed the council in the governor's absence.

39. TJ, JM, and the Executive Council to Benjamin Harrison, Oct. 29, 1779, below.

40. See TJ, JM, and the Executive Council to Richard Henry Lee, July 17, 1779, below, and TJ, JM, and the Executive Council to Richard Caswell, June 22 and 30, 1779, below.

41. Board of War to Governor-in-Council, Nov. 16, 1779, in *PTJ*, III, pp. 190-91.

42. See TJ, JM, and the Executive Council's Proclamation of July 1, 1779, below.

rivers, to Richmond.[43] They also welcomed a French consul to Williamsburg and assured him that Virginia would receive the French armed forces with the utmost cordiality and cooperation.[44]

With Virginia's military commitments stretching from the Mississippi in the West to the Continental army in the East, from troops dispatched to Charleston in the South to George Rogers Clark in the Northwest, the assembly authorized the Governor-in-Council to appoint an officer in every county to recruit men for the duration of the war; if there were not enough volunteers, a draft was authorized to fill the ranks.[45] In a frank letter to General Washington, Jefferson, Madison, and the Executive Council confessed that "we have at present very pressing calls to send additional numbers of men to the Southward. No inclination is wanting in either the legislative or Executive powers to aid them, or to strengthen you: but we find it very difficult to procure men."[46]

The governor and council also worked with the Board of War on other defense measures. Together they formulated orders for the defense of the western frontier and sent appropriate instructions to county lieutenants.[47] To deal with the friendly Cherokees contiguous to Virginia and the two Carolinas, they proposed the apportionment of responsibility among the three states, with South Carolina negotiating with the southern Indian settlements, North Carolina with the middle, and Virginia with the northern. "The attachment which each settlement will by these means acquire to the particular state which is it's immediate patron and benefactor, will be a bond of peace, and will lead to a separation of that powerful people."[48] When the Board of War recommended the appointment of a general with "full powers concentrated in one man" to "accelerate and give energy to military preparations," however, the Governor-in-Council refused, noting that "they are not authorized by Law to appoint a general Officer till an invasion or insurrection has actually taken place, and three Battalions at least of the Militia embodied."[49]

To cap off the frustration of Jefferson's first six months in office, he and the council had to cope with food shortages caused by "the most unfavorable Harvest ever known Since the Settlement of this Country." Instead of export-

---

43. See TJ, JM, and the Executive Council to Thomas Whiting, June 26, 1779, below. The letter is in JM's handwriting.

44. TJ, JM, and the Executive Council to the chevalier D'Anmours, Nov. 10, 1779, below, and TJ, JM, and the Executive Council to Benjamin Harrison, Nov. 23, 1779, below.

45. See TJ, JM, and the Executive Council to the Board of War, Nov. 12, 1979, below, and TJ, JM, and the Executive Council to David Shepherd, Nov. 13, 1779, below. The legislation is in Hening, X, pp. 23–27, 82–83.

46. TJ, JM, and the Executive Council to George Washington, Nov. 28, 1779, below.

47. See TJ, JM, and the Executive Council Issue Orders for the Defense of the Western Frontier, July 23, 1779, below; and TJ, JM, and the Executive Council to John Bowman, Nov. 6, 1779, below; and TJ, JM, and the Executive Council to Certain County Lieutenants, Nov. 6, 1779, below.

48. TJ, JM, and the Executive Council to Richard Caswell, Nov. 11, 1779, below.

49. TJ, JM, and the Executive Council to the Board of War, Nov. 18, 1779, below.

ing flour, Virginia was obliged "for our own subsistence, to purchase it from the neighboring States of Maryland and Pensylvania to whom we have until this year furnished large Quantities."[50] To deal with the shortages, the Governor-in-Council proclaimed an embargo on shipments by land or water of beef and pork, wheat, corn, and grain as well as flour and meal.[51] In one case, however, the governor and council waived the rule, authorizing the grain trade with the enemy island of Bermuda, theoretically on grounds of humanitarianism but actually in exchange for salt to be used in curing meat.[52]

Cumbersome as the procedures of the Executive Council were, the daily meetings of governor and councillors made it possible for Jefferson and Madison, working endless hours together, to become well acquainted. Together they and the other councillors went over every purchase order, every military order, and every communication to and from the assembly, Board of War, Board of Trade, Virginia delegates in Congress, and county courts involved in transacting the state's business. The letters of the Governor-in-Council include many brief notes that may seem unimportant. Cumulatively, however, these papers, both the brief notes and the longer letters, demonstrate as no other existing evidence does the range of issues with which the council dealt when Jefferson and Madison first had lengthy meetings on a daily basis. The papers reveal the diligence and meticulous care of the Governor-in-Council in dealing not only with broad matters of policy, but also with a vast array of details.[53]

In less than six months, Jefferson concluded that Madison was a master of both, and he drew increasingly on "the rich resources of his [Madison's] luminous and discriminating mind, and of his extensive information," as he later recalled. It is clear that Jefferson was not alone in his appraisal, since Madison's growing reputation for industry, sound judgment, and "the powers and polish of his pen" led the Virginia assembly to elect him a delegate to the Continental Congress in December 1779,[54] a belated response to General Washington's plea that Virginia send her "ablest and best men to Congress."[55]

50. TJ, JM, and the Executive Council to Bernardo de Gálvez, Nov. 8, 1779, below.

51. See the Proclamation of Embargo, Nov. 30, 1779, below.

52. See TJ, JM, and the Executive Council to St. George Tucker, June 22, 1779, below, when an earlier embargo was lifted for this purpose.

53. For a careful appraisal of the executive's efforts to meet its wartime responsibilities, see Emory G. Evans, "Executive Leadership in Virginia, 1776–1781: Henry, Jefferson, and Nelson," in *Sovereign States in an Age of Uncertainty*, ed. Ronald Hoffman and Peter J. Albert (Charlottesville, 1981), pp. 181–225. After almost five months of incessant labor, JM and the members of the Executive Council advised Jefferson that, when the council did not have a quorum, Jefferson should take action on a wide variety of routine issues without waiting for the council's consent. See JM and the Executive Council to TJ, Nov. 13, 1779, below.

54. TJ, "Autobiography," in *Thomas Jefferson: Writings*, ed. Merrill D. Peterson (New York, 1984), p. 37.

55. George Washington to Benjamin Harrison, Dec. 30, 1778, in George Washington, *The Writings of George Washington*, ed. John C. Fitzpatrick, 37 vols. (Washington, 1931–1940), XII, p. 466.

# The Letters[*]

*Jefferson, Madison, and the Executive Council to the French Minister to the United States, Conrad Alexandre Gérard*

Williamsburg June 8, 1779

SIR

The General Assembly of Virginia at their first Session which was held after the conclusion of the Treaties of Alliance and Commerce between his most Christian Majesty and the American Congress, tho' seeing that fortunate event in all its importance, yet omitted to give it their particular approbation, entertaining a daily hope that the Confederation of the united States would be acceded to by all the parties, and that the Ratification of their Congress would then be the most proper and complete confirmation, and the most satisfactory to the Mind of their great and good Ally. But as that has not yet taken place they have now thought it their Duty no longer to pretermit their particular Sense of it and so far as their Interests and powers extend, to declare it obligatory; and have accordingly instructed me to communicate to the Minister of his most Christian Majesty resident at Philadelphia their Note of ratification; which I now have the honor to inclose to you. I obey their Commands with the greater pleasure because I know the grateful Sense which the Individual Members of that Body and the Citizens of this Commonwealth in general entertain of those Treaties, the high Value they set on them, and the disposition they have to convince you in every future instance that Nothing in their power shall be wanting to remove from your mind every cause of dissatisfaction which may at any time arise and to render these Treaties as lasting as to them they have been Safe honourable and pleasing. I have the Honor to be with the most profound respect Your Excellency's Most Obedt. and mo: hble Servt.,

TH: JEFFERSON

ENCLOSURE

In General Assembly
friday the 4th June 1779.

Resolved nemine contradicente, that the treaties of alliance and commerce entered into between His Most Christian Majesty of France, on the one part, and the Congress of the United States of America, on behalf of the said States on the other part, ought to be ratified and confirmed so far as is in the power of this Commonwealth, and the same

---

[*] The letters in this chapter are reprinted from *PTJ*, II and III, by permission of Princeton University Press.

are accordingly hereby ratified, confirmed and declared binding on this Commonwealth.

Resolved, that the Governor be desired to notify to the Minister of His Most Christian Majesty, resident at Philadelphia, the above ratification under the Seal of the Commonwealth.

Archibald Cary, Speaker of the Senate<br>Benjamin Harrison, Speaker of the House of Delegates

Test:
J. Beckley, Clerk of the Senate.
Edmund Randolph, Clerk of the house of delegates.

Virginia to wit

In pursuance of the resolutions of the two Houses of Assembly, I hereby notify their joint ratification of the treaties of Alliance and Commerce entered into between his most Christian Majesty of France on the one part and the Congress of the United States on the other part, as expressed in their resolutions of June 4th 1779. and in testimony thereof have caused the Seal of the Commonwealth to be affixed hereto. Given under my hand this 7th day of June in the Year of Our Lord 1779.

TH: JEFFERSON<br>Governor of the Commonwealth of Virginia

## *Jefferson, Madison, and the Executive Council to Congressman William Fleming*

Williamsburg June 8, 1779

DEAR FLEMING

I received your letter and have now to thank you for it. Some resolutions of Congress came to hand yesterday desiring an authentic state to be sent them of the cruelties said to have been committed by the enemy during their late invasion. The council had already taken measures to obtain such a state. Tho' so near the scene where these barbarities are said to have been committed I am not able yet to decide within myself whether there were such or not. The testimony on both sides is such as if heard separately could not admit a moment's suspension of our faith.[1]

We have lately been extremely disturbed to find a pretty general opinion prevailing that peace and the independance of the thirteen states are now within our power, and that Congress have hesitations on the subject, and delay entering on the consideration. It has even been said that their conduct on this head has been so dissatisfactory to the French minister that he thinks of returning to his own country, ostensibly for better health, but in truth through disgust. Such an event would be deplored here as the most dreadful

---

1. See Elizabeth Cometti, "Depredations in Virginia during the Revolution," in *The Old Dominion: Essays for Thomas Perkins Abernethy*, ed. Darrett B. Rutman (Charlottesville, 1964), pp. 140–41, and Ward, II, p. 867.

calamity. It was in contemplation of some gentlemen who conferred on the subject to propose the re-establishment of our committees of correspondence; others thought this too slow for the emergency and that plenipotentiary deputies should be sent to satisfy the mind of the French minister, and to set on foot proper measures for procuring the genuine sense of the several states. The whole however subsided on a supposition that the information might not be true, and that our delegates in Congress would think no obligations of secrecy under which they may have been laid sufficient to restrain them from informing their constituents of any proceedings which may involve the fate of their freedom and independance. It would surely be better to carry on a ten years war some time hence than to continue the present an unnecessary moment.

Our land office I think will be opened; the sale of British property take place, and our tax bill put on a better footing. These measures I hope will put our finances into a better way and enable us to cooperate with our sister states in reducing the enormous sums of money in circulation. Every other remedy is nonsensical quackery. The house of delegates have passed a bill for removing the seat of government to Richmond. It hesitates with the Senate. We have established a board of war and a board of trade. I hear from your quarter that Genl. Sullivan is marching with a large army against the Indians. If he succeeds it will be the first instance of a great army doing any thing against Indians and his laurels will be greater. We have ever found that chosen corps of men fit for the service of the woods, going against them with rapidity, and by surprize, have been most sucesful.[2] I believe that our Colo. Clarke if we could properly reinforce him would be more likely to succeed against those within his reach than Genl. Macintosh's regular method of proceeding. I shall hope to hear from you often. I put no name to this letter, because letters have miscarried, and if it goes safely you know the hand.

## *Jefferson, Madison, and the Executive Council to Colonel Theodorick Bland*

Williamsburg June 8, 1779

SIR

Your letter to Governor Henry of the 1st. instant came safe to hand yesterday and I immediately laid it before the Council.[3] It gave them pain to

---

2. For the standard account of John Sullivan's successful expedition against the Iroquois, see Barbara Graymont, *The Iroquois in the American Revolution* (Syracuse, 1972), pp. 192–222. Also see Isabel Thompson Kelsay, *Joseph Brant, 1743–1807: Man of Two Worlds* (Syracuse, 1984), pp. 254–68.

3. Theodorick Bland was commander of the troops guarding the convention army, which had been captured at Saratoga and was quartered near Charlottesville; see William M. Dabney, *After Saratoga: The Story of the Convention Army* (Albuquerque, 1954), p. 52.

hesitate on my request from General Phillips whose polite conduct has disposed them to every indulgence consistent with the duties of their appointment.[4] The indiscriminate murther of men, Women and children with the usual circumstances of barbarity practised by the Indian savages, was the particular task of Governor Hamilton's employment, and if any thing could have aggravated the acceptance of such an office and have made him personally answerable in a high degree it was that eager Spirit with which he is said to have executed it and which if the representations before the Council are to be credited seems to have shewn that his own feelings and disposition were in union with his employment. The truth of these representations will be the subject of their inquiry shortly, and the treatment of Governor Hamilton will be mild or otherwise as his conduct shall appear to merit. On a dispasionate examination we trust it must furnish a contemplation rather pleasing to the generous Soldier to see his honourable bravery respected even by those against whom it happens to be inlisted, and discriminated from the cruel and cowardly warfare of the savage, whose object in war is to extinguish human nature.[5]

By a letter dated May 27$^{th}$, you were desired to discharge the militia under your command as soon as you judged it proper; lest that letter should have miscarried, I now enclose you a copy.

Colonel Finnie[6] informs me he had written to you to apply for clothes at Winchester, for the use of your regiment of guards, and of the horse now with you. He yesterday showed me a letter from the continental board of war, giving the same directions; he says also that he had lately written to you on the subject of the articles desired for your particular use, and that he is not yet enabled to procure them more fully.

As to putting the horse now with you on the same pay-roll with the regiment of guards, the council are of opinion that either your own powers are competent to it, or at least that it may be done in concert with the continental paymaster. The regiment of guards is recognized as continental; your horse are continental; the duty they are jointly engaged in its continental; they therefore wish that this matter should go into the continental line altogether, rather than be controlled by their interference, where it is not absolutely necessary. I am your most obedient, humble servant, etc.

TH: JEFFERSON

---

4. Major General William Phillips was the ranking British general captured with Burgoyne's army; see *ibid.*, p. 22. After his capture at Vincennes, Governor Hamilton appealed to Phillips to intercede with Virginia authorities on his behalf; see William Phillips to Theodorick Bland, May 29, 1779, in Bland, I, pp. 130–31.

5. The letter to this point has been printed in *PTJ,* II, pp. 286–87. The complete text has been printed in Bland, I, p. 133, and in McIlwaine, *Official Letters of . . . Thomas Jefferson,* II, pp. 5–6.

6. Colonel William Finnie was deputy quartermaster general of the Southern Department.

## Jefferson, Madison, and the Executive Council to Speaker Benjamin Harrison[7]

[Williamsburg] in Council June 8, 1779

SIR

Since receiving the resolutions of Congress calling for an additional sum of money, which I had the honor of transmitting to you yesterday, the inclosed address relating to the same subject, with the letter accompanying it has come to hand.[8] I take the liberty through you of communicating it to the General assembly, and am Sir with the greatest esteem Your most obedient and most humble servant,

TH: JEFFERSON

## Jefferson, Madison, and the Executive Council to Captain Charles de Klauman

[Williamsburg] in Council June 12, 1779

Capt. de Klauman being already sufficiently authorized to inspect and state the quantity and condition of all military stores within this commonwealth and to require necessary aid from the proper officers, I have only to desire that he will in every instance take from the officer in whose custody any ordnance arms, or other military stores are a certificate thereof signed by such officer; and where any such articles may not be in the custody of a particular officer, Capt. Klaumann is desired to certify under his own hand what and where they are.[9]

TH: JEFFERSON

---

7. Benjamin Harrison was first elected Speaker of the House of Delegates in 1778 and was reelected for several sessions; see Howard W. Smith, *Benjamin Harrison and the American Revolution* (Williamsburg, 1978), pp. 49–52.

8. TJ sent Harrison the "Address to the Inhabitants of the United States of America," adopted by Congress on May 26, 1779, which dealt with state quotas of taxes.

9. De Klauman was a Danish volunteer officer appointed by Governor Patrick Henry on Sept. 4, 1778, to report on the number and condition of arms in Virginia's magazines; see McIlwaine, *Official Letters of . . . Patrick Henry,* I, p. 309. De Klauman's report of July 17, 1779, is printed in *PTJ,* III, p. 254.

## Jefferson, Madison, and the Executive Council Issue an Order Placing Lieutenant Governor Henry Hamilton of Detroit and Others in Irons

[Williamsburg] in Council June 16, 1779

The Board proceeded to the consideration of the letters of Colonel Clarke, and other papers relating to Henry Hamilton, Esq; who has acted some years past as Lieutenant Governour of the settlement at and about Detroit, and commandant of the British garrison there, under Sir Guy Carleton as Governour in Chief; Philip Dejean, Justice of the Peace for Detroit, and William Lamothe, Captain of volunteers, prisoners of war, taken in the county of Illinois.

They find that Governour Hamilton has executed the task of inciting the Indians to perpetrate their accustomed cruelties on the citizens of these states, without distinction of age, sex, or condition, with an eagerness and activity which evince that the general nature of his charge harmonized with his particular disposition; they should have been satisfied from the other testimony adduced that these enormities were committed by savages acting under his commission, but the number of proclamations which, at different times were left in houses, the inhabitants of which were killed or carried away by the Indians, one of which proclamations, under the hand and Seal of Governor Hamilton, is in possession of the Board, puts this fact beyond doubt. At the time of his captivity it appears, that he had sent considerable detachments of Indians against the frontier settlements of the states, and had actually appointed a great council of Indians to meet him at the mouth of the Tanissee, to concert the operations of this present campaign. They find that his treatment of our citizens and soldiers, captivated [captured] and carried within the limits of his command, has been cruel and inhuman; that in the case of John Dodge,[10] a citizen of these states, which has been particularly stated to this Board, he loaded him with irons, threw him into a dungeon, without bedding, without straw, without fire, in the dead of winter and severe climate of Detroit; that in that state he harrassed and wasted him, with incessant expectations of death; that when the rigours of his situation had brought him so low that death seemed likely to withdraw him from their power, he was taken out and attended to till somewhat mended, and then again, before he had recovered abilities to walk, was returned to his dungeon, in which a hole was cut seven inches square only, for the admission of air, and the same load of irons again put on him; that appearing again to be in imminent danger of being lost to them, he was a second time taken from his dungeon, in which he had lain from January to June, with the intermission before-mentioned of a few weeks

10. John Dodge was an Indian trader from Connecticut who was imprisoned by the British in 1776. He escaped in 1778 and testified against Hamilton before Governor Henry and the Virginia Executive Council; see *Kaskaskia Records, 1778–1790,* ed. Clarence W. Alvord, in Illinois State Historical Library Collections 5 (Virginia Series II) (Springfield, 1909), pp. 104–5.

only; that Governour Hamilton gave standing rewards for scalps, but offered none for prisoners, which induced the Indians, after making their captives carry their baggage into the neighbourhood of the fort, there to put them to death, and carry in their scalps to the Governour, who welcomed their return and successes by a discharge of cannon; that when a prisoner brought alive, and destined to death by the Indians, the fire already kindled and himself bound to the stake, was dexterously withdrawn and secreted from them by the humanity of a fellow prisoner; a large reward was offered for the discovery of the victim, which having tempted a servant to betray his concealment, the present prisoner Dejean being sent with a party of soldiers, surrounded the house, took and threw into jail the unhappy victim, and his deliverer, where the former soon expired under the perpetual assurances of Dejean, that he was to be again restored into the hands of the savages, and the latter when enlarged was bitterly and illiberally reprimanded and threatened by Governour Hamilton.

It appears to them that the prisoner Dejean, was on all occasions the willing and cordial instrument of Governour Hamilton, acting both as judge and keeper of the jail, and instigating and urging him by malicious insinuations and untruths, to increase rather than relax his severities, heightening the cruelty of his orders by the manner of executing them; offering at one time a reward to one prisoner to be the hangman of another, threatening his life on refusal, and taking from his prisoners the little property their opportunities enabled them to acquire.

It appears that the prisoner Lamothe, was a Captain of the volunteer scalping parties of Indians and whites, who went out, from time to time, under general orders, to spare neither men, women, nor children.

From this detail of circumstances which arose in a few cases only, coming accidentally to the knowledge of the Board, they think themselves authorized to presume by fair deduction what would be the horrid history of the sufferings of the many who have expired under their miseries (which therefore will remain for ever untold) or who having escaped from them, are yet too remote and too much dispersed to bring together their well grounded accusations against these prisoners.

They have seen that the conduct of the British officers, civil and military, has in its general tenor, through the whole course of this war, been savage and unprecedented among civilized nations; that our officers and soldiers taken by them have been loaded with irons, consigned to loathsome and crouded jails, dungeons, and prison ships; supplied often with no food, generally with too little for the sustenance of nature, and that little sometimes unsound and unwholesome, whereby so many of them have perished that captivity and miserable death have with them been almost synonymous; that they have been transported beyond seas where their fate is out of the reach of our enquiry, have been compelled to take arms against their country, and by a new refinement in cruelty to become the murtherers of their own brethren.

Their prisoners with us have, on the other hand, been treated with moderation and humanity; they have been fed on all occasions with wholesome and plentiful food, lodged comfortably, suffered to go at large within extensive tracts of country, treated with liberal hospitality [and] permitted to live in the families of our citizens, to labour for themselves, to acquire and to enjoy property, and finally to participate of the principal benefits of society while privileged from all its burthens.

Reviewing this contrast which cannot be denied by our enemies themselves in a single point, which has now been kept up during four years of unremitted war, a term long enough to produce well founded despair that our moderation may ever lead them into the practice of humanity, called on by that justice which we owe to those who are fighting the battles of their country, to deal out at length miseries to their enemies, measure for measure, and to distress the feelings of mankind by exhibiting to them spectacles of severe retaliation, where we had long and vainly endeavoured to introduce an emulation in kindness; happily possessed by the fortune of war of some of those very individuals, who having distinguished themselves personally in this line of cruel conduct, are fit subjects to begin on with the work of retaliation, this Board has resolved to advise the Governour that the said Henry Hamilton, Philip Dejean, and William Lamothe, prisoners of war, be put into irons, confined in the dungeon of the publick jail, debarred the use of pen, ink, and paper, and excluded all converse except with their keeper. And the Governour orders accordingly. *(A Copy)*
Attest

ARCHIBALD BLAIR, C.C.


## Jefferson, Madison, and the Executive Council to the Continental Board of War

Williamsburg June 18, 1779

SIR

Inclosed you will receive the information you formerly desired on the subject of the barracks ordered to be built at Frederick. Some difference will appear between the report of some gentlemen formerly appointed for that purpose and Colo. Smith's letter;[11] which difference however may be accounted for by their different dates. It is with concern we find that the continent is likely to lose by the inconsiderate omission of Colo. Kennedy to take security from the undertaker [contractor]. Upon thorough enquiry into the

11. Colonel John Smith, county lieutenant for Frederick County, lived at Hackwood Park near Winchester and was a member of the House of Delegates; see T. K. Cartmell, *Shenandoah Valley Pioneers and Their Descendants: A History of Frederick County, Virginia . . . 1738 to 1908* (Winchester, 1909), p. 296.

best measures which may now be pursued, and from gentlemen in whom we confide, we would take the liberty of recommending, that Mr. Hobday the undertaker be immediately prosecuted for not complying with his contract that the whole management be put into the hands of gentlemen near the place who may be relied on to have the work executed on the best terms possible, for we must observe for a very obvious reason that no one will undertake it for a fixed sum, and that you send a proper plan for the barracks, as we learn that egregious blunders in this way would have been committed had the former contract been complied with. Our only object in having Hobday sued is that an execution may be levied on the timber brought into place which seems to be all the property he has, and will be of worth in the execution of the work; and lest any delay should put it in his power to withdraw this we have recommended to your deputy paymaster here to authorize a suit against him immediately without awaiting your orders, which suit by our laws will be determined at the first court of the county after the expiration of ten days from the service of the writ. We recommend Colo. John Smith and Isaac Zane as proper persons for your full confidence in engaging this work on the best terms. From a knowledge of the country in which this building is to be erected we would advise you strongly to build of stone rather than wood. It will cost as little, perhaps less, in the outset as we are assured on good testimony. The stone is not half a mile distant, the spot itself abounding with limestone, the timber prepared fit for cutting into joists, boards etc. and whenever the determination of the war shall render the building useless for barracks, it will reimburse you in some degree by sale, rent or otherwise. This is submitted altogether to your consideration. You formerly expressed a wish that the executive of this state should ease you of this troublesome business. They then declined it, in hopes that the channel into which you had put it would have had the work effected without trouble to you or them. Seeing now the unlucky turn it has taken and sensible that the common cause will be aided by the assistance of the executive in every state, where a business is become intricate and involved so as to require more of the time of the General council than ought to be so employed, they are willing to take up this matter and have the old contract settled as well as they can and the work carried into execution for you, if you think your distance or other occupations may prevent your being able to take better care of it. In this they will await your orders, and if you confide it to them, expect you shall be particular in your directions as to the plan, of what materials it shall be built and other circumstances of weight.

 Among the prisoners taken at Detroit by Colo. Clarke, were some whose conduct seemed to call for severe treatment. I do myself the honour to inclose you a copy of our resolutions on that subject, containing the reasons of our severity. I have the honour to be Sir Your most obedient and most humble servt.,

       TH: JEFFERSON

## *Jefferson, Madison, and the Executive Council to David Shepherd*[12]

Williamsburg June 18, 1779

SIR

You are desired to give notice to such recruits under the act of Assembly passed last winter as may not yet have marched from your county, to hold themselves in readiness to assemble at your courthouse at a moment's warning from you. An officer will be immediately appointed, from whom you will receive notice of the day on which he will attend at your courthouse to receive them; and the necessities of the service oblige me to conjure your attention to their punctual delivery at the time he shall appoint. I am, Sir, Your very humble Servant,

TH: JEFFERSON

## *Jefferson, Madison, and the Executive Council to General George Washington*

Williamsburg June 19, 1779

SIR

I have the pleasure to enclose you the particulars of Colo. Clarkes success against St. Vincenne as stated in his letter but lately received, the messenger with his first letter having been killed. I fear it will be impossible for Colo. Clarke to be so strengthened as to enable him to do what he desires. Indeed the express who brought this letter gives us reason to fear St. Vincenne is in danger from a large body of Indians collected to attack it and said when he came from Kuskuskies to be within 30 leagues of the place. I also enclose you a letter from Colo. Shelby stating the effect of his success against the seceding cherokees and chuccamogga. The damage done them was killing a dozen, burning 11 Towns, 20,000 bushels of Corn collected probably to forward the expeditions which were to have been planned at the Council which was to meet Governor Hamilton at the mouth of Tenissee, and taking as many goods as sold for £25,000.[13] I hope these two blows coming together and the depriving them of their head will in some measure effect the quiet of our frontieres this summer. We have intelligence also that Colo. Bowman from Kentuckey is in the midst of the Shawnee country with 300 men and hope to hear a good

---

12. David Shepherd was appointed county lieutenant for Ohio County in 1777; see Reuben Gold Thwaites and Louise Phelps Kellogg, *The Revolution on the Upper Ohio, 1775–1777* (Madison, Wis., 1908), p.196.

13. For a discussion of Colonel Evan Shelby's campaign against the Chickamauga towns, see James H. O'Donnell, *Southern Indians in the American Revolution* (Knoxville, 1973), p. 84.

account of him.¹⁴ The enclosed order being in its nature important and generally interesting, I think it proper to transmit it to you with the reasons supporting it. It will add much to our satisfaction to know it meets [your] approbation. I have the honor to be with every sentiment of private respect and public gratitude, Sir Your most obedient and most hble. servant,

THOS. JEFFERSON

P.S. The distance of our north western counties from the scene of Southern service and the necessity of strengthening our Western quarter have induced the Council to direct the new levies from the Counties of Yohogania, Ohio, monongalia, Frederick, Hampshire, Barkly, Rockingham and greenbriar amounting to somewhat less than 300 men to enter into the 9th. Regiment at Pittsburgh. The aid they may give there will be so immediate and important and what they could do to the Southward would be so late as I hope will apologize for their interference.

## *Jefferson, Madison, and the Executive Council to President John Jay*

Williamsburg June 19, 1779

SIR

Our delegates by the last post informed us that we might now obtain blank letters of marque¹⁵ for want of which our people have long and exceedingly suffered.¹⁶ I have taken the liberty therefore of desiring them to apply for fifty, and transmit them by a safe conveyance.

The inclosed order being in it's nature important and generally interesting, I thought it my duty to lay it before Congress as early as possible, with the reasons supporting it; nothing doubting but it will meet with their approbation; it's justice seems to have been confirmed by the general sense of the people here.¹⁷

Before the receipt of your letter desiring a state to be made out of the ravages and enormities, unjustifiable by the usage of civilized nations, committed by the enemy on their late invasion near Portsmouth, I had taken measures for the same purpose meaning to transmit them to you.¹⁸ They are not yet

---

14. For Colonel John Bowman's destruction of the Shawnee towns in Ohio, see Jack M. Sosin, *The Revolutionary Frontier, 1763–1783* (New York, 1967), p. 120, and Otis K. Rice, "The Ohio Valley in the American Revolution," in *The Old Northwest in the American Revolution,* ed. David Curtis Skaggs (Madison, Wis., 1977), pp. 144–45.

15. John Jay served as president of the Continental Congress until Sept. 1779, when he was appointed minister plenipotentiary to Spain.

16. Congress issued letters of marque to private citizens, allowing them to fit out armed vessels as privateers to capture enemy ships.

17. The order related to Henry Hamilton.

18. See Cometti, pp. 140–42.

returned to me. I have given the same orders with respect to their still later proceedings in the county of Northumberland.

Our trade has never been so distressed since the time of Lord Dunmore as it is at present by a parcel of trifling privateers under the countenance of two or three larger vessels who keep our little naval force from doing any thing. The uniform train of events which during the whole course of this war we are to suppose has rendered it improper that the American fleet or any part of it should ever come to relieve or countenance the trade of certain places, while the same train of events has as uniformly rendered it proper to confine them to the protection of certain other parts of the continent is a lamentable arrangement of fortune for us. The same ill luck has attended us as to the disposition of the prizes taken by our navy, which tho' sometimes taken just off our capes, it has always been expedient to carry elsewhere. A British prize would be a more rare phaenomenon here than a comet, because the one has been seen, but the other never was.

I have the pleasure to inclose you the particulars of Colo. Clarke's success against St. Vincenne, as stated in his letter but lately received, the messenger with his first letter having been killed. Also a letter from Colo. Shelby stating the effect of his success against the seceding Cherokees of Chuccamogga. The damage done them was the killing about half a dozen, burning 11 towns, 20,000 bushels of corn probably collected to forward the expeditions which were to have been planned at the council which was to meet Governor Hamilton at the mouth of Tenissee, and taking as many goods as sold for twenty five thousand pounds. I have the honour to be Sir Your most obedient and most humble servt.,

TH: JEFFERSON

## Jefferson, Madison, and the Executive Council to General Charles Scott

Williamsburg June 21, 1779

SIR

Your letter by Colo. Buford is just put into my hand.[19] I observe on that part which relates to the cloathing of your new levies that Colo. Parker has probably not communicated to you my answer of June 10. to his letter on that subject written during your absence. In that I stated fully what was done, doing, and likely to be accomplished in that business. I am now to add that the linen therein mentioned as coming from Petersburgh is come and making up. The issues of shoes to all other persons have been stopped from that time, so that these also are under preparation. Nevertheless, as after every effort it is probable we shall not be able to supply every thing we wish you could compro-

---

19. General Scott commanded a Continental force of Virginia recruits that was to be sent to the relief of South Carolina. When the British invaded the Chesapeake in May, Scott kept his troops in Virginia to defend the capital in case the British moved up the James River from Portsmouth.

mise with as many as possible at the following prices fixed by the assembly the 19th. inst. A coat £23-10—a waistcoat £10-15—a pr. of breeches £9-5—a Shirt £9-8—a hat £5—a pr. of Stockings 30/—a pr. of shoes £5. I desired also from Colo. Parker a return of what the men had received that we might know what to send them.

Colo. Buford will receive here £9000. for reenlisting the soldiers. I would have sent you money also for the compromise above-mentioned but had no given principles to fix on any sum. As it is probable the whole of Buford's money will not be used instantly if he can accomodate you with such sums as you may want your draughts in his favour to replace it shall receive instant honour.

In pursuance of a resolution of assembly we have laid off the Commonwealth into the following districts for the purpose of collecting the new levies still remaining in their counties, and rendesvousing them at the places here named.

Loudoun, Fauquier, Pr. Wm., Fairfx, Stafford, K. George, Culpepper, Spotsylvania, and Orange at Fredericksburgh.
Richmond, Lancaster, Westmoreland and Northumbld. at New-Castle. The officer Capt. Vincent Redman of Richmond.
Essex, K and Queen, K. Wm., Caroline, and Hanover at New-Castle.
Middlesex, Gloster, Eliz. city, Warwick, York, James city and Wmsburgh at Wmsburgh.
Henrico, Goochland, Louisa, Albemarle, Fluvanna at Richmond.
Amherst, Buckingham, Cumberland, Powhatan at Richmond. The officer Lieutt. James Barnett of Amherst.
Princess Anne, Norfolk, Nansemond, Isle of Wight at Petersburgh.
New-Kent, Chas. City, Surry, Pr. George, Dinwiddie, Chestfd. and Amelia at Petersburgh.
Southampton, Sussex, Brunswick at Brunswick Ct. house. The officer Capt. Nathaniel Lucas of Brunswick.
Lunenburgh, Mecklenburgh, Pr. Edwd., Charlotte at Mecklenburgh Ct-house.
Halifx., Bedford, Pittsylva., Henry at Halifx Ct-house. The officer Alexr. Cummings.
Augusta, Rockbridge, Botetourt, Washington, Montgomery at Halifx Ct. h. The officer Lt. Robert Elliot.

We hope you will appoint Continental officers to receive the men at the above places at such times as our officers shall be ready to deliver them.

The levies from Rockingham, Frederick, Hampshire, Shenandoah, Green briar, Ohio, Monongalia, Yohogania, were so distant from the scene of Southern service, were so convenient to the Northern where we are pushed, that we have ordered them to recruit our 9th. regiment at Pittsbgh., and I have written to Genl. Washington on the subject hoping his approbation. A draught is to be ordered against such districts as did not furnish their men. We shall instruct the same officers to make a second collection of them, and hope you will take measures for receiving them by an officer or officers if you should be gone.

I trouble you with our whole scheme because it will enable you [to] judge what force you will receive, and when, and to cooperate with us which I know your cordiality for the public service disposes you to do: and I think it a happiness that we have to arrange this matter with you.

It is with pleasure I learn from Colo. Finnie that you have pleased yourself as to the horse directed to be purchased.[20] The difference of sex is surely not to be regarded. The caparison is preparing, but I fear (when I take a view of our workmen) it will hardly be worthy the givers or receiver. Pistols he think will be difficult to get. We know not whether you received the £500 voted you by the assembly. I shall advise Colo. Buford to enquire at the Treasury and carry it if you did not. I am with great and sincere personal esteem founded as well on our earlier acquaintance as your more recent public merits Your friend and servt.,

TH: JEFFERSON

*Jefferson, Madison, and the Executive Council to St. George Tucker*

[Williamsburg] in Council June 21, 1779

The Governor is advised to inform Mr. St. G. Tucker that he is authorised to permit 1000 Bushels of Corn to be exported to the Island of Bermuda, in such vessels as shall be sent from the Island to receive the same, with Salt in exchange, Bushel for Bushel. The Corn shall be ready stored at the Town of Petg. [Petersburg] where the salt will be expected to be delivered.   *(A Copy)*
A:B: C:C:[21]

*Jefferson, Madison, and the Executive Council to St. George Tucker*

Williamsburg June 22, 1779

DR SIR

As to an undoubted zeal for the cause of the American states you have always added a proper disposition to aid the island of Bermudas in her distresses, we have cast our eyes on you as a proper person to communicate to

20. In appreciation of General Scott's assignment of Continental troops to defend Williamsburg, the assembly presented him with a horse and a gift of £500.
21. St. George Tucker, who was born in Bermuda, studied law at the College of William and Mary in Williamsburg; see Mary Haldene Coleman, *St. George Tucker: Citizen of No Mean City* (Richmond, 1938), p. 29. "A:B:" is Archibald Blair, clerk of the council.

them what we are authorized to do by a recommendation from Congress and resolution of our assembly. For this purpose I take the liberty of inclosing to you three copies of a resolution of council to be forwarded if you please to such person in Bermuda as you think best, and by such different opportunities as may ensure the safe passage of one. It is true the relief is small, but if you can intimate under the rose that they bring Brobdinag bushels of salt, I imagine the same measure might be meted to them.[22] I am Dr. Sir Your very humble servt.,

TH: JEFFERSON

*Jefferson, Madison, and the Executive Council to General William Phillips*

Williamsburg June 25, 1779

SIR

Your favors of the 18th. instant came to hand yesterday. I had written that very day to Col. Bland to allow Lt. Campbell and Capt. Bertling to come to the flag as was desired but no opportunity of sending my letter had occurred. Immediately on receiving your letters and knowing that Lt. Campbell was as far as Richmond on his way a permit was dispatched to him to come to the place where the flag lies and perform the several duties you desired, an officer of the commonwealth being directed to attend also.[23] The interview was fixed to be on the 3d of July which was said to be as early as the superfluous clothing could be got down.

The appointment which has withdrawn me from the society of my late neighbors, in which character I with pleasure considered yourself, General and Madme. de Riedesel for that cause as much as any other is not likely to add to my happiness.[24] The hour of private retirement to which I am drawn by my

22. Congress authorized the exportation of corn to Bermuda "for the relief of the distressed citizens." The Virginia Assembly lifted its embargo on exports for this purpose on June 19, 1779; see *PTJ*, III, p. 13.

23. British officers Campbell and Bertling were prisoners of war. In order to get specie, supplies, clothing, rum, and other necessities to the convention troops quartered near Charlottesville, the British command requested that shipments be sent to them under flags of truce. In this case, the British flag was allowed to sail up the James to the Chickahominy River; see TJ, JM, and the Executive Council to Theodorick Bland, June 18, 1779, in *PTJ*, II, p. 299. For Washington's correspondence on flags of truce with the British generals William Phillips and Sir Henry Clinton, see Fitzpatrick, XIV, pp. 47-48, 57, 107, 171-73; with Governor Henry, see *ibid.*, pp. 104-5, 172-73; and with Colonel Bland, see *ibid.*, XV, pp. 493-94. For an example of a marine passport for a ship carrying a flag of truce, dated Sept. 14, 1779, see *ibid.*, XVI, pp. 284-85.

24. After his election as governor, TJ received congratulations from General William Phillips and General Friedrich von Riedesel, senior officers in the convention army quartered near Charlottesville. Mr. and Mrs. Jefferson had befriended them when they arrived in Albemarle County; see *Baroness von Riedesel and the American Revolution*, ed. Marvin L. Brown (Chapel Hill, 1965), pp. xxxv, 80-87.

nature with a propensity almost irresistible, and which would again join me to the same agreeable circle, will be the most welcome of my life.

Should any event take place which should render your removal necessary, tho' I foresee no probability of such an one, you may be assured of receiving the earliest intelligence which I may be permitted to give according to your desire: and that I shall in every circumstance which shall depend on me endeavor to make the situation of the officers and soldiers of the Convention troops as comfortable as possible, warranted as I have no doubt I shall be, by a continuance of proper conduct within them. This has authorized me particularly to assure you that no impediment can arise on my part to the excursion proposed by your family, and Genl. Reidesell's to the Berkeley springs for your amusement:[25] tho' I foresee that it will lessen the satisfaction of the short recess from business which I have a hope of being able to take within a few weeks.

## Jefferson, Madison, and the Executive Council to Thomas Whiting[26]

[Williamsburg] in Council June 26, 1779

SIR

At the request of the directors of the public Buildings in Richmond, I am to desire that you will provide for them locks of different kinds fit for house doors, hinges for do, window glass, putty, lathing nails and shells. For the quantities I must refer you to the Directors themselves.[27] I am Sir Your humble Servant,

TH: JEFFERSON

ENCLOSURE

Memod. for the Board of Trade.
800 feet of Glass—10 by 12.
300 ℔ Putty
500 ℔ of white lead in Kegs ground.
50 Gallons Linseed oil
250000 4d. Nails for lathing
25000 Floaring 20d. brads:
25,000 20d. Nails.
50,000 6d. do.
20,000 10d. do.

25. TJ authorized the trip to Berkeley Springs; see *ibid*.
26. Thomas Whiting was a member of the Virginia Board of Trade. This letter and the enclosure are in JM's handwriting rather than that of Archibald Cary, the clerk of the Council of State; see *PJM*, I, p. 299.
27. The directors of the public buildings in Richmond were appointed on June 24 to supervise the removal of the capital from Williamsburg; see *PTJ*, III, p. 19.

>Six large strong locks—12 pr. strong HL hinges
>12 good locks for inside doors
>Iron plates.

These the board of Trade is to Send for, on Acct. of the Directors for removeing Seat of Government

June 26th. 1779.                                                              Archd Cary

## *Jefferson, Madison, and the Executive Council to Governor Richard Caswell*[28]

Williamsburg June 22, 1779

SIR

The Washington and Caswell Gallies belonging to this commonwealth originally built for the protection of Ocracock Inlet in conjunction with others proposed to be built by your State being so much out of repair as to render it necessary to incur a considerable expense to refit them for Service, their condition and future station were submitted to the consideration of our General Assembly. Our Trade through that inlet to and from South Quay has from experience been found inconvenient and therefore of itself has got mostly into a different channel, so that the little remaining there from this State will not justify the Expense of keeping those Gallies any longer at their present Station. We are uninformed whether you were diverted from your purpose of building the additional Gallies to act in conjunction with ours by a similar Want of importance in the trade, or of necessaries to build Gallies. If the latter, and you think the Washington and Caswell may be made to answer your purpose, we are authorized by the General Assembly to offer them to you at such fair estimation as may be agreed on between us, I apprehend without difficulty. I shall be obliged by your Answer to this; as early as convenient, as we are directed, if you should not want them, to dispose of them otherwise for the Service of this State. I have the honor to be your Excellency's most obedt and mo: hble Servt,

TH: JEFFERSON

## *Jefferson, Madison, and the Executive Council to Governor Richard Caswell*

Williamsburg June 30, 1779

SIR

Since writing the within, I learn that the Caswell Galley is sunk at her station, that her bottom is eaten out, and her original form such that she could not be hove down to be refitted. The within proposition therefore, your

---

28. Richard Caswell was governor of North Carolina.

Excellency will be pleased to understand as confined to the Washington only.[29]

By direction of the Assembly of this State, I do myself the honor of enclosing their resolution containing a proposition for quieting the minds and possessions of those settlers near our unextended boundary as may have unwarily entered in the one State for lands lying in the other. I hope it will be recommended to your patronage as well by its justice as its tendency to promote that friendly harmony so necessary for our general good, and so agreeable to the dispositions of the Citizens of our particular states towards each other. The within letters to the Speakers of the two Houses of your Assembly contain copies of the same resolution, which I take the liberty of transmitting through your hands to them. I am Sir with the greatest esteem and respect Your mo. ob. and mo. huml Servt.,

TH: JEFFERSON

## Jefferson, Madison, and the Executive Council Issue a Proclamation Expelling British Subjects

[Williamsburg July 1, 1779]

By his Excellency Thomas Jefferson, esquire, Governor or Chief Magistrate of the Commonwealth of Virginia.

### A PROCLAMATION.

Whereas the General Assembly, by their Act passed at their last session, entitled "An Act concerning Escheats and forfeitures from British Subjects," did declare "that (1.) all persons Subjects of his Britannick majesty, who on the nineteenth day of April in the year 1775, when hostilities were commenced at *Lexington,* between the United States of America, and the other parts of the British empire, were resident, or following their vocations in any part of the world other than the said United States, and have not since either entered into public employment of the said States or joined the same, and by Overt Act adhered to them; and (2) all such Subjects, inhabitants of any of the said United States, as were out of the said States on the same day, and have since by Overt Act adhered to the enemies of the said States; and (3) all inhabitants of the said States, who after the same day, and before the commencement of the Act of General Assembly intitled "An Act declaring what shall be treason,"

---

29. The Governor-in-Council's letter to Richard Caswell of June 22, 1779, must have been transmitted with this letter.

departed from the said States, and joined the Subjects of his Britannick Majesty of their own free will; or (4.) who by any County Court within this Commonwealth were declared to be British Subjects within the meaning and operation of the resolution of the General Assembly, of the 19th. day of December 1776, for enforcing the Statute Staple, should be deemed British subjects, And by their resolution of the twenty sixth day of the last month, they "required that all the persons so described, and now resident within this Commonwealth, should be banished from the same, and that proper measures should be taken to prevent their return, as also to exclude thereout all others so described; and not now resident within this Commonwealth," I have therefore thought fit, by and with the advice of the Council of State, to issue this my proclamation, hereby strictly charging and commanding all persons Coming under any one of the descriptions in the said Act, and now being within this Commonwealth to be, and appear before me in Council at Williamsburg, on or before the seventeenth day of August in this present year, in readiness to depart the Commonwealth in such manner as shall there be prescribed to them, as they will answer the contrary at their utmost peril: And I do moreover charge and enjoin all officers civil and military, and all other the good citizens of this Commonwealth, to apprehend and carry securely to the commanding officer of the militia of some County within this Commonwealth, all such persons, whom after the said day, they shall find lurking or being therein; And the commanding officers of the several Counties are in like manner charged and required to receive the said persons, and all others so described, whom by the strictest diligence they shall be able to discover and take, to convey them in safe custody to the public jail in the city of Williamsburg, and to make report of such their proceedings to me. And I do further prohibit all persons so described from entering into this Commonwealth during the continuance of the present war with their prince, under colour of any commission, passport, licence, or other pretence whatsoever; and do publish and make known to such of them as shall presume to violate this prohibition, that they shall be deemed and dealt with as spies, wheresoever they be taken.

   Given at Williamsburg, on the first day of July, in the Year
   of our Lord, One thousand seven hundred and seventy
   nine.

 The County Lieutenants are desired to give personal notice of this proclamation to all those within their Counties, who are hereby required to attend on the Governor and Council.

 A copy of a printed copy in the office of the Executive.
*Attest*
    Sam: Coleman, A.C.C.

## Jefferson, Madison, and the Executive Council Issue Credentials for Peter Penet

[Williamsburg] July 15, 1779

To all to whom these present Letters shall come Greeting:

Whereas the General Assembly by their resolution bearing date the 9th day of December 1778 did empower the Governor with the advice of the Council of State to take such measures as might be necessary and should seem probable for obtaining a Loan of Gold and Silver to this Commonwealth to such extent as they should think expedient, and that the said assembly would make good his Contracts for that purpose. And his Excellency Patrick Henry esqr. late Governor of this Commonwealth by his Commission bearing date the 22d. day of May in this present year did by and with the advice of the Council of State nominate constitute and appoint Peter Penett esqr. of Nante in the Kingdom of France to be agent for this Commonwealth for the purpose of obtaining a loan of Gold and Silver not exceeding the Term of one hundred thousand pounds Sterling for the use of the said Commonwealth and did pledge the faith of the said Commonwealth for the fulfilling and punctual performance of all such agreements as he might make and enter into relative to such loan of Gold and Silver: Now Know ye that I Thomas Jefferson Governor of the said Commonwealth of Virginia by and with advice of the Council of State, do ratify and confirm the said power and authorities so given to the said Peter Penet esqr. by the Commission from the said late Governor Henry and do solemnly pledge the faith of the Commonwealth for the fulfilling and punctual performance of all such agreements made or to be made by the said Peter Penet relative to the said Loan of Gold and Silver in the most full and ample manner. In Witness whereof I have hereunto set my hand and caused the Seal of the said Commonwealth to be affixed at Wmsburg the 15th. day of July in the 4th. year of the Commonwealth and in the year of our Lord 1779.

TH JEFFERSON

## Jefferson, Madison, and the Executive Council to Richard Henry Lee

Williamsburg July 17, 1779

DEAR SIR

This being post morning and many letters to write I must beg leave to refer you for some articles to my letter to the feild officers of Northumberland etc. In order to render our miserable navy of some service orders were some time ago issued for two gallies on the seaboard of the Eastern shore to join the others; another galley heretofore stationed in Carolina (if not purchased by that government as proposed by our assembly) will be called into the bay.

It seems we have few or none which can ride on the middle grounds. It is therefore in contemplation to keep them about the North cape for the protection of the North channel, and for the purpose of descrying such hostile vessels coming into the bay as they may be competent to attack. From a very early period of this contest it has been my uniform opinion that our only practicable defence was naval; and that tho' our first efforts in that way must be small and would probably be unsuccessful, yet that it must have a beginning and the sooner the better. These beginnings have indeed been unsuccesful beyond all my fears. But it is my opinion we should still persevere in spite of disappointment, for this plain reason that we can never be otherwise defended. Impressed with the necessity of this kind of defence, the assembly so long ago as October 1776 were prevailed on to direct two frigates and two large gallies to be built. Being ignorant of these things myself, but having great confidence in the British experience on the water, the proposition only referred as to the frigates to their method, and as to the gallies to the Philadelphia plan. I left the house soon after; some members vain enough to suppose they could correct errors in the construction of British vessels, got the plan changed: their plan was again ventured to be improved on by the navy-board, and the event was £100,000 laid out to not a shilling's benefit. I beleive now we should be gainers were we to burn our whole navy, and build what we should be able on plans approved by experience and not warped to the whimsical ideas of individuals, who do not consider that if their projects miscarry their country is in a manner undone. I am in hopes that Congress are about to correct their long continued habits of neglect to the trade of these Southern states, and to send us some aid. I shall refer to the Council the article of the bounty mentioned in your letter. My own idea is that the recruiting officer should apply here for such sum as he thinks he may want, lodging his bond and security for the due expenditure of it (without which we issue no money on account). As he is a standing officer, and will derive considerable advantage from his success, I think he cannot deem it hard to leave the application to be made by himself. I am Dear Sir with much respect Your most obedt. and most humble servt.,

TH: JEFFERSON

P.S. The council approve of the above method of sending out the recruiting money.

## *Jefferson, Madison, and the Executive Council to General George Washington*

Williamsburg July 17, 1779

SIR

I some time ago inclosed to you a printed copy of an Order of Council, by which Governor Hamilton was to be confined in Irons in close Jail. This has occasioned a letter from General Philips of which the inclosed is a Copy. The General seems to suppose that a prisoner on capitulation cannot be put into close confinement tho his capitulation shall not have provided against it. My idea was that all persons taken in war were to be deemed prisoners of war. That those who surrender on capitulation (or convention) are prisoners of war also subject to the same treatment with those who surrender at discretion, except only so far as the terms of their capitulation or convention shall have guarded them. In the Capitulation of Governor Hamilton (a Copy of which I inclose) no stipulation is made as to the treatment of himself or those taken with him. The Governor indeed when he signs, adds a flourish of reasons inducing him to capitulate, one of which is the generosity of his Enemy. Generosity on a large and comprehensive Scale seems to dictate the making a signal example of this gentleman; but waiving that, these are only the private motives inducing him to surrender, and do not enter into the Contract of Colonel Clarke. I have the highest idea of the sacredness of those Contracts which take place between nation and nation at war, and would be among the last on earth who should do any thing in violation of them. I can find nothing in those Books usually recurred to as testimonials of the Laws and usages of nature and nations which convicts the opinions, I have above expressed, of error. Yet there may be such an usage as General Philips seems to suppose, tho' not taken notice of by these writers. I am obliged to trouble your Excellency on this occasion by asking of you information on this point. There is no other person whose decision will so authoritatively decide this doubt in the public mind and none with which I am disposed so implicitly to comply. If you shall be of opinion that the bare existence of a Capitulation in the case of Governor Hamilton privileges him from confinement, tho there be no article to that effect in the capitulation, justice shall most assuredly be done him. The importance of this question in a public view, and my own anxiety under a charge of a violation of national faith by the Executive of this Commonwealth will I hope apologize for my adding this to the many, many troubles with which I know you to be burthened. I have the honor to be with the most profound respect and esteem Yr. Excellency's mo: obedt. and mo: hble. servt.,

Th: Jefferson

P.S. I have just received a Letter from Colo. Bland containing information of numerous desertions from the Convention Troops (not less than 400 in the last fortnight). He thinks he has reason to believe it is with the connivance of some of their officers. Some of these have been retaken, all of them going northwardly. They had armed themselves with forged passports, and with Certificates of having taken the oath of fidelity to the State, some of them forged, others really given by weak Magistrates. I mention this to your Excellency as perhaps it may be in your power to have such of them intercepted as shall be passing through Pennsylvania and Jersey.

Your letter inclosing the opinion of the board of officers in the case between Allison and Lee is come safe to hand after a long passage. It shall be answered by next post.

TH: J.

## Jefferson, Madison, and the Executive Council to General William Phillips

Williamsburg July 22, 1779

SIR

Your Letter, on the Subject of Lieutenant Governor Hamilton's confinement, came safely to hand. I shall, with great chearfulness, explain, to you, the Reasons on which the advice of Council was founded, since, after the satisfaction of doing what is right, the greatest is that of having what we do approved by those whose opinions deserve esteem.

We think ourselves justified in Governor Hamilton's strict confinement, on the general principle of National retaliation. To state to you the particular facts of British Cruelty to American prisoners, would be to give a melancholy history from the capture of Colo. Ethan Allen, at the beginning of the war, to the present day; a history which I will avoid, as equally disagreeable, to you, and to me.[30] I with pleasure do you the justice to say that I believe these facts to be very much unknown to you, as Canada has been the only Scene of your service, in America, and, in that quarter, we have reason to believe that Sr. Guy Carleton, and the other officers commanding there, have treated our prisoners (since the instance of Colo. Allen) with considerable lenity. What has been done in England, and what in New York, and Philadelphia, you are probably uninformed; as it would hardly be made the subject of epistolary correspondence. I will only observe to you, Sir, that the confinement, and treatment, of our officers, soldiers, and Seamen, have been so rigorous, and cruel, as that a very great proportion of the whole of those captured in the course of this war, and carried to Philadelphia, while in possession of the British army, and to New York, have perished miserably, from that cause only; and that this fact is as well established, with us, as any historical fact which has happened in the course of the War.[31] A Gentleman of this Commonwealth, in public office, and of known and established Character, who was taken on Sea,

---

30. Recent scholars agree that the conditions under which American prisoners were confined were wretched. The fullest discussions are in Charles H. Metzger, *The Prisoners of the American Revolution* (Chicago, 1971); Larry G. Bowman, *Captive Americans: Prisoners during the American Revolution* (Athens, Ohio, 1976); William R. Lindsey, *Treatment of American Prisoners of War during the Revolution*, Emporia State Research Studies, no. 22 (Emporia, Kans., 1973); and Royster, pp. 377–78.

31. Dr. James Thacher, a surgeon in the Continental army, estimated that 11,000 Americans died in British prisons; the most recent estimate is 8,500. See Howard H. Peckham, *The Toll of Independence: Engagements and Battle Casualties of the American Revolution* (Chicago, 1974), p. 132, who nonetheless notes that "Dr. Thacher may not be too far off with his figure."

carried to New York and exchanged, has given us lately a particular information of the treatment of our prisoners there. Officers taken by Land, it seems, are permitted to go on parole within certain limits on Long Island, till suggestions shall be made to their prejudice by some Tory refugee or other equally worthless person, when they are hurried to the Prevot in New York, without enquiring 'whether they be founded upon positive facts, be matter of hearsay, or taken from the reports of interested men.' The example of enquiring into the truth of charges of this nature, according to legal principles of evidence, has surely not been set us by our Enemies. We enquired what these Prevots were, and were told they were the common miserable jails, built for the confinement of Malefactors. Officers [and men] taken by sea are kept in prison ships [infected with malignant disorders which have been brought on by the crowd put into them, and he told us that the deaths among these, when he was there, were] from five to ten a day.[32] When therefore we are desired to advert to the possible consequences of treating prisoners with rigour, I need only ask where did those rigours begin? not with us assuredly. I think you Sir, who have had as good opportunities as any British officer of learning in what manner we treat those whom the fortune of war has put into our hands, can clear us from the charge of rigour as far as your knowledge or information has extended. I can assert that Governor Hamilton's is the first instance which has occurred in my own country, and if there has been another in any of the United States, it is unknown to me; these instances must have been extremely rare, if they have ever existed at all, or they could not have been altogether unheard of by me. When a uniform exercise of kindness to prisoners on our part has been returned by as uniform severity on the part of our enemies, you must excuse me for saying it is high time, by other lessons, to teach respect to the dictates of humanity; in such a case, retaliation becomes an act of benevolence.

But suppose, Sir, we were willing, still longer, to decline the drudgery of general retaliation; yet Governor Hamilton's conduct has been such as to call for exemplary punishment on him personally. In saying this I have not so much in view his particular cruelties to our Citizens, prisoners with him, (which, tho they have been great, were of necessity confined to a small scale) as the general Nature of the service he undertook, at Detroit, and the extensive exercise of cruelties which that involved. Those who act together in war are answerable for each other. No distinction can be made between principal and ally, by those against whom the war is waged. He who employs another to do a deed, makes the Deed his own. If he calls in the hand of the assassin, or murderer, himself becomes the assassin or murderer. The known rule of warfare with the Indian Savages is an indiscriminate butchery of men women and

---

32. Henry Steele Commager and Richard B. Morris state that "the British prison ships probably killed more American soldiers than British rifles; the total estimate runs to 7,000 to 8,000"; see *The Spirit of "Seventy-Six": The Story of the American Revolution As Told by Participants* (Indianapolis, 1958), p. 854. The text within brackets in this sentence and below has been supplied from a transcript made of the original manuscript before it became worn and torn; see *PTJ*, III, p. 49.

children. These Savages, under this well-known Character, are employed by the British nation as allies in the War against the Americans. Governor Hamilton undertakes to be the conductor of the War. In the execution of that undertaking, he associates small parties of the whites under his immediate command with large parties of the Savages, and sends them to act, sometimes jointly, sometimes separately, not against our forts, or armies in the feild, but the farming settlements on our frontiers. Governor Hamilton then is himself the butcher of Men Women and Children. I will not say to what length the fair rules of war would extend the right of punishment against him; but I am sure that confinement, under its strictest circumstances, as a retaliation for Indian devastation and massacre, must be deemed Lenity. I apprehend you had not sufficiently adverted to the expression in the advice of the Council, when you suppose the proclamation there alluded to, to be the one addressed to the Inhabitants of the Illinois, afterwards printed [in the public] papers, and to be affirm[ed to contain 'denunciations of vengeance against the Americans, calls for blood, or threats of general massacres of men, women and children.' The] Proclamation, there alluded to, contained nothing more than an invitation to our Officers and Soldiers to join the British arms against those whom he is pleased to call Rebels and Traitors.[33] In order to introduce these among our people, they were put into the hands of the Indians; and in every house, where they murdered or carried away the family, they left one of these proclamations. Some of them were found sticking on the breasts of the persons murdered, one under the hand and Seal of Governor Hamilton came to our hands. The Indians being the Bearers of proclamations, under the hand and Seal of Governor Hamilton (no matter what was the Subject of them) there can be no doubt they were acting under his direction; and, as including this proof, the fact was cited in the advice of the Council. But if you will be so good as to recur to the address to the Illinois, which you refer to, you will find that, tho' it does not in express terms threaten vengeance, blood and Massacre, yet it proves that the Governor had made for us the most ample provision of all these calamities. He there gives in detail the horrid Catalogue of savage nations, extending from South to North, whom he had leagued with himself to wage combined war on our frontiers: and it is well known that that war would of course be made up of blood, and general Massacres of Men Women and Children. Other papers of Governor Hamiltons have come to our hands, containing instructions to officers going out with scalping parties of Indians and Whites, and proving that that kind of war was waged under his [express orders.] Further proofs in abundance might be adduced, but I suppose the fact too notorious to need them.

33. Throughout the war, the British viewed Americans as rebels and traitors. Only after the American victory at Yorktown did Parliament "enact that American 'rebel prisoners' might be lawfully 'held and detained' in Britain as prisoners of war"; see Olive Anderson, "The Treatment of Prisoners of War in Britain during the American War of Independence," *Bulletin of the Institute of Historical Research* 28, no. 77 (1955): 83.

Your letter seems to admit an inference that, whatever may have been the general conduct of our enemies towards their prisoners, or whatever the personal conduct of Governor Hamilton, yet, as a prisoner by capitulation, you consider him as privileged from strict confinement. I do not pretend to an intimate knowledge of this Subject. My idea is that the term 'prisoners of war' is a genuine one, the specification of which is—1st. Prisoners at discretion: and 2d. prisoners on convention, or capitulation. Thus, in the debate in the house of Commons of the 27th. November last, on the address, the Minister, speaking of General Burgoyne (and in his presence) says he is 'a prisoner' and General Burgoyne calls himself 'a prisoner under the terms of the Convention of Saratoga,' intimating that, tho' a prisoner, he was a prisoner of a particular Species entitled to certain terms. The treatment of the first class ought to be such as is approved by the usage of polished Nations; gentle and humane, unless a contrary conduct in an enemy, or individual, renders a stricter treatment necessary. The prisoners of the 2d Class have nothing to exempt them from a like treatment with those of the 1st. except so far as they shall have been able to make better terms by articles of Capitulation. So far then as these shall have provided for an exemption from strict treatment, so [far] prisoners on C[apitulation ha]ve a right to be distin[guished from those at discretion. I do not propose to rely at all on those instances which history furnishes, where it has been thought justifiable to disregard express articles of capitulation from] certain Causes antecedent thereto; tho' such instances might be produced, from English history too, and in one case where the King himself commanded in person. Marshal Boufflers after the taking of the Castle of Namur, was arrested and detained prisoner of War by King William tho by an Article in the Capitulation it was stipulated that the officers and Soldiers of the Garrison in general, and Marshal Boufflers by name, should be at liberty. However we waive reasoning on this head, because no article in the Capitulation of Governor Hamilton is violated by his confinement. Perhaps not having seen the Capitulation, you were led to suppose it a thing of course, that, being able to obtain terms of surrender, they would first provide for their own treatment. I inclose you a Copy of the Capitulation, by which you will see that the 2d article declares them prisoners of War, and nothing is said as to the treatment they were to be entitled to. When Governor Hamilton signs indeed, he adds a flourish, containing the motives inducing him to capitulate, one of which was confidance in a generous Enemy. He should have reflected that generosity on a large Scale would take side against him. However these were only his private motives, and did not enter into the contract of Colo. Clarke. Being prisoners of War then, with only such privileges as their Capitulation has provided, and that having provided nothing on the Subject of their treatment, they are liable to be treated as other prisoners. We have not extended our order, as we might justifiably have done, to the whole of this Corps. Governor Hamilton, and Captn. Lamothe alone, as leading offenders, are in confinement. The other officers and men are treated as if they had been taken in justifiable War; the officers being at large on their parole, and the men also having their liberty to a certain extent. (Dejean was not included in the Capitulation being taken 8 Days after, on the Wabache *150 miles* from St. Vincennes.)

I hope Sir that, being made more fully acquainted with the facts on which the advice of Council was grounded, and exercising your own good sense in cool and candid deliberation on these facts, and the consequences deducible from them, according to the usage and Sentiments of civilized Nations, you will see the transaction in a very different light from that in which it appeared at the time of writing your Letter, and ascribe the advice of the Council, not to want of attention to the sacred Nature of public Conventions, of which I hope we shall never, in any circumstances, lose sight, but to a desire of stopping the effusion of the unoffending blood of women and Children, and the unjustifiable severities exercised on our captive officers and soldiers in general, by proper severities on our part. I have the honor to be with much personal respect Sir Your most obedt and mo: hble Servant.

## *Jefferson, Madison, and the Executive Council Issue Orders for the Defense of the Western Frontier*

[Williamsburg] in Council July 23, 1779

The Act of General Assembly intituled an act for raising a Body of Troops for the defence of the Commonwealth, having directed that two battalions shall be raised for the Western and two for the Eastern Service, the Board advise the Governor to Order that the men to be raised according to the said act in the Counties of Yohogania, Monongalia, Ohio, Kentucky, Hampshire, Berkley, Frederick, Shenandoah, Rockingham, Rockbridge, Botetourt, Loudoun, Fauquier, Culpeper and Orange, be formed into one Battalion for the Western Service, The men to be raised under this same act in the Counties of Washington, Montgomery, Green Brier, Augusta, Henry, Bedford, Amherst, Albemarle, Fairfax, Prince William, Louisa, Fluvanna, Goochland, Cumberland, Buckingham and Pittsylvania be formed into one other Battalion for the Western Service. And the men to be raised in the Counties to the Eastward of those before named to be formed into two other Battalions for the Eastern Service. That the Western battalion secondly above named be divided and stationed the one half at such Posts and in such numbers as shall be proper for the defence of the Southwestern frontier and the other half at Fort Randolph and such other Posts and in such numbers as shall be proper for the defence of the North Western Frontier.[34]

---

34. Fort Randolph was built in 1776 at the junction of the Kanawha and Ohio rivers, near present-day Point Pleasant, West Virginia.

And in order that proper information may be obtained as to the Posts and Garrisons proper to be established, Genl. Lewis, Wm. Fleming and Wm. Christian Esqrs. are appointed to meet on the last day of August in the present Year at Botetour[t] Court House to concert together what Posts shall be taken on the So. Western frontier, and what number of Men stationed at each of the said posts not exceeding 250 in the whole and report the same to this Board for approbation. And for the same purpose, Sampson Matthews, Abraham Hite, and John Pierce Duvall Esqrs. are appointed to meet on the same day at Shenandoah Court House to concert together what posts shall be taken on the Northwestern Frontier (Fort Randolph to be one) and what number of men stationed at each not exceeding 250 in the whole and report the same to this Board for approbation. Joseph Crockett and James Knox are appointed Lieut. Colos. Commandants, Geo. Walls and Robt. Powell Majors, of the two Western Battalions, Wm. Cherry and Samuel Gill Capts., Thos. Walls and Peter Moor Ensigns in the same Battalions.

The Governor Orders, as he is before advis'd by the Honle. the Council, and further he desires that the Feild Officers of the Counties herein after mentioned, will be pleased to assemble on the summons of their County Lieuts. or other Commanding Officer and recommend to the Executive persons proper for the Commands expressed against the name of their County respectively to wit,

|  | | | |
|---|---|---|---|
| Monongalia | a Capt. | a Lieut. | |
| Ohio | | | an Ensign |
| Kentucky | | a Lieut. | |
| Hampshire | a Capt. | a Lieut. | |
| Berkley | a Capt. | a Lieut. | |
| Frederick | a Capt. | a Lieut. | |
| Shenandoah | a Capt. | | an Ensign |
| Rockingham | | a Lieut. | an Ensign |
| Rockbridge | a Capt. | | |
| Botetourt | a Capt. | | an Ensign |
| Loudoun | a Capt. | a Lieut. | two Ensns. |
| Fauquier | a Capt. | a Lieut. | an Ensign |
| Culpeper | a Capt. | a Lieut. | two Ensns. |
| Orange | | a Lieut. | an Ensign |
| Fairfax | a Capt. | | |
| Prince Wm. | a Capt. | | |
| Louisa | | a Lieut. | an Ensign |
| Goochland | | a Lieut. | |
| Fluvanna | | a Lieut. | |
| Albemarle | a Capt. | | an Ensign |
| Augusta | a Capt. | a Lieut. | an Ensign |
| Green Brier | | a Lieut. | |

| | | | |
|---|---|---|---|
| Washington | a Capt. | | an Ensign |
| Montgomery | | a Lieut. | an Ensign |
| Henry | a Capt. | | an Ensign |
| Pittsylvania | a Capt. | | an Ensign |
| Bedford | a Capt. | a Lieut. | an Ensign |
| Amherst | | a Lieut. | |
| Buckingham | | a Lieut. | |
| Cumberland | | a Lieut. | |

He moreover directs that the men to be raised in the Counties of Fairfax, Prince William, Louisa, Goochland, Fluvanna, Albemarle, Augusta and Green Brier and the Officers which shall be appointed on recommendation from the field Officers of those Counties as also one of the Capts. and both the ensigns appointed by the Council as before mentioned shall be allotted for defence of the posts which shall be established on the north Western Frontier and that the men to be raised in the Counties of Washington, Montgomery, Henry, Pittsylvania, Bedford, Amherst, Buckingham and Cumberland and the Officers which shall be appointed on recommendation from the field Officers of those Counties as also one of the Capts. before appointed by the Council shall be allotted for the defence of the posts which shall be established on the So. Western Frontier.

TH: JEFFERSON

## *Jefferson, Madison, and the Executive Council to Colonel Francis Taylor*

[Williamsburg] in Council Oct. 25, 1779

SIR

When you wrote your letter of the 13th. inst. my last to you was on the road. I now send you one Captain's and three Ensigns commissions, so they will stand thus.

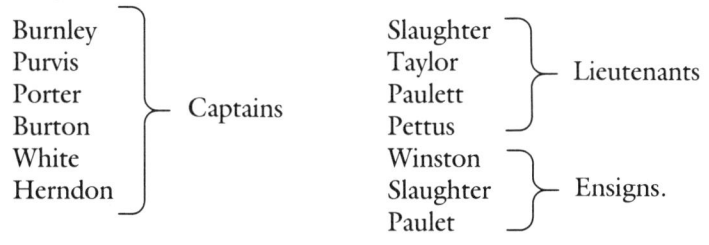

| Captains | Lieutenants | Ensigns |
|---|---|---|
| Burnley | Slaughter | Winston |
| Purvis | Taylor | Slaughter |
| Porter | Paulett | Paulet |
| Burton | Pettus | |
| White | | |
| Herndon | | |

I am sorry to tell you that the throng of business peculiarly incumbent on the council puts it out of their power to do any thing with your requisition for necessaries more than to put it into the hands of the board of war. That board has not set these six weeks; but we are told they will set today and I hope will expedite your requisitions as well of the former as present letter. I am Sir Your very humble servt,

TH: JEFFERSON

## Jefferson, Madison, and the Executive Council to Speaker Benjamin Harrison

[Williamsburg] in Council Oct. 29, 1779

SIR

The Executive in the Month of March 1778, in order to secure the acquisition and proper choice of a supply of Arms, Ordnance, and Military implements sent a Mr. Le Mair of the Kingdom of France their Agent express for that purpose to Europe. He executed his Commission with a zeal and assiduity which we have rarely met with, having traversed for fourteen Months those parts of Europe backwards and forwards where there was a hope of getting the Articles wanted, and after eighteen Months absence returned himself in the last of three Vessels which he charged with Ordnance and other necessaries. His reasonable expences we mean to pay and were about making him a proper pecuniary compensation for his time and great labour but he prays rather to be rewarded with Military rank unattended by either pay or command; expecting to reap greater benefit from this in his own Country to which he is about to return. The Executive apprehending they have no authority to grant brevet Commissions, refer to the general Assembly the expediency of authorising them to give to this Gentleman a Lieutenant Colonels Commission by way of brevet. They shall not indeed then think themselves discharged from making him some pecuniary compensation tho' a much smaller may be given than they had before proposed.[35] I have the honour to be with great respect Sir Your most obedt and most humble servt.,

TH: JEFFERSON

## Jefferson, Madison, and the Executive Council to Speaker Benjamin Harrison

[Williamsburg] in Council Oct. 30, 1779

SIR

In pursuance of a resolution of the last session of General Assembly the Executive proceeded to form a Contract with Messrs. Penet Windel & co. for

---

35. One week later, the assembly authorized TJ to grant Jacques Le Maire a brevet commission; see *PTJ*, III, p. 124.

the establishment of a manufactory of fire arms and foundery of ordnance on James river and for extending navigation through it's falls. The several preliminary papers which passed between them are now transmitted to the General Assembly, that they may be enabled to judge of the obstacles the executive had to encounter, and to see the reasons explained which led them to the several conclusions. These articles also, as ultimately concluded, accompany this, together with a subsequent letter from Mr. Penet and memorial from Mr. Savarit desiring some alterations in two of the articles.

The several objects of this Contract must be admitted of the last importance: The depending on the transportation of arms across an element on which our enemies have reigned, for the defence of our Country, has been already found insecure and distressing. The endeavours of five years aided with some internal manufactures have not yet procured a tolerable supply of arms. To make them within ourselves then as well as the other implements of war, is as necessary as to make our bread within ourselves. The present contract seems really to afford a promising appearance of future supply. Should these Articles meet with ratification from the General Assembly, I must still inform them that obstacles are likely to arise of a very perplexing nature, from an unlucky connection of the public with a certain Mr. Ballendine[36] who has entangled himself into every part of the subjects of this contract. Some of his rights are real, some only pretended. Unless they can be cleared away by legislative authority in a speedy mode, liberal compensation being first allowed him for such of them as shall be found just, the length of time which would be required to follow him through courts of justice in the ordinary course of proceedings, will defeat every hope which might be entertained from this contract. The duty imposed on the Executive by the resolution of assembly led them necessarily to an investigation of this mans rights and pretensions. That the assembly may have proper lights to conduct their enquiries I will analyse his claims as they have appeared to us. They refer to three several subjects, which I will endeavour to keep distinct, to avoid that confusion they might otherwise throw on one another. 1. to the Furnace in Buckingham. 2. to the Foundery at Westham. 3. to the construction of a navigable Canal at the falls of James river.

1. Mr. Ballendine with a partner Mr. Reveley received by order from the assembly £5000 in the year 1776 for the purpose of erecting a furnace in Buckingham and stipulated to repay it in pig iron at Seven pounds ten shillings the ton, which in fact amounted to a contract to pay the public $666\tfrac{2}{3}$ tons of pig iron for it. In December 1777 he received a further sum of £2500. In may 1778 he petitioned the assembly to release him from the obligation of paying his debt in iron @ £7.10/ the ton, and to take it at the market price at the time of delivery of the iron. The assembly resolved that he should be allowed more

36. John Ballendine was an industrialist from Prince William County who promoted several projects between 1755 and 1779, spawning litigation that dragged on until 1809; see Kathleen Bruce, *Virginia Iron Manufacture in the Slave Era* (New York, 1930), *passim.*

than the £7.10. but not the market price at the *time of delivery;* thus signifying their sense that there was some intermediate ground on which they meant to take their stand, but not pointing out what that was. This led us to suppose that the market price of iron at the time of the *paiment of the money* to Ballendine might be what the assembly had probably in view. On settlement of his several accounts with the commissioners whom we appointed according to the resolution of assembly for that purpose and whose report is transmitted herewith, there arose on one of them a balance in his favor for part of 3T-10C-2qr. of pig iron delivered. The commissioners had extended it in money at £30. the ton, and transferred the balance of £42-5 which that produced to the credit of his account for the £5000. or 666⅔ ton of iron. We think they should have credited so much of the 3T-10C-2qr. of iron at £30. as would have balanced that account and transferred the residue, in iron, to the credit of his debt due in iron. This error would have been too trivial to have noted to you, Sir, but as it tended to introduce a false principle into the account, and to prevent us from informing you precisely that of the 666⅔ tons due to the public for the £5000. there has been paid only 1T-3C and nothing paid towards discharging the additional £2500. To secure these balances the lands in which the money was invested were conveyed to the trustees themselves, but under an implied trust, that on payment of the debt conveyances should be made to Ballendine and Reveley: so that it is apprehended they amount in fact to nothing more than mortgages. There is little hope that this balance will ever be paid; an opportunity now occurs not only of making these securities produce to the public the real worth of what was advanced on them, but also of producing it in arms and implements of war, the very articles originally proposed to be obtained by it, and which of all others are most immediately essential to the public safety. But a bill for foreclosing the trust to pass through the usual forms of proceedings in a Court of Chancery will hardly bring us relief till I hope we shall not need it.

  2. The General Assembly in May 1776 having determined to erect a foundery at Westham for casting ordnance appointed commissioners for that purpose. For the Sum of £242.10. which they paid Mr. Ballendine they purchased from him for situating the foundery three acres and an half of land adjacent to a canal he was opening from Westham, and a right to deduce water from the canal for turning a boring Mill and other works necessary for the finishing the cannon. They were also to have free navigation down the canal to the foundery on contributing one moiety to the repairs of that part of the canal; after it should have been once completed, as he bound himself to compleat it. They erected their foundery and found it necessary to make advances of money to Ballendine to enable him to complete his canal and dam on which alone they depended for water. The balance due the Commonwealth on these advances is £2051-2-5½ as appears by one of the accounts transmitted herewith: for securing which payments a mortgage had been taken on 46½ acres of land the whole of the real property of the said Ballendine at that place. So that the

public possessions and interests at this place are 3½ acres of land with the foundery on it, a right to draw off water for working their machines for completing the canon, a common in the navigation, paying one half the expence of keeping that part of the canal in repair, and a mortgage on 46½ acres of land for securing the paiment of £2051-2-5½. But for the state of Mr. Ballendine's dam and canal and the prospect of obtaining water as long as he is to be depended on for it, I beg leave to refer you to the report of the same commissioner.

3. The extending navigation from Westham to Richmond, besides it's other very general importance, being extremely requisite to promote the success of the proposed manufactory, by reducing the difficulty and expence attending the transportation of the bulky articles of coal, wood and other things necessary to be expended at it, and it's own very weighty produce, we were led to enquire by what means Mr. Ballendine had got foothold there and on what pretensions he founds a right of constructing the navigable canal. In 1764. the assembly passed an act authorising the opening the falls of James river by subscriptions of money from individuals and appointing Trustees to take such subscriptions. Some persons accordingly subscribed, but no appearance arising of the work's being ever compleated in this way, the assembly after waiting 8 years, to wit, in 1772. passed another act for putting the business into a different train. They directed that as soon as the former and subsequent subscribers or a majority of them should think a sufficient sum raised, any ten of them, being subscribers of £100. each at least, might appoint a general meeting at which a president and 11 directors should be elected, who should have power to agree with an undertaker to cut the canal proposed, provided such undertaker should first give sufficient security to perform his agreement: they gave to the adventurers authority to carry the canal through any person's lands, paying the worth of them, allowed them certain tolls, and pointed out the precise mode in which they might transfer their shares in the undertaking, to wit, by deed executed by the president, the subscriber having first tendered his share to the directors who were to have the refusal at the same price. Very considerable sums were engaged under this act: but there never was a meeting of the subscribers to elect a president and directors, nor an undertaker employed. While this was in agitation Mr. Ballendine proposing to clear the falls of James river and the falls of Potowmack set on foot subscriptions for enabling him to go to England to learn how to do it. Great sums were subscribed. He went; returned, and brought some workmen. He purchased at the head of the falls of James river the 50 acres of land, three and a half of which were conveyed as before mentioned to the public for the foundery, and the other 46½ mortgaged to them. He opened a canal through this land and then of his own authority, without any act of assembly or even an order of court, as we are told, he made a dam across an arm of James river and drew off 50 feet width of water along his canal. In November 1777. by Petition to the assembly he informs them that the subscribers under the last act of assembly had trans-

ferred their interests to him, that he had made considerable progress in the canal, and should finish it if he met with no interruption from those through whose lands it must pass, and prays an act might pass vesting him with the powers of the former subscribers. Had the allegation in his Petition been true, that the former subscribers had transferred their interests to him, such an act would have been unnecessary, because he would have stood on their footing; but it could not be true, because the transfer being to be executed by the president, after a tender and refusal of the share to the company, and no president having ever been elected, there could have been no such transfer to him as he alledged. I have been thus particular Sir, in order to shew you that Mr. Ballendine has no legal right to the conducting the canal which can stand in the way of the present Contract. He has an equity of redemption in the $46\frac{1}{2}$ acres of land before mentioned, and so far stands on the footing of every other landholder through whose lands the canal must pass. He prayed earnestly that their rights might be sacrificed to him, on his paying them the value: can he then with modesty now say that his rights shall not be sacrificed to others, paying him the value of the injury done him? It is now four years since he begun this canal; he has conducted it about one twentieth part of the whole distance: and this too while his workmen were with him, and his means, if he had any, were fresh. A very simple calculation then will inform us, that, in his hands the completion of this work will require near a century, and then a question arises whether Mr. Ballendine will live so long. I think we may fairly conclude that he will never complete it. It is right that in cases of such general importance, the interests of a few individuals should give way to the general good, full compensation being made them; and as right that Mr. Ballendine's should, as those of the others whose lands were to have been laid open to him. He has had a long enough trial to convince the whole world he never will complete it. Other gentlemen now offer to do it within a reasonable term. As the assembly then after an eight years trial and failure of the act of 1764, made another experiment in 1772. it seems reasonable, after other seven years patience, to try yet other means. It is possible the present Undertakers may not find it necessary to make use of Mr. Ballendine's canal at all, but may take out the water elsewhere. But should they find that it can be taken off no where else, it is submitted to the assembly, whether his having dug a canal along grounds thro' which the navigable canal must necessarily pass, shall privilege those grounds, more than the meadows and grounds of others are privileged, and for ever obstruct the opening that river, and whether there can be any sound objection to the having in his case, as well as in those of others, a just valuation made of the injury he will sustain by the use which shall be made of his canal, and after withholding the £2051.2.5$\frac{1}{2}$ due from him to the public, on that particular account, to pay him the balance if the injury shall be found to exceed that sum.

In stating to you the several obstacles which oppose themselves to the execution of the resolution of assembly, I have been necessarily led to mention circumstances which are to be found among your own journals and acts, and of which therefore you had knowledge before. They were necessary to continue the thread of the relation so as to render it intelligible, and are desired to be considered only as references to your own records for more authentic and precise information. I have the honour to be with the greatest respect Sir Your most obedient and most humble servt.,

Th: Jefferson

## Jefferson, Madison, and the Executive Council to Speaker Benjamin Harrison

Williamsburg Nov. 4, 1779

Sir

According to the pleasure of the House of Delegates signified in their resolution of the 16th. of the last month, I now inclose you a State of the armed Vessels belonging to this Commonwealth, and returns of the Garrison and Artillery regiments, and of such part of the four troops of horse for Eastern service as are raised. What progress is made in raising the four new battalions, is out of my power to say, the returns being very few. Probably the collected information of the Members of General Assembly may enable you to form a Judgment. A Considerable part of the Men for the Illinois troop of horse is raised. Orders were sent in June to Colo. Todd[37] to purchase horses there. The present strength of the Illinois battalion under Colo. Clarke, I am unable to State with accuracy; but from information of Officers from thence not long since, its number was about three hundred.

I also inclose you Sir, returns of the Virginia troops now with the grand army, of Colo. Gibsons regiment at Fort Pitt, of so much of Colo. Baylor's regiment of horse as is with the grand army, and of Colo. Taylors regiment of Guards for the Convention troops. An Express has been sent to General Scott for a return of the new Levies under his command, which we may hope to receive very shortly, and shall be communicated to you the moment it comes. I am sorry that no returns enable me to give you an exact State of the residue of Colo. Baylors horse with the Southern Army, of Colo. Blands horse nor of two independant Companies of infantry under Captns. Ohara and Heath at Fort Pitt, for all of which you are entitled to credit as part of your Continental Quota, according to a resolution of Congress of March 15, 1779 to be found in the printed Journals, but of which no authentic Copy has been received by us. Colo. Taylors regiment on its present establishment seems not to come within the descriptions in the resolution, tho' in Continental service.

I have been much longer in collecting and transmitting to you these

---

37. Colonel John Todd of Kentucky was serving as county lieutenant of Illinois at this time.

returns than I at first hoped. I beg you to be assured that I have not added a moment to those delays which the collecting them has unavoidably occasioned. I have the honour to be with the greatest respect Sir Your most obedient and most humble servt.,

TH: JEFFERSON

## Jefferson, Madison, and the Executive Council to the Board of Trade

[Williamsburg] in Council Nov. 6, 1779

The Board of trade are requested to direct that Major Martin be furnished at the big island with 1000℔ iron 100℔ Steel and a Set of Smiths Tools for the Cherokee nation. Also 100 Gallons of good Whiskey or rum.   (*A Copy*)

ARCH. BLAIR CC

## Jefferson, Madison, and the Executive Council to Colonel John Bowman

Williamsburg Nov. 6, 1779

SIR

I am to ask the favour of you to give notice to the officer recommended by you for the Western Battalions, that as soon as one half his Quota of Men is raised and delivered by you, he shall be entitled to his Commission.[38] These Men are to make part of a Battalion, which will be commanded by Lieut. Colo. Knox, and which is to be stationed this Winter in Powels Valley.[39] As this station is so very far from you, your officer is to march his Men to the falls of Ohio, and there do duty under Major Slaughter this Winter, but he is not actually to march till he shall have heard of Major Slaughters arrival at the Falls; in the mean time let him employ them in the best manner he can for the public service. Money for their Subsistence from the time you deliver them to the officer till he shall have carried them to their Rendezvous, will be lodged with Major Slaughter. The Subsistence account previous to their delivery to the officer you will settle with the auditors here. I am Sir Yr. very hble. Servt.,

TH: JEFFERSON

38. Colonel Bowman was appointed county lieutenant for Kentucky County in 1777; see Otis K. Rice, *Frontier Kentucky* (Lexington, 1975), pp. 91–100.

39. Powell's Valley is between the Kentucky River and the Clinch River, northeast of the Cumberland Gap. TJ also referred to it as Martin's Cabin; see *PTJ*, XIII, pp. 54–55. Sosin locates it properly but mistakenly labels it Martin's Station, which was near present-day Lexington; see Sosin, p. 67.

## Jefferson, Madison, and the Executive Council to Certain County Lieutenants

Williamsburg Nov. 6, 1779

SIR

I am to ask the favor of you to give notice to the Officers recommended by you for the Western Battalions that as soon as one half the quota of one of them is raised and delivered by you he shall be entitled to the Commission for which he was recommended. As soon as that quota is complete and half the next raised another shall be entitled to his commission: and so on where there are more. You will be so good as to decide between the Officers by Lot which shall be first called into Service, he upon whom the first Lot falls is to receive the men from you, til he gets his half quota. Then to march them to the Barracks in Albemarle, after which he who draws the second Lot is to receive the remaining half of the first quota and the half of his own quota when he will become entitled to his Commission and will march them on to the same rendezvous. The last half quota you must send on under a Sergeant as the Commissioned Officers will have left you. Lieut. Colo. Crocket is appointed to the Command of the Battalion of which your men will be. Money for their Subsistence from the time you deliver them to the Officer til he shall have carried them to their rendezvous will be Lodged with Colo. Sampson Matthews of Augusta. The Subsistence Account previous to their delivery to the Officer you will settle with the Auditors here. I am Sir Your very humble servt.,

TH: JEFFERSON

## Jefferson, Madison, and the Executive Council to the Board of Trade

[Williamsburg] in Council Nov. 6, 1779

The board are of opinion payment should be made to Mr. Pollock of all the articles of his account except the draughts by O'Hara, of whom they know nothing, nor by what authority he drew.[40] They would recommend to the board of trade to desire from Mr. Pollock an explanation of O'Hara's draughts and to assure him that if it shall appear they were made on due authority, they shall be immediately replaced. They advise the Governour to write to the Governour of New Orleans for information whether their former application

---

40. Oliver Pollock, a commercial agent for Virginia in New Orleans, had helped finance George Rogers Clark's campaign in Illinois; see James A. James, "Oliver Pollock, Financier of the Revolution in the West," *MVHR* 16 (1929): 67–80, and James's *Oliver Pollock: The Life and Times of an Unknown Patriot* (New York, 1937).

through him for a loan of money from the court of Spain has had success, and if it has, to desire him to pay the demands before allowed of Mr. Pollock; and they recommend to the Board of trade to authorize Mr. Pollock, if he shall not receive the money in that way, to draw on Messrs. Penet & company to that amount, and to take such measures as they can for procuring honour to the bills. They think it will be proper for the board of trade to give Mr. Lindsay a warrant for £2000 on account as agent of trade at New Orleans, notifying Colo. Todd thereof; and approve of the instructions they propose for retaining the merchandise sent to Illinois for the publick use.

TH: JEFFERSON

## Jefferson, Madison, and the Executive Council to Governor Bernardo de Gálvez

Williamsburg Nov. 8, 1779

SIR

By Mr. Lindsay who was sent from our County of Islinois on the Mississippi to New Orleans and lately arrived here on his return by the way of Havanna, we hear that Col. Rogers had left New Orleans and proceeded up the Mississippi; We are anxiously expecting by him your Excellency's answer to the Letters of January 14 1778 by Col. Rogers and January 26th. 1778 by Captain Young from Governor Henry to whom I had the honor of succeeding on his Resignation.[41] The Accession of his most Catholic Majesty, since the Date of those Letters to the Hostilities carrying on by the confederate powers of France and North America against Great Britain, thereby adding to their efforts, the weight of your powerfull and wealthy Empire, has given us, all the certainty of a happy Issue to the present Contest, of which human Events will admit.[42] Our Vicinity to the State over which you immediately preside; the direct channel of Commerce by the River Mississippi, the nature of those Commodities with which we can reciprocally furnish each other, point out the advantages which may result from a close Connection, and correspondence, for which on our part the best Foundations are laid by a grateful Sense of the Favors we have received at your Hands. Notwithstanding the pressure of the present War on our people, they are lately beginning to extend their Settlements rapidly on the Waters of the Mississippi; and we have reason to believe, that on the Ohio particularly, and the Branches immediately communicating

41. Colonel David Rogers headed a military mission to New Orleans at the request of Governor Patrick Henry and the Virginia Council of State. Rogers's instructions and Henry's letter to the governor of Louisiana were issued on JM's first day on the council; see McIlwaine, *Official Letters of . . . Patrick Henry,* I, pp. 226–29.

42. Spain signed a secret treaty with France in Apr. 1779 to enter the war against Great Britain but without recognizing the independence of the United States; see Light Townsend Cummins, *Spanish Observers and the American Revolution, 1775–1783* (Baton Rouge, 1991), pp.113–14, 140–68.

with it, there will in the Course of another Year, be such a number of Settlers, as to render the Commerce an object worth your notice. From New Orleans alone can they be tolerably suppl[ied] with necessaries of European Manufactures, and thither they will carry in Exchange Staves and Peltry immediately, and Flour pork and Beef, as soon as they shall have somewhat opened their Lands. For their Protection from the Indians, we are obliged to send and station among them, a considerable armed Force; the providing of which with cloathing, and the Friendly Indians with necessaries, becomes a matter of great Difficulty with us. For the smaller Forces we have hitherto kept up at Kaskaskia on the Mississippi we have contracted a considerable Debt at New Orleans with Mr. Pollock, besides what is due to your State for the Supplies they have generously furnished, and a Number of Bills from Col. Clarke now lying under protest in New Orleans.[43] We learn by Mr. Lindsay that Mr. Pollock is likely to be greatly distress'd, if we do not immediately make him remittances. The most unfavorable Harvest ever known Since the Settlement of this Country, has put it out of our Power to send flour, obliging us for our own subsistence, to purchase it from the neighboring States of Maryland and Pensylvania to whom we have until this Year furnished large Quantities. The Want of Salt disables us from preparing Beef and Pork for your market. In this Situation of things, we cannot but contemplate the distress of that Gentleman brought on him by Services rendered us, with the utmost Concern. We are endeavoring by Remittances of Tobacco to establish a Fund in France to which we may apply to a certain extent: But the Casualties to which those Tobaccoes are liable in their Transportation; render the Dependence less certain than we could wish for Mr. Pollock's relief; and besides that we have other very extensive occasions for them. Young as we are in Trade and Manufactures, and engaged in war with a Nation whose power on the Sea, has been such as to intercept a great proportion of the Supplies we have attempted to import from Europe, you will not wonder to hear, that we find great Difficulties in procuring either money or Commodities to answer the Calls of our Armies, and therefore that it would be a Circumstance of vast relief to us, if we could leave our deposits in France for the Calls of that part of our State which lies on the Atlantic, and procure a Suspension of the Demands from Your Quarter, for supplies to our Western Forces one, Two, or three Years, or such longer Time as could be obtained; With this view Governor Henry in his Letters of January 14 and 26th 1778 solicited from Your Nation a loan of money which your Excellency was so kind, as to undertake to communicate to Your Court. The Success of this application we expect to learn by Col. Rogers, and should not till then have troubled you with the same Subject, had we not heard of Mr. Pollock's distress. As we flatter ourselves that the Application thro' the intervention of your Excellency may have been successful, and that you may be authorized to advance for us some loans in money, I take the Liberty of soliciting you in such

---

43. For Gálvez's use of Spanish funds "as very secret service money," see John Walton Caughey, "Aid for the American Revolutionists," in his *Bernardo de Gálvez in Louisiana, 1776–1783* (Berkeley, 1934), pp. 85–101.

Case, to advance for us to Mr. Pollock Sixty five Thousand Eight Hundred fourteen and 5/8 Dollars. Encompassed as we are with Difficulties, we may fail in doing as much as our Gratitude would prompt us to, in speedily replacing these Aids; But most assuredly nothing in that way within our Power will be left undone. Our particular prospects for doing it, and the time it may take to accomplish the whole, shall be the Subject of another Letter, as soon as I shall have the Honor to learn from You whether we can be Supplied, and to what extent.

By Col. Rogers I hope also to learn your Excellency's Sentiments, on the Other proposition in the Same Letters, for the establishment of corresponding Posts on Your Side and ours of the Mississippi, near the mouth of the Ohio, for the promotion of Commerce Between us. After returning our most cordial thanks to your Excellency for the friendly Disposition you have personally shewn to us, and, assuring you of our profound Respect and Esteem, beg Leave to Subscribe myself, Your Excellency's most obedient, and most humble Servant,

TH: JEFFERSON

## Jefferson, Madison, and the Executive Council to the Board of War

[Williamsburg] in Council Nov. 9, 1779

Mr. Peyton Clothier General is directed to repair to the Grand Army there to receive and issue to the Officers and Soldiers of the Virginia Line all Cloathing and Stores for them that shall be put into his hands either by the Continental Cloathier General or the Continental State Agents.[44] If the salary annexed to his Office by the Assembly is insufficient, to them the application must be made.

THOS. JEFFERSON

## Jefferson, Madison, and the Executive Council to the Chevalier D'Anmours[45]

[Williamsburg] in Council Nov. 10, 1779

SIR

In compliance with the request which you were pleased to lay before us, I am now to authorize the forces of his most Christian majesty to land in such

---

44. John Peyton was appointed by the assembly as clothier general to the Virginia troops. The "Grand Army" refers to the Continental army under Washington's command; see McIlwaine, *Official Letters of... Thomas Jefferson,* II, p. 58.

45. D'Anmours was appointed French consul in Virginia on July 27, 1779; see TJ, JM, and the Executive Council to Benjamin Harrison, Nov. 23, 1779, below.

place, and his vessels to withdraw into such harbours within this commonwealth as the Admiral or other commanding officer shall think proper and to procure houses for the purpose of hospitals. In determining on the place of his debarkation and encampment, he will be pleased to follow his own judgment; receiving from us this information that the farther he can withdraw his vessels up our rivers into the country, the more it would be in our power to assist in defending them against any attack from the enemy. York river according to our present idea would offer itself as the most defencible but in this or any other we greatly apprehend the difficulties and distresses which may arise from the want of proper houses for hospitals. The board of war will issue orders for their immediate supply of provisions from our magazines, and will aid them with such of our vessels as may be necessary for procuring further supplies, landing their sick and other purposes.

These general measures seem to be all we can take for their present relief, till their wants shall be more particularly laid before us. We beg leave to take this early occasion to assure you that we shall receive into our state the forces of his most Christian majesty with the utmost cordiality and spare nothing which shall be within our power to aid and accommodate them in whatever situation they shall chuse.

I shall take great pleasure in shewing on every occasion which shall occur, my personal gratitude and affection to your nation, and the particular esteem with which I am Sir Your most obedient and most humble servt.

*Jefferson, Madison, and the Executive Council to Governor Richard Caswell*

Williamsburg Nov. 11, 1779

SIR

I have lately received messages and informations from the Cherokee nation of Indians, painting their nakedness and general distress for want of European goods, so strongly as to call for pity and all possible relief. Their several settlements being contiguous to the two Carolinas and to Virginia they have at times received supplies I believe from each of these states. Their great numbers however, and the extent of their settlements, when taken into view by any one of our states, bear a discouraging proportion to the moderate aids we can singly furnish, and render a general distribution of them very troublesome. These considerations have induced me to take the liberty of submitting to your Excellency a proposition (as I do to Governour Rutlege also by a letter of this day's date) to divide the trouble and task of supplying them among our three states. The division of those Indians into Southern, Middle, and Northern settlements, renders the apportionment of them obvious. The protecting from intrusion the lands of the Southern Cherokees and furnishing them with goods seems most convenient to South Carolina; the same friendly offices to the middle settlements seem most within your power, and the Northern settlements are convenient to us. The attachment which each settlement will by these means acquire to the particular state which is it's immediate patron and benefactor, will be a bond of peace, and will lead to a separation of that powerful people.[46] If this distribution should happily meet the approbation of your Excellency and of Govr. Rutlege, we shall do every thing in our power for discharging our duties to the Northern settlement. Knowing your disposition to have these people protected in the possession of their unpurchased lands, I also take the liberty of mentioning to you that the old Tassel in a late message to me complains of intrusions on their lands, and particularly of some attempts to take from them the Great island. This, by the late extension of our boundary, falling, as I understand, within your state, removes the application for protection to your Excellency, whose power alone can extend to the removal of intrusions from thence. As to so much of their lands as lie within our latitudes, as well as the lands of other Indians generally, our assembly now sitting has in contemplation to authorize the Executive to send patroles of the military through them from time to time to destroy the habitations which shall be erected in them by intruders. The bearer of this letter is a Major Martin, our agent residing with the Cherokees, who will be able to inform your Excellency of any particulars you may wish to learn. We have reason to beleive him a good kind of man and worthy of credit.[47]

Intending to fix a post and small garrison in Powell's valley, we have ordered part of a battalion thither to erect a stockade. But as it would be proper for them first to assemble together (being not yet embodied) at a nearer station, and there being a fort and houses at the Great island,[48] we have taken the liberty of appointing their rendezvous at that fort, till there shall be so many embodied as may proceed with safety to Powell's valley. We have reason to expect that their stay at that place will be very short and hope it will not be disagreeable to your Excellency. The necessity of immediate orders, put it out of our power to apply for your previous approbation: we consider the measure still however subject to your pleasure and therefore take this early opportunity of acquainting you with it. I have the honour to be with the greatest respect and esteem Your Excellency's most obedient and most humble servt.

---

46. For a discussion of this proposal, see O'Donnell, pp. 93–94.

47. Joseph Martin was Virginia agent to the Cherokee; see *ibid*. For a brief discussion of Virginia's use of Indian goods in its diplomatic negotiations with the Cherokee, see *ibid*.

48. The Great or Long Island was in the Holston River above the mouth of the Watauga River; see *ibid.*, p. 14, and George M. Waller, *The American Revolution in the West* (Chicago, 1976), p. 18.

## Jefferson, Madison, and the Executive Council to the Board of War

[Williamsburg] in Council Nov. 12, 1779

The Governor is advised to appoint Frederickg., Petersbg., New London, Staunton, and Winchester places of rendezvous for New levies raised under the act of Assembly concerning Officers Soldiers Sailors and marines, and to direct an Officer to meet the recruiting Officers of the several counties at these places at certain times, to wit, Petersburg on the first Day of every other month, beginning in December at New London on the sixth of the same months, at Staunton on the twelve, at Winchester on the eighteenth, and at Fredericksburg on the twenty fourth then and there to review and receive such able bodied men as shall be produced to him by the said recruiting Officers. To appoint also Pittsburg and Wmsburg places of rendezvous for levies of the same kind, and an Officer of the Garrisons at those places to review and receive them at all times when produced to him.

TH: JEFFERSON

## Jefferson, Madison, and the Executive Council to David Shepherd

Williamsburg Nov. 13, 1779

SIR

I am to ask the favour of you to give notice to the Officer recommended by you for the Western Battalions that as soon as one half his [quota] of men is raised and delivered by you, he shall be entitled to his commission and must march the men on to Fort Pitt, the remaining half you must send on under a Serjeant to the same rendezvous. Lieutenant Colo. Knox is appointed to take command of the Battalion of [which] your men will be. But your distance renders it impracticable to join them to their battalion till the Spring. They will do duty under Colonel Gibson this winter. The Subsistence Account previous to their Delivery to the Officer you will settle with the Auditors here. I am Sir Your very humble Servt.,

TH: JEFFERSON

## Madison and the Executive Council to Governor Jefferson

Williamsburg in Council Nov. 13, 1779

SIR

Sickness necessary Business and other Causes often preventing the Attendance of the members of this Board so as that no Council can be held, while many persons are waiting from great distances and at much expense on Business with the Executive; which inconvenience might in a great degree be obviated by a Standing Advice of the Board to the Governor to act during the intervals of their sitting in certain cases where the concurrence of the Council having generally been considered as a matter of course a Special advice woud be of little moment, The Board do Advise his Excellency during the intervals of their sitting to proceed without waiting for a special Advice on the case to countersign certificates from the Board of War for Cloathing due to soldiers under a resolution of the general Assembly, certificates from the same Board for Bounty money due to Soldiers, or enlisting money due or to be advanced to recruiting Officers, Orders from the Board of War for Cloathing to Officers Soldiers Sailors and marines, Orders from the Board of War or Board of Trade for provisions or other necessaries for vessels about to sail, Orders from either of the said Boards in consequence of resolutions approved by the Executive, to Issue military Commissions recommended by the board of War, to Issue commissions for public trading vessels on recommendation from the board of Trade, to issue blank Militia commissions to the County Courts, to Issue commissions of the peace, Inspectors Commissions and Sherifs Commissions on recommendation from County Courts, to order rations and small aids in money to deserters Captives and to discharged and disabled soldiers, to licence Attornies on the report of the commissioners to whom he may refer them for examination and to certify to the Auditors of Accounts where services upon which claims against the State are founded, were performed by Order of the Executive reporting from time to time to the Board his proceedings agreeable to the Above Advice.

## Jefferson, Madison, and the Executive Council to the Board of War

[Williamsburg] in Council Nov. 15, 1779

The board advise the approbation of the proposition from the board of War for building a small magazine at Staunton; but that it be paid for in money, and not by a sale of any of the rifles, these being already ordered to be delivered to the two Western Battalions now raising. They approve also of what is proposed as to the cattle. They advise that no particular supply of Clothing be sent for particular men, but that general supplies be sent to the places of general rendezvous appointed for the two Western Battalions. They approve of engaging Colo. Matthews to have shoes made in the Western Country and furnishing him with money, on Account for that purpose.

TH: JEFFERSON

## *Jefferson, Madison, and the Executive Council to the Board of War*

[Williamsburg] in Council Nov. 15, 1779

The Board advise that one prison ship agreeable to the resolution of Assembly be employed; that she be moored in James river above the windings thereof which form the Peninsula's in Henrico and Chesterfield Counties: that picquetts be erected on the South Side of the same river on such Spot as the Board of War or an Officer to be sent by them to examine grounds for that purpose shall direct; keeping in view the erecting them so near to the moorings of the prisonship as that the same Staff Officers may serve both. The height plan and dimensions of the picquets and block houses they refer to the board of War. The board will of course direct the materials to be of a durable kind, that country Abounding with Cedar proper for picquets.[49]

THOS. JEFFERSON

## *Jefferson, Madison, and the Executive Council to President Samuel Huntington*[50]

Williamsburg Nov. 16, 1779

SIR

Colo. Bland being about to retire from his Command at the Barracks in Albemarle, and desirous to withdraw at the same time the party of his horse which has hitherto been Stationed there, wished that we should supply their place by sending thither about twenty or five and twenty of the horse of this State. Our horse being as yet not very well trained, the Officers represented

---

49. On Nov. 1, 1779, the assembly directed TJ to order a ship for prisoners of war and to authorize construction of a fort to protect it; see *PTJ*, III, p. 187.

50. Samuel Huntington was elected president of the Continental Congress on Sept. 28, 1779, after John Jay was appointed minister plenipotentiary to Spain; see Larry R. Gerlach, *Connecticut Congressman: Samuel Huntington, 1731–1796* (Hartford, 1976), p. 52.

that it would much impede that work, and leave the remaining fragment in a very aukward situation should we divide a troop. We have therefore ordered a complete troop to that Station; but wish congress would be pleased to notify as soon as convenient whether they approve of this or not.

We have hitherto been unable to raise more than about the half of a Battalion of infantry for guarding the convention Troops at the same Post. The deficiencies have been endeavoured to be supplied with Militia. Congress have had too much experience of the radical defects and inconveniences of militia service to need my enumerating them, our Assembly, now sitting, have in contemplation to put the garrison regiment on such a footing as gives us hopes of filling it by the next summer. In the mean time a Battalion which we are raising for our immediate defence may be spared to do garrison duty this winter, and as but a small part of it is raised, as yet, and not probable that it will be completed within any short time, we suppose that with Colo. Taylors regiment it will not exceed the number required to guard the Troops. I woud observe to you that the Captains and Subalterns of this new Battalion are not to be called into service but as their men are raised; so that the burthen which has sometimes been incurred of paying Officers without men need not be apprehended in this instance. We have therefore Ordered this Battalion to rendezvous at the Barracks and do duty there this winter, and that the Battalion shoud be discharged in proportion as these come in. On this measure also we ask the pleasure [of] congress.

The appointment of a successor to Colo. Bland will give us great satisfaction and we hope congress will take it into early consideration. The duties of that post call for respectable Abilities and an uncommon vigilance and firmness of Character.[51] I have the honour to be with the greatest respect and esteem Sir your most obedient humble servt.,

TH: JEFFERSON

*Jefferson, Madison, and the Executive Council to the Board of War*

[Williamsburg] in Council Nov. 18, 1779

The Board are of opinion that until the numbers of an invading enemy and the proposed point of invasion known, neither the numbers of militia proper to be drawn into the field, nor the Counties from which they shall be called can be determined on.[52] They approve of the making ready the Artillery

51. On Dec. 14, 1779, Washington appointed Colonel James Wood to replace Bland as superintendent of the convention troops near Charlottesville; see Fitzpatrick, XVII, pp. 260–61.

52. On Nov. 16, 1779, the Board of War warned the Governor-in-Council that the British might invade Virginia during the winter and suggested various defense measures; see *PTJ*, III, pp. 190–91.

harness's and horses for Artillery, Waggons for the baggage Ammunition forage and for the commissariate, and refer to the Board of War to propose the number proper, taking for granted that the Continental Waggons in this State may be freely called into the Service of the State in case of an invasion and may therefore be counted on as a part of the necessary number: they approve of the repairing immediately the arms in the public Magazines; and with respect to those at Cumberland particularly would recommend that five hundred Stand of them at a time be brought to this place to be repaired and be sent away before others be bought; they approve of having tin Cartridge Boxes made as proposed by the board of War: They approve of recommendations to the County Lieutenants of all the Counties below the blue ridge to have arms of their militia put into good [condition?] as required by Law; but disapprove of the method proposed of getting Cartouch boxes through their intervention: some arms have been heretofore put into the hands of the Lieutenants of the more distant Counties lying on the navigable Waters; the Executive are unwilling for very many reasons to part with more from the public Magazines, and more especially as the exposed Counties not heretofore furnished from them are so convenient as that they may be furnished on very short warning: they approve of the disposition of the three remaining troops of Cavalry, the lookout Boats and ships as proposed: and that express riders be held in readiness for the purpose mentioned by the Board of War.[53] The Executive are of opinion they are not authorized by Law to appoint a general Officer till an invasion or insurrection has actually taken place, and three Battalions at least of the Militia embodied. They recommend to the Board of War to have two heavy Cannon mounted at Hoods on James river, two others at West point on the York river, two others at Hobb's hole on Rappahanock and two others at Alexandria on Potowmack: And if any position lower down the Potowmack can be found where cannon might obstruct the passage of vessels, they woud have two mounted there also: they further recommend that the most vigorous exertions be immediately used to withdraw from the reach of a sudden enterprize of the Enemy all cannon not necessary for the defence of the established batteries: At these Batteries also they wou'd have the Board of War reconsider the number of guns mounted, and where there are more than are necessary for the purpose of the Battery to withdraw in like manner those which are supernumerary: They woud also desire that the prisoners of War at this place, not being commissioned Officers, be removed immediately to the prison Ship and She repair forthwith to her moorings.

TH: JEFFERSON

---

53. The lookout boats in Chesapeake Bay were to notify express riders on the approach of the enemy, and the riders were to carry the word to TJ and the Executive Council "with all possible dispatch"; see *ibid*.

## Jefferson, Madison, and the Executive Council to Speaker Benjamin Harrison

[Williamsburg Nov. 23, 1779]

SIR

There is reason to believe that the appointment of a Consul to reside in this State on the part of his most Christian majesty either has been already or will shortly be made.[54] I must submit to the general Assembly the expediency of considering whether our Laws have settled with precision the prerogatives and jurisdiction to which such a person is entitled by the usage of nations; and putting the Office on the footing they wou'd wish it to rest. The enclosed memorial from a Subject of the same prince is also perhaps worthy the Attention of the Assembly. The expediting judiciary proceedings wherein foreigners are concerned, who come to make only a short stay among us, seems expedient for the preservation of a good understanding with them and for the encouragement of Commerce. The Executive received from Congress some time ago copies of the several proceedings which had taken place between a Subject of the crown of Portugal and the Commander of an American privateer; a part owner of the privateer being a Citizen of this State. They were accompanied by some resolutions of congress desiring that the executive would so far interpose as to have reparation made to the foreigner whose vessel had been taken, pyratically as they supposed, and to have the Offenders proceeded against criminally. The case with all the documents transmitted was submitted to the Attorney General for his opinion which he has lately given us, and I now inclose it. From that you will perceive that if the act complained of were piracy or should any future act of piracy be committed by any of our Citizens, there is no judicature within this State before which it could be tried. Whether the establishment of such a judicature may not be necessary for the preservation of peace with foreign nations is now submitted to the legislature. I have the honour to be with the greatest respect,

TH: JEFFERSON

## Jefferson, Madison, and the Executive Council to General George Washington

Williamsburg Nov. 28, 1779

SIR

Your Excellency's letter on the discriminations which have been heretofore made between the troops raised within this state and considered as part of our quota, and those not so considered, was delivered me four days ago. I immediately laid it before the Assembly, who thereupon came to the resolu-

54. See TJ, JM, and the Executive Council to the chevalier D'Anmours, Nov. 10, 1779, above.

tion I now do myself the honor of inclosing you. The resolution of Congress of Mar. 15. 1779 which you were so kind as to inclose was never known in this state till a few weeks ago when we received printed copies of the journals of Congress. It would be a great satisfaction to us to receive an exact return of all the men we have in Continental service who come within the descriptions of the resolution together with our state troops in Continental service. Colo. Cabell was so kind as to send me a return of Octob. 1779. of the Continental regiments commanded by Lord Sterling,[55] of the 1st and 2d Virginia state regiments, and of Colo. Gist's regiment. Besides these are the following

Colo. Harrison's regiment of artillery:
Colo. Baylor's horse:
Colo. Bland's horse:
General Scott's new levies, part of which are gone to S. Carolina, and part are here:
Colo. Gibson's regiment stationed on the Ohio:
Heath's and O'Hara's independent companies at the same stations:
Colo. Taylor's regiment of guards to the Convention troops: of these we have a return.

There may possibly be others not occurring to me. A return of all these would enable us to see what proportion of the Continental army is contributed by us. We have at present very pressing calls to send additional numbers of men to the Southward. No inclination is wanting in either the legislative or Executive powers to aid them, or to strengthen you: but we find it very difficult to procure men. I herewith transmit to your Excellency some recruiting commissions to be put into such hands as you may think proper for re-enlisting such of our souldiery as are not engaged already for the war. The act of assembly authorising these instructions requires that the men enlisted should be reviewed and received by an officer to be appointed for that purpose; a caution less necessary in the case of men now actually in service, and therefore doubtless able bodied, than in the raising new recruits. The direction however goes to all cases, and therefore we must trouble your Excellency with the appointment of one or more officers of review. Mr. Moss our agent receives orders, which accompany this, to pay the bounty money, and recruiting money, and to deliver the clothing.[56] We have however certain reason to fear he has not any great sum of money on hand: and it is absolutely out of our power at this time to supply him, or to say with certainty when we shall be able to do it. He is instructed to note his acceptances under the draughts and to assure payment as soon as we shall have it in our power to furnish him as the only substitute for

---

55. William Alexander, better known as Lord Stirling, was promoted to major general after the battle of Trenton. His title was never recognized by the House of Lords. The best biography is Paul David Nelson, *William Alexander, Lord Stirling* (University, Ala., 1987).

56. John Moss was state agent for Virginia's Continental troops; see *PTJ,* III, p. 206. The assembly authorized a bounty payment of $750 for soldiers who reenlisted; it also established land bounties for soldiers and officers. See Hening, X, pp. 214, 159-62.

money. Your Excellency's directions to the officer of review will probably procure us the satisfaction of being informed from time to time how many men shall be re-enlisted.

By Colo. Matthews I informed your Excellency fully of the situation of Governour Hamiltoun and his companions. LaMothe and Dejean have given their paroles, and are at Hanover courthouse: Hamiltoun, Hay, and four others are still obstinate. They therefore are still in close confinement, tho their irons have never been on since your second letter on the subject. I wrote full information of this matter to General Philips also, from whom I had received letters on the subject. I cannot in reason beleive that the enemy on receiving this information either from yourself or General Philips, will venture to impose any new distresses on our officers in captivity with them. Yet their conduct hitherto has been most successfully prognosticated by reversing the conclusions of right reason. It is therefore my duty, as well as it was my promise, to the Virginia captives to take measures for discovering any change which may be made in their situation. For this purpose I must apply for your Excellency's interposition. I doubt not but you have an established mode of knowing at all times through your commissary of prisoners, the precise state of those in the power of the enemy. I must therefore pray you to put into motion any such means you may have of obtaining knowledge of the situation of the Virginia officers in captivity. If you shall think proper, as I could wish, to take upon yourself to retaliate any new sufferings which may be imposed on them, it will be more likely to have due weight, and to restore the unhappy on both sides to that benevolent treatment for which all should wish. I have the honour to be with the most perfect esteem and respect Your Excellency's Most obedient and most humble servt.,

TH: JEFFERSON

## *Jefferson, Madison, and the Executive Council Issue a Proclamation of Embargo*
[Williamsburg] Nov. 30, 1779

*By His Excellency* THOMAS JEFFERSON, *Esq; Governour or Chief Magistrate of the commonwealth of* VIRGINIA:

A PROCLAMATION.

Whereas the exportation of provisions from this state will be attended with manifest injury to the United States, by supplying the enemy, and by rendering it difficult for the publick agents and contractors to procure supplies for the *American* troops, and will moreover give encouragement to engrossers and monopolizers to prosecute their baneful practices, I have therefore thought fit, by and with the advice and consent of the Council of State, to issue this my proclamation for laying an embargo on provisions; and I do

THE BEGINNINGS OF FRIENDSHIP, 1779                                    *119*

hereby lay an embargo on provisions, *viz.* On all beef, pork, bacon, wheat, *Indian* corn, pease or other grain, or flour or meal made of the same; to continue until the first day of *May* next. And I do hereby strictly prohibit all mariners, masters, and commanders of vessels, and all other persons whatsoever within this state, from loading on board any vessel for exportation, and from exporting all or any of the above species of provisions, by land or water, from the date hereof, during the term aforesaid, under pain of incurring the penalties inflicted by the act of Assembly intitled *An act to empower the Governour and Council to lay an embargo for a limited time,* except as in the said act is excepted. And I do hereby strictly charge and command all naval officers and others, in their respective departments, to exert their best endeavours to the end that this embargo be strictly observed.

*Given under my hand this* 30*th day of* November, 1779

THOMAS JEFFERSON.

## *Jefferson, Madison, and the Executive Council to the Board of Trade*

[Williamsburg] in Council Dec. 10, 1779

The inclosed resolution for purchasing Slaves to carry on the West Ham Foundary is transmitted to your Board to be carried into execution, as the care of those works rests with you.[57]

TH: JEFFERSON

P.S. Since writing the above another resolution of Assembly is come to hand for purchasing Iron of Mr. Ross.[58] I inclose it to you with a Copy of his Letter proposing the supply, and Governour Henrys Answer.

TH. J.

## *Jefferson, Madison, and the Executive Council to General George Washington*

Williamsburg Dec. 16, 1779

SIR

I take the liberty of putting under cover to your Excellency, some Letters to Generals Philips and Riedesel, uninformed whether they are gone into New York or not, and knowing that you can best forward them in either case.[59]

---

57. On Dec. 3, 1779, the House of Delegates authorized the Executive Council to purchase "labouring Slaves and Tradesmen . . . and if a sufficient number cannot be purchased, to make good the deficiency by Hiring"; see McIlwaine, *Official Letters of . . . Thomas Jefferson,* II, p. 74.

58. David Ross offered to supply the foundry with 250 tons of pig iron; see *ibid.*

59. General William Phillips was the ranking British officer and General Friedrich von Riedesel the ranking German officer captured at Saratoga. Until they were exchanged for captured American

I also trouble you with a Letter from the Master of the Flag in this State to the British Commissary of Prisoners in New York, trusting it will thus be more certainly conveyed than if sent to Mr. Adams. It is my Wish the British Commissary should return his answer through your Excellency or your Commissary of Prisoners, and that they should not propose under this pretext to send another Flag, as the Mission of the present Flag is not unattended by circumstances of Suspicion, and a certain information of the Situation of ourselves and our Allies here might influence the Measures of the Enemy.

Perhaps your Commissary of prisoners can effect the former method of Answer.

I inclose to you part of an Act of Assembly ascertaining the quantities of Land which shall be allowed to the Officers and Soldiers at the close of the War, and providing means of keeping that Country vacant which has been allotted for them.[60]

I am advised to ask the attention of your Excellency to the Case of Colo. Bland late commander at the Barracks in Albemarle. When that Gentleman was applied to, to take that Command, he attended the Executive here, and informed them, that he must either decline it, or be supported in such a way as would keep up that respect which was essential to his Command, without at the same time ruining his private fortune.

The Executive were sensible that he would be exposed to very great and unavoidable expence, they observed that his Command would be in a department separate from any other, and that he actually relieved a Major General from the same Service. They did not think themselves authorized to say what should be done in this case, but undertook to represent the matter to Congress and in the mean time, gave it as their Opinion that a decent table ought to be found for him.

On this he undertook the command, and in the course of it incurred expences, which seemed to have been unavoidable unless he would have lived in such a way as is hardly reconcileable to the Spirit of an Officer, or the reputation of those in whose service he is. Governor Henry wrote on the Subject to Congress. Colo. Bland did the same; but we learn that they have concluded the allowance to be unprecedented and inadmissable, in the case of an officer of his rank. The Commissaries on this have called on Colo. Bland for reimbursement. A Sale of his Estate was about to take place, when we undertook to recommend to them to suspend their demands till we could ask the favor of you to advocate this Matter with Congress so far as you may think it right, otherwise the ruin [of] a very worthy Officer must inevitably follow.[61] I

---

officers in the fall of 1779, they were quartered with the convention army near Charlottesville; see Brown, pp. xxxv, 80–87.

60. The act is in Hening, X, pp. 159–62.

61. Washington wrote to the president of the Continental Congress on Jan. 26, 1780, to support Bland's case; see Fitzpatrick, XVII, pp. 445–47.

have the honor to be with the greatest respect and esteem Your Excellency's Most obedt. and most humble servt.,

TH: JEFFERSON

## Jefferson, Madison, and the Executive Council to President Samuel Huntington

Williamsburg Dec. 16, 1779

SIR

We have information from our Delegates in congress that the detention of some continental arms by the executive of this State during the course of the last summer has given considerable umbrage to congress. I beg leave therefore, thro' you Sir, to lay before that honorable body facts, simply as they occurred hoping that these will satisfy them that, the arms being justly due to this State, necessity alone dictated the measure, and that no sentiment of disrespect to congress entered into the transaction.[62] This State in an early part of the present contest raised at first two, and soon afterwards seven Battalions for its particular defence, finding however that the dangers of our being invaded became less, our legislature made a tender of these Battalions for the continental Service. The tender was accepted of by congress only on condition that We would permit them to carry their Arms with them. They were accordingly marched to the grand army, time after time, as we could get them armed. I think this condition was dispensed with as to two Battalions only which congress, induced by their increasing wants of men, permitted to march on with out their arms. This is one of the Articles of Debt in our Account of Arms against the continent, which I state particularly, in order to bring it into recollection with some of your honorable members, and because, being recollected, it will go far in our justification as to the number of arms retained with us. Since this however, at different times, and for different corps, many smaller parcels of arms have been sent to congress by us. It is a fact, which we are to lament, that, in the earlier part of our Struggles, we were so wholly occupied by the great Object of establishing our rights, that we Attended not at all to those little circumstances of taking receipts, and vouchers, keeping regular Accounts, and preparing subjects for future disputes with our friends. If we

---

62. A congressional committee reported on Oct. 20, 1779, "that in their opinion the State of Virginia had no right to detain the Arms imported on account and for the use of the United States, as thereby the safety and welfare of these States may be essentially endangered." Nonetheless, it recommended that the arms remain in Virginia and that the state "be charged therewith." Although Congress recommitted the report, TJ, JM, and the Executive Council responded in order to justify Virginia's action "to the collective council of our union." Their arguments prevailed, for Congress took no action when the letter was read on Jan. 13, 1780; see W. C. Ford *et al.*, eds., *The Journals of the Continental Congress, 1774–1789*, 34 vols. (Washington, 1904–37), XV, pp. 1190–91, XVI, p. 54.

could have supported the whole continent, I believe we should have done it, and never dishonored our exertions by producing accounts; sincerely assured that, in no circumstances of future necessity or distress, a like free application of any thing theirs would have been thought hardly of or would have rendered Necessary an appeal to Accounts. Hence it has happened that in the present case, the collection of vouchers for the arms furnished by this State has become tedious and difficult. Our board of War has been Attending to this business a considerable time, but have as yet authenticated the loan of only 5664 Stand of Arms and 580 rifles. They seem however to believe that (exclusive of considerable numbers delivered where no receipts were taken and the Officers to whom delivered are dead or not to be found which of course we shall lose) they will be able to establish a right to 10,000 Stand. These arms were most of them of very best quality, imported from Great Britain, by the State, for its own use. After the loan of so many to the continent, the loss of a considerable number put into the hands of the militia during the short invasion of the last Spring, many of which we were never able to recover, and a very recent Loan of 1000 Stand, to be sent on, at the request of congress, to South Carolina, we were reduced to not more than 3000 Stand in all our Magazines. Rumors were spread of an intended invasion by the enemy for the purpose of rescuing the convention Troops; that body of men were in the heart of our Country under a guard not able to furnish centine[ls] for ordinary duty; congress had just recommended to us to prepare for the most immediate and most rigorous operations, and to have our militia ready to march at the Shortest warning; the knolege of the low State of our Magazines had by some means got abroad, and spread a general alarm among our people: in this situation of things a vessel, loaded with arms, seemed to be guided by the hand of providence into one of our harbours. They were it's true the property of our friend, but of friends indebted to us for those very articles. They were for the common defence too, and we were a part of the Body to be defended. An Officer came for the purpose of removing them out of the State. Would circumstances have permited a previous application to congress, tho' not present myself, I so thoroughly know the respect which the executive bears for Congress, that I am safe in affirming that such an Application would most certainly have been made. But had they awaited that ceremony, the arms would have been gone: the continent of course would have been at the expence, and the arms exposed to the injury, and risk of a double transportation: for I cannot but take for granted that congress would on such an Application, in the case of a State so reduced in her magazines, and reduced by Loans to them, have ordered the arms to be replaced. Time however did not Admit of this ceremony; the executive therefore retained 5000 Stand. We shall not draw examples of similar liberties taken by other States; we shall never recapitulate aids granted to, or taken by our brethren from the common Stock, because we wish it to be freely used for their service, and to draw nothing from it for ourselves unless our distresses should at any time be such as to point us out to them as objects needing the common Aid. But we will observe in general, that, between congress and this State, similar freedoms in other articles, had been repeatedly and mutually taken, on many former occasions, and never had been the cause of discontent to either party. This precedent then, strengthened by the existence of an actual Debt, seemed to give a Double sanction to the executive for what they did: nor did any instance occur to them of unreadiness at any time to spare freely on continental requisition any articles within their possession or power, which might expose them to experience in turn the disregard of congress: I flatter myself therefore that that honorable Body whenever this matter shall be the Subject of their deliberations will be of opinion that the proceedings of the Lieutenant Governor and council were substantially justifiable.[63] They hope that no want of ceremony, or other smaller circumstance, may have been matter of Offence to congress. If in this they should be mistaken, feeling the most real respect for that body, impressed with the Idea that its authority can never be wounded without injury to the present union, they are to lament the misapprehension and wish to remove it by assuring you, as they may with truth, that no sentiment of theirs, either on this, or any other occasion, has justified it. A motive of duty and respect to the collective council of our union has led me into this detail to remove all ground of discontent from among us, and to Assure you Sir at the same time that I shall consider as occasions of manifesting my zeal for our sacred cause, those which shall occur of proving how sincerely, I am Sir their and your most Obedient and most humble Servant,

TH: JEFFERSON

63. In TJ's absence, Lieutenant Governor John Page headed the Council of State.

# 4

# "A MOST MELANCHOLY CRISIS,"
# 1780–1781

*I*N THEIR DAILY MEETINGS around the council table at the Capitol in Williamsburg, Jefferson and Madison began a collaboration that would last as long as they lived. When Madison left Williamsburg in December 1779, he and Jefferson had become intimately acquainted, forming a friendship based on mutual respect and affection. At twenty-nine, Madison, the youngest delegate in the Continental Congress, was three years younger than Jefferson had been when he first made his entrance on the Continental stage as a public figure. Like Jefferson, Congressman Madison was constant in attendance, silent in debate, and a workhorse in committee.

Indeed, the two friends had much in common. They came from the same part of Virginia (Montpellier is about twenty-five miles from Monticello). More importantly, they shared basic republican principles and mutual intellectual interests. For almost a decade after their friendship began, Madison later observed, they were "for the most part separated by different walks in public and private life,"[1] but wherever they were, each served as observer and sounding board for the other. From the beginning, they engaged in a lively exchange of correspondence, public and private, one that lasted for more than forty-six years and generated more than 1,250 letters.

Both men were fond of words, and although Madison had not yet gained a reputation for that "peculiar felicity of expression" that characterized Jefferson's writing, he had a latent talent that later led John Marshall to argue that if eloquence included the pure power of reasoned persuasion, Madison was "the most eloquent man I ever heard." Indeed, Jefferson was to recall in his autobi-

---

1. JM to Samuel Harrison Smith, Nov. 4, 1826, in *Letters and Other Writings of James Madison*, (ed. William C. Rives and Philip R. Fendall), 4 vols. (Philadelphia, 1865), III, pp. 533–34.

ography that one of the most impressive things about Madison was the "powers and polish of his pen."[2]

Each man spent long hours at his writing desk, and both knew that their literary legacy lay in their letters. According to Jefferson, "The letters of a person, especially of one whose business has been transacted by letters, form the only full and genuine journal of his life."[3] Madison agreed. "It has been remarked," he wrote late in life, "that the biography of an author must be a history of his writings. So must that of one whose whole life has in a manner been a public life, be gathered from his . . . manuscript papers on public subjects, including letters to as well as from him."[4]

When Madison inaugurated his correspondence with Jefferson in 1780, he picked up where the discussions at the council table in Virginia had so often ended—with financing the Revolutionary War. After leaving Williamsburg for Orange County, Madison had decided to prepare himself for congressional service by studying "the state of Continental affairs, and particularly that of the finances which, owing to the depreciation of paper currency was truly deplorable."[5] In a bold analysis of Hume's and Montesquieu's views that the value of money depended on its quantity, he rejected their economic theory as "manifestly erroneous." Instead, the value of money depended on the credit of the state issuing it, the time of the money's redemption in specie, and public confidence that the money would be redeemed at the time specified. The disastrous depreciation of Continental currency, he concluded, was related to a general promise of redemption at an unspecified date without any provision for taxes to meet that need. Inflation sprang from "distrust of the *public disposition* to fulfill" these obligations. In short, "the discredit of our money" was considered "as an omen of public bankruptcy."[6] To restore faith in Continental currency, Madison favored a loan of specie from abroad, increased taxes by the states to meet wartime expenses, and effective leadership that would demonstrate that the war could be won and that financial obligations would be met.

On March 18, 1780, the day Madison arrived in Philadelphia, Congress chose an option that had not occurred to the Virginia delegate. Congress stopped issuing paper currency, surrendering to the states the responsibility for supporting Continental concerns, including the Continental army. To halt inflation, it devalued the dollar, virtually repudiating the old Continental currency by exchanging it at a ratio of 40 to 1 of specie. But since Congress had

---

2. For Marshall's view, see William Cabell Rives, *History of the Life and Times of James Madison*, 3 vols. (Boston, 1859–68), II, p. 612. For TJ's view, see his "Autobiography," in *Thomas Jefferson: Writings*, ed. Merrill D. Peterson (New York, 1984), p. 37.
3. TJ to Robert Walsh, Apr. 5, 1823, in Jefferson Papers, University of Virginia.
4. Douglass Adair, "James Madison's Autobiography," *WMQ* 2 (1945): 209.
5. *Ibid.*, 200.
6. *PJM*, I, pp. 302–9.

no coin or hard specie, that body authorized new paper money, payable in specie in six years. However, the new money was to be issued not by Congress, which went out of the money business, but by the individual states. As they accepted old bills in payment of state quotas of taxes and returned them to Congress for destruction at the rate of $15 million per month for the next thirteen months, the nominal national debt of $200 million would be reduced to an actual debt of $5 million. But money would still be needed to carry on the war, so new bills were to be issued by the states as the old Continental currency was destroyed. For every $20 turned in, the state could print $1 in new money, redeemable in specie and drawing 5 percent interest payable by the United States six years hence. This would produce $10 million in new paper money that was to be split as it was issued on a 60:40 basis between the states and Congress, with the states spending their $6 million on war supplies and Congress using its $4 million to discharge the states' share of the costs of the war. For the redemption of the new money, the states were to levy taxes in specific commodities. If any state found it impossible to redeem its portion of the new bills, the faith of the United States was pledged for that purpose.[7]

Madison was appalled with the measure and dashed off personal letters to two of his closest friends—his father and Governor Jefferson.[8] That was his only letter to his father for some time, but he pelted Jefferson with five more private letters that, though personal, were essentially reportorial. In the fourth one, he signed his complimentary close as "your friend," and Jefferson reciprocated in his first response, a personal letter to Madison that accompanied an official letter to the Virginia congressional delegation.[9]

Madison's first surviving letter from Philadelphia expressed his "most pungent apprehensions" about relying on the states for currency control. In a melancholy mood, he wrote Jefferson: "If the States do not vigorously proceed in collecting the old money and establishing funds for the credit of the new ... we are undone." Although money was the fundamental problem that faced Congress, Madison ticked off a litany of horrors that made 1780 more critical than any of "the various conjunctures of alarm and distress which have arisen in the course of the revolution":

> Our army threatened with an immediate alternative of disbanding or living on free quarter; the public Treasury empty; public credit exhausted, nay the private credit of purchasing Agents employed, I am told, as far as it will bear, Congress complaining of the extortion of the people; the people of the improvidence of Congress, and the army of both; our affairs requiring the most mature and systematic measures, and the ur-

---

7. See Edmund C. Burnett, *The Continental Congress* (New York, 1941), pp. 426–27; Jack Rakove, *The Beginnings of National Politics: An Interpretive History of the Continental Congress* (Cambridge, Mass., 1979), pp. 212, 277, 284; and E. James Ferguson, *The Power of the Purse: A History of American Public Finance, 1776–1790* (Chapel Hill, 1961), pp. 50–52.

8. JM's first letter to TJ has not survived, but it is mentioned in his second, that of March 27, 1780, below.

9. See JM to TJ, June 6, 1780, below, and TJ to JM, July 26, 1780, below.

gency of occasions admitting only of temporizing expedients and those expedients generating new difficulties. Congress from a defect of adequate Statesmen more likely to fall into wrong measures and of less weight to enforce right ones, recommending plans to the several states for execution and the states separately rejudging the expediency of such plans, whereby the same distrust of concurrent exertions that has damped the ardor of patriotic individuals, must produce the same effect among the States themselves. An old system of finance discarded as incompetent to our necessities, an untried and precarious one substituted and a total stagnation in prospect between the end of the former and the operation of the latter.[10]

Things remained "equally perplexed and alarming" in May and June, when Madison's worries wobbled between "our distress and disgrace." He "feared a most melancholy crisis" unless the states responded promptly to the new financial plan. Recalling the early days when Jefferson had been a member of the Continental Congress, he observed "that the situation of Congress had undergone a total change from what it originally was. Whilst they exercised the indefinite power of emitting money on the credit of their constituents they had the whole wealth and resources of the Continent within their Command, and could go on with their affairs independently and as they pleased. Since the resolution passed for shutting the press, this power has been entirely given up and they are now as dependent on the States as the King of England is on the Parliament. They can neither enlist pay nor feed a single soldier, nor execute any other purpose but as the means are first put into their hands. Unless the legislatures are sufficiently attentive to this change of circumstances and act in conformity to it every thing must necessarily go wrong or rather must come to a total stop."[11]

The war news was as gloomy as the financial. In May, Charleston fell to the British forces commanded by Sir Henry Clinton, the British commander in chief, and General Cornwallis, who captured 5,500 American troops, the most disastrous American loss of the Revolution. The British quickly brought all of South Carolina under their control, joining it to Georgia as a solid base for operations against North Carolina and Virginia. Prospects for a clean sweep north looked so good that General Clinton reported that "if a French or Spanish fleet does not interfere I think a few works if properly reinforced, will give us all between this and Hudson's River."[12]

The French fleet was soon to be joined by a French army in America, but Madison "feared we shall continue to be so unprepared to cooperate with them, as to disappoint their views, and to add to our distress and disgrace." With a sense of national humiliation, he also reported that a mutiny in the army, which was quickly suppressed, had erupted when troops "assembled on the parade with their arms and resolved to return home or satisfy their hunger by the force of the Bayonet." A few days later, Madison hoped that "the arrival

10. JM to TJ, Mar. 27, 1780, below.
11. JM to TJ, May 6, 1780, below, and June 2, 1780, below.
12. Quoted in John R. Alden, *A History of the American Revolution* (New York, 1969), p. 416.

of the French Armament which is hourly expected will place our affairs in a less melancholy situation."[13]

While Madison moaned about the perplexing problems at the Continental level, Jefferson wrestled with baffling issues at the state level that were no less difficult. His first letter to Madison came from Richmond, where the state government had moved in 1780 after the legislature had approved his earlier suggestion.[14] The governor assured Madison that Virginia was complying with the new financial plan by calling in the old paper money in circulation. Because of the slim margin of support in the assembly, however, he thought it "of the utmost consequence to get it into a course of execution before the assembly meets" again.

Virginia had also complied with congressional requests for troops to replace those captured at Charleston. In addition to 3,000 men drafted for service "to the Southward," Jefferson wrote, the state had responded promptly to Congress's request to recruit, remount, equip, and replace the cavalry units decimated by the British in South Carolina. Noting that Congress had addressed its requisitions to both Virginia and North Carolina, Jefferson informed his friend that "the whole has been done by us except as to 200 saddles which the Q[uarter] M[aster] expects to get from the Northward." Knowing that North Carolina's resources were already strained by the British presence in South Carolina, Virginia had acted generously "because we supposed N. Caroline would be considerably burthened with calls for occasional horse."

The one bright spot in their first exchange was Jefferson's report that the newly established law school at the College of William and Mary had won "universal applause" under the leadership of George Wythe. Elected a member of the Board of Visitors when he became governor, Jefferson had been responsible for abolishing three of the college's six professorships—in Oriental languages, Greek and Latin, and divinity—and substituting professorships in modern languages, anatomy and medicine, and law and government. To Madison, he observed that the law school, "by throwing from time to time new hands well principled and well informed into the legislature will be of infinite value." And on a scholarly note, he reminded Madison about the latter's parting promise to obtain for the governor an early map of Virginia from William Smith, former provost of the College of Philadelphia and fellow member of the American Philosophical Society for Useful Knowledge.[15]

Madison also saw a glimmer of hope in patriotic efforts by Philadelphia merchants and bankers to raise funds to supply food to Washington's army, which was as much threatened by famine as by British troops. Indeed, he got

13. JM to TJ, June 2, 1780, below, and June 6, 1780, below.

14. See the article by Rosemarie Zagarri, "Representation and the Removal of State Capitals, 1776–1812," *JAH* 74 (1988): 1239–56, for a fascinating discussion.

15. TJ to JM, July 26, 1780, below. For TJ's role as a member of the college's board of visitors, see Robert Polk Thomson, "The Reform of the College of William and Mary, 1763–1780," *Proceedings of the American Philosophical Society* 115, no. 1 (1971): 187–213.

so carried away, or perhaps he was merely influenced by the astronomical inflation, that he added one zero to the £300,000 and three zeros to the 3,000,000 rations reportedly raised. But he got the 300 hogsheads of rum right.[16]

After this relative flurry of personal correspondence, Madison and Jefferson were so swamped with business that their only exchanges for several months came in official letters between the governor and the Virginia congressional delegation. From Philadelphia, Madison and his colleagues concentrated their efforts on the ratification of the Articles of Confederation, navigation of the Mississippi, and winning the war, while Governor Jefferson, the Executive Council, and the Virginia legislature reciprocated.

As Madison watched the transfer of power from Congress to the states, he joined with his colleague Joseph Jones in trying to reverse the trend by strengthening Congress through ratification of the Articles. Since 1777, Maryland had stalled the ratification process because of a dispute between those states with claims to western lands and those without. Of the seven "landed" states, Virginia's trans-Appalachian territory was largest, stretching west to the Mississippi and northwest to the Great Lakes. Of the six "landless" states, Maryland's opposition was sharpest, and for three years that state had flatly refused to ratify the Articles, which confirmed the claims of the "landed" states.

Maryland argued that the western territory was "common property to be wrested from the common enemy by the blood and treasure of the thirteen states" and should be disposed of for the common benefit. The bond of common ownership would strengthen the Union, tying the states together after the war ended. That laudable view was supported by land speculators in the "landless" states, whose claims were based on Indian treaties or pre-Revolutionary land grants from British officials. Neither of these sources was recognized by Virginia, but they might be if Congress controlled the territory.

The military and financial crises of 1780 finally forced a resolution of the conflict over western lands. With the British army moving from South Carolina towards Virginia and Sir Henry Clinton launching hit-and-run amphibious raids from New York into Chesapeake Bay, both Virginia and Maryland needed military aid from General Washington and the French. When the Maryland congressional delegation requested aid from the Chevalier de la Luzerne, the French ambassador to the United States, he pointed out diplomatically that French ships and soldiers would move more quickly if the Articles of Confederation and Perpetual Union were ratified.

At the same time, New York, in a move designed "to accelerate the federal alliance," agreed to cede to Congress its nebulous claims to western lands. In a united effort to "remove the only obstacle to a final ratification of the articles," Congress then urged the other "landed" states to convey their west-

---

16. JM to TJ, June 23, 1780, below. For JM's use of the extra zeros, see *PTJ*, III, p. 419.

ern lands and pressed Maryland to subscribe to the Confederation constitution. Such action was necessary, Congress argued, in order to support public credit, the army, and "our very existence as a free, sovereign and independent people." By establishing "the federal union on a fixed and permanent basis," ratification would add to the "vigour of our councils and successes of our measures."[17]

Madison and the Virginia delegation promptly proposed a motion respecting any lands "that may be ceded" to Congress and agreed that such lands would be considered "as a common Fund for the use and benefit of such of the United States as have become or shall become members of the confederation." The territory could be formed into separate states and admitted to the Union on the basis of equality with the older states. The Virginians added three provisos: Congress should reimburse the ceding states for expenses in subduing British posts in the West, such as those incurred by George Rogers Clark; land bounties promised to army veterans should be honored; and land claims based on Indian titles made to land companies or private persons were to be deemed as "absolutely void."[18]

Madison took the lead in deliberations about western lands and "the happy establishment of the federal union." He and his colleague Theodorick Bland wrote Governor Jefferson that it was "of the first importance to America."[19] But they warned that the land companies, composed of speculators and "land mongers," would attempt "to extend their influence and support their pretensions . . . in procrastinating that desirable and necessary event."[20] On October 10, 1780, Congress adopted the Virginia delegation's motion but dropped the stipulation relating to claims based on Indian titles. Madison nonetheless urged Virginia to proceed with the cession, insisting that the state could exclude such claims and avoid congressional encroachments by attaching to its cession the proviso voiding private claims.[21] On January 2, 1781, Virginia followed his advice, and one month later Madison and his colleagues reported to Jefferson "unauthenticated information that Maryland has already acceded to the federal Union."[22] Congress set March 1, 1781, as the day that

---

17. The quotations are from W. C. Ford *et al.*, eds., *The Journals of the Continental Congress, 1774–1789*, 34 vols. (Washington, 1904–37), XIV, pp. 619–22; XVII, pp. 806–7.

18. Joseph Jones made the motion and JM seconded it on Sept. 6 1780; see *ibid.*, XVII, p. 808. Also see Thomas Perkins Abernethy, *Western Lands and the American Revolution* (New York, 1937), and Peter S. Onuf, *The Origins of the Federal Republic: Jurisdictional Controversies in the United States, 1775–1787* (Philadelphia, 1983).

19. See JM and the Virginia congressional delegation to TJ, Jan. 1, 1781, below. The phrase "the happy establishment of the federal union" comes from the congressional report on western lands, Sept. 6, 1780, in Ford *et al.*, XVII, pp. 806–7.

20. See JM and the Virginia congressional delegation to TJ, Nov. 22, 1780, below.

21. JM to Joseph Jones, Sept. 19, 1780, and Oct. 17, 1780, in *PJM*, II, pp. 89–90, 136–37.

22. JM and the Virginia congressional delegation to TJ, Jan. 30, 1781, below. Maryland officially agreed to subscribe to the Articles of Confederation on Feb. 2, 1781; see Abernethy, p. 245.

the Articles of Confederation and Perpetual Union were to become effective.[23]

Closely related to the completion of the Confederation were congressional deliberations over a potential treaty of alliance with Spain. Virginia's interest in the West made that state a supporter of the Americans' right to free navigation of the Mississippi River, clashing with Spain's view. But the continuing success of the British army in Georgia and South Carolina heightened the need for Spanish help and weakened Congress's insistence on the free use of the Mississippi. When the Georgia delegation on November 18 recommended that Congress abandon its demand in order to gain Spanish assistance, Madison demanded postponement of the decision until the Virginia delegation received new instructions. Always the forceful advocate of Virginia's western interests, Madison disagreed with his colleague Theodorick Bland, who thought that military aid from Spain might "counterbalance the distant prospect of a free Navigation of that River."[24] In a joint letter to Governor Jefferson, Madison and Bland asked for Virginia's "full and ultimate sense on this point." Although Madison did not think that military necessity meant that "an Alliance with Spain ought to be purchased even at the price of such a cession," he couched his letter to Jefferson in neutral language and requested instructions on what the delegates should do if Congress made concessions without Virginia's consent.[25]

When this request reached Virginia, British forces, after moving through North Carolina, were nearing Richmond, and the assembly modified its instructions, authorizing concessions on navigation "if insisting on the same is deemed an impediment to a treaty with Spain."[26] Although Madison drafted new instructions to John Jay, American minister to Spain, the ambassador did not find it necessary to give up American claims to free navigation of the Mississippi.[27]

During Madison's first year in Congress, the war went badly. After the fall of Charleston, the British routed the southern army, commanded by General Horatio Gates, at Camden, South Carolina, on August 16, the bloodiest defeat of the Revolution. One month later, General Benedict Arnold betrayed his command and his country by attempting to sell to the British America's

---

23. Subsequent arguments over details delayed congressional acceptance of Virginia's cessions until 1784.

24. JM and the Virginia congressional delegation to TJ, Nov. 22, 1780, below. In a letter to Joseph Jones, JM wrote that he would insist on the right of navigation since "Virginia and the United States in general are too deeply interested in the subject of controversy to give it up as long as there is a possibility of retaining it"; see JM to Joseph Jones, Dec. 5, 1780, in *PJM,* II, p. 224.

25. JM and the Virginia congressional delegation to TJ, Dec. 13, 1780, below.

26. The quotation is from the "Instruction from the Virginia General Assembly to Its Delegates in Congress," [Jan. 2, 1781], in *PJM,* II, p. 273, which was transmitted in TJ to JM and the Virginia congressional delegation, Jan. 18, 1781, below.

27. See Richard B. Morris, *The Peacemakers: The Great Powers and American Independence* (New York, 1965), pp. 240–47, and Brant, II, pp. 70–88.

most important fort, West Point, the vital link between New England and the rest of the states. In a letter to Governor Jefferson, Madison and his colleagues called "the sudden defection of Major Genl. Arnold from the American Cause, and his flight to the Enemy" "a most extraordinary and unexpected event." They breathed a sigh of relief, however, noting that the "atrocious and Complicated Vilainy," which had contemplated the seizure of General Washington, Ambassador Luzerne, and General Lafayette, had failed. The stunned delegates then detailed for Jefferson "the Blackest Circumstances of treason and Perfidy." "The General and other Gentlemen above Mentioned arrived at Arnolds Quarters a few minutes after his flight," they wrote, "and he has taken effectual measures to prevent further Mischief." As soon as the news reached Philadelphia, an enraged mob had "burnt the traitor in Effigy," consigning him "to public infamy and odium." And the Virginia delegation quoted Virgil's *Aeneid* to sum up their explanation of Arnold's action: "Cursed greed for gold, to what crimes dost thou not impel the human breast?"[28]

Arnold's treason shocked Americans. But equally shocking was the need to rebuild the southern army following the losses at Charleston and Camden. To General Washington, Jefferson wrote "that after the loss of one army our eyes are turned towards the other." But Jefferson realized that Washington, "being situated between two fires," could not rush reinforcements to the South as long as the British held New York.[29] The governor, therefore, informed the assembly that the burden for opposing British forces in the South rested on Virginia since Georgia and South Carolina were occupied by the British and North Carolina had been "exhausted by the ravages of two armies."[30] To Madison and the congressional delegation he sent an urgent request for "a good supply of Cartridge Paper and Cartouch Boxes," "Muskets being really useless without them." On the whole, he wrote with more than his usual optimism, "the State turns out with a Spirit and alacrity which makes me perfectly happy."[31]

When the delegation informed him that the French fleet might blockade Chesapeake Bay during the winter, a delighted Jefferson sent a lengthy memorandum, suggesting the safest harbors for warships.[32] In their response, Madison and Bland warned Jefferson that a British naval force carrying 2,500 troops had sailed at the end of the year, indicating "a Vigorous effort against the Southern States, this Winter."[33]

Unfortunately, the British arrived in Virginia before Madison's letter did, with Benedict Arnold commanding the invasion. After sweeping up the James

28. JM and the Virginia congressional delegation to TJ, Oct. 5, 1780, below.
29. TJ to George Washington, June 11, 1780, and July 2, 1780, in *PTJ*, III, pp. 433, 478.
30. TJ to Benjamin Harrison, Nov. 24, 1780, *ibid.*, IV, p. 150.
31. TJ to JM and the Virginia congressional delegation, Oct. 27, 1780, below.
32. TJ to JM and the Virginia congressional delegation, Dec. 18, 1780, below.
33. JM and the Virginia congressional delegation to TJ, Jan. 1, 1780, below.

"A MOST MELANCHOLY CRISIS," 1780–1781                133

River as far as Richmond and routing Jefferson and the government, Arnold dropped down the river to Portsmouth and fortified the post. Although Jefferson informed Washington and the president of Congress that the British were "commanded by the parricide Arnold,"[34] Jefferson ignored Arnold in his letter to Madison and his colleagues, except for a passing reference. Indeed, he played down the invasion as "not of any magnitude."[35]

But Madison and Bland were concerned about "the misfortunes our Country has suffer'd from the Invasion under the command of the detestable Arnold," fearing that he would continue to alarm "our State and Maryland, which he has so successfully begun, in order to Harrass our Military, increase our expenses, waste our resources, destroy our Magazines and Stores when he finds it practicable; and by thus distracting us, prevent our sending the necessary succours to the Southern Army."[36] When the delegates heard a rumor that a storm had damaged a number of British warships, forcing the recall of Arnold, they whooped, "Heavenly Storm."[37]

A few days later, Madison and Joseph Jones wrote Jefferson that they hoped a few French warships would sail for Chesapeake Bay "in order to cooperate with our Troops, in taking ample Vengeance on Mr. Arnold, for his treasons, perjuries, Robberies, and depreadations."[38] On March 6, 1781, Madison and Jones informed the governor that Admiral Destouches and the French fleet would transport French troops from Rhode Island to the Chesapeake for a combined operation against Arnold and urged Jefferson to have heavy cannon and mortars ready for a siege.[39] But on the way south, the French fleet encountered a larger British flotilla off the coast of Virginia that forced the French fleet to flee, returning to Narragansett Bay. Thus went any chance of capturing Benedict Arnold, for whom Jefferson had offered a reward of 5,000 guineas alive or 2,000 dead.[40]

Arnold's forays disrupted Virginia's efforts to speed supplies and recruits to the southern army. As Jefferson confessed to General Nathanael Greene, "They have amazingly interrupted both operations. The latter indeed has been totally suspended."[41] To hasten aid to the southern army, the Virginia assembly dispatched Speaker Benjamin Harrison as a special emissary to Congress to plead for assistance. In a letter to Madison and the Virginia delegation, Jefferson referred them to Harrison, who could "so much more fully explain to you

34. TJ to George Washington, Jan. 10, 1781, in *PTJ,* IV, p. 335.
35. TJ to JM and the Virginia congressional delegation, Jan. 18, 1781, below.
36. JM and the Virginia congressional delegation to TJ, Jan. 23, 1781, below.
37. JM and the Virginia congressional delegation to TJ, Feb. 13, 1781, below. The rumor was later proven false.
38. JM and the Virginia congressional delegation to TJ, Feb. [20], 1781, below.
39. JM and the Virginia congressional delegation to TJ, Mar. 6, 1781, below.
40. TJ to J. P. G. Muhlenberg, Jan. 31, 1781, in *PTJ,* IV, pp. 487–88. Muhlenberg was a general in the Virginia Continental line and had been in charge of the defense of Virginia since Mar. 1780.
41. TJ to Nathanael Greene, Jan. 16, 1781, *ibid.,* p. 379.

by words the Steps taken for supporting our Opposition to the common enemy."[42] Harrison had four objectives in addition to military assistance for the South: (1) Continental support of a western campaign against Detroit by George Rogers Clark, who needed four tons of powder at Pittsburgh; (2) transfer of the Saratoga prisoners from Virginia, where they were a tempting target for release by British invaders; (3) assistance in moving French supplies destined for Virginia but diverted to Rhode Island; and (4) continuation of Virginia's trade with Bermuda without giving "umbrage to Congress or the French minister."

Madison and his colleagues in Philadelphia reported to Jefferson that Congress had met Harrison's requests "as far is practicable in the present Situation of affairs."[43] Congress added the Pennsylvania Line to the southern army; recommended an increase in that army to 10,000 men—"all the regular troops, from Pennsylvania to Georgia, inclusive"—with adequate arms, clothing, and supplies; and agreed that the Saratoga prisoners should be moved from Virginia to a northern state.[44] Harrison purchased from the Continental Board of War the gunpowder for Clark's western campaign. On the subject of Virginia's trade with Bermuda, the French ambassador opposed it as "injurious to the common cause," and Harrison referred that issue to Madison and the congressional delegates to resolve. Finally, he made arrangements to have the French arms and supplies, which had been sidetracked to Rhode Island aboard *Le Comité*, forwarded to Virginia on a French warship or perhaps to the Delaware River for transshipment to Fredericksburg.[45] Jefferson also urged Madison and his colleagues to expedite the delivery of supplies from Maryland and Delaware destined for the southern army.[46]

In addition to these major issues of the Revolution, the first year of correspondence between Jefferson and Madison touched on many other matters: money, mutinies in the army, insurrections in Virginia, and the need for a newspaper and printing press in Richmond.[47] In November 1780, Madison and the Virginia delegates sent a three-sentence plea to Governor Jefferson to establish "some stable provision . . . for supplying us with money" in order to cope with "the great depreciation of money and the extravagant prices of every thing."[48]

To combat inflation, Governor Jefferson was especially careful to comply with congressional directives about redeeming the old Continental bills at 40 to 1. When one of Virginia's monthly transactions with the Continental trea-

42. TJ to JM and the Virginia congressional delegation, Jan. 26, 1781, below.
43. JM and the Virginia congressional delegation to TJ, Feb. [20], 1781, below.
44. Ford *et al.,* XIX, pp. 176–78 (Feb. 20, 1781), and 193 (Feb. 24, 1781).
45. Benjamin Harrison to TJ, Feb. 12, 1781, and Feb. 19, 1781, in *PTJ,* IV, pp. 589, 655.
46. TJ to JM and the Virginia congressional delegation, Mar. 8, 1781, below.
47. For efforts to attract a printer to Richmond, see TJ to JM and the Virginia congressional delegation, Feb. [20], 1781, below, and Mar. 20, 1781, below.
48. JM and the Virginia congressional delegation to TJ, [Nov. 5, 1780], below.

sury was erroneously recorded at a 75-to-1 ratio, Jefferson promptly protested, urging Madison and the Virginia delegation to clear the state of any complicity in an action that "would be most destructive to the credit of the new emission, and have a fatal tendency to depreciate it."[49] In another transaction concerning the value of Virginia currency, Jefferson and the Executive Council proposed arbitration to determine whether bills paid by George Rogers Clark to Simon Nathan for military supplies should be accepted at face value in specie or at the value in depreciated currency, and asked Madison and his colleagues to monitor the negotiations.[50] In turn, the congressional delegates requested Jefferson's help in determining Virginia's indebtedness to Baron D'Arendt for his efforts on Virginia's behalf to buy arms and supplies in Prussia while on furlough from the Continental army.[51]

Reports of mutinies in the army and insurrections in Virginia punctuated the correspondence between Madison and Jefferson in 1780–1781, capping an ignominious year of failures and frustrations—wild inflation, military defeats, and treason. Madison described the revolt of the Pennsylvania Line and "the fury of the Mutineers" on New Year's Day, 1781. At the end of the month, he reported similar "commotions" in the New Jersey Line but announced that "prudent and seasonable remedies applied have re-established order and discipline among the troops."[52] Earlier, Jefferson had informed the Virginia delegates of the suppression of "a very dangerous Insurrection" in southwestern Virginia, but he was worried that "this dangerous fire is only smothered: when it will break out [again] seems to depend altogether on events."[53]

--- THE LETTERS ---

*Madison to Jefferson*

Philadelphia Mar. 27 and 28, 1780

DEAR SIR

Nothing under the title of news has occurred since I wrote last week by express[1] except that the Enemy on the 1st. of March remained in the neighbourhood of Charlestown in the same posture as when the preceding account

---

49. TJ to JM and the Virginia congressional delegation, Nov. 17, 1780, below. The quotation is from a congressional report of Nov. 1, 1780, on the transaction; see Ford *et al.*, XVIII, pp. 1003–4.
50. TJ to JM and the Virginia congressional delegation, Mar. 15, 1781, below.
51. JM and the Virginia congressional delegation to TJ, Jan. 1, 1781, below, and Feb. 13, 1781, below; TJ to JM and the Virginia congressional delegation, Jan. 26, 1781, below.
52. JM and the Virginia congressional delegation to TJ, Jan. 9, 1781, below, and Jan. 30, 1781, below.
53. TJ to JM and the Virginia congressional delegation, Oct. 27, 1780, below.

1. This letter, the first one in this historic exchange, has not been found.

came away. From the best intelligence from that quarter there seems to be great encouragement to hope that Clinton's operations will be again frustrated.[2] Our great apprehensions at present flow from a very different quarter. Among the various conjunctures of alarm and distress which have arisen in the course of the revolution, it is with pain I affirm to you Sir, that no one can be singled out more truly critical than the present. Our army threatened with an immediate alternative of disbanding or living on free quarter; the public Treasury empty; public credit exhausted, nay the private credit of purchasing Agents employed, I am told, as far as it will bear, Congress complaining of the extortion of the people; the people of the improvidence of Congress, and the army of both; our affairs requiring the most mature and systematic measures, and the urgency of occasions admitting only of temporizing expedients and those expedients generating new difficulties. Congress from a defect of adequate Statesmen more likely to fall into wrong measures and of less weight to enforce right ones, recommending plans to the several states for execution and the states separately rejudging the expediency of such plans, whereby the same distrust of concurrent exertions that has damped the ardor of patriotic individuals, must produce the same effect among the States themselves. An old system of finance discarded as incompetent to our necessities, an untried and precarious one substituted and a total stagnation in prospect between the end of the former and the operation of the latter: These are the outlines of the true picture of our public situation. I leave it to your own imagination to fill them up. Believe me Sir as things now stand, if the States do not vigorously proceed in collecting the old money and establishing funds for the credit of the new, that we are undone; and let them be ever so expeditious in doing this, still the intermediate distress to our army and hindrance to public affairs are a subject of melancholy reflection. Gen. Washington writes that a failure of bread has already commenced in the army, and that for any thing he sees, it must unavoidably increase. Meat they have only for a short season and as the whole dependance is on provisions now to be procured, without a shilling for the purpose, and without credit for a shilling, I look forward with the most pungent apprehensions. It will be attempted I believe to purchase a few supplies with loan office certificates; but whether they will be received is perhaps far from being certain; and if received will certainly be a most expensive and ruinous expedient. It is not without some reluctance I trust this information to a conveyance by post, but I know of no better at present, and I conceive it to be absolutely necessary to be known to those who are most able and zealous to contribute to the public relief.

March 28.

Authentic information is now received that the Enemy on their passage to Georgia lost all their Horse, the Defiance of 64 guns which foundered at sea, three transports with troops, although it is pretended these troops and the

---

2. For a brief account of the British siege and capture of Charleston, see Alden, pp. 412–16.

men of the Defiance were saved, and 1 transport with Hessians of which nothing has been heard.³ By a letter from Mr. Adams dated Corunna 16 December there seems little probability that Britain is yet in a humour for peace. The Russian ambassador at that Court has been lately changed, and the new one on his way to London made some stop at Paris whence a rumor has spread in Europe that Russia was about to employ her mediation for peace. Should there be any reality in it, Mr. Adams says it is the opinion of the most intelligent he had conversed with that the independance of the United [States] would be insisted on as a preliminary: to which G. B. would accede with much greater repugnance than the cession of Gibraltar which Spain was determined to make a sine qua non. With respect and regard I am Dr Sir. Yrs sincerely,

JAMES MADISON JR

*Madison to Jefferson*

Philadelphia May 6, 1780

DEAR SIR

I am sorry I can give you no other account of our public situation than that it continues equally perplexed and alarming as when I lately gave you a sketch of it. Our army has as yet been kept from starving and public measures from a total stagnation by draughts on the States for the unpaid requisitions. The great amount of these you may judge of from the share that has fallen to Virginia. The discharge of debts due from the purchasing departments has absorbed a great proportion of them, and very large demands still remain. As soon as the draughts amount to the whole of the monthly requisitions up to the end of March, they must cease according to the new scheme of finance. We must then depend wholly on the emissions to be made in pursuance of that scheme which can only be applied as the old emissions are collected and destroyed. Should this not be done as fast as the current expenditures require, or should the new emissions fall into a course of depreciation both of which may but too justly be feared a most melancholy crisis must take place. A punctual compliance on the part of the States with the specific supplies will indeed render much less money necessary than would otherwise be wanted, but experience by no means affords satisfactory encouragement that due and unanimous exertions will be made for that purpose not to mention that our distress is so pressing that it is uncertain whether any exertions of that kind can give relief in time.⁴ It occurs besides that as the ability of the people to comply with the pecuniary requisitions is derived from the sale of their commodities, a

3. A storm off Cape Hatteras did extensive damage to Sir Henry Clinton's fleet. A transport carrying his artillery sank, and the ship transporting Hessian troops was blown off course, eventually landing in England; see *ibid*.

4. In lieu of money quotas from the states, Congress, in Dec. 1779, requested the states to furnish designated supplies for use by the army; see Burnett pp. 402–5.

requisition of the latter must make the former proportionally more difficult and defective. Congress have the satisfaction however to be informed that the legislature of Connecticut have taken the most vigorous steps for supplying their quota both of money and commodities, and that a body of their principal merchants have associated for supporting the credit of the new paper, for which purpose they have in a public address pledged their faith to the Assembly to sell their merchandise on the same terms for it as if they were to be paid in specie. A similar vigor throughout the Union may perhaps produce effects as far exceeding our present hopes as they have heretofore fallen short of our wishes.

It is to be observed that the situation of Congress has undergone a total change from what it originally was. Whilst they exercised the indefinite power of emitting money on the credit of their constituents they had the whole wealth and resources of the Continent within their Command, and could go on with their affairs independently and as they pleased. Since the resolution passed for shutting the press, this power has been entirely given up and they are now as dependent on the States as the King of England is on the parliament. They can neither enlist pay nor feed a single soldier, nor execute any other purpose but as the means are first put into their hands. Unless the legislatures are sufficiently attentive to this change of circumstances and act in conformity to it every thing must necessarily go wrong or rather must come to a total stop. All that Congress can do in future will be to administer public affairs with prudence vigor and œconomy. In order to do which they have sent a Committee to Head Quarters with ample powers in concert with the Commander in chief and the Heads of the departments to reform the various abuses which prevail and to make such arrangements as will best guard against a relapse into them.[5]

The Papers inclosed herewith contain all the news we have here.[6] With great regard I am Dr Sir Yr Obt Servt,

JAMES MADISON JR

## Madison to Jefferson

Philadelphia June 2, 1780

DEAR SIR

I have written several private letters to you since my arrival here, which as they contained matters that I should be sorry should fall into other hands, I could wish to know had been received. If your Excellency has written any acknowledgements of them, they have never reached me.

5. For a discussion of the congressional committee at Washington's headquarters, see *ibid.*, pp. 445-66.
6. The enclosures have not been found.

Mr. Griffin tells me he has seen several letters just received by Mr. Bingham from Martinique which give information that three successive engagements have taken place between the Fleets in the W. Indies the two first of which were indecisive but that the third was so far in favor of the French that the English had gone into port and left the former entirely master of those Seas: that they were gone in consequence of that towards Barbadoes, and that the general expectation was that both that Island and St. Kitts would speedily be in their possession.[7]

It appears from sundry accounts from the Frontier of N. York and other N. States that the Savages are making the most distressing incursions, under the direction of the British Agents, and that a considerable force is assembling at Montreal for the purpose of wresting from us Fort Schuyler, which covers the N. Western frontiers of N. York. It is probable the Enemy will be but too successful this campaign in exciting their vindictive spirit against us throughout the whole frontier of the United States. The Expedition of Genl. Sullivan against the six nations seems by its effects rather to have exasperated than to have terrified or disabled them. And the example of those nations will add great weight to the exhortations addressed to the more Southern tribes.[8]

Rivington has published a positive and particular account of the surrender of Charlestown on the 12 Ulto: said to be brought to N. York by the Iris which left Charleston five days after. There are notwithstanding some circumstances attending it which, added to the notorious character for lying of the Author, leave some hope that it is fictitious. The true state of the matter will probably be known at Richmond before this reaches you.[9]

We have yet heard nothing further of the Auxiliary Armament from France. However anxiously its arrival may be wished for it is much to be feared we shall continue to be so unprepared to cooperate with them, as to disappoint their views, and to add to our distress and disgrace. Scarce a week, and sometimes scarce a day, but brings us a most lamentable picture from Head Quarters. The Army are a great part of their time on short allowance, at sometimes without any at all, and constantly depending on the precarious fruits of momentary expedients. General Washington has found it of the utmost difficulty to repress the mutinous spirit engendered by hunger and want of pay: and his endeavours could not prevent an actual eruption of it in two Connecticut Regiments who assembled on the parade with their arms and resolved to return home or satisfy their hunger by the force of the Bayonet.

---

7. The results in the West Indies were not as decisive as JM reported, and the French fleet returned to France to refit; see Piers Mackesy, *The War for America, 1775–1783* (London, 1964), pp. 329–33.

8. For an account of frontier warfare in New York in 1780, see Barbara Graymont, *The Iroquois in the American Revolution* (Syracuse, 1972), pp. 230–40.

9. James Rivington was the Loyalist editor of New York's *Royal Gazette*. His account of the British capture of Charleston was correct.

We have no permanent resource and scarce even a momentary one left but in the prompt and vigorous supplies of the States. The State of Pennsylvania has it in her power to give great relief in the present crisis, and a recent act of its Legislature shews, they are determined to make the most of it. I understand they have invested the Executive with a dictatorial Authority from which nothing but the *lives* of their Citizens are exempted. I hope the good resulting from it will be such as to compensate for the risk of the precedent.[10] With great respect I am Yr. Excellency's Most Ob and humb servt,

JAMES MADISON JUNR.


*Madison to Jefferson*

Philadelphia June 6, 1780

DEAR SIR

A Vessel from West Florida has brought to the President of Congress intelligence from Govr. Galvez of the surrender of Mobile. No other particulars than that contained in the inclosed paper are mentioned, except the verbal report of the Capt. that the Garrison consisted of about 800 including inhabitants etc.[11] Seven or eight vessels have just arrived from the W. Indies as you will also observe in the inclosed paper but they bring no satisfactory information concerning the late engagements between the two fleets. The Address from the General Assembly was yesterday immediately on its receipt laid before Congress and referred to a special Committee, on whose report it will probably be considered in a committee of the whole.[12] I flatter myself that the arrival of the French Armament which is hourly expected will place our affairs in a less melancholy situation than their apprehensions seem to paint them. There is little doubt but the Conquest of the Southern States was the object of the operation of the present Campain, but I can not think the Enemy will pursue that object at the manifest risk of N. York. It is more probable they will leave a strong Garrison in Charleston, and carry back to N. York. the residue of their forces. If they shou'd endeavour to extend their acquisitions in the Southern States, it must proceed from an Assurance from England that a superior naval force will follow the french fleet to frustrate their views on the American Coast. I cannot suppose that however intent they may have been on taking post at Portsmouth, that they will venture in the present prospect to spread

10. The Pennsylvania assembly, on June 1, 1780, authorized the governor to commandeer supplies for the Continental army.

11. For a brief account of the Spanish seizure of Mobile, see Alden, pp. 430–31.

12. The Virginia General Assembly, on May 24, 1780, less than two weeks after the fall of Charleston and the capture of 5,500 American troops, urged Congress to send a "speedy and powerful reenforcement of Continental troops" to North Carolina in order to prevent "the conquest of the southern states"; see Hening, X, pp. 539–40.

themselves out in so exposed a situation. With great respect and sincerity I am Dr Sir Yr. friend and Servt.,

     JAMES MADISON JUNR

*Madison to Jefferson*
                 Philadelphia June 23, 1780

DEAR SIR

 Nothing material has taken place since my last. The fact is confirmed that Clinton has returned to N.Y. with part of the Southern army, and has joined Kniphausen. They are at present man[oeuvering] for purposes not absolutely known, but most probably in order to draw Genl. Washington to an action in which they suppose he may be disabled to give the necessary co-operation to the french armament.[13] Could they succeed in drawing him from his strong position, the result indeed ought to be exceedingly feared. He is weak in numbers beyond all suspicion, and under as great apprehension from famine as from the Enemy. Unless very speedy and extensive reinforcements are received from the Eastern States which I believe are exerting themselves, the issue of the Campain must be equally disgraceful to our Councils and disgustful to our Allies. Our greatest hopes of being able [to] feed them are founded on a patriotic scheme of the opulent Merchants of this City who have already subscribed nearly £3,000,000 and will very soon complete that sum, the immediate object of which is to procure and transport to the Army 3,000,000,000 of rations and 300 Hhds of rum.[14] Congress for the support of this bank and for the security and indemnification of the Subscribers, have pledged the faith of the United States and agreed to deposit Bills of Exchange in Europe to the Amount of £150,000 Sterling, which are not however to be made use of unless other means of discharging this debt sho[uld] be inadequate.[15] With sincere regard I am Yr. Obt Servt,

     J. MADISON JUNR

---

13. After capturing Charleston, Clinton returned to New York, leaving Lord Cornwallis in command of the royal forces in the South. Baron von Knyphausen, commander in chief of Hessian and other German troops, was second in command to Clinton in New York; see Alden, pp. 404, 413–17.

14. JM's figures were inflated. They should read £300,000 and 3,000,000 rations; see *PJM,* II, p. 41.

15. The best brief account of the Philadelphia merchants' plan to feed the army is in Charles Page Smith, *James Wilson: Founding Father, 1742–1798* (Chapel Hill, 1956), pp. 142–45, where the author discusses the establishment of the Bank of Pennsylvania to furnish "a supply of provisions for the armies of the United States."

## Jefferson to Madison

Richmond July 26, 1780

DEAR SIR

With my letter to the President I inclose a copy of the bill for calling in the paper money now in circulation, being the only copy I have been able to get. In my letter to the delegates I ask the favor of them to furnish me with authentic advice when the resolutions of Congress shall have been adopted by five other states. In a private letter I may venture to urge great dispatch and to assign the reasons. The bill on every vote prevailed but by small majorities, and on one occasion it escaped by two voices only. It's friends are very apprehensive that those who disapprove of it will be active in the recess of assembly to produce a general repugnance to it, and to prevail on the assembly in October to repeal it. They therefore think it of the utmost consequence to get it into a course of execution before the assembly meets. I have stated in my public letter to you what we shall consider as *authentic advice* lest a failure in that article should increase the delay.[16] If you cannot otherwise get copies of the bill, it would be worth while to be at some extraordinary expence to do it.

Some doubt has arisen here to which quarter our 3000 draughts are to go? As Congress directed 5000 militia to be raised and sent to the Southward including what were ordered there, and these 3000 (which I think will be 3500) draughts are raised in lieu of so many militia, the matter seems clear enough. When we consider that a fourth or fifth of the enemy's force are in S. Carolina, it could not be expected that N. Carolina, which contains but a tenth of the American militia should be left to support the Southern war alone; more especially when the regular force to the Northward and the expected aids are taken into the scale.[17] I doubt more whether the balance of the 1,900,000 Doll. are meant by Congress to be sent Northwardly, because in a resolution of June 17. subsequent to the requisition of the sum before mentioned they seem to appropriate *all* the monies from Maryland Southward to the Southern military chest. We shall be getting ready the balance, in which great disappointments have arisen from an inability to sell our tobacco; and in the mean time wish I could be advised whether it is to go Northward or Southward.[18] The aids of money from this state through the rest of the present

---

16. This letter by TJ to JM and the Virginia congressional delegation has not been found. For information about the five other states' ratification of Congress's 40-to-1 financial plan, see JM and the Virginia congressional delegation's certification of Sept. 5, 1780, below.

17. On June 17, 1780, Congress made two requests for Virginia troops: (1) the state should raise enough additional militia to bring the state's quota in the southern army to 5,000 men; (2) it should also enlist 3,000 more men for instant call. The Virginia assembly authorized the recruitment of 2,500 militia for three-month enlistments to meet the first request and 3,000 men to serve until Dec. 31, 1781, to meet the second; see Hening, X, pp. 221–26, 229, 257–62.

18. Virginia had sent to Philadelphia about three-fourths of its quota of $1.9 million requested by Congress in May 1780. On June 17, Congress had instructed states from Maryland southward to

year will be small, our taxes being effectually anticipated by certificates issued for want of money, and for which the sheriffs are glad to exchange their collections rather than bring them to the treasury. Congress desired N. Carolina and Virginia to recruit, remount, and equip Washington's and White's horse.[19] The whole has been done by us except as to 200 saddles which the Q. M. expects to get from the Northward. This draws from us about six or seven hundred thousand pounds, the half of which I suppose is so much more than was expected from us. We took on us the whole, because we supposed N. Caroline would be considerably burthened with calls for occasional horse, in the present low state of our cavalry; and that the disabled horses would be principally to be exchanged there for fresh.

Our troops are in the utmost distress for clothing, as are also our officers. What we are to do with the 3000 draughts when they are raised I cannot foresee.

Our new institution at the college has had a success which has gained it universal applause. Wythe's school is numerous. They hold weekly courts and assemblies in the capitol. The professors join in it; and the young men dispute with elegance, method and learning. This single school by throwing from time to time new hands well principled and well informed into the legislature will be of infinite value.[20] I wish you every felicity and am Dr. Sir Your friend and servt.,

TH: JEFFERSON.

P.S. You have not lost sight of the map I hope.[21]


## *Governor Jefferson to Madison and the Virginia Congressional Delegation*

Richmond Aug. 31, 1780

GENTLEMEN

We agree to employ Mr. Dunlap according to his proposals inclosed in your Letter of the 15th instant except that we must adhere to our requisition that a complete sheet of his weekly paper shall be kept clear of advertisements,

---

send their money quotas directly to the southern army, and TJ wondered if that directive applied to the $500,000 balance still owed by Virginia under its May quota.

19. Just before the fall of Charleston, British forces had defeated Lieutenant Colonel William Augustine Washington's dragoons at Moncks Corner and Colonel Anthony Walton White's cavalry at Lenud's Ferry; see Henry Lumpkin, *From Savannah to Yorktown: The American Revolution in the South* (Columbia, S.C., 1981), pp. 47–48.

20. See Robert M. Hughes, "William and Mary, the First American Law School," *WMQ* 2d ser., 2 (1922): 40–43.

21. See JM to TJ, Sept. 26, 1780, below.

and reserved for intelligence, essays, etc., except that advertisements from the Legislature or Executive shall be put into the same sheet with the intelligence.[22] The standing salary is to be fixed by the assembly, not by the executive, and we will recommend to them in settling it to consider the utility of the weekly paper and make liberal allowance for that over and above Mr. Dunlaps services in printing the public acts, Journals, proclamations, advertisements, etc. and this we can venture to undertake will be done. As to money which you say Mr. Dunlap will want as soon as he comes we are not in a condition to make him any advances between this and the meeting of assembly but immediately after their meeting we have no doubt it will be in our power. I hope his press will be got to work before they meet. We will give him any aid in our power in procuring a house here, and if we should have any vessels coming from the head of Elk[23] down the bay they shall take in any thing he pleases to have lodged here without charge. I wou'd recommend strongly to Mr. Dunlap that his manager here obtain the postmaster's office of the place. Besides that it will carry custom to his shop it will give him an exemption from militia duties which may otherwise be a considerable interruption. I have the honor to be with every sentiment of respect Gent., Your mo. obedient servant,

TH: JEFFERSON

## Madison and the Virginia Congressional Delegation's Certification to Governor Jefferson That Six States Have Complied with the Congressional Resolution of March 18, 1780, Relative to Public Finances

Philadelphia Sept. 5, 1780

We, Delegates from the Commonwealth of Virginia do certify that Congress have received authenticated copies of Acts of the Legislatures of the following States, complying with their resolutions of the 18th. of March last relative to the public finances, viz.[24]

1. An Act of the Legislature of Maryland passed the 12th. day of June

22. In May 1780, the Virginia assembly had decided that "a good printing press . . . is indispensably necessary for the right information of the people" and authorized the governor to engage a printer to establish a press in Richmond "for the public service"; see Hening, X, p. 313. John Dunlap was publisher of the *Pennsylvania Packet* in Philadelphia.

23. Elkton, Maryland.

24. This certificate, which is not in *PTJ*, can be found in *PJM*, II, pp. 71–72. The Virginia assembly had voted to suspend its enforcement of the 40-to-1 financial plan until "the governor shall have received authentick advices that a majority of the United States of America (except Georgia and South Carolina, whose determination thereupon will probably be suspended until the enemy shall be expelled therefrom) have actually or conditionally approved"; see Hening, X, p. 254. See TJ to JM, July 26, 1780, above, for TJ's request for such "*authentic advice.*"

1780. entitled "An Act for sinking the Quota required by Congress of this State of the bills of credit emitted by Congress."

2. An Act of the Legislature of New Jersey passed the 9th. day of June 1780 entitled "An Act for establishing a fund for sinking and redeeming the proportion of the bills of credit of the United States assigned as the quota of this State."

3. An Act of the Legislature of New York passed the 15th. of June 1780 entitled "An Act approving of the Act of Congress of the 18th. day of March 1780, relative to the finances of the United States, and making provision for redeeming the proportion of this State of the bills of credit to be emitted in pursuance of the said Act of Congress.["]

4. An Act of the Legislature of Massachussets bay passed the 5th. day of May 1780. entitled an "An Act making provision for calling in to be destroyed this State's Quota according to the present apportionment of all the public bills of credit, which have been emitted by Congress, and for making and emitting on the credit of this State other bills of credit not to exceed the sum of four hundred and sixty thousand pounds, and for establishing funds sufficient to secure the redemption of the bills so emitted by the last day of december 1786. as recommended by a resolution of Congress of the 18th. day of March of the present year and in conformity thereto; also for paying annually in specie the interest arising on notes which have been issued upon the credit of the province Colony or now State of Massachussets bay promising to be paid in gold or silver.["]

5. An Act of the Legislature of New Hampshire passed April 29th. 1780 entitled "An Act for complying with and carrying into execution certain resolutions of Congress of the 18th of March 1780 for sinking the bills of public credit now current and for issuing other bills in their stead."

6. A Conditional Act of the Legislature of Pennsylvania passed the first day of June 1780 entitled "An Act for funding and redeeming the bills of credit of the United States of America and for providing means to bring the present war to a happy conclusion.["]

JOS: JONES
JAMES MADISON JUN
JN. WALKER

## *Madison to Jefferson*

Philadelphia Sept. 26, 1780

DEAR SIR

I am at length able to give you some answer on the subject of the map in the hands of Dr. Smith. As the Doctor lived out of Town and it was difficult to know when he was to be found in it, and as I supposed the request would go with greater weight through Mr. Rittenhouse, I asked the favor of him to speak to the Doctor on the subject. Through forgetfulness or want of opportunity he failed to do it till lately and brought me for answer that the Doctor although anxious to oblige you was unwilling to let it go out of his hands, but would suffer any transcript to be taken from it at his house and would even assist in it himself. Yesterday evening I had an opportunity of being introduced to him and renewed the application, that he would spare it till I could get a copy taken, which he again declined by politely assuring me that he was proud of an opportunity of obliging you and that he would have a correct and authentic copy made out by his son for you.[25] I am Dr. Sir Yrs. respectfully,

JAMES MADISON JR.

## Madison and the Virginia Congressional Delegation to Governor Jefferson

[Philadelphia ca. Oct. 5, 1780]

SR

Some overtures having been made to Congress, through Mr. Jay our Commissioner at the Court of Madrid, for Building Frigates in America for and on account of his Catholic Majesty and the Proposals having been referred to the Admiralty to Confer with the Navy Boards of the Eastern and Middle district and obtain from them estimates of what would be the Cost of a frigate of forty Guns, and there being no Navy Board in Virginia it was moved in Congress by the Delegates from that State, that the Admiralty should also lay before Congress Estimates of the Cost etc. of Building such frigates in Virginia in which it would be proper to specify the terms, and the time it would take to Compleat one or more such frigates. We have thought it Proper to inform you thereof, that proper persons may be applyed to, to make out such Estimates for Government, in order that they may be given in to the Admiralty to report upon to Congress, as we are not willing that such lucrative, and advantageous contracts, the Execution of which must in the end be attended with so many advantages should be lost to our state and engrossed by others already so far advanced before us in the Establishing a Marine. This Estimate transmitted as early as possible will put it in the power of the Delegates from Virginia to press

25. William Smith and David Rittenhouse were fellow members with TJ of the American Philosophical Society. Smith moved to Chestertown, Maryland, where he became the founding president of Washington College in 1782; he never did copy the map, but JM found a copy in the Library Company of Philadelphia. See JM to TJ, Mar. 18, 1782, below.

its being transmitted to our Commissioner at Madrid with the Estimates from the Other States, and the subject itself together with a speedy compliance we have no doubt will strike you in the same important light in which it has us.[26] The perfect tranquility which has reigned here with regard to news has been lately disturbed by a most extraordinary and unexpected event, no less than the sudden defection of Major Genl. Arnold from the American Cause, and his flight to the Enemy. [He o]n the [September 25] ultimo Shamefully treacherously and ignominiously deserted the important Post at West point which Garrison he Commanded, after having Concerted Measures with the British Adjutant Genl. Colo. André in the Quality of a spy for delivering it up to the Enemy, with the Blackest Circumstances of treason and Perfidy that ever enterd the heart of any, wretch, but his own. Our Great General Washington, the French Ambassador and the Marquis de la fayette were to have been his Peace offering to the Enemy. But Mr. Andre was accidentally taken, by a small party of Militia and is now in our Hands and has probably before this paid his last tribute of Loyalty to his Royal Master together with his infamous Coadjutor Joseph Smith of N. York, occasioned Arnolds precipitate flight on board a British Man of War, which was ready to receive him in case of Accident. The General and other Gentlemen above Mentiond arrived at Arnolds Quarters a few minutes after his flight, and he has taken effectual measures to prevent further Mischief. Arnold has wrote him a letter dated on Board the Vulture sloop imploring his interposition in favor of his Wife whom he has left behind. His Papers have been seized in this City where he some time ago resided and lay open several scenes of Vilany transacted in the Commercial way while he had the Command here between him and other Miscreants, and have laid a train perhaps for further discoveries. Quid non mortalia pectora cogis Auri Sacra fames? [Cursed greed for gold, to what crimes dost thou not impel the human breast?] Every Mark of horror and resentment has been expressed by the Army at such atrocious and Complicated Vilainy, And the Mob in this City have burnt the traitor in Effigy after Exposing it through the streets with a long purse in one hand and a Mask in the other and labels descriptive of the Character thus [consigned?] to public infamy and odium. Thus with [. . .] faded the laurels of a hero, and the appelat[ion . . .] Arnold must be everlastingly changed for [. . .]tive of the Blackest infa[my].[27]

26. In Congress, JM took the lead in discussions dealing with Spain and the navigation of the Mississippi. On Oct. 6, he became chairman of the committee to draft letters to John Jay in Spain and Benjamin Franklin in France on America's territorial and navigation claims; see Ford *et al.*, XVIII, p. 908. See also Brant, II, pp. 70-88.

27. The brackets indicate the mutilated condition of this letter. For accounts of Arnold's treason, see Willard Wallace, *Traitorous Hero: Benedict Arnold* (New York, 1954), pp. 193-259, and Carl Van Doren, *Secret History of the American Revolution* (New York, 1941), pp. 260-388.

## Governor Jefferson to Madison and the Virginia Congressional Delegation

Richmond Oct. 27, 1780

GENTLEMEN

I must beg the favor of you to solicit the sending on to us immediately a good supply of Cartridge Paper and Cartouch Boxes. Nearly the whole of the former Article which we had bought at Alexandria, Baltimore etc. and what the Board of War sent from Philadelphia has been made up and forwarded to the Southern Army; there remains now but a few Ream to make up. I fear we have lost 2000 cartouch Boxes on the Bay which we had had made at Baltimore. Our distress for these is also very great Muskets being really useless without them. I must entreat the greatest dispatch in forwarding these Articles.

A very dangerous Insurrection in Pittsylvania was prevented a few days ago by being discovered three days before it was to take place. The Ringleaders were seized in their Beds. This dangerous fire is only smothered: when it will break out seems to depend altogether on events. It extends from Montgomery County along our Southern boundary to Pittsylvania and Eastward as far as James River: Indeed some suspicions have been raised of it's having crept as far as Culpepper. The rest of the State turns out with a Spirit and alacrity which makes me perfectly happy. If they had Arms there is no effort either of public or private Enemies in this State which would give any Apprehensions. Our whole Arms are or will be in the hands of the force now assembling: Were any disaster to befall these, We have no other resource but a few scattered Squirrel Guns, Rifles etc. in the Hands of the western People.[28] I am with the greatest esteem Gentlemen Your most obedt. humble servt,

TH: JEFFERSON


## Madison and the Virginia Congressional Delegation to Governor Jefferson

[Philadelphia Nov. 5, 1780]

The great depreciation of money and the extravagant prices of every thing here together with the difficulty of negociating Bills renders it absolutely necessary that some stable provision shoud be made, and some fixed mode

---

28. For a brief account of this insurgency, see Peterson, pp. 193–94. For a fine analysis, see Emory G. Evans, "Trouble in the Back Country: Disaffection in Southwest Virginia during the American Revolution," in *An Uncivil War: The Southern Back Country during the American Revolution*, ed. Ronald Hoffman, Thad W. Tate, and Peter J. Albert (Charlottesville, 1985), pp. 179–212. For William Preston's description of "a most horrid conspiracy amongst the Tories" in Montgomery County, see his letter to TJ, Aug. 8, 1780, in *PTJ*, III, pp. 533–34.

"A Most Melancholy Crisis," 1780–1781                                149

adopted for supplying us with money. Other wise we shall not be able to exist. We shou'd be glad to be informed on this head as soon as possible.[29]

*Governor Jefferson to Madison and the Virginia Congressional Delegation*

Richmond Nov. 14, 1780

GENTLEMEN

I do myself the pleasure of inclosing to you a draught of Mr. Ben: Harrison jur. and co: on Messieurs Turnbull and co: merchants of Philadelphia for 66,666⅔ dollars for which we have had transferred to Mr. Harrison the Auditors warrant of aug. 9. 1780. for £20,000 Virginia money with which you stand charged in their books.[30] I have the honor to be with the greatest esteem and respect Gentlemen, Your most obedient and mo. hble. servant.

*Governor Jefferson to Madison and the Virginia Congressional Delegation*

Richmond Nov. 17, 1780

GENTLEMEN

With respect to the payment made on behalf of Mr. Braxton into the Continental treasury in Part of our Quota of the fifteen Million tax, the Executive having been Charged with the raising and remitting that money, we have thought it unnecessary to lay it before the Legislature.[31] The Sum to be sent, was sent, partly in Money and Partly in Bills. These Bills were drawn in *Continental Dollars,* and paiable in such, and not in Specie. Of this nature was Mr. Braxtons Bill desiring his Correspondent to pay so many Continental Dollars into the Treasury. If the treasurer has received payment in another kind of money at an Arbitrary rate of Exchange, this must have been either under the Rules of his office or against them. The former I can Hardly suppose, and in the latter case it has become his own Private act, and he should be deemed to have received (no[t] £1318-15 hard Money but) 263750. dollars Continental Money as he has I suppose given a discharge on the Bill for so much of its

29. TJ transmitted this plea to Speaker Benjamin Harrison on Nov. 17, calling attention to the inconvenience caused by "precarious remittances"; see *ibid.,* IV, p. 121.

30. Along with the other three Virginia delegates, JM received one-fourth share or $16,666⅔ of this draft; see his public accounts of Sept. 25, 1780, in *PJM,* II, pp. 96–98. The rate of depreciation in Sept. 1780 was 75 to 1.

31. Carter Braxton owed money to Virginia, and Virginia owed money to Congress, so TJ allowed Braxton to discharge his debt to the state by paying the Continental treasury in Philadelphia in Continental currency at the rate of 40 to 1. Under the congressional financial plan of Mar. 18, 1780, the states were to retire $15 million each month; Virginia's monthly share was $2.5 million.

Contents. Had he rejected the Tender of the Hard Money would not Continental dollars have been paid? If they had not, then indeed the demand should have reverted on the State, and we would have fallen on means for compelling payment. We were really concerned on the return of our agent who Carried the Money and Bills that he did not have them regularly protested as there appeard some doubts on them. But he acted for the best in his own Judgment, and in that point of view was to be approved. I am exceedingly sorry that this want of Punctuality has arisen in these remittances. We sold Tobacco for these Bills, which would in Much less time have produced us money here. But the responsibility and known Connection between the drawer and drawee induced us to consider them as were Better than Money which would have been liable to Accidents in transportation. Had a tender of Specie been made to us here we would certainly have rejected it. But the payment being now to be transacted between the Drawee and Congress (passing us over) neither the Tender or receipt can be considerd as our act, but the former the act of the Drawee, and the latter of the Treasurer of Congress. We do not therefore think ourselves concernd immediately in this transaction. If Congress please to Consider the Payment of £1318-15 hard Money as a discharge of 263750 dollars paper which was to be paid by the drawee, well: if not on rejecting it he will make payment in the Specific Money he was Calld on to pay or we will resort to the Drawer and Compell such payment.

Since writing thus far I note more particularly than I had before done, that the treasurers return sais that he had *received from the Commonwealth of Virginia a Sum of Money in Specie* etc. This indeed stating it as the act of this Commonwealth renders it necessary for me to disavow it, which I hereby do. It was the Act of the drawee of which the Commonwealth had neither knowledge or Intimation; and this return fixing the act on the Commonwealth instead of the Drawee is so far wrong.[32]

THOS. JEFFERSON

## *Madison and the Virginia Congressional Delegation to Governor Jefferson*

Philadelphia Nov. 22, 1780

SR.

Mr. Walker, who sets off to Virginia tomorrow, affords us this opportunity of Enclosing your Excellency a Copy of a letter Presented to us the 16th

---

32. The Continental treasury accepted Braxton's payment at the rate of 75 to 1. TJ's protest was laid before Congress on Dec. 19, 1780, and, on JM's motion, Congress directed that the treasury records show the transaction so "that the State of Virginia may not be included in it"; see *PJM,* II, p. 248, and Ford *et al.,* XVIII, p. 1174.

Inst. together with a Copy of our Answer, concerning the affair of the Indiana Company.[33]

It may not be improper to Inform Your Excellency and, (through Your Excellency) the Legislature who we suppose may be now Siting, that every art has been and tis probable may be used, by that Company to extend their influence and support their pretensions, and we are sorry to say that we have Suspicions founded upon more than mere Conjecture that the land Jobbs, of this Company, the Vandalia, and the Illinois Companies, have too great an influence in procrastinating that desireable and necessary event of completing the Confederation, which we hope the Wisdom, firmness, candor and Moderation of our Legislature now in Session will remove every obstacle to.

We Could wish also and we think it a duty we owe to our Constituents to call their attention to a revision of our former instructions relative to the Navigation of the Missisipi that, Should any overtures from Spain be offerd which are advantageous to the United States, and which might contribute not only to releive our present necessities, but promise us peace and a firm establishment of our Independance, it might not be considered as an object that would counterbalance the distant prospect of a free Navigation of that River, with Stipulated ports, which may perhaps under another form or at some more convenient opportunity be obtaind from that Nation in behalf of our Citizens settled on its Bankes and Waters. Having Shewn the above to my Colleague Mr. Madison, he has thought it unnecessary to Join in that Part of it relating to our Instructions on the Subject of the Navigation of the Missisipi. I am sorry to say that notwithstanding the high Idea I entertain of that Gentlemans good sense, Judgment and Candor; I feel myself, irrisistably impelld by a Sense of my duty, to State a Matter and to communicate it through the Proper Channel which *may* eventually affect so greatly the Prosperity and mere existence of the United States at large, and feeling myself willing to receive the Censure of my Constituents if I have done wrong, or their applause if I have done Right in Suggesting to them so important a matter I am under the necessity (as to that matter) of standing alone in my opinion; which I would not wish, should in the Minutest degree, be interpreted, as obtruding or dictating a measure however necessary I as an individual Representative of the State may conceive a relaxation of our instructions on that head to be, nor do I conceive that any Member either of the Executive or Legislature of our State, who is acquainted with my wish to promote the Public good, and to conform to the strict tenor of their instructions, can attribute my suggestion to any wish to swerve from them in my Vote in Congress, having pledged

---

33. Although this letter is signed only by Bland, his use of "we" and "our" and his reference to his disagreement with JM, his only colleague from Virginia after Walker left, makes it clear that he is writing for both. The Indiana Company sought to validate its land claims in the West based upon Indian cessions even though the Virginia assembly had resolved that the company's deed was "utterly void."

myself both in Principle and in promise Steadily to adhere to them on all occasions. I have the Honor to be Yr. Excellys Most obedt. and very H: Svt.,

THEOK. BLAND

*Madison and the Virginia Congressional Delegation to Governor Jefferson*

[Philadelphia ca. Dec. 12, 1780]

SIR,

We have the honor to enclose your Excellency a Resolution of Congress of the 6th instant, relating to the Convention troops,[34] also a copy of a letter from G. Anderson found among the dead letters in the post office and communicated to Congress by the Post Master. If there should be occasion for the original of the latter, it shall be transmitted on the first intimation.[35]

An Irish paper informs us that Henry Laurens Esqr. was committed to the Tower on the 6th of October by a warrant from the Secretary of State, on suspicion of High Treason. All the despatches entrusted to the same conveyance unfortunately fell into the hands of the Enemy at the same time.[36]

A letter from Mr. Jonathan Williams dated at Nantz Oct: 17th confirms an account received several days ago of the *Ariel* commanded by P. Jones Esqr. and containing cloathing etc for the Army, being dismasted and obliged to return into port. The effect of this delay will be severely felt by the troops, who have already but too much reason to complain of the sufferings they have been exposed to from a want of these necessaries.[37]

The same letter from Mr. Williams, as well as some others received within a few days give us reason to believe that Portugal has at length yielded to the solicitations of the Neutral Powers and to the remonstrances of France and Spain, so far as to accede to the general object of the former, and to exclude

34. This letter is not in *PJM* but is summarized in *PTJ*, IV, p. 196. It is in JM's handwriting and is printed in *Calendar of Virginia State Papers*, ed. William P. Palmer, 11 vols. (Richmond, 1875–93), I, p. 395; the last two sentences, which were omitted by Palmer, are from the original letter. On Dec. 6, 1780, Congress ordered that "such of the Convention troops as are not already removed from the barracks near Charlottesville . . . remain at that post until the farther order of Congress"; see *PTJ*, IV, p. 196.

35. George Anderson of Hanover County, Virginia, became involved with a Captain Trott in illicit trade with Bermuda; see TJ to JM and the Virginia congressional delegation, Jan. 15, 1781, below.

36. Henry Laurens, a Charleston merchant and former president of the Continental Congress, was appointed commissioner to the Netherlands in 1779. Captured on the high seas by the British, he was imprisoned in the Tower of London on Oct. 6, 1780, where he stayed until Dec. 31, 1781. His papers included a proposed treaty between the United States and the Netherlands, which led Great Britain to declare war on the Dutch; see Morris, pp. 24–26.

37. Jonathan Williams, a grandnephew of Benjamin Franklin, was an American shipping agent at Nantes; see *ibid.*, p. 9, and *PJM*, II, p. 237.

the English from the privileges which their vessels of War have heretofore enjoyed into their ports.[38]

We have received payment of the Bill drawn by Mr. Benj: Harrison.[39] We are with perfect respect, your Excellency's most obedt. and very humble Servts.

JAMES MADISON JNR:<br>THEOD. BLAND JNR:

*Madison and the Virginia Congressional Delegation to Governor Jefferson*

Philadelphia Dec. 13, 1780

SIR

The complexion of the intelligence received of late from Spain, with the manner of thinking which begins to prevail in Congress with regard to the claims to the navigation of the Mississippi, makes it our duty to apply to our constituents for their precise full and ultimate sense on this point. If Spain should make a relinquishment of the navigation of that river on the part of the United States an indispensable condition of an Alliance with them, and the State of Virginia should adhere to their former determination to insist on the right of navigation, their delegates ought to be so instructed not only for their own satisfaction, but that they may the more effectually obviate arguments drawn from a supposition that the change of circumstances which has taken place since the former instructions were given may have changed the opinion of Virginia with regard to the object of them. If on the other side any such change of opinion should have happened, and it is now the sense of the State that an Alliance with Spain ought to be purchased even at the price of such a cession if it cannot be obtained on better terms it is evidently necessary that we should be authorized to concur in it. It will also be expedient for the Legislature to instruct us in the most explicit terms whether any and what extent of territory on the East side of the Mississippi and within the limits of Virginia, is in any event to be yielded to Spain as the price of an Alliance with her. Lastly it is our earnest wish to know what steps it is the pleasure of our Constituents we should take in case we should be instructed in no event to concede the claims of Virginia either to territory or to the navigation of the abovementioned river and Congress should without their concurrence agree to such concession.

We have made use of the return of the Honble. Mr. Jones to N. Carolina

---

38. Portugal did not join the League of Armed Neutrality until July 24, 1782, well after peace negotiations were under way; see Samuel Flagg Bemis, *The Diplomacy of the American Revolution* (Bloomington, Ind., 1957), p. 162.

39. See TJ to JM and the Virginia congressional delegation, Nov. 14, 1780, above.

to transmit this to your Excellency, and we request that you will immediately communicate it to the General Assembly.[40] We have the honor to be with the most perfect respect and esteem Yr. Excelly's Most obt. and humble servants,

JAMES MADISON JUNR.
THEOK: BLAND

## Governor Jefferson to Madison and the Virginia Congressional Delegation[41]

Richmond Dec. 18, 1780

GENTLEMEN:

I have gathered the information necessary to become acquainted with the roadsteads from which the French warships that will be stationed this winter in our bay can most effectively protect its commerce, be safest, and have the best harbor. Only those of *Hampton* and *York* command the entrance of the Chesapeake; no vessel can enter there without being seen from one or the other of these two places. Hampton roadstead is only an hour's or an hour and a half's sail from the capes and this is very much of an advantage: but other considerations make it very inferior to that of York. In the first of these places ships are not completely protected from gales; nor can they receive any assistance from land against a superior naval force, however slight that superiority may be. A ship of the line can not go farther up stream than about eight miles from *Burwell's Ferry*[42] and a frigate only to *Jamestown,* without unloading; it is true that by doing the latter it can move up even beyond *Hoods*,[43] where it would be in complete safety. On the other hand one may keep an equally good watch on the Bay from Yorktown although one's view from there is a little more distant; the harbor there is completely safe all during winter; the batteries at that site can cooperate to make unnecessary a retreat before a slightly superior force, and if the withdrawal were to be indispensable, there are four fathoms of water as far as *portopotank,* 25 miles above York and 6 below *West-point*[44] where the river is a mile and a half wide, but where the channel is only 150 rods [wide]

---

40. Willie Jones was a North Carolina delegate in Congress.

41. TJ's letter has not been found. This text is printed from *PJM,* II, pp. 245–48; it is not in *PTJ,* IV. This version is a translation of a French version sent by Luzerne to Admiral Destouches, who commanded the French fleet at Newport, Rhode Island. It appears to be a response to a missing letter from JM and Bland about a blockade of the Chesapeake by the French fleet.

42. Burwell's Ferry is about six miles below Jamestown on the James River.

43. Hoods is on the south side of the James River below Flowerdew Hundred Creek.

44. West Point is at the confluence of the Pamunkey and Mattaponi rivers, which create the York River.

and extends the length of the north bank. There is a bar at that place where the water is only 18 feet deep at high tide. This latter depth continues up to *Cumberland* on *the pamunkey* and up to *King and queen Court house* on the mattapany. At Cumberland the river is 100 or 120 yards wide, at King and queen Court house it is 250 and these two places are in the *heart* of the country. In view of this it appears that frigates would have in every respect a secure haven; but that ships of the line or all others drawing over 18 feet of water would not be in the same circumstances. Moreover, necessary supplies can be procured more readily at Yorktown than at Hampton and all these considerations ought to make it the preferred location.[45] I have the h[onor] of b[eing] etc. etc.

signed TH. JEPHERSON

## *Madison and the Virginia Congressional Delegation to Governor Jefferson*

Philadelphia Jan. 1, 1781

SIR

We have been Honored with Your Excellencys favor in answer to ours concerning the Safest and best Harbor etc. etc. which has been duely communicated, through the proper Channel, and we beg leave to inform you that we have endeavord to improve the intended design into a mode for obtaining a more speedy and safe Conveyance of the Cargoe of the Comite to Virginia (should it take place,) than a land Carriage would be and hope it will meet with Your approbation; as it appeared to us the most eligible method, we have venturd to adopt it without particular Instructions for so doing. Monsr. L—— [La Luzerne] has promised to use his endeavors to have our request complied with.[46] We have the Honor of transmiting to Your Excellency a Proposal from a Baron D'Arendt. He Speaks of a Commission with which he is charged but we have not as yet seen his Commission or powers, we have seen Mr. Wm. Lees written request to him to endeavor to negotiate the Sending of Arms, Linen, etc. with Mr. Wm. Lee's promise to him in writing that if he Succeeded he should be handsomely rewarded by the State of Virginia, but if not he should be Entitled to receive from that State twenty five Louis D'ors for his

---

45. TJ later made some of these same points about the James and York rivers in his *Notes on the State of Virginia;* see the edition by William Peden (Chapel Hill, 1955; rpt. New York, 1982), pp. 6–7.

46. In May 1780, *Le Comité*, a ship owned by the Penet Company of France, left Nantes bound for Virginia with munitions and military supplies. Captured by a British ship off Chesapeake Bay, it was recaptured by American privateers and taken to Providence, Rhode Island. Ambassador Luzerne promised to have the cargo shipped to Virginia on a French warship.

trouble; all these things we offer to Your Excellency at his request (being ourselves Ignorant of the whole transaction except as stated above) and wait your orders thereon.[47]

In a letter from his Excy. Genl. Washington dated New Windsor Decr. 27th. 1780 we have the following Intelligence—"Another embarkation has taken place at New York supposed to consist of two thousand five Hundred land forces, whose destination is not yet known. The fleet fell down to the Hooke on Wednesday last." *Our* Conjecture is that they are destined to the Southward, and indeed all the Enemy's political and military manœuvres seem to indicate their Intention of making a Vigorous effort against the Southern States, this Winter.[48] We are Sorry to inform your Excellency that we receive very little Authentic Intelligence of the Steps which are takeing to counteract those vigorous operations, that we are in a great measure uninformed of the progress that has been made in raising the new army, and on what terms, of what has been, and will be, done in establishing Magazines for its Support, and above all, of the measures persuing to cancell the old money and give an effectual Support to the new, by providing for its punctual and final redemption with Specie. This is a crisis at which we concieve a most assiduous application to these great objects to be necessary, and (next to the completion of the Confederacy which is perhaps the Basis of the whole) of the first importance to America therefore highly importing us to know, as the measures of so large a state as ours cannot but have considerable effects on the other states in the Union. We have the honor to be with the greatest respect Yr obt and Humble servants,

JAMES MADISON JUNR.
THEOK. BLAND

*Madison and the Virginia Congressional Delegation to Governor Jefferson*

Philadelphia Jan. 9, 1781

SIR

The inclosed extract of a letter from General Washington No. 1 will give your Excellency a more particular account of the late embarkation from N. York than has been before obtained.

On Thursday last Congress were informed by General Potter and Col.

---

47. Baron D'Arendt was appointed colonel of the German battalion by the Continental Congress in 1777, was twice wounded, and was granted a furlough to return to Prussia; see Ford *et al.*, XIX, pp. 143–44. William Lee was commissioner of Congress for the courts of Berlin and Vienna as well as Virginia's agent in France; see William Lee to TJ, Sept. 24, 1779, in *PTJ,* III, pp. 90–93.

48. The British expedition, commanded by Benedict Arnold, invaded Virginia.

Johnston who came expresses for the purpose that a general mutiny of the Pennsylvania line stationed near Morris Town apart from the rest of the Army had broken out on the morning of New Year's day.[49] Every effort was used by the officers to stifle it on its first appearance but with out effect. Several of them fell victims to the fury of the Mutineers. The next information came from Genl. Wayne who wrote from Princeton whither the troops had marched in regular order on their way to Philada. as they gave out, with a determination not to lay down their arms nor return to their obedience till their grievances should be redressed. They did not suffer any of their officers to remain with them except Genl. Wayne and Colos. Stewart and Butler and these they kept under a close guard, but in every other respect treated with the utmost decorum. The grievances complained of were principally a detention of many in service beyond the term of enlistment and the sufferings of all from a deficient supply of cloathing and subsistance and long arrearage of pay. Several propositions and replies on the subject of redress passed between a deputation of Sergeants on the part of the Troops and General Wayne, but without any certain tendency to a favorable issue. The Affair at length took a very serious aspect and as a great proportion of that line are foreigners and not a few deserters from the British Army, and as they shewed a disposition to continue at Princeton from whence a refuge with the Enemy, who it was said were coming out in force to avail themselves of the situation of things, was very practicable, it was thought necessary to depute a Committee of Congress with powers to employ every expedient for putting a speedy end to it. The President of the State with a number of Gentlemen from this place also went up to interpose their influence. The inclosed copy of a Letter from the Committee No. 2 with the paper No. 3 referred to in it are the last accounts received of the matter. The manner in which the offers and emissary of Clinton were received and treated is a very auspicious circumstance and will probably in its impression on the enemy fully balance the joy and encouragement which this event tended to give them.[50]

Col. Bland being one of the Committee does not join me in this. I have the honor to be with great respect and esteem Yr. Excelly's Obt. and hum servt,

JAMES MADISON JR.

---

49. The best account is Carl Van Doren's *Mutiny in January: The Story of a Crisis in the Continental Army* . . . (New York, 1943). During the uprising, a board of sergeants negotiated with officers and political leaders about their grievances.

50. Paper no. 3 was an address from Sir Henry Clinton, the British commander in chief, "to the Person appointed by the Pennsylvania troops to lead them in the present struggle for their liberties and rights," suggesting that they desert the American cause and join the British in New York; see Henry Clinton, *The American Rebellion: Sir Henry Clinton's Narrative of His Campaigns, 1775–1782,* ed. William B. Willcox (New Haven, 1954), pp. 484–85.

## Governor Jefferson to Madison and the Virginia Congressional Delegation

Richmond Jan. 15, 1781

GENTLEMEN

I called on Mr. Anderson the Writer of the letter to Capt. Trot which you were pleased to inclose to me and desired he would explain the foundation on which he had written that letter. His explanation I now inclose you, from which you will be able to collect only thus much, that his application on behalf of Mr. Trot was utterly rejected and nothing said which could authorize him to suppose we should wink at his loading his Vessel with Corn. He has trimmed up an Answer for me of which I only wish to be acquitted till it can be understood.[51]

I must at the same time acknowledge to you with candor that considering the neutral light in which Congress have placed the Bermudians and the extreme want of Salt here we have at various times permitted them to bring in Salt and exchange it with Government at the rate of one Bushel of Salt for two at first and afterwards three of Corn: and sometimes for Tobacco. We have been rigorous in allowing no more to be carried out than was procured by exchange in this way. You cannot be made more sensible of the necessity which forces us to this Barter, than by being assured that no further back than the Counties adjoining the Blue-ridge Salt has sold lately for from 4 to 500£ the Bushell.[52]

T.J.


## Governor Jefferson to Madison and the Virginia Congressional Delegation

Richmond Jan. 18, 1781

GENTLEMEN

I inclose you a resolution of Assembly directing your Conduct as to the navigation of the Missisippi.[53]

The loss of powder lately sustained by us (about 5 tons) together with the

---

51. Congress allowed the exportation of corn from Virginia in exchange for salt from Bermuda, but only if "the Bermudians come for it"; see TJ to Speaker Harrison, Jan. 29, 1781, in *PTJ*, IV, p. 466. Anderson and Trott apparently wanted to ship the corn in their vessels, a proposal that TJ rejected.

52. See Wilfred B. Kerr's account in his *Bermuda and the American Revolution* (Princeton, 1936).

53. Virginia insisted on free navigation of the Mississippi "as extensively as the territorial possession" of the United States reached and urged the establishment of "a free port or ports below the territory" of the United States. For the resolution, see *PTJ*, IV, pp. 386–88.

quantities sent on to the Southward have reduced our stock very low indeed.[54] We lent to Congress in the course of the last year (previous to our issues for the Southern army) about ten tons of powder. I shall be obliged to you to procure an order from the board of war for any quantity from five to ten tons to be sent us immediately from Philadelphia or Baltimore, and to enquire into and hasten from time to time the execution of it. The Stock of Cartridge paper is nearly exhausted. I do not know whether Capt. Irish or what other officer should apply for this.[55] It is essential that a good stock should be forwarded and without a moments delay. If there be a rock on which we are to split, it is the want of Muskets, bayonets and cartouch boxes.

The occurrences since my last to the President are not of any magnitude. Three little rencounters have happened with the enemy. In the first General Smallwood led on a party of two or three hundred Militia and obliged some armed vessels of the enemy to retire from a prize they had taken at Broadway's,[56] and renewing his attack the next day with a 4 ℔ r. or two (for in the first day he had only muskets) he obliged some of their vessels to fall down from City point to their main fleet at Westover. The enemy's loss is not known. Ours was 4 men wounded. One of the evenings during their encampment at Westover and Berkeley their Light horse surprised a party of about 100 or 150 Militia at Charles City Courthouse killed and wounded 4 and took as has been generally said about 7 or 8. On Baron Steuben's approach towards Hood's they embarked at Westover; the wind which till then had set directly up the river from the time of their leaving James Town, shifted in the moment to the opposite point. Baron Steuben had not reached Hood's by 8 or ten miles when they arrived there. They landed their whole army there in the night Arnold attending in person. Colo. Clarke (of Kaskaskias) had been sent on with 240 men by Baron Steuben, and having properly disposed of them in ambuscade gave them a deliberate fire which killed 17 on the spot and wounded 13. They returned it in confusion by which we had 3 or 4 wounded, and our party being so small and without bayonets, were obliged to retire on the enemy's charging with bayonets. They fell down to Cobham, from whence they carried all the tobacco there (about 60 hhds.) and the last intelligence was that on the 16th they were standing for Newports news. Baron Steuben is of opinion they are proceeding to fix a post in some of the lower Counties. Later information has given us reason to believe their force more considerable than we at first supposed. I think since the arrival of the three transports which had been separated in a storm, they may be considered as about 2000 strong. Their naval force according to the best intelligence is the Charon of 44 guns, Com-

54. British troops under Benedict Arnold destroyed 210 barrels of gunpowder, 26 cannon, and the cannon foundry at Westham; see Clinton, p. 244.
55. Captain Nathaniel Irish served as Continental commissary of military stores in Virginia, and for a month during Arnold's invasion he served in a similar capacity for Virginia.
56. Broadway is near the confluence of the Appomattox and James rivers.

modore Symmonds; the Amphitrite, Iris, Thames and Charles town Frigates, the Fowey of 20 guns, 2 sloops of war, a privateer Ship and 2 brigs. We have about 3700 militia embodied, but at present they are divided into three distant encampments: one under General Weedon at Fredericksburg for the protection of the important works there; another under General Nelson at and near Wmsburg; and a third under Baron Steuben at Cabbin point. As soon as the enemy fix themselves these will be brought to a point.[57] I have the honor to be with very great respect, Gentlemen your most obedt. servt.,

TH: JEFFERSON

## Madison and the Virginia Congressional Delegation to Governor Jefferson

Philadelphia Jan. 23, 1781

SIR

It is with much concern that we have learnt from your Excellency's, and the Baron de Steuben's letters to Congress,[58] the misfortunes our Country has suffer'd from the Invasion under the command of the detestable Arnold, and that he has ventured with impunity even to our Capitol. We have some reason to Imagine that the same plan of operations which induced Clinton to send him there will occasion him to remain in our Bay, and continue that alarm to our State and Maryland, which he has so successfully begun, in order to Harrass our Military, increase our expenses, waste our resources, destroy our Magazines and Stores when he finds it practicable; and by thus distracting us, prevent our sending the necessary succours to the Southern Army. This Sr, is a game we are open to at every period of our short enlistments, and in a great measure exposed to, for want of a militia organized to take the field, a few gunboats or Galleys, and some good fortifications in the most advantageous situations on our Rivers, for defence. But this late event has rendered this so obvious, that we are fully persuaded our Country will now see the necessity of adopting arrangements very different from what have been of late trusted to. We have been anxiously expecting to hear that some steps were taken at Rhode Island, in consequence of our application to the Minister, but it is more probable you will hear before we do, should that event take place, which we have spared no pains to have accomplished; and of this we have little doubt should it be found practicable.[59] Nothing new has happened here since we last wrote.

57. Except for Fredericksburg and Williamsburg, all the places mentioned after Broadway are on the James River.

58. During Arnold's invasion, Major General Steuben, who had been expediting troop reinforcements to the southern army, "descended from the dignity of his proper command," according to TJ, "to direct our smallest movements"; see *PTJ,* IV, p. 335.

59. This is a reference to Virginia's munitions and supplies aboard *Le Comité.*

The Judge of the Admiralty of this State has given us notice that there are three negroes, Tom, Hester and Celia, confined in Joal here, in consequence of a condemnation of the vessel in which they were taken. They say they are the property of a certain Money Godwin of Norfolk in Virginia; that their Master went of[f] with the British fleet under Leslie, and gave them permission to do the same, on which they went on board the vessel in which they were taken. If on enquiry your Excellency shall find these facts to be truly stated, we shall with pleasure execute your instructions for securing the slaves for those to whom shall be adjudged.[60] We have the honor to be, with the utmost respect yr: Excelly's most obt and humble Servants.

JAMES MADISON, JUNR.
THEOK. BLAND

## Governor Jefferson to Madison and the Virginia Congressional Delegation

Richmond Jan. 26, 1781

GENTLEMEN

I shall now beg leave to answer your Letter of the first inst. which inclosed a Paper from Baron de Arendt. Mr. William Lee was some Time ago invested with a special Agency from this State, having received however no instructions from him of his having engaged any other Person to transact any Part of it, we are uninformed as to his Stipulations with Baron de Arendt. If he has left the particular one for twenty five Louis unfulfilled we think ourselves bound to discharge which we will do in such Sum of paper money as may purchase that quantity of hard money in Philadelphia, for there being no hard money here, there is no fixed exchange. If you will therefore settle this Sum with him we will make the Remittance either in money or by answering a Bill, or otherwise, as shall be most practicable.[61] After a variety of Trials to effect the cloathing of our Troops and procuring of military Stores and failing in them all, a particular Institution has been adopted here for those Purposes.[62] Into this Channel all our means must be turned to enable it to be effectual. Our Situation is too well known to suppose we have any thing to spare. It is therefore not in our Power to enter into the Commerce with Prussia proposed by the Baron de Arendt, however desirous we are of opening a Communication with that respectable State and willing under every other Circumstance to effect it by great Sacrifices, were Sacrifices necessary. Should the Subject of

60. On Feb. 3, TJ asked Colonel Thomas Newton of Norfolk to determine the facts in this case; see *PTJ*, IV, p. 521.
61. See JM and the Virginia congressional delegation to TJ, Jan. 1, 1781, above.
62. An act of Oct. 1780 directed every county and incorporated city to contribute a specified number of shirts, overalls, stockings, shoes, and hats for the army; see Hening, X, pp. 338-43.

Prussia chuse to adventure on Private Trade with our Citizens every Facility and encouragement in our Power will be certainly afforded. As the Speaker Harrison sets out within three or four Days for Philadelphia and can so much more fully explain to you by words the Steps taken for supporting our Opposition to the common enemy, I shall decline answering that Paragraph of your Letter and beg leave to refer you to him.[63]

TH. JEFFERSON

P.S. We have no Letters of Marque left. Be so good as to send us some by the first Opportunity.

*Madison and the Virginia Congressional Delegation to Governor Jefferson*

Philadelphia Jan. 30, 1781

SIR

We were honored yesterday with your Excellency's favor of the 15th. inst: inclosing Mr. Anderson's explanation of his letter to Capt. Trott, and that of the 18th. enclosing instructions as to the Mississippi and requesting sundry military supplies, in promoting which no exertions shall be omitted on our part. Your Excellency's letter to Congress on the subject of the Convention Prisoners and the unequal apportionment of the general resources with respect to the two great Departments was also received yesterday and referred to a Committee.[64] The Resolutions of the General Assembly ceding the Territory N. West of the Ohio to the United States was laid before Congress at the same time. Although nothing has been yet done declaratory of their sense of them and although they are not precisely conformable to the recommendations of Congress on the subject, we flatter ourselves that the liberal Spirit which dictated them will be approved and that the public will not be disappointed of the advantages expected from the measure. We have pretty good though unauthenticated information that Maryland has already acceded to the federal Union.

Since the extinguishment of the Mutiny in the Pennsylvania line, some commotions founded on similar complaints have taken place in that [part] of New Jersey. But we have the pleasure to inform you that the prudent and

---

63. Harrison carried this letter to the Virginia delegation.

64. The "two great Departments" referred to the southern army and the northern army under Washington's command. Although the British troops captured at Saratoga were moved from Charlottesville to Maryland in the fall of 1780, Congress directed Virginia to furnish one-half the provisions necessary to feed and supply these troops, with Maryland supplying the other half. TJ asked Congress to revise this request because of the need for Virginia to supply the southern army, "who are to oppose the greater part of the enemy's force in the United States, the subsistence of the German and half the British Conventioneers." The German contingent of the Saratoga troops was still at Charlottesville; see TJ to Samuel Huntington, Jan. 15, 1781, in *PTJ*, IV, pp. 369–70.

seasonable remedies applied have re-established order and discipline among the troops.[65] We have the honor to be with the most perfect esteem and regard Yr. Excelly's. most obt. Servts.,

                    JOS. JONES
                JAMES MADISON, JUNR.
                  THEOK. BLAND

*Governor Jefferson to Madison and the Virginia Congressional Delegation*
                                        Richmond Feb. 7, 1781

GENTLEMEN

    The Courier d'Europe a vessel from Penet & Coy. [Company] having on board military stores for this state was chased into Boston by the enemy in the Summer of 1779. They were principally Artillery Stores, too bulky and heavy for us to think of bringing them on by land. By the loss of our papers we are unable to furnish an invoice of them but they are in the hands of a Mr. J. Bradford in Boston who I suppose can furnish you with one.[66] If you can get them on board any part of the French Fleet which may at any time be coming here, it would be eligible: otherwise I would beg the favour of you to have them disposed of to the best advantage for the public. I am with very great respect and esteem Gentn. Your most Obt. and Most humbl. St.,

                        T.J.

*Madison and the Virginia Congressional Delegation to Governor Jefferson*
                                        Philadelphia Feb. 13, 1781

SIR

    By the Speaker Harrison who arrived here the day before yesterday we were honored with your Excellency's favor of the 26th. Ulto. We shall communicate your answer to the Baron d'Arendt, and if his claim against the State be supported by proper evidence shall take the best steps in our power to discharge it.

    A Vessel just arrived from Cadiz has brought Congress two letters from Mr. Carmichael,[67] from one of which dated Madrid Novr. 28th. 1780. the

---

65. For the mutiny of the New Jersey Continentals and its suppression, see Van Doren, *Mutiny in January*, pp. 206–7.

66. John Bradford was a Continental agent in Boston; see *PJM*, II, p. 9.

67. William Carmichael was secretary for John Jay's mission to Spain from 1780 to 1782; see Morris, pp. 44 and *passim*.

following is extracted: "From the best information I have been able to collect I am sorry to tell you, that the nation (British) will be able to borrow the sum demanded for the expenditures of 1781. which with the usual note of credit at the end of the session will amount to 16 Millions sterling at least. The scheme of the Ministry to effect this is not yet public but I am told it will be on similar conditions to that of the present year. 92,000 men are voted for the marine, and I have reason to think a considerable reinforcement will be sent early to the Southward and that agreeable to a proposition of Sr. J. Amherst[68] the Enemy means to occupy and fortify strongly a port near the Mouth of Chesapeak from which, with a strong Garrison and naval force, they hope to interrupt the navigation of the bay and by frequent incursions prevent the States of Maryland and Virginia from sending supplies of men etc. etc. to the Carolinas. Among the troops mentioned to be embarked there are three regiments of Light Dragoons. Your servants nearer G.B. will however give you more accurate information. I am persuaded that our Ally will take early measures for defeating these designs. This latter information is derived indirectly from conversations with men in a situation to be well informed." Private letters by the same conveyance add that the blockade of Gibraltar was continued with great vigor, and that the Garrison began to be severely distressed. We have the honor to be with great respect and esteem Yr. Excelly's. obt. Huml. Servants,

Jos: Jones<br>
James Madison Junr<br>
Theok. Bland Jr

## Madison and the Virginia Congressional Delegation to Governor Jefferson

Philadelphia Feb. 13, 1781

Sr.

We are Just informd from Genl. Varnum[69] a Member now in Congress from Rhode Island that he has received Certain Intelligence that the Culloden of 74 Guns is drove on Shore and all her Crew except 17 men Perishd. The London of 90 Guns is driven out to Sea dismasted and two other 64 Gun Men

---

68. Sir Jeffrey Amherst, who had commanded the British army in North America during the French and Indian War, served the British ministry as an adviser on military affairs during the American Revolution.

69. General James Mitchell Varnum served as a Continental officer from 1775 to 1780 before being chosen as a delegate to Congress from Rhode Island. His information about the damage done the British fleet in New York by a hurricane was faulty. The *Culloden* was lost, but its crew survived. The *America,* not the *London,* was "supposed to have shared the same fate," as General Clinton noted, but it later limped into New York in need of repairs; see Clinton, pp. 249–50. The omission of JM's signature on this letter indicates that he was momentarily absent when the letter was sealed.

of War Were dismasted entirely and all their Guns thrown over board in the late storm. Since writing the above We have procured the account from Genl. Varnum in his own hand, which We have the Honor to Enclose. It is moreover added that on hearing the above the Enemy at N. York sent orders to Arnold to retreat from Virginia. Heavenly Storm. We are Yr. Exlys Most obedt. Sevts,

Jos: Jones<br>Theok. Bland

*Madison and the Virginia Congressional Delegation to Governor Jefferson*

Philadelphia Feb. [20], 1781

Sr.

Since our last in which we informed Your Excellency of the Arrival of Col: Harrison in this City, his Applications to Congress have been referd to a Special Committee,[70] and the necessary Steps are taking to Answer the wishes and wants of the Southern States, and of our State in particular as far is practicable in the present Situation of affairs. We doubt not but that Gentleman will give you full Information of the Progress he has made in the Special Business for which he has been Sent.

We are happy to Inform you of the Arrival of Capt. Paul Jones in the Ariel, from France. This event would have been a much more pleasing one had he brought the cloathing so long and anxiously expected. His Cargo is however by no means useless as it Consists of about thirty Ton of Powder.[71] It is Conjectured that by this time Count D'Estaing is arrived in the West Indies with twenty two sail of the Line,[72] and we are in great Hopes before this reaches you that a Ship of the Line from the fleet of our Allies in Rhode Island and three frigates will be in our Bay in order to cooperate with our Troops, in taking ample Vengeance on Mr. Arnold, for his treasons, perjuries, Robberies and depreadations, accounts being received in this Town that they saild from Rhode Island immediately after the storm and that Monsr. Des touches had taken effectual measures to Block up the Remaining Vessels of the Enemy in Gardners Bay. We have Sanguine hopes that this Expedition will not be fruitless, and that our Allies will find us in a Condition effectually to cooperate with

70. JM served on the committee of six who conferred with Harrison.

71. One week later, Congress hailed Jones for "his distinguished bravery and military conduct" in the brilliant victory of his *Bonhomme Richard* over the *Serapis* in British waters.

72. Count d'Estaing commanded the French fleet besieging Gibraltar, so this conjecture was incorrect. The remnants of the British fleet that he had defeated straggled into St. Lucia, leading reporters to assume that the clash had occurred in the West Indies.

them, as their aid will enable us to draw our whole force to a point.[73] One of the frigates above mentioned will bring the Arms and Stores which were retaken in the Comite; which will perhaps not be an unseasonable aid.[74] We have enclosed Your Excellency two New York Papers for your perusal containing Arnolds account of his Victories and Captures.

Mr. Hays informed us this morning he should be ready to set out for Virginia with the printing materials in about a week.[75] We are with great respect Your Excelcys obed Servts.,

Jos: Jones<br>James Madison Junr.

P.S. Since writing the above we have authentic information that one seventy four with two Frigates and a Cutter sailed from Rhode Island on the eigth for Chesapeake Bay.

## *Governor Jefferson to Madison and the Virginia Congressional Delegation*

[Richmond] in Council Feb. 22, 1781

GENTLEMEN

The object of the inclosed Memorial of Messrs. Stodder, Kerr and North being attainable by Congress only and proper to be the subject of a representation from them I take the Liberty of transmitting it to you that Justice may be done to the parties interested.[76] I have the honor to be with great respect Gentlemen Your mo. ob. Hble Servant,

Th: Jefferson

P.S. We are and have long been without Letters of Marque.[77]

---

73. Because of the damage done to the British fleet in New York, Admiral Destouches dispatched a ship of the line and three frigates to Chesapeake Bay. But Arnold's vessels sailed out of gunshot range in shoal water, and the French soon returned to Rhode Island; see Lee Kennett, *The French Forces in America, 1780–1783* (Westport, Conn., 1977), pp. 96–97.

74. The frigate carrying the cargo from *Le Comité* did not sail with the French flotilla.

75. James Hayes and John Dunlap had agreed to establish a printing press and newspaper in Richmond, but their first shipment of equipment was captured by the British in Oct. 1780.

76. The memorialists were shipowners and merchants from Norfolk whose ships and cargo were seized by the British in the neutral Dutch port of St. Martin in Aug. 1780. On Mar. 26, 1781, JM moved, and Congress agreed, that a memorial be sent to John Adams at Amsterdam seeking redress from the States General of the Netherlands; see Ford *et al.*, XIX, p. 312.

77. In response to TJ's request of Jan. 26, 1781, Charles Thomson, secretary of Congress, had sent 24 letters of marque on Feb. 19, 1781.

## Madison and the Virginia Congressional Delegation to Governor Jefferson

Philadelphia Mar. 6, 1781

SIR

The Minister of France having imparted to Mr. Jones as Chairman of a Committee appointed to confer with him on some secret matters the intentions of Ct. Rochambeau and Mr. Destouches explained in the inclosed note;[78] we thought it of such consequence that your Excellency should be certainly apprized of them, that notwithstanding the probability of the communication being made through some other channel we determined to guard against all risk of failure by despatching one of the established Expresses.[79] As the success of the Enterprize depends much on secrecy of preparation, and celerity of execution, we beg leave to intimate to your Excellency, that it is the wish of the Minister that no persons should be admitted to a knowledge of it, from whom it can be justifiably concealed, and that such military stores, particularly heavy cannon and mortars, as are in the hands of the State and will be wanted for a siege may be in readiness to go forward at a moments call. The Minister also wishes that some supplies of provision, of beef especially, for the French troops may be included in your general preparations.[80] We are with great respect Yr: Excelys. obed. hum. Servts.,

JOS. JONES
JAS. MADISON JUNR.


## Governor Jefferson to Madison and the Virginia Congressional Delegation

[Richmond] in Council Mar. 8, 1781

GENTLEMEN

The inclosed papers so fully explain themselves, that I need say nothing more to apprize you of the Subject.[81] Should the Governor of Maryland and

---

78. The enclosure has not been found, but it must have responded to a suggestion by a congressional committee, which included JM, that asked Washington to urge a combined operation by the French fleet and army in the Chesapeake; see *ibid.*, p. 179. Lieutenant General Rochambeau commanded the French army in America, and Admiral Destouches headed the French fleet.

79. Samuel Huntington, president of Congress, informed TJ that a French fleet and an army detachment would sail against Benedict Arnold's forces in Virginia; see *PTJ*, V, p. 72.

80. The French fleet, carrying 1,120 French troops, sailed on Mar. 8 and met the British fleet off Chesapeake Bay on Mar. 16. The contest was inconclusive, but the British blocked the bay, and the French decided to return to Rhode Island; see Kennett, pp. 98–101.

81. On Feb. 20, 1781, Congress recommended that the executives of Delaware, Maryland, Virginia, and North Carolina supply the southern army with provisions and arrange "such mode of transportation as will be most convenient and least expensive to the whole"; see Palmer, I, p. 531.

President of Maryland [Delaware] not close with my third proposition,[82] you are hereby authorized to treat with the Delegates of those two States or any other Person appointed by the States and to settle the best method of availing the Southern Army of their Supplies. The proposition from Govr. Lee nor any thing like it can possibly be admitted on our part.[83] I have the Honor to be with great respect and esteem Your, etc.,

T.J.

*Governor Jefferson to Madison and the Virginia Congressional Delegation*

[Richmond] in Council Mar. 15, 1781

GENTLEMEN

A Difference of opinion having taken place between the Executive of this State and Mr. Simon Nathan as to the rate at which certain Bills of exchange should be discharged in paper money, we have agreed with him to refer it to such Gentlemen of Knowledge in the Laws, of established Character and of any other State, as yourselves shall mutually agree on with him.[84] Their award shall be performed by the State, which means to stand in the place as well of the Drawer as Drawee. Mr. Wilson and Mr. Serjeant had been consulted by Mr. Nathan.[85]

I inclose to you Mr. Pendleton's and Wythe's Opinion.[86] You will be pleased to observe that the State of the Case requires from Mr. Nathan actual proof that he took up the Bills at par. Mr. Nathan having agreed with us all the facts as stated, I am to suppose nothing contrary to them will be received. As his Signature here was omitted perhaps it would be best for you to require it

---

82. TJ proposed that each state appoint an agent to procure its quota of supplies "as near as they can to the army, replacing their money by Sale of such Specifics as might be raised within their State by Taxation"; see *PTJ*, V, p. 78.

83. Governor Thomas Sim Lee of Maryland wanted to deliver supplies to Alexandria. Jefferson objected that this location would saddle Virginia with the cost for transporting Maryland's supplies to North Carolina; see *ibid.*, pp. 16, 77–78.

84. The editors of *PJM*, III, p. 21, note that the controversy between Nathan and Virginia begins with a "truth that cannot now be sifted, and ends without a known conclusion of the matter at issue."

85. Nathan was a merchant in Philadelphia who accepted 13 bills of exchange from George Rogers Clark for military supplies used in Clark's Illinois campaign. The issue turned on whether the bills were to be accepted at face value in specie or in depreciated Virginia currency. James Wilson was a leading lawyer in Philadelphia and later an associate justice on the Supreme Court of the United States. Jonathan D. Sergeant was attorney general for Pennsylvania.

86. Edmund Pendleton was a judge of the High Court of Chancery in Virginia, and George Wythe was professor of law at the College of William and Mary. Pendleton argued that his opinion was "in favor of Mr. Nathan." Wythe asserted that Nathan had to prove that he had taken the bills "up at par"; if Nathan could not prove this, there were good reasons "for contravening his demands"; see *PTJ*, V, pp. 7–89, 110–11.

before submission. It is not our Desire to pay off those Bills according to the present Depreciation but according to their actual value in hard money at the time they were drawn with Interest. The state having received value so far it is just it should be substantially paid. All beyond this will be plunder made by some Person or other. The Executive in the most candid manner departed from the advantage which their Tender law gave them in the beginning. It seems very hard to make this the means of obtaining an unjust Gain from the State. I have the Honor to be, etc., etc.

T.J.

*Madison and the Virginia Congressional Delegation to Governor Jefferson*

Philadelphia Mar. 20, 1781

SIR

Since our last nothing new has happend except the Sailing of the French fleet Consisting of (as near as we can obtain intelligence) the Ships and Guns as per list enclosed together with about twelve Hundred of their Chosen troops which we flatter our selves are by this time actively and successfully employd in our Bay; And the departure of the M. de la Fayette with about the same Number of Men (and a fine train of artillery) who we hope is by this time acting in Conjunction with them, against Arnold.[87] We must add to the above intelligence that a report is Current here and generally believed that the British have taken St. Eustatia and Curassau, with all the Dutch and american Vessels in their Harbors, together with a Dutch Line of Battle Ship.[88] The Admiral who Commanded her said to be Slain and tis further added that they have saild up the Texel and Taken a great number of the Duch trading Vessels. This news comes by a Prize brought in here yesterday from Antigua, who has also brought a declaration of Reprisals against Holland by England which we expect will be published in the paper of this day.[89] We are Sr. Yr. Excellys Most obedt. sevts.,

JAMES MADISON JUNR
THEOK. BLAND

87. See JM and the Virginia congressional delegation to TJ, Mar. 6, 1781, above. On Feb. 20, 1781, Lafayette was appointed to command an expedition against Arnold in Virginia. Leaving his troops at Annapolis, he arrived at Yorktown on Mar. 14 before going to Williamsburg to confer with General Steuben and Virginia authorities; see *Lafayette in the Age of the American Revolution, 1776–1790*, ed. Stanley J. Idzerda *et al.*, 5 vols. (Ithaca, 1977–83), III, pp. 395–421.

88. St. Eustatius, a Dutch island in the Caribbean, fell to a British fleet commanded by Admiral Rodney on Feb. 2, 1781; see Mackesy, pp. 378–79, 416–18.

89. England had declared war on the Netherlands in Dec. 1780. The reports of the capture of Curaçao and of British captures in the Texel, the channel between Holland and the offshore island

P.S. Mr. Hays set off a few days ago with his printing implements. We sent by him 50 Copies of the last French Memorial to be distributed as your Excellency thinks best. He has also a number of Skins of parchment for the Assembly.

---

of Texel, were incorrect; see Jan Willem Schulte Nordhalt, *The Dutch Republic and American Independence* (Chapel Hill, 1982), pp. 45–46, and W. M. James, *The British Navy in Adversity: A Study of the War of American Independence* (London, 1926), pp. 249, 254–56. See also Simon Schama, *Patriots and Liberators: Revolution in the Netherlands, 1780–1813* (New York, 1977), pp. 58–63.

# 5

# WARTIME COOPERATION: THE CONGRESSMAN AND THE GOVERNOR, 1781

*P*HILADELPHIA SALUTED the ratification of the Articles of Confederation and Perpetual Union with the army and the navy firing one shot for each of the thirteen states and with the ringing of the Liberty Bell and church bells. John Paul Jones, recently honored by Congress for the victory of his *Bonhomme Richard* over the British frigate *Serapis* and allowed to accept the Cross of Military Merit from Louis XVI, had his ship "beautifully decorated with a variety of streamers in the day and ornamented with a brilliant appearance of lights in the night," firing "a *feu de joie*" to usher in "an elegant exhibition of fireworks." According to the *Pennsylvania Packet,* the first of March would be "memorable in the annals of America to the last posterity." The completion of the Union under the Articles was hailed as a "great event which will confound our enemies, fortify us against their acts of seduction, and frustrate their plans of division."[1]

Madison helped plan the congressional celebration of ratification, joining his colleagues, the French ambassador, members of the assembly and the Supreme Executive Council of Pennsylvania, and officers of the army and navy in raising "a glass of wine [to] 'The United States of America.' " According to the *Journals of the Continental Congress,* the celebrants met in Congress Hall and ate from "a keg of biscuit, in the room of cake." Reading these minutes, Madison added an asterisk, then asked in an impish footnote. "Does it mean in the cake room?"—one of the few humorous quips in the voluminous records of the Continental Congress.[2]

---

1. *Pennsylvania Packet* (Mar. 3, 1781), cited in Brant, II, p. 104; Carl Van Doren, *Mutiny in January: The Story of a Crisis in the Continental Army . . .* (New York, 1943), pp. 239-40.
2. See Feb. 24, 1781, in W. C. Ford *et al.,* eds., *The Journals of the Continental Congress, 1774-1789,* 34 vols. (Washington, 1904-37), XIX, p. 192.

Two weeks later, Madison celebrated his first anniversary in Congress. Although the youngest member of Congress, his reputation for industry and ability made him a leading candidate for the newly created post of secretary of foreign affairs. But he remained in Congress instead, where he supported executive efficiency and cooperated with Robert Morris, superintendent of finance, and Robert R. Livingston, secretary of foreign affairs, whose proposals he often guided through Congress.[3]

On March 16, Madison celebrated his thirtieth birthday. But there was little else to celebrate in the spring of 1781. Inflation raged to new heights, plunging credit to new lows. Arnold's invasion of Virginia discredited the Virginia government headed by Jefferson and revealed a fatal flaw in risking the state's defense to militia. On March 1, the day that the Confederation constitution went into effect, Governor Jefferson called the legislature into special session to determine "whether it be practicable to raise and maintain a sufficient number of regulars to carry on the war." At the same time, he asked the legislature to extend the deadline established in the previous session for fulfilling the state's quota of Continental troops and supplying the army. He reported that "one army of our enemies [was] lodged within our Country, another pointing towards it," and lamented that the state was "without a shilling in the public coffers."[4] Even had there been money in the Virginia treasury, it had depreciated so much that it was not accepted in Philadelphia, according to David Ross, the commercial agent of the state. "Our state money," he wrote, "cannot be Negotiated there on any terms."[5]

Jefferson was hopeful that Arnold's forces could be trapped in Portsmouth, but the attempt failed when the French fleet was forced to return to Rhode Island after an indecisive battle off Chesapeake Bay. Madison moaned about "the Unfortunate consequences which have attended the Naval engagement of Chesapeake . . . as they have snatchd from us the pleasing prospects we had cherished for some time past, of frustrating the Sanguine project of the Enemy (of subjugating most of the Southern States this Campaign)."[6] Jefferson was especially worried about the British forces in Virginia: "Should this Army from Portsmouth come forth and become active," he told Madison and the congressional delegation, interpolating one of his few humorous asides, "(and as we have no reason to believe they came here to Sleep) our Affairs will assume a very disagreable Aspect."[7]

But he worried even more about the main British army in North Carolina advancing towards Virginia under Lord Cornwallis's command. Writing to Lafayette, who had been detached by Washington with 1,200 troops to defend against Arnold's forces, the governor observed that the turncoat might "harass

---

3. Lance Banning, "James Madison and the Nationalists, 1780–1783," *WMQ* 40 (1983): 237–55.
4. TJ to the Speaker of the House of Delegates, Mar. 1, 1781, in *PTJ,* V, pp. 33–37.
5. *PTJ,* V, p. 266.
6. JM and the Virginia congressional delegation to TJ, Apr. 3, 1781, below.
7. TJ to JM and the Virginia congressional delegation, Apr. 6, 1781, below.

and distress us greatly but the Carolinas alone can subdue us. . . . We therefore think it our first Interest to keep them under in that Quarter, considering the war in our own Country but as a secondary Object." If Cornwallis should enter Virginia, however, "our Situation will become dangerous."[8]

Jefferson sent frantic pleas for arms and assistance to Madison and the Virginia congressmen, the president of Congress, and General Washington. To the first, he wrote that the need for arms was urgent and added, "It is impossible to give you an Idea of the Distress we are in for want of Lead."[9] To President Huntington, he stressed "our distress for arms." And to Washington he wrote that "arms and a naval force . . . are what must ultimately save us."[10]

Ever since Speaker Harrison's mission to Congress in February, Madison and the Virginia congressmen had endeavored to hurry military assistance to the southern army. Congress had added the Pennsylvania Line in February, but Harrison had predicted that they would have great difficulty in carrying the resolution into effect, "they being extremely poor and their credit but low."[11] No prediction was ever truer. On April 3, Madison wrote Jefferson that the first 1,000 troops would march south "in a day or two," adding that "when the remainder will follow them is altogether uncertain."[12] But two weeks later, the first detachment was "still detained by the want of money."[13] Not until June 3, however, a day after Jefferson's term as governor had expired, did Madison write that General Anthony Wayne and the Pennsylvania Line had finally begun their march with seven battalions of infantry and one of cavalry.[14]

Moving military supplies to Virginia proved as frustrating as moving troops. Arms, clothing, and other military supplies that had been shipped to Virginia from France in May 1780 on *Le Comité* had been seized by the British, recaptured by American privateers, and unloaded in Rhode Island. Jefferson had been trying to get the military cargo forwarded since September 1780. Madison and the Virginia congressional delegation finally arranged to ship it on a French frigate in the fleet that sailed against Arnold in March 1781. With the failure of that expedition, however, the frigate headed for Philadelphia, where the cargo was unloaded for overland transportation to Virginia.[15] In a personal note to the governor, Madison underscored "the infinite impor-

---

8. TJ to the marquis de Lafayette, Apr. 23, 1781, in *PTJ*, V, p. 541.

9. TJ to JM and the Virginia congressional delegation, Apr. 6, 1781, below. The principal vein of the lead mine in Montgomery County petered out early in 1781; see *PTJ*, V, pp. 199, 232. But within a month of TJ's letter, a new vein was discovered that promised "a very abundant Supply"; see *ibid.*, p. 600.

10. TJ to Samuel Huntington, Apr. 7, 1781, in *PTJ*, V, p. 370; TJ to George Washington, May 9, 1781, *ibid.*, p. 624.

11. Benjamin Harrison to TJ, Feb. 19, 1781, *ibid.*, IV, pp. 655-56.

12. JM to TJ, Apr. 3, 1781, below.

13. JM and the Virginia congressional delegation to TJ, Apr. 17, 1781, below.

14. JM and the Virginia congressional delegation to TJ, June 3, 1781, below. The troops departed on May 26 and joined Lafayette's army in Virginia on June 10.

15. JM and the Virginia congressional delegation to TJ, Mar. 27, 1781, below.

tance" of the military stores for Virginia, "especially since the arrival of a reinforcement to Arnold," and he promised "to forward them by land without loss of time."[16]

But the lack of money delayed shipment. Teamsters demanded "instantaneous payment . . . in specie or the old Continental Currency to the real amount thereof," presenting "an insurmountable obstacle to a speedy execution of our intention," according to Madison. Writing two weeks later, the congressmen apologized for their failure to forward the military stores, citing "the probable emptiness of your Treasury, and the impossibility of our making our requisite advance to the Waggoners here, [which] led us to substitute the other plan of . . . procuring from Congress a warrant for the money necessary for the purpose." Even then, the mortified delegates found "that the stores are not yet on their way." Finally, on April 24, Madison and Bland informed Jefferson that the quartermaster general had forwarded the first of the 1,100 stand of French arms that day. But by the time they arrived, Jefferson had retired from office.[17]

Other military supplies also began moving south in April. Congress directed the Board of War "to Send to the Southward Such Arms Cloathing and Military stores as we are in want of," the Virginia congressmen reported. From New York, General Washington dispatched small arms and clothing for use by Lafayette's detachment and the southern army. In Philadelphia, Madison and his colleagues rummaged around and located 2,000 "Rampart Arms belonging to the U. S." that could be converted from siege weapons to infantry muskets. After these were sawed off and bayonets affixed, the arms were promptly shipped to Virginia.[18] Lafayette pledged his personal credit for shoes, hats, shirts, and "over alls" for his troops.[19] And Virginia's commercial agents in Philadelphia, after arranging "loans from private people," shipped guns and gunpowder and reported for the first time that "there will not be a want of arms."[20] Finally, news of massive military and economic aid from France arrived in May, news that could only be viewed as "important and interesting to America," as Madison and the Virginia congressmen wrote with considerable understatement to Jefferson.[21] Indeed, on the day that the delegates wrote to the governor, General Washington met with General Rochambeau in Wethersfield, Connecticut, to plan the campaign that would ultimately lead to the victory at Yorktown in October.

16. JM to TJ, Apr. 3, 1781, below.
17. *Ibid.*, and JM and the Virginia congressional delegation to TJ, Apr. 3, 1781, below, Apr. 17, 1781, below, and Apr. 24, 1781, below. They reported that the exchange rate between specie and the old Continental currency had slipped in two weeks from 135 to 1 to "150 for 1," with "the depreciation progressive" (Apr. 17, 1781).
18. See Madison and the Virginia congressional delegation to TJ, Apr. 24, 1781, below, Apr. 27, 1781, below, May 1, 1781, below, and May 8, 1781, below.
19. The marquis de Lafayette to George Washington, Apr. 18, 1781, in Fitzpatrick, XXI, p. 494.
20. David Ross to TJ, May 28, 1781, in *PTJ*, VI, p. 27.
21. JM and the Virginia congressional delegation to TJ, May 22, 1781, below.

Just as Jefferson made every effort to strengthen the military forces in Virginia, Madison took the lead in trying to tighten the bonds of union under the Articles of Confederation by coercing delinquent states that had failed to abide by congressional legislation and requisitions. Only twelve days after Congress had celebrated ratification of the Articles, Madison headed a committee appointed "to prepare a plan to invest the United States . . . with full and explicit powers for carrying into execution in the several states all acts and resolutions passed agreeably to the Articles of Confederation." His report asserted that under the Articles, "a general and implied power is vested in the United States . . . to enforce and carry into effect all the Articles . . . against any of the States which shall refuse or neglect to abide by . . . their determinations." To make that implied power explicit, Madison drafted an amendment "to cement and invigorate the federal Union." It provided that if one or more states failed to honor the determinations of Congress or to meet their obligations under the Articles, Congress could "employ the force of the United States as well by sea as by land to compel such State or States to fulfill their federal engagements."[22]

In a lengthy letter to Jefferson, Madison explained "the delicacy and importance of the subject," tying it directly to Virginia's desperate situation:

> The necessity of arming Congress with coercive powers arises from the shameful deficiency of some of the States which are most capable of yielding their apportioned supplies, and the military exactions to which others already exhausted by the enemy and our own troops are in consequence exposed. Without such powers too in the general government, the whole confederacy may be insulted and the most salutary measures frustrated by the most inconsiderable State in the Union. . . .
>
> The expediency however of making the proposed application to the States will depend on the probability of their complying with it. If they should refuse, Congress will be in a worse situation than at present: for as the confederation now stands, and according to the nature even of alliances much less intimate, there is an implied right of coercion against the delinquent party, and the exercise of it by Congress whenever a palpable necessity occurs will probably be acquiesced in.
>
> It may be asked perhaps by what means Congress could exercise such a power if the States were to invest them with it? As long as there is a regular army on foot a small detachment from it, acting under Civil authority, would at any time render a voluntary contribution of supplies due from a State, an eligible alternative. But there is a still more easy and efficacious mode. The situation of most of the States is such, that two or three vessels of force employed against their trade will make it their interest to yield prompt obedience to all just requisitions on them.[23]

Although Madison asked Jefferson's opinion about the coercive amendment, the governor was too occupied with military and money matters to reply. When the British blockaded Chesapeake Bay, diverting commerce to Philadelphia, Jefferson reported with regret that "our Continental Money is

---

22. JM's proposed amendment to the Articles of Confederation, Mar. 12, 1781, in *PJM,* III, pp. 17–19.
23. JM to TJ, Apr. 16, 1781, below.

all gone or going off in that Channel."[24] On April 12, he learned that, at the official rate of 40 to 1, the state treasury had only $950 left.[25] By May, William Grayson, a Virginian in Philadelphia, wrote that "as to the credit of the state, I don't believe anybody would trust her for half a crown."[26]

Things were just as bad at the national level. On April 27, Madison informed his friend that "the Public treasury is at this moment left destitute of a Single Shilling and has large demands on it which have anticipated what will probably come into it for some months." Early in May, the Continental currency collapsed in Philadelphia, sparked by an interstate conflict between New Jersey, which set the rate at 150 to 1, and Pennsylvania, which pegged it at 175 to 1. "The effect of this declaration," the Virginia delegation to Congress informed Jefferson, "has been a confusion among the people of this city approaching nearly to tumult, a total Stop to the circulation of the old money, and a considerable stagnation and increased depreciation of the new."[27] Three days later, the old currency had "depreciated from two hundred to seven, eight, and some say nine Hundred for one," with the new money suffering "in proportion."[28] Within two weeks, the explosive depreciation reached Virginia, reducing public credit so low "that it is a matter of doubt . . . whether the present currency in the State will pass much longer."[29]

In the midst of these difficulties, the British forces at Portsmouth moved out to meet Cornwallis's troops marching up from North Carolina. "We have no Doubt," Jefferson informed Washington, "putting all Circumstances together but that these two Bodies are forming a Junction."[30] Writing to the Speaker of the House of Delegates, he deplored the fact that "a Country so intersected with navigable waters can be defended by naval Force alone." But his message was not read to the General Assembly, which hastily fled Richmond for Charlottesville at "the approach of an hostile army of the enemy."[31] The governor remained in Richmond but in a classic understatement observed that the assembly had adjourned because "the movements of the enemy in the neighbourhood of this place" did not afford "that quiet necessary to the Deliberations of Public Bodies."[32]

On May 15, Jefferson left Richmond for Monticello, transferring the

24. TJ to JM and the Virginia congressional delegation, Apr. 6, 1781, below.
25. *PTJ,* V, p. 428.
26. *Ibid.,* p. 209.
27. JM and the Virginia congressional delegation to TJ, Apr. 27, 1781, below, and May 5, 1781, below.
28. JM and the Virginia congressional delegation to TJ, May 8, 1781, below.
29. *Calendar of Virginia State Papers,* ed. William P. Palmer, 11 vols. (Richmond, 1875–93), II, p. 110; cited in *PJM,* III, pp. 109–10.
30. TJ to George Washington, May 9, 1781, in *PTJ,* V, p. 624.
31. *Journal of the House of Delegates, 1781* (Richmond, 1828), pp. 4–6, 9, 18, 21, May 1781; cited in *PTJ,* V, p. 629.
32. TJ to JM and the Virginia congressional delegation, May 14, 1781, below.

seat of government to Charlottesville, where the assembly was to convene on May 24. One member of the Executive Council resigned, and the others scattered, leaving Jefferson without their services for the rest of his term as governor.[33] On May 28, Jefferson informed Washington that Cornwallis's and Arnold's forces, supplemented by reinforcements from New York, now numbered 7,000 men. Lafayette's troops totaled 3,000, and Jefferson urged Washington "to lend us your personal aid" as the "dernier resort in distress."[34] Jefferson added that he would shortly retire as governor: "A few days will bring to me that period of relief which the Constitution has prepared for those oppressed with the labors of my office, and a long declared resolution of relinquishing it to abler hands has prepared my way for retirement to a private station."

Jefferson's term was to expire on June 2, and the House of Delegates, meeting in Charlottesville, resolved on May 30 to ballot for governor on that day. But on Saturday, June 2, the vote was postponed until Monday, June 4, and Jefferson continued to function as governor on Sunday, June 3, his final day in office.

On June 4, General Banastre Tarleton's dragoons, dispatched by Cornwallis to rout the government at Charlottesville and seize the governor, swept into the area, forcing the assembly to adjourn to Staunton, beyond the Blue Ridge. Warned by John Jouett, a Louisa County militiaman who had seen the British moving west, Jefferson and his family escaped Tarleton's legion, but Cornwallis set up temporary headquarters at Jefferson's Elk Hill plantation.[35]

The timing of Jefferson's retirement could not have been worse. Although he had given notice of his intention to retire as early as September 1780 and had written a personal note to Madison on March 23, 1781 (now missing), he seems never to have made a formal announcement of his intention. Madison regretted Jefferson's decision but accepted it stoically: "Notwithstanding the personal advantages which you have a right to expect from an emancipation from your present labours and the interest you have given me in your leisure by the promise of your correspondence I cannot forbear lamenting that the State is in the present crisis to lose the benefit of your administration. But as you seem to have made up your final determination in the matter and have I doubt not weighed well the reasons on which it is grounded I shall lament it in silence."[36]

After the British withdrew—Jefferson called it "the alarm on the day

---

33. TJ to the Speaker of the House of Delegates, May 28, 1781, in *PTJ,* VI, pp. 28-29.

34. TJ to George Washington, May 28, 1781, *ibid.,* pp. 32-33.

35. Malone, I, pp. 355-57. The Virginia assembly hailed Jouett's "activity and enterprise" in warning the executive and legislature of Tarleton's movements and presented him with "an elegant sword and pair of pistols." See *Journal of the House of Delegates, 1781,* p. 15, May 1781; cited in *PTJ,* VI, p. 89.

36. JM to TJ, Apr. 3, 1781, below. For a discussion of TJ's missing letter of Mar. 23, 1781, see *PTJ,* V, p. 328.

succeeding my exit from office"[37]—the assembly met in Staunton, elected General Thomas Nelson governor, and called for an inquiry "into the Conduct of the Executive for the last twelve Months."[38] Although the executive included the eight members of the Executive Council as well as the governor. Jefferson viewed the vote as a censure of himself. Dumas Malone called the charge "the nadir of the entire public career of Thomas Jefferson,"[39] but Jefferson approached the inquiry as an opportunity to vindicate his governorship. Indeed, even before he rejoined the legislature in December as a member, the assembly had elected him to be a delegate to Congress, a sure indication of his standing with the legislature.[40] When he returned to the assembly in December, the committee appointed to conduct the inquiry concluded that the resolution of July had been based on rumors that were groundless. Instead, the assembly, noting that "tenfold value is added to an approbation founded on cool and deliberate discussion," unanimously adopted a resolution thanking Jefferson for "his impartial, upright, and attentive administration" and praising him for his "Ability, Rectitude, and Integrity as cheif Magistrate." By publicly avowing their opinions, both the assembly and the Senate hoped "to obviate and to remove all unmerited Censure."[41]

--- THE LETTERS ---

*Governor Jefferson to Madison and the Virginia Congressional Delegation*

Richmond in Council Mar. 26, 1781

GENTLEMEN

I beg leave to ask your Sollicitations with Congress for Permission to Colo. William Davies of the Virginia line to accept an Appointment to the War Office of this State without prejudice to his rank and right to half-pay for life, Lands, and Depreciation of pay.[1] I am in Hopes it will be the more easily obtained as by the Discontinuance of appointing full Colonels in the Army[,]

37. TJ to William Fleming, June 9, 1781, *ibid.*, VI, p. 84.
38. *Ibid.*, p. 88.
39. Malone, I, p. 361.
40. *Journal of the House of Delegates, 1781*, pp. 42, 48, Oct. 1781; cited in *PTJ*, VI, p. 137. For TJ's notes on his conduct during the invasion of Virginia (1780–1781), written in Aug. 1805, see Ford, VIII, pp. 363–74, which also includes an undated version.
41. Resolution of Thanks to TJ by the Virginia General Assembly, Dec. 12, 1781, in *PTJ*, VI, pp. 135–37.
1. Colonel William Davis (1749–1812) of Mecklenburg County succeeded Colonel George Muter as commissioner of the Virginia State Board of War; see *PJM*, III, p. 32.

Officers of that rank seem not to be deemed essential. We are told too that instances of similar Indulgence do exist: particularly, that his Excellency Governor Clinton of New York retains his rank of Brigadier General, and the honble Mr McDowall a Delegate in Congress that of Major General in the Continental Army. A speedy answer to our Application is much desired. I have the Honor to be etc.

T.J.

P. S. I will be much obliged to you for the Pennsylvania Act either of Assembly or of the Executive for taking off the Embargo on flour etc. by the first Conveyance.[2]

## *Madison and the Virginia Congressional Delegation to Governor Jefferson*

Philadelphia Mar. 27, 1781

SIR,

On the receipt of your favor of the 22d of February inclosing the Memorial of Mr. Stodder and Kerr with the protests and affidavits annexed, we communicated the matter to Congress, and have obtained an instruction to the Hon'ble Mr. Adams to represent the same to the States General of the United Provinces, and to claim such redress for the Memorialists as justice and the law of Nations require.[3] We have also received your Excellency's favor of the 15th instant relating to Mr. Nathan with the several papers under the same cover and shall carry your Excellency's wishes into execution in the best manner we can.[4]

Capt. de la touche is arrived here from the French fleet, with the stores belonging to Virginia;[5] which were delivered to him at Providence.[6] . . . Capt de La Touche confirms the intelligence of an action between the two fleets on the 16th It does not appear to have been by any means a decisive, though a pretty severe one. The French claim the advantage, and say that the English appeared very willing to decline a renewal of the combat. We have the honor

---

2. TJ raised this question because the Virginia legislature had just extended the act of 1778 authorizing the Governor-in-Council to lay an embargo for a limited time; see *ibid.*, p. 33.

3. See TJ to JM and the Virginia congressional delegation, Feb. 22, 1781, above.

4. See TJ to JM and the Virginia congressional delegation, Mar. 15, 1781, above.

5. The stores were the French military arms and supplies from *Le Comité*, which had been put ashore in Rhode Island in Sept. 1780.

6. Up to this point, this letter is printed from Edmund C. Burnett, ed., *Letters of Members of the Continental Congress*, 8 vols. (Washington, 1921–38), VI, p. 38. The rest of the letter comes from Stan. V. Henkels Catalogue No. 1078; see *PJM*, III, pp. 39–40.

to be with the most perfect respect and esteem y'r Excellency's Obt. and humble Servants

     JAMES MADISON JUNR.
     THEO'K BLAND

ENCLOSURE
*[Motion on Stodder, Kerr, and North]*

[Mar. 26 1781]

 A letter, of 22 February, from the governor of Virginia, was read, with a memorial enclosed from Messrs. Stodder, Kerr and North; Whereupon,

 On motion of Mr. [James] Madison, seconded by Mr. M[eriwether] Smith,

 *Ordered,* That authenticated copies of the said memorial, protests and affidavits, be transmitted to the hon. John Adams, and that he be instructed to represent the case to which they relate to their High Mightinesses the States General of the United Provinces of the Netherlands, and to claim such redress for the memorialists as justice and the law of nations require.

## *Madison to Jefferson*

Philadelphia Apr. 3, 1781

DEAR SIR

 I have received your favor of the 23d. of March.[7] The publication of which you wish to have a copy for your private use is not yet finished; as soon as it is I shall take care to provide one for you. I have repeatedly reminded Dr. Smith of his promise with respect to the map, but have never obtained any thing more than a repetition of the promise. He is at present an inhabitant of Maryland. Just before he left this City he assured me that he should soon send me what you wanted. I have not since heard from him and have very little hope that I ever shall on that subject. It is not improbable that he calculates the value of the Chart on its being the single one remaining, and thinks the issuing of copies would depreciate it. The genius of the man and the manner of his behaviour in the course of my applications to him justify such a surmize.

 Notwithstanding the personal advantages which you have a right to expect from an emancipation from your present labours and the interest you have given me in your leisure by the promise of your correspondence I cannot forbear lamenting that the State is in the present crisis to lose the benefit of your administration. But as you seem to have made up your final determination in the matter and have I doubt not weighed well the reasons on which it is grounded I shall lament it in silence.[8]

 The letter from the Delegation by the last post informed you of the arrival

---

7. Letter not found.

8. This paragraph clearly indicates that TJ's letter of Mar. 23 announced his decision to retire as governor at the end of his term.

of the Stores here which were to have been delivered in Virginia by one of the French Ships. The infinite importance of them to the State, especially since the arrival of a reinforcement to Arnold of which we are just apprized by the Marquis [de Lafayette] has determined the Delegates to forward them by land without loss of time. This will be attempted in the first instance in the channel of the Q. Master's department and if it cannot be effected in that mode without delay we propose to engage private waggons for the purpose on the credit of the State. Should the latter alternative be embraced, I find it will be necessary to stipulate instantaneous payment from the Treasury on the arrival of the waggons at Richmond in specie or the old Continental Currency to the real amount thereof. I mention this circumstance that you may be prepared for it. The expence of the transportation will be between five and six hundred pounds Virginia Money. The exchange between specie and the old paper here at present is about 135 for 1.[9]

The Delegates having understood that the Refugees taken by Capt. Tilly on his return to New Port from Chesapeak consisted chiefly of persons who formerly lived in Virginia some of whom were traitors who deserved exemplary punishment, and others vindictive enemies to the State thought proper to make the inclosed application to the French Minister.[10] By conversation I have since had with him on the subject I doubt whether it will be deemed consistent with their general rules of conduct to give up to be punished as malefactors any of the captives made by their fleet which does not serve like their land army as an auxiliary to the forces of the United States. If these persons had been taken by their land forces which serve as auxiliaries under the Commander in chief it seems there would have been no difficulty in the case. However the application will certainly prevent the exchange or release to which it refers, if the Executive think it expedient to do so. On the least intimation I am persuaded the Apostates would be even sent over to France and secured in the most effectual manner during the war. Perhaps this would not be amiss as being not our Prisoners no use can be made of them in redeeming our Citizens from captivity.

About one thousand of the Pennsylvania line will march in a day or two from York Town for the Southern service.[11] When the remainder will follow them is altogether uncertain. The detachment under the Marquis is still at Annapolis. The orders of General Washington will govern their movements. Whatever his intentions mig[ht have] been at first, I flatter myself the embarkat[ion at] N. York of which he must have been soon [informed?] and which is

---

9. Later that day, Congress, acting on a recommendation of the Board of Trade, approved a warrant for $995 to have the military stores taken to Virginia, "for which the said state is to be accountable" when federal/state war accounts were settled; see *PJM*, III, p. 47.

10. See the enclosure, below.

11. "York Town" refers to York, Pennsylvania. The brackets that follow restore words, some conjectural, that were destroyed when a fragment of the last page of this letter was torn off; see *PTJ*, V, p. 328.

now lodged in Chesapeak has det[ermined] him not to withdraw them from a service [which is] now more in need of them than ever.

The Ordinance published in the Newspaper [of this?] day will be an answer to your request by Col. Harr[ison]. It contains the[?] sense of Congress on one of the subjects to which it rela[tes. The] flagrant abuses which were covered by those indul[gences] and the offensive light in which they were justly viewed by our Ally called loudly for their abolition.[12] I am Dr Sir Yr. Sincere friend and servant,

JAMES MADISON JUNR.

ENCLOSURE
*[Madison and the Virginia Congressional Delegation to the French Minister Luzerne]*

SIR                                                                                      Philadelphia Apr. 2, 1781

The Underwritten Delegates from the State of Virginia have been informed that there are among the refugees taken by Capt: Tilly commanding his M.C. Majesty's ship l'Eveillé on his return to New Port from Chesapeak Bay, a considerable number who were formerly inhabitants of Virginia. As some of these persons according to the laws of that State fall under the description of Traiterous Citizens and consequently are not proper subjects of exchange, and others, although they do not fall under that description may if exchanged or released be very prejudicial to the State during the operations against it by giving information and counsel to the Enemy and by their seductions among the people, the Delegates abovementioned wish that no steps may be taken for exchanging or releasing them until the fact shall have been communicated to his Excellency the Governor of Virginia. With this view they ask the favor of you, Sir, to intimate this circumstance to the Commander of his M.C. Majesty's Squadron at New Port, and to obtain from him a list of the names of such of his captives as were formerly inhabitants of Virginia.

The paper inclosed herewith will inform you of the pretensions of three persons Citizens of the State of Virginia founded on their having been on board the Eveillé in the character of Pilots during her expedition into Chesepeak bay, in which a number of prizes were taken. We leave it with you Sir to determine on the justice of them, and to direct the mode in which they ought to be pursued. We wish to be enabled to give the claimants a proper and satisfactory answer, as future operations may render their services again necessary to us, and the facility of commanding them may depend on the temper in which they are now dismissed:

## *Madison and the Virginia Congressional Delegation to Governor Jefferson*

Philadelphia Apr. 3, 1781

SIR

We have been favord with Your Excellencys enclosing a State of the affair between Mr. Nathan and the Commonwealth of Virginia which we are en-

12. The ordinance published on Apr. 3, which dealt with nonintercourse with Great Britain, ended Virginia's illicit trade with Bermuda for salt.

deavoring to put in train for a decision on the Principles you have been pleased to direct, the event of which Your Excellency shall be informd of as soon as tis decided. The Unfortunate consequences which have attended the Naval engagement of Chesapeake on the 16th Ultimo, we feel with unspeakeable regret, as they have snatched from us the pleasing prospects we had cherished for some time past, of frustrating the Sanguine project of the Enemy (of subjugating most of the Southern States this Campaign) and thrown our Country into a Situation which must require her utmost exertions, with all the aid that can be sent her to extricate her from. This we shall leave no means unessayed to effect, on our parts.

The same unhappy event, has deprived us of the immediate Use of the Arms and Stores, which were to have gone from Rhode Island (the Cargoe of the Comite) on board a french frigate, but we have the satisfaction to Inform your Excellency that they are safe arrived at this place, in the Frigate which was to have Carried them to Virginia. We have ordered them to be landed and have taken the necessary steps to forward them with all possible dispatch by a safe Route to Virginia, having committed them to the Care of Colo. Febiger, under the direction of the board of War but it is with much concern that we find on this as well as on many other occasions where we might yield considerable service to our Country on pressing emergencies, the want of small sums of Money is frequently an insurmountable obstacle to a speedy execution of our intention, and the important matters which engage our attention in Congress, interferes with the necessary attention required by such objects when the ready means of executing them are no[t in our hands.] The Remedies to these inconveniencies we leave to the Wisdom of Your Excellency and the Legislature. We have the Honor to be Yr. Excellys Most obedt. Svts.,

JAMES MADISON JUNR
THEOK. BLAND

*Governor Jefferson to Madison and the Virginia Congressional Delegation*

Richmond in Council Apr. 6, 1781

GENTLEMEN

I have received your letter informing us of the Arrival of our Arms etc. from Rhode Island at Philadelphia, and must pray you immediately to send forward the packages within mentioned containing Arms, etc., engaging Waggons for that Purpose who shall be paid on their arrival here the price you contract to give them and be protected from Impresses while in this State.[13] Tho' we do not know the force of the Enemy now at Portsmouth yet the

13. This protection against "Impresses" guaranteed that teamsters hauling the military stores would not have their wagons conscripted for use by the army.

lowest Accounts make them 4,000. This will satisfy you how urgent is our want of those Arms. It is impossible to give you an Idea of the Distress we are in for want of Lead. Should this Army from Portsmouth come forth and become active (and as we have no reason to believe they came here to Sleep) our Affairs will assume a very disagreable Aspect. The want of Arms and military Stores cannot be compensated by Numbers of Militia as that of regular Souldiers may.

Very considerable Debts of a year or two's standing are due from Colo. Finnie and his former Deputies. The present Quarter Master refuses to pay them. Colo. Finnie gives himself no trouble about them. His former Deputies are anxious to pay them, and we willing to advance Monies to those Deputies for this Purpose if Congress will give us their Sanction. You will observe nothing was ever done by our legislature in Consequence of the resolution of Congress of 26th May 1780.[14] Will you be so good as to obtain the Sanction of Congress for our paying these very clamorous and injured Creditors through the former Deputy Quarter Master and this to be done immediately.[15]

Mr. Ross our Commercial Agent since the shutting up our bay finds it necessary to establish funds as far as possible in Philadelphia from which place all our Cloathing and necessaries for the Army must come. We ask the favour of you to be attentive to aid him whenever any remittance of Money shall be intended to the Southward to have them paid to Mr. Ross's Agent there and draw on him for the Amount which shall be paid here and to give them every other possible Assistance in that way. He is furnished so largely with Tobacco and State Money as to leave no doubt of a want of punctuality.[16]

To what a deplorable State shall we be reduced if the Bay continues blocked up. Commerce both Public and private is already taking it's Turn to Philadelphia, our Continental Money is all gone or going off in that Channel and no other resources for remittances to that place. I am etc.,

T.J.

---

14. The resolution of May 26, 1780, recommended that state legislatures empower collectors of Continental taxes due prior to Mar. 1, 1780, to accept as payment certificates issued for provisions, forage, and other supplies for the army. Since Virginia did not enact such legislation, TJ asked Colonel William Finnie to obtain special warrants validating payment, refusing in the meantime to pay for Continental debts on vouchers that might not be sanctioned by Congress; see *PJM*, III, pp. 59-60.

15. JM copied this paragraph, which was read in Congress on Apr. 23 and referred to the Board of the Treasury. The board reported three days later, and Congress directed the board to issue a warrant on the Virginia treasury, as TJ had requested, in order to pay "part of the money due from the said State prior to the first day of March, 1780"; see *ibid.*, p. 60.

16. David Ross served as commercial agent for Virginia from December 1780 until May 1782. He had informed TJ that neither tobacco nor Virginia money could be negotiated in Philadelphia "on any terms"; see *ibid.*

## Governor Jefferson to Madison and the Virginia Congressional Delegation

[Richmond] in Council Apr. 9, 1781

GENTLEMEN

Since my letter of the 6th. I received Information that two Parcels of Medicines marked C V (which we construed Commonwealth of Virginia) were consigned on private Account to Monsieur Coulaux la Vigne, and with other Parts of the Cargo of Le Comité were considered as ours; Be so good as to cause Delivery of them to be made to Monsr. Coulaux la Vigne, he paying all reasonable Charges. I am etc.,

T.J.


## Madison and the Virginia Congressional Delegation to Governor Jefferson

[Philadelphia ca. Apr. 10, 1781][17]

with no Difficulty in arbitrating [the dis]pute, as he admitted the Facts state[d as] agreed between you; and acquiesced in the Gentleman proposed, but contrary to our Expectation we received a Letter from him a Copy of which is enclosed and also our answer to it. You [will] see by these Letters the Turn this [af]fair has taken; and we must wait your further Instructions. Mr. Nathan urges that he may be indulged in the Choice of Merchants to arbitrate th[e dis]pute; if you approve of his Req[uest] you will be pleased to signify your pleasure.

Your favour of the 26th. of [March] came to hand yesterday. We shall attend to what you have mention'd therein respecting Col. Davis, and give you as speedy an Answer as possible
[A] Packet had arrived at New York from England, bringing Advice of the Sailing of the French Fleet for America. It is very probable the Acct. is true. We have the Honour to be, with very great Respect Your Excellency's Most obedient Servants.

JAMES MADISON JUNR.

---

17. For the dating of this fragment of a letter, see *ibid.*, p. 65. It is not in *PTJ*.

### Governor Jefferson to Madison and the Virginia Congressional Delegation

[Richmond] in Council Apr. 13, 1781

SIR

Your letter of the 3d inst. came to hand yesterday. You will by this Time have received letters from me desiring you to do what you have done as to the Arms and in some measure as to the refugees. It would be more agreable to us that they should be sent to France than delivered up to us. I beg leave to add to the Names of those I before mentioned one Cranmer who is said to be the most mischievous of the whole. There may be others, whom it would be desireable to have removed with them, were their names known to us.[18]

I inclose you a Copy of an intercepted letter from a Captain Thomas of the British in which you will find a Display of the present plan of the Enemy as to Chesapeake Bay and it's waters, and Copies of Letters from Captain Reade, and Colonel Richard Henry Lee, shewing that the plan is now in a Course of execution.[19] I trouble you with them as they may enable you to avail us of any Opportunity which may occur of getting the bay scoured. I also inclose an extract of a letter from General Greene to Baron Steuben, to shew you what are the Apprehensions for the Want of lead since the failure of our Mine. I am etc.,

T.J.


### Madison to Jefferson

Philadelphia Apr. 16, 1781

DEAR SIR

The inclosed paper is a copy of a report from a Committee now lying on the table of Congress for Consideration.[20] The delicacy and importance of the subject makes me wish for your judgment on it before it undergoes the final decision of Congress.

The necessity of arming Congress with coercive powers arises from the

---

18. "Cranmer" may be John Cramond, a Norfolk merchant from Scotland who was captured by the French fleet at Lynnhaven Bay in Feb. 1781. He was later taken to France but escaped in 1782 and finally settled in Jamaica; see *ibid.*, p. 69.

19. A British squadron moved into the Potomac in Apr. 1781 to block Lafayette's troops at Annapolis from moving by water to Alexandria. See *ibid.;* see also *PTJ,* V, p. 394.

20. JM's amendment to the Articles of Confederation proposed "full and explicit powers for carrying into execution in the several states" all acts passed by Congress, arguing that "there is an implied right of coercion" that authorized the use of "the force of the United States as well by sea as by land" to compel defaulting states "to fulfill their federal engagements"; see Brant, II, p. 108; *PJM,* III, pp. 17-19, and *PTJ,* V, pp. 471, 474.

shameful deficiency of some of the States which are most capable of yielding their apportioned supplies, and the military exactions to which others already exhausted by the enemy and our own troops are in consequence exposed. Without such powers too in the general government, the whole confederacy may be insulted and the most salutary measures frustrated by the most inconsiderable State in the Union. At a time when all the other States were submitting to the loss and inconveniency of an embargo on their exports, Delaware absolutely declined coming into the measure, and not only defeated the general object of it, but enriched herself at the expence of those who did their duty.

The expediency however of making the proposed application to the States will depend on the probability of their complying with it. If they should refuse, Congress will be in a worse situation than at present: for as the confederation now stands, and according to the nature even of alliances much less intimate, there is an implied right of coercion against the delinquent party, and the exercise of it by Congress whenever a palpable necessity occurs will probably be acquiesced in.

It may be asked perhaps by what means Congress could exercise such a power if the States were to invest them with it? As long as there is a regular army on foot a small detachment from it, acting under Civil authority, would at any time render a voluntary contribution of supplies due from a State, an eligible alternative. But there is a still more easy and efficacious mode. The situation of most of the States is such, that two or three vessels of force employed against their trade will make it their interest to yield prompt obedience to all just requisitions on them. With respect to those States that have little or no foreign trade of their own it is provided that all inland trade with such States as supply them with foreign merchandize may be interdicted and the concurrence of the latter may be enforced in case of refusal by operations on their foreign trade.

There is a collateral reason which interests the States who are feeble in maritime resources, in such a plan. If a naval armament was considered as the proper instrument of general Government, it would be both preserved in a respectable State in time of peace, and it would be an object to mann it with Citizens taken in due proportions from every State. A Navy so formed and under the orders of the general Council of the States, would not only be a guard against aggressions and insults from abroad; but without it what is to protect the Southern States for many years to come against the insults and aggressions of their N. Brethren. I am Dear Yr. sincere friend and obt. servt.,

J. MADISON JUNR

## Madison and the Virginia Congressional Delegation to Governor Jefferson

Philadelphia Apr. 17, 1781

SIR

The inclosed resolution of Congress answers your Excellency's letter of the 26th ulto., relating to the appointment of Col: Davies to the War Office of Virginia. You will observe that it determines his rank in the Army alone, to be the bar to his acceptance of a civil office. Should Col: Davies be willing to give up that, and his place be supplied by one of the supernumerary Colonels, So that no additional expence would accrue to the United States, Congress we believe would not hesitate to let him retire, without forfeiting any of the emoluments to which he is at present entitled. General McDougal was lately appointed by Congress to a civil Office under the like circumstances with Col: Davies, and as he did not chuse to part with his rank in the Army, the appointment was annulled.

We have been favored with your Excellency's two letters of the 6th and 7th instant.[21] The steps already taken by us and of which you will have been informed, will, we flatter ourselves accomplish your wishes with regard to the Refugees taken on board the Romulus.

Your Excellency will also have seen, by our late letters, that we have not been unmindful of the distressed state of Virga., for want of the stores lately brought hither by the French Frigate. We wish however, that our efforts to forward them had been more successful. Our first plan for the purpose, was the one suggested by your letter. The probable emptiness of your Treasury, and the impossibility of our making our requisite advance to the Waggoners here, led us to substitute the other plan of placing the Stores in the Quarter Masters Channel, and procuring from Congress a warrant for the money necessary for the purpose. He at the same time engaged the attention of Colo. Febiger to the business, who has been very alert in expediting the supplies for the Southern Service. Notwithstanding these precautions we have the mortification to find, that the stores are not yet on their way. Since the receipt of your letter, we have determined to recur to our first plan.

The Q. Master and Colo. Febiger assure us that every exertion shall be used to execute it. They say however, it will be several days, before the waggons can possibly be on the road. According to an estimate of the Q. Master, we shall be obliged to draw on your Excellency for near £500 specie or, as much paper as will be equal to it, at the current exchange, to be paid on the arrival of the waggons. The only paper they will receive is the old Continental bills. The Exchange here is 150 for 1; and the depreciation progressive. Your Excellency's other requests relating to the debts left by Col: Finnie in his

---

21. TJ's letter of Apr. 7 has not been found.

department, and the accommodation of Mr. Ross with funds in this place, shall have all the attention we can give them.

The Extract of a letter from Genl: Washington, herewith enclosed, contains all the Authentic information received since our last, on the subject of another embarkation from N. York. For some days of late the report has died away into a general disbelief. Some persons just come out of N. York have revived it, with this variation, that it has a Southern object.

We are extremely concerned to inform your Excellency, that the detachment of the Pennsylvania Line, on which our expectations have been so long fixed, are still detained by the want of money. Every expedient within our invention has been tried, without avail, to remove the obstacles to their march; and we have no encouragement that the resources of the State will put them in motion, in less than 8 or 10 days, at the nearest.[22] The detachment under the Marquis de la Fayette, is, we understand, again moving Southward. But we have great reason to apprehend, that the general cause of our embarrassment will at least retard their progress. The Extract above referred to, will give an idea, how far the Commander in Cheif is likely to be in a condition to spare other detachments from the Troops immediately under him. By a return lately transmitted to Congress, it appears that he had not received five hundred effective recruits from all the States whose levies were assigned to the Northern Department.

It is pretty certain we believe that the British fleet under Arbuthnot is arrived at N. York from Chesapeak. That of our Ally has certainly returned into N. Port [Newport].

On receipt of yr: Excellency's letter of the 8th ult: respecting a plan to be concerted with the States of Maryland and Delaware, for the transportation of supplies to the Southward, we communicated the matter to the Delegates from those States, but they have never been furnished with any power or instructions relative to it.

The Acts of this State, taking off the embargo, are under the same cover with this. We have the honor to be, with sentiments of the highest respect, Yr: Excellency's obt and hble Servants.

[J. MADISON JUR]
[THEO. BLAND]
[MERIWETHER SMITH][23]

---

22. Anthony Wayne's troops finally left York, Pennsylvania, on May 26, 1781. The best biography of Wayne is Paul David Nelson's *Anthony Wayne: Soldier of the Early Republic* (Bloomington, Ind., 1985).

23. Both *PTJ*, V, pp. 481–83, and *PJM*, III, p. 77, print the text from *Calendar of Virginia State Papers*, II, p. 50, noting that that copy is unsigned, although it gives the names of the signers in the heading as listed here.

## Madison and the Virginia Congressional Delegation to Governor Jefferson

Philadelphia Apr. 24, 1781

SIR

We were yesterday Honord with your Excellency's of the 13th Inst. with its enclosures. You may be assured that our utmost endeavors have been exerted in forwarding the arms and stores mentioned in our last, but insurmountable difficulties have prevented their seting off untill now, but we are happy to inform you that the first of them will go on to day as the Quarter Master assures us. We have anticipated the circumstance mentiond in the Extract of Genl. Greenes letter to the Baron, by urging the board of War with every argument for the necessity of a speedy supply which they are taking measures to procure but I fear with little prospect of immediate effect. Neither theirs nor our exertions will be slackend on that head but we cannot advise a reliance on the success.[24] Your desire concerning the Prisioners, has been communicated to the Minister of France who has expressed his fears that such a step could not be Justified on the Common principles adopted by European nations at War, but at the same time thinks there will be no difficulty of complying with your desire signified in your last letter (13th) now before us. A late letter from the Commander in Chief, gives us some reason to think that the British have a serious intention of makeing a descent in Delaware Bay at least to forage, and secure all the Provision they can on the Peninsula that lays below new Castle and the head of Elk if Possible. In Consequence of which measures have been taken to remove all the flower, Cattle and short forage on that Peninsula calld the Eastern shore, out of their Reach, and also from the Jersey shore Bordering on Delaware Bay, for which purpose the Board of War are vested with powers by Congress, and the Executives of Jersey, Pennsyvania, Delaware, Maryland and Virginia are request[ed] to send their assistance to aid in the execution of this necessary measure. Authentic Accounts have arrived here that Don Galvez has enterd the Bay of Pensacola with a considerable sea and Land force, has made good his landing, and been Joind by a large body of troops on the 25th of March, and there is little doubt but that important place will soon be in the hands of Spain.[25] By the same account we are informed that a detachment of Rodneys fleet consisting of seven ships were seen standing towards that place and immediately the Spanish Admiral Put to sea from the Havannah with sixteen sail of men of War of the line and five or six thousand land forces to intercept the British and secure success to the assailants.[26] A report prevails here which gains credit that the fleet from

---

24. General Greene had mentioned his need for lead to Baron Steuben.

25. Bernardo de Gálvez led a Spanish force from Louisiana that captured the British fort at Pensacola on May 9, 1781.

26. The report about Admiral Rodney sending a British squadron from St. Eustasius to Pensacola was false. The Spanish squadron did reinforce Gálvez's troops in April; see *PJM*, III, pp. 83–84.

Corke consisting of two or three men of War and 120 ships under their Convoy, had fallen in with a french Squadron of twelve or fourteen ships of the line, and that very few of the Convoy escaped falling into the hands of our Ally,[27] and a Vessel from Cadiz informs us that War was declared by that nation against the British and that a Manifesto had been Publishd by Holland at that Port authorizing the Dutch to make reprisals on the English Nation before he left Cadiz.[28] We have the honor to be with sentiments of the highest respect and esteem Yr. Excelly's Most ob and hum: servts.,

J. MADISON JUNR
THEOK. BLAND

P.S. We are happy to inform Yr. Excy. that a large detachment of the Pennsylva. line are at length in motion towards Virginia and we hope will arrive in time to Check the Progress of the Enemy in that State. We have accounts that the Confederacy is taken by the Roebuck and Orpheus off this Coast.

*Madison and the Virginia Congressional Delegation to Governor Jefferson*

Philadelphia Apr. 27, 1781[29]

SR.

Having discovered that there were a considerable number of Rampart Arms belonging to the U. S. at this place, which have long lain dormant, (having been supposed useless for the Field,) we have found on enquiry that with a small alteration, and fixing Bayonettes to them they are capable of being renderd [into] exceeding good Field Arms; and knowing the necessity of the State for a Supply of that article we have been extreemely desireous to have them alterd and Sent on with all possible dispatch; we flatterd ourselves that this might have been done expeditiously by the Intervention of some Virginia Merchants who had money in this City which they offerd to dispose of for the purchase of the Arms from the Continent; to have them fitted and transported at their own expence, and on their arrival in Virginia giving the State the offer of them upon terms yeilding them a reasonable Profit for their trouble and expence in so doing; but when they gave in their proposals to us in writing, we were extreemely sorry to find that what would yield them a profit, (far short as they informed us of what might be obtained by vesting their money in other Articles of Commerce,) greatly exceeded any allowance we thought ourselves Justifiable in agreeing they shd. receive, especially when we considered the low condition of the treasury of the State, and that we must engage the faith of the State for the Immediate advance of one half the Money, and the payment of

---

27. This report was also false.

28. This garbled message confirmed the fact that the Netherlands had been at war with Great Britain since Dec. 1780.

29. This letter, which is summarized in *PTJ*, V, pp. 566-67, is printed in *PJM*, III, pp. 88-90.

the other half on the delivery of the Arms. This determined us to embrace an Alternative, which we hope in the End will prove more Eligible; we have in consequence of that determination procured an Order of Congress to the board of War to have two thousand Stand immediately alterd and fitted up for field Service, to be forwarded with all possible expedition to Virginia and the remainder to be sent to Maryland and North Carolina. In order to accelerate this operation, we must entreat your Excellency to devise some means of furnishing to the amount of 1,300 Pounds hard money or its Value in Paper, such as will Circulate in this State; without which we find it will absolutely be impracticable to carry into execution a measure which will be productive of the greatest advantage to the Southern States, for want of some fund in this City we have often found ourselves greatly embarrassed, and frequently absolutely prevented from expediting Succours of whose consequences we are fully apprized to the Southward, and are extremely mortified to find frequently that a very small Sum which would, by being advanced to Waggoners etc. set them at work; it is neither in our power to advance nor procure, either on our own or the States Credit—it being absolutely impracticable to negotiate a Bill we cannot but think it highly proper to fix an Agent for the State in this City, to be furnished with remittances for such purposes, and to transact many other usefull pieces of Business for the State which not only lays greatly out of the line of the delegates duty, but frequently prevents them from bestowing the necessary attention to the more important interests of the State and of the Union in General. Your Excellency will be at no loss to concieve why a remittance of the above Sum for the present occasion is highly necessary and expedient when we inform you that from the tardiness of the States in general to pay in their arrearages of taxes, from the impediments to the Issuing the money according to the Resolution of the 18th of March 1780, and from the daily expenditures for carrying on the war the Public treasury is at this moment left destitute of a Single Shilling and has large demands on it which have anticipated what will probably come into it for some months. We are with the greatest respect Yr. Excy's most obedt. Srts

> JAMES MADISON JUNR.
> THEOK. BLAND
> M. SMITH

We have enclosed yr. Excy. a Copy of the agreement we have been necessitated to enter into in order to ensure and expedite a measure which we are Sensible is of the utmost importance to the State

## Madison and the Virginia Congressional Delegation to Governor Jefferson

Philadelphia May 1, 1781

Sir

We enclose herewith a letter from Oliver Pollock Esqr. which will inform your Excellency of a very large claim which may soon be expected on the Treasury of Virginia.[30]

Mr. Nicholson Agent for Mr. Ross arrived here yesterday. We fear it will not be possible for him to get some of the most essential articles even if an exchange of his funds can be negociated, and that the difficulty of such an exchange will be a great obstacle to his getting such articles as are to be had. As far as our efforts can avail him they will not be spared. We had previous to his coming taken some measures which we flatter ourselves will yield about 2000 good muskets in about two weeks. The transportation is not included otherwise than by a naked order of Congress and must now be referred to Mr. Nicholson.[31]

The 1100 Stand belonging to the State have at length gone forward, with most of the other Articles brought hither with them. The 8th. of this month is the day fixed we understand for the march of the Pennsylvania line from York Town.

The *report* from N. York is that Clinton is disembarking his troops.[32]

We also inclose herewith an extract of a letter from Genl. Washington which needs no comment. We have the honor to be with the highest respect and regard Yr. Excellys obt. and hmble Servts.,

J. Madison Junr.
Theok. Bland
M. Smith


## Madison to Jefferson

Philadelphia May 1, 1781

Dr. Sir

On the receipt of your request as to the map I procured a copy with one of the pamphlets and have put it under the care of Col. Febiger who will have it

---

30. Oliver Pollock served as agent of the Continental Congress and of Virginia in New Orleans, financing much of George Rogers Clark's military expeditions in Kentucky and the Northwest Territory and racking up claims of 54,981 "milled Dollars"; see James A. James, *Oliver Pollock: The Life and Times of an Unknown Patriot* (New York, 1937), pp. 131–78.

31. George Nicholson served as assistant to David Ross, commercial agent for Virginia.

32. General Clinton had detached 1,500 British troops to be convoyed to Virginia, but their departure was delayed until late in May.

conveyed. It is effectually secured against injury on its passage.[33]

I inclose your Excellency a letter from Mazzei although indeed its contents are of no great moment. I have not received the antecedant one referred to in it. The Executive have probably received more particular information from him relative to the object of his mission.

Congress have received a good deal of information from Europe within a few days past. I can only say in general that it is favorable. Indeed whatever consideration the powers of Europe may have for us, the audacious proceedings of our Enemy in all quarters must determine them to abridge a power which the greatest dangers and distresses cannot inspire with moderation or forbearance.

I hope your Excellency has received my letter inclosing a copy of a plan reported to Congress for arming them with co-ercive authority. Your first leisure moments will I flatter myself favor me with your idea of the matter. With great respect I am Dr Sir Yr. Ob friend and servant,

J MADISON JUNR

*Madison to Jefferson*

Philadelphia May 5, 1781

DEAR SIR

In compliance with your request I have procured and now send you a copy of the Constitutions etc. published by order of Congress.[34] I know not why the order in which they stand in the Resolution was varied by the Committee in binding them up. The encomium on the inhabitants of Rhode Island was a flourish of a Delegate from [that] State who furnished the Committee with the account of its Constitution, and was very inconsiderately suffer[ed] to be printed.[35] I am Dear sir, yr sincere friend,

J. MADISON JUNR.

33. In his missing letter of Apr. 7, 1781, TJ probably requested "A New Map of the Western parts of Virginia, Pennsylvania, Maryland and North Carolina" by Thomas Hutchins since he notes in his account book on that date that he had sent JM £150 "to buy Huthcen's map." See *PTJ*, V, p. 585; see also *PJM*, III, p. 98.

34. On Dec. 29, 1780, Congress had authorized the publication of 200 copies of *The Constitutions of the Several Independent States of America; the Declaration of Independence; the Articles of Confederation between the said States; the Treaties between His Most Christian Majesty and the United States;* see *PJM*, III, p. 108.

35. James Mitchell Varnum was the Rhode Island delegate; see *ibid.*, p. 107.

## Madison and the Virginia Congressional Delegation to Governor Jefferson

Philadelphia May 5, 1781

SIR

The Executive of New Jersey in consequence of authority vested in them by the Legislature for that purpose by an Act of the 27th. Ulto. established the rate of exchange between the old Continental currency and the bills issued pursuant to the Act of Congress of the 18th. of March 1780. to be 150 for 1. The speculation arising from this measure to the prejudice of this State with the other reasons stated in the inclosed publication by the Executive Council led to their act of the 2d instant therein referred to declaring the rate between the two kinds of money abovementioned to be 175 for 1.[36] The effect of this declaration has been a confusion among the people of this City approaching nearly to tumult, a total Stop to the circulation of the old money, and a considerable stagnation and increased depreciation of the new. The difference between the latter and hard money is at present vibrating from 4 to 1 downwards. Should the circulation of the former therefore revive, its value cannot exceed 1/700 of that of hard money. The opportunity which this circumstance gives and which we have reason to beleive many are already taking measures to improve, of fraudulent speculation not only on the Citizens of Virginia, but on the State itself, is so obvious and alarming that we thought it our duty to set an Express in immediate motion to put you on your guard against the mischief.[37]

The inclosed list of prisoners taken by Capt: Tilly has been communicated to us by the Minister of France in consequence of our application. We shall select such of the names as have already been mentioned by your Excellency as obnoxious and dangerous to the State, and put them into the hands of the Minister, who as well as the French Commander is entirely disposed to *secure* the State from all further apprehension from their malice. If there are any other names which you would wish to add to your former list we beg to be informed of them by the first opportunity. If there are any of the Prisoners who are not considered as objects of *much* dread, particularly of those who hold commissions we beleive our Allies would chuse not to be deprived of the use of them as subjects of exchange. We have the honor to be with the highest

---

36. New Jersey set the rate at 150 to 1 when the legal rate in Pennsylvania was 75 to 1, setting off a wave of speculation by New Jerseyites, who could double their old Continental money by redeeming it in Pennsylvania. The Executive Council of Pennsylvania tried to reverse the flow by setting the rate at 175 to 1; see *ibid.*, p. 109.

37. Despite this warning, the Continental paper depreciated rapidly in Virginia in May and June. The collapse coincided with the British invasion of the state that forced Governor Jefferson and the legislature to leave Richmond. After the expiration of TJ's term, the legislature abandoned the Continental currency as legal tender except for payment of taxes or other public debts; see *ibid.*

respect and esteem Yr. Excellency's obt. and humble Servts., (By order of the Delegation)

J. MADISON JUNR.


## Madison and the Virginia Congressional Delegation to Governor Jefferson

Philadelphia May 8, 1781

SIR

Having so lately and so often wrote to your Excellency we have little new to Communicate at present; the confusion respecting money still continues in this City, tho with less commotion than could be expected as in a few days the old Continental money has depreciated from two hundred to seven, eight, and some say nine Hundred for one, the new money has of course suffered in proportion. What this Convulsion will end in, it is difficult to Surmise. In the mean time we are in infinite distress as may be easily supposed; the Currency of the old money has been stopp'd for some days past and it is said to day that the new is about to share the same fate. In the midst of these misfortunes we have the pleasure to transmit to Your Excellency a Copy of a letter from Genl. Cornell one of the members of the board of War, who has been directed by Congress to visit the Magazines, and if possible to send to the Southward such Arms Cloathing and Military stores as we are in want of.[38] The Extract is as follows

"Inclosed is a return of Clotheing now on the Road and orderd to be sent immediately from this Place to the care of the board of War, for the Use of the Marquises detachment and the Southern Army, to which may be added one thousand Stand of good small arms orderd forward immediately by the Commander in Chief for the use of the Militia of the Southern States as the board of War shall direct. Early to Morrow morning I shall go to fish Kill with General Knox from which Place the General thinks two or three thousand Cartouch Boxes can be movd.[39] If so they will be forwarded Immediately to the Southward. I Expect to be able to forward for the same Purpose two thousand Small Arms from Springfield exclusive of the Rampart Muskets, my prospects at present are better than I expected. New Windsor[40] April 30th 1780 [1781]." *(A Copy)*

38. Ezekiel Cornell (1732–1800), a Rhode Island member of Congress and a member of the Board of Trade, was granted a six-weeks' leave of absence to expedite the shipment of military supplies to the southern front; see *ibid.,* p. 114. The omission of JM's signature on this letter indicates that he was momentarily absent when the letter was sealed.

39. Fishkill is 45 miles north of New York City. It was a supply base for the northern army. Brigadier General Henry Knox commanded the Continental artillery.

40. New Windsor, about 10 miles south of Newburgh, New York, served as Washington's headquarters.

We have also the pleasure to acquaint your Excellency that about three thousand Suits of Cloathing are safely arrived at Boston from Spain, which our Friend the King of Spain has Enabled our Minister at that Court to procure. We are with the greatest respect Yr. Excelly's most obedt. Servts,

M. SMITH
THEODK: BLAND

N.B. About 400 of the Rampart arms to be made into good Muskets and fixd with Bayonettes for the State as advised in ours of last week are finishd and will be sent forward immediately and the others are finishing with all possible Expedition.

## *Governor Jefferson to Madison and the Virginia Congressional Delegation*

[Richmond] in Council May 10, 1781

GENTLEMEN

A small Affair has taken Place between the British commanding Officer in this State (Genl. Phillips) and the Executive which as he may endeavour to get Rid of through the medium of Congress, I think it necessary previously to apprise you of it.

General Scott obtained Permission from the Commandant at Charlestown for vessels with necessary Supplies to go from hence to them,[41] but instead of sending the Original sent only a Copy of the Permission taken by his Brigade Major. I applied to Genl. Phillips to supply this Omission by furnishing a Passport for the vessel. Having just before taken great Offence at a Threat of Retaliation in the Treatment of Prisoners he inclosed his answer to my Letter under this Address 'To Thos. Jefferson Esqr. American Governor of Virginia.' I paused on receiving the Letter and for some time would not open it. However when the miserable Condition of our Brethren in Charlestown occurred to me, I could not determine that they should be left without the necessaries of Life while a Punctilio should be discussing between the British General and myself: and knowing that I had an Opportunity of returning the Compliment to Mr. Phillips in a Case perfectly corresponding, I opened the Letter.[42]

---

41. Brigadier General Charles Scott of Virginia was captured by the British when Charleston, South Carolina, fell in May 1780. He handled supplies and money forwarded from the Old Dominion for relief of prisoners of war from Virginia who had also surrendered at Charleston; see *PJM,* III, pp. 117-18.

42. TJ seems to have been particularly put out by the conduct of Phillips, whom he had entertained at Monticello while the general was housed with the convention army near Charlottesville. After his exchange, Phillips returned to active duty, serving as the British commanding officer in Virginia. He died three days after this letter was written; see *ibid.*

Very shortly after I received as I expected the Permission of the Board of War for the British Flag vessel then in Hampton Road with Cloathing and Refreshments to proceed to Alexandria. I inclosed and addressed it 'To William Phillips Esqr. commanding the British Forces in the Commonwealth of Virginia.' Personally knowing Phillips to be the proudest man of the proudest Nation on Earth I well know he will not open this Letter; but having Occasion at the same Time to write to Capt. Gerlach the Flag master, I informed him that the Convention Troops in this State should perish for want of necessaries before any should be carried to them through this State till Genl. Phillips either swallowed this Pill of Retaliation or made an Apology for his rudeness.[43] And in this, should the matter come ultimately to Congress, we hope for their Support. He has the less right to insist on the expedition of his Flag because his Letter instead of inclosing a Passport to expedite ours, contained only an Evasion of the Application by saying he had referred it to Sir Henry Clinton and in the mean time he has come up the river and taken the vessel with her Loading which we had chartered and prepared to send to Charlestown and which wanted nothing but the Passport to enable her to depart. I would further observe to you that this Gentleman's letters to Baron Steuben first, and afterwards to the Marquis Fayette, have been in a stile so intolerably insolent and haughty, that both these Gentlemen have been obliged to inform him that if he thinks proper to address them again in the same spirit all Intercourse shall be discontinued.[44] I am with very great Respect and Esteem Gentlemen Your mo: obt. Servt,

TH: JEFFERSON


## *Governor Jefferson to Madison and the Virginia Congressional Delegation*

[Richmond] in Council May 10, 1781[45]

SIR,

The papers of the Executive having been almost wholly lost in the visit which was made by General Arnold to this place, we are endeavouring to

---

43. The British flag vessel brought supplies, "necessaries," and pay for the convention army. Since the German troops had been moved from Charlottesville to Winchester and the British prisoners to Maryland, the flag vessel requested clearance for Alexandria, the closest port for both camps; see *ibid.*

44. TJ's letter was read in Congress late in May and referred to the Board of War. But the board took no action because of Phillips's death and the expiration of TJ's term as governor; see *PTJ*, V, pp. 633–34.

45. The same letter was sent to Washington, with appropriate textual alterations—"your Excellency" was substituted for "Congress" in the second sentence. The version here is from *PJM*, III, p. 119; the version to Washington is in *PTJ*, V, pp. 634–35.

procure Copies of as many of them as we can. As the Correspondence with *Congress* is among the most important I am to solicit the Favor of you to give permission [to] the Bearer hereof Mr. Granville Smith to take Copies of any Letters with which they have been pleased to honour the Executive or have received from them previous to the Commencement of the present year.[46] Besides the General Importance of preserving the Memorial of Public Events, it is natural for those who have had a Share in the Administration to wish that under every possible Circumstance the records of their proceedings may guard them against Misrepresentation or Mistake.[47] Mr Smith has been particularly chosen to execute this Office because of his approved Discretion, and we think ourselves safe in assuring you that he may confidentially be relied on. I have etc.

THO JEFFERSON

## *Governor Jefferson to Madison and the Virginia Congressional Delegation*

Richmond May 14, 1781

GENTLEMEN

I have received your Favor of the 5th. Inst. and am obliged to you for the notification of the State of the Continental Money of which we shall endeavour to avail ourselves to prevent Loss to the State.

We are much obliged to his Excellency the Chevalier de la Luzerne for his Readiness to secure us against the malice of the prisoners taken on Board the Romulus. We would beg Leave to add the name of Jonathan Eelbeck to the others whom we consider as capable of doing us particular Mischief and would not lessen further the Subjects of Exchange in the Hands of our Allies.[48]

The movements of the enemy in the neighbourhood of this place not admitting of that quiet necessary to the Deliberations of Public Bodies, the General Assembly have adjourned themselves to meet at Charlottesville on the 24th inst. I rather expect that the want of Accomodations there will oblige them to adjourn again to some other place. I am etc.,

THO JEFFERSON

---

46. Granville Smith of Louisa County was quartermaster of the Virginia state troops; see *PJM*, III, p. 119.

47. Arnold carried off all of Governor Jefferson's letter books. The only known copy is in the British Museum Library.

48. Jonathan Eilbeck was a merchant in Norfolk who joined Lord Dunmore as a Loyalist in 1775. He returned as a civilian with General Leslie's invasion in 1780 and was captured by the French in Mar. 1781 aboard the *Romulus*. As a civilian, his incarceration by the French would not affect the exchange of American war prisoners for British soldiers; see *PJM*, III, pp. 120–21.

*Madison and the Virginia Congressional Delegation to Governor Jefferson*

Philadelphia May 22, 1781[49]

SIR

Mr. Nicholson we presume will communicate to your Excellency or his principal[50] the State of the business committed to his care. He has we believe been greatly embarrass'd for want of money, and it has not been in our power to afford him assistance, although our endeavours have been exerted for the purpose.

The Chevr. Luzerne has received within a few days past Dispatches from his Court. The Contents of them have not yet transpired, but we expect they will in a day or two be communicated to Congress. No doubt but from the present State of Affairs in Europe, they must be important and interesting to America.[51] Mr. Carmichael writes the Committee of Correspondence, that Mr. Cumberland had left Spain, and returned to England through France, but notwithstanding his negociations are at an end in consequence of his departure, Mr. Carmichael conjectures conferences will be soon opend for the accommodation of the disputes between the belligerent powers, under the mediation of the [Holy Roman] Emperor. He gives this as his conjecture and not from Official authority.[52]

Ct. Rochambeau, in consequence of advices receivd by his Son who arrived in the Ship that brought over the Admiral to take command of the French Fleet at Rhode Island, requested a Conference with General Washington. They are now together and the Operations of the ensuing Campaign will we expect be digested, and we hope the forces of our Ally be put in motion.[53] We are really reduced to extremities for want of money. The State paper passes under great depreciation and not willingly received by the people. Specie appears to be the money chiefly in circulation. How the State will furnish us with that article we know not, unless the Assembly will authorize Mr. Ross their Agent to purchase flour for the Southern Department and exchange it for the Specific supply of Maryland, so far as to answer our exigencies. The Maryland flour may be deliverd at the Head of Elk, and we apprehend disposd of for gold and Silver. Unless something is done to furnish us with money to bear our

---

49. This letter never reached TJ. It was intercepted by the British and forwarded to Lord George Germain; see *ibid.*, p. 130.

50. George Nicholson's "principal" was David Ross, commercial agent for Virginia.

51. Louis XVI promised financial assistance in the form of a subsidy and loans.

52. Richard Cumberland was a British agent in Spain; see Samuel Flagg Bemis, *The Hussey-Cumberland Mission and American Independence* (Princeton, 1931).

53. Admiral Barras and Rochambeau's son informed General Rochambeau that the French fleet commanded by Admiral de Grasse would leave the Caribbean for the Virginia coast in the summer. Washington met with Rochambeau at Wethersfield, Connecticut, the day this letter was written; they agreed on a campaign plan that led to the victory at Yorktown in October.

reasonable expences in this place we must sell what little property we possess here or return to Virginia. Your Excellency will pardon our giving you the trouble of representing to the Assembly any matter that particularly respects ourselves, but our present Situation will we hope apologize for Your Obt. Servts.,

Jos: Jones
James Madison Junr.
Theodk. Bland
M. Smith

## *Madison and the Virginia Congressional Delegation to Governor Jefferson*

[Philadelphia ca. June 3, 1781][54]

D'r S'r

... The delegates have done all they could to hasten Wayne as well as to forward other assistance to our State foreseeing what occasion you would have for aid but could only get the Pen[nsy]lvanians under March very lately and a Resolution a few days past to send forward some Militia from this State and our Neighbour Maryland. Your situation no doubt you have occasionally communicated to the Commander in Chief and [we] must refer you to him for such consolation as he has in prospect. The Delegates endeavours to second your efforts in that quarter have not been wanting and we have no doubt the General will do all in his Power.

[P.S.] 7 Battalions of Militia-Infantry in the whole and 1 Do Horse. ...

## *Jefferson to Madison*

Monticello Sept. 30, 1781

Dear Sir

I beg leave to introduce to your acquaintance the bearer Mr. Short who comes to Philadelphia in hopes of being able to prosecute in greater quiet there than he can here the studies in which he is engaged: and I chearfully add to what you may already have heard of him my testimony of his genius, learning and merit.[55] I do this the rather as it gives me an opportunity of saving the

---

54. This extract from a three-page letter is in *PTJ,* V, pp. 76–77; *PJM,* III, pp. 144–45; and Burnett, VI, p. 110. The letter itself has not been found.

55. William Short (1759–1849), a graduate of the College of William and Mary in 1779, was tutored in law by TJ. Short decided not to pursue his legal studies in Philadelphia because of

right of correspondence with you which otherwise might be lost by desuetude, acknoledging not to have written to you these five months before and lamenting that the same space has occurred since I heard from you. Tho ours is at present the busy and interesting scene yet I have nothing to communicate to you of the military kind, as I am so far from the scene of action and so recluse that I am persuaded you know every event before I do and more especially as Mr. Short does not set out immediately. I pray you to consider me as being with very sincere respect and esteem Dr. Sir your friend and servt.,

TH: JEFFERSON


*Madison to Jefferson*
Philadelphia Nov. 18, 1781
DEAR SIR

By the conveyance through which you will receive this the Delegates have communicated to the State the proceedings in Congress to which the territorial cessions have given birth. The complexion of them will I suppose be somewhat unexpected, and produce no small irritation. They clearly speak the hostile machinations of some of the States against our territorial claims, and afford suspicions that the predominant temper of Congress may coincide with them. It is proper to recollect however that the report of the Committee having not yet been taken into consideration, no certain inference can be drawn as to its issue, and that the report itself is not founded on the obnoxious doctrine of an inherent right in the U. States to the territory in question, but on the expediency of cloaking them with the title of New York which is supposed to be maintainable against all others. It is proper also to be considered that the proceedings of the Committee which we laboured in vain to arrest, were vindicated not by the pretext of a jurisdiction belonging to Congress in such cases, but alledged to have been made necessary by the conditions annexed to the Cession of Virginia. Although the Cession of Virginia will probably be rejected on the whole, I do not think it probable that all the principles and positions contained in the report of the Committee will be ratified. The Committee was composed of a Member from Maryland, Pennsylvania, N. Jersey, Rhode Island and N. Hampshire all of which States except the last are systematically and notoriously adverse to the claims of the Western territory and particularly those of Virginia. The opinion of the Committee is therefore no just index of the opinion of Congress, and as it is a rule observed since the Confederation was completed, that seven votes are requisite in every question, and there are seldom more than 7. 8. 9. or 10. States present, and

---

Cornwallis's surrender three weeks after TJ wrote this letter to JM, which, therefore, was never delivered. Short was admitted to the Virginia bar on Feb. 18, 1782; see *PJM,* III, pp. 269-70.

even the opinion of a Majority of Congress is a very different thing from a Constitutional vote. I mention these particulars that you may be the better able to counteract any intemperate measures that may be urged in the legislature.[56] I do not hesitate to declare my opinion that the State will not only find in the communications we have made to them ample justification for revoking or at least suspending that Act of Cession, and remonstrating against any interference with respect to cases within their jurisdiction, but that they ought in all their provisions for their future security, importance and interest to presume that the present Union will but little survive the present war. I am equally sensible nevertheless of the necessity of great temper and moderation with respect to the first point, and in the last that they ought to be as fully impressed with the necessity of the Union during the war as of its probable dissolution after it. If the State wishes any particular Steps to be pursued by the Delegates, it would be well for particular instructions to that effect to be given. These will not only be a guide to us, but will give greater weight to whatever is urged by us.

I inclose you a paper containing two of the many letters lately published in New York with the subscription of Mr. Deane's name.

The genuineness of some of them and particularly that to Mr. [Robert] Morris is generally doubted. There are some who think the whole of them spurious. However this may be there is, through another channel indubitable proof that no injustice is done in ascribing to him the sentiments advanced in these letters. Either from pique, interested projects of trade, or a traitorous correspondence with the Enemy, he has certainly apostatized from his first principles.[57]

Colo. Willet has lately defeated and dispersed a party from Canada amounting 6 or 700 few of whom will escape captivity, the sword, or famine in the Wilderness. The action commenced near Johnstown.[58]

The Minister of France has dispatches from [France] by a late arrival which confirms the expedition from Cadiz against Minorca, and the actual landing of the troops on the Island. With great respect and sincere regard I am Dr Sir Yr Obt and hbl Servt.,

J MADISON JUNR.

56. JM directed this letter to Richmond, where he expected TJ to attend the legislative investigation of his conduct as governor. But it arrived after the legislature had adjourned and was forwarded to Monticello in Jan. 1782; see *ibid.*, p. 309.

57. See Julian P. Boyd, "Silas Deane: Death by a Kindly Teacher of Treason?" *WMQ* 16 (1959): 165–87, 319–42, 515–50.

58. For an account of Colonel Marinus Willett's defeat of a combined force of British and Indians in the Mohawk valley, see Christopher Ward, *The War of the Revolution,* 2 vols. (New York, 1952), II, pp. 651–52.

# 6

# FROM FRIENDSHIP TO PARTNERSHIP, 1782–1783

THROUGHOUT THE ORDEAL of the legislative inquiry into Jefferson's term as governor, neither of the friends mentioned the investigation. On September 30, 1781, Jefferson acknowledged that he had not written to Madison for five months, but he took the opportunity of introducing a law student to save "the right of correspondence with you which otherwise might be lost by desuetude."¹ Madison responded in November and briefed his friend on congressional opposition to Virginia's western land claims. Although Madison was worried about Congress's probable rejection of Virginia's cession of its claims, he pointed out that Congress had not adopted "the obnoxious doctrine of an inherent right in the U. States to the territory in question." Even so, he thought that there was ample justification for the Virginia legislature to revoke or suspend its cession and to remonstrate against any interference within Virginia's jurisdiction since he doubted "that the present Union will but little survive the present war." But he urged moderation and asked Jefferson, who would be in Richmond to defend himself, "to counteract any intemperate measures that may be urged in the legislature," arguing "that they ought to be as fully impressed with the necessity of the Union during the war as of its probable dissolution after it."²

Strange as it may seem, neither wrote the other about the surrender of Lord Cornwallis and the British army at Yorktown in October 1781, although both had worked ceaselessly to speed military supplies and troops southward to hasten the ultimate triumph of American arms. Writing as "a private individual," Jefferson sent his congratulations to Washington, hailing the general's "return to your native country, and above all things . . . the important

1. TJ to JM, Sept. 30, 1781, above.
2. JM to TJ, Nov. 18, 1781, above.

success which has attended it."³ After Washington's official report of the victory at Yorktown reached Congress on October 24, Madison marched with the other delegates in procession to the Dutch Lutheran Church in Philadelphia to return "thanks to Almighty God."⁴ In a note to a friend, Madison also toasted "the glorious success of the combined [American and French] arms," sure that "these severe doses of ill fortune" would "cool the phrenzy and relax the pride of Britain."⁵

On Christmas Day, 1781, Madison told a friend that Jefferson's "honorable acquital" gave him great pleasure. "I know his abilities, and think I know his fidelity and zeal for his Country so well, that I am persuaded it was a just one." He also expressed his hope that Jefferson would join the Virginia congressional delegation, "the new service to which he is called."⁶

Instead of again entering public service, however, Jefferson resigned his appointment to Congress, then retreated into retirement at Monticello, refusing for nearly three months to write to Madison or anyone else.⁷ Despite the fact that he had found "neither accuser or accusation" when he attended the legislative inquiry,⁸ he complained that the wound inflicted by the original resolution suggested that he "stood arraigned for treasons of the heart and not mere weakness of the head," charges so serious that they could not be removed by "an exculpatory declaration." These could only be cured, he told James Monroe, "by the all healing grave."⁹ For that reason, he vowed to take "final leave" of public life, confirming his earlier decision to retire to "my farm, my family and books from which I think nothing will ever separate me."¹⁰

The usually mild Madison was critical of Jefferson's withdrawal from public affairs. "Great as my partiality is to Mr. Jefferson," he wrote, "the mode in which he seems determined to revenge the wrong received from his Country, does not appear to me to be dictated either by philosophy or patriotism."¹¹ But Madison was gentler in his letters to Jefferson, observing that "the result of the attack on your administration was so fully anticipated that it made little impression on me." Nonetheless, he was disappointed that his friend had refused election to Congress, for that "would have afforded me both unexpected and singular satisfaction, not only from the personal interest I felt in it but from the important aid which the interests of the state would probably have derived from it."

3. TJ to George Washington, Oct. 28, 1781, in *PTJ*, VI, pp. 129–30.
4. *Pennsylvania Packet* (Nov. 1, 1781), cited in *PJM*, III, p. 292.
5. JM to Edmund Pendleton, Oct. 30, 1781, *ibid.*, p. 296.
6. JM to Edmund Pendleton, Dec. 25, 1781, *ibid.*, pp. 337–38.
7. *PTJ*, VI, pp. 136–37.
8. TJ to Isaac Zane, Dec. 24, 1781, *ibid.*, pp. 143–44.
9. TJ to James Monroe, May 20, 1782, *ibid.*, pp. 184–86.
10. TJ to Edmund Randolph, Sept. 16, 1781, *ibid.*, pp. 117–18.
11. JM to Edmund Randolph, June 11, 1782, in *PJM*, IV, pp. 333–34.

Now that the British had been defeated at Yorktown, Madison no longer made any reference to the possibility that the federal Union might not survive the war. Instead, he turned to the long-range problem of Virginia's western land claims and asked Jefferson to "survey the whole subject." Finally, Madison promised to keep up his end of their correspondence, admitting that he was selfish enough "to hope for some return for it."[12]

When Jefferson broke his self-imposed silence, he wrote first to Madison, observing that their friendly correspondence gave him "great pleasure." He confessed that he had planned to research questions relating to Virginia's land claims, but since his books and manuscripts had been moved for safekeeping before Tarleton's raid on Charlottesville and were still unavailable, he was not yet able "to say any thing on the subject."[13] Instead, he turned to other "literary objects" and began to draft answers to questions asked by the marquis de Barbé-Marbois, secretary of the French legation in Philadelphia, about the state of Virginia. His response, which he asked Madison to convey to Marbois, was the basis for his only book, *Notes on the State of Virginia,* published five years later.[14]

Although Jefferson resumed his correspondence in the spring of 1782, he refused to participate in public affairs. When his Albemarle neighbors again elected him to the House of Delegates, he declined to serve and submitted his resignation.[15] When James Monroe, who had studied law with him, attempted to persuade him to reverse his "retreat from public service,"[16] he defended his right "to retire from public employment" and return to "mere private life," which was both a sanctuary and an "asylum also for rest to the wearied."[17]

There are few intimate glimpses of the Jeffersons' family life at any time, but the marquis de Chastellux, a major general in Rochambeau's army, visited Monticello at this moment and gives a brief but graphic picture of the family: "A gentle and amiable wife, charming children whose education is his special care, a house to embellish, extensive estates to improve, the arts and sciences to cultivate—these are what remain to Mr. Jefferson, after having played a distinguished role on the stage of the New World, and what he has preferred to the honorable commission of Minister Plenipotentiary in Europe."[18]

Shortly after the marquis's visit, Jefferson proudly announced that Martha Jefferson had "added another daughter to our family." But the delivery had

12. JM to TJ, Jan. 15, 1782, below.
13. TJ to JM, Mar. 24, 1782, below.
14. TJ to the marquis de Chastellux, Nov. 26, 1782, in *PTJ,* VI, pp. 203-4; TJ to JM, Mar. 24, 1782, below.
15. *PTJ,* VI, pp. 174-75, 179.
16. James Monroe to TJ, May 11, 1782, *ibid.,* p. 183, and June 28, 1782, pp. 192-93.
17. TJ to James Monroe, May 20, 1782, *ibid.,* pp. 184-86.
18. *Travels in North America in the Years 1780, 1781 and 1782 by the Marquis de Chastellux,* ed. Howard C. Rice, Jr., 2 vols. (Chapel Hill, 1963), II, p. 391. Chastellux visited the Jeffersons from Apr. 13 to 17, 1782.

been difficult, and his wife had been "ever since and still continues very dangerously ill."[19] For four months, Jefferson devotedly attended his wife, his eldest daughter recalled: "As a nurse no female ever had more tenderness and anxiety; he nursed my poor Mother in turn with Aunt Carr and her own sisters setting up with her and administering her medicines and drink to the last." The vigil continued while she lingered, and "he was never out of Calling. When not at her bed side he was writing in a small room which opened immediately at the head of her bed."[20] Throughout the summer, he remained in "the state of dreadful suspence," which ended only with "the catastrophe which closed it"—his wife's death.[21]

Jefferson was devastated by "the unmeasurable loss" of his wife, who had been the source of his "comfort and happiness." In his grief, he wrote that "this miserable kind of existence"—he called it "a gloom unbrightened with one chearful expectation"—"is really too burdensome to be borne," creating a "stupor of mind which ... rendered me as dead to the world as she was whose loss occasioned it."[22]

It was Madison who rescued Jefferson from the disparaging depths of despair. Acting on the assumption that the death of his wife had changed his sentiments "with regard to public life," Madison moved—and Congress unanimously agreed on November 12—to reinstate his friend's appointment as minister plenipotentiary for negotiating peace.[23] Madison seemed confident of Jefferson's acceptance and looked forward to "the pleasure of soon seeing him in Philadelphia."[24]

Madison knew his friend as few others did. Jefferson eagerly accepted the change of scene and promised that he would "lose no time ... in preparing for my departure" for Philadelphia, where he would review dispatches relating to peace negotiations.[25] On the day that he accepted the appointment, he told Chastellux that his only object was "so to hasten over those obstacles which would retard my departure as to be ready" to sail on a French frigate with Chastellux to France.[26] One month later, Jefferson reached Philadelphia with his oldest daughter and began "industriously arming himself for the field of negociation."[27]

It had been three years since Madison and Jefferson had last seen each other in Williamsburg, but they resumed their friendship easily, living in the

19. TJ to James Monroe, May 20, 1782, in *PTJ,* VI, pp. 184–86.
20. Reminiscences of Martha Jefferson Randolph, cited *ibid.,* pp. 199–200.
21. TJ to the marquis de Chastellux, Nov. 26, 1782, *ibid.,* pp. 203–4.
22. TJ to Elizabeth Wayles Eppes, [Oct. 3], *ibid.,* pp. 198–99; TJ to the marquis de Chastellux, Nov. 26, 1782, *ibid.,* pp. 198–99, 203–4.
23. *PJM,* V, pp. 268–69.
24. JM to Edmund Randolph, Nov. 14, 1782, *ibid.,* p. 275.
25. TJ to JM, Nov. 26, 1782, below.
26. *PTJ,* VI, pp. 203–4.
27. JM to Edmund Randolph, Dec. 30, 1782, in *PJM,* V, p. 473.

same boardinghouse, eating at the same table, and conversing on public affairs and personal interests. In less than a month, their friendship became a partnership. Together they perfected a cipher to carry on their correspondence without fear of its being decoded by intercepters on either side of the Atlantic. Together they poured over book catalogues, deciding which volumes Jefferson would search for in France. Together they drew up a list of books for a congressional library, and Madison, as chairman of the committee appointed by Congress to compile the list, recommended the purchase of 1,300 volumes on international law, treaties and diplomatic negotiations, political theory, history, law, and the affairs of the United States.[28] But the economy bloc in Congress prevailed, and Madison's motion lost "by a considerable majority."[29]

After a month in Philadelphia, Jefferson and his daughter left for Baltimore to board a French frigate for France. Delayed by winter ice and a blockade of Chesapeake Bay by the British fleet, he spent a restless month in Maryland, where he had "neither occupation nor amusement" except writing letters.[30] For Madison, he recounted an anecdote about the animosity between Ralph Izard, the U.S. commissioner to Tuscany who was temporarily in Paris, and Benjamin Franklin, American minister to France.[31] Madison reciprocated with his account of John Adams's letters to Congress, which were "not remarkable for any thing unless it be a *display of his vanity, his prejudice against* the *French Court* and *his venom against Doctr. Franklin.*"[32] Although Madison had never met Adams, Jefferson knew him well. "*His vanity,*" Jefferson confessed, "*is a lineament in his character which had entirely escaped me. His want of taste I had observed. Notwithstanding all this,*" he concluded, "*he has a sound head on substantial points, and I think he has integrity. I am glad therefore that he is of the [peace] commission and expect he will be useful in it. His dislike of all parties, and all men, by balancing his prejudices, may give the same fair play to his reason as would a general benevolence of temper. At any rate honesty may be extracted even from poisonous weeds.*"[33]

Since a British fleet of 25 ships was cruising off Chesapeake Bay, Jefferson fretted about running the risk of capture, a fate suffered by Henry Laurens, who had been incarcerated in the Tower of London. He outlined five options and asked for Madison's views, which would have great weight with him: he

---

28. See JM's "Report on Books for Congress," *ibid.*, VI, pp. 62–115, and Fulmer Mood, "The Continental Congress and the Plan for a Library of Congress in 1782–1783," *PMHB* 72 (1948): 3–24. Also see Loren Eugene Smith, "The Library List of 1783: Being a Catalogue of Books Composed and Arranged by James Madison, and Others, and Recommended for the Use of Congress on January 24, 1783, with Notes and Introduction" (Ph.D. diss., Claremont Graduate School, 1969); this item was called to my attention by J. A. Leo Lemay.
29. *PJM,* VI, p. 116.
30. TJ to JM, Feb. 14, 1783, below.
31. TJ to JM, Feb. 7, 1783, below.
32. JM to TJ, Feb. 11, 1783, below. The italicized words in this paragraph were written in code.
33. TJ to JM, Feb. 14, 1783, below.

could (1) go to Boston and embark there; (2) stay in Baltimore until the British fleet left the bay; (3) go to Hampton or Yorktown and await favorable weather; (4) seek a flag of safe conduct from the British and leave from Baltimore; or (5) await a truce.[34] He added that he had just heard a rumor "of peace being actually concluded."

A week later, Madison confirmed that a preliminary peace treaty had been signed and that Congress had adopted a resolution instructing Jefferson to "suspend your voyage until . . . further instruction."[35] Jefferson and his daughter promptly returned to Philadelphia, where, as Madison wrote, "your former quarters will await you."[36]

In Philadelphia, Jefferson found "peace engrossing all conversation."[37] In less than two weeks, the American packet *Washington* arrived from France carrying official copies of the preliminary peace treaty signed on November 30, 1782. Two weeks later, Congress learned that preliminaries for a general peace had been signed at Paris on January 20, 1783, and informed Jefferson that it was "unnecessary for him to pursue his Voyage."[38] On April 11, Congress ratified the preliminary articles of peace between Great Britain and the United States, and Jefferson wrote a letter to John Jay and the American peace commissioners congratulating them "on the singular happiness of having borne so distinguished a part both in the earliest and latest transactions of this revolution. The terms obtained for us are indeed great and are so deemed by your country," concluded the author of the Declaration of Independence. Madison and Congress agreed that the terms granted to an independent America were "on the whole extremely liberal."[39]

## THE LETTERS

### Madison to Jefferson

Philadelphia Jan. 15, 1782

DEAR SIR

Your favor of the [22nd?] day of [Dec.] written on the eve of your departure from Richmond came safe to hand by the last week's post.[1] The result of the attack on your administration was so fully anticipated that it made little

---

34. TJ to JM, Feb. 7, 1783, below.
35. JM to TJ, Feb. 13, 1783, below, and Feb. 15, 1783, below.
36. JM to TJ, Feb. 18, 1783, below.
37. TJ to Edmund Randolph, Mar. 4, 1783, in *PTJ*, VI, p. 254.
38. *Ibid.*, p. 259.
39. TJ to John Jay, Apr. 11, 1783, *ibid.*, pp. 260–61; JM's "Notes on Debates," Mar. 12–15, 1783, in *PJM*, VI, p. 328.
1. This letter has not been found.

impression on me. If it had been consistent with your sentiments and views to engage in the new service to which you were called, it would have afforded me both unexpected and singular satisfaction, not only from the personal interest I felt in it but from the important aid which the interests of the state would probably have derived from it.[2] What I particularly refer to is her claim to Western territory. The machinations which have long been practised by interested individuals against this claim are well known to you. The late proceedings within the walls of Congress in consequence of the territorial cessions produced by their recommendations to the States claiming the Western Country were many weeks ago transmitted for the Legislature by a Capt. Irish. By the same conveyance I wrote to you on the subject. We have the mortification to find by our latest letters from Richmond that this Gentleman had not at the date of them appeared there. As it is uncertain whether that information may not have totally miscarried it will be proper to repeat to you that the States besides Virga. from which the cessions came were Connecticut and N. York. The cession of the former consisted of all her claim west of N. York as far as the Missippi. That of the latter of all her claims beyond a certain western limit drawn on the occasion. The cession of Cont. [Connecticut] extended to the soil only expressly reserving the jurisdiction.[3] That of N.Y. made no reservation. These cessions with that of Virga. and Sundry memorials from the Inda. [Indiana] and other land Companies were referred to a Committee composed of a Member from N.H. R.I. N.J. Pa. and Maryld. The ingredients of this composition prepared us for the complexion of their proceedings. Their first Step was to investigate and discuss the respective titles of the States to the territory ceded. As this was directly in the face of the recommendation of Congress which professed to bury all such discussions and might prejudge future controversies between individual members of the Union, we refused to exhibit any evidence in favor of the title of Va. and endeavoured though in vain to prevail on Congress to interdict the Committee from proceeding in the enquiry. The next step of the Committee was still more obnoxious. They went fully into a hearing of the Memorialists through their Agents, and received all the evidence adduced in support of their pretensions. On this occasion we renewed our remonstrances to the Committee and our complaints to Congress, but with as little effect as on the first occasion. The upshot of the whole was a report to Congress rejecting the Cessions of Virga. and Connt. and accepting that of N.Y.; disallowing also the claims of the Companies N.W. of the Ohio, but justifying that of the Inda. Compy. The report seems to distrust the doctrine hitherto maintained, of territorial rights being incident to the U.S. Collectively which are not comprehended within any individual State;

---

2. Even before the Virginia legislature had completed its investigation of Jefferson's administration as governor, it elected him a delegate to Congress on Nov. 30. After his acquittal, Jefferson resigned from the congressional post on Dec. 19; see *PTJ,* VI, p. 137.

3. A dispute between Connecticut and Pennsylvania prevented Congress from accepting the Connecticut cession until 1786; see Peter S. Onuf, "Toward Federalism: Virginia, Congress, and the Western Lands," *WMQ* 34 (1977): 353–74.

substituting the expedient of recognizing the title of N.Y. stretching it over the whole country claimed by the other ceding States, and then accepting a transfer of it to the U.S. In this state the business now rests. The report having never been taken into consideration, nor do we wish it should, till it shall have undergone the consideration of Virga.[4]

In whatever light the policy of this proceeding may be viewed it affords an additional proof of the industry and perseverance with which the territorial rights of Virga. are persecuted and of the necessity of fortifying them with every precaution which their importance demands. As a very obvious and necessary one we long since recommended to the State an accurate and full collection of the documents which relate to the subject. If the arrival of Capt. Irish had taken place before the adjournment of the Assembly and during your stay with it we flattered ourselves that this recommendation would have been attended to and that the task would have fallen on you. As this was not the case we have no hope at present of being enabled from any other sources than the voluntary aids of individuals to contradict even verbally the misrepresentations and calumnies which are daily levelled against the claims of Va. and which cannot fail to prepossess the public with errors injurious at present to her reputation and which may affect a future decision on her rights. Col. Masons industry and kindness has supplied us with some valuable papers and remarks. Mr. Jones has also received from Mr. Pendleton some judicious remarks on the subject. We are still notwithstanding far from possessing a complete view of it. Will you permit me to ask of you such information as your researches have yielded, with the observations which you have made in the course of them. I would not obtrude such a request on you if the subject were not of public importance and if it could have been addressed with equal prospect of advantage elsewhere. Indeed if you would prevail on yourself to spare as much time as would survey the whole subject, beginning with the original charter, pursuing it thro' the subsequent charters and other public acts of the crown thro' the Governors of Virga. and referring to all the transactions with the Indians which have been drawn into the question, the public utility I am persuaded would sufficiently reward you for the labor.

Pray did you ever receive a letter from me enclosing a proposition declaratory of the coercive power of Congress over the States? It went by an Express while you were at the head of the Executive.

We have not a word of news from Europe. The French are assembling a force in the W. Indies which presages further calamities to the English. The Spaniards are also in motion but their object will probably be both a small and a selfish one. I shall cheerfully send you a line as often as I have a subject for it, tho' I shall be so selfish as to hope for some return for it. I am Dr. Sir Yrs sincerely,

J. MADISON JR.

---

4. See Merrill Jensen, "The Creation of the National Domain, 1781–1784," *MVHR* 26 (1939): 323–42.

## Madison to Jefferson

Philadelphia Mar. 18, 1782

DEAR SIR

In my last to you on the subject of the map in the hands of Dr. Smith I informed you of the little chance of getting a copy of it for you. Nothing has since occurred which affords the least expectation from that quarter. But I have met with a bundle of old pamphlets belonging to the public Library here in which is a map published in 1650 which from this and other circumstances I am pretty confident is of the same impression with that of Doctr. Smith's. It represents the South sea at about 10 days travel from the heads or falls I forget which of James River. From the tenor however of the pamphlet to which it is immediately annexed and indeed of the whole collection there is just ground to suspect that this representation was an artifice to favor the object of the publications which evidently was to entice emigrants from England by a flattering picture of the advantages of this Country, one of which dwelt on in all the pamphlets is the vicinity of the S. Sea, and the facility it afforded of a trade with the Eastern World. Another circumstance which lessens much the value of this map to the Antiquary is that it is more modern by 25 years than those extant in Purchase's pilgrim, which are referred to in the Negociations between the British and French Commissaries touching the bounds of N. Scotia as the first of Authenticity relating to this part of the world. If notwithstanding these considerations you still desire that a copy be taken from the map above described I shall with pleasure execute your orders, or if you wish that a copy of Virga. or of the whole country may be taken from those in Purchase, your orders shall be equally attended to. I much doubt however whether that book be so extremely scarce as to require a transcript from it for the purpose you seem to have in view.[5]

You will find in the inclosed gazette all our latest intelligence both from Europe and the W. Indies. The Ministerial speeches in Parliament as well as other considerations render it pretty certain that the system for recovering America will be changed. A peace with Holland and a suspension of the expensive operations in America are to give their resources full play against France and Spain, whilst all the arts of division and seduction will probably be practised on the U. States.

Congress have taken no step in the business of the Western territory since the report of the Committee of which I have already given you an account, and which we hear arrived at Richmond on the day of the Ajournment of the Assembly. We wish it to undergo their consideration, and to receive their instructions before we again move in it. Mr. Randolph by whom this goes, will probably be present at the May Session and will be possessed of every informa-

---

5. These maps are discussed in *PJM,* IV, p. 102, and in Coolie Verner, "The First Maps of Virginia, 1590–1673," *VMHB* 58 (1950): 3–15.

tion that may be necessary. I refer you to the interview with him which I hope that occasion will afford you for other congressional intelligence.

I am this moment told that pretty certain information is come to hand of the final reduction of St. Kitts. With great regard I am Dr. Sr. Yr. obt. friend and Servt.,

J. MADISON JR.

*Jefferson to Madison*

Monticello Mar. 24, 1782

DR SIR

I have received from you two several favours on the subject of the designs against the territorial rights of Virginia. I never before could comprehend on what principle our right to the Western country could be denied which would not at the same time subvert the rights of all the states to the whole of their territory. What objections may be founded on the Charter of N. York I cannot say, having never seen that charter nor been able to get a copy of it in this country. I had thought to have seized the first leisure on my return from the last assembly to have considered and stated our right and to have communicated to our Delegates or perhaps to the public so much as I could trace, and expected to have derived some assistance from antient M.S.S. which I have been able to collect. These with my other papers and books however had been removed to Augusta [County—i.e., Staunton] to be out of danger from the enemy and have not yet been brought back. The ground on which I now find the question to be bottomed is so unknown to me that it is out of my power to say any thing on the subject. Should it be practicable for me to procure a copy of the charter of N.Y. I shall probably think on it, and would cheerfully communicate to you whatever could occur to me worth your notice. But this will probably be much too late to be of any service before Congress who doubtless will decide ere long on the subject. I sincerely wish their decision may tend to the preservation of peace. If I am not totally deceived in the determination of this country the decision of Congres, if unfavourable, will not close the question. I suppose some people on the Western waters who are ambitious to be Governors etc. will urge a separation by authority of Congress; but the bulk of the people Westward are already thrown into great ferment by the report of what is proposed, to which I think they will not submit. This separation is unacceptable to us in form only and not in substance. On the contrary I may safely say it is desired by the Eastern part of our country whenever their Western brethren shall think themselves able to stand alone. In the mean time on the petition of the Western counties a plan is digesting for rendering their access to government more easy.⁶

I trouble you with the inclosed to Monsr. Marbois.⁷ I had the pleasure of hearing that your father and family were well yesterday, by your brother who is about to study the law in my neighborhood. I shall always be glad to hear from you; and if it be possible for me, retired from public business to find any thing worth your notice, I shall communicate it with great pleasure. I am with sincere esteem Dr Sir Your friend and servt.

## Madison to Jefferson

Philadelphia Mar. 26, 1782

DEAR SIR

A letter has been lately received from you by the President of Congress, accompanied by a bundle of papers procured from the Cherokees by Colonel Campbell. As it appears that these papers were transmitted at the request of the late President, it is proper to apprize you that it was made without any written or verbal sanction, and even without the knowledge of Congress; and not improbably with a view of fishing for discoveries which may be subservient to the aggressions meditated on the territorial rights of Virginia.⁸ It would have been unnecessary to trouble you with this, had it not appeared that Colonel Campbell has given a promise of other papers; which if he should fulfil, and the papers contain any thing which the adversaries of Virginia may make an ill use of, you will not suffer any respect for the acts of Congress to induce you to forward hither.

## Madison to Jefferson

Philadelphia Apr. 16, 1782

DEAR SIR

Your favor of the 24 of March with a letter inclosed for Mr. Marbois came to hand yesterday.

I intreat that you will not suffer the chance of a speedy and final determination of the territorial question by Congress to affect your purpose of tracing the title of Virga. to her claims. It is in the first place very uncertain when a determination will take place, even if it takes place at all; and in the next it will

---

6. See Patricia Watlington, *The Partisan Spirit: Kentucky Politics, 1779–1792* (New York, 1972).

7. TJ's answers to the marquis de Barbé-Marbois became the basis for his *Notes on the State of Virginia.*

8. Colonel Arthur Campbell (1743–1811) was a frontier leader in southwestern Virginia. Congress took no action on the documents forwarded by TJ; see *PJM,* IV, pp. 125–26.

assuredly not be a final one, unless Virga. means to be passive and silent under aggression on her rights. In every event therefore it is proper to be armed with every argument and document that can vindicate her title. Her adversaries will be either the U. States, or N.Y. or both. The former will either claim on the principle that the vacant country is not included in any particular State and consequently falls to the whole, or will cloath themselves with the title of the latter by accepting its cession. In both cases it will be alledged that the Charter of 1609 was annulled by the resumption of it into the hands of the Crown, and that the subsequent grants to Maryland etc. denote this to have been the construction of it; that the Proclamation of 1763 has constituted the Allegheny Ridge the Western limit of Virga. and that the letter of Presidt. Nelson on the subject of a New Colony on the Ohio relinquishes on the part of Virga. all interference with the Authority of the Crown beyond that limit.[9] In case the title of N.Y. should alone be opposed to that of Virginia, it will be further alledged against the latter that the treaties of 1684. 1701. 1726. 1744. and 1754 between the Government of the former and the 6 nations have annexed to it all the Country claimed by those nations and their tributaries, and that the expence of N. York in defending and protecting them ought in equity to be reimbursed by this exclusive advantage. The original title of N.Y. is indeed drawn from the charter to the Duke of York in 1663-4, renewed after the treaty of Westminster in 1674. But this Charter will not I believe reach any territory claimed by Virga.

Much stress will also be laid on the Treaty of Fort Stanwix particularly as a bar to any corroboration of the Claim of Virga. from the Treatys of Lancaster and Loggstown. It is under this Treaty that the companies of Ind[ian]a. and Vandalia shelter their pretensions against the claims of Virga. etc. etc. see the pamphlets entitled "Public good" and "plain facts."[10] As these pretensions can be of no avail unless the Jurisdiction of Congress or N. York at least can be established, they no otherwise deserve notice than as sources of calumny and influence in public councils; in both which respects it is the interest of Virga. that an antidote should be applied.

Mr. Randolph during his stay here was very industrious and successful in his researches into the territorial claims of all the States, and will be able to furnish you with many valuable hints. Your visit to Richmond in May will give him an opportunity.[11]

Our information from Europe has been peculiarly defective of late. It

---

9. William Nelson (1711-72) served as president of the governor's council of colonial Virginia, becoming acting governor for a year following Governor Botetourt's death in 1770. The "New Colony on the Ohio" was the proposed settlement to be made by the Walpole Company; see *ibid.*, p. 156.

10. Thomas Paine wrote *Public Good;* Samuel Wharton was the author of *Plain Facts.* See Merrill Jensen, "The Cession of the Old Northwest," *MVHR* 23 (1936): 46-47.

11. JM presumed that TJ would be elected to the House of Delegates, as, indeed, he had been on Apr. 11, but that news could not yet have reached Philadelphia. TJ declined to serve; see *PTJ,* VI, pp. 174-75, 179.

seems little probable that any decisive steps have been or will speedily be taken towards either a partial or general peace. The weight of the war will probably fall on the West Indies at least in the early part of the Campaign. Whither it will then be shifted is altogether uncertain. With very sincere regard I am Dr Sir Yr Obt Servt,

J MADISON JR.


## Jefferson to Madison

Ampthill in Chesterfeild Nov. 26, 1782[12]

DEAR SIR

Your favour by Colo. Basset is not yet come to hand.[13] The intimation through the Attorney I received the day before Colo. Bland's arrival by whom I am honoured with your's of the 14th inst.[14] It finds me at this place attending my family under inoculation. This will of course retard those arrangements of my domestic affairs which will of themselves take time and cannot be made but at home. I shall lose no time however in preparing for my departure; and from the calculation's I am at present enabled to make I suppose I cannot be in Philadelphia before the 20th. of December, and that possibly it may be the last of that month. Some days I must certainly pass there; as I could not propose to jump into the midst of a negotiation without a single article of previous information. From these data you will be enabled to judge of the chance of availing myself of his Excy. the Chev. de la Luzerne's kind offer to whom I beg you to present my thanks for his friendly attention and to let him know I shall use my best endeavors to be in time for the departure of his frigate. No circumstance of a private nature could induce me to hasten over the several obstacles to my departure more unremittingly than the hope of having the Chevalr. de Chattlux as a companion in my voiage.[15] A previous acquaintance with his worth and abilities had impressed me with an affection for him which under the then prospect of never seeing him again was perhaps imprudent. I am with very sincere esteem Dr. Sir Your affectionate friend and humble servt.


12. Ampthill was the estate of Archibald Cary near Richmond.

13. JM's letter of November [10?], 1782, to TJ has not been found.

14. Edmund Randolph was attorney general for Virginia. JM had asked him to inform TJ about the latter's reappointment to the peace mission to France; see JM to Edmund Randolph, Nov. 12, 1782, in *PJM,* V, pp. 272–73. JM's letter to TJ of Nov. 14, with the same news, has not been found.

15. JM's missing letter of Nov. 14 probably mentioned Luzerne's offer of transportation to France with him and Chastellux.

## Jefferson to Madison

Baltimore Jan. 31, 1783[16]

DEAR SIR

A gentleman returning from this place to Philadelphia gives me an opportunity of sending you a line. We reached Newport the evening of the day on which we left you.[17] There we were misled by an assurance that the lower ferry could not be crossed. We therefore directed our course for the Bald friar's: and thence to another ferry 6 miles above.[18] Between these two we lost two days, in the most execrable situation in point of accomodation and society which can be conceived. In short braving all weather and plunging thro' thick and thin we arrived here last night being the fifth from Philadelphia. I saw Monsr. de Villa-brun last night and augur him to be agreeable enough.[19] I learnt (not from him but others) that to embark their sick etc. will keep us three days. Having nothing particular to communicate I will give you an *anecdote* which possibly you may not have heard and which is related to me by *Major Franks*[20] who had it from *Doctr. Franklin* himself. I use the only cypher I can now get at using the paginal numbers in order and not as concerted. *Mr. Z. while at Paris had often pressed the Doctor to communicate to him his several negociations with the court of France which the Doctor avoided as decently as he* could.[21] *At length he received from Mr. Z. a very intemperate letter. He folded it up and put it into a pigeon hole. A second, third and so on to a fifth or sixth he received and disposed of in the same way. Finding no answer could be obtained by letter Mr. Z. paid him a personal visit and gave a loose to all the warmth of which he is susceptible. The Doctor replied I can no more answer this conversation of yours than the several impatient letters you have written me (taking them down from the pigeon hole). Call on me when you are cool and goodly humoured and I will justify myself to you.* They never saw each other afterwards. As I find no A. in the book erase the B in the first A.B. so that 1.1 may denote A. instead of AB.

---

16. This is the first letter in which TJ used the code that he and JM had perfected while they were in Philadelphia. For a discussion of the code, see *PTJ*, VI, pp. x-xi, and *PJM*, IV, pp. 177-79; see also Edmund C. Burnett, "Ciphers of the Revolutionary Period," *AHR* 22 (1916-17): 329-34. All of the italicized words in this letter were written in code. Unless otherwise indicated, I have consistently followed the decoding in *PTJ* or *PJM*.

17. Newport is a village south of Wilmington, Delaware.

18. Bald Friar's ferry was midway between Havre de Grace and Port Deposit, Maryland, on the Susquehanna River.

19. The chevalier de la Villebrune commanded the *Romulus,* the French man-of-war on which TJ hoped to sail.

20. Major David Franks was to accompany TJ to France as his secretary.

21. Brant, II, pp. 266-67, has identified "Mr. Z." as Ralph Izard, who was appointed commissioner to the court of Tuscany in 1777. Because the grand duchy of Tuscany would not receive him in his official capacity, he continued to reside in Paris, where he was a constant critic of Franklin. At the time this letter was written, Izard, a member of the South Carolina congressional delegation, resided at Mrs. House's boardinghouse, as did JM.

I met here the inclosed paper which be so good as to return with my compliments to Miss Kitty.[22] I apprehend she had not got a copy of it, and I retain it in my memory. Be pleased to present me very affectionately to the ladies and gentlemen whose pleasing society I lately had at Mrs. House's and believe me to be Your assured friend,

TH: JEFFERSON

## Jefferson to Madison

Baltimore Feb. 7 and 8, 1783

DEAR SIR

I write by this post to the Minister of foreign affairs, but will repeat to you the facts mentioned to him and some others improper for a public letter, and some reflections on them which can only be hazarded to the ear of friendship. The cold weather having set in the evening of the 30th. Ult. (being the same in which I arrived here) the Chevalr. de Ville-brun was obliged to fall down with his ship and the Guardaloupe to about twelve miles below this; and the ice has since cut off all correspondence with him till yesterday, when I got a boat and attempted a passage. There having passed a small boat before us we got about half way with tolerable ease, but the influx of the tide then happening the ice closed on us on every side and became impenetrable to our little vessel, so that we could get neither backwards nor forwards. We were finally relieved from this situation by a sloop which forced it's way down and put us on board the Romulus, where we were obliged to remain all night. The Chevalr. de Ville-brun communicated to me several letters of intelligence which deserves weight; by which we are informed that the enemy having no other employment at New York, have made our little fleet their sole object for some time, and have now cruising for us nothing less than

1. ship of 64. guns
4.            50
2.            40.
18. frigates from 24 to 30. guns, a most amazing force for such an object.
25

The merchants who intended to have sent their vessels out with us, have so far declined it, that two vessels only go with us. But they are unfortunately the greatest sluggards in the world. The Minister has given Ville-brun leave to remain if he thinks it expedient till the *Middle of March* but politely and kindly offered the Guardaloupe for my passage if I chose to run the risk.[23] I find that

---

22. "Miss Kitty" was Catherine Floyd, daughter of Congressman William Floyd of New York. JM fell in love with her in the fall of 1782; see ch. 7, below.

23. The italicized words in this sentence and below were written in code. The *Guadeloupe* was a British frigate that was scuttled at Yorktown, just before Cornwallis surrendered, to avoid capture

having laid ten months under water she got perfectly sobbed, insomuch that she sweats almost continually on the inside. In consequence of which her commander and several of the crew are now laid up with rheumatisms: but this I should have disregarded had it not appeared that it was giving to the enemy the ship and crew of a friend, and delaying myself in fact by endeavoring at too much haste. I therefore have not made use of the liberty given me by the minister. Ville-brun seems certain he shall not sail till the *first of March* and I confess to you I see no reason to suppose that when that time arrives the same causes will not place our departure as distant as it now seems. What then is to be done? I will mention the several propositions which occur with some reflections on each.

1. To go to Boston and embark thence. Would to God I had done this at first. I might now have been half-way across the Ocean. But it seems very late to undertake a journey of such length, thro' such roads, and such weather: and when I should get there some delay would still necessarily intervene.

Yet I am ready to undertake it if this shall be thought best.

2. To stay here with patience till our enemies shall think proper to clear our coast. There is no certain termination to this object. It may not be till the end of the war.

3. To fall down to York or Hampton and there wait those favourable circumstances of winds and storms which the winter season sometimes presents. This would be speedier than the 2d. but perhaps it may not be approved by the commander for reasons which may be good tho' unknown to me. Should this however be adopted we ought to be furnished by the Marine department with, or authorised to employ one or more swift sailing boats to go out of the capes occasionally and bring us intelligence to York or Hampton wherever we should be.

4. To ask a flag for me from the enemy and charter a vessel here. This would be both quickest and most certain. But perhaps it may be thought injurious to the dignity of the states, or perhaps be thought such a favour as Congress might not chuse to expose themselves to the refusal of. With respect to the last, nothing can be said: as to the first, I suppose, were history sought, many precedents might be found where one of the belligerent powers has received from the other, passports for their plenipotentiaries; and I suppose that Fitzgerald and Oswald got to Paris now under protection of a flag and passport.[24] However these are tender points and I would not wish the sensibility of Congress to be tried on my account, if it would be probably disagreeable.

---

by the French fleet. It was raised in 1782 and joined Villebrune's command; see *PJM,* IV, pp. 205-6.

24. Alleyne Fitzherbert and Richard Oswald were British peace commissioners in Paris who concluded a preliminary peace treaty with the United States on Nov. 30, 1782; see Richard B. Morris, *The Peacemakers: The Great Powers and American Independence* (New York, 1965), pp. 380-82, 409. TJ mistakenly used the name of Fitzgerald instead of Fitzherbert.

5. To await a truce. This cannot take place till after preliminaries signed, if then: and tho' these are not definitive, yet it must be evident that new instructions and new or perhaps inconsistent matter would be introduced with difficulty and discredit.

There is an idle report here of peace being actually concluded. This comes by the way of the W. Indies, and must probably be founded on the settlement of preliminaries, if it has any foundation at all.

Should you think that the interference of Congress might expedite my departure in any of the above ways or any other I have suggested these hasty reflections in hopes that you would do in it whatever you think right. I shall acquiesce in any thing, and if nothing further comes to me I shall endeavor to push the third proposition with the Commander, and if I fail in that shall pursue the 2d. I wish to hear from you as often as you have any thing new. I fear I shall be here long enough to receive many letters from you. My situation is not an agreeable one, and the less so as I contrast it with the more pleasing one I left so unnecessarily. Be so good as to present my esteem to the good ladies and gentlemen of your fireside and to accept yourself the warmest assurances of friendship from Dr. Sir Your friend and servt,

TH: JEFFERSON

Feb. 8.

The preceding was written the last night. Before I close my letter I will ask the favor of you to write me by the return of post and to let me have your own sentiments (whether any thing be, or be not determined authoritatively) which will have great weight with me. I confess that after another night's reflection the 4th. is the plan which appears to me best on the whole, and that the demand from New York is nothing more than what is made at the close of almost every war, where the one or the other power must have a passport: it is no more than asking a flag to New-York. Should this however be disapproved, the 3d seems the only remaining plan which promises any degree of expedition. Perhaps the minister may have a repugnance to venture the Romulus at York or Hampton, in which case if I could receive his approbation I should be willing to fall down there with the Guardaloupe alone and be in readiness to avail ourselves of a Northwesterly snow-storm or other favourable circumstance.

## Madison to Jefferson

Philadelphia Feb. 11, 1783

DEAR SIR

Your favor of the 31 of Jany. was safely brought me by Mr. Thomson. That of the 7. instant came by yesterdays mail. The anecdote related in the first was new to me; and if there were no other key, would sufficiently decypher the implacability of the party triumphed over. In answer to the second I can only say at this time that I feel deeply for your situation: that I approve of the choice you have made among its difficulties, and that every aid which can depend on me shall be excited to relieve you from them. Before I can take any step with propriety however it will be expedient to feel the sentiments of Congress, and to advise with some of my friends. The first point may possibly be brought about by your letter to the Secy. of F. A. which I suppose came too late yesterday to be laid before Congress, but which will no doubt be handed in this morning.[25]

The time of Congress since you left us has been almost exclusively spent on projects for a valuation of the land, as the federal articles require; and yet I do not find that we have got an inch forward towards the object. The mode of referring the task to the States which had at first the warmest and most numerous support seems to be in a manner abandoned; and nothing determinate is yet offered on the mode of effecting it without their intervention. The greatest misfortune perhaps attending the case is that a plan of some kind is made an indispensable preliminary to any other essay for the public relief. I much question whether a sufficient number of States will be found in favor of any [revenue] plan that can be devised, as I am sure that in the present temper of Congress a sufficient number cannot who will agree to tell their Constituents that the law of the Confederation cannot be executed, and to propose an amendment of it.[26] *Congress yesterday received* from *Mr. Adams several letters dated September* not remarkable for any thing unless it be a *display of his vanity, his prejudice against* the *French Court* and *his venom against Doctr. Franklin*. Other preparations for the post do not allow me to use more cypher at present.

I have a letter from Randolph dated Feby. 1. confirming the death of his aunt. You are acquainted no doubt with the course the estate is to take. He seems disposed in case he can make a tolerable compromise with his Father's creditors to resign his appointment under the State and go into the Legislature. His zeal for some continental arrangement as essential for the public honor and safety forms at least one of his motives, and I have added all the fuel to it in my power.

My neglect to write to you heretofore has proceeded from a hope that a letter would not find you at Baltimore; and no subject has occurred for one of sufficient importance to follow you. You shall henceforward hear from me as often as an occasion presents, until your departure forbids it. The Ladies and Gentlemen to whom I communicated your respects, return them with equal sincerity and the former as well as myself very affectionately include Miss Patsy in the object of them.[27] I am Dr. Sir Yr. Sincere friend,

J. MADISON JR.

25. Later that day, TJ's letter to Secretary of Foreign Affairs Robert Livingston was referred to a congressional committee that called off his mission; see *PTJ*, VI, pp. 239-40.
26. For a succinct summary of the revenue system adopted in 1783, see Jack Rakove, *The Beginnings of National Politics: An Interpretive History of the Continental Congress* (Cambridge, Mass., 1979), pp. 310-24. The italicized words in the next sentence were written in code.
27. Patsy was the nickname of TJ's daughter Martha, who was with him in Baltimore.

## Madison to Jefferson

Philadelphia Feb. 12, 1783[28]

MY DEAR SIR

I acknowledged yesterday by the post your two favors of the 30th. ult: and 7th. inst: I add this by Col: Jameson just to inform you that your letter to the Secy. of F. A. has been referred to a Committee consisting of Mr. Jones, Mr. Rutlidge and Mr. Wilson, who are to confer with Mr. Morris as Agent of Marine, and report to Congs. whether any and what remedy can be applied to your embarrassments. I made the first acquainted with the ideas suggested in your last letter, and he will take care to lead the attention of his Colleagues and of Mr. M[orris] to them as far as may be requisite and proper. Mr. Livingston was not here when your letter to him came to hand: but he is now returned. I will take occasion to speak with him before the next post, and will give you the result as well as of the commitment of your letter, if any thing shall have come of it. In the mean time accept of my unfeigned regards.

J. MADISON JR

## Madison to Jefferson

Philadelphia Feb. 13, 1783

DEAR SIR

The Chevr. de la Luzerne having just given me notice that he shall send an Express to the Romulus in ½ an hour I sieze the opportunity of inclosing a copy of the British Kings speech which presages a speedy establishment of peace. What effect this circumstance may have on your mission is at present uncertain. For myself I cannot think that any thing short of a final and authentic ratification ought to be listened to in that view. But I am told that it is the opinion of Mr. Morris that no vessel will sail from any American port whilst the critical uncertainty continues. Whether any and what changes may be produced in the orders to the Romulus will be known from the Commander. Adieu.

J. MADISON JR.

## Jefferson to Madison

Baltimore Feb. 14, 1783

DEAR SIR

Patsy putting the inclosed into my hands obliges me to make a separate letter of it, that while I give it the protection of your address I may yet pay it's

---

28. This letter is not in *PTJ*, but it is printed in *PJM*, VI, p. 228.

postage.²⁹ I suspect by the superscription (which I saw before Majr. Franks amended it) and by what I know of Patsy's hieroglyphical writing that Miss Polly must get an interpreter from Egypt.³⁰ Be so good as to remind the ladies and gentlemen of the house of my affection for them. I am particularly obliged to Mr. Carrol for an introduction to his relation near this, with whom I have been able to pass agreeably some of my heavy hours.³¹ I shall write to E. Randolph on the subject of his going into the legislature and use my interest to promote it. I hope you will be there too when you can no longer be in any more important place. I am with sincere esteem Dr Sir Your friend and servt,

TH: JEFFERSON

## Jefferson to Madison

Baltimore Feb. 14, 1783

DEAR SIR

Yours of the 11th. came to hand last night. *From³² what you mention in your letter I suppose the newspapers must be wrong when they say that Mr. Adams, had taken up his abode with Dr. Franklin. I am nearly at a loss to judge how he will act in the negotiation. He hates Franklin, he hates Jay, he hates the French, he hates the English. To whom will he adhere? His vanity is a lineament in his character which had entirely escaped me. His want of taste I had observed. Notwithstanding all this he has a sound head on substantial points, and I think he has integrity. I am glad therefore that he is of the commission and expect he will be useful in it. His dislike of all parties, and all men, by balancing his prejudices, may give the same fair play to his reason as would a general benevolence of temper. At any rate honesty may be extracted even from poisonous weeds.*

*My stay here has given me opportunities of making some experiments on my amanuensis Franks, perhaps better than I may have in France. He appears to have a good enough heart, an understanding somewhat better than common but too little guard over his lips. I have marked him particularly in the company of women where he loses all power over himself and becomes almost frenzied. His temperature would not be proof against their allurements were such to be employed as engines against him. This is in some measure the vice of his age but it seems to be increased also by his peculiar constitution.*

I wrote to the Chevalier de Ville Brun proposing his falling down to York or Hampton which was one of the measures I suggested in my letter to you, and was the most eligible except that of the flag, in my own opinion. His

---

29. TJ's letters were franked, but he paid postage on his daughter's.
30. Miss Polly was Kitty Floyd's sister.
31. Daniel Carroll was a member of Congress from Maryland; his relation was his cousin, Charles Carroll of Mount Clare, near Baltimore.
32. The italicized words in this letter were written in code.

answer, dated Feb. 12. is in these words. 'Je serois bien de l'avis proposé a votre Excellence d'aller mouiller a York ou Hampton pour etre a portee de profiter des premiers vents de Nord Ouest qui me mettroient loin de la côte dans la nuit, sourtout si je n'avois pas de convoy a conserver. Mais des batiments entrès aujourd'hui raportent avoir eté chassés par quatre fregates jusque sur la Cap Charles et avoir vu au mouillage de Linhaven bay un vaisseau et un fregate qui ont appareillés et pris un Brig qui navigoit avec eux. De plus York et Hampton n'ont pas un canon monté, si l'ennemi, tres superieur, entreprenoit de venir nous y forcer, il y auroit peu de sureté.

Peut etre conviendroit-il autant d'attendre, comme le propose M. de la Luzerne, jusqu'au Mois prochain, des nouvelles d'Europe, ou l'arrivée d'une division des Antilles promise par M. de Vaudreuil, ou bien encore quel'ennemi fatigué ne fut obligé de rentrer a New-York.'[33] *The last basis [basket] is relish and furnishes matter for doubt how far the departure of the Romulus is a decided measure.*[34] *It seems not unlikely.*[35] *So for a purpose wherein time is the most pressing circumstance the idea of going in her is to be abandoned.* To go to Boston would be the most œconomical plan. But it would be *five weeks* from my leaving this place before I could expect to sail from thence. Of course I may from here be *in France* by the time I should be sailing from *Boston*. *Five weeks,* in a crisis of *negotiation* may be much. Should I accept of the *Guadaloupe* and she should be lost, it would under present circumstances draw censure. Moreover in this or the former case, besides losing the vessel, what will be my situation? That of a prisoner certainly. From what has been done in Laurence's case they would not release me; in expectation of a high exchange; or if they did, it would only be on parole, in which case I could neither act nor communicate.[36] This plan would have in it's favour œconomy and a possibility (a bare one) of dispatch. That of the flag still appears best. It is favoured by the circumstances of dispatch, safety, and the preservation of my papers. But when I think of the expence I feel myself annihilated in comparison with it. A vessel may be got

---

33. "Indeed I would adopt your Excellency's suggestion to proceed to an anchorage at York or Hampton where I could avail myself of the first northwest winds to take me at night far off the coast, especially if I would not have to protect a convoy. But several vessels arriving today report that they were pursued by four frigates even within Cape Charles and that a Brig in their company was captured by a vessel and frigate which had left and returned to their anchorage in Linhaven bay. Moreover, without a serviceable cannon at York or Hampton, we would have little security there, if the very much stronger enemy should try to approach and board us.

"Perhaps, as M. de La Luzerne advised, it would be better to wait until next month for news from Europe, or for the arrival from the West Indies of the fleet promised by M. de Vaudreuil, or, better still, for the wearied enemy to be obliged to return to New York"; see *PJM,* VI, p. 239.

34. The editors of *PJM* insert "basket" for Boyd's conjectural "basis" and state that TJ's metaphor meant that "La Villebrune's final suggestion was a condiment designed to conceal unpalatable facts"; see *ibid.,* p. 240.

35. The editors of *PJM* decode the word "unlikely" as "unlucky."

36. Henry Laurens, who was captured by the British in 1780 en route to the Netherlands to negotiate a loan and a commercial treaty, was imprisoned in the Tower of London until he was exchanged for Lord Cornwallis at the end of 1781.

here, but I question if for less than *a thousand* or *two thousand* pounds. Besides can a passport be obtained from New York without naming the vessel, the crew etc.? If not it would take long to furnish these circumstances from hence. The Delaware would be more eligible in that case. Otherwise this place is. If this should be adopted, what would be the extent of the protection of the flag to the papers I should carry? These, so far as this question would affect them, would be of three descriptions. 1. my own commission, instructions and other documents relative to my mission. 2. public letters to the Consuls, ministers and others on other business. 3. private letters. I have no means of satisfying myself on these points here. If therefore this measure should be adopted I should thank you for your opinion on them, as you can, where you are doubtful, make enquiry of others. I am exceedingly fatigued with this place, as indeed I should [be] with any other where I had neither occupation nor amusement. I am very particularly indebted here to the politeness and hospitality of Genl. La Vallette who obliges me to take refuge in his quarters from the tedium of my own, the latter half of every day. You are indebted to him too as I should make my long letters much longer and plague you with more cypher were I confined at home all day. I beg you to be assured of my warmest wishes for your happiness.

TH: JEFFERSON

Feb. 15. [Feb. 14] 9. o'clock P.M. After sealing up this letter I received yours of yesterday inclosing the King's speech, for which I thank you much. The essential information conveyed to us by that is that the preliminary for our independance (which we before knew to have been agreed between the plenipotentiaries) has been provisionally ratified by him. I have thought it my duty to write the inclosed letter which after reading you will be so good as to stick a wafer in and deliver. I wish no supposed inclination of mine to stand in the way of a free change of measure if Congress should think the public interest required it. The argument of œconomy is much strengthened by the impossibility (now certain) of going but in an express vessel. The principal matters confided to me were. 1. the new instruction; which perhaps may have been sent by Count Rochambeau,[37] or may yet be sent. 2. the details of the financier's department which Mr. Morris not chusing to trust to paper had communicated verbally. These in the event of peace or truce may safely go in paper. 3. the topics which supp[ort] our right to the fisheries, to the Western country, and the navigation of the Missisipi. The first of these is probably settled: the two latter should only come into discussion in the Spanish negociation, and therefore would only have been the subject of private conversation with Mr. Jay, whose good sense and knolege of the subject will hardly need any suggestions.

I forgot to mention to you in my letter that Mr. Nash arrived here the day

---

37. General Rochambeau sailed for France in Jan. 1783.

before yesterday on his way to N. Carolina, and that Mr. Blunt is not yet arrived, but is weekly expected.[38] I am yours affectionately,

TH: JEFFERSON

## Madison to Jefferson

Philadelphia Feb. 15, 1783

DEAR SIR

The Committee, to whom was referred your letter to Secretary Livingston, reported to Congress yesterday that they had conferred with Mr. Morris who was of opinion that no vessel would sail from American ports after the arrival of the British King's speech until the suspence produced by it should be removed, and that if your immediate embarkation were still wished by Congress it would be proper to obtain for that purpose a Frigate from the Chevr. de la Luzerne. He informed the Committee that there was a fit vessel in this river which would have sailed for France but for the prospect of peace afforded by the Speech; and which I suppose will still proceed if that prospect should fail. The effect of this information to Congress and of a request from the Committee to be instructed on the subject was, a resolution directing the Secy. of F. A. to acquaint you that it was the pleasure of Congress, considering the present situation of things, that you should suspend your voyage until their further instruction. This resolution will I suppose be forwarded by the post which conveys this. I do not undertake to give any advice as to the steps which may now be proper for you, but I indulge with much pleasure the hope that a return to this place for the present may be the result of your own deliberations.[39] I am Dear Sir with Sincerity Yr. friend and Servt.,

J. MADISON JR.

## Madison to Jefferson

Philadelphia Feb. 18, 1783

DEAR SIR

Your two favors of the 14th. one of them inclosing a letter to Miss Floyd were received by yesterday's mail.

The last paper from N.Y. as the inclosed will shew you has brought us another token of the approach of peace. It is somewhat mysterious neverthe-

---

38. Abner Nash and William Blount were members of the North Carolina congressional delegation.
39. TJ and his daughter returned to Philadelphia on Feb. 26, 1783; see *PTJ*, VI, p. 253.

less that the preliminaries with America should be represented by Secy. Townsend as *actually signed* and those with France as *to be signed,* as also that the signing of the latter would constitute a general peace.[40] I have never been without my apprehensions that some tricks would be tried by the British Court notwithstanding their exterior fairness of late, and these apprehensions have been rendered much more serious by the *tenor of some letters* which *you have seen* and particularly by the *intimation of minister of France to Mr. Livingston.*[41] These considerations have made me peculiarly solicitous that your mission should be pursued as long as a possibility remained of *your sharing in* the *object of it.*

Your *portrait of your am*[*anuensis*] is I conceive drawn to *the life.* For all un*confidential services he is a convenient instrument.* For any*thing farther* ne *sutor ultra* cre*pidam* [let the cobbler stick to his last].

The turn which your case has for the present taken makes it unnecessary to answer particularly the parts of your letter which relate to the expediency of a flag and the extent of its protection. On the first point I am inclined to think that the greatest objection with Congress would have been drawn from the risk of a denial. On the second I have no precise knowledge, but the principle would seem to extend to every thing appertaining to the mission as well as to the person of the Minister. Nor can I conceive a motive to the latter indulgence which would admit of a refusal of the former.

I am impatient to hear of the plan which is to dispose of you during the suspense in which you are placed. If Philada. as I flatter myself, is to be your abode, your former quarters will await you. I am Dear Sir Yr. Affecte. friend,

J. MADISON JR.

An answer to Miss Patsy's letter is in the same mail with this.

40. The italicized words in this sentence were underlined by TJ rather than encoded.
41. The italicized words in this sentence and in the rest of the letter were in code.

# 7

# FROM WAR TO PEACE, 1783

WHILE JEFFERSON WAS IN PHILADELPHIA preparing for his diplomatic mission, he watched Madison fall in love with Catherine ("Kitty") Floyd, the teen-aged daughter of Congressman and Mrs. William Floyd of New York, whose family roomed at Mrs. Mary House's boardinghouse with Madison, Jefferson, and a covey of congressmen. After Jefferson moved to Baltimore to await transportation to France, he asked Madison to convey his "compliments to Miss Kitty," expressing his "warmest wishes for your happiness."[1] When his mission was suspended, he returned to Mrs. House's, where he encouraged the romance after conversations with Miss Floyd confirmed *"that she possessed every sentiment"* in Madison's favor. Indeed, the resident matchmaker freely admitted his hopes that Madison would marry the vivacious girl, settle in Virginia, and *"give me a neighbour whose worth I rate high."* Such a match, he told his friend, *"will render you happier than you can possibly be in a singl*[e] *state."*[2]

Once Jefferson had returned to Monticello, Madison pursued his love affair, became engaged, made *"definitive"* wedding plans, and set the date for the fall, after his term in Congress would have expired. "The *interest which your friendship takes on this occasion in my happiness,"* he confessed to Jefferson, *"is a pleasing proof that* the *disposetions which I feel are reciprocal."*[3]

A week later, Madison accompanied Miss Floyd and her parents, en route to their home in New York, as far as Brunswick, New Jersey.[4] For the next three months, he planned a quick visit to Virginia to make arrangements for housing before going to New York for the wedding. But Madison was never to see Kitty again. Once she was home, she broke the engagement with "a profession of indifference," as Madison told Jefferson, one of "several dilatory cir-

1. TJ to JM, Jan. 31, 1783, above, and Feb. 14, 1783, above.
2. TJ to JM, Apr. 14, 1783, below. The italicized words in this chapter were written in code.
3. JM to TJ, Apr. 22, 1783, below.
4. JM to TJ, May 6, 1783, below. For an account of Madison's courtship, see Brant, II, pp. 283–87.

cumstances on which I had not calculated." "It would be improper by this communication to send particular explanations," he wrote, but he added philosophically that it was "one of those incidents to which such affairs are liable."[5]

Jefferson also tried to be philosophical about the broken romance: "I sincerely lament the misadventure which has happened, from whatever cause it may have happened. Should it be final however, the world still presents the same and many other resources of happiness, and you possess many within yourself. Firmness of mind and unintermitting occupations will not long leave you in pain. No event," he added, "has been more contrary to my expectations, and these were founded on what I thought a good knowledge of the ground. But of all machines ours is the most complicated and inexplicable."[6]

To take Madison's mind off his private misery, Jefferson pelted him with questions about public policy: "What is become of the mutineers? What of the Secretaryship of foreign affairs? What of the commercial treaty with Gr. Britain?"[7] These questions and a complicated cluster of issues involving demobilization, foreign affairs, and the perennial problem of finance dominated the period of transition from war to peace in 1783. For Madison and Jefferson, the central issue confronting the United States was the replacement of the eight-year bond of wartime cooperation with a peacetime program that would preserve the Confederation and allow the states and Congress to adopt adequate revenue measures and establish a program to ensure domestic tranquility. Both men agreed on the need to strengthen the Confederation. Both also knew that this goal called for the minor miracle of unanimity that wartime necessity had failed to produce. Madison was convinced that unless the powers of Congress were extended and the finances of the Confederation provided for, "a dissolution of the union will be inevitable."[8] Jefferson thought that the problem could be solved by "strengthening the band which connects us. We have substituted a Congress of deputies from every state to perform this task," he wrote while camped out in Baltimore, "but we have done nothing that will enable them to enforce their decisions." He was especially worried about "the pride of independance taking deep and dangerous hold on the hearts of the individual states." For that reason, he urged that the Confederation be strengthened "before we forget the advantages of union, or acquire a degree of ill-temper against each other which will daily increase the obstacles to that good work."[9]

Madison took the lead in Congress to extend the powers of the Confederation, which could neither tax nor compel the states to meet congressional

---

5. JM to TJ, Aug. 11, 1783, below.
6. TJ to JM, Aug. 31, 1783, below.
7. *Ibid.*
8. JM to Edmund Randolph, Feb. 25, 1783, in *PJM,* VI, p. 287.
9. TJ to Edmund Randolph, Feb. 15, 1783, in *PTJ,* VI, pp. 248–49.

requisitions. Instead of trying to implement his view that Congress had an implied power to coerce delinquent states to meet revenue requests, however, he revived a revenue proposal of 1781. He had then supported a move to amend the Articles by giving Congress the power to lay a 5 percent duty on imports. Although twelve states ratified the proposal, refusal by Rhode Island in 1782 "pretty thoroughly blasted" any hope for federal revenue from that source, according to Madison.[10] Dismayed but not dissuaded, Congress decided "to persist in the attempt for permanent revenue" and appointed Madison, Alexander Hamilton of New York, and Thomas FitzSimons of Pennsylvania to report on additional revenue measures.[11] After three years in Congress, Madison concluded that continued reliance on the states for revenue constituted a growing danger to the federal Union. "Experience," he declared, "has sufficiently demonstrated that a punctual and unfailing compliance by 13 separate and independent Governments with periodical demands of money from Congress, can never be reckoned upon with the certainty requisite to satisfy our present creditors, or to tempt others to become our creditors in future." He, therefore, pressed for "a general revenue operating throughout the United States under the superintendence of Congress." The alternative would be continued reliance on state requisitions or state diversion of "the revenue required by Congress to the payment of its own Citizens and troops, creditors of the United States." But if the states were to assume this federal function, he asked, "what then would become of the confederation? What would be the authority of Congress? What the tie by which the States could be held together?"[12]

In February, Madison introduced a series of proposals that became central to the revenue system of 1783.[13] His ideas were referred to a committee of five, and on March 6 he reported his comprehensive plan for "restoring and obtaining from the States substantial funds for funding the whole debt of the United States."[14] After Congress enacted a much amended version of his "Report on Restoring Public Credit," Madison wrote an eloquent "Address to the States" recommending approval, which Congress adopted by a unanimous vote. Each of the states, he argued, needed to ratify the plan for the sake of "justice, good faith, honor," and the preservation of "the harmony and tranquility of the Confederacy."[15]

To meet the objections of Rhode Island and states' rights advocates, the

10. JM to Edmund Randolph, Nov. 19, 1782, in *PJM,* V, p. 289.

11. See JM, "Notes on Debates in Congress," Dec. 24, 1782, *ibid.,* p. 442. For a lucid account of Rhode Island's opposition to the impost, see Irwin H. Polishook, *Rhode Island and the Union, 1774–1795* (Evanston, Ill., 1969), pp. 53–80.

12. JM, "Notes on Debates in Congress," Jan. 28, 1783, in *PJM,* VI, pp. 144–45.

13. JM, "Notes on Debates in Congress," Feb. 21, 1783, *ibid.,* pp. 270–74.

14. See JM, "Report on Restoring Public Credit," *ibid.,* pp. 311–16.

15. See JM, "Notes on Debates in Congress," Apr. 25 and 26, 1783, and his "Address to the States by Congress," *ibid.,* pp. 487–98.

congressional plan, which again proposed a 5 percent impost on foreign importations, limited the grant of power to twenty-five years and specified that the duties be collected by state officials according to regulations drafted by Congress. The plan also requested that the states raise annually for twenty-five years an additional $1.5 million from whatever sources they preferred. Then Madison added inducements of interest to different states, which he described to Jefferson as "bait" to gain the concurrence of all.[16] To meet the demands of the "landless states," those with western land claims that had not yet ceded land to Congress should do so while those that had ceded land should revise or reaffirm the cessions already made. For states that had been overrun by the enemy, the plan proposed to have their costs of war abated. Congress would also assume "all reasonable military expences separately incurred by the States." Finally, the Articles of Confederation should be modified to make population rather than land values the basis for apportioning federal expenses, with slaves being enumerated according to a three-fifths ratio—the first appearance in American history of that fateful concept.[17]

Madison had briefed Jefferson on the revenue plan while they were together in Philadelphia, and he forwarded a progress report while Jefferson was in Baltimore.[18] When Jefferson's mission was suspended in February, the disappointed diplomat hurried from Baltimore and arrived in Philadelphia on the day Madison called for the comprehensive revenue plan.[19] Together from the end of February until mid-April, the two spent most of their time discussing state and national politics. Even the possibility, or perhaps the likelihood, of his returning to Congress was, as Jefferson recalled, "sometimes the subject of *our conversation*."[20]

When Madison presented his revenue report to Congress on March 6, he also prepared a three-page summary so that Jefferson might understand the tensions and conflict of state interests affected by the measure.[21] On the eve of Jefferson's departure from Philadelphia, Madison annotated for his friend a printed copy of the "Report on Restoring Public Credit" to indicate the changes that had been made by Congress since he had submitted his original proposal.[22] But he noted that during the debate on the bill for funding "the

---

16. JM to TJ, Apr. 22, 1783, below.

17. *PJM*, VI, pp. 311-16, 397-402, 407-8, 424-25. See also Jack Rakove, *The Beginnings of National Politics: An Interpretive History of the Continental Congress* (Cambridge, Mass., 1979), pp. 310-24, and Harold A. Ohline, "Republicanism and Slavery: Origins of the Three-Fifths Clause in the United States Constitution," *WMQ* 28 (1971): 563-84.

18. JM to TJ, Feb. 11, 1783, above.

19. *PTJ*, VI, p. 253, and *PJM*, VI, pp. 289-97.

20. TJ to JM, May 7, 1783, below. They also devised a new code to replace the more laborious one that they had perfected in January; see *PTJ*, VI, p. 262, and *PJM*, VI, p. 459.

21. JM's memorandum for TJ on a revenue plan, [ca. Mar. 6, 1783], below.

22. See JM's annotations for TJ on the "Report for Restoring Public Credit," [ca. Mar. 26, 1783], below.

National debt," Congress had dropped two of the major features—abatement for war-ravaged states and federal assumption of state debts—and he expressed his fear that the plan as passed held "no bait for Virg[ini]a."[23]

Although Madison regretted the rejection of abatement and assumption—he called Jefferson's attention to "the mutilation of the plan"[24]—he wrote a powerful "Address to the States" that Congress adopted unanimously, a poignant plea to establish "the provision recommended for the national debt." A firm financial footing, based on "justice, good faith, honor, gratitude, and all the other Qualities which ennoble the character of a nation," would set an example "which can not but have the most favorable influence on the rights of mankind."[25]

Despite the plan's shortcomings, Madison told Jefferson, it had three necessary ingredients, and he hoped "not only that the revenue may be established, but that the fœderal rule of dividing the burdens may be changed [from land values to population], and the territorial disputes accomodated."[26] Jefferson agreed with his friend, and on his trip from Philadelphia to Monticello he stopped in Richmond to try to persuade state legislators to support the Madisonian measures for strengthening Congress's powers. Although he regretted Congress's failure to include federal assumption of state war debts—it was, he wrote, "one palatable ingredient at least in the pill *we* were to swallow"—he urged ratification of the revenue plan and listed for Madison the delegates favoring acceptance or rejection. Patrick Henry, he noted, "as usual is *involved in mystery:* should the *popular tide run strongly* in either *direction, he* will fall *in with it.* Should it *not,* he will have a *struggle between his enmity to the Lees, and his enmity* to everything *which may give influence to* Cong[res]s."[27]

Less than a month later, Jefferson wrote Madison that "Mr. Henry has declared in favour of the impost. This will ensure it."[28] But within two weeks, Henry was vascillating, and Jefferson's hopes for adoption "of the Congressional propositions here have lessened exceedingly."[29] By August, only Delaware had ratified the revenue plan "in toto," Madison told his friend; "New Jersey and Maryland have adopted the impost, the other funds recommended being passed for one year only by one of these States, and postponed by the other." He confessed that "this picture of our affairs is not a flattering one," but he had not given up "the consolations of hope."[30]

To establish proper arrangements for the transition from war to peace,

23. JM to TJ, Apr. 22, 1783, below, and May 13, 1783, below.

24. JM to TJ, May 20, 1783, below.

25. JM, "Address to the States by Congress," Apr. 26, 1783, in *PJM,* VI, pp. 488–94.

26. JM to TJ, May 20, 1783, below.

27. TJ to JM, May 7, 1783, below.

28. TJ to JM, June 1, 1783, below.

29. TJ to JM, June 17, 1783, below.

30. JM to TJ, Aug. 11, 1783, below. For the lengthy debate over an impost, see Jackson Turner Main, *The Antifederalists: Critics of the Constitution, 1781–1788* (Chapel Hill, 1965), pp. 72–102, and, by the same author, *Political Parties before the Constitution* (Chapel Hill, 1973), *passim.*

Congress appointed Madison and four other members to recommend plans for a peacetime government. "The object," he said, "was to provide a system for foreign affairs, for Indian affairs, for military and naval peace establishments; and also to carry into execution the regulation of weights and measures and other articles of the Confederation not attended to during the war."[31]

Army reorganization—everything from back pay for wartime service to a peacetime establishment—dominated the early discussions, raising "several nice and interesting questions," as Madison informed Jefferson. For instance, were the soldiers who had enlisted for the war entitled to a discharge before a definitive peace treaty replaced the preliminary one? "At least half of the army under Genl. Washington," Madison observed, "are under this description and are urgent for such a construction of their engagements."[32] But before being discharged, the soldiers wanted to be paid. Jefferson had been in Philadelphia when Congress received a memorial from the army complaining that "the uneasiness of the Soldiers, for want of pay, is great and dangerous."[33] He and Madison undoubtedly discussed "the discontents and designs of the army" in relation to the revenue plan for funding the national debt.[34] In June, when a group of mutinous troops marched from Lancaster to Philadelphia and surrounded Congress Hall, demanding a settlement of accounts, Congress abandoned Philadelphia as the capital of the new nation, going to Princeton, as Madison told Jefferson, because of the failure of Pennsylvania authorities "to exert force against insults offered to Congress."[35] One month later, Madison reported that "Congress remain at Princeton utterly undecided both as to their ultimate seat and their intermediate residence." But the discussions about the location of a new national capital soon became heated. To accommodate what one critic called "the itinerant Genius of Congress," a majority in the fall of 1783 proposed a plan to construct two capitals, one on the Delaware River and the other on the Potomac, with Congress in the meantime alternating meetings between Annapolis and Trenton.[36]

During his final months in Congress, Madison showed particular interest

---

31. JM, "Notes on Debates in Congress," Apr. 4, 1783, in *PJM,* VI, pp. 432–33. See Merrill Jensen, "The Politics of Demobilization," in *The New Nation: A History of the United States during the Confederation, 1781–1789* (New York, 1950), pp. 54–84, for an excellent account of that subject.

32. JM to TJ, Apr. 22, 1783, below.

33. *PJM,* V, pp. 474–75.

34. JM used this phrase in his letter to Edmund Randolph on Feb. 25, 1783, the day before TJ returned to Philadelphia from Baltimore; see *ibid.,* VI, p. 286.

35. JM to TJ, July 17, 1783, below. TJ was so outraged by the failure of the Pennsylvania authorities to protect Congress that he drafted a resolution on the privileges and immunities of Congress, asserting that "the United States in Congress assembled represent the sovereignty of the whole Union" and should "on all occasions have precedence of all other bodies and persons"; their right to deliberate "unawed and undisturbed," therefore, should not be violated. See *PTJ,* VI, pp. 368–69.

36. JM to TJ, Aug. 11, 1783, below; *Boston American Herald,* Apr. 5, 1784, cited in Rakove, p. 335. See also Eugene R. Sheridan and John M. Murrin, eds., *Congress at Princeton: Being the Letters of Charles Thomson to Hannah Thomson, June–October 1783* (Princeton, 1985).

in two measures: state territorial cessions to Congress and the permanent location of the nation's capital. "I am utterly unable to foretell how either of these points will be determined," he told Jefferson. "It is not impossible that an effective vote may be found attainable on neither; in which case the Winter must be spent in this village where the public business can neither be conveniently done, the members of Congress decently provided for, nor those connected with Congress provided for at all." On accommodations in Princeton, he spoke from experience, complaining that "I am obliged to write in a position that scarcely admits the use of any of my limbs: Mr. Jones and myself being lodged in a room not 10 feet square and without a single accommodation for writing."[37]

As Madison's term in Congress drew to a close, the Virginia assembly elected Jefferson to Congress "at the head of the delegation," according to Edmund Randolph, "not without his approbation." Madison was "exceedingly pleased to find Mr. Jefferson's name at the head of the new Delegation."[38] To prepare for his new assignment, Jefferson asked to peruse Madison's "Congressional notes with leave to take notes from them, as they will better than any thing else possess me of the business I am to enter on."[39] Madison, who had already prepared a memorandum for Jefferson on the revenue plan, now sketched another on Congress's place of residence.[40]

Madison had earlier asked Jefferson to ascertain if Chancellor George Wythe, a leading member of Congress in 1776, had preserved any "of his amendments or notes on the Confederation."[41] Although Wythe had not, Jefferson had, and he sent Madison copies of his record of "the debates in Congress on the subjects of Independance, Voting in Congress, and the Quotas of money to be required from the states." He also enclosed "a copy of the original of the declaration of Independance" as well as "the alterations it underwent."[42]

As Madison began his preparations for leaving Congress, he summarized things for Jefferson in August and September. After moving to Princeton, Congress had transacted "very little business of moment . . . , except a ratification of the Treaty with Sweden. In particular nothing [has] been done as to a foreign establishment." Indeed, the position of secretary of foreign affairs remained vacant from May 1783, when Robert R. Livingston resigned because

---

37. JM to TJ, Sept. 20, 1783, below. Joseph Jones was a delegate from Virginia.

38. Edmund Randolph to JM, June 28, 1783, in *PJM,* VII, p. 201, and JM to Edmund Randolph, June 17, 1783, *ibid.,* p. 159.

39. TJ to JM, Aug. 31, 1783, below. TJ had examined the notes earlier that year in preparation for his mission to France; see JM to TJ, Sept. 20, 1783, below.

40. See JM's notes for TJ on Congress's place of residence [ca. Oct. 14, 1783], below. Also see Lawrence D. Cress, "Whither Columbia: Congressional Residence and the Politics of the New Nation, 1776-1787," *WMQ* 32 (1975): 581-600.

41. See TJ to JM, May 7, 1783, below.

42. TJ to JM, June 1, 1783, below.

of the low pay, until December 1784, when John Jay succeeded him. "With regard to an internal peace establishment," he continued, "though it has been treated with less inattention, it has undergone little discussion."[43]

In his final appraisal for Jefferson, Madison noted that "the supposed contrariety of interests among the states and the impotence of the fœderal Government" had led Great Britain to refuse to negotiate a commercial treaty with the United States, since "the ready admission she found into our commerce without paying any price for it has suggested the policy of aiming at the entire benefit of it, and at the same time saving the carriage of the W[est] India trade[,] the price she at first bid for it. . . . The other nations of Europe seem to have more honorable views towards our commerce, sundry advances having been made to our Ministers on that subject."

"Congress," he concluded, "have come to no decision even as yet on any of the great branches of the peace establishment. The military branch is supported and quickened by the presence of the Commander in chief but without any prospect of a hasty issue. The department of foreign affairs both internal and external remains as it has long done. The election of a Secretary has been an order of the day for many months without a vote being taken. The importance of the marine department has been diminished by the sale of almost all the Vessels belonging to the U.S. The department of Finance is an object of almost daily attack and will be reduced to its crisis on the final resignation of Mr. [Robert] M[orris] which will take place in a few months. The War office is connected with the Military establishment and will be regulated I suppose in conformity to what that may be. Among other subjects which divide Congress, their Constitutional authority touching such an establishment in time of peace is one. Another still more puzzling is the precise jurisdiction proper for Congress within the limits of their permanent seat. As these points may possibly remain undecided till Nov[embe]r[,] I mention them particularly that your aid may be prepared."[44]

While Jefferson was supporting Madison's moves to strengthen the Confederation, he also revived his efforts to revise the Virginia Constitution of 1776. During his stopover in Richmond in May 1783 to push Madison's reforms, Jefferson concluded that there would soon be a call for a convention to remodel the state constitution. Within four weeks after his arrival at Monticello on May 15, 1783, he had drafted a new fundamental law for Virginia and enclosed it in his letter of June 17 to Madison.[45] Jefferson later appended it to his *Notes on the State of Virginia,* observing that the constitution of 1776 had been "formed when we were new and unexperienced in the science of government. It was the first too which was formed in the whole United States.

---

43. JM to TJ, Aug. 11, 1783, below.
44. JM to TJ, Sept. 20, 1783, below. The congressional year began on the first Monday in November; see W. C. Ford *et al.,* eds., *The Journals of the Continental Congress, 1774–1789,* 34 vols. (Washington, 1904–37), XIX, p. 215.
45. TJ to JM, June 17, 1783, below, and JM to TJ, July 17, 1783, below.

No wonder then that time and trial have discovered very capital defects in it." The chief defects were the lack of ratification by the people and the failure to make the legislative, executive, and judicial branches sufficiently separate and distinct. According to the former governor of the Old Dominion, that meant that "all the powers of government, legislative, executive, and judiciary, result to the legislative body. The concentrating these in the same hands is precisely the definition of despotic government. . . . An *elective despotism*," he concluded "was not the government we fought for" in the American Revolution; it would protect neither the public money nor public liberty.[46]

––––––––––––––––––––– THE LETTERS –––––––––––––––––––––

*Madison's Memorandum for Jefferson on a Revenue Plan*

[Philadelphia ca. Mar. 6, 1783]

Plan proposed consists of 1st. permanent revenue. 2. abatements in favor of the States distressed by the war—3. common mass of all reasonable expences incurred by the States without sanction of Congress—4. territorial cessions.[1]

Manner in which the interests of the several States will be affected by these objects.[2]

He had in view the followg. objects—1. the abatements proposed by Mr. Hamilton. 2. a transfer into the common mass of expences of all separate expences incurred by the States in their particular defence. 3. an acquisition to the U. States of the vacant territory. The plan thus extended would affect the interest of the States as follows. viz.; N. Hampshire would approve the estab-

46. Thomas Jefferson, *Notes on the State of Virginia by Thomas Jefferson*, ed. William Peden (Chapel Hill, 1955; rpt. New York, 1982), pp. 118–21. In introducing his draft in his *Notes*, TJ added the following:

> In the Summer of the Year 1783, *it was expected, that the* ASSEMBLY OF VIRGINIA *would call a* CONVENTION *for the Establishment of a* CONSTITUTION. *The following* DRAUGHT *of a* FUNDAMENTAL CONSTITUTION *for the* COMMONWEALTH OF VIRGINIA *was then prepared, with a Design of being proposed in such Convention, had it taken place.*

The Virginia Constitution of 1776 was not revised until the constitutional convention of 1829; see *PTJ,* VI, pp. 278–82. For JM's critique of TJ's draft constitution, one that found fault with many of its provisions, see Madison's Observations on Jefferson's Draft of a Constitution for Virginia, [New York, ca. Oct. 15, 1788], below.

1. When JM first called for a comprehensive revenue plan on Feb. 26, 1783, he wrote a long footnote about his proposal in his "Notes on Debates in Congress" for that day; see *PJM,* VI, pp. 290–92. This note formed the basis for his memorandum to TJ, although he consistently substituted the expression "permanent revenue" for "general revenue," except in one instance; see *ibid.,* p. 310.

2. For detailed explanations of JM's observations on the impact of the plan on each of the states, see *ibid.,* pp. 295–97.

lishment of a permanent revenue, as tending to support the confederacy, to remove causes of future contention, and to secure her trade against separate taxation from the States thro which it is carried on. She would also approve of a share in the vacant territory. Having never been much invaded by the Enemy her interest would be opposed to abatements, and throwing all the separate expenditures into the common mass. The discharge of the public debts from a common treasury would not be required by her interest, the loans of her citizens being under her proportion.[3]

Massachusetts is deeply interested in the discharge of the public debts. The expedition to Penobscot alone interests her, she supposes, in making a common mass of expences: her interest is opposed to abatements. The other objects wd. not peculiarly affect her.

Rhode Island as a weak State is interested in a permanant revenue as tending to support the confederacy and prevent future contentions, but against it as tending to deprive Her of the advantage afforded by her situation of taxing the commerce of the contiguous States, as tending to discharge with certainty the public debts, her proportion of loans interest her rather against it. Having been the seat of the war for a considerable time, she might not perhaps be opposed to abatements on that account. The exertions for her defence having been *previously* sanctioned, it is presumed in most instances, she would not be agst. a common mass of expences. In the acquisition of vacant territory she is deeply and anxiously interested.

Connecticut is interested in a permanent revenue as tending to protect her commerce from separate taxation by N. York and Rhode Island: and somewhat as providing for loan office creditors. Her interest is strenuous agst. abatements—in favor of a common mass of expences having often employed militia without sanction of Congss. Since the condemnation of her title to her

---

3. In his long footnote of Feb. 26, JM had included his calculation of the Confederation debt as of Jan. 1, 1783, basing his figures on those submitted to Congress by Robert Morris, superintendent of finance. He omitted this information in his memorandum to TJ, but it totaled $11,437,410.80:

| | *Specie Dollars* | |
|---|---|---|
| NH. | 336.579.58.7 | |
| Mas: | 2.361.866.66.5 | |
| R. Island | 699.725.37.4 | This it is to be observed is only the list of loan office debts. The unliquidated debts and liquidated debts of other denominations due to individuals will vary inexpressibly the relative quantum of credits of the several States. It is to be further observed that this only shews the original credits, transfers having been constant. Heretofore they have flowed into Pa. Other states may hereafter have an influx. |
| Cont. | 1.270.115.30 | |
| N. York | 949.729.57.5 | |
| N. Jersey | 658.883.69 | |
| Pena. | 3.948.904.14.4 | |
| Delaware | 65.820.13.7 | |
| Maryland | 410.218.30 | |
| Virga | 313.741.82.3 | |
| N.Carolina | 113.341.11.1 | |
| S.Carolina | 90.442.10.1 | |
| | 11.437.410.80 | |

Due to an error that he made in transcribing his figures, JM's column totals $11,219,367.80 instead of $11,437,410.80; see *ibid.*, p. 297.

Western claims, she may perhaps consider herself interested in the acquisition of the vacant lands. In other respects she wd not be peculiarly affected.

N. York is exceedingly attached to a permanent revenue as tending to support the confederacy and prevent future contests among the States. Although her citizens are not lenders beyond the proportion of the State, yet individuals of great weight are deeply interested. In making a common mass also interested, and since the acceptance of her cession, interested in those of other States.

N. Jersey is interested as a smaller State in a permanent revenue as tendg to support the confederacy, and to prevent future contests and to guard her commerce agst. the separate taxation of Pensylvania and N.Y. The loans of her Citizens are not materially disproportionate. Although this State has been much the theatre of the war, she wd. not perhaps be interested in abatements. Having had a previous sanction for particular expenditures, her interest wd. be opposed to a common mass. In the vacant territory, she is deeply and anxiously interested.

Penna. is deeply interested in a permanent revenue, the loans of her Citizens amounting to more than ⅓ of that branch of the public debt. As far as a general impost on trade would restrain her from taxing the trade of N. Jersey it would be against her interest. She is not interested in abatements nor common mass, but has espoused both. In the vacant territory she is also interested.

Delaware is interested by her weakness in a permanent revenue as tending to support the confederacy and future tranquility of the States; but not materially by the credits of her Citizens: Her interest is opposed to abatements and to a common mass. To the vacant territory she is firmly attached.

Maryland. Having never been the Seat of war and her Citizens being creditors below her proportion, her interest lies agst. a permanent revenue, otherwise than as she is interested in common with others in the support of the Confederacy and tranquility of the U.S. but against abatements, and against a common mass. The vacant lands are a favorite object to her.

Virga. in common with the Southern States as likely to enjoy an opulent and defenceless trade is interested in a permanent revenue, as tending to secure her the protection of the Confederacy agst. the maritime superiority of the E. States; but agst it as tending to discharge loan office debts and to deprive her of the occasion of taxing the commerce of N. Carolina. It is uncertain how the credits of her citizens may stand in a liquidatioin of their claims vs. U. S.—interested somewhat perhaps in abatements—and particularly so in a common mass—not only her excentric expenditures being enormous but many of them which have been similar to those allowed to other States, having rcd. no sanction of Congs. Her cession of territory would be considered as a sacrifice.

N. Carolina. interested in a permanent revenue as tending to ensure the protection of the Confederacy agst. the maritime superiority of the E. States and to guard her trade from separate taxation by Virginia and S. Carolina. The loans of her Citizens are inconsiderable. Their claims for supplies must be great. In abatements and in a common mass she is essentially interested. In the article of territory, she would have to make a sacrifice.

South Carolina is interested as a weak and exposed State in a permanent revenue as tending to secure to her the protection of the confederacy agst. enemies of *every* kind, and as providing for the public creditors, her citizens being not only loan office creditors beyond her proportion, but having immense unliquidated demands agst. U. States. As restraining her power over the commerce of N. Carolina, a permanent revenue is opposed by her interests. She is also materially interested in abatements, and in a common mass. In the article of territory her sacrifice wd. be inconsiderable.

Georgia as a feeble, an opulent, and frontier State is peculiarly interested in a permanent revenue, as tending to support the confederacy. She is also interested in it somewhat by the credits of her Citizens. In abatements She is also interested, and in a common mass, essentially so. In the article of territory she would make an important sacrifice.

To make this plan still more complete for the purpose of removing all present complaints, and all occasions of future contests, a recommendation is to be included for substituting numbers in place of the value of land as the rule of apportionment. In this all the States are interested if proper deductions be made from the number of Slaves.

## *Madison's Annotations for Jefferson on the Report for Restoring Public Credit*

[Philadelphia ca. Mar. 26, 1783]

Resolved that it be recommended to the several States as indispensably necessary to the restoration of public credit and the punctual and honorable discharge of the public debts, to vest in the U. S. in Congress assd. a power to levy for the use of the U. S., a duty of 5 PerCt. ad valorem, at the time and place of importation, upon all goods wares and merchandizes of foreign growth and manufactures, which may be imported into any of the said States, from any foreign port, island or plantation, except arms, ammunition, cloathing and other articles imported on account of the United States or any of them, except wool cards, cotton cards and wire for making them, and also except salt during the war:

Also a like duty of 5 PerCt. ad valorem on all prizes and prize goods condemned in the Court of Admiralty of any of these States as lawful prize:

Also to levy a duty of $1/8$ of a dollar per Bushel on all Salt imported as aforesaid after the war. $1/15$ of a dollar per Gallon on all wines $1/30$ of a dollar per Gallon on all rum and brandy $2/3$ of a dollar per 112 lbs. on all brown sugars,

1 dollar per 112 lbs. on all powdered, lump and clayed sugars other than loaf sugars, 1 ⅓ dollar on all loaf sugars ¹⁄₃₀ of a dollar Per lb. on all Bohea Tea and ¹⁄₁₅ of a dollar per lb on all finer India Teas, imported as aforesaid, after       , in addition to the five per cent above mentioned.⁴

Provided that none of the said duties shall be applied to any other purpose than the discharge of the interest or principals of the debts which shall have been contracted on the faith of the U.S. for supporting the present war, nor be continued for a longer term than 25 years; and provided that the collectors of the said duties shall be appointed by the States within which their offices are to be respectively exercised; but when so appointed shall be amenable to, and removeable by the U. S. in Congs. assd. alone and in case any State shall not make such appt. within       ⁵ after notice given for that purpose, the appointmt may then be made by the U. S. in Congs. assd.

That it be further recommended to the several States to establish for a like term not exceeding 25 years, and to appropriate to the discharge of the Interest and principal of the debts which shall have been contracted on the faith of the U.S. for supporting the present war, substantial and effectual revenues of such nature as they may respectively judge most convenient to the amount of       ⁶ and in the proportions following, viz.

That an annual account of the proceeds and application of the aforementioned revenues shall be made out and transmitted to the several states distinguishing the proceeds of each of the specified articles, and the amount of the whole revenue received from each State.⁷

the said revenues to be collected by persons appointed as aforesaid; but to be carried to the separate credit of the States within wch. they shall be collected, and be liquidated and adjusted among the States according to the quotas which may from time to time be allotted to them:

That none of the preceding resolutions shall take effect untill all of them shall be acceded to by every State, after Which unanimous accession, however, they shall be considered as forming a mutual compact among all the States, and shall be irrevocable, by any one or more of them without the concurrence of the whole, or of a majority of the U. S. in Congs. assembd.; provided that after the unanimous accession to all the said preceding resolutions, the proposed alteration in the 8th. of the Articles of Confederation shall not hereafter be revoked or varied otherwise than as is pointed out in the 13th. of the Said articles.

That as a further mean[s] as well of hastening the extinguishment of the

4. JM handed TJ an annotated copy of the printed report on or about Mar. 26, 1783. In the left margin opposite this paragraph, JM wrote, "Tuesday Mar: 11. on motion of Mr. Dyer, amendt. agreeably to the Resolution of 16 day of decmr"; see *ibid.*, p. 397.

5. JM wrote, "Within the blank space . . . [insert] 'one month' "; see *ibid.*

6. JM wrote, "2. mi. drs. annuly." Congress later changed the requisition to $1.5 million; see *ibid.*

7. At the end of the paragraph, JM added these words; "According to such rule as is or may be prescribed by the Arts. of Confederation"; see *ibid.*

debts, as of establishing the harmony of the U. States it be recommended to the States which have passed no acts towards complying with the Resolutions of Congs. of the 6 of Sepr. and 10 of Ocr. 1780, relative to territorial cessions, to make the liberal cessions therein recommended, and to the States wch. may have passed acts complying with the said resolutions in part only, to revise and complete such compliances.

That in order to remove all objections agst. a retrospective application of the constitutional rule of proportioning to the Several States the charges and expences which shall have been supplied for the common defence or general welfare, it be recommended to them to enable Congress to make such equitable exceptions and abatements as the particular circumstances of the States from time to time during the war may be found to require.

That conformably to the liberal principles on which these recommendations are founded, and with a view to a more amicable and complete adjustment of all accounts between the U. S. and individual States, all reasonable expences which shall have been incurred by the States, without the sanction of Congress, in their defence agst. or attacks upon British or Savage Enemies, either by sea or by land, and which shall be supported by satisfactory proofs, shall be considered as part of the common charges incident to the present war, and be allowed as such;

That as a more convenient and certain rule of ascertaining the proportions to be supplied by the States respectively to the common Treasury, the following alteration in the articles of confederation and perpetual Union between these States, be and the same is hereby agreed to in Congress, and the several States are advised to authorize their respective Delegates to subscribe and ratify the same as part of the said instrument of Union, in the words following to wit:

"So much of the 8th. of the Articles of Confederation and perpetual Union between the 13 States of America, as is contained in the words following to wit., 'all charges of war etc. [to the end of the paragraph'] is hereby revoked and made void; and in place thereof it is declared and concluded, the same having been agreed to in a Congress of the U. States; 'that all charges of war and all other expences that shall be incurred for the common defence or general welfare, and allowed by the United States in Congress assembled shall be Defrayed out of a common treasury, which shall be supplied by the several states in proportion to the number of inhabitants of every age, sex and condition, except Indians not paying taxes in each State; which number shall be triennially taken and transmitted to the U. S. Congs. assd. in such mode as they shall direct and appoint; provided always, that in such numeration no persons shall be included who are bound to servitude for life according to the laws of the State to which they belong, other than such as may be between the ages of     [' "]

## Jefferson to Madison

Susquehanna Apr. 14, 1783

DEAR SIR

Meeting at our quarters with a Mr. Levi going to Philadelphia and having no other employment, I write by him just to say that all is well, and that having made our stages regularly and in time we hope to make better way than Mr. Nash did. The Carolina letter bearer is here also. We pass one another two or three times a day. I never saw Mr. Ingles to speak to him about my books. Will you be so obliging as to make my acknowledgements to him for his undertaking and to ask him to send them to Richmond to the care of James Buchanan. Be pleased to make my compliments affectionately to the gentlemen and ladies. *I desire them to Miss Kit*[t]*ly particularly*[8] *Do you know that the ra*[il]*lery you sometimes experienced from our family strengthened by my own observation gave me hopes there was some foundation for it   I wished it to be so as it would give me a neighbour whose worth I rate high* [,] *and as I know it will render you happier than you can possibly be in a singl*[e] *state   I often made it the subject of conversation* [,] *more* [,] *exhortation with her and was able to convince my*[self] *that she possessed every sentiment in your favor which you could wish   But of this no more without your leave*   I am with much affection Dr. Sir Your sincere friend

TH: JEFFERSON


## Madison to Jefferson

Philadelphia Apr. 22, 1783

DEAR SIR

Your favor of the 14. inst: written on the Susquehanna with the several letters inclosed were safely delivered to me. I did not fail to present as you desired your particular compliments to *Miss K*[9] *Your inference on that subject was not groundless   Before you left us I had sufficiently ascertained her sentiments   Since your departure* the *affair has been pursued   Most preliminary arrangements although definitive will be postponed untill* the *end of* the *year in congress   At some period of* the *intervail I shall probably make a visit to Virginia*   The *interest which your friendship takes on this occasion in my happiness is a pleasing proof that* the *disposetions which I feel are reciprocal*[10]

The report on funds etc. passed Congress on Saturday last with the dissent of R. Island and the division of N. York only. The latter vote was lost by the rigid adherence of Mr. Hamilton to a plan which he supposed more per-

---

8. These italicized words and those in the rest of the letter were written in code; see *ibid.*, p. 459.

9. These italicized words and those in the rest of the letter were written in code.

10. JM later retrieved this letter and crossed out the coded portion, then wrote "Undecypherable" on it. But Mrs. Irving Brant managed to decode it in 1948; see Brant, II, pp. 283–84.

fect.[11] The clause providing for unauthorized expenditures, could not be reinstated, and consequently no attempt was made to link all the parts of the act inseparably together.[12] As it now stands it has I fear no bait for Virga. which is not particularly interested either in the object or mode of the revenues recommended, nor in the territorial cessions, nor in the change of the constitutional rule of dividing the public burdens. A respect for justice, good faith and national honor is the only consideration which can obtain her compliance.[13]

We have received no intelligence from abroad which deserves to be noted, since your departure. The interval between the preliminary and definitive Treaties, has produced several nice and interesting questions. One is whether laws prohibiting commerce with British Ports during the war, have expired with the cessation of Hostilities. A similar one is whether the soldiers enlisted for the war are entitled to a discharge. At least half of the army under Genl. Washington are under this description and are urgent for such a construction of their engagements. A third question is whether the preliminary treaty between F. and G.B. has given such effect to the provisional articles between the latter and the U.S. as to require an execution of the stipulations in the 6 and 7 articles or whether a definitive Treaty only can produce this effect.

The system for foreign affairs is not yet digested: and I apprehend will be long on the anvil, unless the actual return of our Ministers from Europe should stimulate Congress on the subject. I am charged with many compliments from the whole family for yourself and Miss Patsy, which you will accept with an assurance of sincere friendship from Yr Obt. and Hbl Servt.,

J. MADISON JR.

## Madison to Jefferson

Philadelphia May 6, 1783

DEAR SIR

Your favor of the 21. Ult. written at Col: Pendleton's was brought to hand by the post of last week.[14] Col: Floyd's family did not set out untill the day after it was received. I accompanied them as far as Brunswick, about 60 Miles from this, and returned hither on friday evening. Mr. Jones will attend the Assembly, and proposes to begin his journey this afternoon, if the present rain should cease. Mr. Lee also means to set out for the same purpose in a few days.

---

11. Ironically, in 1783 Hamilton opposed assumption of state debts by the Confederation, a proposal that he supported in 1790. Both JM and TJ supported assumption in 1783 and opposed it in 1790; see *PTJ,* VI, pp. 263–64, and *PJM,* VI, pp. 487–88. For the most careful untangling of JM's and Hamilton's positions, see Lance Banning, "The Hamiltonian Madison: A Reconsideration," *VMHB* 92 (1984): 3–28.

12. Since TJ had a copy of JM's annotations of the printed report, he knew which clause JM meant.

13. JM incorporated this phraseology in his "Address to the States," which was adopted on Apr. 26, 1783; see *PJM,* VI, p. 494.

14. TJ's letter has not been found; the italicized words in this letter were written in code.

*Congress have received a long and curious epistle from Mr. Adams dated in February addressed to the president not to the secretary for foreign affairs. He animadverts on the revocation of his commission for a treaty of commerce with Great Britain[,] presses the appointment of a minister to that court with such a commission[,] draws a picture of a fit character in which his own likeness is ridiculously and palpable studi*[e]*d*[,] *finaly praising and recomending Mr. Jay for the appointment provided injustice must be done to an older servant.*

Letters from the Marquis de la Fayette and Mr. Carmichael shew that the Court of Spain has become pretty tractable since the acknowledgment of our Independence by G.B. The latter has been treated with due respect. And the Court has agreed to accede to the territorial limit fixed for W. Florida in the provisional Articles. The navigation of the Mississippi remains to be settled.

My absence from Congs. the past week disables me from giving you the exact information of their latest proceedings. I am told that in consequence of Mr. A—— *letter the secretary of foreign affairs has been instructed to project a treaty of commerce with Great Britain* which will *probably bring the attention of Congress to the general department of foreign affairs.*

Under the same cover with this are two letters for Miss Patsy, one from Mrs. Trist, the other from Miss Floyd with the copy of a song.[15] I beg that my compliments may be accepted along with them. I am Dear Sir Your sincere friend,

J. MADISON JR.

## Jefferson to Madison

Tuckahoe May 7, 1783

DEAR SIR

I received your favor of Apr. 22. and am not a little concerned at the alterations which took place in the Report on the impost etc. after I left you. The article which bound the whole together I fear was essential to get the whole passed; as that which proposed the conversion of state into federal debts was one palatable ingredient at least in the pill *we* were to swallow. This proposition being then hopeful, I never consulted you whether the paiment of our Western expenditures, annexed as a condition to our passing the articles recommended, would not be acceded to by Congress, more especially when one of those articles is the cession of that very territory for the acquisition and defence of which these expenditures have been incurred.[16] If I recollect

---

15. TJ's daughter was corresponding with Polly Floyd, not Kitty.

16. Like JM, TJ had expected "the conversion of state into federal debts," with Congress assuming each state's unauthorized but reasonable war expenses. The Virginia cession of the Northwest Territory proposed in 1781 specified that Congress would repay Virginia for charges incurred in defending the area during the Revolution.

rightly, Congress offered this in their first proposition for a cession. I beg your sentiments however on this subject by return of the first post. Notwithstanding the unpromising form of these articles I have waited a fortnight in the neighborhood of Richmond that I might see some of the members. I passed yesterday *in associating and conversing with as* many of them *as I could.*[17] The *Attorney*[18] has *cooperated* in this work. This is the view I form at present of *the leaders. Dr. Lee, R. H. Lee M. Page, Taylor* will be *against* them. So will *Thruston and White if elected,* and even an *A. Campbell* is thought *worthy of being named* with these as having some *influence in the S. Western* quarter. In their *favour will probably be Tyler Tazewell, Genl. Nelson, W. Nelson, Nicholas* and a *Mr. Stewart a young man* of *good talents* from the *Westward. Henry* as usual is *involved in mystery:* should the *popular tide run strongly* in either *direction, he* will fall *in with it.* Should it *not,* he will have a *struggle between his enmity to the Lees, and his enmity* to everything which *may give influence to* Congs. *T. Mason* is a *meteor* whose *path cannot* be *calculated.* All the powers of *his mind* seem at present *concentrated* on one *single object,* the *producing* a *Convention* to *new model* the [Virginia] *Constitution.* This *is a subject* much *agitated,* and seems the *only one* they will have to *amuse themselves* with *till* they shall *receive* your *propositions.*[19] *These should* be *hastened; as* I think the session will be short.

I have seen Mr. Wythe. He has none of his amendments or notes on the Confederation.

*Mr. Short has desired me to* suggest *his name* as that of a *person willing* to become a *legatine secretary* should these *offices be continued. I have apprised him of* the possibility that they may not. You know *my high opinion of his abilities and merits.* I will therefore only add that a *peculiar talent* for *prying into facts* seems to mark *his character as proper for* such a *business. He* is *young* and little *experienced in business* tho well *prepared for it.* These defects will *lessen daily.* Should *persons* be *proposed less proper* on the whole you *would* on motives of public good, *knowing his willingness* to *serve, give him* a *nomination* and do justice to *his character.*

*I rejoice* at the information that *Miss K. and yourself concur* in *sentiments. I rejoice* as it will *render you happier* and will give *to me a neighbor on whom I shall set high value.*[20] *You* will be continued in *your* delegation till the end of three years from the completion of the Confederation. *You* will therefore *model your measures accordingly.* You say nothing of the time when you shall pay your visit to

---

17. The italicized words in this sentence and those in the rest of the letter were written in code.

18. Edmund Randolph. The men referred to in the rest of this paragraph are Dr. Arthur Lee, Richard Henry Lee, Mann Page, John Taylor, Charles Thruston, Alexander White, Arthur Campbell, John Tyler, Henry Tazewell, General Thomas Nelson, William Nelson, George Nicholas, Archibald Stuart, Patrick Henry, and Stevens Thomson Mason.

19. "Your *propositions*" referred to the report on credit and JM's "Address to the States," which were mailed by President Boudinot on May 9, 1783; see Edmund C. Burnett, *Letters of Members of the Continental Congress,* 8 vols. (Washington, 1921–38), VII, pp. 160–61, and *PJM,* VII, p. 17.

20. After Miss Floyd broke off her engagement, JM tried to scratch out this passage, but both *PTJ* and *PJM* deciphered it, as did Brant, II, p. 284.

*Virginia:* I hope you will *let me know* of your *arrival* as soon as *it happens.* Should the *call* be made *on me,* which was sometimes the subject of *our conversation,* and be *so timed with your* visit *as that you may* be the *bearer of* it *I shall* with great pleasure accomodate *my movements to yours* so as to *accompany you on your return to Philadelphia.*

I set out this morning for Monticello. My affectionate compliments to the ladies and gentlemen of the house, and sincere friendship to yourself. Adieu.

## Madison to Jefferson

Philadelphia May 13, 1783

DEAR SIR

*Marbois lately took occasion in our family to complain of ungenerous proceedings of the British against individuals as well as against their enemies at large and* finally signified that *he was no stranger to the letter transmited to Congress which he roundly avered to be spurious.*[21] His *information came from Boston* where [the] *incident is said to be no secret* but *whether* [it] *be the echo of letters from Philadelphia or has transpired from the correspondence of Mr. Adams to his private friends is* uncertain.[22] This *conversation passed during my absence in New Jersey but was related to me by Mr. Carrol*

*A project for a treaty of commerce with Britain has been reported by Secretary foreign affairs and is now in the hands of a committee The objects most at heart are first a direct trade between this country and the West Indies Second a right of carrying between the later and other parts of the British empire Third*ly *a right of carrying from West Indies to all other parts of the world As the price of these* advantages *it is proposed that we shall ad*[mit] *British subjects to equal privileges with our own citizens. As to the* [first] *object it may be observed that the bil*[l] *lately brought in British parliament renders it probable that it may be obtained without such a* [con]*cession.*[23] as to the *second that it concerns eastern states* cheifly and as *to the third that it concerns them alone.* Whilst the *privilege to be ceded* will cheifly if not alone *affect the southern states* The interest of these *seems to require that they should retain at least the faculty of giveing any* encouragement *to their own merchants ships or mariners which may be necessary to prevent relapse under scotch monop-*

21. The italicized words in this sentence and those in the rest of the letter were written in code.

22. Barbé-Marbois had visited Mrs. House's boardinghouse while JM made his trip with Kitty Floyd and her family. Despite his claim that the letter attributed to him was spurious, he had written to Vergennes on Mar. 13, 1782, lamenting the terms of peace that Congress sought. The British intercepted his letter and gave a copy to the American peace negotiators, who sent it to Congress; see Richard B. Morris, *The Peacemakers: The Great Powers and American Independence* (New York, 1965), p. 325, and *PJM,* VII, p. 40.

23. The earl of Shelburne, who advocated free trade, had been forced to resign in Feb., and his bill failed.

*oly* or *to* acquire *a maritime importance*  The *eastern states need no such precaution.*

Genl. Washington and Genl. Carlton have had an interview on the subject of arrangements for executing the provisional Treaty. It was interrupted by the sudden indisposition of the latter. In the conversation which took place he professed intentions of evacuating New York and all the posts in the U.S. held by British Garrisons as soon as possible, but did not authorize any determinate or speedy expectations. He confessed that a number of Negroes had gone off with the Refugees since the arrival of the Treaty, and undertook to justify the permission by a palpable and scandalous misconstruction of the Treaty, and by the necessity of adhering to the proclamations under the faith of which the Negroes had eloped into their service. He said that if the Treaty should be otherwise explained, compensation would be made to the owners and to make this the more easy, a register had been and would be kept of all Negroes leaving N.Y. before the surrender of it by the British Garrison. This information has been referred by Congress to a Committee.[24] But the progress already made in the discharge of the prisoners, the only convenient pledge by which fair dealing on the other side could be enforced, makes it probable that no remedy will be applied to the evil.

I have sent Mr. Randolph a pamphlet comprehending all the papers which are to be laid before the States relative to the National debt etc., and have desired him to let you have the reading it. The fewness of the copies made it impossible for me to get one for each of you.[25] I am Dr Sir your sincere friend

J. MADISON JR.

## *Madison to Jefferson*

Philadelphia May 20, 1783

DEAR SIR

In obedience to your request I am to answer by this post your favor of the 7. inst. received yesterday. My brevity will therefore be excused.

For the tenor of the conditions on which Congress were formerly willing to accept the Cession of Virga. I beg leave to refer to their resolutions of the 6 of Sepr. and 10 of Ocr. 1780. I take it granted you have their Journals. The expunging of the article relative to State expences was a subject of no less regret with me than it is with you and for the same reason. But I acknowledge that

---

24. Washington's interview with Carleton took place on May 6, 1783. JM chaired the committee that considered Washington's report.

25. The pamphlet was entitled *Address and Recommendations to the States, by the United States in Congress assembled*. This is one of the first times that JM used the phrase "National debt."

considering the probable defect of vouchers in Virga.[26] and the ardor with which the clause was supported from some other quarters, mine was much diminished in the course of the discussion. On the last trial there were but two or three states besides Virga. that favored it. *S. Carolina's* opposition to it had great weight. After this clause was expunged it was thought improper to retain the connective clause as Virga. will now be at liberty to confine her accession to the revenue part of the plan, without enlarging her territorial cession or being deprived of the opportunity of annexing any conditions she may think fit. The connective clause however could not have been carried I believe either before or after the mutilation of the plan. Notwithstanding this disappointment I adhere to my wishes not only that the revenue may be established, but that the fœderal rule of dividing the burdens may be changed, and the territorial disputes accomodated. The more I revolve the latter subject, the less inducement I can discover to a pertinacity on the part of Virga. and the more interesting it appears to the Union.

I am sorry your departure from Richmond became necessary before more of the members were assembled. I make no doubt that useful impressions have been left with those who were so and were susceptible of them. I shall keep in mind the intimation relative to Mr. Short. The idea of adding the fraction of a year to my Congressial service is totally new, and even if it should prevail, will not as far as I can now see, coincide with my private conveniency.

Since my last I have been able to procure for you a copy of pamphlet which I herewith enclose. If in consequence of the provisional steps I before took it should prove a duplicate I shall thank you to forward one of them to my father. The ladies and gentlemen join me in complimts. to Miss Patsy and to yourself. Adieu.


*Jefferson to Madison*

Monticello June 1, 1783

DEAR SIR

The receipt of your letter of May 6. remains unacknoleged. I am also told that Colo. Monroe has letters for me by post tho' I have not yet received them. I hear but little from our assembly. Mr. Henry has declared in favour of the impost. This will ensure it. How he is as to the other questions of importance I do not learn.

On opening my papers when I came home I found among them the inclosed cyphers which I had received from either Mr. Morris's or Mr. Livingston's office. Will you be so good as to return them for me? The confusion into

---

26. Many vouchers had been destroyed by the British during the campaigns of 1781. JM may also have had in mind the claims submitted by Oliver Pollock and Simon Nathan for military supplies furnished to Virginia troops in Kentucky and the Northwest Territory; see *PJM,* VII, p. 57.

which my papers had got going to and from Baltimore and left there for some time will I hope apologize for my having overlooked them when I returned the other papers. I send you inclosed the debates in Congress on the subjects of Independance, Voting in Congress, and the Quotas of money to be required from the states. I found on looking that I had taken no others save only in one trifling case. As you were desirous of having a copy of the original of the declaration of Independance I have inserted it at full length distinguishing the alterations it underwent.[27]

Patsy increases the bundle inclosed with her correspondence. My compliments attend my acquaintances of the family. Patsy's letter to Miss Floyd will need a safe more than speedy conveyance for which she trusts to your goodness. Our friendship for that family as well as your interest in it will always render any news of them agreeable. I am with the sincerest esteem Dr. Sir your affectionate friend,

TH: JEFFERSON

P.S. I inclose for your perusal the account of the Pain de singe[28] which I mentioned. Be so good as to communicate it to Dr. Shippen who had not heard of it. My compliments attend him and [his lady].

*Madison to Jefferson*

Philadelphia June 10, 1783

MY DEAR SIR

Congress have received two letters from Mr. *Laurens* dated one the *fifteenth of March* the *other fifth of April*.[29] In the former he *persists in* the *jealousy* expressed in *his letter of* the *thirtieth of December of* the *British Councils. He says* that *Shelburne* had *boasted of his success in gaining the provisional treaty without the concurrence of France and of the good effect he expected to draw from that advantage.* Mr. *L.'s remark was* that *admitting* the *fact which he did not* altho' it *might disgrace* and even *prove fatal to the American Ministers,* It *could have no such effects on the United States.* His *second letter* expresses more *confidence in the D. of Portland and Mr. Fox.* These *ministers have* withdrawn the subject of Commerce with the U.S. from Parliament and mean to open negociations for a

---

27. TJ enclosed a forty-nine-page transcript of notes he had taken in 1776. This copy was printed in *The Papers of James Madison,* ed. Henry D. Gilpin, 3 vols. (Washington, 1840), I, pp. 9-39. The copy of the Declaration of Independence that TJ made for JM is printed in Julian P. Boyd, *The Declaration of Independence: The Evolution of the Text As Shown in Facsimiles of Various Drafts by Its Author, Thomas Jefferson* (Princeton, 1945), p. 28.

28. "Pain de singe" is also known by its popular name, "monkey bread," made from the edible fruit of the African baobab tree; see *PJM,* VII, p. 105.

29. These italicized words and those in the rest of the letter were written in code.

Treaty with their Ministers in Europe.[30] Mr. Fox asked Mr. L. whether these had powers for that purpose: his answer was that he believed so. That he had seen a revocation of Mr. Adams' commission noticed in the Gazettes but that he considered the paragraph as spurious. From this it would seem that *Mr. A. had never communicated this* diminution of *his power to his colleagues.* These letters leave us in the suspence in which they found us as to the definitive Treaty. Mr. L. thinks that no such event could have been relied on under Shelburnes Administration. He was on the 5th. of Apl. setting out for Paris with Mr. David Hartley[31] successor to Mr. Oswald, from whence he should proceed to America unless a definitive Treaty was near being concluded. Notwithstand[ing] the daily arrivals from every quarter we get not a line on the subject from our Ministers at Versailles.

Mr. Dumas has inclosed to Congress sundry papers from which it appears that the *Dutch indulge a* violent animosity *against the French court* for *abandoning their interests and the* liberty of *navigation by a premature concluding of the preliminaries.* Complaints on this head are *made through Dumas to Mr. Adams* with *enquiries whether the American ministers had powers to* concert engagements *with the United Provinces, His Most Christian Majesty, and His Catholic Majesty*[32] *for maintaining the rights asserted by the neutral confederation*[33] or if the two last *decline with United Provinces alone. The answer of Mr. A.* is not *included, but references to it import it was satisfactory and* that *negociations were to be opened accordingly.* It is certain notwithstanding that no *powers equal to such a transaction* were *ever given generally to the ministers* and that as far as they were given they were *superceded by the commission to Mr. Dana.*[34] This correspondence commenced in Jany. and is brought down to late in March and yet no *intimation whatever* concerning it has been *received from the ministers themselves.*

Congress have lately sent instructions to the Ministers in Europe to *contend* in *the final treaty for such* amendment of the *article relating to British debts* as will *suspend payment for three years after the war and expressly exclude interest during the war.*[35]

Mr. Livingston has taken his final leave of the department of Foreign

---

30. The duke of Portland succeeded the earl of Shelburne as prime minister on Apr. 1, 1783. Charles James Fox became foreign secretary; see Morris, p. 426.

31. David Hartley held a commission for negotiating the definitive peace treaty as well as a treaty of commerce with the United States.

32. The Netherlands, the king of France, and the king of Spain, respectively.

33. The League of Armed Neutrality.

34. Francis Dana was minister designate to the court of St. Petersburg. Only three weeks earlier, Congress had told him that the return of peace made it unnecessary for him to press for the admission of the United States to the League of Armed Neutrality for fear that it would entangle the United States with the politics of Europe. Nor should he conclude a commercial treaty unless it was limited to a period of fifteen years and subject to approval by Congress; see the "Instructions" of May 22, 1783, and the "Report on Rights of Neutral Nations," in *PJM,* VII, pp. 65-66, 137-40.

35. See Emory G. Evans, "Private Indebtedness and the Revolution in Virginia, 1776-1796," *WMQ* 28 (1971): 357-67.

Affairs. He would have remained if such an augmentation of his Salary had been made as would have secured him against future expence. But besides the disinclination of several members to augment salaries, there was no prospect of a competent number of States for an appropriation of money, until he must have lost the option of the Chancellorship of N.Y. No successor has been yet nominated, altho' the day for a choice has passed. I am utterly at a loss to guess on whom the choice will ultimately fall. *A.L.* will be *started* if the *defection of a respectable competitor* should be *likely to force votes upon him*.[36] No such has yet been *a subject of conversation in my particular presence*.

The general arrangement of the foreign system has been suspended by the thinness of Congress in part, and partly by the desire of further information from Europe. I fear much the delay will be exceedingly protracted. Nothing but final resignation of the Ministers abroad and the arrival of Foreign Ministers here, will effectually stimulate Congress into activity and decision on the subject. How far and at what time the first cause will operate is precarious. The second seems less so. Mr. Van Berkel has sent directions for proper provisions for his reception in the next month. A Sweedish Gentleman recommended by Dr. Franklin as a Philosopher, and by the Ct. de Vergennes as an intended Minister has been here for some time. From the temper of Spain, a mission from that Court also is not improbable.[37]

The Treaty of Comerce with G.B. is another business suspended by the same cause. The Assembly have instructed us to reserve to Congress a revisal after it shall have been settled in Europe. This will give force to the doctrine of caution hitherto maintained by us. The time of my setting out for Virga. continues to be uncertain, but cannot now be very distant. The prospect of seeing you, I need not assure you, enters much into the pleasure I promise myself from the visit. Mrs. House and Mrs. Trist charge me with their very sincere and respectful compliments to you and beg that they may be remembered very affectionately to Miss Patsy. I am Dear Sir Your sincere friend,

J. MADISON JR.

## *Jefferson to Madison*

Monticello June 17, 1783

DEAR SIR

Your favours of the 13th. and 20th. Ult. came to hand about a week ago. I am informed the assembly determined against the capacity of reelection in those gentlemen of the delegation who could not serve a complete year. I do not know on what this decision could be founded. My hopes of the success of

---

36. "*A.L.*" was Arthur Lee.
37. Pieter Johan van Berckel was minister plenipotentiary from the Netherlands, and the Baron de Kermelin represented Sweden; see *PJM,* VII, p. 132.

the Congressional propositions here have lessened exceedingly. Mr. Henry had declared in favor of the impost: but when the question came on he was utterly silent. I understand it will certainly be lost if it be not already. Instead of ceding more lands to the U.S. a proposition is made to revoke the former cession. Mr. Henry is for bounding our state reasonably enough, but instead of ceding the parts lopped off he is for laying them off into small republics. What further his plan is I do not hear. However you get the parliamentary news so much more directly from Richmond that it is idle for me to give it you from hence.

A Convention for the amendment of our Constitution having been much the topic of conversation for some time, I have turned my thoughts to the amendments necessary. The result I inclose to you. You will have opportunities during your stay in Philadelphia of enquiring into the success of some of the parts of it which tho' new to us have been tried in other states. I shall only except against your communicating it to any one of my own country, as I have found prejudices frequently produced against propositions handed to the world without explanation or support. I trust that you will either now or in some future situation turn your attention to this subject in time to give your aid when it shall be finally discussed. The paper inclosed may serve as a basis for your amendment, or may suggest amendments to a better groundwork. I further learn that the assembly are excluding members of Congress from among them. Whether the information they may derive from their presence, or their being marked by the confidence of the people, is the cause of this exclusion I cannot tell. Be pleased to present me with affection to my acquaintances of the house and to receive yourself the sincerest assurances of the esteem with which I am Dr. Sir Your friend and servt,

TH: JEFFERSON

P.S. I will take the first opportunity of forwarding the pamphlet to your father.

E N C L O S U R E<br>
[Jeffersonn's Draft of a Constitution for Virginia]

[Monticello May–June 1783][38]
To the citizens of the Commonwealth of Virginia, and all others whom it may concern, the Delegates of the said Commonwealth send greeting.

It is known to you and to the world that the government of Great Britain, with which the American states were not long since connected, assumed over them an

---

38. Except for the bracket in the paragraph on clerks of courts, all brackets in the draft are TJ's. In the bracket in the paragraph on a council of state, TJ offered alternatives for the term of office; in his *Notes,* he opted for a seven-year term. For JM's appraisal of TJ's draft, made five years later when Kentuckians were thinking about forming a state constitution, see Madison's Observations on Jefferson's Draft of a Constitution for Virginia, [New York ca. Oct. 15, 1788], below. See Merrill D. Peterson's *Jefferson and Madison and the Making of Constitutions* (Charlottesville, 1987), pp. 4–7, for a brilliant analysis of this topic.

authority which to some of them appeared unwarrantable and oppressive; that they endeavoured to enforce this authority by arms, and that the states of New Hampshire, Massachusets, Rhode island, Connecticut, New York, New Jersey, Pennsylvania, Delaware, Maryland, Virginia, North Carolina, South Carolina and Georgia, considering resistance, with all it's train of horrors, as a lesser evil than abject submission, closed in the appeal to arms. It hath pleased the sovereign disposer of all human events, to give to this appeal an issue favourable to the rights of these states, to enable them to reject for ever all dependance on a government which had shewn itself so capable of abusing the trusts reposed in it, and to obtain from that government a solemn and explicit acknowlegement that we are free, sovereign and independant states. During the progress of that war through which we had to labour for the establishment of our rights, the legislature of the commonwealth of Virginia found it necessary to establish a form of government for preventing anarchy and pointing our efforts to the two important objects of war against our invaders and peace and happiness among ourselves. But this, like all other their acts of legislation, being subject to be changed by subsequent legislatures, possessing equal powers with themselves, it has been thought expedient that it should receive those amendments which time and trial have suggested, and be rendered permanent by a power superior to that of the ordinary legislature. The General assembly therefore of this state recommended it to the good people thereof to chuse delegates to meet in General convention with powers to form a constitution of government for them, to which all laws present and future shall be subordinate; and in compliance with this recommendation they have thought proper to make choice of us, and to vest us with powers for this purpose.

We therefore the Delegates chosen by the said good people of this state for the purpose aforesaid, and now assembled in General convention do, in execution of the authority with which we are invested, establish the following Constitution of government for the said state of Virginia.

The said state shall hereafter for ever be governed as a Commonwealth.

The LEGISLATIVE, EXECUTIVE, and JUDICIARY departments shall be separate and distinct, so that no person, or collection of persons of any one of them shall exercise any power properly belonging to either of the others, except in the instances hereinafter expressly permitted.

### Legislature.

The LEGISLATURE shall consist of two distinct branches, the concurrence of both of which expressed on three several readings, shall be necessary to the passage of a law. One of these branches shall be called the HOUSE OF DELEGATES, the other the SENATE, and both together the GENERAL ASSEMBLY.

### H. of Delegates.

DELEGATES for the General assembly shall be chosen on the Monday preceding the 25th. day of December which shall be in the year 178  and thenceforwards triennially. But if an election cannot be concluded on that day, it may be adjourned from day to day till it can be concluded.

The number of delegates shall be so proportioned to the number of qualified electors in the whole state that they shall never exceed 300. nor be fewer than 100. Whenever such excess or deficiency shall take place, the house of delegates so deficient or excessive, shall, notwithstanding this continue in being during it's legal term; but they shall during that term, re-adjust the proportion so as to bring their number within the limits beforementioned at the ensuing election. If any county be reduced in it's qualified electors below the number necessary to send one delegate, let it be annexed to some adjoining county.

*Senate.*

For the election of SENATORS, let the several counties be allotted by the Senate from time to time into such and so many districts as they shall find best, and let each county at the time of electing it's delegates chuse Senatorial electors, qualified as themselves are, and four in number for each delegate their county is entitled to send, who shall convene and conduct themselves in such manner as the legislature shall direct with the Senatorial electors from the other counties of their district, and then chuse by ballot one Senator for every six delegates which their district is entitled to chuse. Let the Senatorial districts be divided into two classes, one of which shall be dissolved at the first ensuing general election of Delegates, the other at the next and so on alternately for ever.

All free male citizens of full age and sane mind, who for one year before shall have been resident in the county, or shall through the whole of that time have possessed therein real property of the value of       or shall for the same time have been enrolled in the militia, and no others, shall have right to vote for delegates for the said county, and for Senatorial electors for the district. They shall give in their votes personally and by balot.

*General Assembly*

The General assembly shall meet at the place to which they shall have last adjourned themselves on the 14th. day after the day of the election of Delegates, and thenceforward at any other time or place on their own adjournment. But if they shall at any time adjourn for more than one year, such adjournment shall be void and they shall meet on that day twelve-month. Neither house without the concurrence of the other shall adjourn for more than one week, nor to any other place than the one at which they are sitting. The Governor shall also have power, with the advice of the council of state, to call them at any other time to the same place, or to a different one where that shall have become since the last adjournment, dangerous from an enemy or from infection.

A majority of either house shall be a Quorum and shall be requisite for doing business: but any smaller numbers which from time to time shall be thought expedient by the respective houses, shall be sufficient to call for and to punish their non-attending members and to adjourn themselves for any time not exceeding one week.

The members during their attendance on General assembly and for so long a time before and after as shall be necessary for travelling to and from the same shall be privileged from all personal restraint and assault, and shall have no other privilege whatsoever. They shall receive during the same time daily wages in gold or silver equal to the value of two bushels of wheat. This value shall be deemed one dollar by the bushel till the year 1790. in which and in every tenth year thereafter the General court at their first sessions in the year shall cause a special jury of the most respectable merchants and farmers to be summoned to declare what shall have been the averaged value of wheat during the last ten years; which averaged value shall be the measure of wages for the ten subsequent years.

Of this General assembly the Treasurer, Attorney General, Register, Ministers of the Gospel, officers of the regular armies of this state or of the United states, persons receiving salaries or emoluments from any power foreign to our Confederacy, those who are not resident in the counties for which they are chosen Delegates or districts for which they are chosen Senators, persons who shall have committed treason, felony or such other crime as would subject them to infamous punishment or who shall have been convicted by due course of law of bribery or corruption in endeavouring to procure an election to the said assembly, shall be incapable of being members. All others not herein elsewhere excluded who may elect, shall be capable of being elected thereto, and none else.

Any member of the said assembly accepting any office of profit under this state, or the United states, or any of them shall thereby vacate his seat, but shall be capable of being re-elected.

Vacancies occasioned by such disqualifications, by death, or otherwise, shall be supplied by the electors on a writ from the Speaker of the respective house.

The General assembly shall not have power to infringe this constitution; to abridge the civil rights of any person on account of his religious belief; to restrain him from professing and supporting that belief, or to compel him to contributions, other than those he shall himself have stipulated, for the support of that or any other: to ordain death for any crime but treason or murder, or offences in the military line: to pardon or give a power of pardoning persons duly convicted of treason or felony, but instead thereof they may substitute one or two new trials and no more: to pass laws for punishing actions done before the existence of such laws: to pass any bill of attainder, of treason or felony: to prescribe torture in any case: nor to permit the introduction of any more slaves to reside in this state, or the continuance of slavery beyond the generation which shall be living on the 31st. day of December 1800; all persons born after that day being hereby declared free.

The General assembly shall have power to sever from this state all of any part of it's territory Westward of the Ohio or of the meridian of the mouth of the Great Kanhaway, and to cede to Congress 100 square miles in any other part of this state, exempted from the jurisdiction and government of this state so long as Congress shall hold their sessions therein or in any territory adjacent thereto which may be ceded to them by any other state.

They shall have power to appoint the Speakers of their respective houses, Treasurer, Auditors, Attorney general, Register [all General officers of the military] their own clerks, and serjeants and no other officers, except where in other parts of this constitution such appointment is expressly given them.

*Executive Governor*

The EXECUTIVE powers shall be exercised by a Governor who shall be chosen by joint balot of both houses of assembly, and when chosen shall remain in office five years, and be ineligible a second time. During his term he shall hold no other office or emolument under this state or any other state or power whatsoever. By Executive powers we mean no reference to those powers exercised under our former government by the crown as of it's prerogative; nor that these shall be the standard of what may or may not be deemed the rightful powers of the Governor. We give him those powers only which are necessary to carry into execution the laws, and which are not in their nature [either legislative or] Judiciary. The application of this idea must be left to reason. We do however expressly deny him the praerogative powers of erecting courts, offices, boroughs, corporations, fairs, markets, ports, beacons, lighthouses, and seamarks; of laying embargoes, of establishing precedence, of retaining within the state or recalling to it any citizen thereof, and of making denizens, except so far as he may be authorized from time to time by the legislature to exercise any of these powers. The powers of declaring war and concluding peace, of contracting alliances, of issuing letters of marque and reprisal, of raising or introducing armed forces, of building armed vessels, forts or strongholds, of coining money or regulating it's value, of regulating weights and measures, we leave to be exercised under the authority of the Confederation; but in all cases respecting them which are out of the said confederation, they shall be exercised by the Governor under the regulation of such laws as the legislature may think it expedient to pass.

The whole military of the state, whether regular or militia, shall be subject to his directions; but he shall leave the execution of those directions to the General officers [appointed by the legislature.]

His salary shall be fixed by the legislature at the session of assembly in which he shall be appointed, and before such appointment be made; or if it be not then fixed, it shall be the same which his next predecessor in office was entitled to. In either case he may demand it quarterly out of any money which shall be in the public treasury, and it shall not be in the power of the legislature to give him less or more, either during his continuance in office, or after he shall have gone out of it. The lands, houses, and other things appropriated to the use of the Governor, shall remain to his use, during his continuance in office.

### Council of State.

A COUNCIL OF STATE shall be chosen by joint balot of both houses of assembly, who shall hold their offices [during good behavior, 7. years and be ineligible a second time,] and who, while they shall be of the said council shall hold no other office or emolument under this state or any other state or power whatsoever. Their duty shall be to attend and advise the Governor when called on by him, and their advice in any case shall be a sanction to him. They shall also have power and it shall be their duty to meet at their own will and to give their advice, tho' not required by the Governor, in cases where they shall think the public good calls for it. Their advice and proceedings shall be entered in books to be kept for that purpose and shall be signed as approved or disapproved by the members present. These books shall be laid before either house of assembly when called for by them. The said council shall consist of eight members for the present: but their numbers may be increased or reduced by the legislature whenever they shall think it necessary; provided such reduction be made only as the appointments become vacant by death, resignation, disqualification, or regular deprivation. A majority of their actual number and not fewer shall be a Quorum. They shall be allowed for the present 500.£ each by the year, paiable quarterly out of any money which shall be in the public treasury. Their salary however may be increased or abated from time to time at the discretion of the legislature; provided such increase or abatement shall not by any ways or means be made to affect either then or at any future time any one of those then actually in office. At the end of each quarter their salary shall be divided into equal portions by the number of days on which during that quarter a council has been held, or required by the governor or their own adjournment, and one of those portions shall be withheld from each member for every of the said days which without cause allowed good by the board he failed to attend, or departed before adjournment without their leave. If no board should have been held during the quarter there shall be no deduction.

### *President.*

They shall annually chuse a President who shall preside in council in the absence of the governor, and who in case of his office becoming vacant by death or otherwise shall have authority to exercise all his functions, till a new appointment be made, as he shall also in any interval during which the Governor shall declare himself unable to attend to the duties of his office.

### *Judiciary.*

The Judiciary powers shall be exercised by County courts and such other inferior courts as the legislature shall think proper to erect, and by four Superior courts, to wit, a court of Admiralty, a General court of common law, a High court of Chancery and court of Appeals.

The judges of the HIGH COURT OF CHANCERY, GENERAL COURT and COURT OF ADMIRALTY shall be four in number each, to be appointed by joint balot of both houses of assembly, and to hold their offices during good behavior. While they continue judges they shall hold no other office or emolument under this state or any other state or power whatsoever, except that they may be delegated to Congress, receiving no additional allowance.

These judges assembled together shall constitute the COURT OF APPEALS.

A majority of the members of either of these courts, and not fewer, shall be a Quorum; but in the court of Appeals nine members shall be necessary to do business. Any smaller numbers however may be authorized by the legislature to adjourn their respective courts.

They shall be allowed for the present 500.£ each by the year, paiable quarterly out of any money which shall be in the public treasury. Their salaries however may be increased or abated from time to time at the discretion of the legislature: provided such increase or abatement shall not by any ways or means be made to affect, either then or at any future time, any one of those then actually in office. At the end of each quarter their salary shall be divided into equal portions by the number of days on which during that quarter their respective courts sat, or should have sat, and one of these portions shall be withheld from each member for every of the said days which without cause allowed good by his court, he failed to attend or departed before adjournment without their leave. If no court should have been held during the quarter there shall be no deduction.

There shall moreover be a court of IMPEACHMENTS to consist of three members of the Council of state, one of each of the Superior courts of Chancery, Common law, and Admiralty, two members of the House of Delegates and one of the Senate, to be chosen by the body respectively of which they are. Before this court any member of the three branches of government, that is to say, the Governor, any member of the Council, of the two houses of legislature or of the Superior courts may be impeached by the Governor the Council, or either of the said houses or courts for such misbehavior in office as would be sufficient to remove him therefrom: and the only sentence they shall have authority to pass shall be that of deprivation and future incapacity of office. Seven members shall be requisite to make a court and two thirds of those present must concur in the sentence. The offences cognisable by this court shall be cognisable by no other, and they shall be judges of fact as well as law.

The Justices or judges of the inferior courts already erected, or hereafter to be erected shall be appointed by the Governor on advice of the Council of state, and shall hold their offices during good behavior or the existence of their court. For breach of the good behavior they shall be tried according to the laws of the land before the court of Appeals, who shall be judges of the fact as well as of the law. The only sentence they shall have authority to pass shall be that of deprivation and future incapacity of office, and two thirds of the members present must concur in the sentence.

All courts shall appoint their own clerks, who shall hold their offices during good behavior or the existence of their court: they shall also appoint all other their attending officers to continue during their pleasure. Clerks appointed by the Superior courts shall be removeable by their respective courts: those to be appointed by other courts shall have been previously examined and certified to be duly qualified by some two members of the General court and shall be removeable for breach of the good behavior by the court of Appeals only, who shall be judges of the fact as well as of the law, [and] two thirds of the members present must concur in the sentence.

The justices or judges of the inferior courts may be members of the legislature.

The judgment of no inferior court shall be final in any civil case of greater value than 50. bushels of wheat as last rated in the General court for settling the allowance to the members of the General assembly, nor in any case of treason, felony, or other crime which would subject the party to infamous punishment.

In all causes depending before any court, other than those of Impeachments, of Appeals and Military courts facts [put in issue] shall be tried by jury, and in all courts whatever witnesses shall give their testimony vivâ voce in open court wherever their attendance can be procured; and all parties shall be allowed Counsel and compulsory process for their witnesses.

Fines, amercements and terms of imprisonment left indefinite by the law other than for Contempts shall be fixed by the jury triers of the offence.

### *Council of Revision.*

The Governor, two Counsellors of state, and a judge from each of the Superior courts of Chancery, Common law and Admiralty, shall be a council to revise all bills which shall have passed both houses of assembly; in which council the Governor, when present, shall preside. Every bill, before it becomes law, shall be presented to this council, who shall have a right to advise it's rejection, returning the bill with their advice and reasons in writing to the house in which it originated, who shall proceed to reconsider the said bill. But if after such reconsideration two thirds of the house shall be of opinion the bill should pass finally, they shall pass and send it with the advice and written reasons of the said council of revision to the other house, wherein if two thirds also shall be of opinion it should pass finally, it shall thereupon become law: otherwise it shall not.

If any bill presented to the said Council be not within one week (exclusive of the day of presenting it) returned by them with their advice of rejection and reasons to the house wherein it originated, or to the clerk of the said house in case of it's adjournment over the expiration of the week, it shall be law from the expiration of the week and shall then be demandeable by the clerk of the house of Delegates to be filed of record in his office.

The bills which they approve, shall become law from the time of such approbation <*or week's omission,*> and shall then be returned to or demandeable by the clerk of the House of Delegates to be filed of record in his office.

A bill rejected on advice of the Council of revision may again be proposed during the same session of Assembly with such alterations as will render it conformable to their advice.

The members of the said Council of revision shall be appointed from time to time by the board or court of which they respectively are. Two of the Executive and two of the Judiciary members shall be requisite to do business. And to prevent the evils of non-attendance, the board and courts may at any time name all or so many as they will of their members in the particular order in which they would chuse the duty of attendance to devolve from preceding to subsequent members, the preceding failing to attend. They shall have additionally for their services in this council the same allowance as members of assembly have.

### *Delegates to Congress*

The Confederation is made a part of this constitution, subject to such future alterations as shall be agreed to by the legislature of this and by all the other confederating states. The DELEGATES TO CONGRESS shall be five in number. They shall be appointed by joint balot of both houses of assembly for any term not exceeding one year, subject to be recalled at any time within the term by joint vote of both the said houses. They may at the same time be members of the Legislative or Judiciary departments.

### *Hab. corp.*

The benefits of the writ of Habeas corpus shall be extended by the legislature to every person within this state and without fee, and shall be so facilitated that no person may be detained in prison more than ten days after he shall have demanded and been refused such writ by the judge appointed by law, or if none be appointed, then by any judge of a superior court; nor more than ten days after such writ shall have been served on the person detaining him and no order given on due examination for his remandment or discharge.

### *Military.*

The MILITARY shall be subordinate to the civil power.

### *Printing.*

PRINTING PRESSES shall be subject to no other restraint than liableness to legal prosecution for false facts printed and published.

### *Convention*

Any two of the three branches of government concurring in opinion, each by the voices of two thirds of their whole existing number, that a Convention is necessary for altering this Constitution or correcting breaches of it, they shall be authorized to issue writs to every county for the election of so many delegates as they are authorized to send to the General assembly, which elections shall be held and writs returned as the laws shall have provided in the cases of elections of Delegates to assembly, mutatis mutandis, and the said delegates shall meet at the usual place of holding assemblies three months after the date of such writs, and shall be acknoleged to have equal powers with this present Convention. The said writs shall be signed by all the members approving of the same.

To INTRODUCE THIS GOVERNMENT the following special and temporary provision is made.

This Convention having been authorized only to amend those laws which constituted the form of government, no general dissolution of the whole system of laws can be supposed to have taken place; but all laws in force at the meeting of this Convention and not inconsistent with this Constitution, remain in full force, subject to alterations by the ordinary legislature.

The present General assembly shall continue till the Monday preceding the 25th. day of December in this present year. The several counties shall then, by their electors qualified as provided by this constitution, elect delegates which for the present shall be in number one for every      militia of the said county according to the latest returns in possession of the Governor, and shall also chuse Senatorial electors in proportion thereto, which Senatorial electors shall meet on the 7th. day after the day of their election at the court house of that county of their present district which would stand first in an Alphabetical arrangement of their counties, and shall chuse Senators in the proportion fixed by this Constitution.

The elections and returns shall be conducted in all circumstances not hereby particularly prescribed by the same persons and under the same form and circumstances as prescribed by the present laws in elections of Senators and Delegates of assembly. The said Senators and Delegates shall constitute the first General assembly of the new government, and shall specially apply themselves to the procuring an exact return from every county of the number of it's qualified electors, and to the settlement of the number of Delegates to be elected for the ensuing General assembly.

The present governor shall continue in office to the end of the term for which he was elected.

All other officers of every kind shall continue in office as they would have done had their appointment been under this constitution, and new ones, where new are hereby called for, shall be appointed by the authority to which such appointment is referred. One of the present judges of the General court, he consenting thereto, shall by joint ballot of both houses of assembly at their first meeting be transferred to the High court of Chancery.

## Madison to Jefferson

Philadelphia July 17, 1783

DEAR SIR

Your two favors of the 1 and 17 of June, with the debates of Congress and the letter for Miss Floyd and the Cyphers inclosed in the former, and your amendments to the Constitution inclosed in the latter, have been duly received. The latter came by yesterdays mail. I feel too sensibly the value of these communications to omit my particular acknowledgments for them.

The usual reserve of our Ministers has kept us in entire suspence since my last with regard to the definitive Treaty and every thing else in Europe. The only incident produced in this interval has been that which removed Congress from this City to Princeton.[39] I have selected the Newspaper which contains the Report of a Committee on that subject, from which you will collect the material information. Soon after the removal of Congress the Mutineers surrendered their arms and impeached some of their officers, the two principal of whom have escaped to sea. Genl. Howe with a detachment of Eastern troops is here and is instituting an enquiry into the whole plot, the object and scheme of which are as yet both involved in darkness. The Citizens of this place seem to disavow the alledged indisposition to exert force against insults offered to Congress, and are uniting in an address rehearsing the proofs which they [have] given of attachment to the fœderal authority, professing a continuance of that attachment, and declaring the utmost readiness on every occasion, to support the dignity and privileges of Congress if they should deem this place the fittest for transacting the public business until their permanent residence shall be fixed. What effect this address backed by the scanty accomodations of Princeton will have on Congress is uncertain. The prevailing disposition seemed to be that a return to their former residence as soon as the way should be decently opened would be prudent in order to prevent any inferences abroad of disaffection in the mass of so important a state to the revolution or the fœderal Government. Others suppose that a freer choice among the seats offered to Congress could be made here than in a place where the necessity of a speedy removal would give an undue advantage to the seat happening to be in greatest readiness to receive them. The Advocates for Anapolis appear to be sensible of the force of this consideration, and probably will if they can, detain Congress in Princeton until a final choice be made. N. Jersey will probably be tempted to concur in the plan by the advantage expected from actual possession. Other Members are extremely averse to a return to Philada. for various reasons.

I have been here during the week past engaged partly in some writing which, my papers being all here could not be so well done elsewhere, partly in some preparations for leaving Congress. The time of my setting out depends on some circumstances which in point of time are contingent. Mr. Lee arrived here two days ago and proceeds today to Princeton.[40] Mr. Mercer is gone to the Seaboard in N. Jersey for his health.[41] I shall probably return to Princeton next week, or sooner if I should have notice of any subject of consequence

39. On the flight to Princeton, see V. L. Collins, *The Continental Congress at Princeton* (Princeton, 1908); Edmund Cody Burnett, *The Continental Congress* (New York, 1941), pp. 575–80; and Brant, II, pp. 293–95.
40. Arthur Lee replaced Joseph Jones on the Virginia congressional delegation.
41. John Francis Mercer was a member of the Virginia congressional delegation.

being taken up by Congress. Subjects of consequence, particularly a ratification of the Treaty with Sweden have been long waiting on their table for 9. states. I am Dr. Sir Yr. sincere friend,

J. MADISON JR.


*Madison to Jefferson*

Philadelphia Aug. 11, 1783

MY DEAR SIR

At the date of my letter in April I expected to have had the pleasure by this time of being with you in Virginia. My disappointment has proceeded from several dilatory circumstances on which I had not calculated. [One of them was the uncertain state into which the object I was then pursuing had been brought by one of those incidents to which such affairs are liable. The result has rendered the time of my return to Virga. less material, as the necessity of my visiting the State of N.Jy: no longer exists. It would be improper by this communication to send particular explanations, and perhaps needless to [trou]ble you with them at any time. An      agst      is in general an impediment of      to them.      character will      etc.      which every      the      of being demanded of them. Toward the capricious[?]      for a profession of indifference at what has happened, I      do not      forward and have faith in a day of some more propitious turn of fortune:]⁴² My journey to Virga. tho' still somewhat contingent in point of time cannot now be very long postponed. I need not I trust renew my assurances that it will not finally stop on this side of Monticello.

The reserve of our foreign ministers still leaves us the sport of misinformations concerning the definitive Treaty. We all thought a little time ago that it had certainly arrived at N. York. This opinion however has become extinct, and we are thrown back on the newspaper evidence which as usual is full of contradictions. The probability seems to be that the delay arises from discussions with the Dutch. Mr. Dana has been sorely disappointed in the event of his announcing himself to the Court of Russia. His written communications obtain verbal answers only and these hold up the Mediation to which the Empress with the Emperor of G——y have been invited as a bar to any overt transaction with the U.S. and even suggest the necessity of new powers from the latter of a date subsequent to the acknowledgment of their sovereignty by G.B.⁴³ Having not seen the letters from Mr. Dana myself, I give this idea of them at second hand, remarking at the same time that it has been taken from such passages only as were not in Cypher; the latter being not yet translated.

42. After retrieving this letter at a later date, JM scratched out the portion, enclosed in brackets, relating to his romance with Kitty Floyd. Brant, II, p. 286, prints a facsimile of the defaced page containing this portion. The deciphering here follows *PTJ*, VI, p. 334, and *PJM*, VII, p. 268.

43. The "Emperor of G——y" was Joseph II, archduke of Austria and the Holy Roman emperor.

Congress remain at Princeton utterly undecided both as to their ultimate seat and their intermediate residence. Very little business of moment has been yet done at the new metropolis, except a ratification of the Treaty with Sweden. In particular nothing [has] been done as to a foreign establishment. With regard to an internal peace establishment, though it has been treated with less inattention, it has undergone little discussion. The Commander-in-chief has been invited to Princeton with a view to obtain his advice and sanction to the military branches of it, and is every day expected [t]here. The Budget of Congress is likely to have the fate of many of their other propositions to the States.[44] Delaware is the only one among those which have bestowed a consideration on it that has acceded in toto. Several Legislatures have adjourned without giving even that mark of their [co]ndescension. In the Southern States a jealousy of Congressional usurpations is likely to be the bane of the system: in the Eastern an aversion to the half pay provided for by it. New Jersey and Maryland have adopted the impost, the other funds recommended being passed for one year only by one of these States, and postponed by the other. Pa. has hitherto been friendly to liberal and fœderal ideas and will continue so, unless the late jar with Congress should give a wrong bias of which there is some danger. Masts. has in the election of Delegates for the ensuing year stigmatized the concurrence of those now in place, in the provision for half-pay, by substituting a new representation; and has sent a Memorial to Congress which I am told is pregnant with the most penurious ideas not only on that subject but on several others which concern the national honor and dignity.[45] This picture of our affairs is not a flattering one; but we have been witnesses of so many cases in which evils and errors have been the parents of their own remedy, that we cannot but view it with the consolations of hope. Remind Miss Patsy of my affection for her and be assured that I am Dr Sir Yr. Sincere friend,

J. MADISON JR.


## Jefferson to Madison

Monticello Aug. 31, 1783

DEAR SIR

Your favor of July 17. which came to hand long ago remains still unacknoleged, as from the time of it's receipt I had constant hope that you would be on the road for Virginia before an answer could reach you. That of the 11th. inst. I received yesterday, and leaves the time of your visit as unfixed as ever, and excites some fear that I shall miss of you. I propose to set out for Congress about the middle of October, unless they should be returned to Philadelphia

---

44. "The Budget of Congress" refers to the plan for restoring public credit.
45. See Stephen Patterson, "After Newburgh: The Struggle for the Impost in Massachusetts," in *The Human Dimensions of Nation Making,* ed. James Kirby Martin (Madison, 1976), pp. 218-42.

in which case I shall take at home the week I meant otherwise to pass at Philadelphia on my way to Congress. I wish it had been possible for your journey to have been so timed as that your return could have been when I go: for I still suppose you mean to pass the winter there as you told me at a time when it seemed to have no object but that of prosecuting your studies more at leisure. I sincerely lament the misadventure which has happened, from whatever cause it may have happened. Should it be final however, the world still presents the same and many other resources of happiness, and you possess many within yourself. Firmness of mind and unintermitting occupations will not long leave you in pain. No event has been more contrary to my expectations, and these were founded on what I thought a good knowlege of the ground. But of all machines ours is the most complicated and inexplicable.

Either here or in Philadelphia I must ask a perusal of your Congressional notes with leave to take notes from them, as they will better than any thing else possess me of the business I am to enter on. What is become of the mutineers? What of the Secretaryship of foreign affairs? What of the commercial treaty with Gr. Britain? These and many other questions I hope for the pleasure of having answered by you at Monticello. Be so good as to present my compliments to Mrs. House and Mrs. Trist and to ask whether the pleasure of lodging in their house may be counted among the circumstances which will render Philadelphia agreeable to me in case of the return of Congress thither. Should Congress not return thither, would it be possible for you to engage me a tolerable birth wherever they are? A room to myself, if it be but a barrack, is indispensable. In either event of my being or not being in Philadelphia I propose to place Patsy there; and will ask the favor of Mrs. Trist to think for me on that subject, and to advise me as to the person with whom she may be trusted. Some boarding school of course, tho' I am not without objections to her passing more than the day in such a one.

The want of public occurrences worth detailing has filled my letter you find with private and unimportant subjects. I wish you every possible felicity and am with sincere esteem Dr. Sir your friend and servt.,

TH: JEFFERSON

## Madison to Jefferson

Princeton Sept. 20, 1783

DEAR SIR

Your favor of the 31 ult: came to hand yesterday. As the reason which chiefly urged my departure for Virga. has ceased I have been led to protract my attendance on Congress by the interest I felt in some measures on foot, and the particular interest which my Constituents have in them. Two of these were the territorial cession and the permanent seat of Congress. The former was a few days ago put into a form which I hope will meet the ultimatum of Virginia.

The first Monday in next month is fixed for a decision of the latter; after which it may still be necessary to choose a temporary residence untill the permanent one can be made ready. I am utterly unable to foretell how either of these points will be determined. It is not impossible that an effective vote may be found attainable on neither; in which case the Winter must be spent in this village where the public business can neither be conveniently done, the members of Congress decently provided for, nor those connected with Congress provided for at all. I shall lose no time in looking out for quarters for you and entering into provisional engagements in your favor. Your other request relative to Miss Patsy shall be equally attended to as soon as I go to Philada. which will probably be towards the end of next week.

It will give me real concern if we should miss of one another altogether in the journies before us; and yet I foresee the danger of it. Mr. Jones and myself will probably be on the road by the middle of next month or a few days later. This is the time about which you expect to commence your journey. Unless therefore we travel the same road a disappointment of even an interview will be unavoidable. At present our plan is to proceed thro' Baltimore Alexandria and Fredericksbg. and we may possibly be at the races of the second place.[46] I am at a loss by what regulation I can obey your wishes with regard to the notes I have on hand; having not yet made any copy of them, having no time now for that purpose, and being unwilling for several reasons to leave them all behind me. A disappointment however will be of the less consequence, as they have been much briefer and more interrupted since the period at which you run them over, and have been altogether discontinued since the arrival of Congress here.

My plan of spending this winter in Philada. in close reading was not entirely abandoned untill Congress left that City and shewed an utter disinclination to returning to it. The prospect of agreeable and even instructive society was an original consideration with me; and the subsequent one of having yours added to it would have confirmed my intention after the abortive issue of another plan, had not the solicitude of a tender and infirm parent exacted a visit to Virga. and an uncertainty of returning been thereby incurred. Even at present if Congress should make Philada. their seat this winter and I can decline a visit to Virga. or speedily get away from it my anxiety on the subject will be renewed.

Our last information from Europe is dated the 27th. July. France and Spain were then ready for the definitive signing of the Peace. Holland was on the point of being so. The American Plenipos. had done nothing on the subject and in case of emergency could only sign the provisional Treaty as final. Their negociations had been spent chiefly on commercial stipulations from which G.B. after very different professions and appearances, altogether drew back. The ready admission she found into our commerce without paying any price for it has suggested the policy of aiming at the entire benefit of it, and

---

46. The Jockey Club of Alexandria had races scheduled to begin on Oct. 21, 1783; see *PJM,* VII, p. 355.

at the same time saving the carriage of the W. India trade the price she at first bid for it. The supposed contrariety of interests among the states and the impotence of the fœderal Government are urged by the ministerial pamphleteers as a safeguard against retaliation. The other nations of Europe seem to have more honorable views towards our commerce, sundry advances having been made to our Ministers on that subject.

Congress have come to no decision even as yet on any of the great branches of the peace establishment. The military branch is supported and quickened by the presence of the Commander in chief but without any prospect of a hasty issue.[47] The department of foreign affairs both internal and external remains as it has long done. The election of a Secretary has been an order of the day for many months without a vote being taken. The importance of the marine department has been diminished by the sale of almost all the Vessels belonging to the U.S. The department of Finance is an object of almost daily attack and will be reduced to its crisis on the final resignation of Mr. M. [Morris] which will take place in a few months. The War office is connected with the Military establishment and will be regulated I suppose in conformity to what that may be. Among other subjects which divide Congress, their Constitutional authority touching such an establishment in time of peace is one. Another still more puzzling is the precise jurisdiction proper for Congress within the limits of their permanent seat. As these points may possibly remain undecided till Novr. I mention them particularly that your aid may be prepared. The investigation of the Mutiny ended in the condemnation of several Sergeants who were stimulated to the measure without being apprised of the object by the two officers who escaped. They have all received a pardon from Congress. The real plan and object of the mutiny lies in profound darkness. I have written this in hopes that it may get to Monticello before you leave it. It might have been made more interesting if I had brought the Cypher from Philada. tho' my present situation required a great effort to accomplish as much as I have. I am obliged to write in a position that scarcely admits the use of any of my limbs: Mr. Jones and myself being lodged in a room not 10 feet square and without a single accommodation for writing. I am Dear Sir Your sincere friend and obt servt.,

J. MADISON JR.


## *Madison to Jefferson*

Philadelphia Sept. 30, 1783

DEAR SIR

My last was written on the supposition that Mr. Jones and myself would be on our way to Virga. by the middle of Ocr. and that my best chance of an

---

47. Washington arrived in Princeton on Aug. 23 and stayed until Nov. 9, 1783, to discuss plans for a peacetime army.

interview with you might be at Alexandria at the time of the races.[48] On further thought I fear that you may be led by that suggestion to suspend your setting out longer than you proposed, and that I may not find it practicable to leave this place finally before it will be practicable for you to reach it by pursuing your own plan. One circumstance which increases the uncertainty of my movements is a melancholy event in Mr. Jones family which may [a]ffect his plans, to which I shall as far as necessary make mine su[bservi]ent. It will rather therefore be my wish that you should ha[sten] than retard your journey, if it be a matter of indifference to y[o]u tho' not that you should do either if it be not so.

I have laid a train at Princeton which I hope will provide as commodious quarters as could be expected. If these should become necessary in Philada. Mrs. House's disposition towards you will be a sure resource. Mrs. Trist concurs in your idea of a boarding school; that it may be expedient for Miss Patsey for hours of instruction but no farther. She will enquire and think for you on the subject as far as her preparations for a voyage to the Mississippi will admit. She and Mrs. House make a tender of their respectful regards for yourself and Miss Patsey. I have nothing to add to my last on public subjects, nor to the above any thing but that I am Dr. Sir Yr. sincere friend and obt. Servt.,

J. MADISON JR.

As the latest papers are very barren I inclose a former one containing No. 1. of N. American, leaving the Author to your conjectures.[49]

*Madison's Notes for Jefferson on Congress's Place of Residence*

[ca. Oct. 14, 1783]

Permanent seat of Congress[50]

North River—recommended for the permanent seat of Congs. chiefly by its security against foreign danger[51]

48. The Jockey Club of Alexandria had races scheduled to begin on Oct. 21, 1783; see *PJM,* VII, p. 355.

49. Irving Brant, *James Madison: The Nationalist, 1780–87* (Indianapolis, 1948), pp. 302–5, argues that JM wrote the *North American* Numbers 1 and 2, strongly nationalist essays covering "the great subjects to which Madison devoted himself for nearly four years in Congress." But the editors of *PJM,* VII, pp. 319–46, "are of the opinion that JM most probably was not the 'North-American.'" After an elaborate comparative analysis of expressions used by JM, Richard Peters of Philadelphia (1743–1828), and *North American,* they conclude that Peters was "far more likely than JM . . . the anonymous essayist."

50. JM probably handed these notes to TJ when the latter stopped in Philadelphia from Oct. 29 until Nov. 3, 1783, before going to Princeton.

51. Kingston, New York, is 90 miles north of New York City on the Hudson River.

Falls of Potowmac—By 1. geographical centrality—2. proximity to western Country already ceded—3. inducement to further Cessions from N.C. S.C. and Georgia. 4 remoteness from the influence of any overgrown commercial city.

Falls of Delaware—By 1. centrality with regard to number of inhabitants. 2 centrality as to no. of States and of Delegates. 3 facility of obtaining intelligence from sea.

### Temporary seat of Congress

Princeton—in favor of it, 1. its neighbourhood to the Permanent [se]at, 2. inconveniency of a removal. 3. beneficial effect of a frug[al] situation of Congs. on their popularity throughout the States. 4 the risque in case of removal from Princeton of returning under the commercial and corrupt influence of Philada.—against it—1. unfitness for transacting the public business. 2 deficiency of accomodation, exposing the attending members to the danger of indignities and extortions, discouraging perhaps the fitest men from undertaking the service and amounting to a prohibition of such as had families from which they would not part.

Trenton. argts. in favor and agst. it similar to those respecting Princeton. It was particularly remarked that when the option lay with the President and committee between Trenton and Princeton the latter was preferred as least unfit to receive Congs. on their removal from Philada.

Philada. In favor of it. 1. its unrivalled conveniency for transacting the public business, and accomodating Congress. 2 its being the only place where all the public offices particularly that of Finance could be kept under the inspection and controul of and proper intercourse with Congs. 3. its conveniency for F. Ministers, to which, cæteris paribus, some regard would be expected. 4. the circumstances which produced a removal from Philada. which rendered a return as soon as the insult had been expiated, expedient for supporting in the eyes of foreign nations the appearance of internal harmony, and preventing an appearance of resentment in Congs. agst. the State of Pa. or City of Philada. an appearance which was very much strengthened by some of their proceedings at Princeton—particularly by an unnecessary and irregular declaration not to return to Phi[l]a. In addition to these overt reasons, it was concluded by sundry of the members who were most anxious to fix Congs. permanently at the falls of the Potowmac that a temporary residence in Philada. would be most likely to prepare a sufficient number of votes for that place in preference to the Falls of Delaware, and to produce a reconsideration of the vote in favor of the latter—Agst. Philada. were alledged. 1. the difficulty and uncertainty of getting away from it at the time limited. 2. the influence of a large comercial and wealthy city on the public Councils. In addition to these objections, the hatred agst. Mr. M. and hope of accelerating his final r[esigna]tion were latent motives with some, as perhaps envy of the prom[inence of] Philada. and dislike of the support of Pa to obnoxious recomendations of Congs. were with others.[52]

Annapolis—in favor of it. 1st. its capacity for accomodating Congs. and its conveniences for the public business. 2. the soothing tendency of so Southern a position on the temper of the S. States.—agst. it, 1st. the preposterousness of taking a temporary station so distant from the permanent seat fixed on, especially as better accomodations were to be passed by at Philada. which was less than ⅘ths of the distance from the Permanent Seat. 2d. the peculiar force such a step would give to the charge agst. Congs. of being swayed by improper motives. Besides these considerations it was the opinion of some that a removal of Congs. to Annapolis would inspire Maryland with hopes that wd. prevent a cooperation in favor of George town, and favor the commerce of that State at the expence of Virginia

52. "Mr. M." was Superintendent of Finance Robert Morris.

# 8

# "THE JUSTLINGS OF STATES": THE PARTNERS CHANGE PLACES, 1783–1784

*T*HROUGHOUT THE SUMMER OF 1783, Madison and Jefferson worked on plans to rendezvous in Virginia or Philadelphia. While they were together in the winter and spring of 1783, they had discussed the possibility of trading places, with Jefferson replacing Madison in Congress and Madison going into the Virginia legislature to revive Jefferson's constitutional and legal reforms. As early as February, Jefferson had urged Edmund Randolph to resign as attorney general and enter the state legislature, adding that he hoped Randolph would "be joined e'er long by Madison and [William] Short."[1]

In one of his first letters after leaving Philadelphia, Jefferson reminded Madison that he was willing to serve in Congress, "should the *call* be made *on me*," noting that the idea "was sometimes the subject of *our conversation*." If his election should coincide with Madison's projected trip to Virginia, Jefferson said that he would "with great pleasure accomodate *my movements to yours* so as to *accompany you on your return to Philadelphia*."[2] Although Madison's plans remained "somewhat contingent in point of time" after Catherine Floyd broke their engagement, Madison assured his friend that his trip, once he started on it, "will not finally stop on this side of Monticello."[3]

Throughout the summer, both men fretted that they might miss each other, as Jefferson headed north and Madison south. "I wish," Jefferson wrote at the end of August, "it had been possible for your journey to have been so

1. TJ to Edmund Randolph, Feb. 15, 1783, in *PTJ*, VI, p. 247.
2. TJ to JM, May 7, 1783, above; the italicized words were written in code. Also see TJ's letter from Philadelphia to Abner Nash, Mar. 11, 1783, in *PTJ*, VI, p. 256.
3. JM to TJ, Aug. 11, 1783, above.

"THE JUSTLINGS OF STATES," 1783–1784

timed as that your return could have been when I go: for I still suppose you mean to pass the winter there [in Philadelphia] as you told me at a time when it seemed to have no object but that of prosecuting your studies more at leisure." It was imperative that they meet either at Monticello or in Philadelphia, Jefferson thought, so that he could review Madison's notes on the congressional debates.[4] Unless they coordinated their trips and traveled the same road, Madison suggested, "a disappointment of even an interview will be unavoidable."[5]

When it became clear that Madison would serve until the end of his appointment in November, he suggested that they might rendezvous in Philadelphia, while Jefferson checked out a boarding school for his daughter.[6] After a leisurely trip of almost two weeks, Jefferson and his daughter Patsy arrived in Philadelphia on October 29, where they stayed for nearly a week.[7] By that time, Congress had decided to move from Princeton to Annapolis, and Jefferson grumbled "that I have had and shall have the trouble of travelling near 400 miles more than would have been necessary."[8]

Jefferson was not the only one to complain about Congress's move to Annapolis. The prestige of the Confederation government dropped with each itinerant move. "The high and mighty and most *gracious* Sovereigns the C[ongres]s," a Boston newspaper jeered, "not being stars of the *first* magnitude, but rather partaking of the nature of *inferior* luminaries, or *wandering* comets, again appear in their wandering orb, assuming various directions and courses, sometimes regular and uniform, at other times, vain and retrograde."[9]

Although the political plight of Congress was depressing, the recess created by the move yielded two personal benefits for Jefferson, who returned to "his family" at Mrs. House's boarding establishment, where Madison had reserved quarters for him. "I leave Patsy here," he wrote, "having had it in my power to procure for her the best tutors in French, dancing, music, and drawing."[10] And he spent almost a month with Madison, their final meeting until Jefferson returned from France in 1789.

Jefferson skipped the opening session of Congress, "knowing that the first day of the new Congress in Princetown would be employed in chusing their president and other formalities of no public consequence."[11] On November 4, he arrived in Princeton, visited a barber, and joined Congress for its second meeting. "That evening," he reported, "they adjourned from that

4. TJ to JM, Aug. 31, 1781, above.
5. JM to TJ, Sept. 20, 1783, above.
6. JM to TJ, Sept. 30, 1783, above.
7. *PTJ,* VI, p. 349, and Edward Dumbauld, *Thomas Jefferson, American Tourist* (Norman, Okla., 1946), p. 53.
8. TJ to Francis Eppes, Philadelphia, Nov. 10, 1783, in *PTJ,* VI, pp. 349–50.
9. *Boston Evening Post* (Nov. 22, 1783), cited in Jack Rakove, *The Beginnings of National Politics: An Interpretive History of the Continental Congress* (Cambridge, Mass., 1979), p. 335.
10. TJ to James Monroe, Nov. 18, 1783, in *PTJ,* VI, p. 355.
11. TJ to Francis Eppes, Nov. 10, 1783, *ibid.,* p. 349.

place" to meet in Annapolis on November 26.[12] He then returned to Philadelphia on November 6, where he remained with Madison until November 22. That morning, just before they left for Annapolis, the official copy of the definitive peace treaty, which had been signed on September 3, reached the city. Rejoicing at this good news, they arrived at the new capital three days later "without any accident and in as good health," Jefferson told his daughter, "as when I left Philadelphia."[13]

While the two friends were together in Philadelphia, they reviewed Madison's notes on congressional debates and his memorandum summarizing Congress's recent actions on the temporary and permanent seats of government under the Confederation (both men favored the falls of the Potomac or the Georgetown area).[14] Jefferson's letter to Governor Harrison about the future residence of Congress was written from Philadelphia and was based, as he acknowledged, on "the information of others," an obvious reference to Madison.[15] Jefferson and Madison also discussed the current status of Virginia's cession of its western lands to Congress and Madison's appointment to a committee considering a proposal "to erect a district of the western territory into a distinct government." After the population was large enough, the settlers could adopt a permanent constitution based on republican principles before being admitted into the Union as the "citizens of a free, sovereign, and independent State."[16] Jefferson then reviewed the Virginia cession with General Washington, whom he saw at Princeton for the first time in seven years.[17]

Madison also briefed Jefferson on the need to counteract British regulation of American trade in the postwar period. Madison and the Virginia congressmen had just warned Governor Harrison that "the cruel and pernicious restraint on our Commerce" required the United States to "regain the reputation of mutual confidence and concertion . . . which have heretofore rendered us superiour to force, machination or intrigue."[18] To buttress their warning, they cited John Adams's dispatch as "uncontrovertible." "If the United States do not soon show to the world," the New England diplomat had written from France, "a proof that they can command a common revenue to satisfy their creditors at home and abroad, that they can act as one people, as one nation, as

---

12. For the peripatetic wanderings of Congress, see Lawrence D. Cress, "Whither Columbia: Congressional Residence and the Politics of the New Nation, 1776-1787," *WMQ* 32 (1975): 581–600.

13. TJ to Martha Jefferson, Nov. 28, 1783, in *PTJ*, VI, p. 359.

14. See JM's notes for Jefferson on Congress's place of residence, [ca. Oct. 14, 1783], above.

15. TJ to Benjamin Harrison, Nov. 11, 1783, in *PTJ*, VI, pp. 351–53.

16. JM and the Virginia congressional delegation had discussed these matters in their letter to Governor Harrison, Nov. 1, 1783, in *PJM*, VII, p. 395. In TJ's first letter to Governor Harrison, Nov. 11, 1783, he referred to "the establishment of new states"; see *PTJ*, VI, pp. 351–53.

17. *Ibid.*

18. JM and the Virginia congressional delegation to Benjamin Harrison, Nov. 1, 1783, in *PJM*, VII, p. 393. See also Benjamin Harrison to TJ, Nov. 14, 1783, in *PTJ*, VI, p. 354.

one man, in their transactions with foreign nations, we shall be soon so far despised that it will be but a few years, perhaps but a few months only, before we are involved in another war."[19]

Although politics and diplomacy dominated their agenda, Madison and Jefferson also had time to roam around Philadelphia. Once again, they combed the bookstores and discussed scientific subjects that ran the gamut from weather observations to Buffon's theory of the central heat of the earth. Jefferson bought the only thermometer in Philadelphia for Isaac Zane and later requested Madison to obtain one so that they could exchange climatic information. The American Philosophical Society for Useful Information was collecting meteorological information on the recent winter storms,[20] and Jefferson, without Madison's knowledge, nominated his friend for membership in that learned organization while they were together in Philadelphia.[21]

On November 27, Madison left for Virginia and a self-imposed study of law and ancient confederacies, while Jefferson attacked the problems that bedeviled Congress, quickly replacing his friend as the dominant figure in the Confederation. That was no small accomplishment. Madison had served in Congress for almost four years, longer than any other member, and he had played an increasingly important role on matters of finance, foreign policy, land cessions, and strengthening the Confederation. The chevalier de la Luzerne, French minister to the United States from 1779 until 1784, rated Madison first among the members of Congress:

James Madison junior—of a sound and just mind. A man of learning, who desires to do good works and improve himself, but who is not overly ambitious. Of honest principles, zealous, without going to excess, for the honor of the thirteen states. He is not free from prejudices in favor of the various claims of Virginia, however exaggerated they may be; but that is a general failing. He appears to be devoted to us, and it is said that his behavior in Congress proves it. He is regarded as the man of the soundest judgment in Congress. He did not begin to take part in debate until he had been there two years and he speaks nearly always with fairness and wins the approval of his colleagues.[22]

Jefferson also had the highest regard for Madison's judgment. Writing to a nephew studying near Montpellier, Jefferson recommended that he find means of attracting "the notice and acquaintance of my friend Mr. Madison lately returned to your neighborhood from Congress.... His judgment is so

---

19. Adams's letter is printed in Francis Wharton, ed., *The Revolutionary Diplomatic Correspondence of the United States,* 6 vols. (Washington, 1889), VI, pp. 560-62, cited in *PJM,* VII, p. 397.

20. Brooke Hindle, *The Pursuit of Science in Revolutionary America, 1735-1789* (Chapel Hill, 1956), p. 348.

21. When the results of the Jan. 1784 election were announced, JM's name was not listed as a new member; see TJ to Francis Hopkinson, Feb. 18, 1784, in *PTJ,* VI, p. 542. For Hopkinson's explanation of the oversight, see *ibid.,* p. 556. For JM's election to the society, see the letter to JM, Jan. 21, 1785, in *PJM,* VIII, p. 236.

22. Luzerne, "Liste des Membres du Congrès depuis 1779 jusqu'en 1784," in Archives des Affaires Etrangères, trans. and cited by Brant, II, p. 14.

sound and his heart is so good that I would wish you to respect every advice he would be so kind as to give you, equally as if it came from me."[23]

As he had promised his successor, Madison stopped on his way home for a visit with George Mason to discuss state and federal politics.[24] *"I found him much less opposed to the general impost than I had expected,"* Madison informed his friend. Mason also favored Virginia's cession of western lands as well as the *"defence of our trade against British machinations."* Even on the issue of *"a convention* for *revising our form of government"* in Virginia, the author of the Constitution of 1776 *"was sound and ripe and, I think would not decline a* participation *in the work. His heterodoxy,"* Madison concluded, *"lay chiefly in being too little impressed with* either the *necessity* or the *proper means of preserving the* confederacy."[25]

Unlike Mason, Jefferson was impressed with the necessity of preserving the Confederation and viewed prompt ratification of the definitive peace treaty as the proper means of accomplishing that goal. But he was also depressed by the dilatory attendance record of the state delegations. Throughout its stay in Annapolis, Congress seldom had a quorum of seven states to transact routine business, much less the nine necessary to ratify the peace treaty. As the chairman of the committee appointed to report on the Treaty of Paris, Jefferson fumed that Congress had only had representatives from six states for ten days in a row, a situation that led some congressmen to advocate fudging a quorum of seven states in order to ratify the treaty "under the sanction of our seal (without letting our actual state appear)." But the Virginian, who had drafted the official instrument of ratification, consistently opposed such action as "a breach of faith in us, a prostitution of our seal," which would probably "be rejected by the other contracting party as null and unauthorized."[26]

There the matter rested until January 14, 1784, when nine state delegations finally arrived in Annapolis and promptly rallied to ratify the treaty, even though the time limit specified in that document had by then expired. Unfortunately, Congress could not afford to pay a courier to carry the instrument of ratification to England. Instead, the French minister to America, the chevalier de la Luzerne, paid a British sea captain to take the news of the congressional action on the Peace of Paris to London and France, a tardy confirmation of American independence.[27]

Appropriately enough, Thomas Jefferson, the author of the Declaration of Independence, was also the author of the congressional proclamation con-

23. TJ to Peter Carr, Annapolis, Dec. 11, 1783, in *PTJ,* VI, p. 380.
24. JM to TJ, Dec. 10, 1783, below, and TJ to JM, Dec. 11, 1783, below.
25. JM to TJ, Dec. 10, 1783, below. The italicized words were written in code.
26. See TJ to JM, Dec. 11, 1783, below and Feb. 20, 1784, below. The latter enclosed TJ's "Resolution Opposing Ratification of the Definitive Treaty by Less Than Nine States," [Dec. 27, 1783], below.
27. William C. Stinchcombe, *The American Revolution and the French Alliance* (Syracuse, 1969), p. 210.

firming the official recognition of the achievement of the revolutionary goal of independence.[28] After the momentary majority of nine states in January 1784, Jefferson complained that "there have never been 9 states on the floor but for the ratification of the treaty and a day or two after." Congress again marked time, seldom convening. "We have not sit above 3. days I beleive in as many weeks," he told Madison late in February.[29] Yet there was much to do, as Jefferson reported to Governor Benjamin Harrison:

1. authorizing our Foreign ministers to enter into treaties of alliance and commerce with the several nations who have desired it.
2. arranging the Domestic administration.
3. establishing Arsenals within the states, and posts on our Frontier.
4. Disposing of Western territory.
5. treaties of peace and purchase with the Indians.
6. Money.[30]

On the question of money, Jefferson had two complaints. On the federal front, he was exasperated that Congress spent so much time debating "the most trifling money propositions," and he asked Madison for the latter's expert thoughts on the subject. On a personal note, he observed that he "had been from home four months and had expended 1200 Dollars before I received one farthing. By the last post we received about seven weeks allowance. In the mean time some of us had had the mortification to have our horses turned out of the livery stable for want of money. There is really no standing this."[31] Two months later, he grumbled about Virginia paying its congressional delegates less than $4 a day. "The predicament in which this places us," he wrote Madison, "is well known to you. It is inconceivably mortifying."[32]

Jefferson also called on his experienced friend to clarify a point of congressional jurisdiction. He recalled a conversation in which Madison had argued "that Congress had no authority to decide any cases between two differing states, except those of disputed territory." However, Jefferson was sure that "every cause of difference" could be "submitted to a federal court" and asked Madison for his considered opinion.[33]

Despite his criticisms of the Confederation, Jefferson nevertheless thought it important that America's most promising young statesmen should be elected to Congress. There they would "see the affairs of the Confederacy from a high ground; they learn the importance of the Union and befriend federal measures when they return" to their states. "Those who never come here, see our affairs insulated, pursue a system of jealousy and self interest, and

---

28. For TJ's proclamation of Jan. 14, 1784, announcing ratification, see *PTJ*, VI, pp. 462–63.
29. TJ to JM, Feb. 20, 1784, below.
30. TJ to Benjamin Harrison, Jan. 16 [17], 1784, in *PTJ*, VI, pp. 468–69.
31. TJ to JM, Feb. 20, 1784, below.
32. TJ to JM, Apr. 25, 1784, below.
33. TJ to JM, Feb. 20, 1784, below.

distract the Union as much as they can." In short, Congress "is a good school for our young statesmen. It gives them impressions friendly to the federal government instead of those adverse which too often take place in persons confined to the politics of their state."[34]

In a long letter of March 16, 1784, Madison responded to Jefferson's questions with a brilliant discussion of constitutional issues under the Confederation. He agreed that "the project of affixing the Seal of the U. S. by 7 States" to the Treaty of Paris, "tho' it might have produced a temporary deception abroad, must have been immediately detected at home, and have finally dishonored the fœderal Councils everywhere." He backed his statement with research notes he had made from the files of Congress while looking "for such lights as the history of the Confederation might furnish."

Madison also reviewed the practice of Congress in drawing a distinction between the "appropriation" of money and the "expenditure" of appropriated funds, noting that if none were drawn, it would require the vote of nine states to "buy quills or wafers." Although he had contended that the authority of Congress—the federal court—was restricted to territorial disputes, he quickly admitted that he had been mistaken "in the opinion I had formed. Whence I got it," he confessed with disarming charm, "I am utterly at a loss to account."

The two friends also exchanged views on the western territories, commerce, and the location of the nation's capital. They had long collaborated on policies for the West, beginning with Governor Jefferson's transmittal to Congress of Virginia's original cession in January 1781, through Madison and the congressional delegation's opposition to the pretensions of land companies, to the insistence on the creation of republican states admitted to the Union on the basis of equality with the original republics.

Working with congressmen who had been Madison's colleagues, Jefferson became the chairman of a succession of committees that dealt with the western territories, quickly demonstrating, as David Howell of Rhode Island observed, that he was "one of the best members I have ever seen in Congress."[35] Under his leadership, Congress executed a deed not only for Virginia's cession, but for all western territory, ceded or to be ceded, converting it into the national domain.[36] For Madison, he sketched his ideas for the entire trans-Appalachian West, including the Northwest Territory already ceded and lands south of the Ohio River still claimed by Virginia, North Carolina, South Carolina, and Georgia. West of the original thirteen states in the area bounded by the Great Lakes to the north, the Mississippi River to the west, and the

---

34. *Ibid.*, Apr. 25, 1784, below.

35. JM to TJ, Mar. 16, 1784, below, and David Howell to Jonathan Arnold, Feb. 21, 1784, cited in *PTJ*, VI, p. 585.

36. Two basic articles are by Merrill Jensen: "The Cession of the Old Northwest," *MVHR* 23 (1936): 27–48, and "The Creation of the National Domain, 1781–1784," *MVRH* 26 (1939): 323–42. Another article of importance is Peter Onuf's "Toward Federalism: Virginia, Congress, and the Western Lands," *WMQ* 34 (1977): 353–74.

Spanish territory to the south would be fourteen new republics arranged in two tiers, the western tier bounded by the Mississippi and the other tier situated between this western row and the original eastern states. Two lines of longitude—one through "the rapids of Ohio" (Louisville, Kentucky) and the other through "the Mouth of the Gr. Kanhaway [River]" (Point Pleasant, West Virginia) on the Ohio—would create the two tiers, and parallels of latitude would allow "to each state an extent of 2°. from N. to South," thus meeting Virginia's condition that the new states be no less than 100 nor more than 150 miles square.[37]

After Congress passed the Ordinance of 1784, Jefferson sent Madison a copy, sketching the steps from temporary territorial government to statehood and showing "how and when they shall be taken into the union. . . . The minuter circumstances of selling the ungranted lands will be provided in an ordinance already prepared but not reported."[38] The movement to statehood involved three stages. The settlers, either by means of their own petition or by order of Congress, could meet to form a temporary government by adopting the constitution and laws of one of the original states. When the population reached 20,000 free inhabitants, the settlers could receive authority from Congress to call a convention "to establish a permanent constitution and government for themselves." Finally, when the population of a territory equaled the least numerous of the original states, it would be admitted into the Union on an equal footing with the thirteen original states.[39]

The territorial governments were to (1) remain forever a part of the United States, (2) be subject to Congress and the Articles of Confederation in all cases in which the original states were so subject, (3) be republican in form, (4) be liable for a proportionate share of the federal debt, (5) never admit as a citizen any person with a hereditary title, and (6) prohibit slavery and involuntary servitude after 1800. The last two clauses, Jefferson informed Madison with regret, were struck out of the report. "The 1st. was done not from an approbation of such honours, but because it was thought an improper place to encounter them. The 2d. was lost by an individual vote only."[40]

While Jefferson settled into his assignment in Congress, Madison quietly pursued his goals in Virginia, undertaking an intensive "course of law read-

---

37. TJ to JM, Feb. 20, 1784, below. Boyd traces the development of TJ's ideas for a "Plan for Government of the Western Territory" in *PTJ*, VI, pp. 571–617.

38. TJ to JM, Apr. 25, 1784, below.

39. *Ibid.*, with the enclosed ordinance, below. For two excellent discussions of the Ordinance of 1784, see Robert K. Berkhofer, Jr., "Jefferson, the Ordinance of 1784, and the Origins of the American Territorial System," *WMQ* 29 (1972): 231–62, and Reginald Horsman, "Thomas Jefferson and the Ordinance of 1784," *Journal* (Illinois State Historical Society) 79 (1986): 99–112. The best presentation of maps is in Lester J. Cappon, Barbara B. Petchenik, and John H. Long, eds., *Atlas of Early American History: The Revolutionary Era, 1760–1790* (Princeton, 1976), pp. 60–61, 128–30.

40. TJ to JM, Apr. 25, 1784, below. See also David Brion Davis, "The Significance of Excluding Slavery from the Old Northwest in 1787," *Indiana Magazine of History* 84 (1988): 75–87.

ing." It was a self-assigned project or, as he phrased it, one "with which I have tasked myself." He also devoted careful study to the science of government, and Jefferson instructed his steward to allow Madison free use of his library at Monticello.[41] Jefferson also promised to buy books for Madison, who was particularly interested in "whatever may throw light on the general Constitution and droit public of the several confederacies which have existed."[42] He singled out "the Duch, the German, and the Helvetic" confederacies, observing that "the operations of our own must render all such lights of consequence. Books on the Law of N. and N. [Nature and Nations]," he wrote, "fall within a similar remark."[43]

A severe winter with heavier snows than usual created what Madison called "the winter blockade," allowing him a great deal of time for reading and study. The standard legal treatise, Sir Edward Coke's *Institutes of the Laws of England*, "and a few others from the same shelf," he reported, "have been my chief society during the Winter."[44] Shortly after he returned home, he agreed to serve in the legislature, "if the suffrage of my County should destine me for that service, which I am made to expect will be the case."[45] On April 25, 1784, he informed Jefferson that he had been elected along with Charles Porter, the candidate who had defeated him in 1777 when he refused to treat the voters to whiskey.

Madison's private preparation in law and political science was tied to his public goals. His reasons for reentering the Virginia legislature were to push the revision of the laws of Virginia introduced by Jefferson in 1779, to try to launch a move to revise the Virginia Constitution of 1776,[46] and to promote a "Plan for giving greater Powers to the federal Government"[47] in order, he later confessed, to bring about "a rescue of the Union and the blessings of liberty staked on it from an impending catastrophe."[48]

Although Madison had been out of the state for four years, his reputation as a congressman assured him of a leadership role in an assembly split among the followers of Patrick Henry, Richard Henry Lee, and Speaker John Tyler. In the first postwar legislature, wrote Attorney General Edmund Randolph, "the increase of new members has introduced some of the children of the revolution," who disdained the old leaders and factions. "This renders it probable," he informed Jefferson, "that our friend of Orange will step earlier into

---

41. TJ to John Key, Annapolis, Nov. 26, 1783, in *PTJ*, VI, p. 358.
42. JM used "droit public" (public law) in contrast to "droit gens" (international law); see *PJM*, VIII, p. 6.
43. JM to TJ, Mar. 16, 1784, below.
44. JM to Edmund Randolph, Mar. 10, 1784, in *PJM*, VIII, p. 3.
45. *Ibid.*
46. JM to TJ, Feb. 11, 1784, below.
47. See William Short to TJ, May 14 [15], 1784, in *PTJ*, VII, pp. 256-58, in which Short describes a coffeehouse meeting between JM, Patrick Henry, and Joseph Jones for this purpose.
48. JM, *The Papers of James Madison*, ed. Henry D. Gilpin, 3 vols. (Washington, 1840), II, pp. 693-94.

the heat of battle, than his modesty would otherwise permit. For he is already resorted to, as a general, of whom much has been preconceived to his advantage."[49] William Short, Jefferson's protégé who served on the governor's council, agreed that members of the assembly "have formed great Hopes of Mr. Madison, and those who know him best think he will not disappoint their most sanguine Expectations."[50]

Although Madison served on several committees, including Religion, his sole chairmanship was that of the Committee on Commerce. Before leaving Congress, Madison had read the earl of Sheffield's pamphlet, which argued that Great Britain could continue to dominate American commerce without changing its restrictive navigation laws since "the interests of the States are so opposite in matters of Commerce, and the authority of Congress so feeble that no defensive precautions need be feared on the part of U. S." Unless Congress and the states could agree on a defensive plan, Madison argued, "it will prove such an inefficacy in the Union as will extinguish all respect for it and reliance on it."[51]

Madison's experience at home confirmed the views he had formed in Congress. After an absence of four years, he was shocked by economic conditions in Virginia. In his first letter to Jefferson after returning home, he complained that "the situation of the commerce of this country as far as I can learn is even more deplorable than I had conceived." Between the dominance of Philadelphia and Baltimore—and he later emphasized a resurgence of trade with Britain—Virginia paid a premium of more than 30 or 40 percent on all its exports and imports, "a tribute which if paid into the treasury of the State would yield a surplus above all its wants."[52]

Virginia needed to emancipate itself from such economic bondage, and the chairman of the Commerce Committee introduced a sweeping port bill in May 1784 in an attempt to establish economic independence and "reduce the trade of G[reat] B[ritain] to an equality with that of other nations."[53] Before Madison had headed home, he and Jefferson had discussed the need to restrict Virginia's foreign trade to Norfolk in an effort to dismantle the pre-Revolutionary system of decentralized river commerce that had led to "British monopoly and diffusive credit."[54] Commercial pressure in the state assembly quickly added Alexandria in the north to Norfolk in the south as the only two

---

49. Edmund Randolph to TJ, May 15, 1784, in *PTJ,* VII, p. 260.

50. William Short to TJ, May 14 [15], 1784, *ibid.,* p. 257.

51. JM to Edmund Randolph, Aug. 30, 1784, in *PJM,* VII, pp. 295–96, and Sept. 13, 1784, *ibid.,* p. 315.

52. JM to TJ, Dec. 10, 1783, below.

53. This blunt statement is quoted from JM's draft letter to TJ of Aug. 20, 1784. It is printed in *PJM,* VIII, pp. 102–10, "to illustrate the striking differences between JM's first ideas and the final letter." The recipient's copy, which JM sent to TJ on Aug. 20, 1784, omitted this statement; see below. For JM's port bill, June 8, 1784, see *PJM,* VIII, pp. 64–65.

54. JM to TJ, Aug. 20, 1784, below, and TJ to JM, Dec. 8, 1784, below. Also see TJ, "On the Port of Norfolk," [May 1784], in *PTJ,* VII, pp. 215–16, which was written before JM introduced his bill in the Virginia legislature.

port cities, but continual political logrolling finally forced the legislature to enumerate five ports, one on each of Virginia's major rivers. "We made a warm struggle for the establishment of Norfolk and Alexandria as our only ports," the committee chairman informed the congressman, "but were obliged to add York[town], Tappahannock, and Bermuda hundred."[55]

The port bill was an attempt to solve Virginia's economic problems without waiting for Congress to establish alternative trade routes by means of commercial treaties. It was designed to create a native merchant marine, a native merchant class, and an urban market in the port cities as well as to restrict foreign merchants to the roles of wholesalers and bankers.[56] By concentrating trade at a few ports, Jefferson observed, the legislation would "bring to a point the proper subjects of taxation and reduce the army of taxgatherers almost to a single hand."[57]

For all its merits, the port bill produced the "most agitation and discussion" after the legislature adjourned because it restrained foreign trade to the enumerated ports. Madison described the opposition for Jefferson:

Those who meditate a revival of it on the old plan of British monopoly and diffusive credit, or whose mercantile arrangements might be disturbed by the innovation, with those whose local situations give them, or are thought to give them an advantage in large vessels coming up the rivers to their usual stations, are busy in decoying the people into a belief that trade ought in all cases to be left to regulate itself, that to confine it to particular ports is to renounce the boon with which Nature has favoured our country, and that if one sett of men are to be importers and exporters, another set to be carryers between the mouths and heads of the rivers and a third retailers, trade, as it must pass through so many hands all taking a profit, must in the end come dearer to the people than if the simple plan should be continued which unites these several branches in the same hands.[58]

Because these objections, "tho' unsound, are not altogether unplausible," Madison feared continuing opposition within the state to the port bill. But he easily steered through the legislature a bill to invest Congress with a new power to control commerce for fifteen years, by retaliating against any nation that excluded American vessels from any of its ports. Aimed at Great Britain for barring American ships from its West Indian ports, the bill could not go into effect until it was ratified by all the other states, an action that never materialized.

Two other aspects of Virginia's trade on its ribbon of rivers attracted Madison's and Jefferson's attention: canal routes between "the Western waters and [the] Atlantic," which "promises us almost a monopoly of the Western

55. JM to TJ, July 3, 1784, below.
56. See Drew R. McCoy, "The Virginia Port Bill of 1784," *VMHB* 83 (1975): 288–303, and Robert B. Bittner, "Economic Independence and the Virginia Port Bill of 1784," in *Virginia in the American Revolution*, ed. Richard A. Rutyna and Peter C. Stewart (Norfolk, 1977), pp. 73–92.
57. TJ to JM, Dec. 8, 1784, below.
58. JM to TJ, Aug. 20, 1784, below.

and Indian trade," and a negotiation to resolve Maryland's claim of exclusive jurisdiction over the Potomac River. On the first, Jefferson urged prompt action by Virginia to link the Ohio and the Potomac. "I think the opening [of] this navigation is an object on which no time is to be lost," or Pennsylvania would "get possession of the commerce." Once this channel was opened, the other major rivers in Virginia could be connected by canals with interior rivers, starting with the "James river and so on through the whole successively. Genl. Washington," he told Madison, "has that of the Patowmac much at heart. The superintendance of it would be a noble amusement in his retirement and leave a monument of him as long as the waters should flow."[59]

On the subject of the Potomac, Madison took the lead. Citing Lord Baltimore's charter of 1632, he observed that Maryland's boundary was "the *Southern Shore* of the Potowmac*,*" with Virginia retaining *"only the free navigation and use"* of the river. If Virginia had no jurisdiction, he asked, "will not such a construction be fatal to our own port regulations on that side and otherwise highly inconvenient?" He warned Jefferson that "no time should be lost in fixing the interest of Virginia." "What will be the best course to repair the error?" he asked rhetorically, before ticking off several approaches: "to extend our laws upon the River, making Maryland the plaintiff if she chooses to contest their authority—to state the case to her at once and propose a settlement by negociation—or to propose a mutual appointment of Commissioners for the general purpose of preserving a harmony and efficacy in the regulations of both sides." He favored the last course and suggested that Jefferson, taking advantage of "the good humour into which the cession of the back lands must have put Maryland," take up the subject in Annapolis.[60] Jefferson liked Madison's proposal and promptly conversed with Thomas Stone, a Maryland congressman who agreed to sponsor it jointly with Jefferson.[61] Thus was set in motion a course of action that led to the Mt. Vernon Conference in 1785, the Annapolis Convention in 1786, and, ultimately, the Constitutional Convention in Philadelphia in 1787.[62]

At the beginning of the legislative session, Madison found Patrick Henry "strenuous for invigorating the federal Government"[63] because "a bold Example set by Virginia would have influence on the other States." Indeed, Henry "saw Ruin inevitable unless something was done to give Congress a compulsory Process on delinquent States."[64] Jefferson also wrote Madison that "Virginia must do something more than she has done to maintain any degree of

---

59. TJ to JM, Feb. 20, 1784, below.
60. JM to TJ, Mar. 16, 1784, below.
61. TJ to JM, Apr. 25, 1784, below.
62. JM was appointed a member of Virginia's Potomac River Commission to meet with Maryland's commissioners; see JM to TJ, July 3, 1784, below.
63. JM to TJ, May 15, 1784, below.
64. William Short to TJ, May 14 [15], 1784, in *PTJ,* VII, p. 257.

respect in the Union and to make it bearable to any man of feeling to represent her in Congress."⁶⁵

Accordingly, the Virginia legislature declared for full compliance with federal requisitions and recommended that amounts owed to the United States be collected "by distress on the property of the defaulting states or their citizens."⁶⁶ But when the legislature moved to pay—belatedly—three-fourths of its 1781 requisition, Henry rammed through a moratorium on tax collection. Madison managed to obtain passage of a stamp tax and to designate its receipts for the foreign creditors of Virginia, but he informed Jefferson that tax receipts "will be much short of what they [Congress] need, and of what might be expected from the declarations with which we introduced the business of the Session."⁶⁷

Henry and Madison disagreed on two other major measures, both close to Jefferson's heart. The first involved revision of the Virginia Constitution of 1776, a wartime creation that had been enacted by the legislature, sitting as an ad hoc convention, but never submitted to the people for ratification. Knowing Henry's opposition to innovation, Madison at first decided not to raise the issue. But with the arrival of Richard Henry Lee, second only to Henry in the House, "we thought it might not be amiss to stir the matter." "Unluckily," he confessed to Jefferson, "R. H. L. was obliged by sickness to leave us the day before the question came on in Committee of the whole, and Mr. Henry shewed a more violent opposition than we expected. The consequence was that after two days Debate, the Report was negatived, and the majority[,] not content with stopping the measure for the present availed themselves of their strength to put a supposed bar on the Journal against a future possibility of carrying it," declaring that the assembly had no power to call a convention "until a majority of all the free people shall direct a reform thereof."⁶⁸

In the case of a general tax assessment for the support of the Christian religion, Patrick Henry and other supporters persuaded the Committee on Religion to report that petitions favoring that policy were "reasonable." Although "the friends of the measure did not chuse to try their strength in the House," Madison told his friend in Annapolis, they kept the measure alive by holding it over for another session. "Extraordinary as such a project was," he concluded, "it was preserved from a dishonorable death by the talents of Mr. Henry."⁶⁹

In one case, Madison and Henry collaborated happily but lost to the Lee faction. Jefferson had urged Madison to persuade the Virginia legislature "to

65. TJ to JM, May 8, 1784, below.
66. Hening, XI, pp. 401–2, 415.
67. JM to TJ, July 3, 1784, below.
68. *Ibid.*, July 3, 1784, below. See also the *Journal of the House of Delegates, May 1784* (Richmond, 1828), pp. 70–71, June 21, 1784; cited in *PJM,* VIII, p. 77.
69. JM to TJ, July 3, 1784, below.

do something" for Thomas Paine, the author of *Common Sense,* as an expression of "the grateful impressions which his services have made on our minds." New York had made him a present of a farm, and Jefferson urged a Virginia gift of "2000 guineas, or an inheritance worth 100 guineas a year."[70] Washington also backed action "in our assembly for poor Paine."[71] Patrick Henry headed a special committee and Madison prepared a bill making Paine a gift of a farm on the eastern shore of Virginia. Although the prospect was at first flattering, Madison thought, "a sudden opposition was brewed up which put a negative on every form which could be given to the proposed remuneration."[72]

One legislative project Madison made all his own. While snowbound during the winter, he had recalled his pledge to Jefferson to revive work on the revision of Virginia laws that had been inaugurated in 1776 but had been stalled in the legislature since 1779. "I have been thinking," he told the chief revisor, "whether the present situation of the Report of the Revisors of the Laws does not render the printing of it for public consideration advisable." Jefferson quickly endorsed the idea. Just before the state legislature met, he wrote Madison: "The more I have reflected on your proposition for printing the Revisal the more I have liked it."[73]

Madison's resolution pointed out that the revision, which proposed "material changes in our legal Code," had been "executed with great Labour and Care" and should be distributed "throughout the Community" for examination by the citizens at large. When the legislature agreed, he sent Jefferson a happy note, even though he grumbled that "a frivolous œconomy restrained the number of copies to 500." But he observed that the legislature had generously recalled the "three Revisor's labours" and had belatedly voted them £500 each for their work, subject to the exigencies of the state treasury. The stipend, he added, was "to be paid out of the first unappropriated money in the Treasury, which renders its value very precarious unless the Treasurer should be willing to endorse it 'receivable in taxes' which he is not obliged to do."[74]

When they were not discussing politics and constitutional issues, Jefferson and Madison explored scientific topics and talked of their next get-together. If the printing of the revision of the laws passed, Jefferson said that he would have to make "a short trip to Virginia, as from the loss of the originals I beleive my copies must often be wanting." Whenever he returned to Monticello, he added, he hoped that Madison would settle nearby:

70. TJ to JM, May 25, 1784, below.

71. George Washington to JM, June 12, 1784, in *PJM,* VIII, pp. 67–68.

72. JM to TJ, July 3, 1784, below. The bill of June 28, 1784, is in *PJM,* VIII, p. 88. For JM's note that Arthur Lee killed the bill by citing Paine's authorship of a pamphlet opposing Virginia's western land claims, see *ibid.,* p. 92.

73. For JM's letter of Feb. 11 and TJ's responses of Feb. 20 and Apr. 25, 1784, see below.

74. For JM's resolution on printing the report about the revision of the Virginia statutes and paying the revisors, see *PJM,* VIII, pp. 48–49. For his explanation about the stipend for each revisor, see JM to TJ, July 3, 1784, below.

Monroe is buying land almost adjoining mine. Short will do the same. What would I not give [if] you could fall into the circle. With such a society I could once more venture home and lay myself up for the residue of life, quitting all it's contentions which grow daily more and more insupportable. Think of it. To render it practicable only requires you to think it so. Life is of no value but as it brings us gratifications. Among the most valuable of these is rational society. It informs the mind, sweetens the temper, chears our spirits, and promotes health.[75]

Such proximity would make it possible for them to join together in the pursuit of science. Madison recalled their conversation about the French scientist Buffon's theory of the central heat of the earth. Even though his trunk with Buffon's book had not yet arrived, he utilized the work of two other scientists to devise a test to prove the validity of Buffon's theory as Jefferson had explained it.[76] On further reflection about Buffon's hypothesis, however, Jefferson revised his opinion, concluding that the scientist's theory was wrong.[77] A chastened Madison replied that Jefferson's new explanation of Buffon's theory had "rectified my misconception of it, and I forbear as I ought perhaps formerly to have done making any further remarks on it, at least till I have seen the work itself."[78]

In his omnivourous reading, Madison filed away obscure references as footnotes to share with Jefferson, particularly if they touched on matters discussed by Jefferson in his manuscript that later became his only book, *Notes on the State of Virginia*. He sent a citation to "grinders of the Incognitum which were found in Brasil and Lima" and were now preserved in the British Museum. "If I do not misremember your Hypothesis," he wrote, "it supposes no bones of that animal to have been met with so far to the South."[79] Jefferson thought that the authority cited was respectable and, therefore, concluded that it was "unsafe to deny the fact; but I think it may well be doubted." Until more remains were found, he suggested, the ones referred to might "still be beleived to have been first carried there either previous to the emigration of the Spaniards when there was doubtless a communication between the Ind[ia]ns. of the two continents, or after that emigration when an intercourse between the Spaniards of N. and S. Amera. took place."[80]

Madison also wrote that Philip Mazzei, Jefferson's former neighbor in Albemarle County, before returning to Europe, had reported the discovery of a subterranean city in Siberia. While he was in Paris, Mazzei had visited Buf-

75. TJ to JM, Feb. 20, 1784, below. For JM's response, see his letter of Mar. 16, 1784, below.
76. JM to TJ, Dec. 10, 1783, below.
77. TJ to JM, Jan. 1, 1784, below.
78. JM to TJ, Feb. 17, 1784, below.
79. JM to TJ, Feb. 11, 1784, below.
80. TJ to JM, Feb. 20, 1784, below. In this letter, TJ also expressed his wish that JM had a thermometer in Orange County so that JM could send comparative readings to him and to JM's cousin, the Reverend James Madison, president of the College of William and Mary.

fon, who had received from Catherine the Great of Russia a piece of golden chain from the site. It was "so exquisitely wrought" that no artist in Paris could equal the workmanship.[81] After receiving this letter, Jefferson wrote promptly to Francis Hopkinson, a fellow member of the American Philosophical Society, about the discovery.[82]

As Congress moved towards adjournment in Annapolis before migrating northward to Trenton for its fall session, its members accepted John Jay's resignation as one of its European ministers, appointed him to the long-vacant post of secretary of foreign affairs, and named Jefferson as his successor to join Benjamin Franklin and John Adams "on the foreign commercial negotiations."

"I am now to take my leave of the justlings of states," he informed Madison happily, "and to repair to a feild where the divisions will be fewer but on a larger scale." But he promised that he would continue his correspondence and asked Madison to reciprocate. "At the close of every session of assembly a state of the general measures and dispositions, as well as of the subordinate politics of parties or individuals will be entertaining and useful. During recesses other objects will furnish matter sufficient for communication."

As a measure of their friendship, Jefferson charged Madison, in whom he placed "unlimited confidence," with "a tender legacy"—the educational oversight of two of his nephews, Peter Carr and Dabney Carr, Jr. They were the sons of his widowed sister and "the dearest friend I knew, who had fate reversed our lots, would have been a father to my children."[83]

Jefferson quickly reactivated the plans for a long absence that had brought him to Philadelphia eighteen months earlier. He returned to Philadelphia to collect his daughter Patsy, pack for the long-delayed trip abroad, and await his secretary, William Short, and his servant, James Hemmings. While he was in Philadelphia, Jefferson tried to have his manuscript printed but decided instead to wait "till I shall cross the water where I will have a few copies struck off." He spent one morning combing every bookstore but one for books Madison had requested. Then he headed north, visiting the principal towns in Connecticut, Rhode Island, Massachusetts, and New Hampshire "in order to acquire what knowlege I could of their commerce and other circumstances." From Massachusetts, he reported that the state was preparing a bill to give Congress power over commerce. And in his farewell note to Madison, he observed that he had found "the conviction growing strongly that nothing can preserve our Confederacy unless the band of Union, their common council[,] be strengthened."[84]

81. JM to TJ, Apr. 25, 1784, below.
82. *PTJ,* VII, p. 227.
83. TJ to JM, May 8, 1784, below.
84. TJ to JM, May 25, 1784, below, and July 1, 1784, below.

──────── THE LETTERS ────────

## Madison to Jefferson

Orange Dec. 10, 1783

DEAR SIR

My journey from Annapolis was so much retarded by rains and their effect on the water courses that I did not complete it till the ninth day after I left you. I took *Col. Mason* in my *way and had an evening's conversation with him. I found him much less opposed to the general impost than I had expected.* Indeed *he disclaimed all opposition to the measure itself but had taken up a vague* apprehension that *if adopted at this crisis it might embarras* the *defence of our trade against British machinations.* He seemed upon the whole to *acquiesce in the territorial cession* but *dwelt much on the* expediency of the *guaranty.* On the article of a convention for *revising our form of government*[1] *he was sound and ripe and, I think would not decline a* participation *in the work. His heterodoxy lay chiefly in being too little impressed with* either the *necessity* or the *proper means of preserving the* confederacy.

The situation of the commerce of this country[2] as far as I can learn is even more deplorable than I had conceived. It can not pay less to Philada. and Baltimore if one may judge from a comparison of prices here and in Europe, than 30 or 40 Per Ct. on all the exports and imports, a tribute which if paid into the treasury of the State would yield a surplus above all its wants. If the Assembly should take any steps towards its emancipation you will no doubt be apprized of them as well as of their other proceedings from Richmond.

I am not yet settled in the course of law reading with which I have tasked myself and find it will be impossible to guard it against frequent interruptions. I deputed one of my brothers to Monticello with the draught on your library, but Capt. Key was down at Richmond.[3] As soon as he returns I propose to send again. My Trunk with Buffon etc. has come safe to Fredg. so that I shall be well furnished with materials for collateral reading. In conversing on this author's Theory of Central heat I recollect that we touched upon, as the best means for trying its validity, the comparative distances from the Earths center of the summits of the highest mountains and their bases or the level of the sea. Does not the oblate figure of the earth present a much more extensive and perhaps adequate field for experiments? According to the calculations of Martin grounded on the data of Maupertius etc.

1. George Mason was the author of the Virginia Declaration of Rights and the Virginia Constitution of 1776. The italicized words were written in code.
2. Virginia.
3. John Key was TJ's manager at Monticello from 1782 to 1784; see Edwin M. Betts, ed., *Thomas Jefferson's Farm Book*... (Princeton, 1953), p. 149.

> The Equatorial diameter of the Earth is 7942.2. Eng: Miles
> The polar diam: 7852.4. E.M.
> 
> difference between Eq: and pol: diameter 89.8. E.M.

The difference then of the semidiameters is 44.9 E. Miles, that is $1/87.94$ of the mean semidiameter, calling this difference in round numbers 45 Miles, and disregarding the small variations produced by the elliptical form of the Earth, the radii will be shortened ½ of a mile by each degree from the Equator to the poles. It would seem therefore that the difference of distance from the center at the Equator and at the highest latitude that may [be] visited must be sufficient to produce a discoverable difference in the degrees of any heat emitted equally in every direction from the center: and the experiments might be sufficiently diversified to guard against illusion from any difference which might be supposed in the intermediate density of different parts of the earth. The distance even between the Equator and the polar circle produces a difference of no less than 33⅙ miles i.e. $1/119$ of the mean distance from the center; so that if the curiosity of the two setts of French Philosophers employed in ascertaining the figure of the earth, had been directed to this question, a very little additional trouble and expence might perhaps have finally solved it. Nay the extent of the U.S. computing from the 31°. of lat: to the 45°. only makes a difference of 7 miles in the distance from the center of the Earth; a greater difference I suppose than is afforded by the highest mountains or the deepest mines or both put together.[4]

On my delivering you the draught on Mr. Ambler I remember you put into my hands a note which I never looked into, supposing it to relate to that circumstance. In examining my papers I perceive that I have lost it and mention it to put you on your guard in case the note should fall into bad hands and be capable of being abused.[5] Present my respects to Mr. Mercer and the other Gentlemen of the Delegation and be assured that I am Yrs Sincerely,

J. MADISON JR.

You will be so good as to give the inclosed a safe conveyance to Mrs. House.

## Jefferson to Madison

Annapolis Dec. 11, 1783

DEAR SIR

Your determination to avail yourself of the fine weather proved I fear a very unfortunate one. I pitied your probable situation in the tempestuous season which immediately succeeded your departure. It is now above a fort-

---

4. For JM's calculations relating to Buffon's, see *PJM,* VII, pp. 404–5.

5. TJ's note acknowledged a loan made to him by JM in the form of a draft on Jacquelin Ambler, the treasurer of Virginia; see *ibid.,* pp. 405–6.

night since we should have met, and six states only appear. We have some hopes of Rhodeisland coming in to-day, but when two more will be added seems as insusceptible of calculation as when the next earthquake will happen. We have at length received the Definitive treaty with a joint letter from all our Commissioners. Not a tittle is changed in the treaty but the preamble and some small things which were of course. The Commissioners write that the riot of Philadelphia and departure of Congress thence made the most serious impressions in Europe, and have excited great doubts of the stability of our confederacy, and in what we shall end. The accounts were greatly exaggerated, and it is suspected that Gr. Br. wished to sign no treaty.

You have seen G.M. [George Mason] I hope and had much conversation with him. What are his sentiments as to the amendment of our constitution? What amendments would he approve? Is he determined to sleep on, or will he rouze and be active? I wish to hear from you on this subject, and at all times on any others which occupy your thoughts. I see Bradford advertizes Smith's history of N. York.[6] As I mean to write for one for myself, and think I heard you say you had it not, I shall add one for you. Our news from the good family we left is not agreeable. Mrs. Trist is much agitated by the doubts and difficulties which hang over her and impede her reunion with Mr. Trist. They are without lodgers except those we left there, and the ladies we left there propose soon to depart. We hear some circumstances of rudeness in Mr. S. inconsistent with the inoffensiveness of character we had given him credit for. I wish you much happiness and am with the sincerest esteem Dr. Sir, Your friend and servt,

TH: JEFFERSON

P.S. I have taken the liberty of putting under cover to you a book for my nephew Peter Carr who is at Mr. Maury's in your neighborhood.

*Jefferson to Madison*

Annapolis Jan. 1, 1784

DEAR SIR

Your favour of the 10th. Dec. came to hand about a fortnight after it's date. It has occasioned me to reflect a little more attentively on Buffon's central heat than I did in the moment of our conversation and to form an opinion different from what I then expressed. The term 'central heat' does of itself give us a false idea of Buffon's hypothesis. If it meant a heat lodged in the center of the earth and diffusing it's warmth from thence to the extremities, then certainly it would be less in proportion to the distance from that center, and of course less under the equator than the poles, on high mountains than in

---

6. For Smith's history, see the edition by Michael Kammen, ed., *The History of the Province of New York, by William Smith, Jr.* (Ithaca, 1972).

deep vallies. But Buffon's theory is that this earth was once in a state of hot fusion, and that it has been, and still continues to be, cooling. What is the course of this process? A heated body being surrounded by a colder one whether solid or fluid, the heat, which is itself a fluid, flows into the colder body equally from every point of the hotter. Hence if a heated spheriod of iron cools to a given degree, in a given space of time, an inch deep from it's surface, in one point, it has in the same time done the same in any and every other point. In a given time more, it will be cooled all round to double that depth, so that it will always be equally cooled at equal depths from the surface. This would be the case of Buffon's earth if it were a smooth figure without unevennesses. But it has mountains and vallies. The tops of mountains will cool to greater depths in the same time than the sides of mountains and than plains in proportion as the line a. b. is longer than a.c. or d.e. or f. g. In the valley the line h.i. or depth of the same temperature will be the same as on a plain. This however is very different from Buffon's opinion. He sais that the earth being thinnest at the poles will cool sooner there than under the equator where it is thicker. If my idea of the process of cooling be right his is wrong and his whole theory in the Epochs of nature is overset.

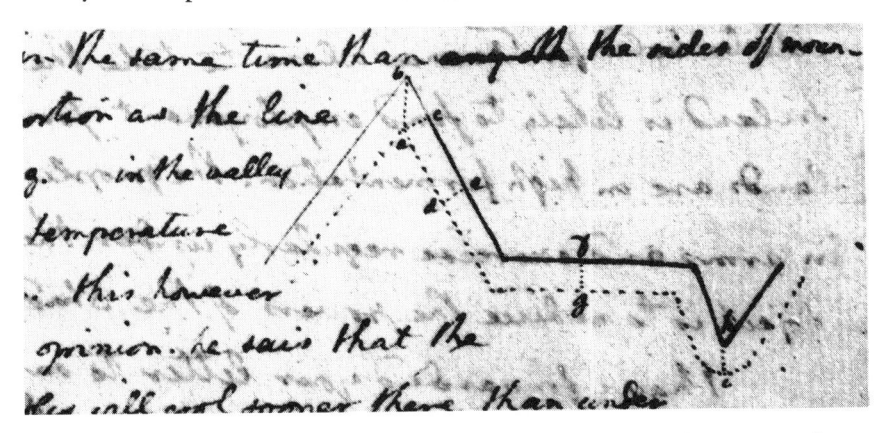

The note which I delivered you contained an acknowlegement of my having borrowed from you a draught for 333⅓ dollars and a promise to repay it on demand. This was exclusive of what I had borrowed in Philadelphia.

We have never yet had more than 7. states, and very seldom that, as Maryland is scarcely ever present, and we are now without a hope of it's attending till February. Consequently having six states only, we do nothing. Expresses and letters are gone forth to hasten on the absent states that we may have 9. for a ratification of the definitive treaty. Jersey perhaps may come in, and if Beresford will not come to Congress, Congress must go to him to do this one act.[7] Even now it is full late. The critical situation in which we are like to be gave birth to an idea that 7. might ratify. But it could not be supported.

---

7. Richard Beresford of South Carolina was ill in Philadelphia. He finally arrived on Jan. 14, 1784, rounding out the nine state delegations necessary to ratify the definitive peace treaty.

I will give you a further account of this when it shall be finally settled.

The letters of our ministers inform us that the two empires have formed a league defensive against Christian powers and offensive against the Turks. When announced by the Empress to the K. of Prussia he answered that he was very sensible on it as one is when informed of important things. If Prussia will join France perhaps it may prevent the war: if he does not, it will be bold for France alone to take the aid of the Turks on herself.[8] Ireland is likely to find employment for England.[9] The United Netherlands are in high fermentation. The people now marshall themselves in arms and exercise regularly under the banners of their towns. Their object is to reduce the powers of the Stadtholder.[10]

I have forwarded your letter to Mrs. House. Mrs. Trist I expect left Philadelphia about the 18th. of Dec. for Pittsburgh. I had a letter from her in which she complained of your not having written and desired me to mention it to you. I made your excuse on the good grounds of the delays you must have experienced on your journey and your distance from the post road: but I am afraid she was gone before my letter reached Philadelphia. I have had very ill health since I have been here and am getting rather lower than otherwise. I wish you every felicity and am with sincere affection Your friend and servt.,

TH: JEFFERSON

*Madison to Jefferson*

Orange Feb. 11, 1784

DEAR SIR

Your favor of the 11. of Decr. ulto. came safe to hand after a very tedious conveyance. Mr. W. Maury having broken up his school in this Neighbourhood in order to attempt a superior one in Williamsburg and his pupils being dispersed, I have sent the book for Mr. P. Carr into the neighbourhood of Doctr. Walker whence I supposed it would most easily find its way to him. I thank you for the mark of attention afforded by your order for Smith's Hist: of N.Y. for me. If it should be in every respct convenient I could wish a copy of Blairs Lectures to be added to it.[11]

---

8. The two empires were Russia under Catherine the Great and the Holy Roman Empire under Joseph II of Austria. In 1780, they formed an alliance against Turkey that finally led to war in 1787.

9. Parliament had granted Ireland legislative independence in 1782, but a Grand National Convention in Dublin in November 1783 pressed for additional reforms; see R. R. Palmer, *The Age of the Democratic Revolution: A Political History of Europe and America, 1760–1800*, 2 vols. (Princeton, 1959–64), I, pp. 287–94, 303–8.

10. For the Dutch patriot movement against the Stadtholder, see *ibid.*, pp. 324–40.

11. Hugh Blair, *Lectures on Rhetoric and Belles Lettres* (London, 1783).

We have had a severer season and particularly a greater quantity of snow than is remembered to have distinguished any preceding winter. The effect of it on the price of grain and other provisions is much dreaded. It has been as yet so far favorable to me that I have pursued my intended course of *law*-reading with fewer interruptions than I had presupposed: but on the other hand it has deprived me entirely of the philosophical books which I had allotted for incidental reading: all my Trunks sent from Philada. both by myself, and by Mr. House after I left it, being still at Fredericksg.

I have been thinking whether the present situation of the Report of the Revisors of the Laws does not render the printing of it for public consideration advisable. Such a step would not only ensure the preservation of the work and gain us credit abroad, but the sanction which it would probably procure to the Legislature might incline them to adopt it the more readily in the gross. If any material objections occur to you, you will be so good as to mention them. I sincerely sympathize with the worthy family left behind us in Philada. but am not without hopes that the vacances produced by our departure were of short duration. If a visit to Miss Patsy should carry you to Philada. I beg you to remember me in the most affectionate terms to the old lady and to Mrs. Trist if the persecutions of fortune should have so long frustrated her meditated voyage. You will also be so good as to tender my respects to Mr. Mercer if he be at Annapolis and to your other Colleagues, and to be assured of my sincerest wishes for your happiness. I am Dr. Sir Your friend and servt.,

J. Madison Jr.

In the Supplement to the 45. vol. of the Universal Magazine page 373. I find it mentioned by Doctr. Hunter that there are in the British Museum grinders of the Incognitum which were found in Brasil and Lima. If I do not misremember your Hypothesis it supposes no bones of that animal to have been met with so far to the South.

## *Madison to Jefferson*

Orange Feb. 17, 1784

Dear Sir

I wrote to you a few days ago by the post acknowledging your favor of the 10th. [11th] of Decr. Mr. Maury has since afforded me an opportunity which I cannot omit to acknowledge that of the first of Jany. which has just come to hand, and to express the concern I feel at the account it gives of your ill health. I hope earnestly that this will find it in a better state and that I may soon receive a confirmation of such a favorable change. Your explanation of Buffon's hypothesis has rectified my misconception of it, and I forbear as I ought perhaps formerly to have done making any further remarks on it, at least till I have seen the work itself. I forgot to mention to you in my last that I had received a letter from Mazzei dated at *Richmond,* apprising me of a proposed visit to Orange from whence he meant to proceed to Annapolis.[12] As I wish in a little time to make an effort to import some law-books, and shall probably hereafter extend the plan to other books, particularly from France, I must beg the favor of you to obtain the name and address of a fit Bookseller both in London and Paris if the means of such information should at any time fall in your way. I have committed to Mr. Maury's care another letter to my worthy friend Mrs. House, which in case he should not proceed to Philada. he will put into your hand. I am my dear Sir with the sincerest wishes for the reestablishment of your health and every other happiness, your Obt. friend and servant,

J. MADISON JR.

## *Jefferson to Madison*

Annapolis Feb. 20, 1784

DEAR SIR

Your favour of the 11th. inst. came to hand this day. I had prepared a multitude of memorandums of subjects whereon to write you, but I will first answer those arising from your letter. By the time my order got to Philadelphia every copy of Smith's history of New York was sold. I shall take care to get Blair's lectures for you as soon as published, and will attend to your presumed wishes whenever I meet with any thing rare and of worth. I wish I knew better what things of this kind you have collected for yourself, as I may often doubt whether you have or have not a thing. I know of no objections to the printing the revisal; on the contrary I think good will result from it. Should this be decided I must make a short trip to Virginia, as from the loss of originals I beleive my copies must often be wanting. I had never met with the particular fact relative to the grinders of the incognitum found in Brasil and Lima and deposited in the British museum which you mention from Dr. Hunter. I know it has been said that in a very few instances such bones have been found in S. America. You will find a collection of these in 2. Buff[on] Epoq. de la nature 187. but they have been so illy attested, so loosely and ignorantly described, and so seldom even pretended to have been seen, that I have supposed their identity with the Northern bones, and perhaps their existence at all not sufficiently established. The authority of Hunter is respectable: but if this be the only well attested instance of those bones brought from S. Amera., they may still be beleived to have been first carried there either previous to the emigration of the Spaniards when there was doubtless a communication between the

12. For Philip Mazzei, see Margherita Marchione, ed., *Philip Mazzei: Jefferson's "Zealous Whig"* (New York, 1975), and Howard R. Marraro, *Memoirs of the Life and Peregrinations of the Florentine, Philip Mazzei, 1730–1816* (New York, 1942).

Indns. of the two continents, or after that emigration when an intercourse between the Spaniards of N. and S. Amera. took place. It would be unsafe to deny the fact; but I think it may well be doubted. I wish you had a thermometer. Mr. Madison of the college[13] and myself are keeping observations for a comparison of climate. We observe at Sunrise and at 4. o'clock P.M. which are the coldest and warmest points of the day. If you could observe at the same time it would shew the difference between going North and Northwest on this continent. I suspect it to be colder in Orange or Albemarle than here.

I think I informed you in my last that an attempt had been made to ratify the Definitive treaty by seven states only, and to impose this under the sanction of our seal (without letting our actual state appear) on the British court. Reade, Williamson and Lee were violent for this, and gave notice that when the question should be put they would call the yeas and nays, and shew by whose fault the ratification of this important instrument should fail, if it should fail. I prepared the inclosed resolution by way of protest and informed them I would place that also on the journals with the yeas and nays, as a justification of those who opposed the proposition. I beleive this put a stop to it. They suffered the question to rest undecided till the 14th. of Jan. when 9. states appeared and ratified. Colo. Harmar and Colo. Franks were immediately dispatched to take passages to Europe with copies of the ratification. But by the extraordinary severity of the season we know they had not sailed on the 7th. inst. The ratification will not therefore arrive in time. Being persuaded I shall be misrepresented within my own state, if any difficulties should arise, I inclose you a copy of the protest containing my reasons.[14] Had the question been put there were but two states who would have voted for a ratification by seven. The others would have been in the negative or divided. I find Congress every moment stopped by questions whether the most trifling money propositions are not above the powers of seven states as being appropriations of money. My idea is that the estimate for the year and requisition grounded on that, whereon the sums to be allowed to each department are stated, is the general appropriation which requires 9. states, and that the detailing it out provided they do not go beyond these sums may be done by the subordinate officers of the federal government or by a Congress of 7. states. I wish you to think of this and give me your thoughts on the subject. We have as yet no Secretary of Foreign affairs. *Lee*[15] avows himself a candidate. The plan of Foreign affairs likely to take place is to commission Adams, Franklin and Jay to conclude treaties with the several European powers, and then to return, leaving the feild to subordinate characters. Messrs. Adams and Jay have paid a visit to the court of London unordered and uninvited. Their reception has been

13. The Reverend James Madison, president of the College of William and Mary.
14. See TJ's "Resolution Opposing Ratification of the Definitive Treaty by Less Than Nine States," enclosure, [Dec. 27, 1783], below.
15. This italicized word and those in the rest of the letter, except for the one cited in n. 20, below, were written in code.

forbidding. *Luzerne leaves* us in August, whether *recalled* or on *his own request* is not known. This information comes from *himself* tho' is not as yet *spoken* of *publicly*.[16] *Lee* finding no *faction* among the *men* here, entered into that among the *women* which rages to a very high degree. A *ball* being appointed by the one party on a certain *night* he undertook to *give* one, and fixed it precisely on the same *night*. This of course has placed him in the midst of the mud. He is *courting Miss Sprig* a *young girl* of *seventeen* and of *thirty thousand pounds* expectation. I have no doubt from some conversations with *him* that there is a design agitating to sever the *Northern Neck* and add it to this *state*. He supported in conversation with me the propriety and necessity of such a general measure, to wit of enlarging the *small states* to interest them in the *union*. He deserves to be well *watched* in our state. *He* is extremely soured with it and is not cautious in betraying his hostility *against it*.[17] We cannot make up a Congress at all. There are 8. states in town, 6 of which are represented by two members only. Of these two members of different states are confined by the gout so that we cannot make a house. We have not sit above 3. days I beleive in as many weeks. Admonition after admonition has been sent to the states, to no effect. We have sent one to day. If it fails, it seems as well we should all retire. There have never been 9 states on the floor but for the ratification of the treaty and a day or two after. Georgetown languishes. The smile is hardly covered now when the federal towns are spoken of. I fear that our chance is at this time desperate. Our object therefore must be if we fail in an effort to remove to Georgetown, to endeavor then to get to some place off the waters of the Chesapeak where we may be ensured against Congress considering themselves as fixed. My present expectations are, that as soon as we get a Congress to do business, we shall attend to nothing but the most pressing matters, get through them and adjourn, not to meet again till November, leaving a Committee of the states. That Committee will be obliged to go immediately to Philadelphia to examine the offices and of course they will set there till the meeting in November. Whether that meeting will be in Philada. or Trenton will be the question and will in my opinion depend on the vote of *New York*. Did not you once suppose in conversation with me that Congress had no authority to decide any cases between two differing states, except those of disputed territory? I think you did. If I am not mistaken in this I should wish to know your sense of the words which describe those cases which may be submitted to a federal court. They seem to me to comprehend every cause of difference.

We have received the act of our assembly ceding the lands North of Ohio and are about executing a deed for it. I think the territory will be laid out by passing a meridian through the Western cape of the Mouth of the Gr. Kanha-

---

16. Luzerne left in June; see William E. O'Donnell, *Chevalier de La Luzerne* (Bruges, 1938), pp. 247–49.
17. Arthur Lee was courting Sophia Sprigg, daughter of Richard Sprigg of Anne Arundel County, Maryland. She married John Francis Mercer in 1785; see *PJM*, VII, p. 430.

way from the Ohio to L. Erie, and another through the rapids of Ohio from the same river to Michigan and crossing these by the parallels of latitude 37°. 39°. 41°. etc. allowing to each state an extent of 2°. from N. to South. On the Eastern side of the meridian of Kanhaway will still be one new state, to wit, the territory lying between that meridian, Pennsylva., the Ohio and L. Erie.[18] We hope N. Carola. will cede all beyond the same meridian of Kanhaway, and Virginia also. For god's sake push this at the next session of assembly. We have transmitted a copy of a petition from the people of Kentucky to Congress praying to be separated from Virginia.[19] Congress took no notice of it. We sent the copy to the Governor desiring it to be laid before the assembly. Our view was to bring on the question. It is for the interest of Virginia to cede so far immediately; because the people beyond that will separate themselves, because they will be joined by all our settlements beyond the Alleghaney if they are the first movers. Whereas if we draw the line those at Kentucky having their end will not interest themselves for the people of Indiana, Greenbriar, etc. who will of course be left to our management, and I can with certainty almost say that Congress would approve of the meridian of the mouth of Kanhaway and consider it as the ultimate point to be desired from Virginia. I form this opinion from conversation with many members. Should we not be the first movers, and the Indianians and Kentuckians take themselves off and claim to the Alleghaney I am afraid Congress would secretly wish them well. Virginia is extremely interested to retain to that meridian: 1. Because the Gr. Kanhaway runs from North to South across our whole country forming by it's waters a belt of fine land, which will be thickly seated and will form a strong barrier for us. 2. Because the country for 180 miles beyond that is an absolute desart, barren and mountainous which can never be inhabited, and will therefore be a fine separation between us and the next state. 3. Because the government of Virginia is more convenient to the people on all the upper parts of Kanhaway than any other which will be laid out. 4. Because our lead mines are in that country. 5. Because the Kanhaway is capable of being made navigable, and therefore gives entrance into the Western waters to every part of our latitude. 6. Because it is not now navigable and can only be made so by expensive works, which require that we should own the soil on both sides. 7. Because the Ohio, and it's branches which head up against the Patowmac affords the shortest water communication by 500. miles of any which can ever be got between the Western waters and Atlantic, and of course promises us almost a monopoly of the Western and Indian trade. I think the opening this navigation is an object on which no time is to be lost. Pennsylva. is attending to the Western commerce. She has had surveys made of the river Susquehanna and of the grounds

18. Congress accepted the Virginia cession on Mar. 1, 1784, creating the national domain. For the deed of cession, see *PTJ*, VI, pp. 571–80. For maps depicting the boundaries of "each state," see *ibid.*, pp. 581–93, and Cappon *et al.*, pp. 60, 128.

19. For Kentucky politics, see Patricia Watlington, *The Partisan Spirit: Kentucky Politics, 1779–1792* (New York, 1972), pp. 65–78.

thro' which a canal must pass to go directly to Philadelphia. It is reported practicable at an expence of £200,000 and they have determined to open it. What an example this is! If we do not push this matter immediately they will be beforehand with us and get possession of the commerce. And it is difficult to turn it from a channel in which it is once established. Could not our assembly be induced to lay a particular tax which should bring in 5. or 10,000£ a year to be applied till the navigation of the Ohio and Patowmac is opened, then James river and so on through the whole successively. Genl. Washington has that of the Patowmac much at heart. The superintendance of it would be a noble amusement in his retirement and leave a monument of him as long as the waters should flow. I am of opinion he would accept of the direction as long as the money should be to be emploied on the Patowmac, and the popularity of his name would carry it thro' the assembly. The portage between Yohogania and the N. branch of Patowmac is of 40 or 50 miles. Cheat river is navigable far up. It's head is within 10 miles of the head of the North branch of Patowmac and I am informed offers the shortest and best portage. I wish in the next election of delegates for Congress, Short could be sent. His talents are great and his weight in our state must ere long become principal. I see the best effects produced by sending our young statesmen here. They see the affairs of the Confederacy from a high ground; they learn the importance of the Union and befriend federal measures when they return. Those who never come here, see our affairs insulated, pursue a system of jealousy and self interest, and distract the Union as much as they can. Genl. Gates would supply Short's place in the council very well, and would act. He is now here. What will you do with the council? They are expensive, and not constantly nor often necessary; yet to drop them would be wrong. I think you had better require their attendance twice a year to examine the Executive department and see that it be going on rightly, advise on that subject the Governor or inform the legislature as they shall see occasion. Give them 50. guineas each for each trip, fill up only 5 of the places, and let them be always subject to summons on great emergencies by the Governor, on which occasions their expences only should be paid. At an expence of 500 guineas you will thus preserve this member of the constitution always fit for use. Young and ambitious men will leave it and go into the assembly, but the elderly and able who have retired from the legislative feild as too turbulent will accept of the offices. Among other legislative subjects *our*[20] distresses ask notice. I had been from home four months and had expended 1200 Dollars before I received one farthing. By the last post we received about seven weeks allowance. In the mean time some of us had had the mortification to have our horses turned out of the livery stable for want of money. There is really no standing this. The supply gives us no relief because it was mortgaged. We are trying to get something more effectual from the treasury, having sent an express to inform them of our predicament. I shall endeavour to place as

20. TJ's italics.

much in the Philadelphia bank as will repay your kindness unless you should alter your mind and chuse to take it in the Virginia treasury. I have hunted out *Chastellux'* journal and had a reading of it. I had never so falsely estimated the character of a book. There are about six sentences of offensive bagatelles which are all of them publicly known. Because having respected individual characters they were like carrion for the buzzard curiosity. All the rest of the book (and it is a 4to. of 186 pages) is either entertaining, or instructive and would be highly flattering to the Americans. He has visited all the principal feilds of battle, enquired minutely into the detail of the actions, and has given what are probably the best accounts extant of them. He often finds occasion to criticize and to deny the British accounts from an inspection of the ground. I think to write to him, recommend the expunging the few exceptionable passages and publication of the rest.[21] I have had an opportunity here of examining Bynkershoek's works. There are about a fourth part of them which you would like to have. They are the following tracts. Questiones juris publici, de lege Rhodiâ, de dominio maris,[22] du Juge competent des Ambassadeurs, for this last if not the rest has been translated into French with notes by Barbeyrac.[23] I have had from Boinod and Gaillard a copy of Mussenbroeck's cours de Physique.[24] It is certainly the most comprehensive and most accurate body of Natural Philosophy which has been ever published. I would recommend you to get it, or I will get that and any other books you want from Boinod or elsewhere. I hope you have found access to my library. I beg you to make free use of it. Key, the steward is living there now and of course will be always in the way. Monroe is buying land almost adjoining me. Short will do the same. What would I not give [if] you could fall into the circle. With such a society I could once more venture home and lay myself up for the residue of life, quitting all it's contentions which grow daily more and more insupportable. Think of it. To render it practicable only requires you to think it so. Life is of no value but as it brings us gratifications. Among the most valuable of these is rational society. It informs the mind, sweetens the temper, chears our spirits, and promotes health. There is a little farm of 140 as. adjoining me, and within two miles, all of good land, tho' old, with a small indifferent house on it, the whole worth not more than £250. Such a one might be a farm of experiment and support a little table and houshold. It is on the road to Orange and so much nearer than I am. It is convenient enough for supplementary supplies from thence. Once more think of it, and Adieu.

---

21. See *Travels in North American in the Years 1780, 1781 and 1782 by the Marquis de Chastellux,* ed. Howard C. Rice, Jr., 2 vols. (Chapel Hill, 1963), I, p. 26.

22. Cornelius van Bynkershoek published this volume at The Hague in 1703; see *PJM,* VII, p. 435.

23. Jean Barbetrac's translation of Bynkershoek's work was published at The Hague in 1723; see *ibid.*

24. Daniel Boinod and Alexander Gaillard were Philadelphia booksellers; see *ibid.*

ENCLOSURE
*[Resolution Opposing Ratification of the Definitive Treaty of Peace by Less Than Nine States]*

[Annapolis Dec. 27, 1783]

Resolved that however earnestly and anxiously Congress wish to proceed to the ratification of the Definitive treaty, yet consisting at present of seven states only they ought not to undertake that ratification without proper explanations.

1. Because by the usage of modern nations it is now established that the ratification of a treaty by the sovereign power is the essential act which gives it validity; the signature of the ministers, notwithstanding their plenipotentiary commission, being understood as placing it, according to the phrase of the writers on this subject, sub spe rati,[25] only, and as leaving to each sovereign an acknoleged right of rejection.

2. Because ratification being an act of so much energy and substance, the authority to perform it is reserved to nine states by those words in the ninth article of Confederation which declare that Congress 'shall not enter into any treaty, unless nine states assent to the same.'

3. Because by the terms 'enter into a treaty' the Confederation must have intended that the assent of nine states should be necessary to it's completion as well as to it's commencement; the object having been to guard the rights of the Union in all those important cases wherein it has required the assent of nine states: whereas by admitting the contrary construction, seven states containing less than one third of the citizens of the Union in opposition to six containing more than two thirds may fasten on them a treaty, commenced indeed under commission and instructions from nine states, but concluded in express contradiction to such instructions and in direct sacrifice of the interests of so great a majority.

4. Because if 7. states be incompetent generally to the ratification of a treaty they are not made competent in this particular instance by the circumstances of the ratification of the provisional articles by nine states, the instructions to our ministers to form a definitive one by them and their actual agreement in substance: for either these circumstances are in themselves a ratification, or are not: if they are, nothing further is requisite than to give attested copies of them in exchange for the British ratification; if they are not, then we remain where we were, without a ratification by 9. states or a competency to ratify by seven.

5. Because the seven states now present in Congress saw this question in the same point of view only 4 days ago when by their *unanimous*[26] resolution they declared that the assent of nine states was requisite to ratify this treaty and urged this as a reason to hasten forward the absent states.

6. Because such a ratification would be rejected by the other contracting party as null and unauthorized, or, if attested to them by the seal of the states without apprising them that it has been expedited by order of seven states only, it will be a breach of faith in us, a prostitution of our seal, and a future ground, when that circumstance shall become known, of denying the validity of a ratification into which they shall have been so surprised.

7. Because there being still 67. days before the exchange of ratifications is requisite,

---

25. "In a state of hoped-for ratification"; see *ibid.*, VIII, p. 13.
26. TJ's italics.

and two states only wanting to render us competent, we have the strongest presumptions that the measures taken by Congress will bring them forward in time for ratification and for it's passage across the Atlantic.

And 8 because should we be disappointed in this hope, the ratification will yet be placed on more honourable and defensible ground if made by 9. states as soon as so many shall be present, and then sent for exchange, urging in it's support the small importance of an exchange of ratifications, a few days sooner or later, the actual impossibility of an earlier compliance, and that failures produced by circumstances not under the controul of the parties, either in points so immaterial, as to call for no compensation, or in those which are material and admit of compensation, can never affect the validity of the treaty itself.

## Madison to Jefferson

Orange Mar. 16, 1784

DEAR SIR

Your favour of the 20. Ult. came duly to hand a few days ago. I cannot apprehend that any difficulties can ensue in Europe from the involuntary and immaterial delay of the ratification of the peace, or if there should that any imputations can be devised which will not be repelled by the collective force of the reasons in the intended protest; some of which singly taken are unanswerable. As you no doubt had recourse to authorities which I have no opportunity of consulting, I probably err in supposing the right of the Sovereign to reject the act of his plenipotentiary to be more circumscribed than you lay it down. I recollect well that an implied condition is annexed by the usage of Nations to a Plenipotentiary commission, but should not have extended the implication beyond cases where some palpable and material default in the Minister could be alledged by the Sovereign. Waving some such plea, the language both of the Commission and of reason seems to fix on the latter as clear an engagement to fulfil his *promise* to ratify a treaty, as to fulfil the *promises* of a treaty which he has ratified. In both cases one would pronounce the obligation equally personal to the Sovereign, and a failure on his part without some absolving circumstance, equally a breach of faith. The project of affixing the Seal of the U. S. by 7 States to an Act *which had been just admitted to require nine,* [27] must have stood self-condemned; and tho' it might have produced a temporary deception abroad, must have been immediately detected at home, and have finally dishonored the fœderal Councils everywhere. The competency of 7 states to a Treaty of Peace has often been a subject of debate in Congress and has sometimes been admitted into their practice, at least so far as to issue fresh instructions. The reasoning employed in defence of the doctrine has been "that the cases which require 9 States, being exceptions to the general

27. These words and the two italicized words above were not written in code, but were underlined by JM.

authority of 7 States ought to be taken strictly; that in the enumeration of the powers of Congress in the first clause of art. 9. of the Confederation, the power of entering into treaties and alliances is contradistinguished from that of determining on peace and war and even separated by the intervening power of sending and receiving ambassadors; that the excepting clause therefore in which "Treaties and Alliances" ought to be taken in the same confined sense, and in which the power of determining on peace is omitted, cannot be extended by construction to the latter power; that under such a construction 5 States might continue a war which it required nine to commence, though where the object of the war has been obtained, a continuance must in every view be equipollent to a commencement of it; and that the very means provided for preserving a state of peace might thus become the means of preventing its restoration." The answer to these arguments has been that the construction of the fœderal articles which they maintain is a nicety which reason disclaims, and that if it be dangerous on one side to leave it in the breast of 5 States to protract a war, it is equally necessary on the other to restrain 7 states from saddling the Union with any stipulations which they may please to interweave with a Treaty of peace. I was once led by this question to search the files of Congress for such lights as the history of the Confederation might furnish, and on a review now of my papers I find the evidence from that source to consist of the following circumstances: In Doctr. Franklin's "Sketch of Articles of Confederation" laid before Congress on 21 day of July 1775. no number beyond a majority is required in any cases. In the plan reported to Congress by the Committee appointed 11. June 1776. the general enumeration of the powers of Congress in Art: 18. is expressed in a similar manner with the first clause in the present 9th art:, as are the exceptions in a subsequent clause of the 18 art: of the report, with the excepting clause as it now stands; and yet in the Margin of the Report and I believe in the same hand writing, there is a "Qu: If so large a majority is necessary in concluding a Treaty of Peace." There are sundry other marginal queries in the report from the same pen. Hence it would seem that notwithstanding the preceding discrimination between the powers of "determining on peace" and "entering into Treaties" the latter was meant by the Committee to comprise the former. The next form in which the articles appear is a printed copy of the Report as it had been previously amended, with sundry amendments, erasures and notes on the printed copy itself in the hand of Mr. Thomson. In the printed text of this paper art: 14. the phraseology which defines the general powers of Congress is the same with that in art: 18 of the manuscript report. In the subsequent clause requiring nine States, the text as printed ran thus: "The United States in Congress assembled shall never engage in a war nor grant letters of marque and reprisal in time of peace, nor enter into any Treaties or alliances except for peace," the words *except for peace* being erased, but sufficiently legible through the erasure. The fair inference from this passage seems to be 1. that without those words 9 States were held to be required for concluding peace, 2. that an attempt had been made to render 7 States competent to such an Act, which attempt must have succeeded either on a preceding discussion in Congress or in a Committee of the whole, or a special Committee, 3. that on fuller deliberation the power of making Treaties of peace was meant to be left on the same footing with that of making all other Treaties. The remaining papers on the files have no reference to this question. Another question which several times during my service in Congress exercised their deliberations was whether 7 States could revoke a Commission for a Treaty issued by nine States, at any time before the faith of the Confederacy should be pledged under it. In the instance of a proposition in 1781 to revoke a Commission which had been granted under peculiar circumstance in 1779 to *J. Adams*[28] to form *a treaty of Commerce with G. B.* the competency of 7 States was resolved on (by 7 States indeed) and a revocation took place accordingly. It was however effected with much difficulty, and some members of the minority even contested the validity of the proceeding. My own opinion then was and still is that the proceeding was equally valid and expedient. The circumstances which had given birth to the commission had given place to others totally different; not a single step had been taken under the commission which could affect the honour or faith of the U. S. and it surely can never be said that either the letter or spirit of the Confederation requires the same majority to decline as to engage in foreign treaties. The safest method of guarding against the execution of those great powers after the circumstances which dictated them have changed, is to limit their duration, trusting to renewals as they expire, if the original reasons continue. My experience of the uncertainty of getting an affirmative vote even of 7 States had determined me before I left Congress always to contend for such limitations.

I thought the sense of the term "appropriation" had been settled by the latter practice of Congress to be the same as you take it to be. I always understood that to be the true, the parliamentary and the only rational sense. If no distinction be admitted between the "appropriation of money to general uses" and "expenditures in detail" the Secretary of Congress could not buy quills or wafers without a vote of nine States entered on record, and the Secretary of the Committee of the States could not do it at all. In short unless one vote of appropriation can extend to a *class* of objects, there must be a physical impossibility of providing for them, and the extent and generality of such classes can only be determined by discretion and conveniency. It is observable that in the specification of the powers which require 9 States, the single technical word "appropriate" is retained. In the general recital which precedes, the word "apply" as well as "appropriate" is used. You were not mistaken in supposing I had in conversation restrained the authority of the fœderal Court to territorial disputes, but I was egregiously so in the opinion I had formed. Whence I got it I am utterly at a loss to account. It could not be from the Confederation itself

---

28. This name and subsequent words and names in italics in this sentence were written in code.

for words could not be more explicit. I detected the error a few days ago in consulting the articles on another subject, and had noted it for my next letter to you. I am not sure that I comprehend your idea of a cession of the territory beyond the Kanhaway and on this side the Ohio. As all the *soil*[29] of value has been granted out to individuals a cession in that view would be improper, and a cession of the *jurisdiction* to Congress can be proper only where the Country is vacant of settlers. I presume your meaning therefore to be no more than a separation of that country from this, and an incorporation of it into the Union; a work to which all three must be parties. I have no reason to believe there will be any repugnance on the part of Virga. The effort of Pena. for the western commerce does credit to her public Councils. The commercial genius of this State is too much in its infancy I fear to rival the example. Were this less the case, the confusion of its affairs must stifle all enterprize. I shall be better able however to judge of the practicability of your hint when I know more of them. The declension of George Town does not surprize me tho' it gives me regret. If the competition should lie between Trenton and Philada. and depend on the vote of *New York* it is not difficult to foresee into which scale it will be thrown, nor the probable effect of such decision on our Southern hopes.

I have long regarded the Council as a grave of useful talents, as well as objectionable in point of expence.[30] Yet I see not how such a reform as you suggest can be brought about. The Constitution, tho' readily overleaped by the Legislature on the spur of an occasion, would probably be made a bar to such an innovation. It directs that 8 members be kept up, and requires the sanction of 4 to almost every act of the Governor. Is it not to be feared too, that these little meliorations of the Government may turn the edge of some of the arguments which ought to be laid to its root? I grow every day more and more solicitous to see this essential work begun. Every days delay settles the Government deeper into the habits of the people, and strengthens the prop which their acquiescence gives it. My field of observation is too small to warrant any conjecture of the public disposition towards the measure; but all with whom I converse lend a ready ear to it. Much will depend on the politics of Mr. H[enry] which are wholly unknown to me. Should they be adverse, and G. M[ason] not in the Assembly hazardous as delay is, the experiment must be put off to a more auspicious conjuncture.

The Charter granted in 1732 [1632] to Lord Baltimore makes, if I mistake not, the *Southern Shore* of the Potowmac, the boundary of Maryland on that side. The constitution of Virginia cedes to that State "all the territories contained within its charter with all the rights of property, *jurisdiction and Govern-*

---

29. This word and subsequent words in italics were not written in code, but were underlined by JM.

30. JM refers to the Executive Council of Virginia, which combined the council members with the governor for the making of executive decisions. TJ's 1783 draft of a proposed new state constitution continued the council but modified its powers.

*ment and all other rights whatsoever,* which might at any time have been claimed by Virginia, excepting *only the free navigation and use* of the Rivers Potowmac and Pokomoque etc." Is it not to be apprehended that this language will be constructed into an entire relinquishment of the Jurisdiction of these rivers, and will not such a construction be fatal to our port regulations on that side and otherwise highly inconvenient? I was told on my journey along the Potowmac of several flagrant evasions which had been practised with impunity and success, by foreign vessels which had loaded at Alexandria. The jurisdiction of half the rivers ought to have been expressly reserved. The terms of the surrender are the more extraordinary, as the patents of the N. Neck place the whole river potowmac within the Government of Virginia; so that we were armed with a title both of prior and posterior date, to that of Maryland. What will be the best course to repair the error?—to extend our laws upon the River, making Maryland the plaintiff if she chooses to contest their authority—to state the case to her at once and propose a settlement by negociation—or to propose a mutual appointment of Commissioners for the general purpose of preserving a harmony and efficacy in the regulations on both sides. The last mode squares best with my present ideas. It can give no irritation to Maryld. It can weaken no plea of Virga. It will give Maryland an opportunity of stirring the question if she chooses, and will not be fruitless if Maryland should admit our jurisdiction. If I see the subject in its true light no time should be lost in fixing the interest of Virginia. The good humour into which the cession of the back lands must have put Maryland, forms an apt crisis for any negociation which may be necessary. You will be able probably to look into her charter and her laws, and to collect the leading sentiments relative to the matter.

The winter has been so severe that I have never renewed my call on the library of Monticello, and the time is now drawing so near when I may pass for a while into a different scene, that I shall await at least the return to my studies. Mr. L. Grymes told me a few days ago that a few of your Books which had been borrowed by Mr. W. Maury, and ordered by him to be sent to his brother's the clergyman, on their way to Monticello, were still at the place which Mr. M. removed from. I desired Mr. Grymes to send them to me instead of the Parson, supposing as the distance is less, the books will probably be sooner out of danger from accidents, and that a conveyance from hence will not be less convenient. I calculated also on the use of such of them as may fall within my plan. I lately got home the Trunk which contained my Buffon, but have barely entered upon him. My time begins already to be much less my own than during the winter blockade. I must leave to your discretion the occasional purchase of rare and valuable books, disregarding the risk of duplicates. You know tolerably well the objects of my curiosity. I will only particularize my wish of whatever may throw light on the general Constitution and droit public of the several confederacies which have existed. I observe in Boinauds' Catalogue several pieces on the Duch, the German, and the Helvetic. The operations of our own must render all such lights of consequence. Books on the Law of N. and N. [Nature and Nations] fall within a similar remark. The tracts of Bynkershoek which you mention I must trouble you to get for me and in french if to be had rather than latin. Should the body of his works come nearly as cheap, as these select publications perhaps it may [be] worth considering whether the whole would not be preferable. Is not Wolfius also worth having? I recollect to have seen at Pritchards a copy of Hawkin's Abridgt. of Co: Litt: [Coke on Littleton] I would willingly take it if it be still there and you have an opportunity.[31] A copy of Deane's letters which were printed in New York and which I failed to get before I left Philada. I should also be glad of.[32] I use this freedom in confidence that you will be equally free in consulting your own conveniency whenever I encroach upon it; I hope you will be so particularly in the request I have to add. One of my parents would be considerably gratified with a pair of good spectacles which can not be got here. The particular readiness of Dudley to serve you inclines me to think that an order from you would be well executed. Will You therefore be so good as to get from him one of his best pebble and double jointed pair, for the age of fifty five or thereabouts with a good case; and forward them by the first safe conveyance to me at Orange or at Richmond as the case may be.[33] If I had thought of this matter before Mr. Maury set out, I might have lessened your trouble. It is not material whether I be repayed at the bank of Philada. or the Treasury of Virginia, but I beg it may be at neither till you are made secure by public remittances. It will be necessary at any rate for £20 or 30 [to] be left in your hands or in the bank for little expenditures which your kindness is likely to bring upon you.

 The Executive of S. Carolina, as I am informed by the Attorney, have demanded of Virginia the surrender of a citizen of Virga. charged on the affidavit of Jonas Beard Esqr. whom the Executive of S. C. represent to be "a Justice of the peace, a member of the Legislature, and a valuable good man," as follows: that "three days before the 25th. day of Octr. 1783 he (Mr. Beard) was violently assaulted" by G. H. [George Hancock] during the sitting of the Court of General sessions, without any provocation thereto given, who beat him (Mr. B) with his fist and switch over the face head and mouth, from which beating he was obliged to keep his room until the said 25th. day of Octr. 1783. and call in the assistance of a physician."[34] Such is the case as collected by Mr. Randolph from the letter of the Executive of S. C. The questions which arise

31. For JM's "Report on Books proper for the use of Congress," see *PJM,* VI, pp. 65–115. Under the heading "Law of Nature and Nations," JM listed fifty-one titles, including Wolfius, Grotius, Pufendorf, Vattel, and Burlamaqui.

32. From the fall of 1776 until the fall of 1777, when he was recalled by Congress, Silas Deane served as one of the American commissioners to the court of France along with Benjamin Franklin and Arthur Lee. His *Paris Papers; or, Mr. Silas Deane's late intercepted Letters, to his Brothers, and other Intimate Friends, in America* was published by a Loyalist press in New York in 1782.

33. Benjamin Dudley was a craftsman in Boston; see *PJM,* VIII, p. 15.

34. The best discussion of the accusation of Jonas Beard against George Hancock is in *PTJ,* VII, pp. 39–40, which corrects the account in Brant, II, pp. 311, 453.

upon it are 1. Whether it be a charge of high misdemesnor within the meaning of the 4 art: of confederation. 2. Whether in expounding the terms high misdemesnor the Law of S. Carolina, or the British Law as in force in the U. S. before the Revolution, ought to be the Standard. 3. If it be not a casus fœderis what the law of Nations exacts of Virginia? 4. If the law of Nations contains no adequate provision for such occurrences, Whether the intimacy of the Union among the States, the relative position of some, and the common interest of all of them in guarding against impunity for offences which can be punished only by the jurisdiction within which they are committed, do not call for some supplemental regulations on this subject. Mr. R. thinks Virginia not bound to surrender the fugitive untill she be convinced of the fact by more substantial information, and of its amounting to a high misdemesnor, by inspection of the law of S. C. which, and not the British law, ought to be the criterion. His reasons are too long to be rehearsed.

I know not my dear Sir what to reply to the affectionate invitation which closes your letter. I subscribe to the justness of your general reflections. I feel the attractions of the particular situation you point out to me; I can not altogether renounce the prospect; still less can I as yet embrace it. It is far from being improbable that a few years more may prepare me for giving such a destiny to my future life; in which case the same or some equally convenient spot may be commanded by a little augmentation of price. But wherever my final lot may fix me be assured that I shall ever remain with the sincerest affection and esteem Yr. friend and servant,

J. MADISON JR.


## *Jefferson to Madison*

Annapolis Mar. 16, 1784

DEAR SIR

I received yesterday by Mr. Maury your favor of Feb. 17. That which you mention to have written by post a few days before is not yet come to hand. I am induced to this quick reply to the former by an alarming paragraph in it, which is that *Mazzei* is coming to Annapolis. I tremble at the idea. I know he will be worse to me than a return of my double quotidian head-ach. There is a resolution reported to Congress by a Committee that they will never appoint to the office of minister, chargé des affaires, consul, agent etc. (describing the foreign emploiments) any but natives. To this I think there will not be a dissenting vote: and it will be taken up among the first things. Could you not, by making him acquainted with this divert him from coming here? A *consulate* is his object, in which he will assuredly fail. But his coming will be attended with evil. He is the violent enemy of *Franklin* having been some time at *Paris*. From my knolege of the man I am sure he will have emploied himself in collecting on the spot facts true or false to *impeach* him. You know there are people here who on the first idea of this, will take him to their bosom and turn all Congress topsy turvy. For god's sake then save us from this confusion if you can.[35]

We have eight states only and 7. of these represented by two members. Delaware and S. Carolina we lost within these two days by the expiration of their powers. The other absent states are N. York, *Maryland*[36] and Georgia. We have done nothing and can do nothing in this condition but waste our time, temper, and spirits in debating things for days or weeks and then losing them by the negative of one or two individuals.

We have letters from Franklin and Marq. Fayette of the 24th. and 25th. of Dec. They inform us that North and Fox are out, Pitt and Temple coming in, that whole nation extremely indisposed towards us, and as having not lost the idea of reannexing us, the Turks and Russians likely to be kept quiet another year, the Marquis coming to America this spring, Mr. Laurence [Laurens] then about sailing for America, Mr. Adams leaving England for the Hague, Mr. Jay at Bath but about returning to Paris. Our ratification tho' on board two different vessels at N. York in the hands of officers as early as the 20th. of Jan. did not sail thence till the 17th. of Feb. on account of the ice. I will attend to your desire about the booksellers. I am considerably mended in my health and hope a favourable change in the weather which seems to be taking place will reestablish me.

I wish you would keep a diary under the following heads or columns. 1. *day of the month.*[37] 2. thermometer at sunrise. 3. barometer at sunrise. 6. thermom. at 4. P.M. 7. barometer at 4. P.M. 4. direction of wind at sunrise. 8. direction of wind at 4. P.M. 5. the weather viz. rain, snow, fair at sunrise, etc. 9. weather at 4. P.M. 10. shooting or falling of the leaves of trees, of flours, and other remarkeable plants. 11. appearance or disappearance of birds, their emigrations etc. 12. Miscellanea. It will be an amusement to you and may become useful. I do not know whether you have a thermometer or barometer. If you have not, those columns will be unfilled till you can supply yourself. In the miscellaneous column I have generally inserted Aurora boreales, and other unclassed rare things.[38] Adieu Adieu Yours affectionately.

The above columns to be arranged according to the order of the numbers as corrected.

---

35. All the italicized words in this paragraph were written in code. Philip Mazzei was as critical of Franklin as JM was of John Adams. TJ feared that Mazzei would revive the factionalism that divided Congress in 1779. For the imbroglio of that year, see "Factional Conflict and Foreign Policy" in Rakove, pp. 243–74; for the situation in 1784, see "Dilemmas of Foreign Policy," *ibid.*, pp. 342–52.
36. TJ's italics.
37. TJ's italics.
38. Although JM had neither thermometer nor barometer, he began keeping a weather log on Apr. 1, 1784; see *PJM,* VIII, p. 17. For the entries for 1784–1786, see *ibid.*, pp. 514–44.

## Madison to Jefferson

Orange Apr. 25, 1784

DEAR SIR

Your favor of the 16th. of March came to hand a few days *before Mazzei called on me.*[39] His *plan was* to have *proceeded hence* directly *to Annapolis.* My *conversation led him to promise a visit to Mr. Henry* from whence *he proposed to repair to Richmond and close his affairs with the Executive. Contrary* to my *expectation he returned hither* on *Thursday last,* proposing to continue *his circuit thro' Gloucester, York* and *Williamsburg* recommended *by Mr. Henry for obtaining from* the *former members of the Council* certain *facts relating to his appointment* of which the *vouchers have been lost.* This *delay* with the expectation of *your adjournment* will probably *prevent his visit to Congress.* Your letter gave me the first information both of *his view towards a consulate* and of *his enmity towards Franklin.* The first was not betrayed to *me by any conversation* either before or after *I made known to him* the determination *of Congress to confine such appointments to natives of America.* As to the second *he was unreserved* alledging at the same time that the *exquisite cunning of the old fox* has so *enveloped his iniquity* that its reality cannot be *proved by those who are thoroughly satisfied of it.* It is evident from several circumstances stated *by himself that his enmity has been embittered* if not wholly *occasioned by incidents of a personal nature.* Mr. *Adams is the only public man* whom *he thinks favorably of* or seems to *have associated with. A circumstance which* their mutual *characters may perhaps account for.* Notwithstanding these sentiments *towards Franklin and Adams his hatred of England* remains *unabated* and does not *exceed his partiality to France* which with many other considerations, which need not be pointed out, persuade me that however dreadful an actual *visit from him might* be to *you in a personal view* it would not produce the *public mischiefs you apprehend from it.* By his interview with Mr. *Henry I learn* that the present *politics of* the *latter* comprehend very friendly *views towards the Confederacy, a* wish tempered with much caution for *an amendment of our own Constitution, a* patronage *of* the *payment of British debts* and *of a scheme of a general assessment.*

The want of both a Thermometer and Barometer had determined me to defer a meteorological diary till I could procure these instruments. Since the receipt of your letter I have attended to the other columns.

I hope the letter which had not reached you at the date of your last did not altogether miscarry. On the 16 of March I wrote you fully on sundry points. Among others I suggested to your attention the case of the Potowmac, having in my eye the river below the head of navigation. It will be well I think to *sound* the *ideas of Maryland* also as to the upper parts of the N. branch of it. The *policy of Baltimore* will probably thwart as far as possible the *opening of it;* and without a very favorable construction of the *right of Virginia* and even the

---

39. The italicized words in this letter were written in code.

privilege of using the *Maryland Bank* it would seem that the *necessary works could not be* accomplished.

Will it not be good policy to suspend further Treaties of Commerce, till measures shall have been taken place in America which may correct the idea in Europe of impotency in the fœderal Government in matters of Commerce? Has Virginia been seconded by any other State in her proposition for arming Congress with power to frustrate the unfriendly regulations of G. B. with regard to her W. India islands? It is reported here that the late change of her Ministers has revived the former liberality which seemed to prevail on that subject. Is the Impost gaining or losing ground among the States? Do any considerable payments come into the Continental Treasury? Does the settlement of the public accounts make any comfortable progress? Has any resolution been taken by Congress touching the old Continental currency? Has Maryland foreborne to take any step in favor of George Town? Can you tell me whether any question in the Court of Appeals has yet determined whether the war ceased on our coast on the 3d of March or the 3d. of April. The books which I was told were still at [the] place left by Mr. W. Maury, had been sent away at the time Mr. L. Grymes informed of them.

Mr. Mazzei tells me that a subterraneous city has been discovered in Siberia, which appears to have been once populous and magnificent. Among other curiosities it contains an equestrian Statue around the neck of which was a golden chain 200 feet in length, so exquisitely wrought that Buffon inferred from a specimen of 6 feet sent him by the Empress of Russia, that no artist in Paris could equal the workmanship. Mr. Mazzei saw the specimen in the hands of Buffon and heard him give this opinion of it. He heard read at the same time a letter from the Empress to Buffon in which she desired the present to be considered as a tribute to the man to whom Nat: Hist: was so much indebted. Monsr. Faujas de St. Fond thought the City was between 72 and 74°. N. L. The son of Buffon between 62 and 64°. Mr. M. being on the point of departure had no opportunity of ascertaining the fact. If you should have had no better account of the discovery this will not be unacceptable to you and will lead you to obtain one.

I propose to set off for Richmond towards the end of this week. The election in this County was on thursday last. My colleague is Mr. Charles Porter. I am your affecte. friend,

J. MADISON JR.


## *Jefferson to Madison*

Annapolis Apr. 25 and 30, 1784

DEAR SIR

My last to you was of the 16th. of March, as was the latest I have received from you. By the proposition to bound our country to the Westward I meant no more than passing an act declaring that that should be our boundary from the moment the people of the Western country and Congress should agree to it. The act of Congress now inclosed to you will shew you that they have agreed to it, because it extends not only to the territory ceded, but *to be ceded;*[40] and shews how and when they shall be taken into the union. There is no body then to consult but the people to be severed. If you will make your act final as to yourselves so soon as those people shall have declared their assent in a certain manner to be pointed out by the act, the whole business is settled. For their assent will follow immediately. One of the conditions is that they pay their quota of the debts contracted. Of course no difficulty need arise on this head: as no quota has been fixed on us unalterably. The minuter circumstances of selling the ungranted lands will be provided in an ordinance already prepared but not reported. You will observe two clauses struck out of the report, the 1st. respecting hereditary honours, the 2d. slavery. The 1st. was done not from an approbation of such honours, but because it was thought an improper place to encounter them. The 2d. was lost by an individual vote only. Ten states were present. The 4. Eastern states, N. York, Pennsva. were for the clause. Jersey would have been for it, but there were but two members, one of whom was sick in his chambers. South Carolina Maryland and !Virginia! voted against it. N. Carolina was divided as would have been Virginia had not one of it's delegates been sick in bed.[41]

The place at which Congress should meet in Nov. has been the subject of discussion lately. Alexandria, Philada. and Trenton were proposed. The first was negatived easily. Trenton had the 4. East. states, N.Y., N.J., and Pennsylva. We expect Georgia and Delaware shortly, in which case it will become possible that Philada. may be determined on. The question is put off to be considered with the establishment of a committee of the states, which to my astonishment would have been negatived when first proposed had not the question been staved off. Some of the states who were against the measure, I believe because they had never reflected on the consequences of leaving a government without a head, seem to be come over.[42] Dr. Lee is appointed an Indian Commissioner. He is not present, but is known to have sought it, and of course will accept. This vacates his seat here. I wish Short could be sent in his room. It is a good school for our young statesmen. It gives them impressions friendly to the federal government instead of those adverse which too often take place in persons confined to the politics of their state.

40. TJ's italics. The enclosure was the Land Ordinance of 1784, which Congress had passed on Apr. 23, 1784; see below.

41. TJ's effort to prohibit slavery in the territories was defeated because John Beatty, a delegate from New Jersey, was ill; the vote was 6 states to 3. James Monroe was also ill or Virginia would have been divided, with Monroe joining TJ for retaining the prohibition and Samuel Hardy and John Francis Mercer for deleting it; see *PJM,* VIII, p. 27, and *PTJ,* VI, p. 612.

42. See Edmund C. Burnett, "The Committee of the States, 1784," in *AHA Annual Report for the Year 1913,* 2 vols. (Washington, 1915), I, pp. 141–52.

I like the method you propose of settling at once with Maryland all matters relative to Patowmac. To introduce this the more easily I have conversed with Mr. Stone (one of their delegates) on the subject and finding him of the same opinion have told him I would by letters bring the subject forward on our part. They will consider it therefore as originated by this conversation.

*Mercer* is *acting* a very *extraordinary part*.[43] *He* is a *candidate* for the *secretaryship* of *foreign affairs* and tho' *he will not* get the *vote of one state*, I beleive *he expects* the *appointment*. *He* has been *endeavoring* to *defeat* all *foreign treaties* to force the *nations* of *Europe* to *send ministers* to *treat here* that *he* may have the *honor* of *fabricating* this *whole business*. Tho' *he could* not *change* the *vote* of *his state, he intrigued* with a *young fool* from *North Carolina* and an *old* one from *New York, got* them to *divide* their *states* by *voting* in the *negative*, and there being but *eleven states present, one* of *which* was *known* before to be *divided* the *whole set* of *instructions* were *rejected*, tho *approved* by *twenty one* out of *twenty five members present*. The *whole business* has been in *the dust* for a *month* and whether it can be *resumed* and *passed depends* on the incertainty of *Delaware* or *Georgia coming* on. *Vanity* and *ambition seem* to be the *ruling passions* of this *young man* and as *his objects* are *impure,* so also are *his means. Intrigue* is a *principal one* on *particular occasions* as *party attachment* is in the *general*. *He takes* now about *one half* of the *time of Congress* to *himself* and in *conjunction* with *Read* [and] *Spaight obstruct business inconc*[*e*]*ivably*. The *last* is of *North Carolina* and no otherwise of *consequence than* as by *his vote he* can *divide his state*.[44]

The more I have reflected on your proposition for printing the Revisal the more I have liked it. I am convinced too from late experiments it cannot be passed in the detail. One of the Eastern states had their laws revised and then attempted to pass them thro' their legislature, but they got so mangled that all consistence was destroyed and I beleive they dropped them altogether. Should this be printed I will ask you to send me half a dozen copies wherever I shall be.

Would it not be well for Virginia to empower persons privately to buy up her quota of old Continental money. I would certainly advise this were I not afraid that the possession of her quota on such easy terms would tempt her to refuse justice to the other states on this matter. For surely there would be no justice in wiping off her part of this debt by so much smaller a contribution than the others. If she would avail herself of it only to sheild herself against injustice and to enable her from an high ground to declare and do what is right, I should much wish to see her adopt secret measures for the purchase. I think some other states will do this, and I fear with unjust views. You know that many gentlemen of this state had money in the hands of merchants in England. I am well informed that these merchants have uniformly refused to pay them interest, saying the money was always ready if they would have called

---

43. The italicized words in this sentence and in the rest of the letter were written in code.

44. The *"young fool"* was Richard Dobbs Spaight of North Carolina and the *"old"* one" was Ephraim Paine of New York. Jacob Read was from South Carolina; see *PJM*, VIII, p. 27.

for it. This adds another to the many good reasons we had before against paying interest during the war.

I inclose herewith the spectacles you desired, price 13⅔ Dollars. I have as yet done nothing on your commission either general or particular for books, because I am in constant expectation of a short trip to Philadelphia and can so much better execute it on the spot. The money hitherto remitted us amounts to about 4. Dollars a day. The predicament in which this places us is well known to you. It is inconceivably mortifying. I expect daily to hear from the Treasurer. As soon as I do it will enable me to give some directions on the subject of your money. I have not heard lately from Mrs. House. Mrs. Trist got safely to Fort Pitt through much distress. Congress hope to adjourn by the last of May. The estimate and requisitions for the year, the arrangements for the land office, and Foreign treaties are subjects they will endeavor to complete. Vermont is pressed on them by N. York and a day declared beyond which they will await no interposition but assert their right of government. The Chevalr. Luzerne has taken his leave of us. He makes a tour to the lakes before he leaves the continent. Marbois acts as Chargé des affaires till the arrival of a successor.

As it is certain that Congress will shortly adjourn, to meet again in Nov. it is desireable that the assembly should at as early a day as convenient appoint their delegates for the ensuing year, in order that such gentlemen as shall be continued, may receive notice of it while here, as this will enable them to take measures for their accomodation at the next meeting, determine them whether to send their baggage Northwardly or Southwardly etc.

Apr. 30.

A London ship is arrived here which left that port the 25th. of March. Pitt was still in place, supported by the King, Lords, and nation in general. The city of London enthusiastically in his favor. Still there was a majority of 12 in favor of Fox who was supported by the Prince of Wales. It was thought the parliament would be dissolved. Congress has determined to adjourn on the 3d of June to meet in November at Trenton. Adieu Your's affectionately,

TH: JEFFERSON

ENCLOSURE
*[The Ordinance of 1784]*

[Annapolis Apr. 23, 1784]

Congress resumed the consideration of the report of a committee on a plan for a temporary government of the western territory, which being amended, was agreed to as follows:

Resolved, That so much of the territory ceded or to be ceded by individual states to the United States, as is already purchased or shall be purchased of the Indian inhabitants, and offered for sale by Congress, shall be divided into distinct states in the following manner, as nearly as such cessions will admit; that is to say, by parallels of latitude, so that each state shall comprehend from north to south two degrees of latitude, beginning to count from the completion of forty five degrees north of the equator; and by meridians of longitude, one of which shall pass through the lowest point of the rapids of Ohio, and the other through the western cape of the mouth of the great Kanhaway; but the territory eastward of this last meridian, between the Ohio, Lake Erie, and Pennsylvania, shall be one state, whatsoever may be its comprehension of latitude. That which may lie beyond the completion of the 45th degree between the said meridians shall make part of the state adjoining it on the south; and that part of the Ohio, which is between the same meridians coinciding nearly with the parallel of 39° shall be substituted so far in lieu of that parallel as a boundary line.

That the settlers on any territory so purchased and offered for sale shall, either on their own petition or on the order of Congress, receive authority from them, with appointments of time and place, for their free males of full age within the limits of their state to meet together, for the purpose of establishing a temporary government, to adopt the constitution and laws of any one of the original states; so that such laws nevertheless shall be subject to alteration by their ordinary legislature; and to erect, subject to a like alteration, counties, townships, or other divisions, for the election of members for their legislature.

That when any such state shall have acquired twenty thousand free inhabitants, on giving due proof thereof to Congress, they shall receive from them authority with appointments of time and place, to call a Convention of representatives to establish a permanent constitution and government for themselves. Provided that both the temporary and permanent governments be established on these principles as their basis.

First. That they shall for ever remain a part of this confederacy of the United States of America.

Second. That they shall be subject to the articles of confederation in all those cases in which the original states shall be so subject, and to all the acts and ordinances of the United States in Congress assembled, conformable thereto.

Third. That they in no case shall interfere with the primary disposal of the soil by the United States in Congress assembled, nor with the ordinances and regulations which Congress may find necessary for securing the title in such soil to the bona fide purchasers.

Fourth. That they shall be subject to pay a part of the federal debts contracted or to be contracted, to be apportioned on them by Congress, according to the same common rule and measure by which apportionments thereof shall be made on the other states.

Fifth. That no tax shall be imposed on lands the property of the United States.

Sixth. That their respective governments shall be republican.

Seventh. That the lands of non resident proprietors shall in no case be taxed higher than those of residents within any new state, before the admission thereof to a vote by its delegates in Congress.

That whensoever any of the said states shall have of free inhabitants, as many as shall then be in any one the least numerous of the thirteen original states, such state shall be admitted by its delegates into the Congress of the United States, on an equal footing with the said original states; provided the consent of so many states in Congress is first obtained as may at the time be competent to such admission. And in order to adapt the said articles of confederation to the state of Congress when its numbers shall be thus increased, it shall be proposed to the legislatures of the states, originally parties thereto, to require the assent of two thirds of the United States in Congress assembled, in all those cases wherein by the said articles, the assent of nine states is now required, which being agreed to by them shall be binding on the new states. Until such admission by their Delegates into Congress, any of the said states after the establishment of their temporary government shall have authority to keep a member in Congress, with a right of debating, but not of voting.

That measures not inconsistent with the principles of the confederation, and necessary for the preservation of peace and good order among the settlers in any of the said new states, until they shall assume a temporary government as aforesaid, may from time to time be taken by the United States in Congress assembled.

That the preceding articles shall be formed into a charter of compact; shall be duly executed by the President of the United States in Congress assembled, under his hand, and the seal of the United States; shall be promulgated; and shall stand as fundamental constitutions between the thirteen original states, and each of the several states now newly described, unalterable from and after the sale of any part of the territory of such state, pursuant to this resolve, but by the joint consent of the United States in Congress assembled, and of the particular state within which such alteration is proposed to be made.

Charles Thomson, Secretary

## Jefferson to Madison

Annapolis May 7, 1784

DEAR SIR

The inclosed resolutions on the subject of commerce are the only things of consequence passed since my last.[45] You will be surprised to receive another pair of spectacles. The paper with them will explain the error. If you can dispose of the supernumerary pair do so, and I will remit the money to Dudley; if you cannot, return them by the next post and I will return them to him.

Congress is now *on foreign treaties.*[46] *Mercer* has *devised* new expedients for *baffling* the measure. *He has* put it into *Read's head* to *think* of being *appointed* a *foreign minister* and has by *his intrigues defeated* every proposition which did not proceed on that *ground. He is very mischievous. He is under no moral restraint. If he* avoids *shame* he *avoids* wrong according to *his system.* His fondness for *Machiavel* is *genuine* and founded on a true *harmony* of *principle.*

---

45. The missing enclosure probably included resolutions adopted on Apr. 30, 1784, recommending that the states authorize commercial retaliation against nations that had not concluded commercial treaties with the United States. The first resolution would have prohibited the importation or exportation of goods carried in vessels from such nations; the second would have prohibited foreign merchants from importing items manufactured or produced in countries other than their own; see Rakove, pp. 345–47.

46. The italicized words in this sentence and in the rest of the letter were written in code.

## Jefferson to Madison

Annapolis May 8 and 11, 1784

DEAR SIR

I will now take up the several enquiries contained in your letter of Apr. 25. which came to hand yesterday.

'Will it not be good policy to suspend further treaties of commerce till measures shall have taken place in America, which may correct the idea in Europe of impotency in the federal government in matters of commerce?' Congress think such measures requisite, and have accordingly recommended them as you will perceive by my last. In the mean time they seem to think that our commerce is got and getting into vital agonies by our exclusion from the West Indies, by late embarrasments in Spain and Portugal, and by the dangers of the Mediterranean trade. These you observe form the aggregate of our valuable markets. They think that the presumption of one or two countries should not be a reason for suspending treaties with all countries; and that the prospect of effect from their recommendations on commerce will perhaps drive on the treaties. The present favourable disposition of the piratical states on the Barbary coast has been repeatedly urged by our ministers as a circumstance which may be transient and should therefore be seised to open the Mediterranean to us.

'Has Virginia been seconded etc. in her proposition for arming Congress with powers to frustrate the unfriendly regulations of Great Britain?' Pennsylvania and Maryland offered much larger powers. Those of Virginia might have been defeated by the British king repealing his proclamation one day and renewing it the next. Yet the powers and plans from all these states were different; and it was visible they would authorize no single measure. Therefore Congress recommended a uniform measure.

'Is the impost gaining or losing ground?' Gaining, most certainly. Georgia, North Carolina, New York, Connecticut and Rhode island are yet to pass it. The three first are supposed to be willing to do it. Connecticut has held off merely to try whether Congress would not rescind the commutation. Finding a firmness on this point it is said and beleived that at their next session they will come into it. Howell has often told me that R. I. will not accede to it as long as any other state holds off; but when every other shall have adopted it, she will.

'Does the settlement of the public accounts make any comfortable progress?' They are going on, but slowly I beleive. However they go on, and of course approach their term.

'Has any resolution been taken by Congress touching the old Continental currency?' That question has been debated by a grand Committee upwards of a month. They yesterday came to the inclosed resolution. It was decided by only 6. votes against 5. I think it will gain strength in the House. The Southern and middle states I beleive are for it, and I think one or two of the Eastern may perhaps come over. Yet there is far from being a certainty of this.[47]

'Has [Maryland] forborne to take any step in favor of [Georgetown]?' Their object was certainly not the same with ours. Yet they have not openly set their faces against us. They have one delegate, honest and disinterested, who certainly will in no case do it.

'Whether the war ceased in March or April?' I think no decision has taken place on that subject in our court of Appeals. Our ministers write that it is no question on that side the water but that it ended in March.

The produce of our slave tax being nearly equal to the Continental requisitions, can you not get it appropriated to that purpose, and have it all paid in money? Virginia must do something more than she has done to maintain any degree of respect in the Union and to make it bearable to any man of feeling to represent her in Congress. The public necessities call distressingly for aid, and very ruinous circumstances proceed from the inattention of the states to furnish supplies in money. S. Carolina is the foremost state in supplies notwithstanding her distresses. Whence does this proceed? From a difference of spirit solely; from a pride of character; from a rejection of the unmanly supineness which permits personal inconveniency to absorb every other sentiment. There is no man who has not some vice or folly the atoning of which would not pay his taxes.[48]

I am now to take my leave of the justlings of states and to repair to a feild where the divisions will be fewer but on a larger scale. Congress yesterday joined me to Mr. Adams and Dr. Franklin on the foreign commercial negotiations. I shall pursue there the line I have pursued here, convinced that it can never be the interest of any party to do what is unjust, or to ask what is unequal. Mr. Jay was to sail for America this month. His health has obliged him to return to try his native air. He is appointed Secretary for Foreign affairs. I pray you to continue to favor me with your correspondence. At the close of every session of assembly a state of the general measures and dispositions, as well as of the subordinate politics of parties or individuals will be entertaining and useful. During recesses other objects will furnish matter sufficient for communication. On my part I shall certainly maintain the correspondence. If moreover you can at any time enable me to serve you by the execution of any particular commission I shall agree that my sincerity may be judged by the readiness with which I shall execute it. In the purchase of books, pamphlets etc. old and curious, or new and useful I shall ever keep you in my eye. Whether I shall procure for you the books you have before desired at Philadelphia or Paris shall be decided according to circumstances when I get to Philadelphia, from which place I will write to you.

---

47. For the enclosed resolution, see TJ's "Report concerning Continental Bills of Credit," [May 7, 1784], below.

48. For a comparison of South Carolina's and Virginia's payments of their quotas of congressional requisitions, see E. James Ferguson, *The Power of the Purse: A History of American Public Finance, 1776–1790* (Chapel Hill, 1961), pp. 181–83.

I have a tender legacy to leave you on my departure. I will not say it is the son of my sister, tho her worth would justify my resting it on that ground; but it is the son of my friend, the dearest friend I knew, who, had fate reversed our lots, would have been a father to my children. He is a boy of fine dispositions, and sound masculine talents. I was his preceptor myself as long as I staid at home, and when I came away I placed him with Mr. Maury. On his breaking up his school I desired Mr. Short to dispose of him, but Mr. Short I expect will go with me to Europe. I have no body then but you to whose direction I could consign him with unlimited confidence. He is nearly master of the Latin, and has read some Greek. I beleive he is about 14. years of age. I would wish him to be employed till 16. in completing himself in latin, Greek, French, Italian and Anglosaxon. At that age I mean him to go to the college. I have written to my sister of the application I make to you and she will be very happy to have your advice executed. My steward Mr. Key will furnish money to his tutors etc. on your order. There is a younger one, just now in his Latin rudiments. If I did not fear to overcharge you I would request you to recommend the best school for him. He is about 10. years old, and of course ceteris paribus, of any two schools, that nearest his mother would be most agreeable. You will readily understand I am speaking of the sons of Mr. Carr.

I think Colo. Monroe will be of the Committee of the states. *He wishes a correspondence with you;* and I suppose his situation will render him an useful one to you. The scrupulousness of his honor will make you safe in the most confidential communications. A better man cannot be. I think your two loans to me amounted to $503\frac{1}{3}$ Dollars. I paid for the first pair of spectacles $13\frac{2}{3}$ Doll. and shall pay the same for the 2d. unless they should be returned. I now inclose you an order on the Treasurer for $407\frac{1}{3}$ Dollars which will leave in my hand a balance of $68\frac{2}{3}$ Dollars due to you which is about the sum you desired.

May 11.

Many considerations have determined me to go on to Boston and take shipping from thence. This was a conclusion of yesterday. All my letters dated previous to that will state me as purposing to sail from N. York. I leave this place to-day; expect to stay in Philadelphia till the 25th. and to be at Boston about the 3d. of June. I am with the sincerest esteem Dr. Sir Your affectionate friend and servt.,

TH: JEFFERSON

ENCLOSURE
*Report concerning Continental Bills of Credit*

Resolved[49]                                                                                    [Annapolis May 7, 1784]

That all sums of Continental bills of credit *paid by or to any State* on account of the United states shall be credited or debited in account according to the specie value of

---

[49]. TJ enclosed his handwritten copy of the report, which he had drafted as chairman of the Grand Committee. By the time Congress acted on the committee report, TJ had left Annapolis to prepare for his trip to France; see *PTJ,* VII, p. 223.

such bills at the time of paiment, as settled by the legislature of the same state in their table of depreciation constructed for the use of their state: and where none such has been constructed, an average shall be taken from those of the states adjoining wherein such tables have been constructed,[50] on which paiments an interest shall be allowed at the rate of 6. per cent. per annum from the time of paiment.

That all such bills *now in the Treasury*[51] of any state, if received before the 18th. of March 1780. shall be credited to such state according to their value on that day as declared by Congress in their resolutions of          and if received after that day shall be credited at their specie value at the time to be settled as directed in the preceding resolution, and if after the last day to which such table descends, they shall then be credited at the rate at which they were purchased or received, or if not purchased or received at any particular rate, then at the market value of such bills within the state at the time, to be estimated on the best evidence which may be obtained: on which sums also a like interest of 6. per cent from the time of receipt shall be allowed: and the affidavit of the Treasurer receiving the said bills shall be evidence of the time and rate at which they were received.

That all such bills *now in the hands of individuals* shall be redeemed at the same rates allowed for those in the Treasury of their state: that the holders of such bills shall be at liberty to carry them to the Loan officer of the U.S. within their state who shall give them in exchange for the same a certificate expressing the sum in specie which the U.S. owe in lieu thereof and the time from which it bears interest, which time shall be the 18th of Mar. 1780. for all those received before that day, and the time of actual receipt for all those received after. The Loan officer shall require from the holder the best evidence of the time of his receiving them which the nature of the case will admit, viz. that of circumstances and disinterested persons where to be had, and where not to be had to his satisfaction, then resorting to the examination of the party himself on oath, and giving to the same so much credit as in his conscience he shall think it deserves: and in all cases of importance and difficulty shall associate to himself two honest and able persons to assist him in the examination and judgment. These certificates shall be funded and paid as the other debts of the United States. But no certificate shall be issued for a less sum than thirty specie dollars.

That the Superintendant of finance direct the form and mode of issuing the aforesaid certificates, and take order for destroying the Continental bills of credit brought in.

## Madison to Jefferson

Richmond May 8, 1784

Near a whole week has already passed without the meeting of a house. 79 are requisite for business, of which about 60 have arrived. . . . Not a single idea can as yet be formed of the politics which will predominate.[52]

50. For the minor textual changes made during the congressional debates, see *ibid*.

51. TJ's italics, as are the rest of the italics in this report.

52. This fragment of a letter, taken from the Stan. V. Henkels Catalogue no. 712 (Dec. 14, 1893), will appear in a forthcoming Supplement to *PTJ;* it was called to my attention by John Catanziriti and Eugene Sheridan.

## Madison to Jefferson

Richmond May 15, 1784

DEAR SIR

Your favor of the 7th. inst: with another pair of Spectacles inclosed came safe to hand on thursday last. I shall leave the person for whose use they were intended to take choice of the most suitable and will return the other pair to Mr. Dudley by the first conveyance, unless I meet with a purchaser which I do not expect. The arrangement which is to carry you to Europe has been made known to me by Mr. Short who tells me he means to accompany or follow you. With the many reasons which make this event agreeable, I cannot but mix some regret that your aid towards a revisal of our State Constitution will be removed. I hope however for your licence to make use of the ideas you were so good as to confide to me, so far as they may be necessary to forward the object. Whether any experiment will be made this Session is uncertain. Several members with whom I have casually conversed give me more encouragement than I had indulged. As Col: Mason remains in private life, the expediency of starting the idea will depend much on the part to be expected from R. H. L. and P. H.[53] The former is not yet come to this place, nor can I determine any thing as to his politics on this point. The latter arrived yesterday and from a short conversation I find him strenuous for invigorating the federal Government though without any precise plan, but have got no explanations from him as to our internal Government. The general train of his thoughts seemed to suggest favorable expectations. We did not make a House till Wednesday last, and have done nothing yet but arrange the Committees and receive petitions. The former Speaker was re-elected without opposition. If you will either before or after your leaving America point out the channel of communication with you in Europe, I will take the pleasure of supplying you from time to time with our internal transact[ions] as far as they may deserve your attention, and expect that you will freely command every other service during your absence which it may be in my power to render. Wishing you every success and happiness I am Dr. Sir Your affecte. friend,

J. MADISON [JR.]


## Jefferson to Madison

Philadelphia May 25, 1784

DEAR SIR

Your favors of the 8th. and 15th. came to hand yesterday. I have this morning reviewed your former letters to see what commissions it would be

---

53. Richard Henry Lee and Patrick Henry.

best for me to execute here for you. In that of Feb. 17. you desire a recommendation of a fit bookseller in Paris and London. This certainly I can better do from the spot. In the mean time address yourself to me as your bookseller for either place, because at whichever I shall be I can easily order books to be sent you from the other. In the letter of March 16. you wish for any good books on the Droit public or constitutions of the several existing confederacies and on the Law of Nature and Nations. There are some books at Boinod's on the first of these subjects but I have not time to examine them. I can do this so conveniently in Paris, get them on so much better terms, have them bound, and send them so speedily that I will refer the execution of this commission till I get there. Bynkershoeck and Wolfius I will also examine there and send you such parts of their works as I think you will like. Boinod will receive very soon the following books which he wrote for me. Should you chuse any of them you will write to him and he will send them to you.

Les troubles des pais bas de Grotius.
Wicquefort des ambassadeurs.
Memoires de l'Amerique.
Barrington's miscellanies.
Scheele's chemical observations on air and fire.
Whatever has been written on air or fire by Fontana, Priestly, Ingenhouse, Black, Irvine, or Crawford.

I have searched every bookshop in town this morning for Deane's letters and Hawk' abr' Co. Lit.[54] except Bell's. It is in none of them. Pritchard had sold Zane's copy. I shall examine Bell's also before I leave town and if I get them they shall come with Blair's lectures which I purchased for you of Aitken and have desired him to send to Richmond to the care of James Buchanan.

Mr. Zane is probably with you. Pray deliver my friendly compliments to him, tell him I have written three letters to him and find him unpunctual, having answered none of them. I am very anxious to receive the thermometrical trials I asked him to make in his cave. I wish they could be sent to me immediately to Paris. I could not get my notes printed here and therefore refer it till I shall cross the water where I will have a few copies struck off and send you one. The assembly of N. York have made Payne the author of Common sense a present of a farm. Could you prevail on our assembly to do something for him. I think their quota of what ought to be given him would be 2000 guineas, or an inheritance worth 100 guineas a year. It would be peculiarly magnanimous in them to do it; because it would shew that no particular and smaller passion has suppressed the grateful impressions which his services have made on our minds. Did I ever inform you that Genl. Washington would accept the superintendance of the clearing the Patowm' and Ohio, if put on a

---

54. For the fuller titles of the works on air or fire, see *PJM,* VIII, p. 44. The "Hawk" abbreviation stands for Hawkins's abridgment of Coke on Littleton.

hopeful footing? Two vessels are arrived here in 24 and 25 days passage from London. They say the elections are going in favor of the ministry. Mrs. House is well and her lodgings well accustomed. Poor Mrs. Trist is in a situation which gives us much pain. Her husband is dead, and she without knowing it is proceeding down the Ohio and Missisipi in hopes of joining him. There is a possibility only that letters sent from hence may overtake her at the Falls of Ohio and recall her to this place. I am obliged to put a period here to my letter being desired to assist in a consultation on a very disagreeable affair. A Frenchman of obscure and worthless character having applied to Mr. Marbois to give him the Consular attestations to a falsehood and being refused, attacked him in the streets a day or two after and beat him much with his cane.[55] The minister has taken up this daring insult and violation of the law of nations in the person of the Secretary to their embassy and demands him to be given up (being a subject of France) to be sent there for punishment. I doubt whether the laws of this state have provided either to punish him sufficiently here or to surrender him to be punished by his own sovereign: and the ——[56] of this state is so indecisive that no defects of law will be supplied by any confidence of his in the justification of his assembly when they shall meet. They have not yet declared what they can or will do, and the scoundrel is going at large on bail, sending anonymous letters to the minister and Marbois with threats of assassination etc. if the prosecution be not discontinued. The affair is represented to Congress who will have the will but not the power to interpose. It will probably go next to France and bring on serious consequences. For god's sake while this instance of the necessity of providing for the enforcement of the law of nations is fresh on men's minds, introduce a bill which shall be effectual and satisf[act]ory on this subject. Consuls you will always have. Ministers may pass occasionally through our country. Members of Congress must pass through it. Should Congress sit in or near the state, frequent instances of their members and public ministers entering the state may occur.[57] I wish you every possible felicity and shall hope to hear from you frequently. I am with sincere esteem Dr. Sir Your friend and servt,

TH: JEFFERSON

---

55. The Frenchman of "worthless character" was Charles Julien Longchamps; see Alfred Rosenthal, "The Marbois-Longchamps Affair," *PMHB* 63 (1939): 294–95, and G. S. Rowe and Alexander W. Knott, "The Longchamps Affair (1784–86), the Law of Nations, and the Shaping of Early American Foreign Policy," *Diplomatic History* 10 (1986): 199–220.

56. John Dickinson, president of the Supreme Executive Council of Pennsylvania; see *PTJ,* VII, p. 290.

57. Both Pennsylvania and Virginia passed legislation to punish violations of the law of nations; see *PJM,* VIII, pp. 44–45.

## Jefferson to Madison

Boston July 1, 1784

DEAR SIR

After visiting the principal towns through Connecticut, Rhodeisland, this state and N. Hampshire in order to acquire what knowledge I could of their commerce and other circumstances I am returned to this place and shall sail the day after tomorrow in the Ceres bound for London: but my purpose is to get on shore in some boat on the coast of France and proceed directly to Paris. My servant being to set off to-day, and much on hand to prepare for my journey I have no time for any particular communications. Indeed there are few I should have to make unless I were to enter into a detail which would be lengthy as to the country and people I have visited. The lower house of this state have passed a bill giving Congress the powers over their commerce which they had asked; it has had two readings with the Senate and meets with no opposition. I find the conviction growing strongly that nothing can preserve our Confederacy unless the band of Union, their common council be strengthened. I inclose you a letter from Mrs. Trist and a new pamphlet.[58] Since I came here I have received from Mr. Harrison a bill of John Pirkman on John J. Bogert Philadelphia for $333\frac{1}{3}$ Dollars. This being for part of the money included in my draught on the Treasurer in your favor, and which at the time of that draught I did not know had been forwarded for me, I now inclose the bill to Mr. Saml. House in Philadelphia and desire him to receive and lodge the money in the bank in your name, and to give you advice of it that you may know when it may be safely drawn for. You shall hear from me as soon as I reach the other side the Atlantic. In the mean time I am with truth Dr. Sir Your affectionate friend and servt.,

TH: JEFFERSON

P.S. I inclosed you by Genl. Gates from N. York Deane's letters which I could not get in Philada.


## Madison to Jefferson

Richmond July 3, 1784

DEAR SIR

The Assembly adjourned the day before yesterday. I have been obliged to remain here since on private business for my Countymen with the auditor's and other departments. I had allotted towards the close of the Session to undertake a narrative for you of the proceedings, but the hurry on which I did

---

58. The pamphlet was by Brian Edwards, *Thoughts on the late Proceedings of Government respecting the Trade of the West India Islands with the United States of North America* (London and Boston, 1784).

not sufficiently calculate rendered it impossible, and I now find myself so abridged in time that I cannot fulfil my intentions. It will however be the less material, as Mr. Short by whom this goes, will be possessed of almost every thing I could say. I inclose you a list of the acts passed excepting a few which had not received the last solemnity when the list went to the press.[59] Among the latter is an Act under which 1 per ct. of the land tax will be collected this fall and will be for Congress. This with the 1 ½ per ct. added to the impost on trade, will be all that Congress will obtain on their last requisition for this year. It will be much short of what they need, and of what might be expected from the declarations with which we introduced the business of the Session. These declarations will be seen in the Journal, a copy of which I take for granted will be carried by Mr. Short. Another act not on the list lays duties on law proceedings, on alienations of land, on probats of Wills, administration and some other transactions which pass through official hands. This tax may be considered as the basis of a stamp-tax; it will probably yield £15 or 20,000 at present; which is set apart for the foreign Creditors of this State.

We made a warm struggle for the establishment of Norfolk and Alexandria as our only ports; but were obliged to add York, Tappahannock and Bermuda hundred, in order to gain any thing and to restrain to these ports foreigners only. The footing on which British debts are put will appear from the Journal noting only that a law is now in force which forbids suits for them. The minority in the Senate have protested on the subject. Having not seen the protest I must refer to Mr. Short who will no doubt charge himself with it.

A trial was made for a Convention, but in a form not the most lucky. The adverse temper of the House and particularly of Mr. Henry had determined me to be silent on the subject. But a Petition from Augusta having among other things touched on a Reform of the Government and R. H. L.[60] arriving with favorable sentiments, we thought it might not be amiss to stir the matter. Mr. Stuart from Augusta accordingly proposed to the Committee of propositions, the Resolutions reported to the House as per Journal. Unluckily R. H. L. was obliged by sickness to leave us the day before the question came on in Committee of the whole, and Mr. Henry shewed a more violent opposition than we expected. The consequence was that after two days Debate, the Report was negatived, and the majority not content with stopping the measure for the present availed themselves of their strength to put a supposed bar on the Journal against a future possibility of carrying it. The members for a Convention with full powers, was not considerable for number, but included most of the young men of education and talents. A great many would have concurred in a Convention for specified amendments, but they were not disposed to be active even for such a qualified plan.

Several Petitions came forward in behalf of a General Assessment which

---

59. The enclosure is missing.
60. Richard Henry Lee.

was reported by the Committee of Religion to be reasonable. The friends of the measure did not chuse to try their strength in the House. The Episcopal Clergy introduced a notable project for re-establishing the independance of the laity. The foundation of it was that the whole body should be legally incorporated, invested with the present property of the Church, made capable of acquiring indefinitely, empowered to make canons and by laws not contrary to the laws of the land, and incumbents when once chosen by vestries to be irremoveable otherwise than by sentence of the Convocation. Extraordinary as such a project was, it was preserved from a dishonorable death by the talents of Mr. Henry. It lies over for another Session.

The public lands at Richmond not wanted for public use are ordered to be sold and the money, aided by subscriptions, to be applied to the erection of buildings on the Hill as formerly planned. This fixes the Government which was nearly being made as vagrant as that of the U.S. by a coalition between the friends of Williamsbg. and Stanton. The point was carried by a small majority only.

The lands about Williamsbg. are given to the University, and are worth Mr. H. Tazewell thinks £10,000 to it. For the encouragement of Mr. Maury's School, licence is granted for a lottery to raise not more than £2000.

The revisal is ordered to be printed. A frivolous œconomy restrained the number of copies to 500. I shall secure the number you want and forward them by the first opportunity. The three Revisor's labour was recollected on this occasion, and £500 voted for each. I have taken out your warrant in five parts, that it may be the more easily converted to use. It is to be paid out of the first unappropriated money in the Treasury, which renders its value very precarious unless the Treasurer should be willing to endorse it "receivable in taxes" which he is not obliged to do. I shall await your orders as to the disposition of it.

An effort was made for Paine and the prospect once flattering. But a sudden opposition was brewed up which put a negative on every form which could be given to the proposed remuneration. Mr. Short will give you particulars.

Col: Mason, the Attorney, Mr. Henderson and myself are to negotiate with Maryland if she will appoint Commissioners to establish regulations for the Potowmac. Since the receipt of yours of May 8. I have made diligent enquiry concerning the several schools most likely to answer for the education of your Nephews. My information has determined me finally to prefer that of Mr. W. Maury as least exceptionable: I have accordingly recommended it to Mrs. Carr and on receiving her answer shall write to Mr. Maury pointing out your wishes as to the course of study proper for Master Carr. I have not yet made up any opinion as to the disposition of your younger Nephew, but shall continue my enquiries till I can do so. I find a greater deficiency of proper schools than I could have supposed, low as my expectations were on the subject. All that I can assure of is that I shall pursue your wishes with equal pleasure and faithfulness.

Your hint for appropriating the slave-tax to Congress fell in precisely with the opinion I had formed and suggested to those who are most attentive to our finances. The existing appropriation of one half of it however to the military debt was deemed a bar to such a measure. I wished for it because the slave holders are Tobacco makers, and will generally have hard money as alone will serve for Congress. Nothing can exceed the confusion which reigns throughout our Revenue department. We attempted but in vain to ascertain the amount of our debts, and of our resourses, as a basis for something like a system. Perhaps by the next Session the information may be prepared. This confusion indeed runs through all our public affairs, and must continue as long as the present mode of legislating continues. If we cannot amend the constitution, we must at least call in the aid of accurate penmen for extending Resolutions into bills, which at present are drawn in manner that must soon bring our laws and our Legislature into contempt among all orders of Citizens.

I have communicated your request from Philada. May 25. to Mr. Zane. He writes by Mr. Short and tells me he is possessed of the observations which he promised you. I found no opportunity of broaching a scheme for opening the Navigation of the Potowmac under the auspices of Genl. Washington, or of providing for such occurrences, as the case of Marbois. With the aid of the Attorney perhaps something may be done on the latter point next Session. Adieu My dear friend,

J. MADISON JR.

# 9

# "THE DARK SIDE OF OUR COMMERCIAL AFFAIRS": THE MINISTER TO FRANCE AND THE VIRGINIA LEGISLATOR, 1784–1785

*J*EFFERSON LEFT BOSTON with his daughter and servant on July 5, 1784, and "had a most favourable run" across the Atlantic.[1] "We had a lovely passage in a beautiful new ship . . . ," Patsy reported, "a fine sun shine all the way, with a sea which was as calm as a river."[2] After landing in England briefly, they took a ship to Le Havre before moving on to Paris, where Jefferson joined Benjamin Franklin and John Adams as minister plenipotentiary to negotiate treaties of amity and commerce with European nations.

In Paris, the Revolutionary trio, who had not met since collaborating on the Declaration of Independence, worked as well together in France as they had in the Continental Congress. "We proceed with wonderful harmony, good humor, and unanimity," Adams reported.[3] The Adamses—Jefferson had met Abigail Adams in Boston just before she sailed to join her husband—welcomed their new colleague warmly. Mrs. Adams called him "one of the choice ones of the earth," and Adams agreed.[4] "He is an old Friend," he reported, "with whom I have often had occasion to labour at many a knotty

---

1. TJ to John Adams, on board the *Ceres* off Scilly, July 24, 1784, in Cappon, I, p. 17.

2. Martha Jefferson to Elizabeth Trist, cited in Marie Kimball, *Jefferson: The Scene of Europe, 1784 to 1789* (New York, 1950), p. 3.

3. Peterson, p. 298.

4. Abigail Adams to Mrs. Richard Cranch, May 8, 1785, in Abigail Adams, *Letters of Mrs. Adams, the Wife of John Adams,* ed. Charles Francis Adams, 2 vols. (Boston, 1841), II, p. 45.

Problem, and in whose Abilities and Steadiness I have always found great Cause to confide."⁵

By the spring of 1785, the reunion had ended, with Congress recalling the venerable Franklin, appointing Jefferson as his successor as minister to France, and sending Adams to London as the first American minister to the Court of St. James's. Adams wrote Jefferson that leaving "all our Friends in and about Paris, make[s] the journey rather triste." In her farewell note, Mrs. Adams told Jefferson that he was "the only person with whom my Companion could associate with perfect freedom, and unreserve." Jefferson confessed that "the departure of your family has left me in the dumps," adding that "my afternoons hang heavily on me."⁶

While Jefferson was settling in at his new post with his colleagues in the fall of 1784, Madison fired off five letters before hearing from Jefferson, keeping him informed on important events in Richmond and the nation as well as less significant developments at home. Jefferson relished both. On the first, he wrote: "I thank you very much for the relation of the proceedings of assembly. It is the most grateful of all things to get those details when one is so distant from home." On the second, he observed: "I am obliged to you for your information as to the prospects of the present year in our farms. It is a great satisfaction to know it, and yet it is a circumstance which few correspondents think worthy of mention."⁷

While he was in Congress, Jefferson had helped draft two basic statements on commerce that became instructions to American diplomats negotiating trade treaties. In both, his object was to strengthen the American Union. The first stated emphatically that the United States should "be considered in all such treaties and in every case arising under them as one nation upon the principles of the federal Constitution."⁸ Implicitly, this provision rejected state authority to the extent that commerce was covered by treaties. By action as one nation, the United States could develop an economic system based on commercial freedom and, at the same time, strengthen the ties binding the Union. The second statement built upon this concept, calling upon the states to "vest Congress with so much power over their commerce as will enable them to retaliate on any nation who may wish to grasp it on unequal terms."⁹

As soon as Jefferson joined Franklin and Adams in Paris, he explained that he had had difficulty in getting Congress to accept his article about the United States being considered one nation. It was "an extreme[ly] delicate point in America where a great party are jealous of their separate [state] independence. . . . The majority however is for strengthening the band of Union," he informed his colleagues; "they are the growing party, and if we can do anything

---

5. John Adams to James Warren, Aug. 27, 1784, cited in *PTJ*, VII, p. 382.
6. John Adams to TJ, May 11, 1785, in Cappon, I, p. 22; Abigail Adams to TJ, June 6, 1785, *ibid.*, p. 28; TJ to John Adams, May 25, 1785, *ibid.*, p. 23.
7. TJ to JM, Dec. 8, 1784, below, and Nov. 11, 1784, below.
8. "Report on Letters from American Ministers in Europe," Dec. 20, 1783, in *PTJ*, VI, p. 394.
9. TJ to Horatio Gates, May 7, 1784, *ibid.*, VII, p. 225.

to help them, it will be well."[10] On another occasion, Jefferson emphasized that "my primary object in the formation of treaties is to take the commerce of the states out of the hands of the states, and to place it under the superintendance of Congress, so far as the imperfect provisions of our constitution will admit, and until the states shall by new compact make them more perfect." Although Congress had no original or inherent power over the commerce of the states, he argued, it could negotiate treaties of commerce. "The moment these treaties are concluded," he added, "the jurisdiction of Congress over the commerce of the states springs into existence, and that of the particular states is superceded so far as the articles of the treaty may have taken up the subject."[11]

Until these treaties were concluded, however, Jefferson welcomed such state action as Madison's port bill for Virginia, which restricted foreign trade to enumerated ports. "This act of our assembly," he informed his friend, "has been announced in all the gazettes of Europe with the highest commendations," indicating that the Continental nations looked forward to liberal commercial arrangements with America.[12]

Like Jefferson, who wanted "to prevent Great Britain from applying her navigation acts against us separately," Madison opposed "the old plan of British monopoly" and welcomed Jefferson's suggestion to "shew that we are capable of foregoing commerce with them, before they will be capable of consenting to an equal commerce." Madison noted that one of the "fruits of Independence," brought about by increased trade with Europe, was a big jump in the price of tobacco, which had "brought more specie into the Country than it ever before contained at one time." The price of hemp was down and the wheat crop scanty, but Madison predicted that the corn crop "will be exuberent, and will afford plentiful supplies for the W. India Islands if their European Masters will no longer deny themselves the benefit of such a trade with us."[13]

Jefferson thought that nothing would bring England to reason "but physical obstruction, applied to their bodily senses. . . . They allow our commodities to be taken from our own ports to the W. Indies in their vessels only. Let us allow their vessels to take them to no port."[14] He reported that the move "to invest Congress with the regulation of our commerce" and "to defeat the avidity of the British government, grasping at our carrying business," had produced "a wonderful sensation in England" and a new "respect towards the United states in . . . Europe."[15]

10. TJ, "Notes for Consideration of the Commissioners to Negotiate Treaties," [Sept. 4–Nov. 10, 1784], *ibid.*, pp. 478–79.
11. TJ to James Monroe, June 17, 1785, *ibid.*, VIII, pp. 230–31.
12. TJ to JM, Nov. 11, 1784, below.
13. JM to TJ, Aug. 20, 1784, below, and TJ to JM, Mar. 18, 1785, below. For TJ's opposition to the British Navigation Act, see *PTJ*, VII, p. 478.
14. TJ to JM, Mar. 18, 1785, below.
15. TJ to JM, Sept. 1, 1785, below.

Madison agreed that "if any thing should reconcile Virga. to the idea of giving Congress a power over her trade, it will be that this power is likely to annoy G.B. against whom the animosities of our Citizens are still strong." But he worried about "the dark side of our commercial affairs," despairing because Virginians seemed "to have less sensibility to their commercial interests" than did merchants in the northern states. Although he favored "a general retaliation on G.B.," he seemed to fear a commercial crisis that might lead to "*a breach in our confederacy.*"[16] In the absence of a general power over commerce, "the more suffering States are seeking relief from partial efforts which are less likely to obtain it than to drive their trade into other channels, and to kindle heart-burnings on all sides."[17]

Throughout Jefferson's tenure as negotiator of trade treaties, Madison stressed the need for a treaty with Spain. His concern about the western settlements and Spain's control of the Mississippi was rooted in his earlier role in Congress. He reaffirmed his view that Spain could "no more finally stop the current of trade down the river than she can that of the river itself," but he feared "an impolitic and perverse attempt in Spain to shut the mouth of the Mississippi against the inhabitants above."[18] Even on a leisurely "ramble into the Eastern States," where he met Lafayette by accident, he pressed his views on the marquis, who volunteered to write to the French foreign minister to urge the latter to divert Spain from its policy.[19]

After meeting with Lafayette, who had returned to the United States for the first time since the end of the war for independence, Madison scrapped his trip to Boston and joined the Revolutionary hero on a western swing to Fort Schuyler, New York, where a treaty with the Indians was to be negotiated. Wherever Lafayette went, Madison informed his friend, "he receives the most flattering tokens of sincere affection from all ranks." In addition, "his presence has furnished occasion for fresh manifestation of these sentiments towards France which have been so well merited by her, but which her enemies pretended would soon give way to returning affection for G. Britain."[20]

After spending nearly a month with the marquis, Madison gave Jefferson his measured appraisal of the international hero. "With great *natural frankness of temper he unites much address;* with very *considerable talents, a* strong *thirst of praise and popularity.* In *his politics he* says *his three hobby-horses are the alliance between France and the United States,* the *Union of the latter* and the *manumission* of the *slaves.* The two former are the *dearer to him* as *they are connected* with *his personal glory.* The last *does him real honor,* as it is a *proof of his humanity.* In a word, I take *him to be as amiable a man* as *his vanity will admit,* and as *sincere an*

16. JM to TJ, Aug. 20, 1785, below. The italicized words in this chapter were written in code.
17. JM to TJ, Oct. 3, 1785, below.
18. *Ibid.,* and Aug. 20, 1784, below.
19. JM to TJ, Sept. 7, 1784, below.
20. JM to TJ, Sept. 7, 1784, below, and Sept. 15, 1784, below.

# "THE DARK SIDE OF OUR COMMERCIAL AFFAIRS," 1784-1785     329

*American as any Frenchman can be;* one *whose past services gratitude* obliges *us to acknowledge* and *whose future friendship* prudence *requires us to cultivate.*"[21] Jefferson agreed that Lafayette was a man of *"unmeasured ambition"* but reassured Madison that "the *means he uses* are *virtuous.*"[22]

Just before Lafayette returned to France, he visited Richmond, giving Madison "further opportunities of *penetrating his character"* and of revising his earlier appraisal. "Though *his foibles did* not *disappear* all the *favorable traits* presented themselves in a *stronger light.* On *closer inspection he* certainly possesses *talents which might figure in any line.* If *he is ambitious* it is rather of the *praise* which virtue *dedicates to merit* than *of the homage* which *fear renders to power. His disposition is* naturally *warm and affectionate* and *his attachment to the United States* unquestionable.[23] Unless *I am grossly deceived* you will *find his zeal sincere* and *useful* wherever it can be *employed* in behalf *of the United States without opposition* [to] *the essential interests of France.*"[24]

Acting on his new view, Madison persuaded the Virginia assembly to authorize the casting of two busts of Lafayette, "late Commander in Chief of the Army of the United States in Virginia," as a lasting monument to the marquis' merit and the gratitude of Virginia's citizens.[25] When the hero returned to France, Jefferson reported that the marquis was *"fraught* with *affection* to *America* and *disposed* to render every *possible service.*"[26]

Madison kept Jefferson posted on Confederation politics. While he was in Congress, Jefferson had proposed that a "Committee of the States," with one representative per state, exercise executive powers during the recess of Congress, a move designed to strengthen the Confederation by giving it a continuing executive presence in the capital in the absence of the legislature. Such a committee was appointed in June 1784; but on his ramble northward in the summer, Madison discovered that the committee had dispersed, leaving "an entire interregnum of the fœderal Government for some time, against the intention of Congress . . . as well as against every rule of decorum."[27] When Jefferson asked him to "unriddle the *dissolution of the committee*," Madison reported that "*the abrupt departure of* some of the *Eastern delegates,* which *destroyed the quorum* . . . proceeded *partly from irritations among the committee, partly from dislike to the place of their session* and *partly from an impatience to get*

21. JM to TJ, Oct. 17, 1784, below. For JM's later views, see the notes to this letter, below.
22. TJ to JM, Mar. 18, 1785, below.
23. Before he returned to France at the end of 1784, Lafayette was made an honorary American citizen by Congress. For a fine study, see Anne C. Loveland, *Emblem of Liberty: The Image of Lafayette in the American Mind* (Baton Rouge, 1971).
24. JM to TJ, Aug. 20, 1785, below.
25. *PJM,* VIII, pp. 162-63. The bust presented to the city of Paris was destroyed during the French Revolution, but the other, by Houdon, is on display in Richmond in the Virginia Capitol near Houdon's statue of Washington. Virginia later made Lafayette a citizen of the commonwealth; see JM to TJ, Jan. 22, 1786, below.
26. TJ to JM, Mar. 18, 1785, below.
27. JM to TJ, Sept. 7, 1784, below.

*home,* which prevailed over *their regard* for *their private characters* as well as *for their public duty*."[28] In fact, the secretary of Congress informed Jefferson that "this invisibility of a federal head will have . . . an ill aspect in the eyes of European Nations . . . which will require all your address and abilities to remove."[29]

When Madison took his second summer trip to the northward in 1785, he visited with the Virginia congressional delegation in New York, where the Confederation government had gravitated. He told Jefferson that the affairs of Congress had not yet been "redeemed from the confusion which has so long mortified the friends to our national honor and prosperity. Congress have kept the Vessel from sinking," he conceded, "but it has been by standing constantly at the pump, not by stopping the leaks which have endangered her." He suggested four measures to correct the shortcomings revealed "by our past experience and our present situation":

1. a final discrimination between such of the unauthorised expences of the States, as ought to be added to the common debt, and such as ought not; 2. a constitutional apportionment of the common debt, either by a valuation of the land, or a change of the article which requires it; 3. a recognition by the States of the authority of Congress to enforce payment of their respective quotas; 4. a grant to Congress of an adequate power over trade.

Madison concluded that "the present plan of federal Government reverses the first principle of all Government. It punishes not the evildoers, but those that do well." His proposed solution for enforcing payment of state requisition was based on "a fortunate circumstance for the U.S." The use of coercion against the states, "or such provision as would render the use of it unnecessary, might be made at little expence and perfect safety. A single frigate under the orders of Congress could make it the interest of any one of the Atlantic States to pay its just Quota. With regard to such of the Ultramontane States, as depend on the trade of the Mississippi, as small a force would have the same effect; whilst the residue trading thro' the Atlantic States might be wrought upon by means more indirect indeed, but perhaps sufficiently effectual."[30]

In addition to Continental news, Madison sent Jefferson detailed reviews of legislative action in Richmond. With the elevation of Patrick Henry to governor in the fall of 1784, the latent opposition to Madison's program lacked "both a mouth and a head" at the October session. Madison was appointed chairman of the Committee for Courts of Justice, a post usually assigned to a lawyer, and he quickly revived a bill "originally penned in 1776 by Mr. [Edmund] Pendleton" who, with Jefferson and George Wythe, had been on the Committee of Revisors. It established courts of assize—circuit courts—in an effort to cut down on crowded dockets and eliminate the necessity of

---

28. JM to TJ, Aug. 20, 1785, below.
29. Charles Thomson to TJ, Oct. 1, 1784, in *PTJ,* VII, p. 432.
30. JM to TJ, Oct. 3, 1785, below.

carrying all appeals from the county courts to the state capital. Although the bill was opposed by solidly entrenched courthouse cliques, Madison pushed it through the assembly "without any direct and open opposition" by rallying "the discontented extremities of the State"—the Eastern Shore and the western counties.[31]

Madison also noted that "the Revisal"—the "Report of the Committee of Revisors on the Revision of the Laws"—had been published and the £500 stipend for each of the revisors funded, though he did not mention his role in achieving this belated result. He did report, however, on the successful tactic used by Patrick Henry's followers to sidetrack passage of Jefferson's bill to establish religious freedom, one of the major bills in the revisal report. Instead of that bill, the assembly had debated Henry's proposal for a general tax assessment "for a legal provision for the 'teachers of Christian Religion,' " a move that Madison viewed as "obnoxious on account of its dishonorable principle and dangerous tendency." Although Madison opposed the bill with "great Learning and Ingenuity,"[32] Henry's measure came close to passage. But at the last moment, on the third reading, Madison joined a small majority in a delaying tactic, voting to have the bill printed for public distribution, with an invitation to the citizens of Virginia to comment on the proposal.

Madison also informed Jefferson about the other major issues at the October 1784 session of the General Assembly: internal improvements and canal companies for the Potomac, James, and Elizabeth rivers; boat navigation and ship construction, and Washington's passionate interest in all such measures; incorporation of the Protestant Episcopal Church; payment of British creditors; authorization of an impost; and taxation.[33]

On the personal front, Madison watched out for his absent friend's reputation, and he promptly reported a rumor that linked Jefferson to a land-speculation scheme in Kentucky.[34] Jefferson's reply traced his two attempts to invest in western lands, neither of which was carried to fruition. "I can with truth therefore declare to you, and wish you to repeat it on every proper occasion, that no person on earth is authorized to place my name in any adventure for lands on the Western waters, that I am not engaged in any one speculation for that purpose at present, and never was engaged in any, but the two before mentioned."[35]

31. JM to TJ, Jan. 9, 1785, below. Although the law passed, it never went into effect, being first postponed until 1787, then until 1788, when it was repealed; see *PJM,* VIII, pp. 163–64.

32. JM to TJ, Jan. 9, 1785, below; Beverley Randolph to James Monroe, Nov. 26, 1784, cited in *PJM,* VIII, p. 196. For the text of Henry's proposed "Bill Establishing a Provision for Teachers of the Christian Religion, 1784," see Thomas E. Buckley, *Church and State in Revolutionary Virginia, 1776–1787* (Charlottesville, 1977), pp. 188–89.

33. JM to TJ, Jan. 9, 1785, below. For Washington's vision of "a more perfect union" based on linking the nation's waterways by canals, see John Seelye, *Beautiful Machine: Rivers and the Republican Plan, 1755 1825* (New York, 1991).

34. JM to TJ, Aug. 20, 1784, below.

35. TJ to JM, Nov. 11, 1784, below.

In the transatlantic exchange of knowledge and information, Jefferson sent Madison books, gadgets, and diplomatic reports, along with his impressions of politics and society in the Old World. He mailed a steady stream of books, sending 45 volumes in the first shipment, which included 37 volumes of the *Encyclopédie méthodique,* Madison's first choice for books needed by Congress, made almost two years earlier.[36] A massive shipment in September 1785 included an additional 207 volumes, costing more than 1,154 livres.[37]

Jefferson's first letter from Paris also included a shipment of the latest gadgets and curiosities that had caught his attention in the French capital: phosphorous matches—"by having them at your bedside with a candle, the latter may be lighted at any moment of the night without getting out of bed"; the new Argand cylinder lamp—"thought to give a light equal to six or eight candles"; "a pamphlet on Animal magnetism"—a government report on mesmerism; and a pamphlet on ballooning—"an account of Robert's last voiage thro' the air."[38]

The usually undemonstrative Madison found the gadgets and pamphlets "a great treat to my curiosity." Intrigued by the Argand lamp, he asked Jefferson to find other gadgets, such as a new pocket compass, "in case of a ramble into the Western Country," and a telescope fitted inside a hollow cane. But he reserved his special thanks for Jefferson's "attention to my literary wants. All the purchases you have made for me," he assured his friend, "are such as I should have made for myself with the same opportunities." Recalling Jefferson's offer to procure for him "such books as may be 'either old and curious or new and useful,'" Madison renewed his request for treatises on ancient and modern federal republics, the law of nations, and the history of America and the New World, "to which I will add such of the Greek and Roman authors where they can be got very cheap, as are worth having and are not on the common list of School classics."[39]

One other volume loomed large in the correspondence between Madison in Virginia and Jefferson in France. It was Jefferson's only book, *Notes on the State of Virginia.* He had begun it in the final troubled months of his term as wartime governor and in the gloomy aftermath of his early retirement from office. "To apologize for this by developing the circumstances of the time and place of their composition," he wrote in the preface to his book, "would be to open wounds which have already bled enough." Because the costs of publication in Philadelphia were prohibitive, he had postponed publication "till I shall cross the water where I will have a few copies struck off."[40] It was perhaps appropriate that the book was first published in France because Jefferson wrote

---

36. *Ibid.*
37. TJ to JM, Sept. 1, 1785.
38. TJ to JM, Nov. 11, 1784, below. Also see TJ, "Autobiography," in *Thomas Jefferson: Writings,* ed. Merrill D. Peterson (New York, 1984), p. 55.
39. JM to TJ, Apr. 27, 1785, below.
40. TJ to JM, May 25, 1784, above.

it, after the signing of the Franco-American alliance of 1778, in response to the request of the French government for information concerning the American states.

Jefferson's *Notes* became his best-known commentary on political economy, history, philosophy, and the arts, an intellectual and literary landmark of the early republic. It was both a description and a vindication of American natural and civil history—of America's flora and fauna, its laws and institutions, it land and its people, a carefully argued rebuttal of European theories of biological degeneracy in the New World popularized by the Comte de Buffon, the Abbé Raynal, and others.[41] It was also a rebuttal of some of the social and economic theories of the philosophes:

> The political œconomists of Europe have established it as a principle that every state should endeavour to manufacture for itself: and this principle, like many others, we transfer to America, without calculating the difference of circumstance which should often produce a difference of result. In Europe the lands are either cultivated, or locked up against the cultivator. Manufacture must therefore be resorted to of necessity not of choice, to support the surplus of their people. But we have an immensity of land courting the industry of the husbandman. Is it best then that all our citizens should be employed in its improvement, or that one half should be called off from that to exercise manufactures and handicraft arts for the other? Those who labour in the earth are the chosen people of God, if ever he had a chosen people, whose breasts he has made his peculiar deposit for substantial and genuine virtue. It is the focus in which he keeps alive that sacred fire, which otherwise might escape from the face of the earth. Corruption of morals in the mass of cultivators is a phænomenon of which no age nor nation has furnished an example. It is the mark set on those, who not looking up to heaven, to their own soil and industry, as does the husbandman, for their subsistance, depend for it on the casualties and caprice of customers. Dependance begets subservience and venality, suffocates the germ of virtue, and prepares fit tools for the designs of ambition. This, the natural progress and consequence of the arts, has sometimes perhaps been retarded by accidental circumstances: but, generally speaking, the proportion which the aggregate of the other classes of citizens bears in any state to that of its husbandmen, is the proportion of its unsound to its healthy parts, and is a good-enough barometer whereby to measure its degree of corruption. While we have land to labour then, let us never wish to see our citizens occupied at a work-bench, or twirling a distaff.[42]

Jefferson's early contact with the landless poor in France seemed to confirm the views he had set forth in his *Notes*. In a sober letter to Madison, he commented on the plight of the laboring and idle poor in Europe and the need to prevent the development of a similar class in America. Only two

---

41. The best edition of Jefferson's *Notes* is the one edited by William Peden (Chapel Hill, 1955). For Buffon, see Gilbert Chinard, "Eighteenth Century Theories on America As a Human Habitat," *Proceedings* (American Philosophical Society) 91 (1947): 28–57; Henry Steele Commager and Elmo Giordanetti, *Was America a Mistake?: An Eighteenth Century Controversy* (Columbia, S.C., 1968); and Paul Merrill Spurlin, *The French Enlightenment in America: Essays on the Times of the Founding Fathers* (Athens, Ga., 1984), pp. 68–75.

42. TJ, *Notes*, pp. 164–65.

months after his arrival in Paris, he met a poor woman, a day laborer, whose conversation on the lack of bread led him "into a train of reflections on that unequal division of property which occasions the numberless instances of wretchedness which I had observed in this country." Land ownership was concentrated "in a very few hands," and much of the land was kept idle "for the sake of game" and hunting by the owners. He conceded that the "equal division of property is impracticable," but he recurred to his contest against primogeniture in Virginia and suggested that "legislators cannot invent too many devices for subdividing property, only taking care to let their subdivisions go hand in hand with the natural affections of the human mind. The descent of property of every kind therefore to all the children, or to all the brothers and sisters, or other relations in equal degree is a politic measure, and a practicable one." He also thought that progressive taxation of land might lessen the inequality of property. "Whenever there is in any country, uncultivated lands and unemployed poor, it is clear that the laws of property have been so far extended as to violate natural right."

The earth had been given as a common stock for man to labor and live on, and "if, for the encouragement of industry we allow it to be appropriated, we must take care that other employment be furnished to those excluded from the appropriation. If we do not the fundamental right to labour the earth returns to the unemployed."

From his French experience, Jefferson extended his observations to his native land. Although it was "too soon yet in our country to say that every man who cannot find employment but who can find uncultivated land, shall be at liberty to cultivate it, paying a moderate rent," it was "not too soon to provide by every possible means that as few as possible shall be without a little portion of land. The small landholders," he concluded, repeating the statement in his *Notes on the State of Virginia,* "are the most precious part of a state."[43]

The first person in the United States to learn of the publication of Jefferson's *Notes* was Madison, who had read the book in manuscript. The day after the book was printed in Paris, Jefferson sent two copies to America—one for Madison, the other for James Monroe. "I beg you to peruse it carefully," he told Madison, "because I ask your advice on it and ask nobody's else." He hoped to distribute it to the students at the College of William and Mary but would defer to Madison's judgment since "there are sentiments on some subjects"—his criticism of slavery and the Virginia Constitution of 1776 were two examples—"which I apprehend might be displeasing to the country perhaps to the assembly or to some who lead it."[44]

Madison read the book carefully "and consulted several judicious friends in confidence." They praised the book "in *terms which* I must *not repeat to you*"

---

43. TJ to JM, Oct. 28, 1785, below. For JM's response, see JM to TJ, June 19, 1786, below. For an interesting analysis of this exchange, see Drew R. McCoy, "Jefferson and Madison on Malthus: Population Growth in Jeffersonian Political Economy," *VMHB* 88 (1980): 259–76, and Edmund S. Morgan, "Slavery and Freedom: The American Paradox," *JAH* 59 (1972): 11–12.

44. TJ to JM, May 11, 1785, below.

for fear of turning the author's head. Charles Thomson, secretary of the Confederation Congress, was more forthright, calling the *Notes* "a most excellent Natural History not merely of Virginia but of North America and possibly equal if not superior to that of any country yet published."[45]

George Wythe, professor of law at William and Mary, cautioned against an indiscriminate distribution of the book to students at the college. It would not only exhaust the supply quickly, but would also run the risk of offending narrow-minded parents. Madison agreed that several copies might better go on the reserve shelf at the college library, allowing the professors to assign it to "the Students as they successively come in."[46]

Knowing Madison's standing in Richmond, Jefferson used him as an intermediary in his dealings with the directors of public buildings in Virginia, who had asked Jefferson to "have drawn for them plans of sundry buildings, and in the first place of a Capitol." Jefferson's standing at home as a student of architecture meant that he would take the assignment seriously, "as it's object is to improve the taste of my countrymen, to increase their reputation, to reconcile to them the respect of the world and procure them it's praise." His choice of a model for the state Capitol building was based on his research in architectural books, and he fell in love with the Maison Carrée at Nîmes, "the best morsel of antient architecture now remaining," in a book published recently in Paris by Charles Clérisseau, an architect whom he commissioned to prepare a plaster model. Built in the Roman classical style, the Maison Carrée was thoroughly appropriate for the new republic. "It has obtained the approbation of fifteen or sixteen centuries," he told Madison, "and is therefore preferable to any design which might be newly contrived." Indeed, Jefferson, who had not yet seen the building, but had studied Clérisseau's drawings, thought it "one of the most beautiful, if not the most beautiful and precious morsel of architecture left us by antiquity . . . and has the suffrage of all the judges of architecture who have seen it, as yeilding to no one of the beautiful monuments of Greece, Rome, Palmyra and Balbec. . . . It is very simple, but it is noble beyond expression" and would do honor "to our country as presenting to travellers a morsel of taste in our infancy promising much for our maturer age." Indeed, he was sure that "it will be superior in beauty to any thing in America, and not inferior to any thing in the world."[47]

When he learned that work was about to begin on a less worthy and more costly plan, he was so "much mortified" that he urged Madison to stop the project. If the contractors were "afraid to undo what they have done," he suggested that Madison "encourage them to it by a recommendation from the assembly." Otherwise, he asked, "how is a taste in this beautiful art to be formed in our countrymen, unless we avail ourselves of every occasion when

---

45. JM to TJ, Nov. 15, 1785, below, and Charles Thomson to TJ, Mar. 6, 1785, in *PTJ,* VIII, p. 16. Thomson based his judgment on his reading of the manuscript copy.
46. JM to TJ, Nov. 15, 1785, below.
47. TJ to JM, Sept. 1, 1785, below, and Sept. 20, 1785, below.

public buildings are to be erected, of presenting to them models for their study and imitation?" Economic expediency should not decide the choice between "the satisfaction of seeing an object and proof of national good taste" and the "mortification of erecting a monument of our barbarism which will be loaded with execrations as long as it shall endure." In a moment of self-analysis, he told Madison: "You see I am an enthusiast on the subject of the arts."[48]

Jefferson was also enthusiastic about having Madison move to "the neighborhood of Monticello." He was convinced that "agreeable society is the first essential in constituting the happiness and of course the value of our existence," and he hoped that Madison would join Monroe and Short near Monticello to make it a "partie quarree": "I view the prospect of this society as inestimable." Instead of rambling in "the woods of America," Madison might also consider visiting his friend in France. Jefferson urged him to travel abroad and issued a generous invitation: "You shall find with me a room, bed and plate, if you will do me the favor to become of the family." There Madison could meet the men of France, study the arts, attend the theater and public entertainments, and purchase "the knowlege of another world." If costs were an objection, Jefferson offered to finance the visit to France or the move to Albermarle from "the money which the assembly have given me for my share in the revisal."[49]

When Jefferson heard that Madison had been nominated as American minister to Spain, his hopes soared of seeing his friend in Europe. "I need not tell you," he told Madison, "how much I shall be pleased with such an event." But he suspected that Madison would not accept the appointment, for he added: *"I want you* in the *Virginia Assembly* and also in *Congress* yet we cannot have *you everywhere.* We must therefore be contented to have *you where you chuse."*[50]

Madison chose to remain in Virginia and push the legal reforms first proposed by Jefferson and his fellow revisors during the Revolution. In June 1785, he wrote his "Memorial and Remonstrance" against religious assessments, which was circulated throughout the state as a powerful petition opposing such levies and favoring religious freedom and separation of church and state. Although he kept his authorship of the remonstrance secret until 1826,[51] he told Jefferson that *"I drew up the remonstrance"* and sent him a copy, "one of the truly epoch-making documents in the history of American Church-State separation."[52]

48. TJ to JM, Sept. 20, 1785, below.
49. TJ to JM, Dec. 8, 1784, below.
50. TJ to JM, Mar. 18, 1785, below.
51. He acknowledged his role in his letter to the grandson of George Mason, July 14, 1826, cited in *PJM,* VIII, p. 295.
52. JM to TJ, Aug. 20, 1785, below. See also Anson Phelps Stokes, *Church and State in the United States,* 3 vols. (New York, 1950), I, p. 391. For JM's "Remonstrance," see JM to TJ, Aug. 20, 1785, below.

## THE LETTERS

*Madison to Jefferson*

Orange Aug. 20, 1784[1]

DEAR SIR

Your favor of the 1st. July written on the eve of your embarkation from Boston was safely delivered by your Servant Bob about the 20th. of the same month. Along with it I received the pamphlet on the W. India trade, and a copy of Deane's letters. My last was written from Richmond on the adjournment of the General Assembly and put into the hands of Mr. Short. It contained a cursory view of legislative proceedings, referring to the bearer for a more circumstancial one. Since the adjournment I have been so little abroad that I am unable to say with certainty how far those proceedings harmonize with the vox populi. The opinion of some who have better means of information is that a large majority of the people either from a sense of private justice or of national faith, dislike the footing on which British debts are placed. The proceedings relative to an amendment of the State Constitution seem to interest the public much less than a friend to the scheme would wish. The act which produces most agitation and discussion is that which restrains foreign trade to enumerated ports. Those who meditate a revival of it on the old plan of British monopoly and diffusive credit, or whose mercantile arrangements might be disturbed by the innovation, with those whose local situations give them, or are thought to give them an advantage in large vessels coming up the rivers to their usual stations, are busy in decoying the people into a belief that trade ought in all cases to be left to regulate itself, that to confine it to particular ports is to renounce the boon with which Nature has favoured our country, and that if one sett of men are to be importers and exporters, another set to be carryers between the mouths and heads of the rivers and a third retailers, trade, as it must pass through so many hands all taking a profit, must in the end come dearer to the people than if the simple plan should be continued which unites these several branches in the same hands. These and other objections, tho' unsound, are not altogether unplausible, and being propagated with more zeal and pains by those who have a particular interest to serve than proper answers are by those who regard the general interest only, make it very possible that the measure may be rescinded before it is to take effect. Should it escape such a fate, it will be owing to a few striking and undeniable facts, namely, that goods are much dearer in Virginia, than in the States where trade is drawn to a

1. For the draft version of this remarkable letter, which was designed to persuade TJ of the importance of opening the Mississippi to American shipping, see *PJM,* VIII, pp. 100–1. During his months in Congress, TJ had concentrated "primarily on developing the Potomac route to tap northwestern trade and bring it to Virginia ports"; see *PTJ,* VII, p. 408.

general mart, that even goods brought from Philada. and Baltimore to Winchester and other W. and S. W. parts of Virginia are retailed cheaper, than those imported directly from Europe are sold on tide water, that generous as the present price of our Tobacco appears, the same article has currently sold 15 or 20 per Ct. at least higher in Philada. where being as far from the ultimate market it cannot be intrinsically worth more; that scarce a single vessel from any part of Europe, other than the British Dominions, comes into our ports, whilst vessels from so many other parts of Europe, resort to other ports of America, almost all of them too in pursuit of the Staple of Virginia. The exemption of our own citizens from the restriction is another circumstance that helps to parry attacks on the policy of it. The warmest friends to the law were averse to this discrimination which not only departs from its principle, but gives it an illiberal aspect to foreigners, but it was a necessary concession to prevailing sentiments. The like discrimination between our own citizens and those of other States contrary to the fœderal articles is an erratum which was omitted to be rectified, but will no doubt be so. Notwithstanding the languor of our direct trade with Europe, this Country has indirectly tasted some of the fruits of Independence. The price of our last crop of Tobacco has been on James River from 36/ to 42/6 per Ct. and has brought more specie into the Country than it ever before contained at one time. The price of hemp however has been reduced as much by the peace as that of Tobacco has been raised, being sold I am told as low as 20/. per Ct. beyond the mountains. Our crops of wheat have been rather scanty, owing partly to the rigors of the winter, partly to an insect[2] which in many places has destroyed whole fields of that grain. The same insect has since the harvest fallen upon the Corn with considerable damage; but without some very unusual disastre to that article the crop will be exuberent, and will afford plentiful supplies for the W. India Islands if their European Masters will no longer deny themselves the benefit of such a trade with us. The crop of the Tobacco now on the ground will if the weather continues favorable be tolerably good, though much shortened on the whole by the want of early seasons for transplanting and an uncommon number of the insects which prey upon it in its different stages. It will be politic I think for the people here to push the culture of this article whilst the price keeps up, it becoming more apparent every day that the richness of soil and fitness of climate on the western waters will in a few years, both reduce the price and engross the culture of it. This event begins to be generally foreseen and increases the demand greatly for land on the Ohio. What think you of a guinea an acre being already the price for choice tracts with sure titles? Nothing can delay such a revolution with regard to our staple, but an impolitic and perverse attempt in Spain to shut the mouth of the Mississippi against the inhabitants above. I say *delay*[3] because she can no more finally stop the current of trade down the river than she can that of the river itself. The importance of this

2. The chinch bug.
3. JM's italics.

matter is in almost every mouth. I am frequently asked what progress has been made towards a treaty with Spain and what may be expected from her liberality on this point, the *querists*[4] all *counting on an early ability* in the *western settlements to apply to other motives if necessary*. My answers have both from ignorance and prudence been evasive. I have not thought fit however to cherish unfavorable impressions, being more and more led by revolving the subject, to conclude that Spain will never be so mad as to persist in her present ideas. For want of better matter for correspondence, I will state the grounds on which I build my expectations.

First. *Apt as* the policy of *nations* is to *disregard justice* and the *general rights of mankind I deem* it no *small advantage* that these *considerations are in our* favour. They must *be felt in* some *degree* by the *most corrupt councils* on a *question whether* the interest of *millions shall be sacrificed* to *views concerning* a *distant and paltry settlement*. They are *every day* acquiring weight *from the progress of philosophy* and *civilization* and they must *operate on* those *nations of Europe* who have *given us a title* to *their friendly offices* or who may wish to *gain a title to ours*.

Secondly. May not something be hoped from the *respect which Spain may feel for consistency* of *character on an appeal* to the *doctrine maintained* by *herself in the year* 1609, touching the *Scheld* or at least from the *use which may be made* of that fact by the *powers disposed to favor our views*.

Thirdly. The *interest* of *Spain* at *least ought to claim her attention*. (1) A *free trade down* the Mississippi would *make new Orleans one* of the *most flourishing emporiums in the world* and deriving its *happiness* from the *benevolence of Spain* would *feel a* firm *loyalty* to *her government*. At present it is *an expensive establishment settled* chiefly by *French,* who *hate* the *government which oppresses them,* who already *covet a trade* with the *upper country,* will become *every day more* sensible of the *rigor which denies it to them* and will *join in any attempt which may be made against their masters*. (2) A generous *policy on* the *part of Spain toward the U.S.* will be the *cement of friendship and lasting peace with them*. A *contrary one* will *produce immediate heart burnings* and *sow the seeds*[5] *of inevitable hostility*. The *U.S. are already a power not to be despised by Spain*. The time *cannot be distant when, in spite of all precautions* the *safety of her possessions in* this *quarter of* the *globe must depend more on our peaceableness than her own power*. (3) In another *view it is against the interest of Spain* to throw *obstacles in the way of our Western settlements*. The part *she took* during the *late war shews that she* apprehended *less from the power growing up in her neighborhood in a state of independance* than as *an instrument in* the *hands of Great Britain*. If in this *she calculated* on the *impotence of* the *U.S.* when *dismembered* from the *British empire she saw but little way into futurity:* if on the *pacific temper of republics* unjust *irritations* on *her part* will soon *prove to her that these* have *like passions* with *other governments*. Her *permanent security* seems to *lie in* the *complexity of our federal government* and the

---

4. This word and the italicized words in the rest of the letter, except for those that pertain to n. 5, below, were written in code.

5. JM's italicization of the word "seeds."

*diversity of interests among* the *members of it which* render *offensive* measures *improbable in council* and *difficult in execution.* If *such be the case when thirteen States compose* the *system* ought *she not to* wish *to see* the *number enlarged to three and twenty?* A source of *temporary security to her is* our *want of naval strength.* Ought *she not* then *to favor* those *emigrations to* the *western land* which as long as *they* continue will *leave no supernumerary hands for the sea.*

Fourthly. Should none of *these circumstances affect her councils she can not* surely so *far disregard* the *usage of nations as to* contend that *her possessions* at the *mouth of* the Mississippi *justify a total denial of* the *use of it to the* inhabitants *above when possessions much less dis*proportionate *at* the *mouth of other rivers* have been admitted only as *a title to a moderate toll.* The case of the *Rhine the Maese and the Scheld as well as of the Elbe and Oder* are if *I mistake not in point here.* How far *other rivers* may *afford parralel cases I cannot say.* That of *the Missisipi is probably the strongest in the world.*

Fifthly. Must not the general *interest of Europe* in all cases *influence the* determinations of any particular *nation in Europe and* does not that *interest in the* present *case clearly lie* on *our side.* (1) All the *principal powers* have in a *general view* more to *gain than to lose* by denying a *right of those* who *hold the mouths of rivers to intercept a communication* with *those above. France Gr. Brit.* and *Sweden* have no opportunity of *exerting such a right* and must wish a *free passage for their merchandize in every country. Spain her*self has no such *opportunity and* has *besides* three of *her principal rivers* one of *them the seat of her metropolis runing* thro' *Portugal. Russia* can have nothing to *lose by denying this pretension* and is *bound to* do so *in favor of her* great *rivers* the *Neiper* the *Niester* and the *Don which mouth in the black sea* and of the *passage thro' the Dardanelles* which *she extorted from* the *Turks.* The *Emperor in* common with the *inland states of Germany* and moreover by *his possessions on the Maese and the Scheld* has a *similar interest.* The *possessions of* the *King of Prussia* on the *Rhine the Elbe and the Oder* are *pledges for his orthodoxy.* The *U. Prs. hold* it is true the *mouths of the Maese* the *Rhine and the Scheld* but a general *freedom of trade* is so much *their policy and they now* carry on so much *of it through the channel of rivers flowing through* different *dominions* that their *weight can hardly be thrown into* the *wrong scale.* The only *powers that* can have an *interest in opposing* the *American doctrine* are the *Ottoman* which has already *given up the point to Russia, Denmark* which is suffered to *retain* the *entrance of the Baltic, Portugal* whose principal *rivers head in Spain, Venice* which *holds the* mouth *of the Po* and *Dantzick* which commands *that of the Vistula* if it is yet to be considered as a *sovereign city.* The prevailing disposition of *Europe* on this *point once fru*strated an *attempt of Denmark to* exact *a toll* at the mouth of the *Elbe* by means of a *fort* on *the holstein side,* which commands it. The *fact is mentioned in Salmon's* gazeteer, under the *head of Gluckstadt.* I have *no opportunity* of ascertain*ing the circumstances of the case or* discovering *like cases.* (2) In a more important view the settlement of the *Western country* which will *much depend on the free use of the Missisipi* will be *beneficial to all nations* who either directly or indirectly *trade with the U.S.* By a *free expan-*

*sion* of our *people* the establishment of *internal manufactures* will not only be *long delayed:* but the *consumption of foreign manufactures* long *continued* increasing: and at the same time all the *productions of the American soil* required by *Europe in return for her manufactures*, will *proportionably increase*. The vacant land of the United States lying on the *waters of the Missisipi is perhaps equal in extent to the land actually settled*. If no *check be given to* emigrations from *the latter to the former* they will probably keep *pace* at least *with the incr*ease of our people, till the *population of both* becomes *nearly equal*. For *twenty or twenty five years* we shall consequently have *as few internal manufactures* in proportion to *our numbers as at present* and *at the end of* that *period* our *imported manufactures* will *be doubled*. It may be observed too, that as the *market for* these *manufactures* will *first incr*ease *and the* provision *for supplying it* will *follow* the *price of supplies* will naturally *rise* in *favor of* those who *manufacture them*. On the other hand as the *demand for the tobacco indigo rice corn etc.* produced by *America for exportation* will neither *precede* nor *keep pace with their increase*, the *price* must naturally *sink in favor also of* those who *consume them*. Reverse the case by supposing the *use of the Missisipi denied to us* and the consequence is that many of our *supernumerary hands* who in the *former case* would be *husbandmen* on the *waters of the Missisipi* will on the *latter supposition be manufacturers* on those of *the Atlantic* and even those who may not *be discouraged from seating the vacant lands* will be obliged by the *want of vent* for the *produce of the soil* and of the *means of purchasing foreign manufactures* to *manufacturing in* great measure *for themselves*.

 Should Spain yield the point of the navigation of the Mississippi, but at the same time *refuse us the use of her shores* the *benefit will be ideal* only. I have conversed with *several persons* who have a *practical knowlege of the* subject, all of whom *assure me* that not only the *right of fastening to the Spanish shore* but that of *holding an entrepot of our own* or of *using New Orleans as a free port* is *essential* to a *trade thro' that channel*. It has been said that *sea vessels can get up as high as latitude thirty two to meet* the *river craft* but it will be with so much *difficulty and dis*advantage *as to amount to a prohibition*. The idea has also been *suggested of large magazines constructed for floating* but if this *expedient* were *otherwise* admissible the hurricanes which in *that quarter frequently demolish edifices* on *land forbid* the least *confidence in* those which would have no *foundation but water*. Some *territorial privileges* therefore seem to be as indispensable to the *use of the river as this is to* the prosperity of *the western country*. A place *called* "The *Englishman's turn*" on the *island of* about *six leagues below the town of New O.* is I am told the *fittest for our* purpose and that the lower *side of the* pen*insula* is *the best*. *Batton rouge* is also *mentioned as a* convenient *station*, and *point coupé* as the *highest to* which *vessels* can *ascend* with tolerable ease. Information *however of this from men* who judge from *a general and superficial view only* can never be *received as accurate*. If *Spain be* sincerely *disposed to gratify us* I hope *she will be* sensible it can not be *done effectually* without *allowing a* previous *survey and deliberate choice*. Should it be *impossible to* obtain *from her a portion of ground* by other means, would it *be unadvisable to attempt it by purchase*. The *price de-*

*manded* could not well *exceed* the benefit *to be obtained;* and a *reimbursement of* the public *advance* might easily be *provided* for *by the sale to individuals* and the *conditions* which might be *annexed to their tenures.* Such a *spot* could not fail in a *little time to equal in value* the same *extent in London or Amsterdam.* The most intelligent of those with whom I have conversed think that on whatever *footing our trade may be allowed* very judicious *provision will be necessary* for a fair adjustment of *disputes between the Spaniards* and *the Americans, disputes* which must be not only *noxious to trade* but *tend to embroil the two nations.* Perhaps a joint *tribunal* under some *modification or other* might answer the purpose. There is a *precedent I see* for *such an establishment in the twenty first article* of the *treaty of Munster in* 1648 *between Spain and the United Provinces.* I am informed that sometime after *New O.* passed *into the hands of Spain her Governor* for*bid all British vessels navigating* under the *treaty of Paris to fasten to the shore* and caused such as *did so to be cut loose.* In consequence of this *practice a British frigate went up near the town, fastened to the shore, and* set *out guards to fire on* any who might *attempt to cut her loose.* The *Governor after trying* in vain *to remove the frigate by menaces acquiesed,* after which *British vessels* indiscriminately *used the shore* and even the *residence of British merchants* in the *town of New O., trading clandestinely* with the *Spaniards* as well as *openly* with *their own people winked at.* The *treaty of* 1763 *stipulated to British* subjects, as well as *I recollect,* no *more than the right of navigating* the *river* and if *that of using* was *admitted* under *that stipulation* the latter *right* must have been *admitted to be included in* the former.

When you were about leaving America as a Commissioner for peace you intimated to me that a report was in circulation of *your being a party to* jobbing for *Kentucky lands* and authorized me to contradict the report. I have some reason to believe that the credit of *your name* has been *made use of* by some who are making *purchases* or *locations in that quarter.* If they have done *it without sanction* it may not be amiss to *renew my authority.*

In consequence of my letter to Mrs. Carr I have been called on by your elder Nephew, who is well satisfied with the choice made of Williamsbg. for his future studies. I have furnished him with letters to my acquaintance there and with a draught on your steward for £12. He will be down by the opening of Mr. Maury's school at the close of the vacation which lasts from the begining of August to the end of Sepr. I have the greater hopes that the preference of this School will turn out a proper one, as it has received the approbation of the literary gentlemen of Williamsbg. and will be periodically examined by Mr. Wythe and others. Your younger Nephew is with Majr. Callis, who will keep [him] some time longer. I am at a loss as yet where to fix him, but will guard as much as possible against any idle interval. I am very affectly, Dear Sir, Yr friend and servt.,

J. MADISON JR.

*Madison to Jefferson*

Philadelphia Sept. 7, 1784

DEAR SIR

Some business, the need of exercise after a very sedentary period, and the view of extending my ramble into the Eastern States which I have long had a curiosity to see have brought me to this place. The letter herewith enclosed was written before I left Virginia and brought with me for the sake of a conveyance hence.[6] Since the date of it I have learned that Mr. Short who was to be the bearer of the letter to which it refers has not yet left Richmond. The causes of his delay are unknown to me. At Baltimore I fell in with the Marquis de la Fayette returning from a visit to Mount Vernon. Wherever he passes he receives the most flattering tokens of sincere affection from all ranks. He did not propose to have left Virginia so soon but Genl. Washington was about setting out on a trip to the Ohio, and could not then accompany him on some visits as he wished to do. The present plan of the Marquis is to proceed immediately to New York, thence by Rhode Island to Boston, thence through Albany to Fort Stanwix where a treaty with the Indians is to be held the latter end of this month, thence to Virginia so as to meet the Legislature at Richmond. I have some thoughts of making this tour with him, but suspend my final resolution till I get to N.Y. whither I shall follow him in a day or two.

The *relation*[7] *in* which *the Marquis stands to France* and *America has induced me to enter into a free conversation* with *him on the* subject *of the Missisipi.* I have *endeavored emphatically to impress* on *him* that the *ideas of America and of Spain irreconciliably clash, that unless the mediation of France be effectually exerted* an *actual rupture is near at hand, that in such an event the connection between France and Spain* will *give the enemies of the former in America the fairest opportunity of involving her in our resentments against the latter* and *of introducing Great Brit. as a party with us against both, that America can not possibly be diverted* from *her object and therefore France is bound to set every engine at work to divert Spain from hers* and *that France has besides a* great *interest in a trade with the western country thro the Missisipi.* I thought *it not amiss also to suggest to him* some of the *considerations which seem to appeal to the prudence of Spain. He admitted the force of every thing I said, told me he would write in the most* [favorable] *terms to the Count de Vergennes by the packet* which will probably *carry this and let me see his letter at N. York before he sends it. He thinks that Spain is bent on excluding us from the Mississippi and mentioned* several *anecdotes* which *happened while he was at Madrid in proof of it.*

The Committee of the States have dispersed. Several of the Eastern members having, by quitting it, reduced the number below a quorum, the impotent remnant thought it needless to keep together. It is not probable they will be

6. JM to TJ, Aug. 20, 1784, above.
7. This word and the italicized words in the rest of the letter were written in code.

reassembled before Novr. so that there will be an entire interregnum of the fœderal Government for some time, against the intention of Congress I apprehend, as well as against every rule of decorum.

The *Marquis this moment stepped into my room and seeing my cyphers before me dropped* some *questions* which *obliged me* in order *to avoid reserve to let him know* that *I was writing to you*. I *said nothing of the* subject, but *he will probably infer from our conversation that the Missisipi is most in my thoughts.*

Mrs. House charges me with a thousand compliments and kind wishes for you and Miss Patsy. We hear nothing of Mrs. Trist since her arrival at the Falls of Ohio on her way to N. Orleans. There is no doubt that she proceeded down the river thence unapprised of her loss. When and how she will be able to get back since the Spaniards have shut all their ports against the U.S. is uncertain and gives much anxiety to her friends. Browze has a windfall from his grandmother of £1000 Sterling[8] Present my regards to Miss Patsy and to Mr. Short if he should be with you, and accept yourself Dear Sir, the sincerest affection of your friend and servant,

J. MADISON JR.


## Madison to Jefferson

New York Sept. 15, 1784

DEAR SIR

In pursuance of my intentions as explained in my last dated in Philada. I came to this City on Saturday last. The information I have here received convinces me that I can not accomplish the whole route I had planned within the time to which I am limited, nor go from this to Boston in the mode which I had reckoned upon. I shall therefore decline this part of my plan, at least for the present, and content myself with a trip to Fort Schuyler, in which I shall gratify my curiosity in several respects, and have the pleasure of the Marquis's Company.[9] We shall set off this afternoon in a Barge up the North River. The Marquis has received in this city a continuation of those marks of cordial esteem and affection which were hinted in my last. The gazettes herewith enclosed will give you samples of them. Besides the personal homage he receives, his presence has furnished occasion for fresh manifestation of these sentiments towards France which have been so well merited by her, but which her enemies pretended would soon give way to returning affection for G. Britain. In this view a republication of those passages in the Gazettes of France

---

8. Mrs. Trist's son, Hore Browse Trist, was Mrs. House's grandson; see Drew R. McCoy, *The Last of the Fathers: James Madison and the Republican Legacy* (New York, 1989), pp. 209–14.

9. Rome, New York, is located on the site of Fort Schuyler, which, before the Revolution, was named Fort Stanwix.

may be of advantage to us. They will at least give a pleasure to the friends of the Marquis. We have an account from Canada, how far to be relied on I can not say, that the Indians have surprized and plunderd fort Michellmackinac where the English had a great amount of Stores and Merchandize, and that they have refused to treat with Sr. Jno. Johnson. Being in danger of losing the conveyance by the packet which is just sailing, I subscribe in haste Yrs sincerely,

J: MADISON JR.

The M. has shewn me a passage in his letter to the Ct. de V. in which he sketches the idea relative to the Miss: he says he has not had time to dilate upon it, but that his next letter will do it fully.

## Madison to Jefferson

New York Oct. 11, 1784

DEAR SIR

My last dated from this place on the 14. ult. informed you of my projected trip to Fort Schuyler. I am this moment arrived so far on my return to Virginia. My past delay requires so much hurry now that I can only drop a few lines for the packet which is to sail on the 15th. inst: The Marquis and myself were overtaken at Albany by Mr. de Marbois on the same errand with ourselves.[10] We reached Fort S. on the 29. and on the next day paid a visit to the Oneida Nation 18 miles distant. The Commissioners did not get up till the Saturday following. We found a small portion only of the Six nations assembled: nor was the number much increased when we quitted the scene of business. Accounts however had come of deputies from more distant tribes being on the way. The Marquis was received by the Indians with equal proofs of attachment as have been shewn him elsewhere in America. This personal attachment with their supposed predilection for his nation, and the reports propagated among them that the Alliance between F. and U.S. was transient only, led him with the sanction of the Commissioners to deliv[er] a speech to the Indian cheifs coinciding with the object of the Treaty.[11] The answers were

10. The marquis de Barbé-Marbois was the French chargé d'affaires who had posed the questions that led TJ to write his *Notes on the State of Virginia*. For the marquis's account of the trip, see Eugene P. Chase, ed., *Our Revolutionary Forefathers: The Letters of François de Barbé-Marbois* (New York, 1929).

11. For an account of Lafayette's dramatic speech, see Louis Gottschalk, *Lafayette between the American and the French Revolutions, 1783–1789* (Chicago, 1950), pp. 96–108; the text is also in *PTJ*, VIII, pp. 448–51. For an account of the Fort Stanwix treaty, which was negotiated after JM and Lafayette left, see Reginald Horsman, *Expansion and American Indian Policy, 1783–1812* (East Lansing, Mich., 1967), and Randolph C. Downes, *Council Fires on the Upper Ohio* (Pittsburgh, 1940), p. 291, who quotes the commissioners as telling the Indians "You are mistaken in supposing that . . . you are become a free and independent nation. . . . You are a subdued people. . . . We shall now, therefore declare to you the conditions on which you can be received into the peace and protection of the United States."

very favorable in their general tenor. Copies of both will be sent to Mons. de Vergennes and the M. de Castres by Mr. Marbois and be within the reach of your curiosity. The originals were so much appropriated to this use during my stay with the Marquis that I had no opportunity of providing copies for you. What the upshot of the Treaty will be is uncertain. The possession of the posts of Niagara etc. by the British is a very inauspicious circumstance. Another is that we are not likely to make a figure otherwise that will impress a high idea of our power or opulence. These obstacles will be rendered much more embarrassing by the instructions to the Commissioners which I am told leave no space for negociation or concession, and will consequently oblige them in case of refusal in the Indians to yield the ultimate hopes of Congress to break up the Treaty. But what will be [the] consequence of such an emergency? Can they grant a peace with out cessions of territory—or if they do must not some other price hereafter purchase them. A Truce has never I believe been introduced with the Savages, nor do I suppose that any provision has been made by Congress for such a contingency. The perseverance of the British in retaining the posts produces various conjectures. Some suppose it is meant to enforce a fulfilment of the Treaty of peace on our part. This interpretation is said to have been thrown out on the other side. Others that it is a salve for the wound given the Savages who are made to believe that the posts will not be given up till good terms shall be granted them by Congress. Others that it is the effect merely of omission in the B. Government to send orders. Others that it is meant to fix the fur trade in the B. channel and it is even said that the Governor of Canada has a personal interest in securing a monopoly of at least the Crop of this season. I am informed by a person just from Mic[hili]mackinac that this will be greater than it has been for several seasons past or perhaps any preceding season, and that no part of it is allowed by the British Commanders to be brought thro' the U. S. From the same quarter I learn that the posts have been lately well provisioned for the winter, and that reliefs if not reinforcements of the Garrisons will take place. Col: Monroe had passed Oswega when last heard of and was likely to execute his plan.[12] If I have time and opportunity I will write again from Philada. for which I set out immediately; if not, from Richmond. The Marquis proceeded from Albany to Boston from whence he will go via R. Island to Virga. and be at the Assembly. Thence he returns into the N. States to embark for Europe. I am Yrs. affecly.,

J. MADISON JR.

---

12. For Monroe's western trip, see Harry Ammon, *James Monroe: The Quest for National Identity* (New York, 1971), pp. 45-48.

## Madison to Jefferson

Philadelphia Oct. 17, 1784

DEAR SIR

On my arrival here I found that Mr. Short had passed through on his way to N. York and was there at the date of my last. I regret much that I missed the pleasure of seeing him. The inclosed was put into my hands by Mrs. House, who received it after he left Philada. My two last, neither of which were in cypher, were written as will be all future ones in the same situation, *in expectation of their being read by* the *postmasters*.[13] I am well assured that this is the fate of all letters at least to *and from public persons* not only in *France but all the other Countries of Europe*. Having now the *use of my cypher I can write without restraint.* In my last I gave you a sketch of what past at Fort Schuyler during my stay there, mentioning in particular that the *Marquis had made a speech to* the *Indians with the sanction of the Commissioners, Wolcot, Lee, Butler.*[14] The question will probably occur how *a foreigner and a private one,* could *appear on the theatre of a public treaty* between *United States and the Indian nations* and how *the Commissioners could lend a sanction to it.* Instead of offering *an opinion of the measure* I will state the *manner in which it* was *brought about.* It seems that most of the *Indian tribes* particularly *those of the Iroquois retain a strong predilection for the French* and most of *the latter an enthusiastic idea of the marquis.* This idea has resulted from *his being a Frenchman, the* figure *he has made during the war* and the arrival of several important *events which he foretold to* them soon after *he came to this country.* Before *he went to Fort Schuyler* it had been suggested, either in *compliment or sincerity* that his *presence and influence* might be of *material service to the treaty.* At *Albany* the *same thing had been said to him by general Wolcot.* On *his arrival at Fort S. Mr. Kirkland*[15] recommended an exertion of *his influence as of essential consequence to the treaty,* painting in the strongest colours the *attachment of the* Indians *to his person,* which seemed indeed to be *verified by their caresses* and the artifices employed by the *British partizans to frustrate the objects of the treaty,* among which was a pretext that the *alliance between the United States and France* was *insincere and transitory* and consequently the respect of *the Indians for the later ought to be no motive for their respecting the former.* Upon these *circumstances the M. grounded a written message to the Commissioners* before *they got up* intimating *his disposition to render the United States* any *service his small* influence *over the Indians* might *put in his power* and *desiring to know* what *the Commissioners would chuse him to say.* The *answer in Mr. Lee's hand* consisted of *polite acknowledgments* and information that the *Commissioners would be happy in affording him an opportunity of saying what ever he*

---

13. These words and the italicized words in the rest of the letter were written in code.
14. The commissioners were Oliver Wolcott from Connecticut, Arthur Lee from Virginia, and Richard Butler from Georgia.
15. Samuel Kirkland was missionary to the Oneidas and secretary of the negotiating conference.

*might wish* forbearing to *advise or suggest what it would be best for him to say. The M. perceived the caution but imputed it to Lee alone.* As his stay however *was to be very short* it was *necessary for him to take provisional measures* before *the arrival of the commissioners* and particularly for *calling in the Oneida Cheifs* who were *at their town.* It fell *to my lot to be consulted in his dilemma. My advice was* that *he should invite the* chiefs *in such a way as* would *give him an opportunity of addressing* them *publicly,* if on a *personal interview with the Commissioners* it should be judged expedient; or *of satisfying their expectations* with a friendly *entertainment in return for the civilities his visit to their town* had met with. This *advice was approved;* but the *Indians* brought with *them such ideas of his importance as* no *private reception* would *probably have been equal to.* When *the Commissioners arrived the M. consulted them in person.* They were *reserved, he was embarrassed.* Finally *they changed their plan* and *concurred* explicitly *in his making a Speech in form.* He accordingly *prepared one, communicated it to the Commissioners* and *publicly pronounced it, the Commissioners premising* such an one as was thought proper *to introduce his.* The *answer of the sachems,* as well as the *circumstances of the audience* denoted the *highest reverence for the orator.* The cheif of *the Oneidas said* that the *words which he had spoken to them early in the war* had *prevented them from being misled to the wrong side of it.* During this *scene* and even during *the whole stay of the M. he* was *the only conspicuous figure.* The *Commissioners were eclipsed.* All of *them probably felt it. Lee complained to me of the im*moderate *stress laid on the* influence *of the M.,* and evidently *promoted his departure.* The *M. was not insensible of it, but consoled himself* with the *service* which *he thought the Indian speech* would witness that *he had rendered to the United States.* I am persuaded that the *transaction* is also *pleasing to him in another view as* it will *form a bright column in the gazettes of Europe,* and that *he will be impatient for its appearance there* without seeing *any mode in* which it *can happen of course.* [16] As it is *blended with the proceedings of the Commissioners,* it will probably not be *published in America very soon, if at all.* [17] *The* time I have lately *passed with the M. has given me a* pretty thorough *insight into his character.* With great *natural frankness of temper he unites much address;* with very *considerable talents, a* strong *thirst of praise and popularity.* [18] In *his politics he* says *his three hobby-horses* are the *alliance between France and the United States,* the *Union of the latter* and the *manumission* of the *slaves.* The two former are the *dearer to him* as *they are connected* with *his personal glory.* The last *does him real honor,* as it is a *proof of his humanity.* In a word, I take *him to be as amiable a man* as *his vanity*

16. Sometime after Lafayette's triumphal visit to the United States in 1824, JM tried to revise his text to soften this early characterization of the legendary leader, scratching out the words in this sentence following the comma. Julian P. Boyd restored the original wording in *PTJ,* VII, pp. 446, 451. See also *PJM,* VIII, pp. 118–22.

17. JM tried to delete the last three words of this sentence, which Boyd restored. Lafayette's speech was published in Philadelphia newspapers before the commissioners submitted their report to Congress; see *PTJ,* VII, p. 447, and Gottschalk, p. 107.

18. JM tried to delete the words following the semicolon, but Boyd restored the original language.

*will admit,* [19] and as *sincere an American as any Frenchman can be;* one *whose past services gratitude* obliges *us to acknowledge* and *whose future friendship* prudence requires *us to cultivate.*

The Committee of the States have never reassembled. The case of Longchamps has been left both by the Legislature and Executive of this State to its Judiciary course. He is sentenced to a fine of 100 Crowns, to 2 years imprisonment, and Security for good behaviour for 7 years. On teusday morning I set off for Richmond, where I ought to be tomorrow, but some delays have put it out of my power. The ramble I have taken has rather inflamed than extinguished my curiosity to see the Northern and N.W. Country. If circumstances be favorable I may probably resume it next Summer. Present my compliments to Miss Patsy, for whom as well as yourself Mrs. House charges me with hers. She has lately received a letter from poor Mrs. Trist, every syllable of which is the language of affliction itself. She had arrived safe at the habitation of her deceased husband, but will not be able to leave that Country till the Spring at the nearest. The only happiness she says she is capable of there is to receive proofs that her friends have not forgotten her. I do not learn what is likely to be the amount of the effects left by Mr. T. Former accounts varied from 6 to 10,000 dollars. I am Dear Sir Yrs. very affectly.,

J. MADISON JR.


## *Jefferson to Madison*

Paris Nov. 11, 1784

DEAR SIR

Your letters of Aug. 20. Sep. 7. and 15. I received by the last packet. That by Mr. Short is not yet arrived. His delay is unaccountable. I was pleased to find by the public papers (for as yet I have no other information of it) that the assembly had restrained their foreign trade to four places. I should have been more pleased had it been to one. However I trust that York and Hobbs' hole will do so little that Norfolk and Alexandria will get possession of the whole. Your letter first informs me of the exception in favor of citizens, an exception which by the contrivance of merchants will I fear undo the whole. The popular objection which you mention that the articles passing thro' so many hands must come at a higher price to the consumer, is much like the one which might be made to a pin passing thro' the hands of so many workmen. Each being confined to a single operation will do it better and on better terms. This act of our assembly has been announced in all the gazettes of Europe with the highest commendations.

---

19. For the preceding five words, JM tried to substitute "as can be imagined," but Boyd restored the original wording. See his explanation in *PTJ*, VII, p. 451.

I am obliged to you for your information as to the prospects of the present year in our farms. It is a great satisfaction to know it, and yet it is a circumstance which few correspondents think worthy of mention. I am also much indebted for your very full observations on the navigation of the Missisipi. I had thought on the subject, and sketched the anatomy of a memorial on it, which will be much aided by your communications.

You mention that my name is used by some speculators in Western land jobbing, as if they were acting for me as well as themselves. About the year 1776 or 1777 I consented to join Mr. Harvey and some others in an application for lands there: which scheme however I beleive he dropped in the threshold, for I never after heard one syllable on the subject. In 1782. I joined some gentlemen in a project to obtain some lands in the Western parts of North Carolina. But in the winter of 1782. 1783. while I was in expectation of going to Europe and that the title to Western lands might possibly come under the discussion of the ministers, I withdrew myself from this company. I am further assured that the members never prosecuted their views. These were the only occasions in which I ever took a single step for the acquisition of Western lands, and in these I retracted at the threshold. I can with truth therefore declare to you, and wish you to repeat it on every proper occasion, that no person on earth is authorized to place my name in any adventure for lands on the Western waters, that I am not engaged in any one speculation for that purpose at present, and never was engaged in any, but the two before mentioned. I am one of eight children to whom my father left his share in the loyal company; whose interests however I never espoused, and they have long since received their quietus. Excepting these, I never was nor am now interested in one foot of land on earth, off of the waters of James river.[20]

I shall subjoin the few books I have ventured to buy for you. I have been induced to do it by the combined circumstances of their utility and cheapness. I wish I had a catalogue of the books you would be willing to buy, because they are often to be met with on stalls very cheap, and I would get them as occasions should arise. The subscription for the Encyclopedie is still open. Whenever an opportunity offers of sending you what is published of that work (37 vols) I shall subscribe for you and send it with the other books purchased for you. Probably no opportunity will occur till the spring when I expect the packets will be removed from L'Orient to Havre. The communication between this place and l'Orient is as difficult as it is easy with Havre. From N. York packages will be readily sent to Richmond by the care of Mr. Neill Jamieson, a very honest refugee now living at New York but who certainly ought to be permitted to return to Norfolk. Whatever money I may lay out for you here in books, or in any thing else which you may desire, may be replaced, crown for crown (without bewildering ourselves in the Exchange) in Virginia,

---

20. For the use of TJ's name by Thomas Walker in his petition to the Virginia legislature in 1784 and 1785, see *ibid.*, p. 507.

by making paiments for the instruction or boarding of my nephews, and I wish you to be assured that this will be as perfectly convenient to me as the replacing the money here, that you may with freedom order any thing from hence of which you have occasion. If the bearer Colo. Le Maire[21] can take charge of a pamphlet on Animal magnetism, another giving an account of Robert's last voiage thro' the air, and of some Phosphoretic matches, I will send them to you. These matches consist of a small wax taper, one end of which has been dipped in Phosphorus, and the whole is inclosed in a glass tube hermetically sealed. There is a little ring on the tube to shew where it is to be broken. First warm the phosphorized end (which is the furthest one from the ring) by holding it two or three seconds in your mouth, then snap it at or near the ring and draw the phosphorized end out of the tube. It blazes in the instant of it's extraction. It will be well always to decline the tube at an angle of about 45°. (the phosphorized end lowest) in order that it may kindle thoroughly. Otherwise though it blazes in the first instant it is apt to go out if held erect. These cost about 30 sous the dozen. By having them at your bedside with a candle, the latter may be lighted at any moment of the night without getting out of bed. By keeping them on your writing table, you may seal three or four letters with one of them, or light a candle if you want to seal more which in the summer is convenient. In the woods they supply the want of steel, flint and punk. Great care must be taken in extracting the taper that none of the phosphorus drops on your hand, because it is inextinguishable and will therefore burn to the bone if there be matter enough. It is said that urine will extinguish it. There is a new lamp invented here lately which with a very small consumption of oil (of olives) is thought to give a light equal to six or eight candles. The wick is hollow in the middle in the form of a hollow cylinder, and permits the air to pass up thro' it. It requires no snuffing. They make shade candlesticks of them at two guineas price, which are excellent for reading and are much used by studious men.

Colo. Le Maire, whom you know, is the bearer of this. He comes to Virginia to obtain the 2000 acres of land given him for his services in procuring us arms, and what else he may be entitled to as having been an officer in our service. Above all things he wishes to obtain the Cincinnatus eagle, because it will procure him here the order of St. Louis, and of course a pension for life of 1000 livres. He is so extremely poor that another friend and myself furnish him money for his whole expences from here to Virginia. There I am in hopes the hospitality of the country will be a resource for him till he can convert a part of his lands advantageously into money. But as he will want some small matter of money, if it should be convenient for you to furnish him with as much as ten guineas from time to time on my account I will invest that sum in books or any thing else you may want here by way of paiment. He is honest and grateful,

---

21. Colonel Jacques Le Maire served in Virginia during the Revolution and became a member of the Society of the Cincinnati in the State of Virginia; see *PJM,* VIII, p. 131.

and you may be assured that no aid which you can give him in the forwarding his claims will be misplaced.

The lamp of war is kindled here, not to be extinguished but by torrents of blood. The firing of the Dutch on an Imperial vessel going down the Scheld, has been followed by the departure of the Imperial minister from the Hague without taking leave. Troops are in motion on both sides towards the Scheld, but probably nothing will be attempted till the spring. This court has been very silent as to the part they will act. Yet their late treaty with Holland, as well as a certainty that Holland would not have proceeded so far without an assurance of aid furnish sufficient ground to conclude they will side actively with the republic. The king of Prussia it is beleived will do the same. He has patched up his little disputes with Holland and Dantzic. The prospect is that Holland, France, Prussia and the Porte will be engaged against the two Imperial courts. England I think will remain neuter. Their hostility towards us has attained an incredible height. Notwithstanding the daily proofs of this, they expect to keep our trade and cabotage to themselves by the virtue of their proclamation. They have no idea that we can so far act in concert as to establish retaliating measures. Their Irish affairs will puzzle them extremely. We expect every moment to hear whether their Congress took place on the 25th Ult. Perhaps before I seal my letter I may be enabled to inform you. Should things get into confusion there, perhaps they will be more disposed to wish a friendly connection with us.

There is a dictionary of law, natural, civil and political in 13. vols. 4to. published here. It is well executed, by Felice, Jaurat, De la lande and others. It supplies the diplomatic dictionary of which you saw some volumes in Philadelphia and which degenerated into a trifling thing. This work costs half a guinea a volume. If you want De Thou, I can buy it on the stalls in perfect condition, 11. vols. 4to. in French @ 6. livres a vol. Moreri is to be bought cheap on the stalls.

The inclosed papers being put into my hands by Mr. Grand I cannot do better than to forward them to you and ask your attention to the case should the party present himself to you.[22] I am with great sincerity Your affectionate friend and servt.,

TH: JEFFERSON

Address your letters À Monsr. Monsr. Jefferson ministre plenipotentiaire des etats unis de l'Amerique à Paris, Cul-de-sac Tetebout.

Books bought for you
Historia de España por Mariana. 2 vol. fol. (old) 15 livres.
Le Dictionnaire de Trevoux. 5. vol. folio. in good condition 28. livres.
Wicquefort de l'Ambassadeur. 2. vols. 4to. good condition 7. livres 4. sous.

---

22. Ferdinand Grand was a banker in Paris who handled accounts for Virginia and the United States during the Revolution. The papers involved "Massieu's case," which is otherwise unidentified; see *PTJ*, VII, p. 507.

Traité de Morale. a new and good publication 12 mo.
l'Encyclopedie 37. vols. some thing above 300 livres.

8 counties only sent deputies to the Congress in Dublin. They came to resolutions on the reform of parliament etc. and adjourned to the 20th. of Jan. recommending to the other counties to send deputies then.

## Jefferson to Madison

Paris Dec. 8, 1784

DEAR SIR

In mine of Nov. 11. I acknoleged the receipt of yours of Aug. 20. Sep. 7. and 15. Since that, the one of Oct. 11. by the packet has come to hand as also that of July 3. by Mr. Short who came in the packet, was actually in N. York when you passed through it and had waited there several days in hopes of seeing you. I thank you very much for the relation of the proceedings of assembly. It is the most grateful of all things to get those details when one is so distant from home. I like to see a disposition increasing to replenish the public coffers, and so far approve of the young stamp act. But would it not be better to simplify the system of taxation rather than to spread it over such a variety of subjects and pass the money thro' so many new hands. Taxes should be proportioned to what may be annually spared by the individual. But I do not see that the sale of his land is an evidence of his ability to spare. One of my reasons for wishing to center our commerce at Norfolk was that it might bring to a point the proper subjects of taxation and reduce the army of taxgatherers almost to a single hand. The simplest system of taxation yet adopted is that of levying on the land and the labourer. But it would be better to levy the same sums on the produce of that labour when collected in the barn of the farmer; because then if through the badness of the year he made little, he would pay little. It would be better yet to levy it only on the surplus of this produce above his own wants. It would be better too to levy it, not in his hands, but in those of the purchaser; because tho' the farmer would in fact pay it, as the purchaser must deduct it from the original price of his produce yet the farmer would not be sensible that he paid it. This idea would no doubt meet it's difficulties and objections when it should come to be reduced to practice: yet I suspect it would be practicable and expedient. Your taxgatherers in Virginia cost as much as the whole civil list besides. What a comfort to the farmer to be allowed to supply his own wants before he should be liable to pay any thing, and then to pay only out of his surplus.

The proposition for a Convention has had the result I expected. If one could be obtained I do not know whether it would not do more harm than good. *While Mr. Henry lives*[23] another bad constitution would be formed, and

---

23. These words and the italicized words in the rest of the letter were written in code.

saddled for ever on us. What we have to do I think is *devoutly to pray* for *his death,* in the mean time to *keep alive* the *idea* that the present is *but* an *ordinance* and to *prepare* the *minds* of the *young men.* I am glad the *Episcopalians* have again shewn their teeth and fangs. The *dissenters* had almost forgotten them. I still hope something will be done for Paine. He richly deserves it; and it will give a character of littleness to our state if they suffer themselves to be restrained from the compensation due for his services by the paltry consideration that he opposed our right to the Western country. Who was there out of Virginia who did not oppose it? Place this circumstance in one scale, and the effect his writings produced in uniting us in independence in the other and say which preponderates. Have we gained more by his advocation of independance than we lost by his opposition to our territorial right? Pay him the balance only.

I look anxiously to the approaching and improving the navigation of the Patowmac and Ohio, the actual junction of that of Big-beaver and Cayahoga by a Canal; as also that of Albermarle sound and Elizabeth through the dismal [swamp]. These works will spread the feild of our commerce Westwardly and Southwardly beyond any thing ever yet done by man.

I once hinted to you the project of seating yourself in the neighborhood of Monticello, and my sanguine wishes made me look on your answer as not absolutely excluding the hope. Monroe is decided in settling there and is actually engaged in the endeavor to purchase. Short is the same. Would you but make it a 'partie quarree' I should beleive that life had still some happiness in store for me. Agreeable society is the first essential in constituting the happiness and of course the value of our existence: and it is a circumstance worthy great attention when we are making first our choice of a residence. Weigh well the value of this against the difference in pecuniary interest, and ask yourself which will add most to the sum of your felicity through life. I think that weighing them in this balance, your decision will be favourable to all our prayers. Looking back with fondness to the moment when I am again to be fixed in my own country, I view the prospect of this society as inestimable.

I find you thought it worth while to pass the last summer in exploring the woods of America, and I think you were right. Do you not think the men, and arts of this country would be worth another summer. You can come in April, pass the months of May, June, July, August and most of September here, and still be back to the commencement of real business in the Assembly following, which I would not have you absent from. You shall find with me a room, bed and plate, if you will do me the favor to become of the family. As you would be here only for the summer season, I think your out-fit of clothes need not cost you more than 50 guineas, and perhaps the attendance on the theatres and public entertainments with other small expences might be half a guinea or three quarters a day. Your passage backwards and forwards would I suppose be 60. or 70 guineas more. Say that the whole would be 200 guineas. You will for that have purchased the knowlege of another world. I expect Monroe will come in the Spring and return to Congress in the fall. If either this object, or the one preceding for settling you near Monticello can be at all promoted by the use of the money which the assembly have given me for my share in the revisal, make use of it freely, and be assured it can in no otherway be applied so much to my gratification. The return of it may wait your perfect convenience. Should you have no occasion for it, either Mr. Eppes or Mr. Nichs. Lewis will receive it and apply it according to my general directions.

I wrote you there would be war. At that time there was no symptom which could indicate any thing else. We know of none as yet on the part either of the Emperor or Dutch. I still expect it and found my expectation on the character of the Emperor, which I collect from his public acts. These certainly shew him far above the level of common men. He would of course during the winter encourage the hopes of those who wish for peace. At present it is the general beleif here, and that even of some people who approach the men in office, that the matter will be accomodated. They found this expectation too on the character of the emperor, who they say is bizarre, and eccentric, and particularly in the dog-days. He stands in a dangerous predicament. If he sheaths the sword, he proves himself to the world a trifling personage; if he draws it, his ruin is well nigh sealed. It will not be known ultimately till the season for taking the feild. I have reason to think that before the January packet sails we shall make a short trip to England. If so, you will hear from me from thence. Both here and there I pray you to try to make me useful to you, as nothing will be more pleasing to me than to prove to you in every situation the sincere friendship I bear you. Adieu.

## *Madison to Jefferson*

Richmond Jan. 9, 1785

DEAR SIR

My last was dated in Philada. Octr. 17. I reached this place the 14th. day after that fixed for the meeting of the Assembly and was in time for the commencement of business. Yesterday put an end to the tedious Session. According to my promise I subjoin a brief review of its most material proceedings.

An act for the establishment of Courts of Assize. This act was carried through the House of Delegates against much secret repugnance, but without any direct and open opposition. It luckily happened that the latent opposition wanted both a mouth and a head. *Mr. Henry*[24] had been previously *elected governor* and was *gone for his family*. From *his conversation since I* surmise that *his presence* might have *been fatal*. The act is formed precisely on the English pattern, and is nearly a transcript from the bill originally penned in 1776 by

24. These words and the italicized words in the rest of the letter were written in code.

Mr. Pendleton except that writs sent blank from the clerk of general court are to issue in the district but returned to General Court. In the Senate it became a consideration whether the Assize Courts ought not to be turned into so many Courts of independent and complete jurisdiction, and admitting an appeal only to the Courts of Appeals. If the fear of endangering the bill had not checked the experiment, such a proposition would probably have been sent down to the House of Delegates, where it would have been better relished by many than the assize plan. The objections made to the latter were that as it required the issues to be made up and the judgments to be awarded in the General Court it was but a partial relief to suitors, and might render the service of double setts of Lawyers necessary. The friends of the plan thought these inconveniences, as far as they were real, outweighed by the superior wisdom and uniformity of decisions incident to the plan; not to mention the difference in the frequency of appeals incident to the different plans.[25] In order to leave as few handles as possible for cavil the bill omitted all the little regulations which would follow of course, and will therefore need a supplement. To give time for this provision as well as by way of collecting the mind of the public, the commencement of the law is made posterior to the next Session of Assembly. The places fixed for the Assize Courts are Northumberland Court House, Williamsbg., Accomack Ct. House, Suffolk, Richmond, Petersburg, Brunswick Ct. House, King and Queen Ct. House, Prince Edwd. Ct. H., Bedford Ct. H., Montgomery and Washington Ct. Hs. alternately, Staunton, Charlottesville, Fredericksbg., Dumfries, Winchester and Monongalia Ct. H. Besides the juridical advantages hoped from this innovation, we consider it as a means of reconciling to our Government the discontented extremities of the State.

An act for opening and extending the navigation of Potowmac river. An act for d[itt]o. d[itt]o. of James river. The subject of clearing these great rivers was brought forward early in the Session under the auspices of General Washington, who had written an interesting private letter on it to Govr. Harrison which the latter communicated to the General Assembly.[26] The conversation of the General during a visit paid to Richmond in the course of the Session, still further impressed the magnitude of the object on sundry members. Shortly after his departure, a joint memorial from a number of Citizens of Va. and Maryland, interested in the Potowmac, was presented to the Assembly, stating the practicability and importance of the work, and praying for an act of incorporation, and grant of perpetual toll to the undertakers of it. A bill had been prepared at the same meeting which produced the memorial, and was transmitted to Richmond at the same time. A like memorial and bill went to Annapolis where the legislature of Maryland were sitting. The Assembly here lent a ready ear to the project, but a difficulty arose from the height of the tolls

---

25. *PJM,* VIII, p. 222, transcribes this word as "places."
26. JM meant that Washington wrote as a private individual to urge public action.

proposed, the danger of destroying the uniformity essential in the proceeding of the two States, by altering them, and the scarcity of time for negociating with Maryland a bill satisfactory to both States. Short as the time was however, the attempt was decided on, and the negotiation committed to Genl. Washington himself. Genl. Gates who happened to be in the way and Col: Blackband were associated with him.[27] The latter did not act the two former pushed immediately to Annapolis, where the sickness of Genl. Gates threw the whole agency on Genl. Washington. By his exertions in concert with Committees of the two branches of the Legislature, an amendment of the plan was digested in a few days, passed thro' both houses in one day with nine dissenting voices only, and despatched for Richmond, where it arrived just in time for the Session. A corresponding act was immediately introduced and passed without opposition. The scheme declares that the subscribers shall be an incorporated body, that there shall be 500 Shares amounting to about 220,000 dollars, of which the States of Va. and Maryd. are each to take 50 shares, that the tolls shall be collected in three portions at the three principal falls, and with the works rest as real estate in the members of the Company, and that the works shall be begun within one year, and finished within ten years under the penalty of entire forfieture.

Previous to the receipt of the act from Annapolis a bill on a different plan had been brought in and proceeded on for clearing James River. It proposed that subscriptions should be taken by Trustees and under their management solemnly appropriated to the object in view, that they should be regarded as a loan to the State, should bear an interest of 10 per ct. and should entitle the subscriber to the double of the principal remaining undischarged at the end of a moderate period; and that the tolls to be collected should stand inviolably pledged for both principal and interest. It was thought better for the public to present this exuberant harvest to the subscribers than to grant them a perpetuity in the tolls. In the case of the Potowmac which depended on another authority as well as our own, we were less at liberty to consider what would be best in itself. Exuberant however as the harvest appeared, it was pronounced by good judges an inadequate bait for subscriptions even from those otherwise interested in the work, and on the arrival and acceptance of the Potowmac plan, it was found advisable to pass a similar one in favor of James River. The circumstancial variations in the latter are 1. the sum to be aimed at in the first instance is 100,000 Dollars only. 2. The shares which are the same in number with those of Potowmac, are reduced to 200 dollrs. each and the number of public shares raised to 100. 3. The tolls are reduced to ½ of the aggregate of the Potowmac tolls. 4. In the case the falls at this place where alone tolls are to be paid, shall be first opened, the Company are permitted to receive the tolls immediately, and continue to do so till the lapse of ten years, within which the

---

27. "Col: Blackband" was Colonel Thomas Blackburn of Prince William County; see *PJM,* VIII, p. 233.

whole river is to be made navigable. 5. A right of pre-emption is reserved to the public on all transfers of shares. These acts are very lengthy, and having passed in all the precipitancy which marks the concluding stages of a Session, abound I fear with inaccuracies.

In addition to these acts joint resolutions have passed the Legislatures of Maryd. and Va. for clearing a road from the head of the Potowmac navigation to Cheat-river or if necessary to Monongalia and 3333 ⅓ Dollars are voted for the work by each State. Pennsylva. is also to be applied to by the Governors of the two States for leave to clear a road thro' her jurisdiction if it should be found necessary, from Potowmac to Yohogania; to which the Assembly here have added a proposition to unite with Maryland in representing to Pena. the advantages which will accrue to a part of her citizens from opening the proposed communication with the sea, and the reasonableness of her securing to those who are to be at the expence, the use of her waters, as a thorough fare to and from the Country beyond her limits, free from all imposts and restrictions whatever, and as a channel of trade with her citizens free from greater imposts than may be levied on any other channel of importation. This Resolution did not pass till it was too late to refer it to Genl. Washington's negociations with Maryland. It now makes a part of the task allotted to the Commissioners who are to settle with Maryd. the jurisdiction and navigation of Potowmac below tide water. By another Resolution of this State, persons are to be forthwith appointed by the Executive to survey the upper parts of Jas. river, the country thro' which a road must pass to the navigable waters of New River, and these waters down to the Ohio. I am told by a member of the Assembly who seems to be well acquainted both with the intermediate ground and with the Western waters in question, that a road of 25 or 30 miles in length will link these waters with Js. river and will strike a branch of the former which yields a fine navigation, and falls into the main stream of the Kenhawha below the only obstructions lying in this river down to the Ohio. If these be facts James River will have a great superiority over Potowmac, the road from which to Cheat river is indeed computed by Genl. Washington at 20 miles only: but he thinks the expence of making the latter navigable will require a continuation of the road to Monongalia, which will lengthen it to 40 miles. The road to Yohogania is computed by the General at 30 miles.

By another resolution Commissioners are to be appointed to survey the ground for a canal between the waters of Elizabeth river and those of N. Carolina, and in case the best course for such a canal shall require the concurrence of that State, to concert a joint plan and report the same to the next Session of Assembly. Besides the trade which will flow thro' this channel from N. Carolina to Norfolk, the large district of Virginia watered by the Roanoak will be doubled in its value by it.

An act vesting in G. Washington a certain interest in the Companies for opening James and Potowmac rivers. The Treasurer is by this act directed to subscribe 50 Shares in the Potowmac and 100 shares in the James river Companies which shall vest in Genl. Washington and his heirs. This mode of adding some substantial to the many honorary rewards bestowed on him was termed least injurious to his delicacy, as well as least dangerous as a precedent. It was substituted in place of a direct pension urged on the House by the indiscreet zeal of some of his friends. Though it will not be an equivalent succour in all respects it will save the General from subscriptions which would have oppressed his finances; and if the schemes be executed within the period fixed, may yield a revenue for some years before the term of his. At all events it will demonstrate the grateful wishes of his Country and will promote the object which he has so much at heart. The earnestness with which he espouses the undertaking is hardly to be described, and shows that a mind like his, capable of great views and which has long been occupied with them, cannot bear a vacancy, and surely he could not have chosen an occupation more worthy of succeeding to that of establishing the political rights of his Country, than the patronage of works for the extensive and lasting improvement of its natural advantages; works which will double the value of half the lands within the Commonwealth, will extend its commerce, link with its interests those of the Western States, and lessen the emigration of its Citizens, by enhancing the profitableness of situations which they now desert in search of better.

An act to discharge the people of this commonwealth from one half of the tax for the year 1775 [i.e., 1785]. Our successive postponements had thrown the whole tax of 1784 on the year 1785. The remission therefore still leaves three halves to be collected. The plentiful crops on hand both of corn and tobacco and the price of the latter which is vibrating on this river between 36/ and 40/. seem to enable the Country to bear the burden. A few more plentiful years with steadiness in our Councils will put our credit on a decent footing. The payments from this State to the Continental treasury between Apl. 83 and Novr. 84 amount to £123,202.11.1½ Va. Curry. The printed report herewith inclosed will give you a rude idea of our finances.[28]

An act giving James Rumsey the exclusive privilege of constructing and navigating certain boats for a limited time. J. Rumsey by a memorial to the last Session represented that he had invented a mechanism, by which a boat might be worked with little labour at the rate of from 25 to 40 miles a day, against a stream running at the rate of 10 miles an hour, and prayed that the disclosure of his invention might be purchased by the public. The apparent extravagance of his pretensions brought a ridicule upon them, and nothing was done. In the recess of the Assembly, he exemplified his machinery to General Washington and a few other gentlemen, who gave a certificate of the reality and importance of the invention, which opened the ears of the Assembly to a second memorial. The act gives a monopoly for ten years, reserving a right to abolish it at any time on paying £10,000. The inventor is soliciting similar acts from other

28. The enclosed report is now missing, but the text is in the *Journal of the* (Virginia) *House of Delegates* for Oct. 1784; see *ibid.*

States, and will not I suppose publish the secret till he either obtains or despairs of them.

An act for punishing certain offences injurious to the tranquility of this commonwealth. This act authorizes the surrender of a citizen to a foreign sovereign within whose acknowledged jurisdiction the citizen shall commit a crime, of which satisfactory proof shall be exhibited to Congress, and for which in the judgment of Congress the law of nations exacts such surrender. This measure was suggested by the danger of our being speedily embroiled with the nations contiguous to the U. States, particularly the Spaniards, by the licentious and predatory spirit of some of our Western people. In several instances gross outrages are said to have been already practised. The measure was warmly patronized by Mr. Henry, and most of the forensic members, and no less warmly opposed by the Speaker [John Tyler] and some others. The opponents contended that such surrenders were unknown to the law of nations, and were interdicted by our declaration of Rights. Vattel however is express as to the case of Robbers, murderers and incendiaries. Grotius quotes various instances in which great offenders have been given up by their proper sovereigns to be punished by the offended Sovereigns. Puffendorf only refers to Grotius. I have had no opportunity of consulting other authorities. With regard to the bill of rights, it was alledged to be no more or rather less violated by considering crimes committed against other laws as not falling under the notice of our own, and sending our Citizens to be tried where the cause of trial arose, than to try them under our own laws without a jury of the vicinage and without being confronted with their accusers or witnesses; as must be the case if they be tried at all for such offences under our own laws. And to say that such offenders could neither be given up for punishment, nor be punished within their own Country, would amount to a licence for every aggression, and would sacrifice the peace of the whole community, to the impunity of the worst members of it. The necessity of a qualified interpretation of the bill of rights was also inferred from the law of the Confederacy which requires the surrender of our Citizens to the laws of other States in cases of treason, felony or other high misdemeanors. The act provides however for a domestic trial in cases where a surrender may not be justified or insisted upon, and in cases of aggressions on the Indians.

An act for incorporating the Protestant Episcopal Church. This act declares the ministers and vestries who are to be triennially chosen in each period a body corporate, enables them to hold property not exceeding the value of £800 per annum, and gives sanction to a Convention which is to be composed of the Clergy and a lay deputy from each parish, and is to regulate the affairs of the Church. It was understood by the House of Delegates that the Convention was to consist of two laymen for each clergyman, and an amendment was received for that express purpose. It so happened that the insertion of the amendment did not produce that effect, and the mistake was never discovered till the bill had passed and was in print. Another circumstance still more singular is that the act is so constructed as to deprive the vestries of the uncontrouled right of electing clergymen, unless it be referred to them by the canons of the Convention, and that this usurpation actually escaped the eye both of the friends and adversaries of the measure, both parties taking the contrary for granted throughout the whole progress of it. The former as well as the latter appear now to be dissatisfied with what has been done, and will probably concur in a revision if not a repeal of the law. Independently of these oversights the law is in various points of view exceptionable. But the necessity of some sort of incorporation for the purpose of holding and managing the property of the Church could not well be denied, nor a more harmless modification of it now obtained. A negative of the bill too would have doubled the eagerness and the pretexts for a much greater evil, a general assessment, which there is good ground to believe was parried by this partial gratification of its warmest votaries. A Resolution for a legal provision for the "teachers of Christian Religion" had early in the Session been proposed by Mr. Henry, and in spite of all the opposition that could be mustered, carried by 47 against 32 votes. Many Petitions from below the blue ridge had prayed for such a law; and though several from the presbyterian laity beyond it were in a contrary Stile, the Clergy of that Sect favoured it. The other sects seemed to be passive. The Resolution lay some weeks before a bill was brought in, and the bill some weeks before it was called for; after the passage of the incorporating act it was taken up, and on the third reading, ordered by a small majority to be printed for consideration. The bill in its present dress proposes a tax of blank per Ct. on all taxable property for support of Teachers of the Christian Religion. Each person when he pays his tax is to name the society to which he dedicates it, and in case of refusal to do so, the tax is to be applied to the maintenance of a school in the county. As the bill stood for some time, the application in such cases was to be made by the Legislature to pious uses. In a committee of the whole it was determined by a majority of 7 or 8 that the word "Christian" should be exchanged for the word "Religious." On the report to the House the *pathetic zeal of the late Governor Harrison* gained a like majority for reinstating discrimination. Should the bill ever pass into a law in its present form it may and will be easily eluded. It is chiefly obnoxious on account of its dishonorable principle and dangerous tendency.

The subject of the British debts underwent a reconsideration on the motion of Mr. Jones. Though no answer had been received from Congress to the Resolutions passed at the last Session, a material change had evidently taken place in the mind of the Assembly, proceeding in part from a more dispassionate view of the question, in part from the intervening exchange of the ratifications of the Treaty. *Mr. Henry was out of the way.* His previous conversation, I have been told, *favored the reconsideration. The speaker,* the other *champion* at the last Session *against the treaty* was at least half *a proselyte.* The proposition rejected interest during the period of blank, and left the periods of payment blank. In this form it was received with little opposition and by a very great majority. After much discussion and several nice divisions the first blank was filled up with the period between the 19 of Apl. 1775, and the 3 of March

1783, the commencement and cessation of hostilities; and the second with seven annual payments. Whilst the bill was depending, some proceedings of the Glascow merchants were submitted to the House of Delegates in which they signified their readiness to receive their debts in four annual payments, with immediate security, and summary recoveries at the successive periods, and were silent as to the point of interest. Shortly after were presented memorials from the merchants of this Town and Petersburg representing the advantage which a compliance with the Glascow overtures would give the foreign over the domestic creditors. Very little attention seemed to be paid by the House to the overtures, tho' as the treaty was not to be litterally pursued, the shadow of assent from the other party was worthy of being attended to. In the Senate the bill met with a diversity of opinions. By a majority of one voice only an attempt to put all our domestic debts on the same footing with British debts was lost. Whether this was sincere or a side blow at the bill I am unable to say. An attempt was next made to put on the same footing all those who left this Country and joined the other side, or who remained within the British territories for one year at any time since the 19 Apl. 1775, or who refused a tender of paper money before Jany. 1779. These discriminations were almost unanimously disagreed to by the House of Delegates. The Senate insisted. The former proposed a conference. The Senate concurred. The Conference produced a proposition from the House of Delegates to which the Senate assented; but before their assent was notified an incident happened which has left the bill in a very singular situation. The delay attending this measure had spun it out to the day preceding the one prefixed for a final adjournment. Several of the members went over to Manchester in the evening, with an intention it is to be presumed of returning the next morning. The severity of the night rendered their passage back the next morning impossible. Without them there was no house. The impatience of the members was such as might be supposed. Some were for stigmatizing the absentees and adjourning. The rest were some for one thing, some for another. At length it was agreed to wait till the next day. The next day presented the same obstructions in the river. A canoe was sent over for enquiry by the Manchester party, but they did not chuse to venture themselves. The impatience increased, warm resolutions were agitated. They ended however in an agreement to wait one day more. On the morning of the third day the prospect remained the same. Patience could hold out no longer and an adjournment to the last day of March ensued. The question to be decided is whether a bill which had passed the House of Delegates, and been assented to by the Senate; but not sent down to the House of Delegates nor enrolled, nor examined, nor signed by the two Speakers and consequently not of record, is or is not a law?[29] A bill for the better regulation of the Customs is in the same situation.

29. It was later held that the debt bill had not been enacted; see Isaac Samuel Harrell, *Loyalism in Virginia: Chapters in the Economic History of the Revolution* (Philadelphia, 1976), pp. 147–48.

After the passage of the Bill for British debts through the House of Delegates a bill was introduced for liquidating the depreciated payments into the Treasury, and making the debtors liable for the deficiency. A foresight of this consequential step had shewn itself in every stage of the first bill. It was opposed by *Governor Harrison principally* and laid asleep by the refusal of the interested members to vote in the question, and the want of a quorum without them.

Among the abortive measures may be mentioned also a proposition to authorize the collection of the impost by Congress as soon as the concurrence of twelve States should be obtained. Connecticut had set the example in this project. The proposition was made by the Speaker and supported by the late Governour. It was disagreed to by a very large majority on the following grounds. 1. The appearance of a schism in the confederacy which it would present to foreign eyes. 2. Its tendency to combinations of smaller majorities of the States. 3. The channel it would open for smuggling; goods imported into Rhode Island in such case might not only be spread by land through the adjacent States, but if slipped into any neighbouring port might thence be carried duty-free to any part of the associated States. 4. The greater improbability of a union of twelve States on such new ground, than of the conversion of Rhode Island to the old one. 5. The want of harmony among the other States which would be betrayed by the miscarriage of such an experiment, and the fresh triumph and obstinacy which R.I. would derive from it.

The French vice Consul in this State has complained to the Assembly that the want of legal power over our Sheriffs, Goalers and prisons both renders his decrees nugatory, and exposes his person to insults from dissatisfied litigants. The Assembly have taken no step whatever on the subject being at a loss to know what ought to be done, in compliance either with general usage, or that of France in particular. I have often wondered that the proposed convention between France and the U.S. for regulating the consular functions, has never been executed. The delay may prove unfriendly both to their mutual harmony and their commerce.[30]

Mr. Henry was elected successor to Mr. Harrison without competition or opposition. The victims to the article requiring a triennial removal of two Counsellors were Merryweather Smith and General Christian. Young Mr. Roane and Mr. Miles Selden take their places. Mr. Shorts place is filled by Mr. Joseph Jones.

Nothing has passed during the Session concerning an amendment of the State Constitution. The friends of the undertaking seem to be multiplying rather than decreasing. Several Petitions from the Western side of the Blue Ridge appeared in favor of it; as did some from the Western side of the Alleghenny praying for a separate Government. The latter may be considered all of

---

30. For the problems of the French vice-consul in Norfolk, see J. Rives Childs, "French Consul Martin Oster Reports on Virginia, 1784–1796," *VMHB* 76 (1968): 31–34; *PTJ*, VII, p. 599; and *PJM*, VIII, p. 233.

them as the children of A[rthur] C[ampbell]'s ambition. The assize Courts and the opening of our Rivers are the best answers to them.

The Revisal has but just issued from the press. It consists of near 100 folio pages in a small type. I shall send you six copies by the first opportunity. £500 was voted at the Spring Session to each of the acting members of the Committee, but no fund having been provided for payment, no use could be made of the warrants. I drew yours however and carried them up to Orange where they now lye. A vote of this Session has provided a fund which gives them immediate value. As soon as I get home I shall send the dead warrants to Mr. Nichs. Lewis who may exchange them for others and draw the money from the Treasury. Mr. Peter Carr is I hear now in Williamsburg. He did not get there so soon as I expected, but I have not heard the circumstances which delayed him. On the best enquiries I could make for a stand for his younger brother I could hear of none preferable to the Academy in Prince Edward and accordingly recommended that in a letter to Mrs. Carr. I have received no answer, but am told by Mr. Underwood her neighbour that he is at school with a very proper man who has lately opened a school very convenient to Mrs. Carr. If this be the case it will be improper to remove him.

I have not yet had the pleasure of a line from you since you left Boston, nor do I know when I shall next find a subject for another to you. As soon as I do you may be assured that you shall hear from me and that I am in the mean time with the sincerest friendship Yrs.,

J. MADISON JR.

Present my respects to Miss Patsy and Mr. Short.


*Madison to Jefferson*

Richmond Jan. 22, 1785

DEAR SIR

I have remained here since the adjournment of the Assembly cheifly with a view of gaining from the Office of the Attorney some insight into the juridical course of practice. This has given me an opportunity of forwarding you 6 copies of the revisal with a few of the late Newspapers under the cover which incloses this. They will go in a vessel belonging to Mr. Alexander the Gentleman who resides in this State as Tobo. Agent for the Farmers Genl. He assures me that due care shall be taken of them. . . .[31]

---

31. Only the top portion of this letter survives, the lower part having been cut away. This has led Boyd to suggest that JM may have mutilated the letter, perhaps to conceal his critical view of Lafayette; see *PTJ*, VII, pp. 614–15. For William Alexander, a Richmond tobacco merchant with international connections, see George Mason, *The Papers of George Mason, 1725–1792*, ed. Robert A. Rutland, 3 vols. (Chapel Hill, 1970), I, pp. xxx–xxxi.

## Jefferson to Madison

Paris Mar. 18, 1785

DEAR SIR

My last to you was dated Dec. 8. Since that yours of Feb. 1. has come to hand;[32] and I am in hopes I shall shortly receive from you the history of the last session of our assembly. I will pray you always to send your letters by the French packet which sails from N. York the 15th. of every month. I had made Neill Jamieson my postmaster general there, who will always take care of my letters and confide them to passengers when there are any worthy of confidence: since the removal of Congress to that place, you can chuse between N. Jamieson and our delegates there, to which you would rather address my letters. The worst conveyances you can possibly find are private hands, or merchant ships coming from Virginia directly to France. These letters either come not at all, or like the histories of antient times they detail to us events after their influence is spent.

Your *character* of the *M. Fayette* is precisely agreeable to the idea I had formed of *him*.[33] I take *him* to be of *unmeasured ambition* but that the *means he uses* are virtuous. *He* is *returned fraught* with *affection* to *America* and *disposed* to render every *possible service*. Of the cause which *separated* the *committee* of the *states* we never have had *an explicit account*. *Hints* and *dark sentences* from newspapers and private letters have *excited* without *satisfying* our *curiosity*. As your *cipher* is safe pray *give me a detail* of it. The navigation of the Scheld had for a great while agitated the politics of Europe and seemed to threaten the involving it in a general war.[34] All of a sudden another subject, infinitely more interesting is brought on the carpet. There is reason to beleive that the Emperor has made an exchange of territories with the Elector of Bavaria, and that while the Scheld has been the ostensible, Bavaria has been the real object of his military preparations.[35] When the proposition was communicated to the *King of Prussia* it is said he declared qu'il mourroit le cul sur la selle rather than see it take effect. *The Dutch* it is thought would be *secretly pleased* with it. And some *think* that certain *places* said to be *reserved* by the *Emperor* on the *borders* of *France* are meant to be *given to the latter* for her *acquiescence*. I am *attending* with *anxiety* to the part she will act on this occasion. I shall change my opinion of *her system* of *policy* if it be not *honorable*. If the Dutch escape a war, they seem still to be in danger of internal revolution. The Stadholder and Aristocracy can carry their differences no further without an appeal to the sword. The people

---

32. TJ received JM's letter of Oct. 17, 1784, on Feb. 1, 1785.

33. The italicized words in this sentence and in the rest of the letter were written in code.

34. Joseph II tried to open the Scheldt by sending a cargo vessel down the river, "only to have it fired on and driven back by the Dutch"; see R. R. Palmer, *The Age of the Democratic Revolution: A Political History of Europe and America, 1760–1800*, 2 vols. (Princeton, 1959–64), I, p. 345.

35. For the proposed exchange of the Austrian Netherlands for Bavarian territory, see Leo Gershoy, *From Despotism to Revolution, 1763–1789* (New York, 1944), pp. 186–88.

are on the side of the *Stadtholder*. The conduct of the *aristocracy* in pushing *their* measures to such extremity is inexplicable but on the *supposition* that *France* has *promised* to *support them* which it is *thought she* was *obliged* to *do before they* would *enter into* the *late treaty*.[36] We hear nothing from England. This circumstance, with the passage of their N.F.-land bill thro' the house of commons, and the sending a Consul to America (which we hear they have done) sufficiently prove a perseverance in the system of managing for us as well as for themselves in their connection with us. The administration of that country are governed by the people, and the people by their own interested wishes without calculating whether they are just or capable of being effected. Nothing will bring them to reason but physical obstruction, applied to their bodily senses. We must shew that we are capable of foregoing commerce with them, before they will be capable of consenting to an equal commerce. We have all the world besides open to supply us with gew-gaws, and all the world to buy our tobacco, for in such an event England must buy it from Amsterdam, l'Orient or any other place at which we should think proper to deposit it for them. They allow our commodities to be taken from our own ports to the W. Indies in their vessels only. Let us allow their vessels to take them to no port. The transportation of our own produce is worth 750,000£ sterl. annually, will employ 200,000 tonnage of ships, and 12,000 seamen constantly. It will be no misfortune that Gr. Br. obliges us to exclude her from a participation in this business. Our own shipping will grow fast under the exclusion, and till it is equal to the object the Dutch will supply us. The commerce with the Eng. W. I. is valuable and would be worth a sacrifice to us. But the commerce with the British dominions in Europe is a losing one and deserves no sacrifice. Our tobacco they must have from whatever place we make it's deposit, because they can get no other whose quality so well suits the habits of their people. It is not a commodity like wheat, which will not bear a double voyage. Were it so, the privilege of carrying it directly to England might be worth something. I know nothing which would act more powerfully as a sumptuary law with our people than an inhibition of commerce with England. They are habituated to the luxuries of that country and will have them while they can get them. They are unacquainted with those of other countries, and therefore will not very soon bring them so far into fashion as that it shall be thought disreputable not to have them in one's house or on their table.

It is to be considered how far an exemption of Ireland from this inhibition would embarrass the councils of Engld. on the one hand, and defeat the regulation itself on the other. I rather beleive it would do more harm in the latter way than good in the former. In fact a heavy aristocracy and corruption are two bridles in the mouths of the Irish which will prevent them from making any effectual efforts against their masters. We shall now *very soon call* for *decisive answers* to certain points *interesting* to the *United States* and *uncon-*

---

36. For the contest between the stadtholder and the Dutch aristocracy, see Palmer, I, pp. 324–40, and Simon Schama, *Patriots and Liberators: Revolution in the Netherlands, 1780–1813* (New York, 1977), pp. 88–100.

nected with the *general treaty* which they have a right to *decline*. I mentioned to you in a former letter a very good dictionary of universal law called the Code d'humanité in 13. vols. 4to. Meeting by chance an opportunity of buying a copy, new, and well bound for 104 livres I purchased it for you. It comes to 8 livres a volume which is a fraction over a dollar and a half, and in England costs 15/ sterl. a volume. I shall have an opportunity of sending this and what other books I have bought for you in May. But new information throws me all into doubt what to do with them. Late letters tell us you are *nominated for* the *court of Spain*. I must depend on further intelligence therefore to decide whether to send them or to await your orders. I need not tell you how much I shall be pleased with such an event. Yet it has it's displeasing sides also. *I want you* in the *Virginia Assembly* and also in *Congress* yet we cannot have *you everywhere*. We must therefore be contented to have *you where you chuse*. Adieu, Yours affectionately etc.


*Madison to Jefferson*

Orange Apr. 27, 1785

Dear Sir

I have received your two favors of Novr. 11 and Decr. 8. Along with the former I received the two pamphlets on animal magnetism and the last aeronautic expedition, together with the phosphoretic matches. These articles were a great treat to my curiosity. As I had left Richmd. before they were brought thither by Col. le Maire, I had no opportunity of attending myself to your wishes with regard to him; but I wrote immediately to Mr. Jones and desired him to watch over the necessities of le Maire. He wrote me for answer that the Executive tho' without regular proof of his claims were so well satisfied from circumstances of the justice of them, that they had voted him £150 for his relief till the assembly could take the whole into consideration. This information has made me easy on the subject though I have not withdrawn from the hands of Mr. Jones the provisional resource. I thank you much for your attention to my literary wants. All the purchases you have made for me, are such as I should have made for myself with the same opportunities. You will oblige me by adding to them the Dictionary in 13 vol. 4º. by Felice and others, also de Thou in French. If the utility of Moreri be not superseded by some better work I should be glad to have him too. I am afraid if I were to attempt a catalogue of my wants I should not only trouble you beyond measure, but exceed the limits which other considerations ought to prescribe to me. I cannot however abridge the commission you were so kind as to take on yourself in a former letter, of procuring me from time to time such books as may be "either old and curious or new and useful." Under this description will fall those particularised in my former letters, to wit treatises on the antient or modern fœderal republics, on the law of Nations, and the history natural and political of the New World; to which I will add such of the Greek and Roman authors where they can be got very cheap, as are worth having and are not on the common list of School classics. Other books which particularly occur, are the translation [French][37] of the Historians of the Roman Empire during its decline by ——, Paschals provincial letters—Don Ulloa in the Original—Lynnæus best edition—Ordinances Marines—Collection of Tracts in french on the Œconomics of different nations. I forget the full title. It is much referred to by Smith on the wealth of nations. I am told a Monsr. Amelot has lately published his travels into China, which if they have any merit must be very entertaining. Of Buffon I have his original work of 31 vol., 10 vol. of Supplemt. and 16 vol. on birds. I shall be glad of the continuation as it may from time to time be published. I am so pleased with the new invented lamp that I shall not grudge two guineas for one of them. I have seen a pocket compass of somewhat larger diameter than a watch and which may be carried in the same way. It has a spring for stopping the vibration of the needle when not in use. One of these would be very convenient in case of a ramble into the Western Country. In my walks for exercise or amusements, objects frequently present themselves, which it might be matter of curiosity to inspect, but which it is difficult or impossible to approach. A portable glass would consequently be a source of many little gratifications. I have fancied that such an one might be fitted into a Cane without making it too heavy. On the outside of the tube might be engraved a scale of inches etc. If such a project could be executed for a few Guineas, I should be willing to submit to the price; if not, the best substitute I suppose will be a pocket-telescope, composed of several tubes so constructed as to slide the lesser into the greater. I should feel great remorse at troubling you with so many requests, if your kind and repeated offers did not stifle it in some measure. Your proposal for my replacing here advances for me without regard to the exchange is liable to no objection except that it will probably be too unequal in my favour. I beg that you will enable me as much as you can to keep those little matters balanced.

The papers from le Grand were sent as soon as I got them to Mr. Jones with a request that he would make the use of them which you wished me to do.

Your remarks on the tax on transfers of land in a general view appear to me to be just but there were two circumstances which gave a peculiarity to the case in which our Law adopted it. One was that the tax will fall much on those who are evading their quotas of other taxes by removing to Georgia and Kentucky: the other that as such transfers are more frequent among those who do not remove, in the Western than the Eastern part of the Country, it will fall heaviest where direct taxes are least collected. With regard to the tax in general on law proceedings, it cannot perhaps be justified if tried by the strict rule which proportions the quota of every man to his ability. Time however will gradually in some measure equalize it, and if it be applied to the support of the Judiciary establishment, as was the ultimate view of the friends of the tax, it

37. JM's bracket.

seems to square very well with the Theory of taxation.

The people of Kentucky had lately a convention which it was expected would be the mother of a separation. I am informed they proceeded no farther than to concert an address for the Legislature on some points in which they think the laws bear unequally upon them. They will be ripe for that event at least as soon as their interest calls for it. There is no danger of a concert between them and the Counties West of the Alleghany which we mean to retain. If the latter embark in a scheme for independance it will be in their own bottom. They are more disunited in every respect from Kentucky than from Virginia.

I have not learnt with certainty whether Genl. Washington will accept or decline the shares voted him by the assembly in the Companies for opening our rivers. If he does not chuse to take to himself any benefit from the donation, he has I think a fine opportunity at once of testifying his disinterested purposes, of shewing his respect for the assembly, and of rendering a service to his Country. He may accept the gift so far as to apply it to the scheme of opening the rivers, and may then appropriate the revenue which it is hereafter to produce, to some patriotic establishment. I lately dropped a hint of this sort to one of his friends and was told that such an idea had been suggested to him. The private subscriptions for Potowmac I hear amount to £10,000 Sterling. I can not discover that those for James River deserve mention, or that the undertaking is pushed with any spirit. If those who are most interested in it let slip the present opportunity, their folly will probably be severely punished by the want of such another. It is said the undertaking on the Susquehannah by Maryland goes on with great spirit and expectations. I have heard nothing of Rumsey or his boats since he went into the Northern States. If his machinery for stemming the current operates on the water alone as is given out, may it not supply the great desideratum for perfecting the Balloons?

I understand that Chase and Jennifer on the part of Maryland, Mason and Henderson on the part of Virginia have had a meeting on the proposition of Virga. for settling the navigation and jurisdiction of Potowmac below the falls, and have agreed to report to the two assemblies, the establishment of a concurrent jurisdiction on that river and Chesapeak. The most amicable spirit is said to have governed the negociation.

The Bill for a Genl. Assesst. has produced some fermentation below the Mountains and a violent one beyond them. The contest at the next Session on this question will be a warm and precarious one. The port bill will also undergo a fiery trial. I wish the Assize Courts may not partake of the danger. The elections as far as they have come to my knowledge are likely to produce a great proportion of new members. In Albemarle young Mr. Fry has turned out Mr. Carter. The late Governor Harrison I hear has been baffled in his own County, but meant to be a candidate in Surry and in case of a rebuff there to throw another die for the borough of Norfolk. I do not know how he construes the doctrine of residence. It is *surmised* that the *machinations of Tyler who fears a rivailship for the chair* are *at the bottom of his difficulties.*[38] *Arthur Lee is elected* in *Prince William. He is said* to have *paved the way by promises* to *overset the port bill* which is *obnoxious* to *Dumfries* and to *prevent the removal [of]*[39] *the assise court* from *this town to Alexandria.*

I received a letter from *the Marquis Fayette* dated on the *eve of his embarcation* which *has the following paragraph.* "*I have much confered with the general upon the Potowmac system. Many people [think] the navigation of the Mississippi is not an advantage but* it *may be the excess of a very good thing viz. the opening of your rivers. I fancy* it *has not changed your opinion* but *beg you will write me on the* subject. *In the meanwhile I hope Congress will act coolly and prudently by Spain who is such a fool that allowance must be made."* It is *unlucky that he should have left America with* such *an idea as to the Mississippi.* It may be *of the worse consequence as* it is *not wholly imaginary, the* prospect of *extending the commerce of the Atlantic states to the western waters having given birth to it.* I can not believe that *many minds are tainted with so illiberal and short sighted a policy.* I have *thought it not amiss to* [write] *the marquis* according to the *request of his letter* and *have stated to* him *the motives and obligations* which must *render* [the] *United States inflexible* on the *subject of the Mississippi, the folly of Spain in contesting it* and *our expectation from the known influence of France over Spain* and *her friendly dispositions toward us.* It is but *justice to the marquis to observe* that *in all our conversations* on *the Mississippi he expressed* with every *mark of sincerity a zeal for our claims* and *a pointed dis*like *to the national character and policy of Spain* and that if *his zeal should be found to abate* I should construe it to be the effect *of a supposed* revolution *in the sentiments of America.*

This would have been of somewhat earlier date but I postponed it that I might be able to include some information relative to your Nephews. My last informed you that your eldest was then with Mr. Maury. I was so assured by Mr. Underwood from his neighbourhood, who I supposed could not be mistaken. I afterwards discovered that he was so, but could get no precise information till within a few days. One of my brothers being called into that part of the Country by business, I wrote to Mrs. Carr and got him to wait on her. The answer with which I have been favored imports that "her eldest son was taken last fall with a fever which with repeated relapses kept him extremely weak and low till about the first of Jany. from which time he was detained at home by delays in equipping him for Williamsbg. till the 1st. of April, when he set out with promises to make up his lost time; that her youngest son had also been detained at home by ill health till very lately, but that he would certainly go on to the academy as soon as a vacation on hand was over, that his time had not been entirely lost as his brother was capable of instructing him whenever his health would admit." Mr. Maury's School is said to be very flourishing. Mr. Wythe and the other gentlemen of the University have examined it from time to time and published their approbation of its management. I can not speak

---

38. The italicized words in this sentence and those in the rest of the letter were written in code.

39. This word and the subsequent words in brackets were omitted in the coded message but were probably inserted by JM after he retrieved his letters following TJ's death; see *PTJ,* VII, p. 116.

with the same authority as to the academy in Prince-Edward. The information which I have received has been favorable to it. In the recommendation of these Seminaries I was much governed by the probable permanency of them; nothing being more ruinous to education than the frequent interruptions and change of masters and methods incident to the private schools of this country.

Our winter has been full of vicisitudes, but on the whole far from being a severe one. The Spring has been uncommonly cold and wet, and vegetation of course very backward; till within a few days during which it has been accelerated by very uncommon heat. A pocket Thermometer which stands on the second floor and the N. W. side of the House was on the 24 inst. at 4 oClock, at 77.°, on the 25. 78., on the 26. 81½., to day 27. at 82. The weather during this period has been fair and the wind S. the atmosphere thick NW. Our Wheat in the ground is very unpromising throughout the Country. The price of that article on tide water is about 6/. Corn sells in this part of the Country at 10/. and under., below at 15/., and where the insect prevailed as high as 20/. It is said to have been raised by a demand for exportation. Tobacco is selling on Rappahannock at 32/. and Richmd. at 37/6. It is generally expected that it will at least get up to 40/. Some of our peaches are killed and most of our Cherries. Our Apples are as yet safe. I can not say how it is with the fruit in other parts of the Country. The mischief to the Cherries etc. was done on the night of the 20. when we had a severe black frost.

I can not take my leave of you without making my acknowledgments for the very friendly invitation contained in your last. If I should ever visit Europe I should wish to do it less stinted in time than your plan proposes. This crisis too would be particularly inconvenient as it would break in upon a course of reading which if I neglect now I shall probably never resume. I have some reason also to suspect that crossing the sea would be unfriendly to a singular disease of my constitution. The other part of your invitation has the strongest bias of my mind on its side, but my situation is as yet too dependant on circumstances to permit my embracing it absolutely. It gives me great satisfaction to find that you are looking forward to the moment which is to restore you to your native Country, though considerations of a public nature check my wishes that such an event may be expedited. Present my best respects to Mr. Short, and Miss Patsy, and accept of the affectionate regards of Dear Sir, Your sincere friend,

       J. MADISON JR.

What has become of the subterraneous City discovered in Siberia?
Deaths Thomson Mason
    Bartholemew Dandridge
    Ryland Randolph [Peyton Randolph?][40]
    Joseph Reed of Philada.

---

40. *PTJ* notes that "one name below that of [Ryland] Randolph's is heavily obliterated; see *ibid.* *PJM* transcribes the name as "Peyton Randolph," referring to Peyton Randolph (1738–1784), who died on May 15, 1784; VIII, p. 272.

## Jefferson to Madison

Paris May 11, 1785

DEAR SIR

Your favor of Jan. 9. came to my hands on the 13th. of April. The very full and satisfactory detail of the proceedings of assembly which it contained, gave me the highest pleasure. The value of these communications cannot be calculated at a shorter distance than the breadth of the Atlantic. Having lately made a cypher on a more convenient plan than the one we have used, I now transmit it to you by a Monsr. Doradour who goes to settle in Virginia. His family will follow him next year. Should he have occasion of your patronage I beg leave to solicit it for him. They yesterday finished printing my notes. I had 200 copies printed, but do not put them out of my own hands, except two or three copies here, and two which I shall send to America, to yourself and Colo. Monroe, if they can be ready this evening as promised. In this case you will receive one by Monsr. Doradour. I beg you to peruse it carefully because I ask your advice on it and ask nobody's else. I wish to put it into the hands of the young men at the college, as well on account of the political as physical parts. But there are sentiments on some subjects which I apprehend might be displeasing to the country perhaps to the assembly or to some who lead it. I do not wish to be exposed to their censure, nor do I know how far their influence, if exerted, might effect a misapplication of law to such a publication were it made. Communicate it then in confidence to those whose judgments and information you would pay respect to: and if you think it will give no offence I will send a copy to each of the students of W.M.C.[41] and some others to my friends and to your disposal. Otherwise I shall only send over a very few copies to particular friends in confidence and burn the rest. Answer me soon and without reserve. Do not view me as an author, and attached to what he has written. I am neither. They were at first intended only for Marbois. When I had enlarged them, I thought first of giving copies to three or four friends. I have since supposed they might set our young students into a useful train of thought and in no event do I propose to admit them to go to the public at large. A variety of accidents have postponed my writing to you till I have no further time to continue my letter. The next packet will sail from Havre. I will then send your books and write more fully. But answer me immediately on the preceding subject. I am with much affection Dr. Sir Your friend and servt.,

TH: JEFFERSON

---

41. The College of William and Mary.

## Madison to Jefferson

Orange Aug. 20, 1785

DEAR SIR

Yours of the 18th. of March never reached me till the 4 inst:. It came by post from N. York, which it did not leave till the 21. of July. My last was dated in April, and went by Mr. Mazzei who picked it up at N. York and promised to deliver it with his own hand.

The machinations of G.B. with regard to Commerce have produced much distress and noise in the Northern States, particularly in Boston, from whence the alarm has spread to New York and Philada. Your correspondence with Congress will no doubt have furnished you with full information on this head.[42] I only know the general fact, and that the sufferers are every where calling for such augmentation of the power of Congress as may effect relief. How far the Southern States and Virginia in particular will join in this proposition cannot be foreseen. It is easy to foresee that the circumstances which in a confined view distinguish our situation from that of our brethren, will be laid hold of by the partizans of G.B., by those who are or affect to be jealous of Congress, and those who are interested in the present course of business, to give a wrong bias to our Councils. If any thing should reconcile Virga. to the idea of giving Congress a power over her trade, it will be that this power is likely to annoy G.B. against whom the animosities of our Citizens are still strong. They seem to have less sensibility to their commercial interests; which they very little understand, and which the mercantile class here have not the same motives if they had the same capacity to lay open to the public, as that class have in the States North of us. The price of our Staple since the peace is another cause of inattention in the planters to the dark side of our commercial affairs. Should these or any other causes prevail in frustrating the scheme of the Eastern and Middle States of a general retaliation on G.B., I *tremble for the event.*[43] A *majority* of *the States* deprived of a *regular remedy for their distresses* by *the want of a fœderal spirit in the minority* must *feel the* strongest *motives to some ir*regular *experiments.* The *danger of such a crisis* makes me surmise that the *policy of Great Britain* results as much from *the hope of effecting a breach in our confederacy as of monopolising our trade.*

Our internal trade is taking an arrangement from which I hope good consequences. Retail stores are spreading all over the Country, many of them carried on by native adventurers, some of them branched out from the principal Stores at the heads of navigation. The distribution of the business however into the importing and the retail departments has not yet taken place. Should

---

42. For the serious commercial depression of 1784-85, see Curtis P. Nettels, *The Emergence of a National Economy, 1775-1815* (New York, 1962), pp. 60-64, and Merrill Jensen, *The New Nation: A History of the United States during the Confederation, 1781-1789* (New York, 1950), pp. 187-90.

43. These italicized words and those in the rest of the letter were written in code.

the port bill be established it will I think quickly add this amendment which indeed must in a little time follow of itself. It is the more to be wished for as it is the only radical cure for credit to the consumer which continues to be given to a degree which if not checked will turn the diffusive retail of merchandize into a nusance. When the Shopkeeper buys his goods of the wholesale merchant, he must buy at so short a credit, that he can venture to give none at all.

You ask me to unriddle the *dissolution of the committee of the states at annapolis.*[44] I am not sure that I am myself possessed fully of the causes, *different members of Congress having differed in their accounts of the matter.* My conception of it is that *the abrupt departure of* some of the *Eastern delegates,* which *destroyed the quorum* and which *Dana* is said *to have been at the bottom of* proceeded *partly from irritations among the committee, partly from dislike to the place of their session* and *partly from an impatience to get home,* which prevailed over *their regard* for *their private characters* as well as *for their public duty.*

Subsequent to the date of *mine in* which I gave my idea of *Fayette* I had further opportunities of *penetrating his character.* Though *his foibles did* not *disappear* all the *favorable traits* presented themselves in a *stronger light.* On *closer inspection he* certainly possesses *talents which might figure in any line.* If *he is ambitious* it is rather of the *praise* which virtue *dedicates to merit* than *of the homage* which *fear renders to power. His disposition is* naturally *warm and affectionate* and *his attachment to the United States* unquestionable. Unless *I am grossly deceived* you will *find his zeal sincere* and *useful* wherever it can be *employed* in behalf *of the United States without opposition* [to] *the essential interests of France.*

The opposition to the general assessment gains ground. At the *instance of some* of *its adversaries I drew up the remonstrance* herewith inclosed.[45] It has been sent thro' the *medium of confidential persons in a number of the upper county*[s] and I am told will be pretty extensively signed. The presbyterian clergy have at length espoused the idea of the opposition, being moved either by *a fear of their laity* or *a jealousy of the episcopalians.* The mutual hatred of these sects has been much inflamed by the late act incorporating the latter. *I am far from being sorry for it* as *a coalition between them* could *alone endanger our religious rights* and a tendency to *such an event had been suspected.* The fate of the Circuit Courts is uncertain. They are threatened with no small danger from the diversity of opinions entertained among the friends of some reform in that department. But the greatest danger is to be feared from those who mask a secret aversion to any reform under a zeal for such a one as they know will be rejected. The Potowmack Company are going on with very flattering prospects. Their subscriptions sometime ago amounted to upwards of four fifths of the whole sum. I have the pleasure also to find by an advertisement from the

---

44. On the collapse of the Committee of the States, see Jack Rakove, *The Beginnings of National Politics: An Interpretive History of the Continental Congress* (Cambridge, Mass., 1979), pp. 351, 356–59.

45. See JM, "A Memorial and Remonstrance . . . ," [ca. June 20, 1785], below.

managers for James River that more than half the sum is subscribed for that undertaking, and that the subscribers are to meet shortly for the purpose of organizing themselves and going to work. I despair of seeing the Revisal taken up at the ensuing Session. The number of copies struck are so deficient (there being not above three for each County) and there has been such delay in distributing them (none of the Counties having received them till very lately and some probably not yet, tho' they were ready long ago) that the principal end of their being printed has been frustrated. Our fields promise very short crops both of Corn and Tobacco. The latter was much injured by the grass hopper and other insects; the former somewhat by the bug in the Southern parts of the State. But both have suffered most from dry weather which prevails at present in this part of the Country, and has generally prevailed I understand in most other parts. It seems certain that no future weather can make a great crop of either, particularly of Tobacco, so great a proportion of the hills being without plants in them, and so many more with plants which must come to nothing. Notwithstanding this prospect, its price has fallen from 36/ to 32 and 30/ on James River and 28/ on Rappahanock. The scarcity of cash is one cause. *Harrison the late governor* was *elected* in *Surry* whither *he previously removed with his family. A contest* for *the chair* will *no* doubt *ensue.* Should *he fail it he* will be *for Congress.*

I have not yet received any of the books which you have been so kind as to pick up for me, but expect their arrival daily, as you were probably soon after the date of your last apprised that I was withdrawn from the nomination which led you to suspend the forwarding them. I am invited by Col: Monroe to an option of rambles this fall, one of which is into the Eastern States. I wish much to accept so favorable an opportunity of executing the plan from which I was diverted last fall; but cannot decide with certainty whether it will be practicable or not. I have in conjunction with a friend here a project of interest on the anvil which will carry me at least as far as Philada. or New York where I shall be able to take my final resolution. Adieu. Yrs. sincerely,

J M Jr.

ENCLOSURE
*[James Madison], A Memorial and Remonstrance to the Honorable the General Assembly of the Commonwealth of Virginia*

[Orange ca. June 20, 1785]

We the subscribers, citizens of the said Commonwealth, having taken into serious consideration, a Bill printed by order of the last Session of General Assembly, entitled "A Bill establishing a provision for Teachers of the Christian Religion," and conceiving that the same if finally armed with the sanctions of a law, will be a dangerous abuse of power, are bound as faithful members of a free State to remonstrate against it, and to declare the reasons by which we are determined. We remonstrate against the said Bill,

1. Because we hold it for a fundamental and undeniable truth, "that Religion or the duty which we owe to our Creator and the manner of discharging it, can be directed

only by reason and conviction, not by force or violence."[46] The Religion then of every man must be left to the conviction and conscience of every man; and it is the right of every man to exercise it as these may dictate. This right is in its nature an unalienable right. It is unalienable, because the opinions of men, depending only on the evidence contemplated by their own minds cannot follow the dictates of other men: It is unalienable also, because what is here a right towards men, is a duty towards the Creator. It is the duty of every man to render to the Creator such homage and such only as he believes to be acceptable to him. This duty is precedent, both in order of time and in degree of obligation, to the claims of Civil Society. Before any man can be considered as a member of Civil Society, he must be considered as a subject of the Governour of the Universe: And if a member of Civil Society, who enters into any subordinate Association, must always do it with a reservation of his duty to the General Authority; much more must every man who becomes a member of any particular Civil Society, do it with a saving of his allegiance to the Universal Sovereign. We maintain therefore that in matters of Religion, no mans right is abridged by the institution of Civil Society and that Religion is wholly exempt from its cognizance. True it is, that no other rule exists, by which any question which may divide a Society, can be ultimately determined, but the will of the majority; but it is also true that the majority may trespass on the rights of the minority.

2. Because if Religion be exempt from the authority of the Society at large, still less can it be subject to that of the Legislative Body. The latter are but the creatures and vicegerents of the former. Their jurisdiction is both derivative and limited: it is limited with regard to the co-ordinate departments, more necessarily is it limited with regard to the constituents. The preservation of a free Government requires not merely, that the metes and bounds which separate each department of power be invariably maintained; but more especially that neither of them be suffered to overleap the great Barrier which defends the rights of the people. The Rulers who are guilty of such an encroachment, exceed the commission from which they derive their authority, and are Tyrants. The People who submit to it are governed by laws made neither by themselves nor by an authority derived from them, and are slaves.

3. Because it is proper to take alarm at the first experiment on our liberties. We hold this prudent jealousy to be the first duty of Citizens, and one of the noblest characteristics of the late Revolution. The free men of America did not wait till usurped power had strengthened itself by exercise, and entangled the question in precedents. They saw all the consequences in the principle, and they avoided the consequences by denying the principle. We revere this lesson too much soon to forget it. Who does not see that the same authority which can establish Christianity, in exclusion of all other Religions, may establish with the same ease any particular sect of Christians, in exclusion of all other Sects? that the same authority which can force a citizen to contribute three pence only of his property for the support of any one establishment, may force him to conform to any other establishment in all cases whatsoever?

4. Because the Bill violates that equality which ought to be the basis of every law, and which is more indispensible, in proportion as the validity or expediency of any law is more liable to be impeached. If "all men are by nature equally free and independent,"[47] all men are to be considered as entering into Society on equal conditions; as

---

46. In the margin, JM cited Article XVI of the Virginia Declaration of Rights of 1776, written by George Mason and amended by JM in his first session in the Virginia legislature.

47. In the margin, JM cited Article I of the Virginia Declaration of Rights.

relinquishing no more, and therefore retaining no less, one than another, of their natural rights. Above all are they to be considered as retaining an "*equal* title to the free exercise of Religion according to the dictates of Conscience."[48] Whilst we assert for ourselves a freedom to embrace, to profess and to observe the Religion which we believe to be of divine origin, we cannot deny an equal freedom to those whose minds have not yet yielded to the evidence which has convinced us. If this freedom be abused, it is an offence against God, not against man: To God, therefore, not to man, must an account of it be rendered. As the Bill violates equality by subjecting some to peculiar burdens, so it violates the same principle, by granting to others peculiar exemptions. Are the Quakers and Menonists the only sects who think a compulsive support of their Religions unnecessary and unwarrantable? Can their piety alone be entrusted with the care of public worship? Ought their Religions to be endowed above all others with extraordinary privileges by which proselytes may be enticed from all others? We think too favorably of the justice and good sense of these denominations to believe that they either covet pre-eminences over their fellow citizens or that they will be seduced by them from the common opposition to the measure.

5. Because the Bill implies either that the Civil Magistrate is a competent Judge of Religious Truth; or that he may employ Religion as an engine of Civil policy. The first is an arrogant pretension falsified by the contradictory opinions of Rulers in all ages, and throughout the world: the second an unhallowed perversion of the means of salvation.

6. Because the establishment proposed by the Bill is not requisite for the support of the Christian Religion. To say that it is, is a contradiction to the Christian Religion itself, for every page of it disavows a dependence on the powers of this world: it is a contradiction to fact; for it is known that this Religion both existed and flourished, not only without the support of human laws, but in spite of every opposition from them, and not only during the period of miraculous aid, but long after it had been left to its own evidence and the ordinary care of Providence. Nay, it is a contradiction in terms; for a Religion not invented by human policy, must have pre-existed and been supported, before it was established by human policy. It is moreover to weaken in those who profess this Religion a pious confidence in its innate excellence and the patronage of its Author; and to foster in those who still reject it, a suspicion that its friends are too conscious of its fallacies to trust it to its own merits.

7. Because experience witnesseth that ecclesiastical establishments, instead of maintaining the purity and efficacy of Religion, have had a contrary operation. During almost fifteen centuries has the legal establishment of Christianity been on trial. What have been its fruits? More or less in all places, pride and indolence in the Clergy, ignorance and servility in the laity, in both, superstition, bigotry and persecution. Enquire of the Teachers of Christianity for the ages in which it appeared in its greatest lustre; those of every sect, point to the ages prior to its incorporation with Civil policy. Propose a restoration of this primitive State in which its Teachers depended on the voluntary rewards of their flocks, many of them predict its downfall. On which Side ought their testimony to have greatest weight, when for or when against their interest?

8. Because the establishment in question is not necessary for the support of Civil Government. If it be urged as necessary for the support of Civil Government only as it is a means of supporting Religion, and it be not necessary for the latter purpose, it

---

48. JM's italics. In the margin, JM cited Article XVI of the Virginia Declaration of Rights. This is the phraseology proposed by JM and adopted in 1776.

cannot be necessary for the former. If Religion be not within the cognizance of Civil Government how can its legal establishment be necessary to Civil Government? What influence in fact have ecclesiastical establishments had on Civil Society? In some instances they have been seen to erect a spiritual tyranny on the ruins of the Civil authority; in many instances they have been seen upholding the thrones of political tyranny: in no instance have they been seen the guardians of the liberties of the people. Rulers who wished to subvert the public liberty, may have found an established Clergy convenient auxiliaries. A just Government instituted to secure and perpetuate it needs them not. Such a Government will be best supported by protecting every Citizen in the enjoyment of his Religion with the same equal hand which protects his person and his property; by neither invading the equal rights of any Sect, nor suffering any Sect to invade those of another.

9. Because the proposed establishment is a departure from that generous policy, which, offering an Asylum to the persecuted and oppressed of every Nation and Religion, promised a lustre to our country, and an accession to the number of its citizens. What a melancholy mark is the Bill of sudden degeneracy? Instead of holding forth an Asylum to the persecuted, it is itself a signal of persecution. It degrades from the equal rank of Citizens all those whose opinions in Religion do not bend to those of the Legislative authority. Distant as it may be in its present form from the Inquisition, it differs from it only in degree. The one is the first step, the other the last in the career of intolerance. The magnanimous sufferer under this cruel scourge in foreign Regions, must view the Bill as a Beacon on our Coast, warning him to seek some other haven, where liberty and philanthrophy in their due extent, may offer a more certain repose from his Troubles.

10. Because it will have a like tendency to banish our Citizens. The allurements presented by other situations are every day thinning their number. To superadd a fresh motive to emigration by revoking the liberty which they now enjoy, would be the same species of folly which has dishonoured and depopulated flourishing kingdoms.

11. Because it will destroy that moderation and harmony which the forbearance of our laws to intermeddle with Religion has produced among its several sects. Torrents of blood have been split in the old world, by vain attempts of the secular arm, to extinguish Religious discord, by proscribing all difference in Religious opinion. Time has at length revealed the true remedy. Every relaxation of narrow and rigorous policy, wherever it has been tried, has been found to assuage the disease. The American Theatre has exhibited proofs that equal and compleat liberty, if it does not wholly eradicate it, sufficiently destroys its malignant influence on the health and prosperity of the State. If with the salutary effects of this system under our own eyes, we begin to contract the bounds of Religious freedom, we know no name that will too severely reproach our folly. At least let warning be taken at the first fruits of the threatened innovation. The very appearance of the Bill has transformed "that Christian forbearance, love and charity,"[49] which of late mutually prevailed, into animosities and jealousies, which may not soon be appeased. What mischiefs may not be dreaded, should this enemy to the public quiet be armed with the force of a law?

12. Because the policy of the Bill is adverse to the diffusion of the light of Christianity. The first wish of those who enjoy this precious gift ought to be that it may be imparted to the whole race of mankind. Compare the number of those who have as yet

---

49. In the margin, JM cited Article XVI again.

received it with the number still remaining under the dominion of false Religions; and how small is the former! Does the policy of the Bill tend to lessen the disproportion? No; it at once discourages those who are strangers to the light of revelation from coming into the Region of it; and countenances by example the nations who continue in darkness, in shutting out those who might convey it to them. Instead of Levelling as far as possible, every obstacle to the victorious progress of Truth, the Bill with an ignoble and unchristian timidity would circumscribe it with a wall of defence against the encroachments of error.

13. Because attempts to enforce by legal sanctions, acts obnoxious to so great a proportion of Citizens, tend to enervate the laws in general, and to slacken the bands of Society. If it be difficult to execute any law which is not generally deemed necessary or salutary, what must be the case, where it is deemed invalid and dangerous? And what may be the effect of so striking an example of impotency in the Government, on its general authority?

14. Because a measure of such singular magnitude and delicacy ought not to be imposed, without the clearest evidence that it is called for by a majority of citizens, and no satisfactory method is yet proposed by which the voice of the majority in this case may be determined, or its influence secured. "The people of the respective counties are indeed requested to signify their opinion respecting the adoption of the Bill to the next Session of Assembly."[50] But the representation must be made equal, before the voice either of the Representatives or of the Counties will be that of the people. Our hope is that neither of the former will, after due consideration, espouse the dangerous principle of the Bill. Should the event disappoint us, it will still leave us in full confidence, that a fair appeal to the latter will reverse the sentence against our liberties.

15. Because finally, "the equal right of every citizen to the free exercise of his Religion according to the dictates of conscience" is held by the same tenure with all our other rights. If we recur to its origin, it is equally the gift of nature; if we weigh its importance, it cannot be less dear to us; if we consult the "Declaration of those rights which pertain to the good people of Virginia, as the basis and foundation of Government,"[51] it is enumerated with equal solemnity, or rather studied emphasis. Either then, we must say, that the Will of the Legislature is the only measure of their authority; and that in the plentitude of this authority, they may sweep away all our fundamental rights; or, that they are bound to leave this particular right untouched and sacred: Either we must say, that they may controul the freedom of the press, may abolish the Trial by Jury, may swallow up the Executive and Judiciary Powers of the State; nay that they may despoil us of our very right of suffrage, and erect themselves into an independent and hereditary Assembly or, we must say, that they have no authority to enact into law the Bill under consideration. We the Subscribers say, that the General Assembly of this Commonwealth have no such authority: And that no effort may be omitted on our part against so dangerous an usurpation, we oppose to it, this remonstrance; earnestly praying, as we are in duty bound, that the Supreme Lawgiver of the Universe, by illuminating those to whom it is addressed, may on the one hand, turn their Councils from every act which would affront his holy prerogative, or violate the trust committed to them: and on the other, guide them into every measure which may be worthy of his

---

50. JM quoted the 1784 resolution that postponed the general-assessment bill until the voters had been canvassed.

51. In the margin, JM cited the title of the Virginia Declaration of Rights.

blessing, may redound to their own praise, and may establish more firmly the liberties, the prosperity and the happiness of the Commonwealth.

## Jefferson to Madison

Paris Sept. 1, 1785

DEAR SIR

My last to you was dated May 11. by Monsr. de Doradour. Since that I have received yours of Jan. 22. with 6. copies of the revisal, and that of Apr. 27. by Mr. Mazzei.

All is quiet here. The Emperor and Dutch are certainly agreed tho' they have not published their agreement. Most of his schemes in Germany must be postponed, if they are not prevented, by the confederacy of many of the Germanic body at the head of which is the K. of Prussia, and to which the Elector of Hanover is supposed to have acceded. The object of the league is to preserve the members of the empire in their present state. I doubt whether the jealousy entertained of this prince, and which is so fully evidenced by this league, may not defeat the election of his nephew to be king of the Romans, and thus produce an instance of breaking the lineal succession. Nothing is as yet done between him and the Turks. If any thing is produced in that quarter it will not be for this year. The court of Madrid has obtained the delivery of the crew of the brig Betsy taken by the Emperor of Marocco. The Emperor had treated them kindly, new-cloathed them, and delivered them to the Spanish minister who sent them to Cadiz. This is the only American vessel ever taken by the Barbary states. The Emperor continues to give proofs of his desire to be in friendship with us, or in other words, of receiving us into the number of his tributaries. Nothing further need be feared from him. I wish the Algerines may be as easily dealt with. I fancy the peace expected between them and Spain is not likely to take place. I am well informed that the late proceedings in America have produced a wonderful sensation in England in our favour. I mean the disposition which seems to be becoming general to invest Congress with the regulation of our commerce, and in the mean time the measures taken to defeat the avidity of the British government, grasping at our carrying business. I can add with truth that it was not till these symptoms appeared in America that I have been able to discover the smallest token of respect towards the United states in any part of Europe. There was an enthusiasm towards us all over Europe at the moment of the peace.[52] The torrent of lies published unremittingly in every day's London paper first made an impression and produced a coolness. The republication of these lies in most of the papers of Europe (done probably by authority of the governments to discourage emigra-

---

52. For a brilliant summary of the impact of the American Revolution on Europe, see Palmer, I, pp. 239–82.

tions) carried them home to the belief of every mind. They supposed every thing in America was anarchy, tumult, and civil war. The reception of the M. Fayette gave a check to these ideas. The late proceedings seem to be producing a decisive vibration in our favour. I think it possible that England may ply before them. It is a nation which nothing but views of interest can govern. If it produces us good there, it will here also. The defeat of the Irish propositions is also in our favor.

I have at length made up the purchase of books for you, as far as it can be done for the present. The objects which I have not yet been able to get, I shall continue to seek for. Those purchased, are packed this morning in two trunks, and you have the catalogue and prices herein inclosed. The future charges of transportation shall be carried into the next bill. The amount of the present is 1154 livres 13 sous which reckoning the French crown of 6. livres at 6/8 Virginia money is £64-3. which sum you will be so good as to keep in your hands to be used occasionally in the education of my nephews when the regular resources disappoint you. To the same use I would pray you to apply twenty five guineas which I have lent the two Mr. Fitzhughs of Marmion, and which I have desired them to repay into your hands. You will of course deduct the price of the revisals and any other articles you may have been so kind as to pay for me. Greek and Roman authors are dearer here than I believe any where in the world. No body here reads them, wherefore they are not reprinted. Don Ulloa in the original not to be found. The collection of tracts on the œconomics of different nations we cannot find; nor Amelot's travels into China. I shall send these two trunks of books to Havre there to wait a conveiance to America; for as to the fixing the packets there it is as incertain as ever. The other articles you mention shall be procured as far as they can be. Knowing that some of them would be better got in London, I commissioned Mr. Short, who was going there, to get them. He is not yet returned. They will be of such a nature as that I can get some gentleman who may be going to America to take them in his portmanteau. Le Maire being now able to stand on his own legs there will be no necessity for your advancing him the money I desired if it is not already done. I am anxious to hear from you on the subject of my Notes on Virginia. I have been obliged to give so many of them here that I fear their getting published. I have received an application from the Directors of the public buildings to procure them a plan for their Capitol. I shall send them one taken from the best morsel of antient architecture now remaining. It has obtained the approbation of fifteen or sixteen centuries, and is therefore preferable to any design which might be newly contrived. It will give more room, be more convenient and cost less than the plan they sent me. Pray encourage them to wait for it, and to execute it. It will be superior in beauty to any thing in America, and not inferior to any thing in the world. It is very simple. Have you a copying press? If you have not, you should get one. Mine (exclusive of paper which costs a guinea a ream) has cost me about 14. guineas. I would give ten times that sum that I had had it from the date of the stamp act. I hope you will be so good as to continue your communications both of the great and small kind which are equally useful to me. Be assured of the sincerity with which I am Dr. Sir Your friend and servt.,

Th: Jefferson

ENCLOSURE
*[A List of Books Purchased by Jefferson for Madison]*

|  | livres sous den |
|---|---|
| Dictionnaire de Trevoux. 5. vol. fol. @ 5f12 | 28– 0–0 |
| La Conquista di Mexico. De Solis. fol. 7f10. relieure 7f | 14– 10 |
| Traité de morale et de bonheur. 12mo. 2. v. in 1. | 2– 8 |
| Wicquefort de l'Ambassadeur. 2. v. 4to. | 7– 4 |
| Burlamaqui. Principes du droit Politique 4to. 3f12 relieure 2f5 | 5– 17 |
| Conquista de la China por el Tartaro por Palafox. 12mo. | 3 |
| Code de l'humanité de Felice. 13. v. 4to. | 104– 0 |
| 13. first livraisons of the Encyclopedie 47. vols. 4to. (being 48f less than subscription) | 348– 0 |
| 14th. livraison of do. 4. v. 4to. | 24– 0 |
| Peyssonel | 2– 0 |
| Bibliotheque physico-œconomique. 4. v. 12mo. 10f4. rel. 3f | 13– 4 |
| Cultivateur Americain. 2. v. 8vo. 7f17. rel. 2f10 | 10– 7 |
| Mirabeau sur l'ordre des Cincinnati. 10f10. rel. 1f5 (prohibited) | 11– 15 |
| Coutumes Anglo-Normands de Houard. 4. v. 4to. 40f rel. 10f | 50– 0 |
| Memoires sur l'Amerique 4. v. 4to. | 24– 0 |
| Tott sur les Turcs. 4. v. in 2. 8vo. 10f. rel. 2f10 | 12– 10 |
| Neckar sur l'Administration des Finances de France. 3. v. 12mo. 7f10 rel. 2f5 | 9– 15 |
| le bon-sens. 12mo. 6f rel. 15s (prohibited) | 6– 15 |

Mably. Principes de morale.

| | | | | |
|---|---|---|---|---|
| 1. v. 12mo. | 3 | 12 | | |
| etude de l'histoire 1. | 2 | 10 | | |
| maniere d'ecrire l'histoire 1. | 2 | 8 | | |
| constitution d'Amerique 1. | 1 | 16 | | |
| sur l'histoire de France. 2. v. | 6 | | relieure de 11 vols. @ | |
| droit de l'Europe 3. v. | 7 | 10 | 15 s. 8f5 | |
| ordres des societies | 2 | | | 41– 1 |
| principes des negotiations | 2 | 10 | | |
| entretiens de Phocion | 2 | | | |
| des Romains | 2 | 10 | | |
| | 32 | 16 | | |

Wanting to complete Mably's works which I have not been able to
    procure
  les principes de legislation
  sur les Grecs
  sur la Pologne.

# "The Dark Side of Our Commercial Affairs," 1784–1785

|  | *livres sous den* |
|---|---|
| Chronologie des empires anciennes de la Combe. 1. v. 8vo. | 5– 0–0 |
|     de l'histoire universelle de Hornot. 1. v. 8vo. 4f | 4– 0–0 |
|     de l'histoire universelle de Berlié 1. v. 8vo. 2f10 rel. 1f5 | 3– 15 |
|     des empereurs Romains par Richer 2. v. 8vo. 8f rel. 2f10 | 10– 10 |
|     des Juifs. 1. v. 8vo. 3f10. rel. 1f5 | 4– 15 |
|     de l'histoire universelle par Du Fresnoy. 2. v. 8vo. 13f rel. 2f10 | 15– 10 |
|     de l'histoire du Nord. par La Combe 2. v. 8vo. 10f. rel. 2f10 | 12– 10 |
|     de France. par Henault. 3. v. 8vo. 12f rel. 3f15 | 15– 15 |
| Memoires de Voltaire. 2. v. in 1. 2f10 rel. 15s | 3– 5–0 |
| Linnaei Philosophia Botanica. 1 v. 8vo. 7f rel. 1f5 | 8– 5 |
|     Genera plantarum 1. v. 8vo. 8f rel. 1f5 | 9– 5 |
|     Species plantarum. 4. v. 8vo. 32f rel. 5f | 37– 0 |
|     Systema naturae 4. v. 8vo. 26f rel. 5f | 31– 0 |
| Clayton. Flora Virginica. 4to. 12f. rel. 2f10. | 14– 10 |
| D'Albon sur l'interet de plusieurs nations. 4. v. 12mo. 12f. rel. 3f | 15– 0 |
| Systeme de la nature de Diderot. 3. v. 8vo. 21f (prohibited) | 21– 0 |
| Coussin histoire Romaine. 2. v. in 1. 12mo. / de Constantinople 8. v. in 10. / de l'empire de l'Occident 2. v. / de l'eglise. 5. v. in 3. } 16. vols. 12mo. | 36– 0–0 |
| Droit de la Nature. por Wolff. 6. v. 12mo. 15f rel. 4f10 | 19– 10 |
| Voyage de Pagét 8vo. 3. v. in 1. | 9 |
| Mirabeau. Ami des hommes 5. v. 12mo. / Theorie de l'impot 2. v. in 1. 12mo. | 12 |
| Buffon. Supplement 11. 12. Oiseaux 17. 18. Mineraux 1. 2. 3. 4. | 24. |
| Lettres de Pascal. 12mo. 2f. rel. 15s. | 2– 15 |
| Le sage à la cour et le roi voiageur (prohibited) | 10– 15 |
| Principes de legislation universelle 2. v. 8vo. | 12– 0 |
| Ordonnances de la Marine par Valin. 2. v. 4to. | 22 |
| Diderot sur les sourds and muets 12mo. / 3f12. sur les aveugles 3f. sur la nature 3f. sur la morale 3f15 } 4. v. 12mo. | 13– 7 |
| Mariana's history of Spain 11. v. 12mo. | 21 |
| 2 trunks and packing paper | 43– 0 |
|  | 1154– 13 |

## Jefferson to Madison

Paris Sept. 20, 1785

Dear Sir

By Mr. Fitzhugh you will receive my letter of the 1'st inst. He is still here, and gives me an opportunity of again addressing you much sooner than I should have done but for the discovery of a great peice of inattention. In that letter I send you a detail of the cost of your books, and desire you to keep the amount in your hands, as if I had forgot that a part of it was in fact your own, as being a balance of what I had remained in your debt. I really did not attend to it in the moment of writing, and when it occurred to me, I revised my memorandum book from the time of our being in Philadelphia together, and stated our account from the beginning lest I should forget or mistake any part of it: I inclose you this state. You will always be so good as to let me know from time to time your advances for me. Correct with freedom all my proceedings for you, as in what I do I have no other desire than that of doing exactly what will be most pleasing to you.

I received this summer a letter from Messrs. Buchanan and Hay as directors of the public buildings desiring I would have drawn for them plans of sundry buildings, and in the first place of a Capitol. They fixed for their receiving this plan a day which was within one month of that on which their letter came to my hand. I engaged an Architect of capital abilities in this business.[53] Much time was requisite, after the external form was agreed on, to make the internal distribution convenient for the three branches of government. This time was much lengthened by my avocations to other objects which I had no right to neglect. The plan however was settled. The gentlemen had sent me one which they had thought of. The one agreed on here is more convenient, more beautiful, gives more room and will not cost more than two thirds of what that would. We took for our model what is called the Maison-quarrèe of Nismes, one of the most beautiful, if not the most beautiful and precious morsel of architecture left us by antiquity.[54] It was built by Caius and Lucius Caesar and repaired by Louis XIV. and has the suffrage of all the judges of architecture who have seen it, as yeilding to no one of the beautiful monuments of Greece, Rome, Palmyra and Balbec which late travellers have communicated to us. It is very simple, but it is noble beyond expression, and would have done honour to our country as presenting to travellers a morsel of taste in

---

53. TJ chose Charles-Louis Clérisseau, "an architect whose taste had been formed on a study of the ancient models of this art"; see TJ to James Buchanan and William Hay, Aug. 13, 1785, in *PTJ*, VII, p. 366. See Thomas J. McCormick, "Clérisseau, Thomas Jefferson, and the Virginia Capitol, 1785–90," in *Charles-Louis Clérisseau and the Genesis of Neo-Classicism* (Cambridge, Mass., 1990), pp. 191–99, for an excellent discussion.

54. TJ had not yet seen the Maison Carrée at Nîmes, deriving his knowledge of it from Clérisseau's 1778 edition of his *Antiquitées de la France;* see *PTJ*, IX, p. xxvii.

our infancy promising much for our maturer age. I have been much mortified with information which I received two days ago from Virginia that the first brick of the Capitol would be laid within a few days. But surely the delay of this peice of a summer would have been repaid by the savings in the plan preparing here, were we to value it's other superiorities as nothing. But how is a taste in this beautiful art to be formed in our countrymen, unless we avail ourselves of every occasion when public buildings are to be erected, of presenting to them models for their study and imitation? Pray try if you can effect the stopping of this work. I have written also to E. R.[55] on the subject. The loss will be only of the laying the bricks already laid, or a part of them. The bricks themselves will do again for the interior walls, and one side wall and one end wall may remain as they will answer equally well for our plan. This loss is not to be weighed against the saving of money which will arise, against the comfort of laying out the public money for something honourable, the satisfaction of seeing an object and proof of national good taste, and the regret and mortification of erecting a monument of our barbarism which will be loaded with execrations as long as it shall endure. The plans are in good forwardness and I hope will be ready within three or four weeks. They could not be stopped now but on paying their whole price which will be considerable. If the Undertakers are afraid to undo what they have done, encourage them to it by a recommendation from the assembly. You see I am an enthusiast on the subject of the arts. But it is an enthusiasm of which I am not ashamed, as it's object is to improve the taste of my countrymen, to increase their reputation, to reconcile to them the respect of the world and procure them it's praise.

I shall send off your books, in two trunks, to Havre within two or three days to the care of Mr. Limozin, American agent there. I will advise you as soon as I know by what vessel he forwards them. Adieu. Your's affectionately,

TH: JEFFERSON

ENCLOSURE
*[A Statement of Account between Jefferson and Madison, 1783–1784]*

J. Madison to Th: J. Dr.

|       |         |         |                      | Dollars |
|-------|---------|---------|----------------------|---------|
| 1783. | Nov. 5. | To paid | Stockdon at Princeton | 9.133   |
|       |         |         | Dr. Wiggins          | 2.333   |
|       |         |         | Laurence             | 4.533   |
|       | 13.     | to cash |                      | 86.666  |
|       |         |         |                      | 102.666 |

---

55. Edmund Randolph.

|  |  |  | Cr. |  |  |
|---|---|---|---|---|---|
|  |  |  |  | *Dollars* |  |
|  | Nov. 2. | By cash |  | 98. |  |
|  | 12. | By do. |  | 4.666 | 102.666 |

|  |  |  | Dr. |  |  |
|---|---|---|---|---|---|
|  |  |  |  | *Dollars* |  |
| 1784. | Apr. 6. | To paid Dudley (by Mr Maury) for a pr. spectacles |  | 13.666 |  |
|  |  | To my assumpsit to do. for a 2d. pr. spectacles |  | 13.666 |  |
|  |  | To my bill on the Treasurer of Virginia for |  | 407.333 |  |
|  |  | Balance in your favour |  | 68.666 | 503.333 |

|  |  |  | Cr. |  |  |
|---|---|---|---|---|---|
| 1783. | Nov. 22. | By cash at Philadelphia |  | 170. |  |
|  | 26. | By bill on the Treasurer of Virginia (given me at Annapolis) |  | 333.333 | 503.333 |

|  |  |  | Dr. |  |  |
|---|---|---|---|---|---|
| 1784. | May 25. | To pd. Aitken for Blair's lectures for you |  | 4.666 |  |
|  |  | Balance in your favor |  | 77.666 | 82.333 |

|  |  |  | Cr. |  |  |
|---|---|---|---|---|---|
| 1784. |  | By balance as above |  | 68.666 |  |
|  |  | By my omission to pay Dudley for the 2d pr of spectacles |  | 13.666 | 82.333 |

|  |  | J. Madison to Th: J.   Dr. |  |  |
|---|---|---|---|---|
|  |  |  | *livres* | *s* |
| 1784. | Sep. 1. | To amount of advances for books etc. as by acct. rendered this day | 1154 | 13 |
|  |  | Testament politique d'Angleterre 12 mo. | 2 | 10 |
|  |  | Memoires de Voltaire 12mo. | 3 | 0 |
|  |  | Frederic le grand. 8vo. | 4 | 0 |
|  |  |  | 1164 | 3 |

## Madison to Jefferson

Philadelphia Oct. 3, 1785

DEAR SIR

In pursuance of the plan intimated in my last I came to this City about three weeks ago, from which I continued my trip to New York. I returned last night and in a day or two shall start for Virginia. Col. Monroe had left Philada. a few days before I reached it, on his way to a treaty to be held with the Indians about the end of this month on the Wabash. If a visit to the Eastern States had been his choice, short as the time would have proved, I should have made an effort to attend him. As it is I must postpone that gratification, with a purpose however of embracing it on the first convenient opportunity. Your favour of the 11 May by Monsr. Doradour inclosing your Cypher arrived in Virga. after I left it, and was sent after me to this place. Your notes which accompanied it, remained behind, and consequently I can only now say on that subject, that I shall obey your request on my return, which my call to Richmond will give me an early opportunity of doing. During my stay at New York I had several conversations with the Virga. Delegates, but with few others, on the affairs of the Confederacy. I find with much regret that these are as yet little redeemed from the confusion which has so long mortified the friends to our national honor and prosperity. Congress have kept the Vessel from sinking, but it has been by standing constantly at the pump, not by stopping the leaks which have endangered her. All their efforts for the latter purpose have been frustrated by the selfishness or perverseness of some part or other of their constituents. The desiderata most strongly urged by our past experience and our present situation are 1. a final discrimination between such of the unauthorised expences of the States, as ought to be added to the common debt, and such as ought not; 2. a constitutional apportionment of the common debt, either by a valuation of the land, or a change of the article which requires it; 3. a recognition by the States of the authority of Congress to enforce payment of their respective quotas; 4. a grant to Congress of an adequate power over trade. It is evident to me that the first object will never be effected in Congress, because it requires in those who are to decide it the spirit of impartial judges, whilst the spirit of those who compose Congress is rather that of advocates for the respective interests of their constituents. If this business were referred to a Commission filled by a member chosen by Congress out of each State, and sworn to impartiality, I should have hopes of seeing an end of it. The 2d. object affords less ground of hope. The execution of the 8th. art. of Confederation is generally held impracticable, and R. Island, if no other State, has put its veto on the proposed alteration of it. Until the 3d. object can be obtained the Requisitions of Congress will continue to be mere calls for voluntary contributions, which every State will be tempted to evade, by the uniform experience that those States have come off best which have done so most. The present plan of federal Government reverses the first principle of all Government. It punishes not the evildoers, but those that do well. It may be considered I think as a fortunate circumstance for the U.S. that the use of coercion, or such provision as would render the use of it unnecessary, might be made at little expence and perfect safety. A single frigate under the orders of Congress could make it the interest of any one of the Atlantic States to pay its just Quota. With regard to such of the Ultramontane States, as depend on the trade of the Mississippi, as small a force would have the same effect; whilst the residue trading thro' the Atlantic States might be wrought upon by means more indirect indeed, but perhaps sufficiently effectual. The fate of the 4th. object is still suspended. The Recommendations of Congress on this subject past before your departure, have been positively complied with by few of the States I believe; but I do not learn that they have been rejected by any. A proposition has been agitated in Congress, and will I am told be revived, asking from the States a general and permanent authority to regulate trade, with a proviso that it shall in no case be exercised without the assent of *eleven*[56] States in Congress. The Middle States favor the measure, the Eastern are Zealous for it, the Southern are divided. Of the *Virginia delegation*[57] the *president*[58] *is* an *inflexible adversary, Grayson unfriendly* and *Monroe* and *Hardy warm on the opposite side*. If the proposition should pass Congress its fate will depend much on the reception it may find in Virga. and this will depend much on the part which may be taken by a few members of the Legislature. The prospect of its being levelled against G. Britain will be most likely to give it popularity. In this suspence of a general provision for our commercial interests, the more suffering States are seeking relief from partial efforts which are less likely to obtain it than to drive their trade into other channels, and to kindle heart-burnings on all sides. Massachussetts made the beginning. Penna. has followed with a catalogue of duties on foreign goods and tonnage, which could scarcely be enforced against the smuggler, if N. Jersey, Delaware and Maryland were to cooperate with her. The avowed object of these duties is to encourage domestic manufactures, and prevent the exportation of coin to pay for foreign. The Legislature had previously repealed the incorporation of the bank, as the cause of the latter and a great many other evils. S. Carolina I am told is deliberating on the distresses of her commerce and will probably concur in some general plan, with a proviso, no doubt against any restraint from importing slaves, of which they have received from Africa since the peace about twelve thousand. She is also deliberating on the emission of paper money, and it is expected she will legalize a suspension of Judicial proceedings which has been already effected by popular combinations. The pretext for these measures is the want of specie occasioned by the unfavorable balance of trade.

Your introduction of Mr. T. Franklin has been presented to me. The arrival of his grandfather has produced an emulation among the different parties here in doing homage to his character. He will be unanimously chosen president of the State, and will either restore to it an unexpected quiet or lose his own. It appears from his answer to some applications that he will not decline the appointment.[59]

On my journey I called at Mount Vernon and had the pleasure of finding

56. JM's italics.
57. These words and the italicized words in the rest of the letter were written in code.
58. Richard Henry Lee was president of Congress.
59. Benjamin Franklin became president of Pennsylvania's Supreme Executive Council in 1785; see Esmond Wright, *Franklin of Philadelphia* (Cambridge, Mass., 1986), p. 339.

the General in perfect health. He had just returned from a trip up the Potowmac. He grows more and more sanguine, as he examines further into the practicability of opening its navigation. The subscriptions are compleated within a few shares, and the work is already begun at some of the lesser obstructions. It is overlooked by Rhumsey the inventor of the boats which I have in former letters mentioned to you. He has not yet disclosed his secret. He had of late nearly finished a boat of proper size which he meant to have exhibited, but the house which contained it and materials for others was consumed by fire. He assured the General that the enlargement of his machinery did not lessen the prospect of utility afforded by the miniature experiments. The General declines the shares voted him by the assembly, but does not mean to withdraw the money from the object which it is to aid, and will even appropriate the future tolls I believe to some useful public establishment if any such can be devised that will both please himself and be likely to please the State. This is accompanied by a letter from our amiable friend Mrs. Trist to Miss Patsy. She got back safe to her friends in Augst. and is as well as she has generally been, but her chearfulness seems to be rendered less uniform than it once was by the scenes of adversity through which fortune has led her. Mrs. House is well and charges me not to omit her respectful and affectionate compliments to you. I remain Dr. Sir Yrs

J. M.

## Jefferson to Madison

Fontainebleau Oct. 28, 1785

DEAR SIR

Seven o'clock, and retired to my fireside, I have determined to enter into conversation with you; this is a village of about 5,000 inhabitants when the court is not here and 20,000 when they are, occupying a valley thro' which runs a brook, and on each side of it a ridge of small mountains most of which are naked rock. The king comes here in the fall always, to hunt. His court attend him, as do also the foreign diplomatic corps. But as this is not indispensably required, and my finances do not admit the expence of a continued residence here, I propose to come occasionally to attend the king's levees, returning again to Paris, distant 40 miles.[60] This being the first trip, I set out yesterday morning to take a view of the place. For this purpose I shaped my course towards the highest of the mountains in sight, to the top of which was about a league. As soon as I had got clear of the town I fell in with a poor woman walking at the same rate with myself and going the same course.

---

60. For a detailed analysis of Paris at this time, see the brilliant detective work by Howard C. Rice, Jr., *Thomas Jefferson's Paris* (Princeton, 1976).

Wishing to know the condition of the labouring poor I entered into conversation with her, which I began by enquiries for the path which would lead me into the mountain: and thence proceeded to enquiries into her vocation, condition and circumstance. She told me she was a day labourer, at 8. sous or 4 d. sterling the day; that she had two children to maintain, and to pay a rent of 30 livres for her house (which would consume the hire of 75 days), that often she could get no emploiment, and of course was without bread. As we had walked together near a mile and she had so far served me as a guide, I gave her, on parting 24 sous. She burst into tears of a gratitude which I could perceive was unfeigned, because she was unable to utter a word. She had probably never before received so great an aid. This little attendrissement, with the solitude of my walk led me into a train of reflections on that unequal division of property which occasions the numberless instances of wretchedness which I had observed in this country and is to be observed all over Europe. The property of this country is absolutely concentered in a very few hands, having revenues of from half a million of guineas a year downwards. These employ the flower of the country as servants, some of them having as many as 200 domestics, not labouring. They employ also a great number of manufacturers, and tradesmen, and lastly the class of labouring husbandmen. But after all these comes the most numerous of all the classes, that is, the poor who cannot find work. I asked myself what could be the reason that so many should be permitted to beg who are willing to work, in a country where there is a very considerable proportion of uncultivated lands? These lands are kept idle mostly for the sake of game. It should seem then that it must be because of the enormous wealth of the proprietors which places them above attention to the increase of their revenues by permitting these lands to be laboured. I am conscious that an equal division of property is impracticable. But the consequences of this enormous inequality producing so much misery to the bulk of mankind, legislators cannot invent too many devices for subdividing property, only taking care to let their subdivisions go hand in hand with the natural affections of the human mind. The descent of property of every kind therefore to all the children, or to all the brothers and sisters, or other relations in equal degree is a politic measure, and a practicable one. Another means of silently lessening the inequality of property is to exempt all from taxation below a certain point, and to tax the higher portions of property in geometrical progression as they rise. Whenever there is in any country, uncultivated lands and unemployed poor, it is clear that the laws of property have been so far extended as to violate natural right. The earth is given as a common stock for man to labour and live on. If, for the encouragement of industry we allow it to be approrpriated, we must take care that other employment be furnished to those excluded from the appropriation. If we do not the fundamental right to labour the earth returns to the unemployed. It is too soon yet in our country to say that every man who cannot find employment but who can find uncultivated land, shall be at liberty to cultivate it, paying a moderate rent. But it is not too soon to provide by every possible means that as few as possible shall be without a little portion of land. The small landholders are the most precious part of a state.

The next object which struck my attention in my walk was the deer with which the wood abounded. They were of the kind called 'Cerfs' and are certainly of the same species with ours. They are blackish indeed under the belly, and not white as ours, and they are more of the chesnut red: but these are such small differences as would be sure to happen in two races from the same stock, breeding separately a number of ages.

Their hares are totally different from the animal we call by that same: but their rabbet is almost exactly like him. The only difference is in their manners; the land on which I walked for some time being absolutely reduced to a honeycomb by their burrowing. I think there is no instance of ours burrowing.

After descending the hill again I saw a man cutting fern. I went to him under the pretence of asking the shortest road to the town, and afterwards asked for what use he was cutting fern. He told me that this part of the country furnished a great deal of fruit to Paris. That when packed in straw it acquired an ill taste, but that dry fern preserved it perfectly without communicating any taste at all. I treasured this observation for the preservation of my apples on my return to my own country. They have no apple here to compare with our Newtown pipping. They have nothing which deserves the name of a peach; there being not sun enough to ripen the plumbpeach and the best of their soft peaches being like our autumn peaches. Their cherries and strawberries are fair, but I think less flavoured. Their plumbs I think are better; so also the gooseberries, and the pears infinitely beyond any thing we possess. They have no grape better than our sweet-water. But they have a succession of as good from very early in the summer till frost. I am tomorrow to go to Mr. Malsherbes (an uncle of the Chevalr. Luzerne's) about 7. leagues from hence, who is the most curious man in France as to his trees. He is making for me a collection of the vines from which the Burgundy, Champagne, Bourdeaux, Frontignac, and other the most valuable wines of this country are made. Another gentleman is collecting for me the best eating grapes, including what we call the raisin. I propose also to endeavor to colonize their hare, rabbet, red and grey partridge, pheasants of different kinds, and some other birds. But I find that I am wandering beyond the limits of my walk and will therefore bid you Adieu. Yours affectionately,

TH: JEFFERSON

## Madison to Jefferson

Richmond Nov. 15, 1785

DEAR SIR

I acknowledged from Philada. your favor of the 11 of May. On my return to Orange I found the copy of your notes brought along with it by Mr. Doradour. I have looked them over carefully myself and consulted several judicious friends in confidence. We are all sensible that the *freedom of your strictures* on some *particular measures* and *opinions* will displease *their respective abettors*.[61] But we equally concur in thinking that this consideration ought not to be weighed against the *utility of your plan*. We think both the facts and remarks which you have assembled too *valuable* not to be made known, at least to those for whom *you destine* them, and speak of them to *one another* in *terms which* I must *not repeat to you*. Mr. Wythe suggested that it might be better to put the number you may allot to the University into the library, rather than to distribute them among the Students. In the latter case the Stock will be immediately exhausted. In the former the discretion of the professors will make it serve the Students as they successively come in. Perhaps too an *indiscriminate gift*[62] might offend *some narrow minded parents*. Mr. Wythe desired me to present you with his most friendly regards. He mentioned the difficulty he experiences in using his pen as an apology for not giving these assurances himself. I postpone my account of the assembly till I can make it more satisfactory, observing only that we are at work on the Revisal, and I am not without hopes of seeing it pass this Session with as few alterations as could be expected. Some are made unavoidable by a change of circumstances. The greatest danger is to be apprehended from the impatience which a certain lapse of time always produces. Mr. W. Maury informs me that Master P. Carr has read at Williamsbg. Horace, some of Tully's select orations, Greek Testament, Æsops fables in Greek, ten books of Homer, and is now beginning Xenophon, Juvenal and Livy. He has been also employed on the French. Your other Nephew is at Hampden Sidney. I have no particular account of him.

---

61. These italicized words and those in the rest of the letter, except for those cited in n. 62, below, were written in code.

62. JM's italics.

# STATE AND NATIONAL REFORMS: THE VIRGINIA LEGISLATOR AND THE MINISTER TO FRANCE, 1785–1786

"CAN YOU SUPPOSE IT POSSIBLE that Madison should shine with more than the usual splendor in this Assembly?" asked one of his colleagues while the Virginia legislature was in session during the fall of 1785. "It is, Sir, not only possible but a fact. He has astonished Mankind and has by means perfectly constitutional become almost a Dictator.... His influence alone has ... carried half ... the Revised Code."[1]

Madison had again taken the lead in pushing the enactment of Jefferson's revised code, which he later labeled "the severest of his [Jefferson's] many intellectual labours," persuading the Virginia assembly to spend three days a week on the task. To his friend in Paris, he confessed that he found the new code "more popular in the assembly than I had formed any idea of, and though it was considered by paragraphs and carried through all the customary forms, it might have been finished at one Session with great ease, if the time spent on motions to put it off, and other dilatory artifices, had been employed on its merits."

Madison singled out "the Bill concerning Religious freedom" with particular pride. Although some amendments "somewhat defaced the composition," they did not affect the substance. Indeed, "the enacting clauses past without a single alteration, and I flatter myself have in this country extinguished for ever the ambitious hope of making laws for the human mind."[2]

---

1. Archibald Stuart to John Breckinridge, Dec. 7, 1785, cited in Ketcham, p. 161.
2. JM to TJ, Jan. 22, 1786, below. For JM's characterization of TJ's work on the revised code, see JM to Nicholas Biddle, May 17, 1827, in Hunt, IX, p. 288. For JM's role in the enactment of the Virginia statute, see Lance Banning, "James Madison, the Statute for Religious Freedom, and the Crisis of Republican Convictions," in *The Virginia Statute for Religious Freedom: Its Evolution and*

The preamble of Jefferson's Bill for Establishing Religious Freedom argued that

> Almighty God hath created the mind free; that all attempts to influence it by temporal punishments or burthens, or by civil incapacitations, tend only to beget habits of hypocrisy and meanness . . . that our civil rights have no dependence on our religious opinions, any more than our opinions in physics or geometry; that therefore the proscribing any citizen as unworthy the public confidence by laying upon him an incapacity of being called to offices of trust and emolument, unless he profess or renounce this or that religious opinion, is depriving him injuriously of those privileges and advantages to which, in common with his fellow-citizens, he has a natural right . . . and finally, that truth is great and will prevail if left to herself, that she is the proper and sufficient antagonist to error, and has nothing to fear from the conflict unless by human interposition disarmed of her natural weapons, free argument and debate; errors ceasing to be dangerous when it is permitted freely to contradict them.[3]

As Rhys Isaac observes, "The Act for Establishing Religious Freedom remade Virginia. In its universal language, indeed, it was remaking America and the world."[4] Lauding his friend's achievement, Jefferson told Madison that "the Virginia act for religious freedom has been received with infinite approbation in Europe and propagated with enthusiasm," appearing in French and Italian translations and being inserted in the new *Encyclopédie*. "In fact," he added, "it is comfortable to see the standard of reason at length erected, after so many ages during which the human mind has been held in vassalage by kings, priests and nobles; and it is honorable for us to have produced the first legislature who has had the courage to declare that the reason of man may be trusted with the formation of his own opinions."[5]

In his usual methodical way, Madison also ticked off the other legislation enacted: the naturalization of Lafayette; Washington's role in the canal companies; the suspension of the courts-of-assize bill passed the year before; the postponement of taxes; the reduction of salaries of state officials; and the imposition of a tonnage tax on British vessels.

Madison had tried strenuously to have the assembly grant Congress the power to regulate commerce since the federal councils had been "instituted for the purpose of managing the interests of the States in cases which cannot so well be provided for by measures individually passed." The two friends had long agreed on a strategy of limiting British access to American markets until

---

*Consequences in American History*, ed. Merrill D. Peterson and Robert C. Vaughn (Cambridge, Eng., and New York, 1988), pp. 109–38.

3. *PTJ*, II, pp. 545–46.

4. Rhys Isaac, " 'The Rage of Malice of the Old Serpent Devil': The Dissenters and the Making and Remaking of the Virginia Statute for Religious Freedom," in *The Virginia Statute for Religious Freedom*, ed. Peterson and Vaughn, p. 139. Also see Thomas E. Buckley, *Church and State in Revolutionary Virginia, 1776–1787* (Charlottesville, 1977), pp. 38–167.

5. TJ to JM, Dec. 16, 1786, below.

British ports were freely opened to American shipping. Madison argued that "the relative situation of the United States, has been found on trial, to require uniformity in their commercial regulations." When the assembly cut his proposed "perpetual" grant of power to thirteen years, however, he opposed the temporary measure, thinking it better "to trust to further experience and even distress, for an adequate remedy."[6]

Jefferson followed these developments from Paris and assumed that Madison's commercial resolutions had passed. "I have heard with great pleasure," he told his friend, "that our assembly have come to the resolution of giving the regulation of their commerce to the federal head. I will venture to assert that there is not one of it's opposers who, placed on this ground, would not see the wisdom of this measure. The politics of Europe render it indispensably necessary that with respect to every thing external we be one nation only, firmly hooped together. Interior government is what each state should keep to itself. If it could be seen in Europe that all our states could be brought to concur in what the Virginia assembly has done, it would produce a total revolution in their opinion of us, and respect for us. And it should ever be held in mind that insult and war are the consequences of a want of respectability in the national character."[7]

On the last day of the session, Jefferson later learned, the assembly had substituted for Madison's state proposal a resolution calling for an interstate conference to recommend a federal plan for regulating commerce. Madison was appointed one of Virginia's commissioners to the commercial convention, which was set to meet at Annapolis in September 1786. He viewed the meeting as "a remedial experiment which ought to command every assent," but he despaired of success. "It is necessary however that something should be tried," he told Jefferson, "and if this be not the best possible expedient, it is the best that could possibly be carried thro' the Legislature here. And if the present crisis cannot effect unanimity," he asked plaintively, "from what future concurrence of circumstances is it to be expected?"[8]

After making another trip north during the summer, where he visited congressional friends in New York, Madison discovered that "many Gentlemen both within and without Congress wish to make this meeting subservient to a plenipotentiary convention for amending the Confederation." Although he favored such a move, he was so depressed by the anarchy of American commerce that he did not extend his views beyond commercial reform. "To speak the truth," he wrote Jefferson, "*I almost despair even of this*."

His pessimism stemmed from the Mississippi question. Spain had closed the river to American navigation in 1784, but John Jay, who had become

---

6. JM to TJ, Jan. 22, 1786, below. See JM's resolution of Nov. 14, 1785, in *PJM,* VIII, pp. 413–14, and JM to George Washington, Dec. 9, 1785, *ibid.,* pp. 438–40.

7. TJ to JM, Feb. 8, 1786, below.

8. JM to TJ, Mar. 18, 1786, below.

secretary of foreign affairs, had inaugurated negotiations in 1785 with Don Diego de Gardoqui, Spanish minister to the United States, in an effort to lift the prohibition. By 1786, Jay had proposed that navigation of the Mississippi be waived for twenty-five or thirty years in exchange for trading privileges with Spain and its American colonies. The proposal created the sharpest sectional division in Congress since the end of the Revolutionary War, threatening to bring the fragile Union to the breaking point. Such a policy, Madison warned, if adopted, might persuade settlers in the West that they had been sold down the river "*by* their *Atlantic brethren*." The resulting animosities between the northern commercial and southern agricultural states might be "*fatal . . . to an augmentation of the federal authority* if not to the *little now existing*. My personal situation," he confided to Jefferson, "is rendered by this business particularly *mortifying*. Ever since I have been *out of Congress I have been inculcating* on our *assembly a confidence* in the *equal attention of Congress* to the *rights and* interests of *every part of the republic* and on the *western members* in particular, the necessity of making the Union *respectable by new powers* to *Congress* if they wished *Congress to negociate with effect for the Mississippi*."⁹

Despite his pessimism, Madison joined Governor Edmund Randolph and the Virginia delegates at the commercial convention in Annapolis in September; he was disappointed when only five other states sent representatives. Before the meeting broke up, however, he joined the other commissioners in issuing a call for another convention, set for Philadelphia in 1787, "to devise such further provisions as shall appear to them necessary to render the Constitution of the federal government adequate to the exigencies of the Union." Writing to Monroe from Annapolis, Madison reported that this was "an *intimation* of the expediency of extending the plan to other defects of the Confederation" in addition to commerce.¹⁰

By the end of the year, Madison informed Jefferson about "the revolution of sentiment which the experience of one year has effected in this country." The Virginia assembly had given its "unanimous sanction" to the call for the Constitutional Convention in Philadelphia. "The evidence of dangerous defects in the Confederation," he wrote, "has at length proselyted the most obstinate adversaries to a reform."¹¹

Jefferson hoped that the Philadelphia convention would produce both "a full meeting in May, and a broader reformation" of the Articles of Confederation than tinkering with a new commercial clause. "To make us one nation as to foreign concerns," he wrote from his diplomatic perspective, "and keep us distinct in Domestic ones, gives the outline of the proper division of powers

---

9. JM to TJ, Aug. 12, 1786, below. The italicized words were written in code. See Frederick W. Marks, *Independence on Trial: Foreign Affairs and the Making of the Constitution* (Baton Rouge, 1973), pp. 25–36, for a discussion of the movement towards the dissolution of the Union.
10. JM to James Monroe, Sept. 12, 1786, in *PJM,* IX, pp. 121–22.
11. JM to TJ, Dec. 4, 1786, below.

between the general and particular governments." But he had specific suggestions based on his experience as chief executive of Virginia and as originator of the Committee of the States in Congress. "To enable the Federal head to exercise the powers given it, to best advantage, it should be organised, as the particular ones are, into Legislative, Executive and Judiciary. The 1st. and last are already separated. The 2d should also be. When last with Congress," he recalled, "I often proposed to members to do this by making of the Committee of the states, an Executive committee during the recess of Congress, and during it's sessions to appoint a Committee to receive and dispatch all executive business, so that Congress itself should meddle only with what should be legislative. But I question if any Congress (much less all successively) can have self-denial enough to go through with this distribution." In that case, "the distribution should be imposed on them then."[12]

Throughout the year, Madison worried about paper money and the "impolitic measures" of postponing taxes. "Our Treasury is empty," he told Jefferson at the end of the year. "No supplies have gone to the federal treasury, and our internal embarrassments torment us exceedingly." But Virginia had not yet succumbed to the paper-money mania. Indeed, "in one instance only the general principles of finance have been departed from," when "the specie part of the tax under collection is made payable in Tobacco."[13]

On the other hand, the "general rage for paper money"—"this fictitious money," as Madison labeled it—had swept the nation like an "epidemic malady." Since it was less valuable than specie, "depreciation is inevitable." "Among the numerous ills with which this practice is pregnant," he told Jefferson, "one I find is that it is producing the same warfare and retaliation among the States as were produced by State regulations of commerce." Madison contrasted these antagonisms with interstate cooperation on river navigation and canal or road construction. "These fruits of the Revolution do great honour to it. I wish," he sighed, "all our proceedings merited the same character."[14]

Madison also wrote a thoughtful reply to Jefferson's reflections on the idle poor of Europe. He concluded that his friend's observations formed "a valuable lesson to the Legislators of every Country, and particularly of a new one." He agreed that one of the causes for the greater comfort of the people of the United States was the absence of feudal landed privileges, but he stressed an additional factor—"our limited population." He thought that the relative sparseness "has probably as large a share in producing this effect as the political advantages which distinguish us. A certain degree of misery," he elaborated, "seems inseparable from a high degree of populousness." He found this princi-

12. TJ to JM, Dec. 16, 1786, below.
13. JM to TJ, Dec. 4, 1786, below.
14. JM to TJ, Aug. 12, 1786, below.

ple disturbing. For even in a republican government, where land was distributed equitably, a large population might create difficult social pressures and problems:

No problem in political Œconomy has appeared to me more puzzling than that which relates to the most proper distribution of the inhabitants of a Country fully peopled. Let the lands be shared among them ever so wisely, and let them be supplied with labourers ever so plentifully; as there must be a great surplus of subsistence, there will also remain a great surplus of inhabitants, a greater by far than will be employed in cloathing both themselves and those who feed them, and in administering to both, every other necessary and even comfort of life. What is to be done with this surplus? Hitherto we have seen them distributed into manufacturers of superfluities, idle proprietors of productive funds, domestics, soldiers, merchants, mariners, and a few other less numerous classes. All these classes notwithstanding have been found insufficient to absorb the redundant members of a populous society.

Part of Madison's puzzlement sprang from "the very reform which appears so necessary and desirable" to reduce these classes of inhabitants. Jefferson's more equal distribution of land in a republican system would, he explained, lead to "a greater simplicity of manners, consequently a less consumption of manufactured superfluities, and a less proportion of idle proprietors and domestics." And this phenomenon would be complicated—indeed, compounded—by "a juster government," which would require "less need of soldiers either for defence against dangers from without, or disturbances from within." The future for a populous republic might be as bad as, or perhaps worse than, any corrupt society, Madison implied. Perhaps this fearful thought caused him to cut off his reflections abruptly, for he concluded his discussion by saying, "But I forget that I am writing a letter not a dissertation."[15]

During the year, both Jefferson and Madison took trips, Jefferson joining John and Abigail Adams briefly in London in an unsuccessful effort to negotiate a trade treaty with Great Britain and Madison going to New York for political and personal reasons. "With this nation," Jefferson wrote from London, "nothing is done; and it is now decided that they intend to do nothing." The king, his ministers, the merchants, and the people presented a solid phalanx of opposition. "They sufficiently value our commerce," Jefferson was convinced, "but they are quite persuaded they shall enjoy it on their own terms."[16]

While he was in London, Jefferson joined Adams in meeting with merchants trading with the United States to discuss prewar debts owed by Americans. The Treaty of Paris stipulated that "creditors on either side shall meet with no lawful impediment to the recovery of the full value in sterling money, of all bona fide debts heretofore contracted." Madison had twice tried to get

15. JM to TJ, June 19, 1786, below.
16. TJ to JM, Apr. 25, 1786, below.

the Virginia assembly to act in conformity with the pledged honor of the United States—first in 1784 and again in 1785. "A Bill was brought in for paying British debts," he informed Jefferson early in 1786, "but was rendered so inadequate to its object by alterations inserted by a Committee of the whole that the patrons of it thought it best to let it sleep."[17]

Jefferson reported that the British merchants were "sensible that it was for the interest of the creditor as well as debtor to allow time for the paiment of the debts to this country." Moreover, he agreed with Adams that the courts should be open to creditors immediately, as Madison's bill would have provided, making "judgments recoverable" and payable in equal and annual installments in order to discharge the debts by 1790. "If our law is not already on this footing," Jefferson urged, not yet having received Madison's note to the contrary, "I wish extremely it were put on it." Despite the broad areas of agreement between Jefferson and Adams and the British merchants, the British foreign minister refused to meet with the American negotiators, and the unofficial conferences, which "were intended as preparatory to authoritative propositions . . . ended in nothing."[18] In his reply, Madison agreed with his friend on the issue of British debts. "The expectations of the British Merchants coincide with the information I had received," he wrote, "as your opinion of the steps proper to be taken by the Assembly do with those for which I have ineffectually contended."[19]

Jefferson's frustrating experience with London officials strengthened his prejudices against England. Before visiting the Adamses, he had chided Mrs. Adams about living in a "rich, proud, hectoring, swearing, squibbing, carnivorous" nation.[20] But when George III, who had received John Adams cordially, snubbed the author of the Declaration of Independence, the humiliated Jefferson concluded that "that nation hates us, their ministers hate us, and their king more than all other men."[21]

With more time on their hands than they had counted on, Jefferson and Adams did what any other sensible visitor to England would do—they embarked upon a leisurely tour of famous country estates and gardens, using Thomas Whately's *Observations on Modern Gardening* as their guide. "The gardening in that country," Jefferson confessed with delight, "is the article in which it surpasses all the earth. I mean their pleasure gardening. This, indeed went far beyond my ideas."[22]

Madison's trip to New York not only allowed him to consult with the

17. JM to TJ, Jan. 22, 1786, below. For JM's bill providing for installment payments on British debts, see *PJM,* VIII, pp. 447-50.
18. TJ to JM, Apr. 25, 1786, below.
19. JM to TJ, Aug. 12, 1786, below.
20. TJ to Abigail Adams, June 21, 1785, in Cappon, I, p. 34.
21. TJ to John Page, May 4, 1786, in *PTJ,* IX, p. 446.
22. *Ibid.* See Edward Dumbauld, "Jefferson and Adams' English Garden Tour," in *Jefferson and the Arts: An Extended View,* ed. William Howard Adams (Washington, 1976), pp. 135-57.

Virginia delegates to Congress on the affairs of the Confederation, but also involved "a plan concerted between Col. Monroe and myself for a purchase of land on the Mohawk" River. He sketched the virtues of the land in glowing terms and invited Jefferson to participate. "We have made a small purchase," he added, "and nothing *but the difficulty of raising a* sufficient *sum restrained us* from *making a large one*." He urged Jefferson to use his *"credit* in *your private capacity . . . for borrowing"* money in France on the collateral of all three at 6 percent interest, payable in full *"within a term* not less than *eight or ten years*."[23] Jefferson replied that he had already discussed borrowing money to aid in opening the Potomac canal, but without success. He thought that Madison's plan might attract more interest, but he considered its chance for success "as only possible, not probable."[24]

In the transatlantic correspondence during 1786, Madison was more productive than Jefferson, who, after a silence of nearly eight months, informed Madison that "an unlucky dislocation of my right wrist has disabled me from using my pen."[25] Although he had learned to write with his left hand, it was "too slow and awkward to be employed but in cases of necessity."[26] What Jefferson did not tell Madison was that he had dislocated his wrist perhaps on a ramble with Maria Cosway, an enchantress twenty years his junior.[27] To another correspondent, he made the mishap a minor mystery: "How the right hand became disabled would be a long story for the left to tell. It was by one of those follies from which good cannot come, but ill can."[28] Although Jefferson never revealed how he sustained his injury, a friend said that it occurred when Jefferson, in a feisty moment, attempted "to leap over a large kettle in a small court yard."[29]

Belatedly, Jefferson informed Madison about a new development in commercial relations with France that made "several advantageous regulations" for the United States. It was the result of a year's negotiations and reflected the joint efforts of Jefferson and Lafayette, who was "so useful an auxiliary that acknowlegements for his cooperation are always due."[30] These included concessions on tobacco (America's leading export to Europe), reduction of export duties on French wines, and the elimination of import duties on many

---

23. JM to TJ, Aug. 12, 1786, below.
24. TJ to JM, Dec. 16, 1786, below. The italicized words were written in code.
25. *Ibid.*
26. TJ to Charles Thomson, Dec. 17, 1786, in *PTJ,* X, pp. 608–10.
27. The best explanation is in L. H. Butterfield and Howard C. Rice, Jr., "Jefferson's Earliest Note to Maria Cosway, with Some New Facts and Conjectures on His Broken Wrist," *WMQ* 5 (1948): 26–33.
28. TJ to William S. Smith, Oct. 22, 1786, in *PTJ,* X, p. 478.
29. Louis-Guillaume Le Veillard to Temple Franklin, Sept. 20, 1786, cited in Marie Kimball, *Jefferson: The Scene of Europe, 1784 to 1789* (New York, 1950), p. 168. For the Cosway affair as TJ's "last romance," see *ibid.,* pp. 156–83, and Helen D. Bullock, *My Head and My Heart: A Little History of Thomas Jefferson and Maria Cosway* (New York, 1945).
30. TJ to JM, Dec. 16, 1786, below.

American items. In reporting this development to Washington, Lafayette praised Jefferson as "a most able and respected representative, and such a man as makes me happy to be his aid de camp. Congress have made a choice very favorable to their affairs."[31]

─────────────── THE LETTERS ───────────────

*Madison to Jefferson*

Richmond Jan. 22, 1786

DEAR SIR

My last dated Novr. 15 from this place answered yours of May 11th. on the subject of your printed notes. I have since had opportunity of consulting other friends on the plan you propose, who concur in the result of the consultations which I transmitted you. Mr. Wythe's idea seems to be generally approved, that the copies destined for the University should be dealt out by the discretion of the Professors, rather than indiscriminately and at once put into the hands of the students, which, other objections apart, would at once exhaust the Stock. A vessel from Havre de Grace brought me a few days ago two Trunks of Books, but without letter or catalogue attending them. I have forwarded them to Orange without examining much into the contents, lest I should miss a conveyance which is very precarious at this season, and be deprived of the amusement they promise me for the residue of the winter.

Our Assembly last night closed a Session of 97 days, during the whole of which except the first seven I have shared in the confinement. It opened with a very warm struggle for the chair between Mr. Harrison and Mr. Tyler which ended in the victory of the former by a majority of 6 votes. This victory was shortly afterwards nearly frustrated by an impeachment of his election in the County of Surry. Having failed in his native County of Charles City, he abdicated his residence there, removed into the County of Surry where he had an Estate, took every step which the interval would admit to constitute himself an inhabitant, and was in consequence elected a representative. A charge of non residence was nevertheless brought against him, decided against him in the Committee of privileges by the casting voice of the Chairman, and reversed in the House by a very small majority. The election of Docr. [Arthur] Lee was attacked on two grounds, 1st. of non-residence, 2dly. of holding a lucrative office under Congress. On the 1st. he was acquitted, on the 2d. expelled, by a large majority.

The revised Code was brought forward pretty early in the Session. It was first referred to Committee of Courts of Justice, to report such of the bills as were not of a temporary nature, and on their report committed to committee

31. The marquis de Lafayette to George Washington, Oct. 26, 1786, in *Letters of Lafayette to Washington, 1777–1799,* ed. Louis Gottschalk (Philadelphia, 1976), p. 314.

of the whole. Some difficulties were raised as to the proper mode of proceeding, and some opposition made to the work itself. These however being surmounted, and three days in each week appropriated to the task, we went on slowly but successfully, till we arrived at the bill concerning crimes and punishments. Here the adversaries of the code exerted their whole force, which being abetted by the impatience of its friends in an advanced stage of the Session, so far prevailed that the prosecution of the work was postponed till the next Session.[1] The operation of the bills passed is suspended untill the beginning of 1787, so that if the code should be resumed by the next assembly and finished early in the Session, the whole system may commence at once. I found it more popular in the assembly than I had formed any idea of, and though it was considered by paragraphs and carried through all the customary forms, it might have been finished at one Session with great ease, if the time spent on motions to put it off, and other dilatory artifices, had been employed on its merits. The *adversaries were* the *speaker, Thruston*—and *Mercer* who *came late in the session, into a vacancy left by* the *death of Col. Brent of Stafford,* and *contributed principally to the mischieve.*[2] The titles in the inclosed List will point out to you such of the bills as were adopted from the Revisal. The alterations which they underwent are too numerous to be specified, but have not materially viciated the work. The bills passed over were either temporary ones, such as being not essential as parts of the System, may be adopted at any time and were likely to impede it at this, or such as have been rendered unnecessary by Acts passed since the epoch at which the revisal was prepared. After the completion of the work at this Session was despaired of it was proposed and decided that a few of the bills following the bill concerning crimes and punishments should be taken up as of peculiar importance. The only one of these which was pursued into an Act is the Bill concerning Religious freedom. The steps taken throughout the Country to defeat the General Assessment had produced all the effect that could have been wished. The table was loaded with petitions and remonstrances from all parts against the interposition of the Legislature in matters of Religion. A general convention of the Presbyterian church prayed expressly that the bill in the Revisal might be passed into a law, as the best safeguard short of a constitutional one, for their religious rights. The bill was carried thro' H. of Delegates, without alteration. The Senate objected to the preamble, and sent down a proposed substitution of the 16th. article of the Declaration of Rights. The H. of D. disagreed. The Senate insisted and asked a Conference. Their objections were frivolous indeed. In order to remove them as they were understood by the Managers of the H. of D. The preamble was sent up again from the H. of D. with one or two verbal alterations. As an amendment to these the Senate sent back a few others; which as they did not

1. Before the next session of the state legislature began in Oct., JM had returned to Congress. His colleague Thomas Mathews reintroduced the remainder of the revised code and managed to get an additional twenty-three bills enacted, but the rest languished; see *PJM,* VIII, p. 481, and *PTJ,* II, pp. 322–24.
2. The italicized words in this sentence and those in the rest of the letter were written in code.

affect the substance though they somewhat defaced the composition, it was thought better to agree to than to run further risks, especially as it was getting late in the Session and the House growing thin. The enacting clauses past without a single alteration, and I flatter myself have in this country extinguished for ever the ambitious hope of making laws for the human mind.[3]

Acts not included in the Revisal

For the naturalization of the Marquis de la fayette. This was brought forward by Col: Henry Lee Jr. and passed without opposition. It recites his merits toward this Country and constitutes him a Citizen of it.

To amend the act vesting in Genl. Washington certain shares in the River Companies. The donation presented to Genl. W. embarrassed him much. On one side he disliked the appearance of slighting the bounty of his Country and of an ostentatious disinterestedness. On the other an acceptance of reward in any shape was irreconcileable with the law he had imposed on himself. His answer to the Assembly declined in the most affectionate terms the emolument allotted to himself, but intimated his willingness to accept it so far as to dedicate it to some public and patriotic use. This Act recites the original Act and his answer, and appropriates the future revenue from the shares to such public objects as he shall appoint. *He has been pleased to ask my* ideas with regard to the *most proper objects. I suggest in* general only a *partition of the fund between* some *institution* which would *please the philosophical world* and some other which may be of *a popular cast.* If your knowledge of the *several institutions, in France* or *elsewhere,* should suggest *models or hints, I could wish for your ideas* on the *case which* no less *concerns the good of the common wealth* than *the character of it's most illustrious citizen.*

An Act empowering the Governor and Council to grant conditional pardons in certain cases. Some of the malefactors consigned by the Executive to labour, brought the legality of such pardons before the late Court of Appeals who adjudged them to be void. This Act gives the Executive a power in such cases for one year. It passed before the bill in the revisal on this subject was taken up, and was urged against the necessity of passing it at this Session. The expiration of this act at the next Session will become an argument on the other side.

An Act giving powers to the Governor and Council in certain cases. This Act empowers the Executive to confine or send away suspicious aliens, on notice from Congress that their sovereigns have declared or commenced hostilities against U.S. or that the latter have declared War against such sovereigns. It was occasioned by the arrival of two or three Algerines here, who having no apparent object were suspected of an unfriendly one. The Executive caused them to be brought before them, but found them unarmed with power to proceed. These adventurers have since gone off.

Act for safekeeping land papers of the Northern Neck. Abolishes the

---

3. For a discussion of the maneuvers by opponents, see *PTJ,* II, pp. 545-46.

quitrent and removes the papers to the Registers office.

Act for reforming County Courts. Requires them to clear their dockets quarterly. It amounts to nothing and is cheifly the result of efforts to render Courts of Assize unnecessary.

Act to suspend the operation of the Act establishing Courts of Assize. The latter act passed at last Session required sundry supplemental regulations to fit it for operation. An attempt to provide these which involved the merits of the innovation drew forth the united exertions of its adversaries. On the question on the supplemental bill they prevailed by 63 votes against 49. The best that could be done in this situation was to suspend instead of repealing the original act, which will give another chance to our successors for introducing the proposed reform. The various interests opposed to it, will never be conquered without considerable difficulty.

Resolution proposing a general meeting of Commissioners from the States to consider and recommend a fœderal plan for regulating Commerce, and appointing as Commissioners from Va. Ed. Randolph, Js. Madison Jr., Walter Jones, St. G. Tucker, M. Smith, G. Mason and David Ross who are to communicate the proposal and suggest time and place for meeting. The necessity of harmony in the commercial regulations of the States has been rendered every day more apparent. The local efforts to counteract the policy of G.B. instead of succeeding have in every instance recoiled more or less on the States which ventured on the trial. Notwithstanding these lessons, The Merchants of this State except those of Alexandria and a few of the more intelligent individuals elsewhere, were so far carried away by their jealousies of the Northern Marine, as to wish for a navigation act confined to this State alone. In opposition to those narrow ideas the printed propositions herewith enclosed was made.[4] As printed it went into a Committee of the whole. The alterations of the pen shew the state in which it came out. Its object was to give Congress such direct power only as would not alarm, but to limit that of the States in such manner as would indirectly require a conformity to the plans of Congress. The renunciation of the right of laying duties on imports from other States, would amount to a prohibition of duties on imports from other foreign Countries, unless similar duties existed in other States. This idea was favored by the discord produced between several States by rival and adverse regulations. The evil had proceeded so far between Connecticut and Massts. that the former laid heavier duties on imports from the latter than from G.B. of which the latter sent a letter of complaint to the Executive here and I suppose to the other Executives. Without some such self-denying compact it will, I conceive be impossible to preserve harmony among the contiguous States. In the Committee of the whole the proposition was combated at first on its general merits. This ground was however soon changed for that of its perpetual duration, which was reduced first to 25 years, and then to 13 years. *Its adversaries* were the *Speaker, Thruston and Corbin. They* were *bitter and illiberal against Congress*

---

4. For JM's resolution on uniform commercial regulations, enclosure, Nov. 14, 1785, see below.

and the *Northern States,* beyond *example. Thruston* considered it as problematical, whether it would not be better to *encourage the British than the Eastern marine. Braxton* and *Smith* were in the same *sentiments* but *absent at* this *crisis of the question.* The limitation of the plan to 13 years so far destroyed its value in the judgment of its friends that they chose rather, to do nothing than to adopt it in that form. The report accordingly remained on the table uncalled for to the end of the Session. And on the last day the resolution above quoted was substituted.[5] It had been proposed by Mr. Tyler immediately after the miscarriage of the printed proposition, but was left on the table till it was found that several propositions for regulating our trade without regard to other States produced nothing. In this extremity the resolution was generally acceded to, not without the *opposition however of Corbin and Smith.* The Commissioners *first named were the Attorney Dr. Jones* and *myself. In the* House of D. *Tucker* [*and*] *Smith were added and* In the Senate *Mason, Ross and Ronald.* The *last does not undertake.*

The port bill was attacked and nearly defeated. An amendatory bill was passed with difficulty thro' the H. of D. and rejected in the Senate. The original one will take effect before the next Session, but will probably be repealed then. It would have been repealed at this, if its adversaries had known their strength in time and exerted it with Judgment.

A Bill was brought in for paying British debts but was rendered so inadequate to its object by alterations inserted by a Committee of the whole that the patrons of it thought it best to let it sleep.

Several petitions (from Methodists cheifly) appeared in favor of a gradual abolition of slavery, and several from another quarter for a repeal of the law which licenses private manumissions. The former were not thrown under the table, but were treated with all the indignity short of it. A proposition for bringing in a Bill conformably to the latter, was decided in the affirmative by the casting voice of the Speaker, but the bill was thrown out on the first reading by a considerable majority.

A considerable itch for paper money discovered itself, though no overt attempt was made. The partizans of the measure, among whom Mr. M. S.[6] may be considered as the most zealous, *flatter themselves,* and *I fear upon too good ground* that it will be *among the measures of the next session.* The unfavorable balance of trade and the substitution of facilities in the taxes *will have dismissed the little specie remaining among us* and strengthened the common *argument for a paper medium.*[7]

Act for postponing the tax of the present year and admitting facilities in

---

5. Unlike JM's proposal, this plan clearly bypassed Congress and relied solely on the states to agree on a uniform system of commercial regulations. Boyd contrasts it with JM's resolution; see *PTJ,* IX, pp. 206–8. Although JM preferred his plan, he thought the other one "better than nothing"; see JM to James Monroe, Jan. 22, 1786, in *PJM,* VIII, p. 483.

6. Meriwether Smith.

7. "Facilities" or "facility notes" were a special kind of negotiable paper that circulated in lieu of specie; see *PJM,* VIII, p. 482.

payment. This tax was to have been collected in Sepr. last and had been in part actually collected in specie. Notwithstanding this and the distress of public credit, an effort was made to remit the tax altogether. *The party was headed by Braxton who was courting an appointment into the council.* On the question for a third reading the affirmative was carried by 52 against 42. On the final question, a vigorous effort on the negative side with a reinforcement of a few new members threw the bill out. The oratory however was not obtained, without subscribing to a postponement instead of remission, and the admission of facilities instead of specie. The postponement too extends not only to the tax which was under collection, and which will not now come in till May, but to the tax of Sepr. next which will not now be in the Treasury till the beginning of next year. The wisdom of seven Sessions will be unable to repair the mischiefs of this single act.

Act concerning the erection of Kentucky into an independent State. This was prayed for by a Memorial from a Convention held in Kentucky, and passed without opposition. It contains stipulations in favor of territorial rights held under the laws of Virga. and suspends the actual separation on the decision of a Convention authorized to meet for that purpose, and on the assent of Congress. The boundary of the proposed State is to remain the same as the present boundary of the district.

Act to amend the Militia law. At the last Session of 1784. an act passed displacing all the militia officers, and providing for the appointment of experienced men. In most counties it was carried into execution, and generally much to the advantage of the militia. In consequence of a few petitions against the law as a breach of the Constitution, this act reverses all proceedings under it, and reinstates the old officers.

Act to extend the operation of the Escheat law to the Northern Neck. From the peculiar situation of that district the Escheat law was not originally extended to it. Its extension at this time was occasioned by a bill brought in by Mr. Mercer for seizing and selling the deeded land of the late lord Fairfax on the ground of its being devized to aliens, leaving them at liberty indeed to assert their pretensions before the Court of Appeals. As the bill however stated the law and the fact, and excluded the ordinary inquest, in the face of pretensions set up even by a Citizen (Martin) to whom it is said the reversion is given by the Will, it was opposed as exerting at least a legislative interference in and improper influence on the Judiciary question.[8] It was proposed to substitute the present act as an amendment to the bill, in a Committee of the whole which was disagreed to. The bill being of a popular cast went thro' the H. of

---

8. Thomas Bryan Martin was executor of the will of Lord Fairfax, holder of a vast pre-Revolutionary grant in northern Virginia. After Fairfax's death in 1781, his will was challenged with the claim that the property of enemy aliens escheated to Virginia. In *Martin* v. *Hunter's Lessee,* the U.S. Supreme Court upheld the validity of Fairfax's division of his property according to his will. See F. Thornton Miller, "John Marshall versus Spencer Roane: A Reevaluation of *Martin* v. *Hunter's Lessee,*" *VMHB* 96 (1988): 297–314. See also William F. Swindler, *The Constitution and Chief Justice Marshall* (New York, 1978), pp. 293–97.

D. by a great majority. In the Senate it was rejected by a greater one, if not unanimously. The extension of the escheat law was in consequence taken up and passed.

"Act for punishing certain offences." To wit, attempts to dismember the State without the consent of the Legislature. It is pointed against the faction headed by A.C.[9] in the County of Washington.

Act for amending the appropriating Act. Complies with the requisition of Congress for the present year, to wit, 1786. It directs 512.000 dollars the quota of this State, to be paid before May next the time fixed by Congress, *altho' it is known* that the *postponement* of the *taxes renders the payment of a shilling impossible.* Our payments last year *gained us a little reputation.* Our conduct *this must stamp us with ignominy.*

Act for regulating the Salaries of the Civil list. Reduces that of the Governor from £1000 to £800 and the others some at a greater and some at a less proportion.

Act for disposing of waste lands on Eastern waters. Meant cheifly to affect vacant land in Northern Neck, erroneously conceived to be in great quantity and of great value. The price is fixed at £25 per Hundred Acres at which not an acre will be sold.

An Act imposing additional tonnage on British vessels, amounting in the whole to 5/. per ton.

Nothing has been yet done with N.C. towards opening a canal thro' the Dismal [Swamp]. The powers given to Commissioners on our part are renewed, and some negociation will be brought about if possible. A certain interest in that State is suspected of being disinclined to promote the object, notwithstanding its manifest importance to the community at large. On Potowmack they have been at work some time. On this river they have about eighty hands ready to break ground, and have engaged a man to plan for them. I fear there is a want of skill for the undertaking that threatens a waste of labour and a discouragement to the interprize. I do not learn that any measures have been taken to procure from Europe the aid which ought [to] be purchased at any price, and which might I should suppose be purchased at a moderate one.

I had an opportunity a few days ago of knowing that Mrs. Carr and her family, as well as your little daughter, were well. I am apprehensive that some impediments still detained your younger nephew from his destination. Peter has been in Williamsburg, and I am told by Mr. Maury that his progress is satisfactory. He has read under him Horace, some of Cicero's Orations, Greek testament, Æsop's fables in Greek, ten books of Homer's Iliad and is now beginning Xenophon, Juvenal and Livy. He has also given some attention to French.

I have paid le Maire ten guineas. He will set out in about three weeks I am

---

9. Arthur Campbell; see *PJM,* VIII, p. 482.

told for France. Mr. Jones has promised to collect and forward by him all such papers as are in print and will explain the situation of our affairs to you. Among these will be the most important acts of the Session, and the Journal as far as it will be printed.

Mr. Wm. Hays, in sinking a well on the declivity of the Hill above the proposed seat of the Capitol and nearly in a line from the Capitol to Belvidere, found about seventy feet below the surface, several large bones apparently belonging to a fish not less than the Shark, and what is more singular, several fragments of potters ware in the stile of the Indians. Before he reached these curiosities he passed thro' about fifty feet of soft blue clay. I have not seen these articles, having but just heard of them, and been too closely engaged; but have my information from the most unexceptionable witnesses who have. I am told by Genl. Russel of Washington County, that in sinking a Salt well in that county he fell in with the hip bone of the incognitum, the socket of which was about 8 inches diameter. It was very soft in the subterraneous State, but seemed to undergo a petrifaction on being exposed to the air. Adieu affecty.

Promotions. Edwd. Carrington and H. Lee Jr. added to R. H. Lee, Js. Monroe, and Wm. Grayson, in the delegation to Congress.
Carter Braxton to the Council.
Jno. Tyler to Court of Admiralty in room of B. Waller resigned.

Prices Current. Tobo. 23s on James River and proportionally elsewhere
Wheat 5s to 6s per Bushel
Corn 15s to 20s per Barrel
Pork 28s to 30s per Ct.

ENCLOSURE
*[Madison's Resolution on Uniform Commercial Regulations]*
In the House of Delegates.[10] November 14, 1785.

Whereas, the relative situation of the United States, has been found on trial, to require uniformity in their commercial regulations, as the only effectual policy for obtaining in the ports of foreign nations a stipulation of privileges reciprocal to those enjoyed by the subjects of such nations in the ports of the United States, for preventing animosities, which cannot fail to arise among the several States from the interference of partial and separate regulations[, and for deriving from commerce, such aids to the public revenue as it ought to contribute];[11] and whereas such uniformity can be best concerted and carried into effect by the Fœderal Councils, which, having been instituted for the purpose of managing the interests of the States in cases which cannot so well be provided for by measures individually pursued, ought to be invested with authority in this case as being within the reason and policy of their institution:

*Resolved,* That the delegates representing this Commonwealth in Congress, be

---

10. For the textual history of this resolution, see *PTJ,* IX, pp. 203–9, where Boyd argues that JM was "the chief architect of this attempt to increase the powers of Congress." See also *PJM,* VIII, pp. 406–10, 413–15.

11. The bracketed portion was deleted in the Committee of the Whole; see *PTJ,* IX, p. 208.

instructed to propose in Congress a recommendation to the States in Union, to authorize that Assembly to regulate their trade[, and to collect a revenue therefrom,][12] on the following principles, and under the following qualifications:

1st, That the United States in Congress assembled, be authorized to prohibit vessels belonging to any [nation, which has no commercial treaty with the United States,][13] from entering any of the ports thereof, or to impose any duties on such vessels and their cargoes, which may be judged necessary; all such prohibitions and duties to be uniform throughout the United States, and the proceeds of the latter to be carried into the Treasury of the State within which they shall accrue.

[2d, That over and above any duties which may be so laid, the United States in Congress assembled, be authorized to collect, in manner prescribed by an Act "To provide certain and adequate funds for the payment of this State's quota of the debts contracted by the United States," an impost not exceeding five *per centum ad valorem*, on all goods, wares, and merchandizes whatsoever, imported into the United States from any foreign ports; such impost to be uniform as aforesaid, and to be carried to the Treasury of the United States.][14]

3d, That no state be at liberty to impose duties on any goods, wares, or merchandizes, imported by land or by water from any other State; but may altogether prohibit the importation from any other state of any particular species or description of goods, wares, or merchandize, [of] which the importation is at the same time prohibited from all other places whatsoever.

4th, That no Act of Congress that may be authorized, as hereby proposed, shall be entered into by less than two-thirds of the Condfederated States, nor be in force longer than[15] —— years, [unless continued by a like proportion of votes within one year immediately preceding the expiration of the said period, or be revived in like manner after the expiration thereof; nor shall any impost whatsoever, be collected by virtue of the authority proposed in the second article, after the year 17   ]. . . .[16]

John Beckley, C.H.D.

## Jefferson to Madison

Paris Feb. 8, 1786

DEAR SIR

My last letters have been of the 1st. and 20th. of Sep. and the 28th. of Oct. Yours unacknoleged are of Aug. 20. Oct. 3. and Nov. 15. I take this the first safe opportunity of inclosing you the bills of lading for your books, and

---

12. The bracketed portion was deleted in the Committee of the Whole; see *ibid*.
13. For the bracketed portion, the Committee of the Whole substituted "foreign nation"; see *ibid*.
14. This bracketed paragraph was deleted in the Committee of the Whole; see *ibid*.
15. The Committee of the Whole inserted "thirteen" instead of JM's longer term of twenty-five years; see JM to TJ, Jan. 22, 1786, above.
16. The bracketed portion was deleted in the Committee of the Whole. The ellipses indicate that four lines relating to the commitment and printing of the resolution have been omitted; see *PTJ*, IX, p. 208.

two others for your name sake of Williamsburgh and for the attorney which I will pray you to forward. I thank you for the communication of the remonstrance against the assessment. Mazzei who is now in Holland promised me to have it published in the Leyden gazette. It will do us great honour. I wish it may be as much approved by our assembly as by the wisest part of Europe. I have heard with great pleasure that our assembly have come to the resolution of giving the regulation of their commerce to the federal head. I will venture to assert that there is not one of it's opposers who, placed on this ground, would not see the wisdom of this measure. The politics of Europe render it indispensably necessary that with respect to every thing external we be one nation only, firmly hooped together. Interior government is what each state should keep to itself. If it could be seen in Europe that all our states could be brought to concur in what the Virginia assembly has done, it would produce a total revolution in their opinion of us, and respect for us. And it should ever be held in mind that insult and war are the consequences of a want of respectability in the national character. As long as the states exercise separately those acts of power which respect foreign nations, so long will there continue to be irregularities committing by some one or other of them which will constantly keep us on an ill footing with foreign nations.

I thank you for your information as to my Notes. The copies I have remaining shall be sent over to be given to some of my friends and to select subjects in the college. I have been unfortunate here with this trifle. I gave out a few copies only, and to confidential persons, writing in every copy a restraint against it's publication. Among others I gave a copy to a Mr. Williamos. He died. I immediately took every precaution I could to recover this copy. But by some means or other a book seller had got hold of it. He had employed a hireling translator and was about publishing it in the most injurious form possible. An Abbé Morellet, a man of letters here to whom I had given a copy, got notice of this. He had translated some passages for a particular purpose: and he compounded with the bookseller to translate and give him the whole, on his declining the first publication. I found it necessary to confirm this, and it will be published in French, still mutilated however in it's freest parts. I am now at a loss what to do as to England. Every thing, good or bad, is thought worth publishing there; and I apprehend a translation back from the French and publication there. I rather believe it will be most eligible to let the original come out in that country; but am not yet decided.

I have purchased little for you in the book way since I sent the catalogue of my former purchases. I wish first to have your answer to that, and your information what parts of those purchases went out of your plan. You can easily say buy more of this kind, less of that etc. My wish is to conform myself to yours. I can get for you the original Paris edition in folio of the Encyclopedie for 620 livres, 35. vols: a good edition in 39. vols 4to, for 380$^{tt}$ and a good one in 39. vols. 8vo. for 280$^{tt}$. The new one will be superior in far the greater number of articles: but not in all. And the possession of the ancient one has more over the advantage of supplying present use. I have bought one for myself, but wait your orders as to you. I remember your purchase of a watch in Philadelphia. If she should not have proved good, you can probably sell her. In that case I can get for you here, one made as perfect as human art can make it for about 24. louis. I have had such a one made by the best and most faithful hand in Paris. She has a second hand, but no repeating, no day of the month, nor other useless thing to impede and injure the movements which are necessary. For 12. louis more you can have in the same cover, but on the backside, and absolutely unconnected with the movements of the watch, a pedometer which shall render you an exact account of the distances you walk. Your pleasure hereon shall be awaited.

Houdon is returned. He called on me the other day to remonstrate against the inscription proposed for Genl. W's statue.[17] He says it is too long to be put on the pedestal. I told him I was not at liberty to permit any alteration, but I would represent his objection to a friend who could judge of it's validity, and whether a change could be authorized. This has been the subject of conversations here, and various devices and inscriptions have been suggested. The one which has appeared best to me may be translated as follows: 'Behold, Reader, the form of George Washington. For his worth, ask History: that will tell it, when this stone shall have yeilded to the decays of time. His country erects this monument: Houdon makes it.' This for one side. On the 2d. represent the evacuation of Boston with the motto 'hostibus primum fugatis.' On the 3d. the capture of the Hessians with 'hostibus iterum devictis.' On the 4th. the surrender of York, with 'hostibus ultimum debellatis.' This is seising the three most brilliant actions of his military life. By giving out here a wish of receiving mottos for this statue, we might have thousands offered, of which still better might be chosen. The artist made the same objection of *length* to the inscription for the bust of the M. de la fayette. An alteration of that might come in time still, if an alteration was wished. However I am not certain that it is desireable in either case. The state of Georgia has given 20,000 acres of land to the Count d'Estaing. This gift is considered here as very honourable to him, and it has gratified him much. I am persuaded that a gift of lands by the state of Virginia to the Marquis de la fayette would give a good opinion here of our character, and would reflect honour on the Marquis. Nor am I sure that the day will not come when it might be an useful asylum to him. The time of life at which he visited America was too well adapted to receive good and lasting impressions to permit him ever to accommodate himself to the principles of monarchical government; and it will need all his own prudence and that of his friends to make this country a safe residence for him. How glorious, how comfortable in reflection will it be to have prepared a refuge for him in case of a reverse. In the mean time he could settle

17. Houdon had returned to Paris from his visit to the United States to prepare a statue of Washington. JM wrote the inscription for the pedestal. See Brant, II, pp. 321-22, and *PTJ*, IX, pp. 270-71. See also H. H. Arnasou, *The Sculptures of Houdon* (New York, 1975).

it with tenants from the freest part of this country, Bretagny. I have never suggested the smallest idea of this kind to him: because the execution of it should convey the first notice. If the state has not a right to give him lands with their own officers, they could buy up at cheap prices the shares of others.

I am not certain however whether in the public or private opinion, a similar gift to Count Rochambeau could be dispensed with. If the state could give to both, it would be better: but in any event I think they should to the Marquis. C. Rochambeau too has really deserved more attention than he has received. Why not set up his bust, that of Gates, Greene, Franklin in your new Capitol? à propos of the Capitol, do my dear friend exert yourself to get the plan begun or set aside, and that adopted which was drawn here. It was taken from a model which has been the admiration of 16. centuries, which has been the object of as many pilgrimages as the tomb of Mahomet; which will give unrivalled honour to our state, and furnish a model whereon to form the taste of our young men. It will cost much less too than the one begun, because it does not cover one half the Area. Ask if you please, a sight of my letter of Jan. 26. to Messrs. Buchanan and Hay, which will spare me the repeating it's substance here.

Every thing is quiet in Europe. I recollect but one new invention in the arts which is worth mentioning. It is a mixture of the arts of engraving and printing, rendering both cheaper. Write or draw any thing on a plate of brass with the ink of the inventor, and in half an hour he gives you copies of it so perfectly like the original that they could not be suspected to be copies. His types for printing a whole page are all in one solid peice. An author therefore only prints a few copies of his work from time to time as they are called for. This saves the loss of printing more copies than may possibly be sold, and prevents an edition from being ever exhausted. I am with a lively esteem Dear Sir your sincere friend and servant,

TH: JEFFERSON

P.S. Could you procure and send me an hundred or two nuts of the Paccan? They would enable me to oblige some characters here whom I should be much gratified to oblige. They should come packed in sand. The seeds of the sugar maple too would be a great present.

## Jefferson to Madison

Paris Feb. 9, 1786

DEAR SIR

In my letter of yesterday I forgot to inclose one I have received on the subject of a debt due to Mr. Paradise,[18] and I wish the present letter may reach

---

18. For John Paradise, see Archibald B. Shepperson, *John Paradise and Lucy Ludwell of London and Williamsburg* (Richmond, 1942).

the bearer of that in time to go by the same conveiance. The inclosed from Doctor Bancroft will explain itself. I add my solicitations to his, not to ask any thing to be done for Mr. Paradise inconsistent with the justice due to others, but that every thing may be done for him which justice will permit. Your assistance in this either by yourself or by interesting such other person in it as may be more in the way to forward it will oblige Dear Sir your friend and servant,

TH: JEFFERSON

## Madison to Jefferson

Virginia Orange Mar. 18, 1786

DEAR SIR

Your two favours of the 1 and 20 Sepr. under the same cover by Mr. Fitzhugh did not come to hand till the 24th. ult: and of course till it was too late for any Legislative interposition with regard to the Capitol. I have written to the Attorney on the subject. A letter which I have from him dated prior to his receipt of mine takes notice of the plan you had promised and makes no doubt that it will arrive in time for the purpose of the Commissioners. I do not gather from his expressions however that he was aware of the change, which will become necessary in the foundation already laid; a change which will not be submitted to without reluctance for two reasons. 1. The appearance of caprice to which it may expose the Commissioners. 2. Which is the material one, the danger of retarding the work till the next Session of Assembly can interpose a vote for its suspension, and possibly for a removal to Williamsburg. This danger is not altogether imaginary. Not a Session has passed since I became a member without one or other or both of these attempts. At the late Session, a suspension was moved by the Williamsburg Interest, which was within a few votes of being agreed to. It is a great object therefore with the Richmond Interest to get the building so far advanced before the fall as to put an end to such experiments. The circumstances which will weigh in the other scale, and which it is to be hoped will preponderate, are the fear of being reproached with sacrificing public considerations to a local policy, and a hope that the substitution of a more œconomical plan, may better reconcile the Assembly to a prosecution of the undertaking.

Since I have been at home I have had leisure to review the literary cargo for which I am so much indebted to your friendship. The collection is perfectly to my mind. I must trouble you only to get two little mistakes rectified. The number of Volumes in the Encyclopedie corresponds with your list, but a duplicate has been packed up by Tom. 1., 1ere. partie of Histoire Naturelle,

Quadrepedes, premiere livraison, and there is left out the 2d. part of the same Tom. which, as appears by the Avis to the 1st. livraison, makes the 1st. Tom. of Histoire des Oiseaux, as well as by the Histoire des oiseaux sent, which begins with Tom. II., 1re. partie, and with the letter F. From the Avis to the sixth livraison I infer that the volume omitted made part of the 5me. livraison. The duplicate volume seems to have been a good deal handled, and possibly belongs to your own Sett. Shall I keep it in my hands or send it back? The other mistake is an omission of the 4th. vol. of D'Albon sur l'interêt de plusieurs nations etc. The binding of the three volumes which are come is distinguished from that of most of the other books by the circumstance of the figure on the back, numbering the volumes, being on a black instead of a red ground. The Authors name above is on a red ground. I mention these circumstances that the binder may supply the omitted volume in proper uniform. I annex a State of our account balanced. I had an opportunity a few days after your letters were received of remitting the balance to the hands of Mrs. Carr with a request that it might be made use of as you direct to prevent a loss of time to her and from occasional disappointments in the stated funds. I have not yet heard from the Mr. Fitzhughs on the subject of your advance to them. The advance to Le Maire had been made a considerable time before I received your countermanding instructions. I have no copying press, but must postpone that conveniency to other wants which will absorb my little resources. I am fully apprized of the value of this machine and mean to get one when I can better afford it, and may have more use for it. I am led to think it would be a very œconomical acquisition to all our public offices which are obliged to furnish copies of papers belonging to them.

A Quorum of the deputies appointed by the Assembly for a Commercial Convention had a meeting at Richmond shortly after I left it, and the Attorney tells me, it has been agreed to propose Annapolis for the place, and the first Monday in Sepr. for the time of holding the Convention. It was thought prudent to avoid the neighbourhood of Congress, and the large Commercial towns, in order to disarm the adversaries to the object of insinuations of influence from either of these quarters. I have not heard what opinion is entertained of this project at New York, nor what reception it has found in any of the States. If it should come to nothing, it will I fear confirm G. B. and all the world in the belief that we are not to be respected, nor apprehended as a nation in matters of Commerce. The States are every day giving proofs that separate regulations are more likely to set them by the ears, than to attain the common object. When Massts. set on foot a retaliation of the policy of G. B. Connecticut declared her ports free. N. Jersey served N. York in the same way. And Delaware I am told has lately followed the example in opposition to the commercial plans of Penna. A miscarriage of this attempt to unite the States in some effectual plan will have another effect of a serious nature. It will dissipate every prospect of drawing a steady revenue from our imports either directly into the federal treasury, or indirectly thro' the treasuries of the commercial States, and of consequence the former must depend for supplies solely on annual requisitions, and the latter on direct taxes drawn from the property of the Country. That these dependencies are in an alarming degree fallacious is put by experience out of all question. The payments from the States under the calls of Congress have in no year borne any proportion to the public wants. During the last year, that is from Novr. 1784 to Novr. 1785, the aggregate payments, as stated to the late Assembly, fell short of 400,000 dollrs., a sum neither equal to the interest due on the foreign debts, nor even to the current expences of the federal Government. The greatest part of this sum too went from Virga. which will not supply a single shilling the present year. Another unhappy effect of a continuance of the present anarchy of our commerce will be a continuance of the unfavorable balance on it, which by draining us of our metals furnishes pretexts for the pernicious substitution of paper money, for indulgences to debtors, for postponements of taxes. In fact most of our political evils may be traced up to our commercial ones, as most of our moral may to our political. The lessons which the mercantile interest of Europe have received from late experience will probably check their propensity to credit us beyond our resources, and so far the evil of an unfavorable balance will correct itself. But the Merchants of G.B. if no others will continue to credit us at least as far as our remittances can be obtained, and that is far enough to perpetuate our difficulties unless the luxurious propensity of our own people can be otherwise checked.

  This view of our situation presents the proposed Convention as a remedial experiment which ought to command every assent; but if it be a just view it is one which assuredly will not be taken by all even of those whose intentions are good. I consider the event therefore as extremely uncertain, or rather, considering that the States must first agree to the proposition for sending deputies, that these must agree in a plan to be sent back to the States, and that these again must agree unanimously in a ratification of it. I almost despair of success. It is necessary however that something should be tried and if this be not the best possible expedient, it is the best that could possibly be carried thro' the Legislature here. And if the present crisis cannot effect unanimity, from what future concurrence of circumstances is it to be expected? Two considerations particularly remonstrate against delay. One is the danger of having the same *game played on our confederacy* by which *Philip managed that of the Grecian states.*[19] *I saw enough during the late assembly* of the *influence of the desperate circumstances of individuals on their public conduct* to *admonish me of the possibility of finding in the council of some one of the states, fit instruments of foreign machinations.* The other consideration is the probability of an early *increase* of the *confederated states which more* than *proportionally impede measures which re-*

---

19. The italicized words in this sentence and in the rest of the letter were written in code.

*quire unanimity as* the *new members may bring sentiments* and *interests less congenial with those of* the *Atlantic states than those of the latter are one with another.*

The price of our Staple is down at 22/. at Richmond. One argument for putting off the taxes was that as it would relieve the planters from the necessity of selling and would enable them to make a better bargain with the purchasers. The price has notwithstanding been falling ever since. How far the event may have proceeded from a change in the Market of Europe I know not. That it has in part proceeded from the very practice of remitting and postponing the taxes may I think be fairly deduced. The scarcity of money must of necessity sink the price of every article, and the relaxation in collecting the taxes increases this scarcity by diverting the money from the public Treasury to the shops of Merchandize. In the former case it would return into circulation. In the latter it goes out of the Country to balance the increased consumption. A vigorous and steady collection of taxes would make the money necessary here and would therefore be a mean of keeping it here. In our situation it would have the salutary operation of a sumptuary law. The price of Indian Corn, in this part of the Country which produced the best crops, is not higher than 2 dollrs. per barrl. It would have been much higher but for the peculiar mildness of the winter. December and Jany. scarcely reminded us that it was winter. February, though temperate, was less unseasonable. Our deepest snow (about 7 inches) was in the present month. I observe the tops of the blue ridge still marked with its remains. My last was dated Jany. 22. and contained a narrative of the proceedings of the Assembly. I shall write you again as soon as a subject and opportunity occur, remaining in the mean time Yr. affecte. friend,

J M

Dr. to T. J.

| | *livrs.* | *sols* |
|---|---|---|
| 1785 Sepr. 1. To amt. of books etc. | 1164 | 3 |

Credit

| | *livrs.* | *sols* |
|---|---|---|
| By balance stated by T.J. 77$^{2/3}$ drs. = | 407 | 15 |
| By advance to Lemaire 10 guins. | 234 | |
| By do. for 6 copies of Revisal at 2½ Drs. | 81 | |
| | 722 | 15 |
| *By £25 Va. Cy. remitted to Mrs. C. | 441 | 8 |
| | 1164 | 3 |

*£25 I discover exceeds the sum extended a few livres which may be carried into the next acct. if it be thought worth while.

*Jefferson to Madison*

London Apr. 25, 1786

DEAR SIR

Some of the objects of the joint commission with which we were honoured by Congress called me to this place about six weeks ago.[20] Tomorrow I set out on my return to Paris. With this nation nothing is done; and it is now decided that they intend to do nothing with us. The king is against a change of measures; his ministers are against it, some from principle, others from attachment to their places, and the merchants and people are against it. They sufficiently value our commerce; but they are quite persuaded they shall enjoy it on their own terms. This political speculation fosters the warmest feeling of the king's heart, that is, his hatred to us. If ever he should be forced to make any terms with us, it will be by events which he does not foresee. He takes no pains at present to hide his aversion. Our commission expiring in a fortnight there is an end of all further attempts on our part to arrange matters between the two countries. The treaty of peace being yet unexecuted it remains that each party conduct themselves as the combined considerations of justice and of caution require. We have had conversations on the subject of our debts with the chairman of the committee of American merchants here. He was anxious for arrangements. He was sensible that it was for the interest of the creditor as well as debtor to allow time for the paiment of the debts to this country, and did not seem to think the time taken by Virginia was more than enough. But we could not help agreeing with him that the courts should be open to them immediately, judgments recoverable, the executions to be divided into so many equal and annual parts as will admit the whole to be paid by the year 1790., and that the paiments should be in money and not in any thing else. If our law is not already on this footing, I wish extremely it were put on it. When we proceeded to discuss the sum which should be paid, we concurred in thinking that the principal and interest preceding and subsequent to the war should be paid. As to interest during the war, the chairman thought it justly demandeable; we thought otherwise. I need not recapitulate to you the topics of argument on each side. He said the renunciation of this interest was a bitter pill which they could not swallow. Perhaps he would have agreed to say noth-

---

20. For TJ's trip to London, see Edward Dumbauld, *Thomas Jefferson, American Tourist* (Norman, Okla., 1946), pp. 69–82. TJ and John Adams, the first American minister to the Court of St. James's, were commissioned to negotiate commercial treaties with England as well as pacts with Tunis, Algiers, and Tripoli; see Malone, II, pp. 27–30, 50–58. Since the British refused to negotiate, the two diplomats did what most tourists in England did then and still do—they toured country houses and gardens; see Dumbauld, "Jefferson and Adams' English Garden Tour," pp. 135–57. Some of the sites are discussed in Robert P. Maccubbin and Peter Martin, eds., *British and American Gardens in the Eighteenth Century* (Williamsburg, 1984), and Peter Martin, *The Pleasure Gardens of Virginia: From Jamestown to Jefferson* (Princeton, 1991), pp. 144–64.

ing about it, not expecting to receive it in most cases, yet willing to take the chance of it where debtors or juries should happen to be favorably disposed. We should have insisted on an express declaration that this interest should not be demandeable. These conferences were intended as preparatory to authoritative propositions; but the minister not condescending to meet us at all on the subject, they ended in nothing. I think the merchants here do not expect to recover interest during the war in general; tho' they are of opinion they are entitled to it.

I wrote you in a former letter on the subject of a Mr. Paradise who owns an estate in Virginia in right of his wife, and who has a considerable sum due to him in our loan office. Since I came here I have had opportunities of knowing his extreme personal worth, and his losses by the late war. He is from principle a pure republican, while his father was as warm a tory. His attachment to the American cause, and his candid warmth brought him sometimes into altercations on the subject with his father, and some persons interested in their variance artfully brought up this subject of conversation whenever they met. It produced a neglect in the father. He had already settled on him a sum of money in the funds; but would do no more, and probably would have undone that if he could. When remittances from Virginia were forbidden, the profits of the Virginia estate were carried into our loan office. Paradise was then obliged to begin to eat his capital in England. From that to part with conveniencies and to run in debt. His situation is now distressing; and would be completely relieved could he receive what is due to him from our state. He is coming over to settle there. His wife and family will follow him. I never ask unjust preferences for any body. But if by any just means he can be helped to his money, I own I should be much gratified. The goodness of his heart, his kindness to Americans before, during and since the war, the purity of his political and moral character, interest me in the events impending over him, and which will infallibly be ruinous if he fails to receive his money. I ask of you on his behalf that in pursuing the path of right you will become active for him, instead of being merely quiescent were his merit and his misfortune unknown to you.

I have put into the hands of Mr. Fulwar Skipwith[21] for you a packet containing some catalogues, which he will forward. I am with very sincere esteem Dr. Sir Your friend and servt.,

TH: JEFFERSON

---

21. Skipwith was a Virginian in London on behalf of his father's tobacco business; see *PTJ*, VIII, p. 358.

## Madison to Jefferson

Orange May 12, 1786

DEAR SIR

My last was of March 18. since which I have been favored with yours of the 8. and 9th. of Feby. Bancroft's application in favor of Paridise inclosed in the latter shall be attended to as far as the case will admit; though I see not how any relief can be obtained. If Mr. P. stands on the list of foreign creditors his agent here may possibly convert his securities into money without any very great loss, as they rest on good funds, and the principal is in a source of payment. If he stands on the domestic list as I presume he does, the interest only is provided for, and since the postponement of the taxes even that cannot be negociated without a discount of 10 per ct. at least. The principal cannot be turned into cash without sinking ¾ of its amount.

Your notes having got into print in France will inevitably be translated back and published in that form, not only in England but in America, unless you give out the original. I think therefore you owe it not only to yourself, but to the place you occupy and the subjects you have handled, to take this precaution. To say nothing of the injury which will certainly result to the diction from a translation first into French and then back into English, the ideas themselves may possibly be so perverted as to lose their propriety. The books which you have been so good as to forward to me are so well assorted to my wishes that no suggestions are necessary as to your future purchases. A copy of the Old edition of the Encyclopedie is desireable for the reasons you mention, but as I should gratify my desire in this particular at the expence of something else which I can less dispense with, I must content myself with the new Edition for the present. The watch I bought in Philada. though a pretty good one, is probably so far inferior to those of which you have a sample, that I cannot refuse your kind offer to procure me one of the same sort; and I am fancying to myself so many little gratifications from the pedometer that I cannot forego that addition. The Inscription for the Statue is liable to Houdons criticism, and is in every respect inferior to the substitute which you have copied into your letter. I am apprehensive notwithstanding that no change can be effected. The Assembly will want some proper ground for resuming the matter. The devices for the other sides of the pedestal are well chosen, and might I should suppose be applied without scruple as decorations of the artist. I counted myself on the addition of proper ornaments, and am persuaded that such a liberty could give offence no where. The execution of your hints with regard to the *Marquis* and *Rochambeau* [22] would be no less pleasing to me than to you. I think with you also that the *setting up the busts of our own worthies* would not be doing more *honor to them than to ourselves.* I foresee however the difficulty of

---

22. The italicized words in this sentence and those in the rest of the paragraph were written in code.

overcoming the popular objection against every measure which involves expence, particularly where the importance of the measure will be felt by a few only; and an unsuccessful attempt, would be worse than no attempt. I have heard nothing as to the Capitol. I mentioned to you in my last that I had written to the attorney on the subject. I shall have an opportunity shortly of touching on it again to him.

A great many changes have taken place in the late elections. The principal acquisitions are Col. G. Mason who I am told was pressed into the service at the instigation of Genl. Washington, Genl. Nelson, Mann Page.[23] In Albemarle both the old ones declined the task. Their successors are George and Jno. Nicholas. Col. Carter was again an unsuccessful candidate. I have not heard how Mr. Harrison has shaped his course. It was expected that he would stand in a very awkward relation both to Charles City and to Surry, and would probably succeed in neither. Munroe lost his election in King George by 6 votes. Mercer did his by the same number in Stafford. Neither of them were present, or they would no doubt have both been elected. Col. Bland is also to be among us. Among the many good things which may be expected from Col. Mason we may reckon perhaps an effort to review our Constitution. The loss of the port bill will certainly be one condition on which we are to receive his valuable assistance. I am not without fears also concerning his federal ideas. The last time I saw him he seemed to have come about a good deal towards the policy of giving Congress the management of Trade. But he has been led so far out of the right way, that a thorough return can scarcely be hoped for. On all the other great points, the Revised Code, the Assize bill, taxation, paper money etc. his abilities will be inestimable. Most if not all the States except Maryld. have appointed deputies for the proposed Convention at Annapolis. The refusal of Maryland to appoint proceeded as I am informed by Mr. Danl. Carrol, from a mistaken notion, that the measure would derogate from the authority of Congress, and interfere with the Revenue system of April 1783, which they have lately recommended anew to the States. There is certainly no such interference, and instead of lessening the authority of Congress, the object of the Convention is to extend it over commerce. I have no doubt that on a reconsideration of the matter it will be viewed in a different light. The internal situation of this State is growing worse and worse. Our specie has vanished. The people are again plunged in debt to the Merchants, and those circumstances added to the fall of Tobacco in Europe and a probable combination among its chief purchasers here have reduced that article to 20/.[24] The price of Corn is in many parts of the Countrey at 20/. and upwards per

23. A bout with gout prevented George Mason from attending the legislative session; see George Mason, *The Papers of George Mason, 1725–1792,* ed. Robert A. Rutland, 3 vols. (Chapel Hill, 1970), II, p. 858.

24. According to Curtis P. Nettels, *The Emergence of a National Economy, 1775–1815* (New York, 1962), p. 49, the United States imported £8 million worth of British goods and exported £2.5 million worth of American products. The deficit "acted like a magnet to draw gold and silver from America to Britain."

barrel. In this part it is not more than 15/. but Spring has been a cool and laterly a dry one. Of course it is a backward one. The first day of April was the most remarkable ever experienced in this climate. It snowed and hailed the whole day in a storm from N.E., and the Thermometer stood at 4 oC.P.M. at 26°. If the snow had fallen in the usual way it would have been 8 or 10 inches deep at least, but consisting of small hard globules mixed with small hail, and lying on the ground so compact and firm as to bear a man, it was less than half of that depth. We hear from Kentucky that the inhabitants are still at variance with their savage neighbours. In a late skirmish several were lost on both sides. On that of the whites Col. W. Christian is mentioned. It is said the scheme of independence is growing unpopular since the Act of our Assembly has brought the question fully before them. Your Nephew, D. Carr, has been some time at the Academy in Prince Edward. The President Mr. Smith speaks favorably of him.[25] With the sincerest affection I remain Dr. Sir your friend and servant,

Js. Madison Jr.

P.S. I have taken measures for procuring the Paccan Nuts and the seed of the Sugar Tree. Are there no other things here which would be acceptable on a like account? You will withold from me a real pleasure if you do not favor me with your commands freely. Perhaps some of our animal curiosities would enable you to gratify particular characters of merit. I can without difficulty get the skins of all our common and of some of our rarer quadrupeds, and can have them stuffed if desired. It is possible also that I may be able to send some of them alive. I lately had on hand a female opossum with 7 young ones, which I intended to have reared for the purpose partly of experiments myself and partly of being able to forward some of them to you, in case of an opportunity and your desiring it. Unfortunately they have all died. But I find they can be got at any time almost in the Spring of the year, and if the season be too far advanced now, they may certainly be had earlier in the next Spring. I observe that in your Notes you number the fallow and Roe-deer among the native quadrupeds of America. As Buffon had admitted the fact, it was, whether true or erroneous, a good argument no doubt against him. But I am persuaded they are not natives of the New Continent. Buffon mentions the Chevreuil in particular as abounding in Louisiana. I have enquired of several credible persons who have traversed the Western woods extensively and quite down to New Orleans, all of whom affirm that no other than our common deer are any where seen. Nor can I find any written evidence to the contrary that deserves notice. You have I believe justly considered our Monax as the Marmotte of Europe. I have lately had an opportunity of examining a female one with some attention. Its weight after it had lost a good deal of blood was 5½ lbs. Its dimensions, shape, teeth, and structure within as far as I could judge corre-

25. The president of Hampden-Sydney Academy was the Reverend John Blair Smith, a classmate of JM's at Princeton. See Wesley Frank Craven, "John Blair Smith," in *Princetonians 1769–1775: A Biographical Dictionary*, ed. Richard A. Harrison (Princeton, 1980), pp. 342–46.

sponded in substance with the description given by D'Aubenton. In sundry minute circumstances a precise correspondence was also observable. The principal variations were 1. in the face which was shorter in the Monax than in the proportions of the Marmotte, and was less arched about the root of the nose. 2. In the feet, each of the forefeet having a fifth nail about ⅓ of an inch long growing out of the inward side of the heel, without any visible toe. From this particular it would seem to be the Marmotte of Poland, called the Bobac, rather than the Alpine Marmotte. 3. In the teats, which were 8 only. The Marmotte in Buffon had 10. 4. In several circumstances of its robe, particularly of that of the belly, which consisted of a short coarse thin hair, whereas this part of Buffon's Marmotte was covered with a thicker fur than the back etc. A very material circumstance in the comparison remains yet to be ascertained. The European Marmotte is in the class of those which are dormant during the winter. No person here of whom I have enquired can decide whether this be a quality of the Monax. I infer that it is of the dormant class not only from its similitude to the Marmotte in other respects, but from the sensible coldness of the Monax I examined compared with the human body, altho' the vital heat of quadrupeds is said in general to be greater than that of man. This inferiority of heat being a characteristic of animals which become torpid from cold, I should consider it as deciding the quality of the Monax in this respect, were it not that the subject of my examination, tho' it remained alive several days in my hands, was so crippled and apparently dying the whole time that its actual heat could not fairly be taken for the degree of its natural heat. If it had recovered I intended to have made a trial with the Thermometer. I now propose to have if I can one of their habitations discovered during the summer, and to open it during some cold day next winter. This will fix the matter. There is another circumstance which belongs to a full comparison of the two animals. The marmotte of Europe is said to be an inhabitant of the upper region of mountains only. Whether our Monax be confined to mountainous situations or not I have not yet learnt. If it is not found as a permanent inhabitant of the level country, it certainly descends occasionally into the plains which are in the neighbourhood of mountains. I also compared a few days ago one of our moles (male) with the male one described in Buffon. It weighed 2 oz. 11 penwt. Its length from the end of its snout to the root of its tail was 5 inch. 3 lines English measure. That described in Buffon was not weighed I believe. Its length was 5 inch. french measure. The external and internal correspondence seemed to be too exact for distinct species. There was a difference nevertheless in two circumstances, one of which is not unworthy of notice, and the other of material consequence in the comparison. The first difference was in the tail, that of the mole here being 10½ English lines only in length, and naked, whereas that of Buffon's mole was 14 French lines in length and covered with hair. If the hair was included in the latter measure, the difference *in the length,* [26] ought scarcely to be noted. The second difference lay

26. JM's italics.

in the teeth. The mole in Buffon had 44. That which I examined had but 33. One of those on the left side of the upper Jaw, and next to the principal Cutters, was so small as to be scarcely visible to the natural eye, and had no visible corresponding tooth on the opposite side. Supposing this defect of a corresponding tooth to be accidental, a difference of 10 teeth still remains. If these circumstances should not be thought to invalidate the identity of species, the mole will stand as an exception to the Theory which supposes no animal to be common to the two Continents, which cannot bear the cold of the region where they join, since according to Buffon this species of mole is not found "dans les climats froids, ou la terre est gelée pendant la plus grande partie de l'annèe [in cold climates, where the ground is frozen for most of the year]," and it cannot be suspected of such a Journey during a short summer as would head the sea which separates the two Continents. I suspect that several of our quadrupeds which are not peculiar to the new Continent will be found to be exceptions to this Theory, if the mole should not. The Marmotte itself, is not an Animal taken notice of very far to the North and as it travels slowly, and is deprived of its locomotive powers altogether by cold, cannot be supposed to have travelled the road which leads from the old to the new world. It is perhaps questionable whether any of the dormant animals if any such be really common to Europe and America can have emigrated from one to the other. I have thought that the cuts of the Quadrupeds in Buffon, if arranged in frames, would make both an agreeable and instructive piece of wall furniture. What would be about the cost of them in such a form? I suppose they are not to be had, coloured to the life, and would besides be too costly. What is the price of Buffon's birds coloured?

Your letter of the 28. October has never come to hand.

## *Madison to Jefferson*

Orange June 19, 1786

DEAR SIR

Since my last which was of the 18th of May[27] I have received your very agreeable favor of the 28th. of Octobr. I began to fear it had miscarried. Your reflections on the idle poor of Europe, form a valuable lesson to the Legislators of every Country, and particularly of a new one. I hope you will enable yourself before you return to America to compare with this description of people in France the Condition of the indigent part of other communities in Europe where the like causes of wretchedness exist in a less degree. I have no doubt that the misery of the lower classes will be found to abate wherever the Government assumes a freer aspect, and the laws favor a subdivision of property. Yet I suspect that the difference will not fully account for the comparative comfort of the mass of people in the United States. Our limited population

27. JM's last letter was dated May 12, 1786.

has probably as large a share in producing this effect as the political advantages which distinguish us. A certain degree of misery seems inseparable from a high degree of populousness. If the lands in Europe which are now dedicated to the amusement of the idle rich were parcelled out among the idle poor, I readily conceive the happy revolution which would be experienced by a certain proportion of the latter. But still would there not remain a great proportion unrelieved? No problem in political Œconomy has appeared to me more puzzling than that which relates to the most proper distribution of the inhabitants of a Country fully peopled. Let the lands be shared among them ever so wisely, and let them be supplied with labourers ever so plentifully; as there must be a great surplus of subsistence, there will also remain a great surplus of inhabitants, a greater by far than will be employed in cloathing both themselves and those who feed them, and in administering to both, every other necessary and even comfort of life. What is to be done with this surplus? Hitherto we have seen them distributed into manufacturers of superfluities, idle proprietors of productive funds, domestics, soldiers, merchants, mariners, and a few other less numerous classes. All these classes notwithstanding have been found insufficient to absorb the redundant members of a populous society, and yet a reduction of most of those classes enters into the very reform which appears so necessary and desirable. From a more equal partition of property must result a greater simplicity of manners, consequently a less consumption of manufactured superfluities, and a less proportion of idle proprietors and domestics. From a juster government must result less need of soldiers either for defence against dangers from without, or disturbances from within. The number of merchants must be inconsiderable under any modification of Society; and that of Mariners will depend more on geographical position, than on the plan of legislation. But I forget that I am writing a letter not a dissertation.

Things have undergone little change here since my last. The scarcity of money, the low price of Tobacco and the high price of bread continue to be the topics of complaint. The last evil is likely to be much increased by a sudden vicisitude in the prospects of wheat. At the date of my last we were praying for rain. Shortly after we had a deluge of it. From the 19th. of May to the 4th. of June, we scarcely saw the sun, had almost incessant rains, and sometimes showers, or rather torrents that threatened to sweep away every thing. The planters pretty generally availed themselves of the Season for getting their Tobacco into the hills. But the farmers have nearly lost their crops of wheat. A great proportion of the heads in this part of the country are blasted, and in many parts it is said the fields will not be worth cutting. Our crops of apples also which in common with all other fruits seemed to be abundant, appear to have suffered much from the wet. We are now again suffering from the opposite extreme. We have had no rain since the cessation of the long spell, that is since the 3d. instant, and the earth is as dry and as hard as a brick.

In an answer from the attorney to a late letter, he says "that after great anxiety we have received the plan of the Capitol from Mr. J. and with some difficulty the directors have assented to conform the bricks already laid to that model."

I have a little itch to gain a smattering in Chymistry. Will you be kind eno' to pick up some good elementary treatise for me, with a good dictionary of moderate size, unless the Chymical volume in the Encyclopedie should be judged a competent provision. Morveau's Elements I observe are quoted with great respect by Buffon. I wish also to get his two Boxes, called Le Necessaire chemique. They are described in the Bibliotheque physico-Economique for 1784. p. 134. where the Maker in Paris is also referred to. I project this last indulgence on the supposition that the whole apparatus, including the contents of the Bottles will not cost more than a couple of Louis.

I observe that in your analysis of the Revisal p. 251. of your notes, a Bill is mentioned for consigning our roads to Undertakers instead of the present vicious plan of repairing them. No such provision is comprized in the Road bill reported and printed. If it be any where in existence, I wish you could put me on the means of getting a sight of it. I conceive such a reform to be essential and that the Legislature would adopt it, if presented in a well digested form.

I lately sent you some particulars relating to our Mole. In enumerating the distinctions between our Mole and the common one of Europe, I find I omitted the difference of colour. You know the colour of ours, which is pretty remote from black, tho' somewhat darkish.[28] For want of something better to fill the remainder of my paper, I will now add the result of my examination two days ago of another of our minor quadrupeds. I mean a Weasel. It was a female and came to my hands dead. Its colour corresponded with the description given by D'Aubenton of the Belette and Roselet or Hermine when in its summer dress, excepting only that the belly etc. which in the European animal was white, was in ours of a lightish yellow, save only the part under the lower jaws which was white for about ½ an inch back from the under lip. The little brown spots near the corners of the mouth mentioned by D'Aubenton, were peninsular. The tail was of the color of the back etc. all but the end which was black. The ears were extremely thin, had a fold or duplication on the lower part of the tongue about 2 lines deep, and at the margin all around were covered with a very fine short hair or fur of the colour nearly of the back. The rest of the ear was in a manner naked, and of a lightish color. The forefeet were tipped and spotted with white. The hind feet were also tipped with white, and one of them a little spotted. It had five toes on each foot, the fifth on each being very short and at some distance from the end of the foot. Its smell was a sort of rankish musk, but not so strong as to be very offensive. It had no visible teats. Its weight, dimensions etc. compared with those of Buffon's Belette and Hermine were as follows:

---

28. The two preceding sentences were added by JM as a marginal note for insertion here.

|  | Weasel oz. pwt. gns. | | | Belette oz. | | Hermine oz. pwt. | |
|---|---|---|---|---|---|---|---|
| Weight § | 7 | 17 | 13 | 2.* | | 7. | 10 |
|  | Inch | Lines | | Inch | Lines | Inch | Lines |
| Length from muzzle to root of tail |  | 7 | 9 | 6 | 6 | 9 | 6 |
| of the trunk of the tail |  | 3 | 6 | 1 | 3 | 3 | 10 |
| Height before |  | 1 | 11 | 1 | 5 | 2 | 8 |
| behind |  | 2 | 6 | 1 | 6 | 3 | 10 |
| Distance from muzzle to lower corner of the eye |  |  | 5 |  | 5 |  | 7 |
| from upper corner of eye to the ear |  |  | 4½ |  | 5 |  | 7 |
| from one corner to the other of the eye |  |  | 3 |  | 2¼ |  | 3½ |
| Length of the ear perpendicularly |  |  | 4½ |  | 3 |  | 4 |
| Width of the ear horizontally |  |  | 4 |  |  |  |  |
| Distance between the ears at bottom |  |  | 10½ |  | 9 |  | 1 |
| Length of the neck |  | 1 | 1½ |  | 11 | 1 | 4 |
| Circumference of neck |  | 2 | 5 | 2 |  | 2 | 6 |
| of body behind forelegs |  | 2 | 10 | 2 | 3 | 3 | 4 |
| before hindlegs |  | 3 | 3 | 2 | 2 | 3 | 4 |
| of head between eyes and ears |  | 2 | 9 | 2 | 6 | 3 | 3 |
| Length of foreleg from knee to heel |  |  | 10½ |  | 9 | 1 | 2 |
| from heel to the nails |  |  | 9 |  | 7 | 1 | 1 |
| of hind leg from knee to heel |  | 1 | 4 |  | 11 | 1 | 20 |
| Width of forefoot |  |  | 3½ |  | 3 |  | 3½ |
| of hindfoot |  |  | 3½ |  |  |  |  |
| Length of nails of forefoot |  |  | 2 |  | 2 |  | 3 |
| of hindfoot |  |  | 1½ |  |  |  |  |
| of hair of the body |  |  | 3½ |  | 3 |  | 6 |
| at end of tail |  |  | 6½ |  | short | 3 |  |
| Distance between anus and vulva |  |  | 3 |  | 1 |  |  |
| Spleen, length of |  | 1 | 3 |  | 11 |  |  |
| width of in middle |  |  | 3½ |  | 4 |  |  |
| Kidneys, long |  |  | 7½ |  | 5½ |  |  |
| wide |  |  | 4½ |  | 4 |  |  |
| thick |  |  | 3 |  | 3 |  |  |
| Heart, long |  |  | 6½ |  | 4 |  |  |
| round |  | 1 | 4½ | 1 | 3 |  |  |
| Tongue, long from end to the filêt |  |  | 3½ |  | 2½ |  |  |
| wide |  |  | 2¾ |  | 2 |  |  |
|  | | Number | | | no. | | no. |
| Teeth |  | | 34 | | 34 | | 34 |
| Ribbs |  | | 14 | | 14 | | 14 |
| Vertebrae of tail |  | | 14 | | 14 or 15 | | 19 |
| Palate, furrows of |  | | 6 | | 6 | | 6 |

§The weight and measure of the Weasel are English, those of the Belette and Roselet french.
*The belette of this weight was but 6 in. 5 lines in length.

The Gall bladder was empty. The membrane of the Bladder very thin, and the last two furrows of the palate broken in the middle. In the Weasel as noted in the Belette, and the contrary not noted in the Hermine.

The spleen was of the same color on both sides in the weasel. In the Hermine it was of a reddish brown as in the weasel, on one side, and of a very pale hue on the other. Nothing is said as to this circumstance in the description of the Belette.

The right Kidney in the weasel was advanced a little only before the left, as in the Belette, and not its whole length as in the Hermine.

The attempt to examine whether the number of false ribs in the weasel was 4 as in the Belette or 3 as in the Hermine, was frustrated.

On a review of the differential characters of the Belette and the Hermine, and a comparison of the weasel with both, it appears: 1. That the weasel stands between the two in point of size, but much less removed from the former than the latter, unless the individual here examined was much under the ordinary size. It having no visible teats seems to be an indication that it was young. Another *probable* indication was the smallness of the hindmost teeth both in the upper and lower Jaws, those in the lower being not bigger than the head of a small pin; and those in the upper disproportionate to the contiguous tooth. 2. That it resembles the Hermine in the length of the trunk of the tail, and in the blackness of its end. But the Belette in the number of vertebra in the Trunk, and in the shortness of the hair at the end of the tail. 3. That it resembles the Hermine in the colour of its feet, and the Belette in that of the margin of the ears. 4. That it resembles the Belette and not the Hermine in the Relative position of the Kidneys. 5. That it differs from the Hermine in being an inhabitant of warm climates. Whether it resembles the Belette in not being an inhabitant of cold climates remains for enquiry. 6. That it differs from both in never becoming white during the winter, if this change be well founded with regard to the Belette. Buffon asserts that there are instances of it, but it may be questioned whether they were not mere albinos of the species.

The figure of the head of the Weasel when reduced to the naked bone resembled rather that of the Beletta than that of the Hermine in the skeletons represented by Buffon. In its entire state it resembled most the head in the cut of the Hermine given by Buffon. Indeed the entire cut of the Hermine was a much stronger likeness of the Weasel than the cut of the Belette.

The result of the comparison seems to be that notwithstanding the blackness of the end of the tail and whiteness of the feet, which are regarded as characteristics of the Hermine contradistinguishing it from the belette, our weasel cannot be of the former species, and is nothing more than a variety of the latter. This conclusion is the stronger, as the manners of our weasel correspond more nearly with those of the Belette, than with those of the Hermine. And if it be a just conclusion, it may possibly make one exception to Buffons position that no animal is common to the two Continents that cannot bear the climate where they join; as it certainly contradicts his assertion that of the animals common to the two continents, those of the new are in every instance smaller than those of the old. But he seems to have given up this point himself. Supplemt. tom. 8. p. 329. "L'imperfection de nature qu'il [M.P. l'auteur des recherches sur les Americains] reproche gratuitement a l'Amerique en general ne doit porter que sur les animaux *de la partie meridionale* de ce continent lesquels etc."

My next will probably be dated in Philada. or rather in N. York to which I am called by some business of a private nature in which I am concerned jointly with Col. Monroe. In the meantime I remain Yrs. very affectionately,

Js. Madison Jr.

## Madison to Jefferson

Philadelphia Aug. 12, 1786

Dear Sir

My last of the 19th. of June intimated that my next would be from N. York or this place. I expected it would rather have been from the former which I left a few days ago, but my time was so taken up there with my friends and some business that I thought it best to postpone it till my return here. My ride through Virga. Maryd. and Pena. was in the midst of harvest. I found the crops of wheat in the upper parts of the two former considerably injured by the wet weather which my last described as so destructive in the lower parts of those States. The computed loss where I passed was about one third. The loss in the Rye was much greater. It was admitted however that the crops of both would have been unusually large but for this casualty. Throughout Pena. the wheat was unhurt, and the Rye very little affected. As I came by the way of Winchester and crossed the Potowmac at Harpers Ferry I had an opportunity of viewing the magnificent scene which nature here presents. I viewed it however under great disadvantages. The air was so thick that distant objects were not visible at all, and near ones not distinctly so. We ascended the mountain also at a wrong place, fatigued ourselves much in traversing it before we gained the right position, were threatened during the whole time with a thunder storm, and finally overtaken by it. Had the weather been favorable the prospect would have appeared to peculiar advantage, being enriched with the harvest in its full maturity, which filled every vale as far as the eye could reach. I had the additional pleasure here of seeing the progress of the works on the Potowmac. About 50 hands were employed at these falls or rather rapids, who seemed to have overcome the greatest difficulties. Their plan is to slope the fall by opening the bed of the river, in such a manner as to render a lock unnecessary, and by means of ropes fastened to the rocks, to pull up and ease down the boats where the current is most rapid. At the principal falls 150 hands I was told were at work, and that the length of the canal will be reduced to less than a mile, and carried through a vale which does not require it to be deep. Locks will here be unavoidable. The undertakers are very sanguine. Some of them, who are most so, talk of having the entire work finished in three years. I can give no particular account of the progress on James River, but am told it is very flattering. I am still less informed of what is doing with North Carolina towards a canal between her and our waters. The undertaking on the Susquehannah is said to be in such forwardness as to leave no doubt of its success. A negociation is set on foot between Pena. Maryd. and Delaware for a canal from the head of Chesapeak to the Delaware. Maryd. as I understand heretofore opposed the undertaking, and Pena. means now to make her consent to it a condition on which the opening of the Susquehannah within the limits of Pena. will depend. Unless this is permitted the opening undertaken within the limits of Maryland will be of little account. It is lucky that both parties are so dependent on each other as to be thus mutually forced into measures of general utility. I am told that Pena. has complied with the joint request of Virga. and Maryland for a Road between the head of Potowmac and the waters of the Ohio and the secure and free use of the latter through her jurisdiction. These fruits of the Revolution do great honour to it. I wish all our proceedings merited the same character. Unhappily there are but too many belonging to the opposite side of the account. At the head of these is to be put the general rage for paper money. Pena. and N. Carolina took the lead in this folly. In the former the sum emitted was not considerable, the funds for sinking it were good, and it was not made a legal tender. It issued into circulation partly by way of loan to individuals on landed security, partly by way of payment to the public creditors. Its present depreciation is about 10 or 12 per Ct. In N. Carolina the sums issued at different times has been of greater amount, and it has constantly been a tender. It issued partly in payments to military creditors, and latterly in purchases of Tobacco on public account. The Agent I am informed was authorized to give nearly the double of the current price, and as the paper was a tender, debtors ran to him with their Tobacco and the Creditors paid the expence of the farce. The depreciation is said to be 25 or 30 per Ct. in that State. S. Carolina was the next in order. Her emission was in the way of loans to individuals, and is not a legal tender. But land is there made a tender in case of suits, which shuts the courts of Justice, and is perhaps as great an evil. The friends of the emission say that it has not yet depreciated, but they admit that the price of commodities has risen, which is evidently the form in which depreciation will first shew itself. New Jersey has just issued £30,000 (dollar at 7/6). in loans to her Citizens. It is a legal tender. An addition of £100,000 is shortly to follow on the same principles. The terror of popular associations stifles as yet an overt discrimination between it and specie; but as this does not operate in Philada. and N. York where all the trade of N.J. is carried on, its depreciation has already commenced in those places and must soon communicate itself to N.J. New York is striking £200,000 (dollr. at 8s) on the plan of loans to her citizens. It is made a legal tender in case of suits only. As it is but just issuing from the press, its depreciation exists only in the foresight of those who reason without prejudice on the subject. In Rhode Island £100,000 (dolr. at 6s.) has lately been issued in loans to individuals. It is not only made a tender, but severe penalties annexed to the least attempt direct or indirect to give a preference to specie. Precautions dictated by distrust in the rulers, soon produced it in the people. Supplies were witheld from the Market, the Shops were shut, popular meetings ensued, and the State remains in a sort of convulsion. The Legislature of Massts. at their last session rejected a paper emission by a large majority. Connecticut and N. Hampshire also have as yet foreborne, but symptoms of the danger it is said begin to appear in the latter. The Senate of Maryd. has hitherto been a bar to paper in that State. The clamor for it is now universal, and as the periodical election of the Senate happens at this crisis, and the whole body is unluckily by their constitution to be chosen at once, it is probable that a paper emission will be the result. If in spite of the zeal exerted against the old Senate a majority of them should be reelected, it will require all their firmness to withstand the popular torrent. Of the affairs of Georga. I know as little as of those of Kamskatska. Whether Virga. is to remain exempt from the epidemic malady will depend on the ensuing assembly. My hopes rest chiefly on the exertions of Col. Mason, and the failure of the experiments elsewhere. That these must fail is morally certain; for besides the proofs of it already visible in some states, and the intrinsic defect of the paper in all, this fictitious money will rather feed than cure the spirit of extravagance which sends away the coin to pay the unfavorable balance, and will therefore soon be carried to market to buy up coin for that purpose. From that moment depreciation is inevitable. The value of money consists in the uses it will serve. Specie will serve all the uses of paper. Paper will not serve one of the essential uses of specie. The paper therefore will be less valuable than specie.

Among the numerous ills with which this practice is pregnant, one I find is that it is producing the same warfare and retaliation among the States as were produced by the State regulations of commerce. Massts. and Connecticut have passed laws enabling their Citizens who are debtors to Citizens of States having paper money, to pay their debts in the same manner as their Citizens who are Creditors to Citizens of the latter States are liable to be paid their debts.

The States which have appointed deputies to Annapolis are N. Hampshire, Massts., R. Island, N.Y., N.J., Pena., Delaware and Virga. Connecticut declined not from a dislike to the object, but the idea of a Convention, which it seems has been rendered obnoxious by some internal conventions which embarrassed the Legislative Authority. Maryd. or rather her Senate negatived an appointment because they supposed the measure might interfere with the plans or prerogatives of Congress. N. Carolina has had no Legislative meeting since the proposition was communicated. S. Carolina supposed she had sufficiently signified her concurrence in a general regulation of trade by vesting the power in Congress for 15 years. Georgia

Many Gentlemen both within and without Congress wish to make this meeting subservient to a plenipotentiary convention for amending the Confederation. Tho' my wishes are in favor of such an event, yet I despair so much of its accomplishment at the present crisis that I do not extend my views beyond a Commercial Reform. To speak the truth *I almost despair even of this.* [29] You will find the *cause in a measure* now before *Congress of which you will receive* the *details* from *Col. Monroe*. I content myself with *hinting* that it is a *proposed treaty with Spain,* [in][30] one *article of* which *she shuts the Mississippi for twenty five or thirty years*. Passing by the other *southern States, figure* to yourself the *effect of such a stipulation* on the *assembly of Virginia* already *jealous* of *northern policy* and which will be composed of about *thirty members from the western waters;* of a majority of others attached to the *western country from interests* of their *own, of their friends, or their constituents* and of many others who though indifferent to the *Mississippi will zealously* play off the *disgust of* its *friends against federal measures*. Figure to yourself its effect on the *people at large* on the *western waters* who are impatiently waiting for a *favorable result* to *negociation with Guardoqui* and who will consider themselves as *sold by* their *Atlantic brethren*. Will it be an unnatural consequence if they consider *themselves as absolved* from every *federal tie* and *court some protection* for their *betrayed rights?* This *protection* will appear more attainable from the *maritime power* of *Britain* than any from *any other quarter;* and *Britain* will be *more ready than any other nation* to *seize an opportunity of embroiling our affairs*. What may be the motive *with Spain to satisfy her self* with a *temporary occlusion* of the *Mississippi* at the same time that *she holds forth* our *claim to it as absolutely inadmissible is matter* of *conjecture only*. The *patrons* of the *measure in Congress* contend that the *Minister* who at present *governs* the *Spanish Councils* means only to *disembarrass himself at the expence* of *his successors*. I should rather suppose *he means to work a total* separation of *interest and affection between* the *western and eastern settlements* and to *foment* the jealousy *between the eastern and southern states*. By the former the *population of* the *western country* it may be expected will be *checked* and the *Mississippi so far secured;* and by both the general *security of Spanish America* be promoted. As far as I can learn the *assent of nine states* in *Congress* will not at this time be *got to the proposed treaty*. But an *unsuccessful attempt* by *six or seven* will *favor the views of Spain* and be *fatal I fear* to an *augmentation of* the *federal authority* if not to the *little now existing*. My personal situation is rendered by this business particularly *mortifying*. Ever since I have been *out of Congress I have been inculcating* on our *assembly a confidence* in the *equal attention of Congress* to the *rights and* interests of *every part of the republic* and on the *western members* in particular, the necessity of making the Union *respectable by new powers* to *Congress* if they wished *Congress to negociate with effect for the Mississippi*. I leave to Col. Monroe the giving you a particular account of the Im-

---

29. The italicized words in this sentence and in the rest of the letter were written in code.
30. JM omitted this word.

post. The Acts of Penna. Delaware and N. York must be revised and amended in material points before it can be put in force, and even then the fetters put on the collection by some other States will make it a very awkward business.

Your favor of 25th. of April from London found me here. My letter from Richmd. at the close of the Assembly will have informed you of the situation in which British debts stand in Virga. Unless Congress say something on the subject I do not think any thing will be done by the next Session. The expectations of the British Merchants coincide with the information I had received, as your opinion of the steps proper to be taken by the Assembly do with those for which I have ineffectually contended. The merits of Mr. P.[31] will ensure every attention from me to his claim as far as general principles will admit. I am afraid that these will insuperably bar his wishes. The Catalogues sent by Mr. Skipwith I do not expect to receive till I get back to Virga. If you meet with "Græcorum Respublicæ ab Ubbone Emmio descriptæ," Lugd. Batavorum, 1632, pray get it for me.

My trip to N.Y. was occasioned chiefly by a plan concerted between Col. Monroe and myself for a purchase of land on the Mohawk. Both of us have visited that district, and were equally charmed with it. The soil is perhaps scarcely inferior to that of Kentucky, it lies within the body of the Atlantic States, and at a safe distance from every frontier, it is contiguous to a branch of Hudson's River which is navigable with trifling portages which will be temporary, to tide-water, and is not more than ten, 15 or 20 miles from populous settlements where land sells at £8 and £10 per Acre. In talking of this Country sometime ago with *General Washington* he considered it in the same light with Monroe and myself, intimating that if he had money to spare and was disposed to deal in land, this is the very spot which his fancy had selected out of all the U.S. We have made a small purchase, and nothing *but the difficulty of raising a sufficient sum restrained us from making a large one.* In searching for the *means of overcoming this difficulty* one has occurred which we have agreed that *I should mention to you,* and which if *you should think as we do* is *recommended* by the prospect of *advantage to yourself as well as to us.* We mention it *freely because we trust* that *if it does* not *meet your sanction you will as freely tell us so.* It is that the *aid of your credit* in *your private capacity* be *used for borrowing* say *four or five thousand louis* more or less on the *obligation of Monroe* and myself with *your suretyship,* to be laid out by *Monroe and myself* for *our triple emolument;* an *interest* not *exceeding six per cent* to be *paid annually* and the *principal within a term* not less than *eight or ten years.* To guard against accidents a private *instrument* might be *executed among ourselves specifying* all necessary *covenants.* We have not taken the resolution of *submitting this plan without well examining* the expediency of *your becoming a party to it* as well as the *prospect of its succeeding.* There can certainly be *no impropriety in your* taking *just means of bettering your fortune.* Nor can *we discover any in your doing this on* the *Mohawk,* more than *on*

---

31. JM later wrote in "Paradise."

*James River.* For the prospect of *gain by the rise of* the *land beyond* the *interest of the money we calculate* on the present *difference of price* between the *settled and vacant land* far beyond any *possible* difference in the *real value.* The former as has been noted *sells for eight or ten pounds per acre.* The latter distinguished only by its being a little *higher up* the *river* and its being *uninhabited* was *bought by us for* one *dollar and a half* and there is little doubt that *by taking a larger* quantity, still *better bargains may be got.* This comparative *cheapness* proceeds from causes which are accidental and temporary. The *lands in question* are chiefly in the *hands of men who hold large quantities* and who are either *in debt* or *live in* the *city at an expence* for which *they have no other resource* or are *engaged in transactions* that *require money.* The scarcity of *specie which* enters *much into the cheapness* is probably but temporary also. As it is the *child of extravagance* it will become the *parent of economy* which will regain us our due share of the *universal medium.* The same vicisitude which can only be retarded by our *short lived substitutes of paper* will be attended also by such a *fall in the rate of exchange* that *money drawn by bills* from *Europe now* and *repaid a few years hence* will probably *save one years interest at least* and I will only add that scarce an instance has happened in which *purchases of new land of good quality* and *in good situations* have not *well rewarded the adventurers.* With these remarks which determine *our judgments, we submit to your better one* the *project to which they relate.* Wishing you every possible happiness I remain Dr. Sir your affectionate friend and Servt.,

Js. Madison Jr.

Mrs. House and Mrs. Trist desire to be particularly remembered to yourself and Miss Patsy. I left with Col. Monroe letters for you both from Mrs. T. which will probably go by the same packet with this.

*Madison to Jefferson*

Richmond Nov. 25, 1786

Dear Sir

The inclosed letter did not get to my hands till very lately though it was covered by one from Mrs. Carr dated Aug: 21. I conferred a few days ago with Mr. Wythe on the subject of your Nephew in Williamsburg, and had the pleasure of receiving the most favorable account of his capacity, his diligence and his disposition. He is now in the College and enjoys the advantage of Mr. Wythe's valuable patronage and instructions. Mr. Wythe assures me that he is an excellent Latin Scholar, and from the Greek classics which he has read and is reading, he must shortly merit the same character in the latter language. I have communicated to Mr. Wythe the plan of education which you wished t[o b]e pursued, and can count with perfect assurance on every attention on his part which the most zealous friendship to you and a particular affection to your

Nephew can inspire. The evidence in favor of your younger Nephew is of the negative kind only, no late information having been received concerning him. Mr. D. Fitzhugh is here a member of the Assembly. He has not yet put into my hands the small sum which I was authorized to receive.[32] He intimated to me a few days ago that he regretted the delay, and that he had a prospect of shortly putting an end to it. This letter goes by Mr. Chevalier who sets out tomorrow morning for N.Y. where he takes the packet on the 15th. prox. I do not include any public matters, because I expect to bring them down to a later period in a letter which will reach N.Y. in time for the same conveyance. Ad[ie]u.

       Js. Madison Jr.

32. TJ had lent money to Theodorick and Daniel McCarty Fitzhugh when they toured Europe in 1785; see *PTJ,* IX, pp. 25–27, 657–58; X, p. 605.

# 11

# MIRACLE IN PHILADELPHIA, 1787

LATE IN 1786, James Madison was reelected to the Confederation Congress, one of the few delegates to return under the rule that prohibited congressmen from serving more than three out of every six years. His first letter to Jefferson from New York did not give "any general view of American affairs" since "information of this sort must fall within your correspondence with the office of foreign affairs." But not much had changed during Madison's absence of three years. His revenue plan of 1783, which had called for an import duty, supplemental state funds appropriated for the use of Congress, and a proposal that population replace land values as the basis for allocating the nation's expenses, had not been ratified by the states. Congress, therefore, continued to rely on requisitions on the state legislatures, and the sporadic remittances never offset obligations. A Massachusetts delegate lamented that "there is not much pleasure in being a member of Congress, unless a man can bear duning very well."[1]

Nor had Congress made much progress in dealing with major matters of foreign policy. It could not compel Spain to open the Mississippi River to American navigation, nor could it persuade Great Britain or France to dismantle the discriminatory restrictions they had imposed on American commerce after the war.[2] Old markets in the West Indies were closed to Americans, and one of Jefferson's correspondents observed that Britain seemed "determined to pursue the same ruinous line of conduct that guided her through the late war" in her efforts to keep her former colonies in commercial bondage.[3] Finally, Congress was unable to force Great Britain to relinquish the military forts it held within America's Northwest Territory.[4] Indeed, an impoverished Congress could not maintain military forces capable of defending America's

---

1. Samuel Holten to Samuel Adams, Apr. 11, 1785, cited in Jack Rakove, *The Beginnings of National Politics: An Interpretive History of the Continental Congress* (Cambridge, Mass., 1979), p. 340.

2. Frederick W. Marks, *Independence on Trial: Foreign Affairs and the Making of the Constitution* (Baton Rouge, 1973), pp. 52-95.

3. John Langdon to TJ, Dec. 7, 1785, in *PTJ,* IX, p. 84.

4. Charles R. Ritcheson, *Aftermath of Revolution: British Policy toward the United States, 1783-1795* (Dallas, 1969), pp. 164-84.

frontiers. One delegate complained that the Board of Treasury had confessed "their utter inability to make [a] pitiful advance" of $1,000 to transport ammunition to military posts along the Ohio.[5]

After Madison's return to Congress, Jefferson shared with him his appraisal of public figures so that his friend could form "a just estimate" of them. He concentrated on diplomatic characters in the United States and France and stressed his view that "nothing should be spared on our part to attach this country to us. It is the only one on which we can rely for support under every event. It's inhabitants love us more I think than they do any other nation on earth. This is very much the effect of the good dispositions with which the French officers returned" from service in the American Revolution.[6]

Jefferson confessed that Madison's earlier criticism had shaken his favorable opinion of John Adams, convicting him of "a degree of *vanity*, and of a *blindness* to it, of which no germ *had appeared* in Congress," when Jefferson first knew him. After serving with Adams for seven months in France and visiting with the Adamses for seven weeks in London, however, he concluded that John Adams "*is vain, irritable and a bad calculator* of the force and probable effect of the motives which govern men." But that was "*all* the *ill* which can possibly be *said of him*. He is as disinterested as the being which made him: he is profound in his views: and accurate in his judgment *except where knowledge of the world* is necessary to form a judgment. He is so amiable, that I pronounce you will love him if ever you become acquainted with him."

Jefferson had shrewd and incisive comments on Lafayette: "a most valuable *auxiliary to me*"; Vergennes: "It is impossible to have a clearer, better *organised head* but *age* has *chilled his heart*"; Reyneval: "*he* is rather *cunning* than *wise*"; William Carmichael, American agent in Madrid: he "can do *more than* any other *person who* could be *sent there*," although "very little *known* in *America*"; William Bingham, wealthy merchant from Philadelphia, who was "not in *diplomatic office* yet . . . he wishes to be": "*He* will make *you believe he* was on the most intimate footing with the first *characters in Europe* and versed in the *secrets* of every *cabinet.* Not a word of this *is true*."[7]

In Congress, Madison quickly regained his position of leadership, concentrating his attention on the Mississippi question, violations of the peace treaty with Great Britain, the sale of western lands, the Northwest Ordinance of 1787, the final settlement of Revolutionary War accounts between the Union and the States, and the recruitment of troops to quell Shays's Rebellion.

Before he got caught up in the affairs of Congress, however, Madison gave his friend a final sketch of Virginia's legislative proceedings. The revised code, carried over from the previous session, had been "prosecuted pretty far towards its conclusion," consuming a great deal of time because its opponents contested "every innovation inch by inch." In fact, the bill for proportioning

---

5. Rufus King to Elbridge Gerry, June 18, 1786, cited in Rakove, p. 353.
6. TJ to JM, Jan. 30, 1787, below.
7. *Ibid.* The italicized words above were written in code.

capital crimes and punishments, a reform designed to ease the cruel and sanguinary penal laws of the past, was lost by a single vote because of "the rage against Horse stealers," Madison reported. "Our old bloody code is by this event fully restored."[8]

One of Jefferson's favorite proposals in the revised code—he called it the most important one in 1786—was the Bill for the More General Diffusion of Knowledge, designed to promote liberal education and "to illuminate, as far as practicable, the minds of the people at large."[9] "No other sure foundation," he told George Wythe, "can be devised for the preservation of freedom, and happiness."[10] "Above all things," he later wrote Madison, "I hope the education of the common people will be attended to; convinced that on their good sense we may rely with the most security for the preservation of a due degree of liberty."[11] Madison, of course, agreed, and so did most of the legislators, who admitted "the necessity of a systematic provision on the subject." But they were also parsimonious, complaining of the expense as well as the difficulty of establishing schools "in the present sparse settlement of the Country." So the bill languished without a third reading.

Instead, the education bill and the residual portions of the revised code not yet passed were turned over to a committee to prepare a supplemental revision of the laws to be presented later. For the portion of the code already adopted but not yet incorporated into law as a unified body of legislation, Madison and "the friends of the Revisal" hit upon a scheme to put the adopted bills out of the reach of a succeeding assembly—and of Patrick Henry, if he reentered it: they voted to implement the parts of the new code thus far enacted, without waiting for the completion of the unfinished portions.[12]

Late in life, Jefferson praised "the unwearied exertions of Mr. Madison" in getting the main body of the code adopted, despite "endless quibbles, chicaneries, perversions, vexations and delays of lawyers and demi-lawyers."[13] Although he never mentioned it to Madison, he also persuaded the editor of the *Encyclopédie méthodique* to praise Madison for his eloquence, his wisdom, and his genius.[14] However, Jefferson's secretary, William Short, called Madison's attention to his mention in "the Article *Etats-Unis* in the new Encyclopedia" and observed that "the *Philosophical legislation* of Virginia is in the mouths of all the learned of this place, and quoted by all the advocates of the *lumieres de*

---

8. JM to TJ, Dec. 4, 1786, below, and Feb. 15, 1787. The reform bill is printed in *PTJ*, II, pp. 492–507.

9. *Ibid.*, pp. 526–35.

10. TJ to George Wythe, Aug. 13, 1786, *ibid.*, X, p. 244.

11. TJ to JM, Dec. 20, 1787, below.

12. JM discussed the revised code in his letters to TJ of Dec. 4, 1786, below, and Feb. 15, 1787, below.

13. TJ, "Autobiography," in *Thomas Jefferson's Writings*, ed. Merrill D. Peterson (New York, 1984), p. 40.

14. The section of the *Encyclopédie* on "Economie politique et diplomatique," which includes the article on the United States, is cited in *PTJ*, X, p. 64. Also see Brant, II, pp. 56–57.

*la Philosophie.*" If Virginia had achieved "a degree of eclat and of honor of which it is difficult to form an idea," Short continued, "it is but just to mention it to you Sir, who have contributed so much by your exertions in the legislature, to the fame she has acquired in every part of Europe—even in England."[15]

Madison was only partially successful in his other efforts. He had to admit defeat on one of his favorite measures—the attempt to reform the state court system. Realizing that his proposal of assize courts was doomed, he substituted a plan for district courts that he thought, in December, would "probably though not certainly be adopted." Instead, "after a great struggle they were lost in the House of Delegates by a single voice."

But the legislature had faced up to the need to levy taxes for both state and federal purposes. Early in the session, Madison had written Jefferson that the state treasury was empty and that the state was delinquent in its federal contribution. But after learning of Shays's Rebellion, a taxpayers' revolt in western Massachusetts that seemed to Madison to threaten the tranquility of the Union,[16] the legislature defeated attempts to reduce taxes and instead levied new ones.[17]

Jefferson was impatient to learn Madison's views of Shays's Rebellion. Jefferson's first impression was that it did "not appear to threaten serious consequences." Whatever the provocation, however, he thought the rebellious acts "absolutely unjustifiable." Nevertheless, he hoped "they will provoke no severities from their governments." His view of the armed uprising of hard-pressed democratic farmers was colored by his reaction to the oppressions of monarchy—"it is a government of wolves over sheep," he observed. He, therefore, defended "a little rebellion now and then" in a republic; revolts were "as necessary in the political world as storms in the physical." "Honest republican governors" might, indeed, punish rebellions, but it should be so mild "as not to discourage them too much. It is a medicine," he argued, "necessary for the sound health of government."[18]

Madison had not received this letter when he took his seat in Congress in February 1787. By that time, Shays's Rebellion was "on the point of being extinguished," but he strongly supported congressional enlistment of troops until "the spirit of insurrection was subdued."[19] Viewing the rebellion from the perspective of the Confederation's effort to assist a "suffering member of

---

15. William Short to JM, May 12, 1787, in *PJM,* IX, pp. 411–13. For the influence of the *Encyclopédie,* see Robert Darnton, *The Business of Enlightenment: A Publishing History of the Encyclopédie* (Cambridge, Mass., 1979).

16. See JM's speech in Congress, Feb. 19, 1787, in *PJM,* IX, p. 278.

17. JM to TJ, Feb. 15, 1787, below.

18. TJ to JM, Jan. 30, 1787, below.

19. JM and the Virginia congressional delegation to Edmund Randolph, Feb. 12, 1787, in *PJM,* IX, p. 278. See John L. Brooke, "To the Quiet of the People: Revolutionary Settlements and Civil Unrest in Western Massachusetts," *WMQ* 46 (1989): 425–62.

the federal body," he argued that the action of "internal enemies" in Massachusetts constituted a threat to "the tranquility of the Union." And he cited the impact of the disturbance in Massachusetts on the Virginia legislature while he was a member only a month earlier, when "that very consideration inspired the ardor which voted towards their quota" to Congress in the form of a tax on tobacco. Such action, the veteran of Virginia politics stated with more passion than usual, "would not have been granted for scarce any other purpose whatever."[20]

Madison went even further in his letters to Jefferson, labeling the rebellion as treason. Although the insurgents had been disarmed and disfranchised for a limited time, he reported, a military corps "is to be raised to the amount of 1000, or 1500 men, and to be stationed in the most suspected districts," a true indication "of the temper of the Government." Even so, Madison was worried that the offenders remained insolent, wearing "badges of their character" and courting popular favor.[21] By the time he received Jefferson's views, "vigorous measures" had dispersed the rebels. But he still feared that they would adopt new tactics in an effort to "promote their views under the auspices of Constitutional forms," now that John Hancock had again been elected governor of Massachusetts. "His general character," Madison assured Jefferson, "forbids a suspicion of his patriotic principles; but as he is an idolator of popularity, it is to be feared that he may be seduced by this foible into dishonorable compliances."[22]

Jefferson dropped the subject of Shays's Rebellion in his correspondence with Madison, but he pursued it with his friends from Massachusetts, Abigail and John Adams, and William Stephens Smith, the Adamses' son-in-law. "I like a little rebellion now and then," he wrote to Mrs. Adams.[23] And later he told Smith that "the tree of liberty must be refreshed from time to time with the blood of patriots and tyrants. It is its natural manure."[24]

The disagreement between Madison and Jefferson over interpreting Shays's Rebellion had no influence on Madison's preparation for the Philadelphia convention, which he had essentially completed by the time he received Jefferson's views late in April.[25] But it did underscore their differing perspec-

20. See JM's speech in Congress, Feb. 19, 1787, in *PJM, IX,* p. 278.

21. JM to TJ, Mar. 19, 1787, below.

22. JM to TJ, Apr. 23, 1787, below. For Shays's Rebellion, see Van Beck Hall, *Politics without Parties: Massachusetts, 1780–1791* (Pittsburgh, 1972); Robert Feer, "Shays's Rebellion and the Constitution: A Study in Causation," *New England Quarterly* 42 (1969): 388–410; David P. Szatmary, *Shays' Rebellion: The Making of an Agrarian Insurrection* (Amherst, 1980); Richard D. Brown, "Shays's Rebellion and the Ratification of the Federal Constitution in Massachusetts," in *Beyond Confederation: Origins of the Constitution and American National Identity,* ed. Richard Beeman, Stephen Botein, and Edward C. Carter II (Chapel Hill, 1987), pp. 113–27; and Robert A. Gross, ed., *In Debt to Shays: The Bicentennial of an Agrarian Revolution* (Charlottesville, 1992).

23. TJ to Abigail Adams, Feb. 22, 1787, in Cappon, I, p. 173.

24. TJ to William Smith, Nov. 13, 1787, in *PTJ,* XII, p. 356.

25. JM acknowledged TJ's letter of Jan. 30 on Apr. 23, 1787, below.

tives on the persistent issues of liberty and power that had dominated the constitutional debates during the pre-Revolutionary, the Revolutionary, and the post-Revolutionary years. Both favored a stronger national government in 1787, but they differed in their views on the extent of the needed reform. Madison's was an insider's view throughout the critical period, but Jefferson's had become an outside view, shaped as much by European as by American fears. As early as 1785, Jefferson had anticipated "a new compact" to correct "the imperfect provisions" of the Articles of Confederation and, thus, to create a "more perfect" constitution.[26] After three years in France, however, he saw American problems from an international perspective. He grieved over the fact that "all respect for our government" under the Articles of Confederation "is annihilated on this side of the water, from an idea of its want of tone and energy." He, therefore, advocated new powers that would strengthen the Confederation so that it could command more respect abroad as well as at home. But, as he watched the early stages of the French Revolution unfold in Paris, where the king had not convened the representative Estates General since 1614, he feared power as a threat to liberty and concentrated almost solely on the shortcomings of the American government in the field of international affairs. "To make us one nation as to foreign concerns," he told Madison on the eve of the Constitutional Convention, "and keep us distinct in Domestic ones, gives the outline of the proper division of powers between the general and particular governments."[27]

Madison agreed on the need to make America one nation regarding its foreign concerns. But on the domestic scene, he thought that the division of powers between the federal and state governments needed reform as well. His was a double-barreled approach: the Confederation was too weak; the state governments were too strong. Instead of wanting to amend the Articles of Confederation, he wished to replace America's first constitution with a new one, creating a more powerful central government founded on the people, not on the states. In short, Madison viewed power granted by the people, if adequately checked and balanced, as a protector of liberty.[28]

Madison's careful preparation made him the leading theoretician as well as the foremost strategist of constitutional reform, the catalytic converter who transformed the earlier debates on the shortcomings of the Confederation into a discussion of the shortcomings of the republican experiment in America at both the state and federal levels.

His first position paper, "Notes on Ancient and Modern Confederacies," had been compiled in 1786 from the "literary cargo" shipped to him by Jefferson. Scribbled on small sheets of notepaper that would fit into his pocket, it was thirty-nine pages long and documented with almost 200 footnotes. In the

---

26. TJ to James Monroe, June 17, 1785, in *PTJ,* VIII, pp. 230–31.

27. See TJ to JM, Dec. 16, 1786, below.

28. See Jack N. Rakove, "From One Agenda to Another: The Condition of American Federalism, 1783–1787," in *The American Revolution: Its Character and Limits,* ed. Jack P. Greene (New York, 1987), pp. 80–103, for a brilliant summary of JM's role in this area.

spring of 1787, he prepared his second memorandum, "Vices of the Political System of the United States." Together, these essays have been labeled by a leading historian as "probably the most fruitful piece of scholarly research ever carried out by an American."[29] Despite the existence of thirteen separate state sovereignties and the Confederation government, Madison viewed America's political system as a single system and the problem of reform—at both the state and federal levels—as a single problem. He first listed the defects of the Confederation, especially its lack of sanctions, which effectively subordinated the central authority to the state sovereignties: failure of the states to meet the financial requisitions of the Confederation Congress; state encroachments on powers specifically delegated to the Confederation government; state trespasses on the rights of neighboring states; state violations of the treaties of the United States and of the law of nations; lack of concert among the states in matters of common interest, such as regulation of trade; and the absence of a guarantee to the states of their republican constitutions and laws against internal violence.

Although this indictment turned, for the most part, on the shortcomings of the Confederation, analyzing the proper relationship between the central authority and the states or among the several states, it was but a prelude to Madison's concluding section, which was an even stronger blast at the evils flowing from legislative sovereignty within the states individually. As early as 1785, he had lamented the lack of wisdom and steadiness in state legislation, "the grievance," he noted, "complained of in all our republics." By 1787, he listed additional grounds for complaint: the multiplicity of laws, "a nuisance of the most pestilent kind"; the mutability of laws, a clear mark of "vicious legislation"; and, finally, the injustice of some state legislation, which brought "into question the fundamental principle of republican government, that the majority who rule in such governments are the safest guardians both of public good and private rights."

This concentration of power in the state legislature, "drawing all power into its impetuous vortex," as Madison later phrased it in *The Federalist*, created a legislative sovereignty dominated by a simple majoritarianism that threatened individual liberty through "unjust violations of the rights and interests of the minority, or of individuals." "In developing the evils which viciated the political system of the United States," he wrote (with Shays's Rebellion clearly in mind), "it is proper to include those which are found within the States individually, as well as those which directly affect the States collectively, since the former class have an indirect influence on the general malady and must not be overlooked in forming a compleat remedy."[30]

Madison's ideas were incorporated in the Virginia Plan, which he

---

29. Douglass Adair, "James Madison, Philosopher and Father of the Constitution," in *The Lives of Eighteen from Princeton*, ed. Willard Thorp (Princeton, 1946), p. 150.

30. See the "Vices" essay in *PJM*, IX, pp. 348–58, at p. 353. For a recent review of the movement for the Constitution, see Richard B. Morris, *The Forging of the Union, 1781–1789* (New York, 1987).

sketched for Jefferson two months before the convention met in Philadelphia. "The mortal diseases of the existing constitution" were well known to Jefferson, he thought; and instead of summarizing them, he stressed his conclusion that they were so alarming they would bring "from the votaries of liberty every concession in favor of stable Government not infringing fundamental principles." His chief goal was to establish "a new system" and to lay its foundation "in such a ratification by the people themselves of the several States as will render it clearly paramount to their Legislative authorities." Second, substantial powers should be transferred from the states to the federal government, "such an augmentation . . . as will render it efficient without the intervention of the Legislatures." This change in the power of Congress would require a change in "the principle of Representation in the federal system," one based on population—on the people—not on the states. Third, in addition to "the positive power of regulating trade and sundry other matters," the "federal head" should be armed "with a negative *in all cases whatsoever* on the local legislatures." He was convinced that without this defensive power, "the Legislative sovereignties of the States" would transgress on expanded federal powers, no matter how "clearly their boundaries may be delineated." And, finally, the concept of separation of powers, which characterized most state constitutions, should be introduced at the federal level. "The limited powers now vested in Congress," he concluded, "are frequently mismanaged from the want of such a distribution of them. What would be the case, under an enlargement not only of the powers, but the number, of the federal Representatives?"[31]

By the time Jefferson replied—he had spent three months in the south of France, where he tried the healing effects of the mineral springs on his broken wrist[32]—he skipped over two of Madison's four points, endorsed one, and objected to the other. He liked "the idea of separating the executive business of the confederacy from Congress, as the judiciary is already in some degree," and he reviewed his earlier efforts in creating a Committee of the States to act in an executive capacity when Congress was not in session. But he did not comment on Madison's "new system" that proposed to transfer some significant powers from the states to the federal government and to eliminate the intervention of the state legislatures. Nor did he mention the proposed change in representation in Congress from the states to the people.

Instead, he pounced on the proposed federal negative, something he had not thought of before. "Primâ facie," he said bluntly, "I do not like it. It fails in an essential character, that the hole and the patch should be commensurate." Instead of mending a small hole, the proposed patch would cover the whole garment. As a substitute for such an inclusive negative, he suggested judicial review: "Would not an appeal from the state judicatures to a federal

31. JM to TJ, Mar. 19, 1787, below.
32. See Edward Dumbauld, *Thomas Jefferson, American Tourist* (Norman, Okla., 1946), pp. 83–109.

court, in all cases where the act of Confederation controuled the question, be as effectual a remedy, and exactly commensurate to the defect."[33]

The eager Madison was the first out-of-town delegate to get to Philadelphia for the convention, and he popped Jefferson a quick note, predicting "a pretty full meeting."[34] The failure of the convention to obtain a quorum on the scheduled opening date in May gave Madison and his colleagues in the Virginia delegation time to caucus and agree on the Virginia Plan, which set the framework for discussion of an extended republic at the Constitutional Convention. Once the deliberations began, he listed the delegates for his friend, who was impressed with the caliber of the representatives. "It is really an assembly of demigods," Jefferson told John Adams.[35] Madison also apologized for the rule of secrecy adopted by the convention, noting that it would prevent his sending "even a confidential communication of our proceedings." But he was sure that "the whole Community is big with expectation. And there can be no doubt," he added, "that the result will in some way or other have a powerful effect on our destiny."[36]

Jefferson was miffed about the rule of secrecy. "I am sorry they began their deliberations by so abominable a precedent as that of tying up the tongues of their members," he wrote John Adams. "Nothing can justify this example but the innocence of their intentions, and ignorance of the value of public discussions," he groused. But he had "no doubt that all their other measures will be good and wise."[37]

Madison set the agenda for the Constitutional Convention when Governor Edmund Randolph presented the Virginia Plan, which had been modeled by his colleague. Although the opening paragraph bowed towards the Articles of Confederation by saying that they "ought to be . . . corrected and enlarged," the plan called for a new and more powerful government founded on the people, not on the states, one chosen by them and that acted directly on them.[38] The "supreme national government" was to have a separate executive branch and a national judiciary. Madison's plan also called for a two-house national legislature, the first elected by the people and the other by the first, who would choose from candidates nominated by the state legislatures. It was to enjoy the legislative rights vested in Congress by the Confederation, and it

33. TJ to JM, June 20, 1787, below.
34. JM to TJ, May 15, 1787, below.
35. TJ to John Adams, Aug. 30, 1787, in Cappon, I, p. 196. For TJ's use of the term "demigods," see Douglass Adair, *Fame and the Founding Fathers: Essays by Douglass Adair,* ed. H. Trevor Colbourn (New York, 1974), p. 17.
36. JM to TJ, June 6, 1787, below.
37. TJ to John Adams, Aug. 30, 1787, in Cappon, I, p. 196.
38. Since Rhode Island, which was sometimes referred to during the Confederation period as Rogue's Island, did not send delegates to the Philadelphia convention, it was more than doubtful that an amended Confederation, which required unanimous ratification by the state legislatures, would have been adopted.

was also "to legislate in all cases to which the separate states are incompetent, or in which the harmony of the United States may be interrupted by the exercise of individual Legislation." Finally, the national legislature could "negative all laws passed by the several States, contravening in the opinion of the National Legislature the articles of Union; and to call forth the force of the Union against any member of the Union failing to fulfill its duty under the articles" of the Union.[39]

The Virginia Plan became the basis for the secret deliberations and debates of the Philadelphia convention. Madison's prominent role was quickly recognized by his colleagues. "What is very remarkable" about him, wrote a delegate from Georgia, is that "every person seems to acknowledge his greatness. He blends together the profound politician, with the Scholar. . . . From a spirit of industry and application which he possesses in a most eminent degree, he always comes forward the best informed Man in the Union." Nor was Madison's reputation confined to his colleagues in Congress and the Constitutional Convention. Louis Otto, the French chargé d'affaires, observed that Madison was "well educated, wise, temperate, gentle, studious; perhaps more profound than Mr. Hamilton, but less brilliant; the intimate friend of Mr. Jefferson and sincerely devoted to France. He entered Congress very young and seems to have concerned himself particularly with public affairs."[40]

Madison was also interested in preserving for posterity the fullest record of the proceedings of the Constitutional Convention. "I have taken lengthy notes of every thing that has passed," he informed Jefferson after almost two months of deliberations, "and mean to go on with the drudgery, if no indisposition obliges me to discontinue it."[41] Although he could not reveal any part of the proceedings, he had "little doubt that the people will be as ready to receive, as we shall be able to propose, a Government that will secure their liberties and happiness."[42]

As the convention drew to an end in September, Madison finally lifted the veil of secrecy enough to give Jefferson a glimpse of the Constitution that

---

39. See JM's Virginia Plan, May 29, 1787, in *PJM,* X, pp. 15-17. For differing approaches to the federal convention, see Clinton Rossiter, *1787: The Grand Convention* (New York, 1966; rpt. New York, 1987); Gordon S. Wood, *The Creation of the American Republic: 1776–1787* (Chapel Hill, 1969; rpt. New York, 1972); and Forrest McDonald, *Novus Ordo Seclorum: The Intellectual Origins of the Constitution* (Lawrence, Kans., 1985). For two provocative sets of essays stimulated by the bicentennial of the Constitution, see Richard Beeman, Stephen Botein, and Edward C. Carter II, eds., *Beyond Confederation: Origins of the Constitution and American National Identity* (Chapel Hill, 1987), and Leonard W. Levy and Dennis J. Mahoney, eds., *The Framing and Ratification of the Constitution* (New York, 1987), p. 39.

40. William Pierce of Georgia, "Character Sketches of Delegates to the Federal Convention," in *The Records of the Federal Convention of 1787,* ed. Max Farrand, 4 vols. (New Haven, 1911), III, pp. 94-95. For Otto's views, see Brant, III, p. 14.

41. Robert Rutland and his editorial colleagues on *The Papers of James Madison* observe that JM's "Notes on Debates have become a national treasure, an indispensable source for our knowledge of how the Constitution came into being"; see *PJM,* IX, p. xix.

42. JM to TJ, July 18, 1787, below.

would be submitted "to the *people of* the *states*" for ratification. A president would be clothed with executive power. The two-house legislature would include a House chosen by the people and a Senate elected by the state legislatures. There would be a separate judiciary establishment. The convention had not yet settled the manner of choosing the president nor the length of the term of office. But the House would be based on population and elected by the people of the states, and its members would serve two-year terms. The Senate would include two members from each state, and they would serve six-year terms. "The Legislative power," Madison added, "will *extend to taxation, trade* and sundry other general matters.... The States will be *restricted from paper money* and in a *few other instances*."[43]

Madison surmised that Jefferson might be surprised at the extent of the powers of the federal government. But Jefferson was more than surprised; he was momentarily stunned. He found "things in it which stagger all my dispositions," he confessed to John Adams, his fellow diplomat in London. He had expected only "three or four new articles to be added to the good, old, and venerable fabrick," the Articles of Confederation, "which should have been preserved even as a religious relique." Indeed, Jefferson suspected that the delegates to the Philadelphia convention had overreacted to Shays's Rebellion in Massachusetts and sent up "a kite to keep the hen yard in order."[44]

Although Jefferson at first thought that too much power had been granted the new government, Madison feared that not enough had been assigned. He especially regretted the failure of the convention to include his favorite scheme of a federal negative on state laws, a major disappointment that led him to predict privately that the plan would "neither effectually *answer* its *national object* nor prevent the local *mischiefs* which every where *excite disgusts* against the *state governments*."[45]

But once the Constitutional Convention adjourned on September 17, Madison shook off his pessimism, returned to Congress in New York, and began to plan the strategy for the ratification of the Constitution. There he discovered that his letters of July 18 and September 6, written while the convention was in secret session, had not yet been dispatched. Perhaps for that reason, but more especially because he was still smarting from the rejection of the national negative by the convention, he wrote Jefferson the longest and most important letter in their growing correspondence and included the two earlier letters, even though they were now old news. "I let them go forward nevertheless," he told his friend, ". . . as they will prevent a chasm on my part of our correspondence which I have so many motives to cherish by an exact punctuality."

Madison also enclosed a copy of the Constitution and, in his seventeen-

---

43. JM to TJ, Sept. 6, 1787, below. The italicized words were written in code.
44. TJ to John Adams, Nov. 13, 1787, in Cappon, I, p. 212, and Peterson, p. 359.
45. JM to TJ, Sept. 6, 1787, below. The italicized words were written in code.

page letter, outlined a brief history of the convention, presented a perceptive analysis of the Constitution, and sketched a brilliant theory of republican politics in an extended republic. His extraordinary letter took the good-news/bad-news form, first tracing the remarkable "degree of concord which ultimately prevailed," making the agreement on the Constitution nothing "less than a miracle."[46] But most of the letter is an "immoderate digression" on his keen dissatisfaction with the omission in the Constitution of his protective device of a national negative on state laws.

On the plus side, the convention had discarded the confederation of sovereign states and replaced it with a union based directly on the people, extending to the general government the representative principle that was common to all the states, thus meeting the criticism of "the want of ratification by the people of the articles of Confederation."[47] This new Union was designed "1. to unite a proper energy in the Executive and a proper stability in the Legislative departments, with the essential characters of Republican Government. 2. To draw a line of demarkation which would give to the General Government every power requisite for general purposes, and leave to the States every power which might be most beneficially administered by them. 3. To provide for the different interests of different parts of the Union. 4. To adjust the clashing pretensions of the large and small States."

The second object, the due division of power between the general government and the state governments, "was perhaps of all, the most nice and difficult" problem, and the convention had achieved only a partial reform. There were constitutional restraints on the states: they could not coin money, issue paper currency, or violate contracts. But Madison thought that as valuable as these were, they fell "short of the mark." A national negative, he continued to insist, would have made it possible "1. to prevent encroachments on the General authority, 2. to prevent instability and injustice in the legislation of the States."

On the first point, he argued that "such a check in the whole over the parts" would give either "compleat supremacy" or "a controuling power" by which the general authority could be defended from encroachments by "the subordinate authorities, and by which the latter may be restrained from encroachments on each other." He concluded that the Constitution without the negative had substituted "a feudal system of republics" for "a Confederacy of independent States." His melancholy review of feudal constitutions had convinced him that in all of them there was "a continual struggle between the head and the inferior members," a contest that usually ended in the dominance of

---

46. JM to TJ, Oct. 24, 1787, below. See the important article by John Agresto, "'A System without a Precedent': James Madison and the Revolution in Republican Liberty," *South Atlantic Quarterly* 82 (1983): 129–44.

47. JM had singled out this basic shortcoming of the Confederation in his paper "Vices of the Political System of the United States"; see *PJM*, IX, p. 352. See Robert A. Rutland's editorial note to JM's "Vices" essay, *ibid.*, p. 346, and Gordon S. Wood, "Interests and Disinterestedness in the Making of the Constitution," in *Beyond Confederation*, pp. 69–109.

the latter. In terms of America's experience under the Confederation, he predicted that the dangers of encroachment under the new Constitution were more to be feared from the states than from the general government. Jefferson had suggested that judicial review would keep the states within their proper limits, but Madison would have preferred an early national veto to a later judicial review. It was more preferable "to prevent the passage of a law," he argued, "than to declare it void after it is passed."

On his second point, Madison emphasized that a constitutional negative would remedy "instability and injustice in the legislation of the States." His chief concern here was the federal protection of individual rights. The mutability and injustice of state laws, he told Jefferson, were "so frequent and so flagrant as to alarm the most stedfast friends of Republicanism," who sought "to secure individuals against encroachments on their rights."

In Madison's considered judgment, "the evils issuing from these sources contributed more to that uneasiness which produced the Convention, and prepared the public mind for a general reform, than those which accrued to our national character and interest from the inadequacy of the Confederation to its immediate objects." During his recent service in the Virginia assembly, where majoritarian democracy often threatened minority or individual rights, he had become increasingly critical of the "vicious" character of state legislation, one of "the evils which viciate the political system of the U. S."[48]

Even though the central problem of the Confederation period had been the central government, the reformation of the political system of the United States came not so much from efforts to bolster the central government from above by adding new powers; instead, it came from creeping criticism of state sovereignty from below, from growing denials at the grass-roots level within the states that legislative sovereignty was the same thing as popular sovereignty—that is, denials that the representatives in the state legislatures were the sole or adequate spokesmen for the represented. In short, the attack on state sovereignty was an inside job—one done inside the states. And Madison, one of the leading attackers, spoke from his personal experiences as a member of the Virginia assembly.

The legislatures were not sovereign; the people were. By the exercise of the principle of representation, the people could delegate their authority to expand governmental power and, at the same time, protect individual liberty by reserving individual rights beyond the reach of even a legislative majority. However, Madison's ultimate defense, had it been adopted by the convention, was the national negative on state laws. Without it, the constitutional reform was only a "partial provision"; it was, moreover, "materially defective" since it did not give the general government the ultimate defense for individual liberties.

Even without this ultimate defense, however, individual rights would be

---

48. JM to TJ, Oct. 24, 1787, below; JM, "Vices of the Political System of the United States," pp. 353–54. For JM's growing criticism of state legislation, see JM to TJ, July 3, 1784, above, Jan. 9, 1785, above, Jan. 22, 1786, above, Dec. 4, 1786, below, and Feb. 15, 1787, below.

more secure under the new general government than they were under the state governments—including Virginia's, which contained America's first Declaration of Rights. Why, Madison asked rhetorically, would this be so since both the states and the United States under the new Constitution were founded on the republican principle of majority rule and "are distinguished rather by the extent within which they will operate, than by any material difference in their structure?" He replied with his first extensive exposition to anyone outside the convention of his theory of an extended republic, a brilliant analysis of "the true principles of Republican Government," which would appear a month later, in elaborated form, as *The Federalist* Number 10, the most famous of *The Federalist* papers. Drawing on his observations of legislative abuses throughout the nation and on his frustrating years in the Virginia assembly, which he had summarized in "Vices of the Political System of the United States," he set his firsthand experience in the context of his study of the history of confederacies based on bundles of books shipped by Jefferson, particularly on his reading of David Hume's "Idea of a Perfect Commonwealth."[49]

Conventional political theory from Aristotle to Montesquieu had contended that republics could operate only in small geographical areas. Madison turned the traditional theory upside down. The chief advantage of a large republic over a small one, he argued, was the fact that it encompassed a greater number of interests, groups, parties, and factions scattered over a more extensive geographical sphere of government so that "no common interest or passion will be likely to unite a majority of the whole number in an unjust pursuit" such as encroachment on individual liberties or private rights. "In a large Society," he told Jefferson, "the people are broken into so many interests and parties, that a common sentiment is less likely to be felt, and the requisite concert less likely to be formed, by a majority of the whole." He concluded by arguing that divide and conquer, "the reprobated axiom of tyranny, is under certain qualifications, the only policy, by which a republic can be administered on just principles."

Liberty and justice, Madison believed, were the true ends of republican government, and he thought that "the same security seems requisite for the civil as for the religious rights of individuals." These were basic rights that no government could rightfully disregard. "The great desideratum in Government," he concluded, "is, so to modify the sovereignty as that it may be sufficiently neutral between different parts of the Society to controul one part from invading the rights of another, and at the same time sufficiently controuled itself, from setting up an interest adverse to that of the entire Society. . . . In the extended Republic of the United States, the General Government

---

49. JM to TJ, Oct. 24, 1787, below. See the significant articles by Douglass Adair, " 'That Politics May be Reduced to a Science': David Hume, James Madison, and the Tenth Federalist" and "The Tenth Federalist Revisited," in *Fame and the Founding Fathers,* pp. 3–26, 93–108. For a carefully argued revisionist analysis, see Edmund S. Morgan, "Safety in Numbers: Madison, Hume, and the Tenth *Federalist,*" *Huntington Library Quarterly* 49 (1986): 95–112.

would hold a pretty even balance between the parties of particular States, and be at the same time sufficiently restrained by its dependence on the community, from betraying its general interests."[50]

In his "immoderate digression," Madison linked the national negative to his theory of the extended republic, suggesting that the rejection of the former made the Constitution only a partial reform. His private letter to Jefferson marked his most pessimistic appraisal of the work of the Philadelphia convention.[51] But his momentary disappointment should not obscure the distinctive contribution that he made at the convention. Although his was not a magnetic personality, he had long ago lost his shyness in political discussions. Never a forceful speaker, he was a logical thinker who had analyzed the basic principles of republican government, steeped himself in the history of confederations, prepared himself more thoroughly than any other delegate for debate, and outlined the framework for discussion of a federal government that resulted in agreement on an extended republic.

Despite his doctrinaire and rear-guard defense of the federal negative, he clearly preferred the Constitution to the Confederation, which he feared might not "be kept alive . . . until the new one may take its place." Like Benjamin Franklin, who supported the Constitution "because I expect no better, and because I am not sure, that it is not the best,"[52] Madison quickly embraced the Constitution designed to create a more perfect Union. Three weeks after mailing his letter to Jefferson, he published his first *Federalist* paper, Number 10, which omitted any mention of the national negative and concentrated instead on demonstrating how an enlarged federal republic would "secure the public good, and private rights against the danger" of unjust factions "and at the same time . . . preserve the spirit and form of popular government." The Constitution, he proclaimed, provided "a republican remedy for the diseases most incident to republican government."[53]

In his reply, Jefferson understandably ignored Madison's digression on the national negative since he had already blasted it because the proposed patch did not match the hole. But he also ignored Madison's brilliant and perceptive theory of an extended republic that utilized governmental power as

50. JM to TJ, Oct. 24, 1787, below. See Lance Banning, "The Practicable Sphere of a Republic: James Madison, the Constitutional Convention, and the Emergence of Revolutionary Federalism," in *Beyond Confederation*, pp. 162-87.

51. Charles Hobson's "The Negative on State Laws: James Madison, the Constitution, and the Crisis of Republican Government," *WMQ* 36 (1979): 215-35, is the most thorough treatment of JM's dissatisfaction, but it presses too hard the argument that it demonstrates his consolidationist desires. See Banning, pp. 169-71, 184, and Michael P. Zuckert, "Federalism and the Founding: Toward a Reinterpretation of the Constitutional Convention," *Review of Politics* 48 (1986): 166-210.

52. *Records of the Federal Convention,* Sept. 17, 1787, II, p. 643.

53. *PJM,* X, pp. 263-70. For a brilliant analysis of "Madison's cogency, penetration, knowledge, and range," see the enlarged edition of Bernard Bailyn, *The Ideological Origins of the American Revolution* (Cambridge, Mass., 1992), pp. 321-79, esp. 366-78.

a defense of liberty, perhaps because he was still wedded to the traditional view that republics could only operate in small geographical areas.[54] Skipping over Madison's penetrating analysis, he concentrated instead on what he liked and disliked about the proposed Constitution:

> I like much the general idea of framing a government which should go on of itself peaceably, without needing continual recurrence to the state legislatures. I like the organization of the government into Legislative, Judiciary and Executive. I like the power given the Legislature to levy taxes; and for that reason solely approve of the greater house being chosen by the people directly. For tho' I think a house chosen by them will be very illy qualified to legislate for the Union, for foreign nations etc. yet this evil does not weigh against the good of preserving inviolate the fundamental principle that the people are not to be taxed but by representatives chosen immediately by themselves. I am captivated by the compromise of the opposite claims of the great and little states, of the latter to equal, and the former to proportional influence. I am much pleased too with the substitution of the method of voting by persons, instead of that of voting by states: and I like the negative given to the Executive with a third of either house, though I should have liked it better had the Judiciary been associated for that purpose, or invested with a similar and separate power. There are other good things of less moment.

In sharp contrast to Madison's tough-minded analysis of the nature of liberty and politics, Jefferson responded as a high-minded citizen of the Enlightenment, basing his objections on European standards of conventional wisdom and liberal political theory and stating them bluntly: "I will now add what I do not like." First, the Constitution had no bill of rights, and, second, it abandoned the principle of rotation in office, especially in the case of the president, who "will always be re-elected if the constitution permits it. He is then an officer for life"—in effect an elected monarch.[55] Thinking in traditional Whig terms, he viewed power as a threat to liberty. He seemed puzzled by the dilemma created by the obvious need to strengthen the central government and the threat that new powers might pose for the liberties of the people. He readily conceded the need for "a great addition to the energy" of the national government. But he also confessed, "I am not a friend to a very energetic government. It is always oppressive. The late rebellion in Massachusetts," he continued, recurring to one of his favorite doctrinaire themes, "has

---

54. When the Confederation Congress replaced with fewer and larger states the fourteen small states that TJ had proposed in his western Land Ordinance of 1784, he deplored the move as "reversing the natural order of things. A tractable people may be governed in large bodies," he wrote JM, "but in proportion as they depart from this character, the extent of their government must be less. We see into what small divisions the Indians are obliged to reduce their societies"; see TJ to JM, Dec. 16, 1786, below.

55. TJ to JM, Dec. 20, 1787, below. For a brief discussion of the contrast between TJ's "liberal conventionality" and JM's perceptive analysis, see Bernard Bailyn, "Boyd's Jefferson: Notes for a Sketch," *New England Quarterly* 33 (1960): 388–89, which has been reprinted in his *Faces of Revolution: Personalities and Themes in the Struggle for American Independence* (New York, 1990), pp. 22–41.

given more alarm than I think it should have done. Calculate that one rebellion in 13 states in the course of 11 years, is but one for each state in a century and a half. No country should be so long without one. Nor will any degree of power in the hands of government prevent insurrections." Citing upheavals in France, Turkey, and England, he contrasted "the ferocious depredations of their insurgents with the order, the moderation and the almost self extinguishment of ours."

To guard against oppressive government, Jefferson insisted on additional protection for the liberties of the people. "A bill of rights," he contended, "is what the people are entitled to against every government on earth, general or particular, and what no just government should refuse, or rest on inference." Such a charter should provide "clearly and without the aid of sophisms for freedom of religion, freedom of the press, protection against standing armies, restriction against monopolies, the eternal and unremitting force of the habeas corpus laws, and trials by jury in all matters of fact triable by the laws of the land and not by the law of Nations."

Jefferson knew that Madison had already formed his own judgment on these points. From his distant post in Paris, he could not "pretend to decide what would be the best method of procuring the establishment of the manifold good things in this constitution, and of getting rid of the bad." He was pleased that the Constitution would be "duly weighed and canvassed by the people," since "it is my principle that the will of the Majority should always prevail. If they approve the proposed Convention," he concluded, "I shall concur in it chearfully, in hopes that they will amend it whenever they shall find it work wrong."[56]

As the year of the convention ended, Madison was not sure that the Confederation could last until the new government replaced it. "The Treasury Board," he wrote his friend in France, "seem to be in despair of maintaining the shadow of Government much longer. Without money, the offices must be shut up, and the handful of troops on the frontier disbanded, which will probably bring on an Indian war, and make an impression to our disadvantage on the British Garrisons within our limits." But he was happy to report that two states had ratified the Constitution: Delaware unanimously and Pennsylvania by a 2-to-1 margin.[57]

While Jefferson learned of constitutional developments in America from Madison, he kept his friend informed about political and constitutional issues in France. Following the death of Vergennes, who had guided Franco-American relations for a decade as foreign minister, the comte de Montmorin came into office in 1787. Jefferson thought that "the late changes in the ministry here excite considerable hopes. . . . *I am pleased* with *Montmorin. His* honesty

---

56. TJ to JM, Dec. 20, 1787, below.
57. JM to TJ, Dec. 20, 1787, below.

proceeds from *the heart* as well as *the head and therefore may be more surely counted on.*[58] But he worried that France was "on the eve of a *bankruptcy*,"[59] writing Jay that "this deficiency of the public revenues" made it evident that "some of the wheels of government must stop, unless they can be relieved."[60]

To win support for new taxes, the king called an Assembly of Notables, reviving a long-defunct institution that had not met for 160 years, and his chief minister offered a detailed program designed to save the French monarchy by reforming it. He proposed to introduce an unprecedented land tax proportional to income and payable by persons of all classes, without privileged exemption or exception, a harsh blow to the privileged classes. His second proposal called for the establishment of new representative provincial assemblies to be elected by all landowners, regardless of rank in the three ancient orders—the separate and distinct estates of the clergy, the nobility, and the commoners—a leveling device sure to arouse opposition.

These proposals, which struck at both privilege and aristocracy, won Jefferson's instant support. In letters to Madison and to Jay, which Madison often read in the Foreign Office of the Confederation, Jefferson praised the proposal for popularly elected provincial assemblies as "a fundamental improvement." "Chosen by the people, they will soften the execution of hard laws: and, having a representation to the King, they will censure bad laws, suggest good ones, expose abuses. . . . The hope is that the improvements thus promised" will be maintained "long enough for them to take some root in the constitution."[61] "The nation was in a delirium of joy on the convocation of the Notables," Jefferson wrote, "and on the various reformations agreed on between them and the government."[62]

Even after the ministry reneged on popularly elected provincial assemblies and substituted appointive bodies dominated by the privileged orders, Jefferson viewed the aristocratic revolt against royal absolutism as a defense of political liberty. During the summer of 1787, he informed John Adams "that in the course of three months, the royal authority has lost, and the rights of the nation gained, as much ground, by a revolution of public opinion only, as England gained in all her civil wars under the Stuarts."[63]

Insisting on the principle of consent to taxation, the Parlement of Paris, he informed Madison, "refuse to register any act for a new tax, and require an assembly of the states"—the Estates General, which had not met since 1614. "The object of this assembly is evidently to give law to the king, to fix a

---

58. TJ to JM, June 20, 1787, below. The italicized words here and in the next sentence were written in code.
59. TJ to JM, Aug. 2, 1787, below.
60. TJ to John Jay, June 21, 1787, *ibid.,* pp. 489-90.
61. *Ibid.*
62. TJ to John Jay, Aug. 6, 1787, *ibid.,* p. 697.
63. TJ to John Adams, Aug. 30, 1787, *ibid.,* XII, p. 68.

constitution, to limit expences." Jefferson was not sure that all this could be done peaceably. "An *explosion* of some sort is not impossible," he told Madison. "The *ministry* is alarmed, and the surest reliance at this moment for the *public peace* is on their *two hundred thousand men*" in the army.⁶⁴

The Parlement won the support of the populace for its stand on taxation. On one occasion, Jefferson told Madison, 10,000 people surrounded the parliament house and, on adjournment, greeted the members "with acclamations of joy, took out the horses of the principal speakers and drew their chariots themselves to their hotels." Instead of using troops against the mob, the king exiled the Parlement to Troyes for fear of further demonstrations or "popular commotion."⁶⁵

In the discussion of the French national debt by the Assembly of Notables, Jefferson informed Madison, "our credit here has been ill treated here in public debate, and our *debt* deemed *apocryphal*. We should try to transfer this *debt* elsewhere, and leave nothing capable of exciting ill thoughts between us."⁶⁶ Approximately two-thirds of the foreign debt of the United States had been loaned by the French Crown during the Revolution, and the remainder had been borrowed by John Adams from Dutch bankers on a French guarantee. Adams had also floated additional loans in Holland to pay the interest on old loans and to cover the cost of embassies and diplomacy in Europe, with the United States living from hand to mouth on borrowed money.⁶⁷ Indeed, when the United States defaulted in 1786 on an interest payment due the Dutch, France had assumed payment to 1790.⁶⁸

Jefferson, therefore, suggested that Adams again take the lead in efforts to shift the debt from France to Dutch investors. When Jefferson learned that Charles W. F. Dumas, a Frenchman resident in the Dutch republic who served as a diplomatic correspondent of Congress, had recommended "himself and *me* for the *money negociations in Holland*," Jefferson denied that any such idea had entered his head. "On the contrary it is a *business* which would be the most *disagreeable to me* of all others." The expert was John Adams, who "stands already on ground for that business which *I* could not gain in years."⁶⁹

Jefferson was particularly concerned about payment of congressional pledges to French officers who had fought in the Revolution. "These gentlemen have connections both in and out of office," he reminded Madison, "and these again their connections, so that our default on this article is further known, more blamed, and excites worse dispositions against us than you can

64. TJ to JM, Aug. 2, 1787, below. The italicized words were written in code.
65. TJ to JM, Aug. 15, 1787, below.
66. TJ to JM, June 20, 1787, below. The italicized words were written in code.
67. For Adams's role in the complicated loan negotiations, see Pieter J. Van Winter, *American Finance and Dutch Investment, 1780–1805,* 2 vols. (New York, 1977), I, pp. 82–133.
68. *PTJ,* XIV, p. 195.
69. TJ to JM, June 20, 1787, below. The italicized words were written in code.

conceive. If you think as I do, pray try to procure an order for paying off their capital," both principal and interest. He hoped that this debt could be transferred to Holland also. In fact, he agreed with Adams that if Congress would lay "any certain tax . . . for the paiment of interest, Congress may borrow enough in Holland to pay off their whole debts in France both public and private, to the crown, to the farmers and to Beaumarchais."[70]

Jefferson also viewed the sale of western lands as a "precious fund for the immediate extinction of our debt."[71] He was pleased when Madison told him that they were selling well. He hoped that "they will absorb all the Certificates of our Domestic debt speedily in the first place, and that then offered for cash they will do the same by our foreign one."[72]

——————————— THE LETTERS ———————————

### Madison to Jefferson

Richmond Dec. 4, 1786

DEAR SIR

Your last favor which was of the 25th. of April has already been acknowledged. My last inclosing a letter from Mrs. Carr, was dated a few days ago only. It was put into the hands of Monr. Chevalier who has gone on to N. York, whither I shall forward this to his care. He is to embark in the packet which will sail on the 15th. inst:

The recommendation from the Meeting at Annapolis of a plenipotentiary Convention in Philada. in May next has been well received by the Assembly here. Indeed the evidence of dangerous defects in the Confederation has at length proselyted the most obstinate adversaries to a reform. The unanimous sanction given by the Assembly to the inclosed compliance with the Recommendation marks sufficiently the revolution of sentiment which the experience of one year has effected in this country.[1] The deputies are not yet appointed. It is expected that Genl. Washington, the present Govr. E. Randolph Esqr. and the late one Mr. Henry will be of the number.

The project for bartering the Mississipi to Spain was brought before the Assembly after the preceding measure had been adopted. The report of it having reached the ears of the Western Representatives, as many of them as

---

70. TJ to JM, Aug. 2, 1787, below. For John Adams's letter to TJ of July 10, 1787, see Cappon, I, p. 187.

71. TJ to JM, June 20, 1787, below.

72. TJ to JM, Dec. 20, 1787, below.

1. The enclosure was a newspaper report on the Virginia legislature's unanimous recommendation that delegates be appointed to the Philadelphia convention of 1787; see *PTJ,* X, p. 578, and *PJM,* IX, p. 192.

were on the spot, backed by a number of the late officers, presented a Memorial, full of consternation and complaint, in consequence of which some very pointed resolutions by way of instruction to the Delegates in Congress were *unanimously* entered into by the House of Delegates. They are now before the Senate who will no doubt be also unanimous in their Concurrence.

The question of paper money was among the first with which the Session opened. It was introduced by petitions from two Counties. The discussion was faintly supported by a few obscure patrons of the measure, and on the vote it was thrown out by 85.vs.17. A petition for paying off the public securities according to a scale of their current prices, was *unanimously* rejected.

The Consideration of the Revised Code has been resumed and prosecuted pretty far towards its conclusion. I find however that it will be impossible as well as unsafe to give an ultimate fiat to the System at this Session. The expedient I have in view is to provide for a supplemental revision by a Committee who shall accomodate the bills skipped over, and the subsequent laws, to such part of the Code as has been adopted, suspending the operation of the latter for one year longer. Such a work is rendered indispensible by the al[te]rations made in some of the bills in their passage, by the change of circumstances which call for corresponding changes in sundry bills which have been laid by, and by the incoherence between the whole code and the laws in force of posterior date to the Code. This business has consumed a great deal of the time of two Sessions, and has given infinite trouble to some of us. We have never been without opponents who contest at least every innovation inch by inch. The bill proportioning crimes and punishments, on which we were wrecked last year, has after undergoing a number of alterations got thro' a Committee of the Whole; but it has not yet been reported to the House, where it will meet with the most vigorous attack. I think the chance is rather against its final passage in that branch of the Assembly, and if it should not miscarry there, it will have another guantlet to run through the Senate. The bill on the subject of Education, which could not safely be brought into discussion at all last year, has undergone a pretty indulgent consideration this. In order to obviate the objection from the inability of the County to bear the expence, it was proposed that it should be passed into a law, but its operation suspended for three or four years. Even in this form however there would be hazard in pushing it to a final question, and I begin to think it will be best to let it lie over for the supplemental Revisors, who may perhaps be able to put it into some shape that will lessen the objection of expence. I should have no hesitation at this policy if I saw a chance of getting a Committee equal to the work of compleating the Revision. Mr. Pendleton is too far gone to take any part in it. Mr. Wythe I suppose will not decline any duty which may be imposed on him, but it seems almost cruel to tax his patriotic zeal any farther. Mr. Blair is the only remaining character in which full confidence could be placed.

The delay in the administration of Justice from the accumulation of business in the General Court and despair of obtaining a reform according to the Assize plan have led me to give up this plan in favor of district Courts; which differ from the former in being cloathed with all the powers of the General Court within their respective districts. The bill on the latter plan will be reported in a few days and will probably tho' not certainly be adopted.

The fruits of the impolitic measures taken at the last Session with regard to taxes are bitterly tasted now. Our Treasury is empty, no supplies have gone to the federal treasury, and our internal embarrassments torment us exceedingly. The present Assembly have good dispositions on the subject, but some time will elapse before any of their arrangements can be productive. In one instance only the general principles of finance have been departed from. The specie part of the tax under collection is made payable in Tobacco. This indulgence to the people as it is called and considered, was so warmly wished for out of doors, and so strenuously pressed within that it could not be rejected, without danger of exciting some worse project of a popular cast. As Tobacco alone is made commutable, there is reason to hope the public treasury will suffer little if at all. It may possibly gain.

The Repeal of the port bill has not yet been attempted. Col. Mason has been waited for as the hero of the Attack. As it is become uncertain whether he will be down at all, the question will probably be brought forward in a few days. The repeal were he present would be morally certain. Under the disadvantage of his absence it is more than probable.[2] The question of British debts has also awaited his patronage. I am unable to say what the present temper is on that subject, nothing having passed that could make trial of it. The repeated disappointments I have sustained in efforts in favor of the Treaty make me extremely averse to take the lead in the business again.

The public appointments have been disposed of as follows: The contest for the Chair lay between Col. Bland and Mr. Prentis. The latter prevailed by a majority of near 20 votes. Mr. Harrison the late Speaker lost his election in Surry which he represented last year; and since has been equally unsuccessful in his pristine County Charles City where he made a second experiment. In the choice of a Governor Mr. E. Randolph had a considerable majority of the whole in the first ballot. His competitors were Col. Bland and R. H. Lee, each of whom had between 20 and 30 votes. The delegation to Congress contained under the first choice Grayson, Carrington, R. H. Lee, Mr. Jones and myself. Col. H. Lee of the last delegation was dropt. The causes were different I believe and not very accurately known to me. One of them is said to have been his supposed heterodoxy touching the Mississipi. Mr. Jones has since declined his appointment and Col. Lee has been re-instated by an almost unanimous vote. A vacancy in the Council produced by the Resignation of Mr. Roane is

---

2. The attempt at repeal lost, but two additional entry ports on the Eastern Shore of Virginia were added to the five already authorized; see *PJM,* IX, p. 192.

filled by Mr. Bolling Starke. Cyrus Griffin was a candidate but was left considerably in the rear. The Attorney Generalship has been conferred on Col. Innis. Mr. Marshal had a handsome vote.

Our summer and fall have been wet, beyond all imagination in some places, and much so every where. The crops of corn are in general plentiful. The price up. The country will not exceed 8/ or 10/. In this district it is scarcest and dearest, being already [as] high as 12/ or 15/. The crop of Tobacco will fall short considerably it is calculated of the last year's. The highest and lowest prices in the Country of the new Crop are 25/ and 20/. A rise is confidently expected.

My next will be from N.Y. whither I shall set out as soon as the principal business of the Session is over. Till my arrival there I postpone communications relative to our national affairs, which I shall then be able to make on better grounds, as well as some circumstances relative to the affairs of this State, which the hurry of the present opportunity restrains me from entering into. Adieu.

J. M. Jr.

## *Jefferson to Madison*

Paris Dec. 16, 1786

Dear Sir

After a very long silence, I am at length able to write to you. An unlucky dislocation of my right wrist has disabled me from using my pen for three months. I now begin to use it a little, but with great pain; so that this letter must be taken up at such intervals as the state of my hand will permit, and will probably be the work of some days. Tho' the joint seems to be well set, the swelling does not abate, nor the use of it return. I am now therefore on the point of setting out to the South of France to try the use of some mineral waters there, by immersion. This journey will be of 2. or 3. months.

My last letters to you were of Apr. 25. and May 29. the latter only a letter of recommendation. Yours of Jan. 22. Mar. 18. May. 12. June 19. and Aug. 12. remain unacknowleged.

I inclose you herein a copy of the letter from the Minister of finance to me, making several advantageous regulations for our commerce. The obtaining this has occupied us a twelvemonth.[3] I say us, because I find the M. de la Fayette so useful an auxiliary that acknowlegements for his cooperation are always due. There remains still something to do for the articles of rice, turpentine and shipduties. What can be done for tobacco when the late regulation

---

3. For Calonne's letter on Franco-American trade, Oct. 22, 1786, see *PTJ*, X, pp. 474-78. By "us," TJ included Lafayette; see *ibid.*, p. 606.

expires, is very incertain.[4] The commerce between the U.S. and this country being put on a good footing, we may afterwards proceed to try if any thing can be done to favour our intercourse with their colonies. Admission into them for our fish and flour is very desireable. But unfortunately both these articles would raise a competition against their own.

I find by the public papers that your Commercial Convention failed in point of representation. If it should produce a full meeting in May, and a broader reformation, it will still be well. To make us one nation as to foreign concerns, and keep us distinct in Domestic ones, gives the outline of the proper division of powers between the general and particular governments. But to enable the Federal head to exercise the powers given it, to best advantage, it should be organised, as the particular ones are, into Legislative, Executive and Judiciary. The 1st. and last are already separated. The 2d should also be. When last with Congress, I often proposed to members to do this by making of the Committee of the states, an Executive committee during the recess of Congress, and during it's sessions to appoint a Committee to receive and dispatch all executive business, so that Congress itself should meddle only with what should be legislative. But I question if any Congress (much less all successively) can have self-denial enough to go through with this distribution. The distribution should be imposed on them then. I find Congress have reversed their division of the Western states, and proposed to make them fewer and larger. This is reversing the natural order of things. A tractable people may be governed in large bodies; but in proportion as they depart from this character, the extent of their government must be less. We see into what small divisions the Indians are obliged to reduce their societies. This measure, with the disposition to shut up the Missisipi give me serious apprehensions of the severance of the Eastern and Western parts of our confederacy. It might have been made the interests of the Western states to remain united with us, by managing their interests honestly and for their own good. But the moment we sacrifice their interests to our own, they will see it better to govern themselves. The moment they resolve to do this, the point is settled. A forced connection is neither our interest nor within our power.

The Virginia act for religious freedom has been received with infinite approbation in Europe and propagated with enthusiasm. I do not mean by the governments, but by the individuals which compose them. It has been translated into French and Italian, has been sent to most of the courts of Europe, and has been the best evidence of the falshood of those reports which stated us to be in anarchy. It is inserted in the new Encyclopedie, and is appearing in most of the publications respecting America. In fact it is comfortable to see the standard of reason at length erected, after so many ages during which the human mind has been held in vassalage by kings, priests and nobles; and it is

---

4. TJ referred to the contract for 1785–87 in which the Farmers General gave Robert Morris a monopoly on American tobacco imported into France.

honorable for us to have produced the first legislature who has had the courage to declare that the reason of man may be trusted with the formation of his own opinions. I shall be glad when the revisal shall be got thro'. In the criminal law, the principle of retaliation is much criticised here, particularly in the case of Rape. They think the punishment indecent and unjustifiable. I should be for altering it, but for a different reason: that is on account of the temptation women would be under to make it the instrument of vengeance against an inconstant lover, and of disappointment to a rival.

Are our courts of justice open for the recovery of British debts according to the Septennial act? The principles of that act can be justified; but the total stoppage of justice cannot. The removal of the negroes from New York would only give cause for stopping some of the last paiments, if the British government should refuse satisfaction, which however I think they will not do.

I thank you for your communications in Natural history. The several instances of trees etc. found far below the surface of the earth, as in the case of Mr. Hay's well, seem to set the reason of man at defiance. Another Theory of the earth has been contrived by one Whitford, not absolutely reasonable, but somewhat more so than any that has yet appeared.[5] It is full of interesting facts; which however being inadequate to his theory, he is obliged to supply them from time to time by begging questions. It is worth your getting from London. If I can be useful to you in ordering books from London you know you may command me. You had better send me the duplicate volume of the Encyclopedie. I will take care to send you the proper one. I have many more livraisons for you and have made some other inconsiderable purchases for you in this way. But I shall not send them till the spring, as a winter passage is bad for books. I reserve myself till that time therefore to give you an account of the execution of your several commissions, only observing that the watch will not be finished till the spring and that it will be necessary for me to detain her some time on trial, because it often happens that a watch, looking well to the eye, and faithfully made, goes badly at first on account of some little circumstance which escapes the eye of the workman when he puts her together and which he could easily rectify.

With respect to the proposition about the purchase of lands, I had just before made the experiment desired. It was to borrow money for aiding the opening of the Patowmac, which was proposed to me by Genl. Washington. I had the benefit of his name, and the foundation of a special act of assembly. I lodged the papers in the hands of Mr. Grand to try to obtain money on loan at 6. per cent. assuring him that the securities should be made compleatly satisfactory to the lenders. After long trial he told me it could not be done; that this government has always occasion to borrow more money than can be lent in this country; that they pay 6. percent per annum in quarterly paiments, and

---

5. See JM to TJ, Jan. 22, 1786, above, for the archaeological discoveries in Richmond. TJ meant John Whitehurst, a British archaeologist, not Whitford; see *PTJ*, X, p. 606.

with a religious punctuality; that besides this they give very considerable douceurs to the lenders; that every one therefore would prefer having his money here rather than on the other side the Atlantic, where distance, want of punctuality, and a habitual protection of the debtor would be against them. There is therefore but one way in which I see any chance of executing your views. Monied men sometimes talk of investing money in American lands. Some such might be willing to ensure an advantageous investiture by interesting trustworthy characters in the purchase, and to do this might be willing to advance the whole money, being properly secured. On this head no satisfaction should be wanting, which I could give them; and as persons with these views sometimes advise with me, I shall be attentive to propose to them this plan. I consider it's success however as only possible, not probable.

When I wrote you by the Fitzhughs I informed you I had lent them 600 livres; but after this I received notice of their bill on me in favor of Limozin for 480 livres which I paid in December 1785. so that the sum I would wish you to receive from them is 1080 livres.

The bickerings between Russia and the Porte are again patched up by this court. Those between Spain and Naples never looked towards war. The only danger was that Naples might throw itself into the arms of the house of Austria. This court is labouring at a reconciliation. It will probably end in a settled coolness between the two kings father and son, and the former withdrawing from all interference with the affairs of Naples: while the latter will keep himself clear of new connections. There have been serious fears of a rupture of the equilibrium by a shifting of Prussia into the Austrian scale. This country will certainly support the patriotic party in Holland, even at the expence of a war. It is rather beleived the new king of Prussia will not go so far in favor of the Stadholder, tho much interested for him. This is the only germ at present, the development of which can produce war. I am Dear Sir with sincere esteem your friend and servant,

TH: JEFFERSON

P.S. Since writing the above I have received the deficient volume of the encyclopedie for you. The price of Buffon's plates coloured are

        Oiseaux. 1008. Plates in 42 quires    630 livres
        Quadrupedes 27. quires              194 - 8

They cannot be bought uncoloured separate from the text.

## Jefferson to Madison

Paris Jan. 30 and Feb. 5, 1787

DEAR SIR

My last to you was of the 16th of Dec. since which I have received yours of Nov. 25. and Dec. 4. which afforded me, as your letters always do, a treat on matters public, individual and oeconomical. I am impatient to learn your sentiments on the late troubles in the Eastern states. So far as I have yet seen, they do not appear to threaten serious consequences. Those states have suffered by the stoppage of the channels of their commerce, which have not yet found other issues. This must render money scarce, and make the people uneasy. This uneasiness has produced acts absolutely unjustifiable: but I hope they will provoke no severities from their governments. A consciousness of those in power that their administration of the public affairs has been honest, may perhaps produce too great a degree of indignation: and those characters wherein fear predominates over hope may apprehend too much from these instances of irregularity. They may conclude too hastily that nature has formed man insusceptible of any other government but that of force, a conclusion not founded in truth, nor experience. Societies exist under three forms sufficiently distinguishable. 1. Without government, as among our Indians. 2. Under governments wherein the will of every one has a just influence, as is the case in England in a slight degree, and in our states in a great one. 3. Under governments of force: as is the case in all other monarchies and in most of the other republics. To have an idea of the curse of existence under these last, they must be seen. It is a government of wolves over sheep. It is a problem, not clear in my mind, that the 1st. condition is not the best. But I believe it to be inconsistent with any great degree of population. The second state has a great deal of good in it. The mass of mankind under that enjoys a precious degree of liberty and happiness. It has it's evils too: the principal of which is the turbulence to which it is subject. But weigh this against the oppressions of monarchy, and it becomes nothing. Malo periculosam, libertatem quam quietam servitutem [I would rather have a disturbed liberty than a quiet slavery]. Even this evil is productive of good. It prevents the degeneracy of government, and nourishes a general attention to the public affairs. I hold it that a little rebellion now and then is a good thing, and as necessary in the political world as storms in the physical. Unsuccesful rebellions indeed generally establish the incroachments on the rights of the people which have produced them. An observation of this truth should render honest republican governors so mild in their punishment of rebellions, as not to discourage them too much. It is a medecine necessary for the sound health of government. If these transactions give me no uneasiness, I feel very differently at another piece of intelligence, to wit, the possibility that the navigation of the Missisipi may be abandoned to Spain. I never had any interest Westward of the Alleghaney; and I never will have any. But I have had great opportunities of knowing the character of the people who inhabit that country. And I will venture to say that the act which abandons the navigation of the Missisipi is an act of separation between the Eastern and Western country. It is a relinquishment of five parts out of eight of the territory of the United States, an abandonment of the fairest subject for the paiment of our public debts, and the chaining those debts on our own necks in perpetuum. I have the utmost confidence in the honest intentions of those who concur in this measure; but I lament their want of acquaintance with the character and physical advantages of the people who, right or wrong, will suppose their interests sacrificed on this occasion to the contrary interests of that part of the confederacy in possession of present power. If they declare themselves a separate people, we are incapable of a single effort to retain them. Our citizens can never be induced, either as militia or as souldiers, to go there to cut the throats of their own brothers and sons, or rather to be themselves the subjects instead of the perpetrators of the parricide. Nor would that country quit the cost of being retained against the will of it's inhabitants, could it be done. But it cannot be done. They are able already to rescue the navigation of the Missisipi out of the hands of Spain, and to add New Orleans to their own territory. They will be joined by the inhabitants of Louisiana. This will bring on a war between them and Spain; and that will produce the question with us whether it will not be worth our while to become parties with them in the war, in order to reunite them with us, and thus correct our error? And were I to permit my forebodings to go one step further, I should predict that the inhabitants of the U.S. would force their rulers to take the affirmative of that question. I wish I may be mistaken in all these opinions.

We have for some time expected that the Chevalier de la Luzerne would obtain a promotion in the diplomatic line, by being appointed to some of the courts where this country keeps an Ambassador. But none of the vacancies taking place which had been counted on, I think the present disposition is to require his return to his station in America. He told me himself lately, that he should return in the spring. I have never pressed this matter on the court, tho' I knew it to be desireable and desired on our part: because if the compulsion on him to return had been the work of Congress, he would have returned in such ill temper with them as to disappoint them in the good they expected from it. He would for ever have laid at their door his failure of promotion. I did not press it for another reason, which is that I have great reason to beleive that the character of the Count de Moutier, who would go were the Chevalier to be otherwise provided for, would give the most perfect satisfaction in America.

As you are now returned into Congress it will become of importance that you should form a just estimate of certain public characters; on which therefore I will give you such notes as my knowlege of them has furnished me with. You will compare them with the materials you are otherwise possessed of, and decide on a view of the whole. You know the opinion I *formerly* entertained of *my friend Mr. Adams.* [6] Yourself and the governor were the first who *shook* that opinion. I afterwards saw proofs which *convicted* him of a degree of *vanity,* and of a *blindness* to it, of which no germ *had appeared* in Congress. A *7-months'* intimacy with him *here* and *as* many *weeks* in *London* have given me opportunities of studying him closely. *He is vain, irritable and a bad calculator of* the force and probable effect of the motives which govern men. This is *all* the *ill* which

---

6. The italicized words in this sentence and in the rest of the letter were written in code.

can possibly be *said of him*. He is as disinterested as the being which made him: he is profound in his views: and accurate in his judgment *except where knowledge of the world* is necessary to form a judgment. He is so amiable, that I pronounce you will love him if ever you become acquainted with him. He would be, as he was, a great man in *Congress. Mr. Carmichael* is I think very little *known* in *America*.[7] I never *saw him* and while I was *in Congress I* formed rather a *disadvantageous idea* of him. His letters, received then, shewed him *vain* and more attentive to *ceremony* and *etiquette* than we suppose men *of sense* should be. I have now a constant correspondence with him, and find *him* a little *hypocondriac* and *discontented*. He possesses very *good understanding* tho' not of the *first order. I have* had great opportunities of *searching into* his *character* and have availed myself *of it*. Many persons of different nations *coming* from *Madrid* to *Paris* all speak of *him as* in *high esteem* and *I think* it certain that he has more of the *Count de Florid. B's friendship* than any *diplomatic* character at *that court*. As long as this *minister* is in *office* Carmichael can do *more than* any other *person who* could be *sent there*. You will see *Franks and* doubtless he will be *asking some appointment*. I wish there may be any one for *which* he is *fit*. He is *light, indiscreet,* [*act*]*ive, honest, affectionate*.[8] Tho' *Bingham* is not in *diplomatic office* yet as he wishes to be so I will mention such circumstances of *him as you might* otherwise be *deceived in. He* will make *you believe he* was on the most intimate footing with the first *characters in Europe* and versed in the *secrets* of every *cabinet*. Not a word of this *is true. He* had a rage for being *presented* to *great men* and had no *modesty* in the methods by which he could effect it. If *he obtained access* afterwards, it was with such as who were susceptible of impression from the *beauty of his wife*.[9] I must *except* the *Marquis de Bouilli* who had been an *old acquaintance*. The *Marquis de Lafayette* is a most valuable *auxiliary to me*. His *zeal* is unbounded, and his *we*[*ight*] with those in *power great*. His *education* having been merely *military, commerce* was an unknown feild to him. But his good sense enabling him to *comprehend* perfectly whatever is *explained to him, his agency* has been very *efficacious. He* has a great deal of *sound genius,* is well *remarked* by the *king* and rising in *popularity. He* has nothing against *him* but the *suspicion of republican principles*. I think he will one day *be of* the *ministry*. His *foible* is a *canine appetite for popularity and fame*. But he will get *above* this. *The Count de Vergennes* is *ill*. The possibility of his *recovery* renders it dangerous for *us to express a doubt but* he is *in danger*. He is *a great Minister* in *European affairs* but has very *imperfect ideas* of *ours* [and] *no confidence in* them. His *devotion* to the principles of *pure despotism* render him *unaffectionate to our governments* but *his fear* of *England makes him value us* as a *make weight*. He is

---

7. William Carmichael was the American agent in Madrid; see *PJM*, IV, p. 450.

8. David S. Franks, who served as secretary to the mission to negotiate a treaty with the emperor of Morocco, carried the treaty to the United States, arriving in Apr. 1787; see *PTJ*, XI, pp. 135–36, 305–6.

9. See Robert C. Alberts, *The Golden Voyage: The Life and Times of William Bingham, 1752–1804* (Boston, 1969).

*cool, reserved in political conversation, free* and *familiar* on other *subjects,* and a very *attentive, agreeable person* to *do business with.* It is impossible to have a clearer, better *organised head* but *age* has *chilled his heart.* Nothing should be spared on our part to attach this country to us. It is the only one on which we can rely for support under every event. It's inhabitants love us more I think than they do any other nation on earth. This is very much the effect of the good dispositions with which the French officers returned. In a former letter I mentioned to you the dislocation of my wrist. I can make not the least use of it, except for the single article of writing, tho' it is going on five months since the accident happened. I have great anxieties lest I should never recover any considerable use of it. I shall, by the advice of my Surgeons, set out in a fortnight for the waters of Aix in Provence. I chose these out of several they proposed to me, because if they fail to be effectual, my journey will not be useless altogether. It will give me an opportunity of examining the canal of Languedoc and of acquiring knowlege of that species of navigation which may be useful hereafter: but more immediately it will enable me to take the tour of the ports concerned in commerce with us, to examine on the spot the defects of the late regulations respecting our commerce, to learn the further improvements which may be made on it, and, on my return, to get this business finished. I shall be absent between two and three months, unless any thing happens to recall me here sooner, which may always be effected in ten days, in whatever part of my route I may be. In speaking of *characters* I omitted *those of Reyneval and Henin,* the *two eyes* of *M. de Vergennes.* The *former* is the most important *character because possessing* the most of the *confidence* of the *Count, he* is rather *cunning* than *wise. His* views of things being neither *great* nor *liberal he governs* himself by *principles* which he has *learnt* by *rote* and is *fit only* for the *details* of *execution. His heart* is susceptible of *little passions* but not of *good ones. He* is *brother* in *law* to *M. Gerard* from whom he received *disadvantageous impressions* of *us which* cannot be *effaced. He* has much *duplicity. Henin* is a *philosopher sincere, friendly, liberal, learned, beloved* by every *body,* the *other* by *nobody.* [10] *I think* it a great *misfortune* that the *United States* are in the *department* of the *former.* As particulars of this kind may be useful to you in your present situation, I may hereafter continue the chapter. I know it safely lodged in your discretion.

Feb. 5.
Since writing thus far *Franks* is *returned* from *England.* I *learn* that *Mr. Adams* desires to be *recalled* and that *Smith* should be *appointed charge des affairs* there. It is not for me to decide whether any *diplomatic character* should be *kept* at a *court* which *keeps* none with *us.* You can judge of *Smith's abilities* by *his letters.* They are not of the *first order* but they are *good.* For his *honesty* he is like

---

10. Pierre-Michel Hennin was Vergennes's chief clerk and secretary to the Council of State; see *PJM,* IX, p. 252.

our friend *Monroe.* Turn his *soul* wrong side outwards and there is not a speck on it. *He* has one *foible,* an *excessive inflammability* of *temper,* but he feels it when it comes on, and has *resolution enough* to *suppress* it, and to *remain silent* till it *passes* over.

I send you by Colo. Franks your pocket telescope, walking stick, and chemical box. The two former could not be combined together. The latter could not be had in the form you referred to. Having a great desire to have a portable copying machine, and being satisfied from some experiments that the principle of the large machine might be applied in a small one, I planned one when in England and had it made. It answers perfectly. I have since set a workman to making them here, and they are in such demand that he has his hands full. Being assured that you will be pleased to have one, when you shall have tried it's convenience, I send you one by Colo. Franks. The machine costs 96 livres, the appendages 24. livres, and I send you paper and ink for 12 livres, in all 132 livres. There is a printed paper of directions: but you must expect to make many essays before you succeed perfectly. A soft brush, like a shaving brush, is more convenient than the sponge. You can get as much ink and paper as you please from London. The paper costs a guinea a ream.

## *Jefferson to Madison*

Paris Feb. 7, 1787

DEAR SIR

I leave the inclosed open for your perusal and that of your Collegues and others to whom you may chuse to shew it; only taking care that neither copies nor extracts be taken. Be so good, when you are done with it, as to stick a wafer in it and forward it to the Governor.[11] I am with sincere esteem Dr. Sir your friend and servt.,

TH: JEFFERSON

P.S. I do not know whether you are acquainted with young Bannister who goes by the packet. He is of good understanding and of infinite worth.[12] I have letters and papers to the 15th. of Decemb. yet neither these nor those of any person I can meet with inform us who is President of Congress.[13]

---

11. See TJ to Edmund Randolph, Feb. 7, 1787, in *PTJ,* XI, pp. 104-5, 124-25, about the bust of Lafayette ordered by the Virginia legislature as a gift to the city of Paris.

12. John Banister, Jr., was the son of a former delegate to Congress; see *PJM,* IX, p. 258.

13. Because of a lack of a quorum, Congress did not convene between Nov. 1786 and Feb. 2, 1787; see *ibid.*

## Madison to Jefferson

New York Feb. 15, 1787

DEAR SIR

My last was from Richmond of the 4th. of December, and contained a sketch of our legislative proceedings prior to that date. The principal proceedings of subsequent date relate as nearly as I can recollect 1st. to a rejection of the Bill on crimes and punishments, which after being altered so as to remove most of the objections as was thought, was lost by a single vote. The rage against Horse stealers had a great influence on the fate of the Bill. Our old bloody code is by this event fully restored, the prerogative of conditional pardon having been taken from the Executive by a Judgment of the Court of Appeals, and the temporary law granting it to them having expired and been left unrevived. I am not without hope that the rejected bill will find a more favorable disposition in the next Assembly. 2dly. to the bill for diffusing knowledge. It went through two readings by a small majority and was not pushed to a third one. The necessity of a systematic provision on the subject was admitted on all hands. The objections against that particular provision were 1. the expence, which was alledged to exceed the ability of the people. 2. the difficulty of executing it in the present sparse settlement of the Country. 3. the inequality of the districts as contended by the Western members. The latter objection is of little weight and might have been easily removed if it had been urged in an early stage of the discussion. The bill now rests on the same footing with the other unpassed bills in the Revisal. 3dly. to the Revisal at large. It was found impossible to get thro' the system at the late session for several reasons. 1. the changes which have taken place since its compilement, in our affairs and our laws, particularly those relating to our Courts, called for changes in some of the bills which could not be made with safety by the Legislature. 2. the pressure of other business which tho' of less importance in itself, yet was more interesting for the moment. 3. the alarm excited by an approach toward the Execution Bill which subjects land to the payment of debts. This bill could not have been carried, was too important to be lost, and even too difficult to be amended without destroying its texture. 4. the danger of passing the Repealing Bill at the end of the Code before the operation of the various amendments etc. made by the Assembly could be leisurely examined by competent Judges. Under these circumstances it was thought best to hand over the residue of the work to our successors, and in order to have it made compleat, Mr. Pendleton, Mr. Wythe and Blair were appointed a Committee to amend the unpassed bills and also to prepare a supplemental revision of the laws which have been passed since the original work was executed. It became a critical question with the friends of the Revisal whether the parts of the Revisal actually passed should be suspended in the mean time, or left to take their operation. The first plan was strongly recommended by the advantage of giving effect to the system at once, and by the inconveniency arising from the latter of leaving the old laws to a constructive repeal only. The latter notwithstanding was preferred as putting the adopted bills out of the reach of a succeeding Assembly, which might possibly be unfriendly to the system altogether. There was good reason to suspect Mr. *Henry* who will certainly be *then a member*.[14] By suffering the bills which have passed to take effect in the meantime it will be extremely difficult to get rid of them. 4thly. Religion. The Act incorporating the protestant Episcopal Church excited the most pointed opposition from the other sects. They even pushed their attacks against the reservation of the Glebes etc. to the Church exclusively. The latter circumstance involved the Legislature in some embarrassment. The result was a repeal of the Act, with a saving of the property. 5th. the district Courts. After a great struggle they were lost in the House of Delegates by a single voice. 6thly. taxes; the attempts to reduce former taxes were baffled, and sundry new taxes added; on lawyers ¹⁄₁₀ of their fees, on Clerks of Courts ¼ of do., on doctors a small tax, a tax on houses in towns so as to level their burden with that of real estate in the Country, very heavy taxes on riding carriages, etc. Besides those an additional duty of 2. per Ct. ad valorem on all merchandizes imported in vessels of nations not in treaty with the U.S., an additional duty of 4d. on every gallon of wine except French wines, and of 2d. on every gallon of distilled spirits except French brandies which are made duty free. The exceptions in favor of France were the effect of the sentiments and regulations communicated to you by Mr. Calonne. A printed copy of the communication was received the last day of the Session in a newspaper from N. York and made a warm impression on the Assembly. Some of the taxes are liable to objections, and were much complained of. With the additional duties on trade they will considerably enhance our revenue. I should have mentioned a duty of 6s. per Hhd. on Tobacco for complying with a special requisition of Congress for supporting the corps of men raised for the public security. 7th. The Mississippi. At the date of my last the House of Delegates only had entered into Resolutions against a surrender of the right of navigating it. The Senate shortly after concurred. The States South of Virga. still adhere as far as I can learn to the same ideas as have governed Virginia. N. Jersey one of the States in Congress which was on the opposite side has now instructed her Delegates against surrendering to Spain the navigation of the River even for a limited time. And Pena. it is expected will do the same. I am told that Mr. *Jay* has *not ventured to proceed in his project* and I suppose will *not now do it.* 8th. The Convention for amending the federal Constitution. At the date of my last Virga. had passed an act for appointing deputies. The deputation consists of

---

14. The italicized words in this sentence and in the rest of the letter were written in code.

Genl. Washington, Mr. Henry late Governor, Mr. Randolph present Governor, Mr. Blair, Mr. Wythe, Col. Mason and Js. M. North Carola. has also made an appointment including her present and late Governor. S.C. it is expected by her delegates in Congress will not fail to follow these examples. Maryland has determined I just hear to appoint but has not yet agreed on her deputies. Delaware, Penna. and N. Jy. have made respectable appointments. N. York has not yet decided on the point. Her Assembly has just rejected the impost which has an unpropitious aspect. It is not clear however that she may not yet accede to the other measures.[15] Connecticut has a great aversion to Conventions, and is otherwise habitually disinclined to abridge her State prerogatives. Her concurrence nevertheless is not despaired of. Massts. it is said will concur, though hitherto not well inclined. N. Hampshire will probably do as she does. Rhode Island can be relied on for nothing that is good. On all great points she must sooner or later bend to Massts. and Connecticut.

Having but just come to this place I do not undertake to give you any general view of American affairs, or of the particular state of things in Massts. The omission is probably of little consequence as information of this sort must fall within your correspondence with the office of foreign affairs. I shall not however plead this consideration for a future letter when I hope to be more able to write fully.

Mr. Fitzhugh has paid into my hands for your use £58-6-8. Virga. currency in discharge of 1000 livres advanced to him in France. He was anxious to have settled it according to the actual exchange instead of the legal one of 33 ⅓ on the British standard, and even proposed the addition of interest. I did not hesitate to conclude that I should fulfill your intentions by rejecting both. I have sent to Mrs. Carr £25 for the use of your nephews as you directed. The balance is in my hands subject to your orders tho' I shall venture to apply it in the same way if I should be apprized of its being necessary to prevent interruption to the studies of the young gentlemen. My last informed you of the progress etc. of Master Peter. I have since received from the president of Hampden Sydney a letter containing the following paragraph. "Dabney Carr is a boy of very promising genius and very diligent application. He conducts himself with a good deal of prudence, and I hope will answer the expectations of his friends. I was afraid at first that he was dull or indolent from his appearance, but I find myself agreeably disappointed. His principal study at present is the Latin language, but he is also obliged to pay some attention to his native tongue." I remain Dr. Sir Yr. Affecte. friend,

Js. MADISON JR.

---

15. For the final contest over the impost in New York, see Merrill Jensen, *The New Nation: A History of the United States during the Confederation, 1781–1789* (New York, 1950), pp. 415–21. For the appointment of the New York delegates to the Philadelphia convention, see Linda Grant DePauw, *The Eleventh Pillar: New York State and the Federal Constitution* (Ithaca, 1966), pp. 52–54.

## Madison to Jefferson

New York Mar. 18, 1787

DEAR SIR

My endeavors to obtain for you the peccan Nuts have all been unsuccessful untill a few days ago when I recd. by the post about a dozen of them which I now enclose. They go by a French Gentleman in a vessel bound for England, who will either carry them himself to Paris, or consign them to the care of Mr. Adams. I do not yet despair of being able to possess myself of the full quantity which you wished.[16] My endeavours have been equally unsuccessful as to the seed of the Sugar Maple, notwithstanding the different plans pursued for the purpose. I have begun a letter to you of some length which I allotted for this conveyance, but the short notice I had of it, the tediousness of writing in Cypher, and several unseasonable interruptions make it doubtful whether I shall be able to finish it. If I should it will accompany this. The fear of losing the opportunity for both induces me to send this off without delay. I remain yr. affecte. friend and Servt.

Js. MADISON JR.

## Madison to Jefferson

New York Mar. 19, 1787

DEAR SIR

My last was of the 15th. of Feby, and went by the packet. This will go to England in the care of a French gentleman who will consign it to the care of Mr. Adams.

The appointments for the Convention go on auspiciously. Since my last Georgia, S. Carolina, N. York, Massts. and N. Hampshire have come into the measure. The first and the last of these States have commissioned their delegates to Congress, as their representatives in Convention. The deputation of Massts. consists of Messrs. Gohram, Dana, King, Gerry, and Strong. That of N. York, Messrs. Hamilton, Yates and Lansing. That of S. Carolina, Messrs. J. Rutlidge, Laurens, Pinkney (General)[,] Butler, and Chas. Pinkney lately member of Congress. The States which have not yet appointed are R. Island, Connecticut, and Maryland. The last has taken measures which prove her intention to appoint, and the two former it is not doubted will follow the example of their neighbours. I just learn from the Governor of Virginia that

---

16. This letter, in the Sol Feinstone Collection, Washington Crossing, Pennsylvania, is taken from *PJM,* IX, pp. 313-14; it is not in *PTJ.* The pecan, or "Illinois nut," as TJ called it, was unknown to European botanists; see William Peden, ed., *Notes on the State of Virginia by Thomas Jefferson* (Chapel Hill, 1955; rpt. New York, 1982), p. 39.

Mr. Henry has resigned his place in the deputation from that State, and that Genl. Nelson is put into it by the Executive who were authorised to fill vacancies. The Governor, Mr. Wythe and Mr. Blair will attend, and some hopes are entertained of Col. Mason's attendance. Genl. Washington has prudently authorised no expectations of his attendance, but has not either precluded himself absolutely from stepping into the field if the crisis should demand it. What may be the result of this political experiment cannot be foreseen. The difficulties which present themselves are on one side almost sufficient to dismay the most sanguine, whilst on the other side the most timid are compelled to encounter them by the mortal diseases of the existing constitution. These diseases need not be pointed out to you who so well understand them. Suffice it to say that they are at present marked by symptoms which are truly alarming, which have tainted the faith of the most orthodox republicans, and which challenge from the votaries of liberty every concession in favor of stable Government not infringing fundamental principles, as the only security against an opposite extreme of our present situation.[17] I think myself that it will be expedient in the first place to lay the foundation of the new system in such a ratification by the people themselves of the several States as will render it clearly paramount to their Legislative authorities. 2dly. Over and above the positive power of regulating trade and sundry other matters in which uniformity is proper, to arm the federal head with a negative *in all cases whatsoever*[18] on the local legislatures. Without this defensive power experience and reflection have satisfied me that however ample the federal powers may be made, or however Clearly their boundaries may be delineated, on paper, they will be easily and continually baffled by the Legislative sovereignties of the States. The effects of this provision would be not only to guard the national rights and interests against invasion, but also to restrain the States from thwarting and molesting each other, and even from oppressing the minority within themselves by paper money and other unrighteous measures which favor the interest of the majority. In order to render the exercise of such a negative prerogative convenient, an emanation of it must be vested in some set of men within the several States so far as to enable them to give a temporary sanction to laws of immediate necessity.[19] 3dly. to change the principle of Representation in the federal system. Whilst the execution of the Acts of Congress depends on the several legislatures, the equality of votes does not destroy the inequality of importance and influence in the States. But in case of such an augmentation of

17. Nicholas P. Trist, who married one of TJ's granddaughters, copied this letter on Oct. 1, 1834, and added this marginal note: "that is to say *Monarchy*. This is the obvious meaning. Moreover, in reading the letter to me today, Mr. Madison made a parenthetical remark to that effect"; see *PTJ*, XI, p. 224. For Trist's relationship with JM, see Drew R. McCoy, *The Last of the Fathers: James Madison and the Republican Legacy* (New York, 1989), pp. 132–33, 141–44, 325–28.

18. JM's italics.

19. Trist added this marginal note in 1834: "In reading this Mr. Madison paused here; and said he had subsequently satisfied himself that there would be difficulties, perhaps insuperable, in reducing this idea to practice"; see *PTJ*, XI, pp. 224–25.

the federal power as will render it efficient without the intervention of the Legislatures, a vote in the general Councils from Delaware would be of equal value with one from Massts. or Virginia. This change therefore is just. I think also it will be practicable. A majority of the States concieve that they will be gainers by it. It is recommended to the Eastern States by the actual superiority of their populousness, and to the Southern by their expected superiority. And if a majority of the larger States concur, the fewer and smaller States must finally bend to them. This point being gained, many of the objections now urged in the leading States against renunciations of power will vanish. 4thly. to organise the federal powers in such a manner as not to blend together those which ought to be exercised by separate departments. The limited powers now vested in Congress are frequently mismanaged from the want of such a distribution of them. What would be the case, under an enlargement not only of the powers, but the number, of the federal Representatives?

These are some of the leading ideas which have occurred to me, but which may appear to others as improper, as they appear to me necessary.

Congress have continued so thin as to be incompetent to the despatch of the more important business before them. We have at present nine States and it is not improbable that something may now be done. The report of Mr. Jay on the mutual violations of the Treaty of peace will be among the first subjects of deliberation. He *favors the British claim of interest* but *refers the question to the court.*[20] The amount of the *report which is an able one* is that the *treaty should* be *put in force* as a *law and the exposition of it* left like that *of other laws to the ordinary tribunals.*

The *Spanish project sleeps. A* perusal of the *attempt of seven states* to make a *new treaty by repealing* an *essential condition of the old* satisfied me that Mr. *Jay's caution* would *revolt at so irregular a sanction.* A late accidental conversation with *Guardoqui proved to me* that the *negociation is arrested.* It may appear strange that a member of *Congress should be indebted to a foreign minister* for *such information.*[21] Yet *such* is the *footing on which* the *intemperance* of *party has put the matter* that it rests wholly with *Mr. Jay how far he* will *communicate with Congress* as well as *how far he will negociate with Guardoqui.* But although it appears that the intended *sacrifice of* the *Missisipi will not be made,* the *consequences of the intention* and the *attempt are likely to be very serious.* I have already made known to you the light in which the subject was *taken up by Virginia.* Mr. *Henry's disgust exceeded all measure* and I am not singular in ascribing his refusal to *attend the Convention* to the *policy of keeping himself free* to *combat or espouse the*

20. The italicized words in this sentence and in the rest of the letter were written in code.

21. JM's lengthy interview with the Spanish minister was hardly accidental but instead was part of a series of discussions by congressmen, especially from the Virginia delegation, with foreign ministers in the nation's capital. JM was accompanied by William Bingham on this trip, which he summarizes in his "Notes" for Mar. 13, 1787; see *PJM,* IX, pp. 309–11. For a discussion of JM's efforts to line up support by middle states' delegates, see Drew McCoy, "James Madison and Visions of American Nationality in the Confederation Period," in *Beyond Confederation,* pp. 239–43.

*result of it according* to the result *of the Missisipi business among other circumstances. North Carolina also* has given *pointed instructions* to *her delegates*. So has New Jersey. A *proposition* for the *like purpose* was a *few days ago made in the legislature of Pennsylvania* but went off without a *decision on its merits. Her delegates in Congress are equally divided* on the subject. The tendency of this *project* to *foment distrusts among the Atlantic states* at a *crisis when harmony* and *confidence ought to have been* studiously *cherished* has not been more *verified than* [by] *its predicted effect* on the *ultramontane settlements*. I have credible information that the people *living on the Western waters are already in great agitation and are* taking *measures, for uniting their consultations*. The *ambition* of *individuals* will *quickly mix itself* with the *original motives of resentment and interest*. A *communication will gradually* take place *with their British neighbors*. They will be *led to set up for themselves,* to *seise on the vacant lands,* to *entice* [emigrants][22] *by bounties,* and an *exemption from federal burdens,* and in all respects to *play the part of Vermont on a larger theatre*. It is *hinted to me* that *British partisans* are already *feeling the pulse* of some of the *Western settlements*. Should these *apprehensions not be imaginary Spain may have equal reason* with the *United States to rue the unnatural attempt to shut the Missisipi. Guardoqui has been admonished* of *the danger* and I believe *is not insensible to it tho'* he *affects to be otherwise* and *talks* as if the dependance of *Britain on the commercial favors of his court* would *induce her to play into the hands of Spain*. The eye of *France also can not fail to watch over the Western prospects*. I learn from those who *confer here with Otto and de la forest* that they *favor the opening of the Missisipi* disclaim[ing][23] *at the same time any authority to* speak the *sentiments of their court*. I find that the *Virginia delegates during the Missisipi discussions* last *fall entered into very confidential interviews with these gentlemen*. In one of them the *idea was communicated to Otto* of *opening the Missisipi for exports* but *not for imports* and *of giving to France and Spain* some *exclusive privileges in the trade*. He *promised* to transmit it to *Vergennes to obtain his sentiments* on the *whole matter* and *to communicate them to the delegates*. Not long *since Grayson called on him* and *revived the subject*. He *assured G       that he had recieved no answer* [from][24] *France* and signified his *wish that you might pump the count de Vergennes observing that he would deny to you his having recieved any information from America*. I *discover thro* several *channels that it would be* very *grateful to the French politicians here to see our negociations with Spain shifted into your hands* and *carried on under the mediating auspices of their court*.[25]

Van Berkel has remonstrated against the late acts of Virginia giving privileges to French wines and brandies in French bottoms, contending that the Dutch are entitled by their treaty to equal exemptions with the most favored nation without

22. At a later time, JM supplied this word, which he had omitted when encoding this sentence.
23. At a later time, JM supplied the ending.
24. At a later time, JM supplied this word.
25. On Apr. 18, 1787, JM introduced a motion proposing that TJ be authorized to negotiate with Madrid; see JM to TJ, Apr. 23, 1787, below.

*being subject to a compensation for them.* Mr. *Jay has reported against this construction* but considers the *act of Virginia as violating the treaty.* First *because it appears to be gratuitous,* not *compensatory on the face of it.* Secondly *because the states have no right to form tacit compacts with foreign nations.* No decision of Congress has yet taken place on the subject.

The expedition under General Lincoln against the insurgents has effectually succeeded in dispersing them. Whether the calm which he has restored will be durable or not is uncertain. From the precautions taking by the Government of Massts. it would seem as if their apprehensions were not extinguished. Besides disarming and *disfranchising*[26] for a limited time those who have been in arms, as a condition of their pardon, a military corps is to be raised to the amount of 1000, or 1500 men, and to be stationed in the most suspected districts. It is said that notwithstanding these specimens of the temper of the Government, a great proportion of the offenders chuse rather to risk the consequences of their treason, than submit to the conditions annexed to the amnesty, that they not only appear openly on public occasions but distinguish themselves by badges of their character, and that this insolence is in many instances countenanced by no less decisive marks of popular favor than elections to local offices of trust and authority.

A proposition is before the Legislature of this State now sitting for renouncing its pretensions to Vermont, and urging the admission of it into the Confederacy. The different parties are not agreed as to the form in which the renunciation should be made, but are likely to agree as to the substance. Should the offer be made, and Vermont should not reject it altogether I think they will insist on two stipulations at least, 1st. that their becoming parties to the Confederation shall not subject their boundaries, or the rights of their citizens to be questioned under the 9th. art: 2dly. that they shall not be subject to any part of the public debts already contracted.

The Geographer and his assistants have returned surveys on the federal lands to the amount of about 800,000 acres which it is supposed would sell pretty readily for public securities, and some of it lying on the Ohio even for specie. It will be difficult however to *get the proper steps taken by Congress, so many of the states having* now *lands of their own at mark*[et]. It is supposed that this consideration had *some share in the zeal for shutting the Missisipi. New Jersey* and some others *having no western land* which *favored this measure* begin now to *penetrate the secret.*

A letter from the Governor of Virga. informs me that the project of paper money is beginning to recover from the blow given it at the last Session of the Legislature. *If Mr. H[enry]*[27] *espouses it of which* there is *little doubt I think an emission will take place.* The Governor mentioned the death of Col. A. Cary Speaker of the Senate.

26. JM's italics.
27. JM encoded "H" and late in life completed the name.

This letter will be accompanied by another inclosing a few Peccan nuts. When I sent the latter to the Gentleman who is charged with it, I doubted whether I should be able to finish this in time, and I only succeed by having written to the last moment. Adieu. Yrs. Afy.,

      Js. MADISON JR

## Madison to Jefferson

[New York] Apr. 23, 1787

DEAR SIR

Since my last which was of March 19. I have had the pleasure of yours of Decr. 16. Jany. 30. and Feby. 7. which were handed to me by Col. Franks. Along with them were received the copying machine and other articles referred to in them. You will accept my warmest thanks for all these favors. The packet for the Governor of Virginia under the same cover with your letter of Feby. 7. has been forwarded. The accident to your wrist was first made known to me by these communications. I learnt with satisfaction from Col. Franks that the pain and weakness was apparently going off, and ardently wish that your projected trip to the South of France may produce a radical cure.

  The vigorous measures finally pursued by the Government of Massachusetts against the insurgents, had the intended effect of dispersing them. By some it was feared that they would re-embody on the return of favorable weather. As yet no symptom of such a design has appeared. It would seem that they mean to try their strength in another way; that is, by endeavoring to give the elections such a turn as may promote their views under the auspices of Constitutional forms. How far they may succeed is not yet reducible to certainty. That a great change will be effected in the component members of the government is certain, but the degree of influence imputable to the malcontents can not be well known till some specimen shall be given of the temper of the new rulers. Mr. Hancock takes the place of Mr. Bowdoin. His general character forbids a suspicion of his patriotic principles; but as he is an idolater of popularity, it is to be feared that he may be seduced by this foible into dishonorable compliances. A great proportion of the Senate is also changed, . and a greater proportion of the other branch it is expected will be changed. A paper emission at least is apprehended from this revolution in their councils.

  Congress have agreed to Mr. Jays report on the treaty of peace and to an address which accompanies it. Copies of both will no doubt be sent you from his department. The Legislature of this State which was sitting at the time and on whose account the acts of Congress were hurried through, has adjourned till Jany. next without deciding on them. This is an ominous example to the other states, and must weaken much the claim on Great Britain of an execution of the Treaty on her part as promised in case of proper steps being taken on ours. Virginia we foresee will be among the foremost in seizing pretexts for evading the injunctions of Congress. S. Carolina is not less infected with the same spirit. The present deliberations of Congress turn on 1. the sale of the western lands, 2. the Government of the Western settlements within the federal domain, 3. the final settlement of the Accounts between the Union and its members, 4. the *treaty* [with]²⁸ *Spain*.²⁹

1. Between six and seven hundred thousand acres have been surveyed in townships under the land ordinance, and are to be sold forthwith. The place where Congress sit is fixed for the sale. Its excentricity and remoteness from the premises will I apprehend give disgust. On the most eligible plan of selling the unsurveyed residue Congress are much divided; the Eastern States being strongly attached to that of townships, notwithstanding the expence incident to it; the Southern being equally biassed in favor of indiscriminate locations, notwithstanding the many objections against that mode. The dispute will probably terminate in some kind of compromise, if one can be hit upon.³⁰

2. The Government of the settlements on the Illinois and Wabash is a subject very perplexing in itself; and rendered more so by our ignorance of many circumstances on which a right judgment depends. The inhabitants at those places, claim protection against the savages, and some provision for both criminal and Civil justice. It appears also that land jobbers are among them who are likely to multiply litigations among individuals, and by collusive purchases of spurious titles, to defraud the United States.

3. The settlement of the public accounts has long been pursued in varied shapes, and with little prospect of success. The idea which has long been urged by some of us, seems now to be seriously embraced, of establishing a plenipotentiary tribunal for the final adjustment of the mutual claims on the great and simple principle of equity. An ordinance for this purpose has been reported by the Treasury board and has made some progress through Congress. It is likely to be much retarded by the thinness of Congress, as indeed is almost every other matter of importance.

4. The *Spanish negociation* is in a very *ticklish situation*. You have been already apprized of the *vote of seven states last fall* for *ceding* the *Missisipi* for a *term of years*. From sundry circumstances it was *inferred that Jay was* not *proceeding under this usurped authority*. A late instruction to *him to lay the state* of the *negociation before Congress* has *discovered* that he has *adjusted* with *Guardoqui* an *article* for *suspending* the *use of the Missisipi* by *the citizens of U.S.* The report however leaves it *somewhat doubtful how far U.S.* are *commited by this step* and a *subsequent* [Report]³¹ *of* the *secretary* on the *seizure of Spanish property* in the

---

28. At a later time, JM supplied this word, which he had omitted when encoding this sentence.

29. The italicized words in this sentence and in the rest of the letter were written in code.

30. For proposed systems of land surveys during the Confederation, see Payson J. Treat, *The National Land System, 1785–1820* (New York, 1910), pp. 179–97.

31. At a later time, JM supplied this word, which he had omitted when encoding this sentence.

*western country* and on *information of discontents,* touching the *occlusion of the Mississipi* shews that the probable *consequences of the measure perplex him extremely.* It was nevertheless conceived by the *instructed delegations* to be *their duty to press a revocation* of the *step taken* in some *form which would least offend* Spain and *least irritate* the *patrons of* the *vote* [of][32] *seven states.* Accordingly *a motion was made* to the *following effect*—that the *present state of the negociation with Spain and of the affairs of U.S. rendered it expedient* that *you should proceed under a special commission to Madrid* for the *purpose of making such representations as might at once impress* on that *court our friendly disposition* and *induce it to relax* on the *contested points,* and that the *proper communications* and *explanations* should *be made to Guardoqui relative* to this *change in* the *mode of conducting the negociation.* This *motion was referred* to *Mr. Jay* whose *report disapproves of it.* In this state the *matter lies.* Eight *states only being present no effective vote* is to be *expected.* It may notwithstanding be incumbent *on us to try some question* which will at least *mark the paucity of states who abet* the *obnoxious project. Massachusets* and *New York* alone of the present *states are under that* description; and *Connecticut and New Hampshire alone of the absent. Maryland* and *S. Carolina* have heretofore been on the *right side.* Their *future conduct* is somewhat problematical. The opinion of *New Hampshire* is only *conjectured.* The *conversion of Rhode Island* countenances a *hope that she too* may in this instance *desert the New England standard.*

The prospect of a full and respectable convention grows stronger every day. Rho. Island alone has refused to send deputies. Maryland has probably appointed by this time. Of Connecticut alone doubts are entertained. The antifederal party in that State is numerous and persevering. It is said that the elections which are now going on, are rather discouraging to the advocates of the Convention. Pennsylvania has added Doctor Franklin to her deputation. There is some ground to calculate on the attendance of Genl. Washington. Our Governor, Mr. Wythe, Mr. Blair, and Col. Mason will pretty certainly attend. The last I am informed is renouncing his errors on the subject of the Confederation, and means to take an active part in the amendment of it. Mr. Henry pretty soon resigned the undertaking. Genl. Nelson was put into his place, who has also declined. He was succeeded by R. H. Lee, who followed his example. Docr. McClurg has been since appointed, and as he was on the spot must have been previously consulted.

Considerable changes are taking place I hear in the County elections in Virginia, and a strong itch beginning to return for paper money. Mr. Henry is said to have the measure in contemplation, and to be laying his train for it already. He will however be powerfully opposed by Col. Mason, if he should be elected and be able to serve, by Monroe and Marshal, and Ludwel Lee (son of R. H. L.) who are already elected, and sundry others of inferior rank. Mr.

---

32. At a later time, JM supplied this word, which he had omitted when encoding this sentence.

Harrison the late Governor, has so far regained the favor of Charles City as to be reinstated a representative. The part which he will take is uncertain. From his repeated declarations he ought to be adverse to a paper emission. My next will probably be from Philada. In the mean time with my fervent wishes for your happiness I remain Yr. affecte. friend,

Js. MADISON JR.

Deaths. Archibald Cary Esqr.
Jno. Augustine Washington, brother of Genl. W.

## Madison to Jefferson

Philadelphia May 15, 1787

DEAR SIR

I am just furnished by Mr. Pollock with a box containing a few Peccan Nuts, which Mr. Jno. Vaughan of this City undertakes to forward by a Vessel just sailing for France.

Monday last was the day for the meeting of the Convention. The number as yet assembled is but small. Among the few is Genl. Washington who arrived on Sunday evening admist the acclamations of the people, as well as more sober marks of the affection and veneration which continues to be felt for his character. The Governor, Messrs. Wythe and Blair, and Docr. McClurg are also here. Col. Mason is to be here in a day or two. There is a prospect of a pretty full meeting on the whole, though there is less punctuality in the outset than was to be wished. Of this the late bad weather has been the principal cause. I mention these circumstances because it is possible, this may reach you before you hear from me through any other channel, and I add no others because it is merely possible. Adieu.

Js. MADISON JR.

## Madison to Jefferson

Philadelphia June 6, 1787

DEAR SIR

The day fixed for the meeting of the Convention was the 14th. ult: on the 25th. and not before seven States were assembled. General Washington was placed unâ voce in the chair. The Secretaryship was given to Major Jackson. The members present are from Massachusetts Mr. Gherry, Mr. Ghorum, Mr. King, Mr. Strong. From Connecticut Mr. Sherman, Doct. S. Johnson, Mr.

Elseworth. From N. York Judge Yates, Mr. Lansing, Col. Hamilton. N. Jersey, Governour Livingston, Judge Brearly, Mr. Patterson Attorney Genl. [Mr. Houston and Mr. Clarke are absent members.][33] From Pennsylvania Doctr. Franklyn, Mr. Morris, Mr. Wilson, Mr. Fitzimmons, Mr. G. Clymer, Genl. Mifflin, Mr. Governeur Morris, Mr. Ingersoll. From Delaware Mr. Jno. Dickenson, Mr. Read, Mr. Bedford, Mr. Broom, Mr. Bassett. From Maryland Majr. Jenifer only. Mr. McHenry, Mr. Danl. Carrol, Mr. Jno. Mercer, Mr. Luther Martin are absent members. The three last have supplied the resignations of Mr. Stone, Mr. Carrol of Carolton, and Mr. T. Johnson as I have understood the case. From Virginia Genl. Washington, Governor Randolph, Mr. Blair, Col. Mason, Docr. McClurg, J. Madison. Mr. Wythe left us yesterday, being called home by the serious declension of his lady's health.[34] From N. Carolina, Col. Martin late Governor, Docr. Williamson, Mr. Spaight, Col. Davy.

Col. Blount is another member but is detained by indisposition at N. York. From S. Carolina Mr. John Rutlidge, General Pinkney, Mr. Charles Pinkney, Majr. Pierce Butler. Mr. Laurens is in the Commission from that State, but will be kept away by the want of health. From Georgia Col. Few, Majr. Pierce, formerly of Williamsbg. and aid to Genl. Greene, Mr. Houston.

Mr. Baldwin will be added to them in a few days. Walton and Pendleton are also in the deputation. N. Hamshire has appointed Deputies but they are not expected; the State treasury being empty it is said, and a substitution of private resources being inconvenient or impracticable. I mention this circumstance to take off the appearance of backwardness, which that State is not in the least chargeable with, if we are rightly informed of her disposition. Rhode Island has not yet acceded to the measure. As their Legislature meet very frequently, and can at any time be got together in a week, it is possible that caprice if no other motive may yet produce a unanimity of the States in this experiment.

In furnishing you with this list of names, I have exhausted all the means which I can make use of for gratifying your curiosity. It was thought expedient in order to secure unbiassed discussion within doors, and to prevent misconceptions and misconstructions without, to establish some rules of caution which will for no short time restrain even a confidential communication of our proceedings. The names of the members will satisfy you that the States have been serious in this business. The attendance of Genl. Washington is a proof of the light in which he regards it. The whole Community is big with expectation. And there can be no doubt but that the result will in some way or other have a powerful effect on our destiny.

Mr. Adams' Book which has been in your hands of course, has excited a good deal of attention. An edition has come out here and another is on the

---

33. JM's brackets.
34. Elizabeth Wythe died in Aug.; see *PJM*, X, p. 30.

press at N. York. It will probably be much read, particularly in the Eastern States, and contribute with other circumstances to revive the predilections of this Country for the British Constitution. Men of learning find nothing new in it, Men of taste many things to criticize. And men without either, not a few things, which they will not understand. It will nevertheless be read, and praised, and become a powerful engine in forming the public opinion. The name and character of the Author, with the critical situation of our affairs, naturally account for such an effect. The book also has merit, and I wish many of the remarks in it, which are unfriendly to republicanism, may not receive fresh weight from the operations of our Governments.[35]

I learn from Virginia that the appetite for paper money grows stronger every day. Mr. H—n—y is an avowed patron of the scheme, and will not fail I think to carry it through unless the County[36] which he is to represent shall bind him hand and foot by instructions. I am told that this is in contemplation. He is also said to be unfriendly to an acceleration of Justice. There is good reason to believe *too that* [he is] *hostile* to *the object of the convention* and that *he wishes either a partition or total dissolution of the confederacy.*[37]

I sent you a few days ago by a Vessel going to France a box with peccan nuts planted in it. Mr. Jno. Vaughn was so good as to make the arrangements with the Capt: both for their preservation during the voyage and the conveyance of them afterwards. I had before sent you via England a few nuts sealed up in a letter.

Mr. Wythe gave me favorable accounts of your Nephew in Williamsburg. And from the Presidt. of Hampden Sidney who was here a few days ago I received information equally pleasing as to the genius, progress, and character of your younger nephew.

I must beg you to communicate my affectionate respects to our friend Mazzei, and to let him know that I have taken every step for securing his claim on Dorhman, which I judged most likely to succeed. There is little doubt that Congress will allow him more, than he owes Mr. Mazzei, and I have got from him such a draught on the Treasury board as I think will ensure him the chance of that fund.[38] Dorman is at present in Virga. where he has also some

---

35. John Adams published *A Defence of the Constitutions of Government of the United States of America* in London in 1787 and added two more volumes in 1788; see Page Smith, *John Adams,* 2 vols. (Garden City, N.Y., 1963), II, pp. 690-702, 711, 723-25. See Gordon S. Wood, "The Relevance and Irrelevance of John Adams," in his *The Creation of the American Republic,* pp. 567-92; for a discussion of Adams's role in the international argument over American state constitutions, see R. R. Palmer, *The Age of the Democratic Revolution: A Political History of Europe and America, 1760-1800,* 2 vols. (Princeton, 1959-64), I, pp. 263-82.

36. JM later wrote in "Prince Edward."

37. The italicized words in this sentence were written in code. JM omitted the two words in brackets but inserted them late in life.

38. For Dohrman, the Board of Treasury recommended a cash settlement, back pay, and a title to 640 acres in the Northwest Territory for his services as U.S. agent in Lisbon during the Revolution; see *PJM,* X, p. 31.

claims and expectations, but they are not in a transferrable situation. I intended to have written to Mazzei and must beg his pardon for not doing it. It is really out of my power at this time. Adieu. Yrs. affy.,

J M

## Jefferson to Madison

Paris June 20, 1787

DEAR SIR

I wrote you last on the 30th. of Jan. with a postscript of Feb. 5. Having set out the last day of that month to try the waters of Aix, and been journeying since till the 10th. inst. I have been unable to continue my correspondence with you.[39] In the mean time I have received your several favors of Feb. 15. Mar. 18. 19. and Apr. 23. The last arrived here about the 25th. of May, while those of Mar. 18. and 19. tho' written five weeks earlier arrived three weeks later. I mention this to shew you how incertain is the conveyance thro' England.

The idea of separating the executive business of the confederacy from Congress, as the judiciary is already in some degree, is just and necessary. I had frequently pressed on the members individually, while in Congress, the doing this by a resolution of Congress for appointing an Executive committee to act during the sessions of Congress, as the Committee of the states was to act during their vacations. But the referring to this Committee all executive business as it should present itself, would require a more persevering self-denial than I supposed Congress to possess. It will be much better to make that separation by a federal act. The negative proposed to be given them on all the acts of the several legislatures is now for the first time suggested to my mind. Primâ facie I do not like it. It fails in an essential character, that the hole and the patch should be commensurate. But this proposes to mend a small hole by covering the whole garment. Not more than 1. out of 100. state-acts concern the confederacy. This proposition then, in order to give them 1. degree of power which they ought to have, gives them 99. more which they ought not to have, upon a presumption that they will not exercise the 99. But upon every act there will be a preliminary question. Does this act concern the confederacy? And was there ever a proposition so plain as to pass Congress without a debate? Their decisions are almost always wise: they are like pure metal. But you know of how much dross this is the result. Would not an appeal from the state judicatures to a federal court, in all cases where the act of Confederation

39. For TJ's tour of southern France and northern Italy, see Dumbauld, pp. 83–109. George Green Shackelford's "A Glimpse into Elysium," in *Jefferson and the Arts: An Extended View*, ed. William Howard Adams (Washington, 1976), pp. 237–69, is a superlative analysis of TJ's two-week visit to northern Italy.

controuled the question, be as effectual a remedy, and exactly commensurate to the defect. A British creditor, e.g. sues for his debt in Virginia; the defendant pleads an act of the state excluding him from their courts; the plaintiff urges the Confederation and the treaty made under that, as controuling the state law; the judges are weak enough to decide according to the views of their legislature. An appeal to a federal court sets all to rights. It will be said that this court may encroach on the jurisdiction of the state courts. It may. But there will be a power, to wit Congress, to watch and restrain them. But place the same authority in Congress itself, and there will be no power above them to perform the same office. They will restrain within due bounds a jurisdiction exercised by others much more rigorously than if exercised by themselves.

I am uneasy at seeing that the sale of our Western lands is not yet commenced. That precious fund for the immediate extinction of our debt will I fear be suffered to slip thro' our fingers. Every delay exposes it to events which no human foresight can guard against. When we consider the temper of the people of that country, derived from the circumstances which surround them, we must suppose their *separation possible* at every moment.[40] If they can be *retained til* their governments *become* settled and wise, they will *remain* with us always, and be a precious part of our strength and of our virtue. *But* this affair of *the Missisipi* by shewing that *Congress is capable* of hesitating on a question which proposes a *clear sacrifice* of the *western* to the *maritime states* will with difficulty be *obliterated*. The proposition of *my going to Madrid* to try to *recover* there the ground which has been *lost* at *New York* by the *concession* of the vote of *seven states* I should think desperate. With respect to *myself,* weighing the pleasure of *the journey* and bare possibility of *success* in one scale, and the strong *probability* of *failure* and the public *disappointment directed* on *me* in the other, the latter preponderates. Add to this that *jealousy* might be *excited* in the *breast* of a *person* who could find occasions of making *me uneasy.*[41]

The late changes in the ministry here excite considerable hopes. I think we *gain in them all.* I am particularly happy at the *reentry* of *Malsherbes* into the *council.* His knolege, his integrity render his value inappreciable, and the greater *to me* because while he had no *view* of *office we* had established together the most unreserved *intimacy.* So far too *I am pleased* with *Montmorin. His* honesty proceeds from *the heart* as well as *the head* and therefore may be more surely *counted on. The king* loves *business, oeconomy, order* and *justice. He* wishes sincerely the good of *his people. He* is *irascible, rude* and very *limited in his understanding, religious* bordering only on *bigotry. He* has no *mistress,* loves his *queen* and is too much *governed by her. She is capricious* like *her brother and governed* by *him,* devoted to *pleasure and expence, not remarkable* for any other *vices or virtues. Unhappily the king* shews a propensity for the *pleasures* of the

---

40. The italicized words in this sentence and those in the rest of the letter were written in code.

41. TJ meant Secretary of Foreign Affairs John Jay, who in his negotiations in New York with the Spanish minister, Don Diego de Gardoqui, had agreed to the closing of the Mississippi River for twenty-five years.

*table.* That for *drink* has *increased lately* or at least it is *become more known.* For European news in general I will refer you to my letter to Mr. Jay. Is it not possible that the occurrences in Holland may excite a desire in many of leaving that country and transferring their effects out of it? May make an opening for shifting into their hands the debts due to this country, to it's officers and farmers? It would be surely eligible. I believe Dumas,[42] if put on the watch, might alone suffice: but surely if Mr. Adams should go when the moment offers. *Dumas* has been in the habit of sending his *letters open* to *me* to be *forwarded* to Mr. *Jay.* During my absence they passed through Mr. *Short's* hands who made *extracts* from them by which I see he has been recommending himself and *me* for the *money negociations in Holland.* It might be thought perhaps that *I have* encouraged *him in* this. Be assured, my dear Sir, that no such idea ever entered my head. On the contrary it is a *business* which would be the most *disagreeable to me* of all others, and for which *I am* the most *unfit person living. I do* not understand *bargaining* nor possess the *dexterity* requisite to *make* them. On the other hand Mr. *A.* whom I expressly and sincerely recommended, stands already on ground for that business which *I* could not gain in years. Pray set *me* to rights in the minds of those who may have supposed *me privy* to this proposition. En passant, I will observe with respect to *Mr. Dumas* that the death of the *C.* de *V.* places Congress more at *their* ease how to dispose of *him.* Our credit here has been ill treated here in public debate, and our *debt* deemed *apocryphal.* We should try to transfer this *debt* elsewhere, and leave nothing capable of exciting ill thoughts between us. I shall mention in my letter to Mr. Jay a disagreeable affair in which *Mr. Barclay* has been thrown into [jail] at *Bordeaux.*[43] An honester man cannot be found, nor a *slower* nor more *indecisive one. His affairs* too are so *embarrassed and desperate* that the *public reputation* is every moment in danger of being *compromitted* with *him.* He is perfectly amiable and honest with all *this.*

By the next packet I shall be able to send you some books as also your watch and pedometer. The two last are not yet done. To search for books and forward them to Havre will require more time than I had between my return and the departure of this packet. You did perfectly right as to the paiment by the Mr. Fitzhughs.

Having been a witness heretofore to the divisions in Congress on the

---

42. Charles W. F. Dumas served as unofficial U.S. agent at The Hague.

43. TJ omitted the word "jail," where Barclay spent five days for debt; see *PTJ,* XI, pp. 491–92. Charles Barclay was American consul general in France who had been appointed by TJ and John Adams as agent to negotiate a treaty with the emperor of Morocco. After completing his mission, he was en route to Paris when he was arrested in Bordeaux for a debt contracted in a commercial transaction prior to his diplomatic appointment. A Bordeaux judge released him because of his diplomatic immunity, but this decision was reversed in Paris. Before he could be rearrested, Barclay sailed for the United States. As secretary of state, TJ appointed Barclay consul for Morocco in 1791. As president, he drafted a memorial for Barclay's widow, and Congress compensated her for his services between 1781 and 1787. See *PTJ,* XI, pp. 494–500, and Cappon, I, pp. 53, 57–58, 63–65, 155–57.

subject of their foreign ministers, it would be a weakness in me to suppose none with respect to myself, or to count with any confidence on the renewal of my commission, which expires on the 10th. day of March next: and the more so as, instead of requiring the disapprobation of 7. states as formerly, that of one suffices for a recall when Congress consists of only 7. states, 2 when of 8. etc. which I suppose to be habitually their numbers at present. Whenever I leave this place, it will be necessary to begin my arrangements 6. months before my departure: and these, once fairly begun and under way, and my mind set homewards, a change of purpose could hardly take place. If it should be the desire of Congress that I should continue still longer, I could wish to know it at farthest by the packet which will sail from New York in September. Because were I to put off longer the quitting my house, selling my furniture etc. I should not have time left to wind up my affairs: and having once quitted, and sold off my furniture, I could not think of establishing myself here again. I take the liberty of mentioning this matter to you not with a desire to change the purpose of Congress, but to know it in time. I have never fixed in my own mind the epoch of my return so far as shall depend on myself, but I never suppose it very distant. Probably I shall not risk a second vote on this subject. Such trifling things may draw on one the displeasure of one or two states, and thus submit one to the disgrace of a recall.

I thank you for the Paccan nuts which accompanied your letter of March. Could you procure me a copy of the bill for proportioning crimes and punishments in the form in which it was ultimately rejected by the house of delegates? Young Mr. Bannister desired me to send him regularly the Mercure de France. I will ask leave to do this thro' you, and that you will adopt such method of forwarding them to him as will save him from being submitted to postage, which they would not be worth. As a compensation for your trouble you will be free to keep them till you shall have read them. I am with sentiments of the most sincere esteem Dear Sir Your friend and servt.,

TH: JEFFERSON

## *Madison to Jefferson*

Philadelphia July 18, 1787

DEAR SIR

I lately received and forwarded to Mr. Jno. Banister Jr. a packet which came from you under cover to me. I had an opportunity which avoided the charge of postage.

The Convention continue to sit, and have been closely employed since the Commencement of the Session. I am still under the mortification of being restrained from disclosing any part of their proceedings. As soon as I am at liberty I will endeavor to make amends for my silence, and if I ever have the pleasure of seeing you shall be able to give you pretty full gratification. I have taken lengthy notes of every thing that has yet passed, and mean to go on with the drudgery, if no indisposition obliges me to discontinue it. It is not possible to form any judgment of the future duration of the Session. I am led by sundry circumstances to guess that the residue of the work will not be very quickly dispatched. The public mind is very impatient for the event, and various reports are circulating which tend to inflame curiosity. I do not learn however that any discontent is expressed at the concealment; and have little doubt that the people will be as ready to receive, as we shall be able to propose, a Government that will secure their liberties and happiness.

I am not able to give you any account of what is doing at N. York. Your correspondents there will no doubt supply the omission. The paper money here ceased to circulate very suddenly a few days ago. It had been for some time vibrating between a depreciation of 12. and of 20 Per Ct. The entire stagnation is said to have proceeded from a combination of a few people with whom the Country people deal on market days against receiving it. The consequence was that it was refused in the market, and great distress brought on the poorer Citizens. Some of the latter began in turn to form combinations of a more serious nature in order to take revenge on the supposed authors of the stagnation. The timely interposition of some influencial characters prevented a riot, and prevailed on the persons who were opposed to the paper, to publish their willingness to receive it. This has stifled the popular rage, and got the paper into circulation again. It is however still considerably below par, and must have received a wound which will not easily be healed. Nothing but evil springs from this imaginary money wherever it is tried, and yet the appetite for it, when it has not been tried, continues to be felt. There is good reason to fear that the bitterness of the evil must be tasted in Virga. before the appetite there will be at an end.

The Wheat harvest throughout the Continent has been uncommonly fine both in point of quantity and quality. The crops of corn and Tobacco on the ground in Virginia are very different in different places. I rather fear that in general they are both bad: particularly the former. I have just received a letter from Orange which complains much of appearances in that neighbourhood; but says nothing of them in the parts adjacent. Present my best respects to Mr. Short and Mr. Mazzei. Nothing has been done since my last to the latter with regard to his affair with Dorhman. Wishing you all happiness, I am Dr. Sir Yr. affec. friend and servt.,

Js. Madison Jr.

## Jefferson to Madison

Paris Aug. 2, 1787

DEAR SIR

My last was of June 20. Your's received since that date are May 15. and June 6. In mine I acknoleged the receipt of the Paccan nuts which came sealed up. I have reason to believe those in the box are arrived at Lorient. By the Mary Capt. Howland lately sailed from Havre to N. York I shipped three boxes of books one marked J.M. for yourself, one marked B.F. for Doctr. Franklin, and one marked W.H. for William Hay in Richmond. I have taken the liberty of addressing them all to you as you will see by the inclosed bill of lading, in hopes you would be so good as to forward the other two. You will have opportunities of calling on the gentlemen for the freight etc. In yours you will find the books noted in the account inclosed herewith. You have now Mably's works complete except that on Poland, which I have never been able to get, but shall not cease to search for. Some other volumes to compleat your collection of Chronologies. The 4th. vol. of D'Albon was lost by the bookbinder, and I have not yet been able to get one to replace it. I shall continue to try. The Memoires sur les droits et impositions en Europe (cited by Smith) was a scarce and excessively dear book. They are now reprinting it. I think it will be in three or four quartos of from 9. to 12 a volume. When it is finished I shall take a copy for you. Amelot's travels into China I can learn nothing of. I put among the books sent you, two somewhat voluminous, and the object of which will need explanation; these are the Tableau de Paris and L'espion Anglois. The former is truly a picture of private manners in Paris, but presented on the dark side and a little darkened moreover. But there is so much truth in it's ground work that it will be well worth your reading. You will then know Paris (and probably the other large cities of Europe) as well as if you had been here years. L'Espion Anglois is no Caricature. It will give you a just idea of the wheels by which the machine of government is worked here. There are in it also many interesting details of the last war, which in general may be relied on. It may be considered as the small history of great events. I am in hopes when you shall have read them you will not think I have mis-spent your money for them. My method for making out this assortment was to revise the list of my own purchases since the invoice of 1785, and to select such as I had found worth your having. Besides this I have casually met with and purchased some few curious and cheap things. I have made out the Dr. side of the account, taking for my ground work yours of March 18. 1786. correcting two errors of computation in that which were to your prejudice. The account of the Mr. Fitzhughs stood thus. 1785. Sep. 1. cash 600.$^{tt}$ Nov. 10. paid their bill of exchange in favor of Limozin 480.$^{tt}$ making 1080.$^{tt}$ The money they paid you was worth 1050.$^{tt}$ according to our mode of settling at 18.$^{tt}$ for 20/ Virginia money. The difference of 30.⅛ will never be worth notice unless you were to meet with them by chance, and hardly then. I must trouble you on behalf of a Mr. Thos. Burke at Loughburke near Loughrea in Ireland, whose brother James Burke is supposed to have died in 1785. on his passage from Jamaica, or St. Eustatius to New York. His property on board the vessel is understood to have come to the hands of Alderman Groom at New York. The inclosed copy of a letter to him will more fully explain it. A particular friend of mine here applies to me for information, which I must ask the favor of you to procure and forward to me.[44]

Writing news to others, much pressed in time, and making this letter one of private business, I did not intend to have said any thing to you on political subjects. But I must press one subject. Mr. Adams informs me he has borrowed money in Holland, which if confirmed by Congress will enable them to pay not only the interest due here to the foreign officers but the principal. Let me beseech you to reflect on the expediency of transferring this debt to Holland. All our other debts in Europe do not injure our reputation so much as this. These gentlemen have connections both in and out of office, and these again their connections, so that our default on this article is further known, more blamed, and excites worse dispositions against us than you can conceive. If you think as I do, pray try to procure an order for paying off their capital. Mr. Adams adds that if any certain tax is provided for the paiment of interest, Congress may borrow enough in Holland to pay off their whole debts in France both public and private, to the crown, to the farmers and to Beaumarchais. Surely it will be better to transfer these debts to Holland. So critical is the state of that country that I imagine the monied men of it would be glad to place their money in foreign countries, and that Mr. Adams could borrow there for us without a certain tax for the interest, and saving our faith too by previous explanations on that subject. This country is really supposed on the eve of a *bankruptcy*.[45] Such a spirit has risen within a few weeks as could not have been believed. They see the great deficit in their revenues, and the hopes of oeconomy lessen daily. The parliament refuse to register any act for a new tax, and require an assembly of the states. The object of this assembly is evidently to give law to the king, to fix a constitution, to limit expences. These views are said to gain upon the nation. The *king's passion* for *drink* is *divesting him* of all *respect*. The *queen* is *detested* and an *explosion* of some sort is not impossible. The *ministry* is alarmed, and the surest reliance at this moment for the *public peace* is on their *two hundred thousand men*. I cannot write these things in a public dispatch because they would *get* into a *newspaper* and *come back here*. A final decision of some sort should be made in Beaumarchais' affairs.

44. "Alderman Groom" was John Broome, a New York merchant; see *ibid.,* 668, and XII, p. 138. The "particular friend" was the abbess of the abbey of Pentemont, where TJ's daughter attended school.

45. The italicized word and those in the rest of the letter were written in code.

I am with sentiments of the most perfect esteem Dear Sir Your friend and servt,

TH: JEFFERSON

P.S. The watch and pedometer not done. In the box of books are some for the colleges of Philadelphia and Williamsburg and two vols. of the Encyclopedie for Congress, presented by the author of that part.

ENCLOSURE
*State of account between James Madison esq. and Th: Jefferson Dr.*

|  |  | J: M. to Th: J.    Dr. | *lt* |  |  |
|---|---|---|---|---|---|
| 1785. | Sep. 1. | To amount of books | 1164 – 3 |  |  |
|  |  | Cr. | *lt* |  |  |
|  |  | By balance stated by Th: J. 77⅔ Dollars. | 407 – 15 |  |  |
|  |  | By advance to Le Maire 10. Guineas | 234 – |  |  |
|  |  | By 6. copies of revisal @ 2½ dollars. | 81 – |  |  |
|  |  | By 25£ Virga. currcy. remitted to Mrs. Carr | 441 – 8 | 1164 – 3 |  |
|  |  | James Madison esq. to Th: Jefferson Dr. | *lt* |  |  |
|  |  | To 58£-6s-8 Virga. currency received from the Fitzhughs | 1050 – 0 – 0 |  |  |
| 1785. | Nov. 4. | To repaid Mr. Short for a Spy-glass bought in England | 50 – |  |  |
|  | Nov. 21. | To Limozin at Havre transportation of 2. trunks of books Sep. 1785. | 34 – 8 – 9 |  |  |
| 1786. | Aug. 2. | To paid for an Umbrella cane | 30 – |  |  |
|  |  | a copying press and apparatus, paper and ink | 144 – |  |  |
|  | Oct. 13. | a chemical box | 69 – |  |  |
| 1787. | July 4. | To paid Cabaret for binding books | 46 – 14 |  |  |
|  |  | To paid for books, to wit. |  |  |  |

|  | *lt* | *s* | *d* |  |
|---|---|---|---|---|
| Guerre de 1775 – 83. 4to | 10 – | 0 – | 0 |  |
| Voyage en Suisse par Mayer. 2. v. 8vo. | 7 – | 4 |  |  |
| Ordonnance de marine 8vo. | 4 – | 4 |  |  |
| Voiage aux Alpes par Saussure. 4. v. 8vo. | 18 – |  |  |  |
| Experiences d'Ingenhousz. 8vo. | 4 – 10 |  |  |  |
| Chymie de Fourcroy. 4. v. 8vo. | 24 – 0 |  |  |  |
| Peines infamantes par La Cretelle. 8vo. | 3 – 12 |  |  |  |
| Savary sur l'Egypte 3. v. 8vo. | 15 – 0 |  |  |  |
| Voiages de Volney. 2. v. 8vo. | 10 – 4 |  |  |  |
| la France et les etats Unis par Warville. 8vo | 4 – 10 |  |  |  |
| Loix criminelles par Warville 2. v. 8vo. | 7 – 4 |  |  |  |
| Vie de Turgot par Condorcet. 8vo. | 4 – 10 |  |  |  |
| L'Espion Anglois. 10. v. 12mo. | 25 – 0 |  |  |  |
| Annales Romaines par Macquer. 12mo. | 5 – |  |  |  |
|  | 142 – 18 |  | 1424 – 2 – 9 |  |

|   |   |   | lt s | lt s d |
|---|---|---|---|---|
| | | Brought forward | 142–18 | 1424– 2– 9 |
| | | Troubles de l'Amerique par Soulés. 4. v. 8vo. | 16– 0– | |
| | | Bibliotheque physico-oeconomique (1786) 2. v. 12mo. | 5– 4 | |
| | | Mably. Principes de legislation. 12mo. | 3– | |
| | | —— de la Grece. 12mo. | 2– | |
| | | De Juvigny sur la decadence des lettres. 8vo. | 6– | |
| | | Abregé chronologique d'Angleterre de Salmon. 2. v. 8vo. | 12– | |
| | | Abregé chronol. de l'histoire ecclesiastique | 18– | |
| | | Abregé chronol. de l'Allemagne par Pfeffel. 2. v. 12mo. | 12– | |
| | | Histoire ancienne de Milot. 4. v. 12mo. | 12– | |
| | | Moderne 5. v. 12mo. | 15 | |
| | | de France 3. v. 12mo. | 7–10 | |
| | | De Thou. 11. v. 4to | 55– | |
| | | Bibliotheque Physico-oeconomique. (1787.) 2. v. 12mo. | 5– 4 | |
| | | Pieces interessantes. 4. v. 12mo. | 12– | |
| | | Tableau de Paris 4. v. 12mo. | 13– | |
| | (given) | Demarcation entre l'Espagne et le Portugal en Amerique. | | |
| | | Histoire de Kentuckey. 8vo. | 4– 5 | |
| | | Smith's history of New York. 8vo. | 6– | |
| | | Voiages de Chastellux. 2. v. 8vo. | 11– | |
| | | Memoires de Brandenburgh. 8vo. | 6– | |
| | | Examen de Chastellux par Warville. 8vo. | 2– 8 | |
| | | Hennepin. 12mo. | 2– | |
| | | Vie de Voltaire par l'Abbé Duvernet. 8vo. | 7– 5 | |
| | | | 375–14 | 1424– 2– 9 |

|   |   |   | lt s | lt s d |
|---|---|---|---|---|
| | | Brought forward | 375–14 | 1424– 2– 9 |
| | | Histoire de la Nouvelle France par Lescarbot 8vo. | 2–10 | |
| | | Gibson's Saxon chronicle. 4to. 6/ sterl. | 7– 4 | |
| | | Avantages et desavantages de la decouverte de l'Amerique | 1– 4 | |
| | | Encyclopedie. 16th. 18th. 19th. 20th. 22d. livraisons @ 24 lt. each. 120 15th. 23 lt-10—17th. and 21st. 36 lt-10 each  96–10 | 216–10 | |
| | | *5th. Oiseaux to. 1. part 2. | 7–0 | 610– 2 |
| 1787. Aug. 4. | | To paid Limozin carriage of books to Havre (exclus. of Dr. F's and Hay's) | | 27–14– 9 |
| | | | | 2061–19– 6 |

Graecorum respublicae Ubbonis Emmii (qu. if sent?)  9 lt.

*when your duplicate vol. shall be returned they will give you credit for it.

Cr.

By error in computing the value of 10 Guineas in former account

$$\frac{s\ lt\ \ s\ lt\ \ s}{(20{:}18{::}28{:}25-4)}$$
$$\frac{£\ \ \ \ lt}{}$$
By do. $\overline{25} = \overline{441} - 8$ remitted to Mrs. Carr
$$\frac{£\ \ \ \ lt}{(25 = 450)}$$

| | lt |
|---|---|
| | 18 |
| | 8– 12 |

---

NB. Having been very desirous of collecting the original Spanish writers on American history, I commissioned Mr. Carmichael to purchase some for me. They came very dear, and moreover he was obliged to take duplicates in two instances. I have packed one copy of these in Mr. Madison's box, and will beg the favor of him to sell them for me if he can. I state below the exact prices they cost me in Spain, adding nothing for transportation to France, which was high.

La Florida de Garcilasso de la Vega. fol.  
Historia General de la Florida por De Cadenasz Caro. fol. } 200. reals = 10. Dollars.  
Herrera Historia General 4. v. fol.              500. reals = 25. Dollars.

TH: JEFFERSON<br>Aug. 3. 1787

1784.

Cr.

| | Doll. | lt s | livres sous den. |
|---|---|---|---|
| By balance brought forward 77⅔ @ | 5– 5 | | 407–15– 0 |
| By advance to le Maire 10 Guineas | | | 234– |
| By do. for 6 Revisals at 2½ drs. | | | 81– |
| | | | 722–15– |
| By £25 Va. Currency remitted to Mrs. Carr for use of Peter and Dabney equal to the Balance | | | 441– 8 |
| | | | 1164– 3 |

## Jefferson to Madison

Paris Aug. 15, 1787

DEAR SIR

A gentleman going from hence by Lorient to Boston furnishes me an opportunity of recommending to your care the inclosed letters which I could not get ready for the last packet. Pray inform me in your next whether letters directed to your foreign ministers or franked by them are free of postage. That they ought to be so, is acknoleged substantially by the resolution of Congress allowing us to charge postages. I have sometimes suspected that my letters stagnate in the post-offices.

My letters by the last packet brought down the domestic news of this country to the day in which the bed of justice was held.[46] The day before yesterday the parliament house was surrounded by ten thousand people, who received them, on their adjournment, with acclamations of joy, took out the horses of the principal speakers and drew their chariots themselves to their hotels. The parliament not having taken the desperate step (as far as is known yet) of forbidding the execution of the new tax laws by an Arret de defense sur peine de mort, we presume it is the fear of a popular commotion which has occasioned the king to exile them to Troyes. This is known only this morning. The ministry here have certain information that the English squadron has sailed, and took it's course Westwardly. This is another move towards war. No other important fact has taken place since my letters by the packet. Adieu. Yours affectionately,

TH: JEFFERSON

## Madison to Jefferson

Philadelphia Sept. 6, 1787

DEAR SIR

My last was intended for the Augst. Packet and put into the hands of Commodore Paul Jones. Some disappointments prevented his going, and as he did not know but its contents might be unfit for the ordinary conveyance, he retained it. The precaution was unnecessary. For the same reason the delay has been of little consequence. The rule of secrecy in the Convention rendered that as it will this letter barren of those communications which might otherwise be made. As the Convention will shortly rise I should feel little scruple in disclosing what will be public here, before it could reach you, were it practicable for me to guard by Cypher against an intermediate discovery. But I am deprived of this resource by the shortness of the interval between the receipt of your letter of June 20. and the date of this. This is the first day which has been free from Committee service both before and after the hours of the House, and the last that is allowed me by the time advertised for the sailing of the Packet.

The Convention consists now as it has generally done of Eleven States. There has been no intermission of its Sessions since a house was formed; except an interval of about ten days allowed a Committee appointed to detail the general propositions agreed on in the House. The term of its dissolution cannot be more than one or two weeks distant. A Government will probably be submitted to the *people of* the *states* consisting of a President *cloathed* with *executive power;* a *Senate chosen* by the Legislatures, and another *house chosen* by

---

46. A "bed of justice" is a court session attended by the king or by a prince of the blood as his immediate representative.

the *people of* the *states* jointly *possessing* the *legislative power* and a regular *judiciary* establishment.[47] The mode of constituting the *executive* is among the few points not yet finally settled. The *Senate* will consist of two *members* from each *State* and *appointed sexennially:* The other, of *members appointed biennially* by the *people of* the *states* in proportion to their number. The Legislative power will *extend to taxation, trade* and sundry other general matters. The powers of Congress will be *distributed* according to their *nature among the several departments.* The States will be *restricted from paper money* and in a *few other instances.* These are *the outlines.* The extent of them may perhaps surprise you. I hazard an opinion nevertheless that the *plan should* it *be adopted* will neither effectually *answer* its *national object* nor prevent the local *mischiefs* which every where *excite disgusts* against the *state governments.* The grounds of this opinion will be the subject of a future letter.[48]

I have written to a friend in Congress intimating in a covert manner the necessity of deciding and notifying the intentions of Congress with regard to their foreign Ministers after May next, and have dropped a hint on the communications of Dumas.

Congress have taken some measures for disposing of their public land, and have actually sold a considerable tract. Another bargain I learn is on foot for a further sale.

Nothing can exceed the universal anxiety for the event of the Meeting here. Reports and conjectures abound concerning the nature of the plan which is to be proposed. The public however is certainly in the dark with regard to it. The Convention is equally in the dark as to the reception which may be given to it on its publication. All the prepossessions are on the right side, but it may well be expected that certain characters will wage war against any reform whatever. My own idea is that the public mind will now or in a very little time receive any thing that promises stability to the public Councils and security to private rights, and that no regard ought to be had to local prejudices or temporary considerations. If the present moment be lost it is hard to say what may be our fate.

Our information from Virginia is far from being agreeable. In many parts of the Country the drouth has been extremely injurious to the corn. I fear, tho' I have no certain information, that Orange and Albemarle share in the distress. The people also are said to be generally discontented. A paper emission is again a topic among them. So is an instalment of all debts in some places and the making property a tender in others. The taxes are another source of discontent. The weight of them is complained of, and the abuses in collecting them still more so. In several Counties the prisons and Court Houses and Clerks offices have been wilfully burnt. In Green Briar the course of Justice has been mutinously stopped, and associations entered into against the payment

---

47. The italicized words in this sentence and those in the rest of the letter were written in code.

48. See JM to TJ, Oct. 24, 1787, below.

of taxes. No other County has yet followed the example. The approaching meeting of the Assembly will probably allay the discontents on one side by measures which will excite them on another.

Mr. Wythe has never returned to us. His lady whose illness carryed him away, died some time after he got home. The other deaths in Virga. are Col. A. Cary, and a few days ago, Mrs. Harrison, wife of Benjn. Harrison Junr. and sister of J. F. Mercer. Wishing you all happiness I remain Dear Sir Yrs. affecty.,

Js. MADISON JR.

Give my best wishes to Mazzei. I have received his letter and book and will write by next packet to him. Dorhman is still in Va. Congress have done nothing further in his affair. I am not sure that 9 states have been assembled of late. At present it is doubtful whether there are seven.

## Jefferson to Madison

Paris Sept. 17, 1787

DEAR SIR

My last to you were of Aug. 2. and 15. Since that I have sent to Havre to be forwarded to you by the present packet 3. boxes marked J.M. G.W. and A.D. The two last are for Mr. Wythe in Williamsburgh, and Mr. Alexr. Donald merchant in Richmond. The first contains the books for yourself which shall be noted at the close of my letter, together with the following for Mr. Rittenhouse; viz. la Chymie de Fourcroi 4 vols. 8vo. Connoissance des Tems 1788–1789. and Dissertation de la Sauvagere. I have put into the same box 9. copies of the Notes on Virginia. That of the English edition, and one of the others are for yourself. The 7. remaining are for Mr. Jay, Mr. Thomson, Mr. Hopkinson, Mr. Mercer (late of Congress) Mr. Rittenhouse, Mr. Izard and Mr. Ed. Rutledge, which I will pray of you to have delivered in my name to those gentlemen. I have also put into the box 100 copies of the map of Virginia Pennsylvania etc. which be so good as to put into the hands of any booksellers you please in New York and Philadelphia to be sold at such price as you think proper, ready money only.[49] I have sent some to Virginia to be sold at ⅚ of a dollar. If it should appear that a greater number might be sold, I would have the plate re-touched, and any number struck off which might be desired. It may serve to refund a part of the expences of printing the book and engraving the map.

In my letter of Aug. 2. I troubled you on the case of John Burke. I now inclose you a letter lately received, by which it will appear that Mr. Broom (not

---

49. The map had been included in both the French and English editions of TJ's *Notes on the State of Virginia*. It is based on the 1751 map drawn by Peter Jefferson, TJ's father, and his collaborator, Joshua Fry, and is reproduced as an endpaper in William Peden's edition of the *Notes*.

Groom) of New York paid into the hands of a Capt. William S. Browne of Providence in Rhode island a balance of £56. The property of John Burke deceased, brother to Thos. Burke who writes the letter: that possibly there may be more of his property in Brown's hands: and that it is Brown for whom your enquiries must be directed, and of whom the money must be demanded. If he will pay it on this letter of Thomas Burke, (in real money) it might be placed in the bank of Philadelphia till called for by T. B. If he requires more regular authority, be so good as to inform me what may be necessary and I will give notice to Mrs. Burke the wife of Thomas who lives in France and to whom he has confided the pursuit of this object.

I have received the box you were so kind as to send me with paccans. There were 13. nuts in it, which I mention, because I suspect it had been pillaged. Your situation at New York, and the packets coming from thence to Havre, where Mr. Limozin, agent for the U.S. will take care of any thing for me, may enable you to send me a few barrels of Newtown pippins and cranberries. If you could send me also 50. or 100 grafts of the Newtown pippin they would be very desireable. They should be packed between layers of moss, a layer of moss and a layer of plants alternately, in a box, and the box nailed close, with directions to Limozin to forward them by the Diligence. Red birds for the ladies, and Opossums for the naturalists would be great presents, if any passenger would take charge of them. I must either refer you to my public letter for news, or write you a letter of news if my time will permit. I am with sincere esteem, dear Sir, your friend and servant,

Th: Jefferson

J. Madison esq. to Th: Jefferson Dr.

| | |
|---|---:|
| To paid Frouille for the box marked J.M. No. 1. and packing | 20$^{tt}$ – 0 |
| Memoires sur les impositions de l'Europe 4. v. 4to. | 36 – |
| Loisirs d'Argenson. 2 v. 8vo. | 8 – 10 |
| Charlevoix histoire de la nouvelle France. 3. v. 4to. | 27 |
| American traveller 4to. | 3 |
| Pollucis onomasticon. 4to. | 5 |
| Buffon Mineraux. 5th. 6th. 7th. 8th. volumes | 12 |
| Pieces interessantes. 5th. vol. | 3 |
| Dissertation de la Sauvagere 8vo. | 4 – 12 |
| | 119 – 2 |

Your watch is done, and is in my possession. She costs 3. guineas more than I had told you she would. Two were owing to a mistake of mine in the price of my own, and the other to that of the workman who put that much gold into the case more than he had into mine. Yours costs therefore 600.$^{tt}$ I have worn it a month during which, tho new, it is impossible for a watch to go better. I shall send her by the French minister, Monsieur le comte de

Moustier. I wish the step-counter may be done in time to go by the same conveiance. I have been almost tempted to buy for you one of the little clocks made here mounted on marble columns. They strike, go with a pendulum, a spring instead of a weight, are extremely elegant and can be had for 10. guineas. But I shall wait your orders.

TH: J.

P.S. Will you be so good as to pay Mr. C. Thomson 86.35 dollars for me, and to apologize to him for my not writing, the bearer going off a day sooner than he had told me. The letter to N. Lewis is of great consequence.

*Jefferson to Madison*

Paris Oct. 8, 1787

DEAR SIR

The bearer hereof the count de Moustier, successor to Monsr. de la Luzerne, would from his office need no letter of introduction to you or to any body. Yet I take the liberty of recommending him to you to shorten those formal approaches which the same office would otherwise expose him to in making your acquaintance. He is a great enemy to formality, etiquette, ostentation and luxury. He goes with the best dispositions to cultivate society without poisoning it by ill example. He is sensible, disposed to view things favorably, and being well acquainted with the constitution of England, it's manners and language, is the better prepared for his station with us. But I should have performed only the lesser, and least pleasing half of my task, were I not to add my recommendations of Madame de Brehan. She is goodness itself. You must be well acquainted with her. You will find her well disposed to meet your acquaintance and well worthy of it. The way to please her is to receive her as an acquaintance of a thousand years standing. She speaks little English. You must teach her more, and learn French from her. She hopes by accompanying M. de Moustier to improve her health which is very feeble, and still more to improve her son in his education and to remove him to a distance from the seductions of this country. You will wonder to be told that there are no schools in this country to be compared to ours, in the sciences. The husband of Madame de Brehan is an officer, and obliged by the times to remain with the army. Monsieur de Moustier brings your watch. I have worn her two months, and really find her a most incomparable one. She will not want the little re-dressing which new watches generally do, after going about a year. She costs 600 livres. To open her in all her parts, press the little pin on the edge, with the point of your nail. That opens the chrystal. Then open the dial plate in the usual way. Then press the stem, at the end within the loop, and it opens the back for winding up or regulating. *De Moutier is remarkably communicative.*[50] *With adroitness he may be pumped of any thing. His openness is from character not from affectation. An intimacy with him will on this account be politically valuable.* I am Dear Sir Your affectionate friend and servant,

TH: JEFFERSON

*Madison to Jefferson*

New York Oct. 24 and Nov. 1, 1787

DEAR SIR

My two last, though written for the two last Packets, have unluckily been delayed till this conveyance. The first of them was sent from Philada. to Commodore Jones in consequence of information that he was certainly to go by the packet then about to sail. Being detained here by his business with Congress, and being unwilling to put the letter into the mail without my approbation, which could not be obtained in time, he detained the letter also. The second was sent from Philada. to Col. Carrington, with a view that it might go by the last packet at all events in case Commodore Jones should meet with further detention here. By ill luck he was out of Town, and did not return till it was too late to make use of the opportunity. Neither of the letters were indeed of much consequence at the time and are still less so now. I let them go forward nevertheless as they may mention some circumstances not at present in my recollection, and as they will prevent a chasm on my part of our correspondence which I have so many motives to cherish by an exact punctuality.

Your favor of June 20. has been already acknowledged. The last packet from France brought me that of August 2d. I have received also by the Mary Capt. Howland the three Boxes for W. H. B. F. and myself.[51] The two first have been duly forwarded. The contents of the last are a valuable addition to former literary remittances and lay me under additional obligations, which I shall always feel more strongly than I express. The articles included for Congress have been delivered and those for the two Universities and for General Washington have been forwarded, as have been the various letters for your friends in Virginia and elsewhere. The parcel of rice referred to in your letter to the Delegates of S. Carolina has met with some accident. No account whatever can be gathered concerning it. It probably was not shipped from France. Ubbo's book I find was not omitted as you seem to have apprehended. The charge for it however is, which I must beg you to supply. The duplicate volume of the Encyclopedie, I left in Virginia, and it is uncertain when I shall

---

50. These italicized words and those in the rest of the letter were written in code.
51. "W. H." was William Hay; "B. F." was Benjamin Franklin.

have an opportunity of returning it. Your Spanish duplicates will I fear be hardly vendible. I shall make a trial wherever a chance presents itself. A few days ago I received your favor of the 15 of Augst. via L'Orient and Boston. The letters inclosed along with it were immediately sent on to Virga.

You will herewith receive the result of the Convention, which continued its session till the 17th of September. I take the liberty of making some observations on the subject which will help to make up a letter, if they should answer no other purpose.

It appeared to be the sincere and unanimous wish of the Convention to cherish and preserve the Union of the States. No proposition was made, no suggestion was thrown out in favor of a partition of the Empire into two or more Confederacies.

It was generally agreed that the objects of the Union could not be secured by any system founded on the principle of a confederation of sovereign States. A *voluntary*[52] observance of the federal law by all the members could never be hoped for. A *compulsive*[53] one could evidently never be reduced to practice, and if it could, involved equal calamities to the innocent and the guilty, the necessity of a military force both obnoxious and dangerous, and in general, a scene resembling much more a civil war, than the administration of a regular Government.

Hence was embraced the alternative of a government which instead of operating, on the States, should operate without their intervention on the individuals composing them: and hence the change in the principle and proportion of representation.

This ground-work being laid, the great objects which presented themselves were 1. to unite a proper energy in the Executive and a proper stability in the Legislative departments, with the essential characters of Republican Government. 2. To draw a line of demarkation which would give to the General Government every power requisite for general purposes, and leave to the States every power which might be most beneficially administered by them. 3. To provide for the different interests of different parts of the Union. 4. To adjust the clashing pretensions of the large and small States. Each of these objects was pregnant with difficulties. The whole of them together formed a task more difficult than can be well conceived by those who were not concerned in the execution of it. Adding to these considerations the natural diversity of human opinions on all new and complicated subjects, it is impossible to consider the degree of concord which ultimately prevailed as less than a miracle.[54]

The first of these objects as it respects the Executive, was peculiarly embarrassing. On the question whether it should consist of a single person, or a

52. JM's italics.
53. JM's italics.
54. JM discussed these objectives of the convention in *The Federalist* Number 37.

plurality of co-ordinate members, on the mode of appointment, on the duration in office, on the degree of power, on the re-eligibility, tedious and reiterated discussions took place. The plurality of co-ordinate members had finally but few advocates. Governour Randolph was at the head of them. The modes of appointment proposed were various, as by the people at large—by electors chosen by the people—by the Executives of the States—by the Congress, some preferring a joint ballot of the two Houses—some a separate concurrent ballot allowing to each a negative on the other house—some a nomination of several canditates by one House, out of whom a choice should be made by the other. Several other modifications were started. The expedient at length adopted seemed to give pretty general satisfaction to the members. As to the duration in office, a few would have preferred a tenure during good behaviour—a considerable number would have done so in case an easy and effectual removal by impeachment could be settled. It was much agitated whether a long term, seven years for example, with a subsequent and perpetual ineligibility, or a short term with a capacity to be re-elected, should be fixed. In favor of the first opinion were urged the danger of a gradual degeneracy of re-elections from time to time, into first a life and then a hereditary tenure, and the favorable effect of an incapacity to be reappointed, on the independent exercise of the Executive authority. On the other side it was contended that the prospect of necessary degradation would discourage the most dignified characters from aspiring to the office, would take away the principal motive to the faithful discharge of its duties. The hope of being rewarded with a reappointment, would stimulate ambition to violent efforts for holding over the constitutional term, and instead of producing an independent administration, and a firmer defence of the constitutional rights of the department, would render the officer more indifferent to the importance of a place which he would soon be obliged to quit for ever, and more ready to yield to the incroachments of the Legislature of which he might again be a member.

The questions concerning the degree of power turned chiefly on the appointment to offices, and the controul on the Legislature. An *absolute*[55] appointment to all offices—to some offices—to no offices, formed the scale of opinions on the first point. On the second, some contended for an absolute negative, as the only possible mean of reducing to practice, the theory of a free government which forbids a mixture of the Legislative and Executive powers. Others would be content with a revisionary power to be overruled by three fourths of both Houses. It was warmly urged that the judiciary department should be associated in the revision. The idea of some was that a separate revision should be given to the two departments—that if either objected two thirds; if both three fourths, should be necessary to overrule.

In forming the Senate, the great anchor of the Government, the questions as they came within the first object turned mostly on the mode of ap-

55. JM's italics.

pointment, and the duration of it. The different modes proposed were, 1. by the House of Representatives, 2. by the Executive, 3 by electors chosen by the people for the purpose, 4. by the State Legislatures. On the point of duration, the propositions descended from good behavior to four years, through the intermediate terms of nine, seven, six and five years. The election of the other branch was first determined to be triennial, and afterwards reduced to biennial.

The second object, the due partition of power, between the General and local Governments, was perhaps of all, the most nice and difficult. A few contended for an entire abolition of the States; Some for indefinite power of Legislation in the Congress, with a negative on the laws of the States, some for such a power without a negative, some for a limited power of legislation, with such a negative: the majority finally for a limited power without the negative. The question with regard to the Negative underwent repeated discussions, and was finally rejected by a bare majority. As I formerly intimated to you my opinion in favor of this ingredient, I will take this occasion of explaining myself on the subject. Such a check on the States appears to me necessary 1. to prevent encroachments on the General authority, 2. to prevent instability and injustice in the legislation of the States.

1. Without such a check in the whole over the parts, our system involves the evil of imperia in imperio.[56] If a compleat supremacy some where is not necessary in every Society, a controuling power at least is so, by which the general authority may be defended against encroachments of the subordinate authorities, and by which the latter may be restrained from encroachments on each other. If the supremacy of the British Parliament is not necessary as has been contended, for the harmony of that Empire, it is evident I think that without the royal negative or some equivalent controul, the unity of the system would be destroyed. The want of some such provision seems to have been mortal to the antient Confederacies, and to be the disease of the modern. Of the Lycian Confederacy little is known. That of the Amphyctions is well known to have been rendered of little use whilst it lasted, and in the end to have been destroyed by the predominance of the local over the federal authority. The same observation may be made, on the authority of Polybius, with regard to the Achæan League. The Helvetic System scarcely amounts to a confederacy and is distinguished by too many peculiarities to be a ground of comparison. The case of the United Netherlands is in point. The authority of a Statholder, the influence of a standing army, the common interest in the conquered possessions, the pressure of surrounding danger, the guarantee of foreign powers, are not sufficient to secure the authority and interests of the generality, against the antifederal tendency of the provincial sovereignties. The German Empire is another example. A Hereditary chief with vast independent resources of wealth and power, a federal Diet, with ample parchment

---

56. A government within a government.

authority, a regular Judiciary establishment, the influence of the neighbourhood of great and formidable Nations, have been found unable either to maintain the subordination of the members, or to prevent their mutual contests and encroachments.[57] Still more to the purpose is our own experience both during the war and since the peace. Encroachments of the States on the general authority, sacrifices of national to local interests, interferences of the measures of different States, form a great part of the history of our political system. It may be said that the new Constitution is founded on different principles, and will have a different operation. I admit the difference to be material. It presents the aspect rather of a feudal system of republics, if such a phrase may be used, than of a Confederacy of independent States. And what has been the progress and event of the feudal Constitutions? In all of them a continual struggle between the head and the inferior members, until a final victory has been gained in some instances by one, in others, by the other of them. In one respect indeed there is a remarkable variance between the two cases. In the feudal system the sovereign, though limited, was independent; and having no particular sympathy of interests with the great Barons, his ambition had as full play as theirs in the mutual projects of usurpation. In the American Constitution The general authority will be derived entirely from the subordinate authorities. The Senate will represent the States in their political capacity, the other House will represent the people of the States in their individual capacity. The former will be accountable to their constituents at moderate, the latter at short periods. The President also derives his appointment from the States, and is periodically accountable to them. This dependence of the General, on the local authorities seems effectually to guard the latter against any dangerous encroachments of the former: Whilst the latter within their respective limits, will be continually sensible of the abridgment of their power, and be stimulated by ambition to resume the surrendered portion of it. We find the representatives of counties and corporations in the Legislatures of the States, much more disposed to sacrifice the aggregate interest, and even authority, to the local views of their Constituents, than the latter to the former. I mean not by these remarks to insinuate that an esprit de corps will not exist in the national Government, that opportunities may not occur of extending its jurisdiction in some points. I mean only that the danger of encroachments is much greater from the other side,[58] and that the impossibility of dividing powers of legislation, in such a manner, as to be free from different constructions by different interests, or even from ambiguity in the judgment of the impartial, requires some such expedient as I contend for. Many illustrations might be given of this impossibility. How long has it taken to fix, and how imperfectly is yet fixed the legislative power of corporations,

---

57. JM elaborated on ancient confederacies in *The Federalist* Numbers 18, 19, and 20.
58. JM emphasized the greater danger of state encroachments in *The Federalist* Numbers 45 and 46.

though that power is subordinate in the most compleat manner? The line of distinction between the power of regulating trade and that of drawing revenue from it, which was once considered as the barrier of our liberties, was found on fair discussion, to be absolutely undefinable. No distinction seems to be more obvious than that between spiritual and temporal matters. Yet wherever they have been made objects of Legislation, they have clashed and contended with each other, till one or the other has gained the supremacy. Even the boundaries between the Executive, Legislative and Judiciary powers, though in general so strongly marked in themselves, consist in many instances of mere shades of difference. It may be said that the Judicial authority under our new system will keep the States within their proper limits, and supply the place of a negative on their laws. The answer is that it is more convenient to prevent the passage of a law, than to declare it void after it is passed; that this will be particularly the case where the law aggrieves individuals, who may be unable to support an appeal against a State to the supreme Judiciary, that a State which would violate the Legislative rights of the Union, would not be very ready to obey a Judicial decree in support of them, and that a recurrence to force, which in the event of disobedience would be necessary, is an evil which the new Constitution meant to exclude as far as possible.

2. A Constitutional negative on the laws of the States seems equally necessary to secure individuals against encroachments on their rights. The mutability of the laws of the States is found to be a serious evil. The injustice of them has been so frequent and so flagrant as to alarm the most stedfast friends of Republicanism. I am persuaded I do not err in saying that the evils issuing from these sources contributed more to that uneasiness which produced the Convention, and prepared the public mind for a general reform, than those which accrued to our national character and interest from the inadequacy of the Confederation to its immediate objects. A reform therefore which does not make provision for private rights, must be materially defective. The restraints against paper emissions, and violations of contracts are not sufficient. Supposing them to be effectual as far as they go, they are short of the mark. Injustice may be effected by such an infinitude of legislative expedients, that where the disposition exists it can only be controuled by some provision which reaches all cases whatsoever. The partial provision made, supposes the disposition which will evade it. It may be asked how private rights will be more secure under the Guardianship of the General Government than under the State Governments, since they are both founded on the republican principle which refers the ultimate decision to the will of the majority, and are distinguished rather by the extent within which they will operate, than by any material difference in their structure. A full discussion of this question would, if I mistake not, unfold the true principles of Republican Government, and prove in contradiction to the concurrent opinions of theoretical writers, that this form of Government, in order to effect its purposes must operate not within a small but an extensive sphere. I will state some of the ideas which have occurred to me on this subject. Those who contend for a simple Democracy, or a

pure republic, actuated by the sense of the majority, and operating within narrow limits, assume or suppose a case which is altogether fictitious. They found their reasoning on the idea, that the people composing the Society enjoy not only an equality of political rights; but that they have all precisely the same interests and the same feelings in every respect. Were this in reality the case, their reasoning would be conclusive. The interest of the majority would be that of the minority also; the decisions could only turn on mere opinion concerning the good of the whole of which the major voice would be the safest criterion; and within a small sphere, this voice could be most easily collected and the public affairs most accurately managed. We know however that no Society ever did or can consist of so homogeneous a mass of Citizens. In the savage State indeed, an approach is made towards it; but in that state little or no Government is necessary. In all civilized Societies, distinctions are various and unavoidable. A distinction of property results from that very protection which a free Government gives to unequal faculties of acquiring it. There will be rich and poor; creditors and debtors; a landed interest, a monied interest, a mercantile interest, a manufacturing interest. These classes may again be subdivided according to the different productions of different situations and soils, and according to different branches of commerce and of manufactures. In addition to these natural distinctions, artificial ones will be founded on accidental differences in political, religious and other opinions, or an attachment to the persons of leading individuals.[59] However erroneous or ridiculous these grounds of dissention and faction may appear to the enlightened Statesman, or the benevolent philosopher, the bulk of mankind who are neither Statesmen nor Philosophers, will continue to view them in a different light. It remains then to be enquired whether a majority having any common interest, or feeling any common passion, will find sufficient motives to restrain them from oppressing the minority. An individual is never allowed to be a judge or even a witness in his own cause. If two individuals are under the biass of interest or enmity against a third, the rights of the latter could never be safely referred to the majority of the three. Will two thousand individuals be less apt to oppress one thousand, or two hundred thousand, one hundred thousand? Three motives only can restrain in such cases. 1. A prudent regard to private or partial good, as essentially involved in the general and permanent good of the whole. This ought no doubt to be sufficient of itself. Experience however shews that it has little effect on individuals, and perhaps still less on a collection of individuals, and least of all on a majority with the public authority in their hands. If the former are ready to forget that honesty is the best policy; the last do more. They often proceed on the converse of the maxim: that whatever is politic is honest. 2. Respect for character. This motive is not found sufficient to restrain individuals from injustice, and loses its efficacy in

---

59. In his *Federalist* Number 10, JM deleted his reference to natural and artificial distinctions, replacing it with his observation that "the most common and durable source of factions, has been the various and unequal distribution of property"; see Edmond N. Cahn, "Madison and the Pursuit of Happiness," *New York University Law Review* 27 (1952): 272.

proportion to the number which is to divide the praise or the blame. Besides as it has reference to public opinion, which is that of the majority, the standard is fixed by those whose conduct is to be measured by it. 3. Religion. The inefficacy of this restraint on individuals is well known. The conduct of every popular assembly, acting on oath, the strongest of religious ties, shews that individuals join without remorse in acts against which their consciences would revolt, if proposed to them separately in their closets. When Indeed Religion is kindled into enthusiasm, its force like that of other passions is increased by the sympathy of a multitude. But enthusiasm is only a temporary state of Religion, and whilst it lasts will hardly be seen with pleasure at the helm. Even in its coolest state, it has been much oftener a motive to oppression than a restraint from it. If then there must be different interests and parties in Society; and a majority when united by a common interest or passion can not be restrained from oppressing the minority, what remedy can be found in a republican Government, where the majority must ultimately decide, but that of giving such an extent to its sphere, that no common interest or passion will be likely to unite a majority of the whole number in an unjust pursuit. In a large Society, the people are broken into so many interests and parties, that a common sentiment is less likely to be felt, and the requisite concert less likely to be formed, by a majority of the whole. The same security seems requisite for the civil as for the religious rights of individuals. If the same sect form a majority and have the power, other sects will be sure to be depressed. Divide et impera, the reprobated axiom of tyranny, is under certain qualifications, the only policy, by which a republic can be administered on just principles. It must be observed however that this doctrine can only hold within a sphere of a mean extent. As in too small a sphere oppressive combinations may be too easily formed against the weaker party; so in too extensive a one a defensive concert may be rendered too difficult against the oppression of those entrusted with the administration. The great desideratum in Government is, so to modify the sovereignty as that it may be sufficiently neutral between different parts of the Society to controul one part from invading the rights of another, and at the same time sufficiently controuled itself, from setting up an interest adverse to that of the entire Society. In absolute monarchies, the Prince may be tolerably neutral towards different classes of his subjects, but may sacrifice the happiness of all to his personal ambition or avarice. In small republics, the sovereign will is controuled from such a sacrifice of the entire Society, but it is not sufficiently neutral towards the parts composing it. In the extended Republic of the United States, the General Government would hold a pretty even balance between the parties of particular States, and be at the same time sufficiently restrained by its dependence on the community, from betraying its general interests.[60]

60. The preceding observations on the need for a federal negative on state laws became the basis for *The Federalist* Number 10, once JM had deleted all references to the negative.

Begging pardon for this immoderate digression, I return to the third object abovementioned, the adjustment of the different interests of different parts of the Continent. Some contended for an unlimited power over trade including exports as well as imports, and over slaves as well as other imports; some for such a power, provided the concurrence of two thirds of both Houses were required; some for such a qualification of the power, with an exemption of exports and slaves, others for an exemption of exports only. The result is seen in the Constitution. S. Carolina and Georgia were inflexible on the point of the slaves.

The remaining object, created more embarrassment, and a greater alarm for the issue of the Convention than all the rest put together. The little States insisted on retaining their equality in both branches, unless a compleat abolition of the State Governments should take place; and made an equality in the Senate a sine qua non. The large States on the other hand urged that as the new Government was to be drawn principally from the people immediately and was to operate directly on them, not on the States; and consequently as the States would lose that importance which is now proportioned to the importance of their voluntary compliances with the requisitions of Congress, it was necessary that the representation in both Houses should be in proportion to their size. It ended in the compromise which you will see, but very much to the dissatisfaction of several members from the large States.

It will not escape you that three names only from Virginia are subscribed to the Act. Mr. Wythe did not return after the death of his lady. Docr. MClurg left the Convention some time before the adjournment. The Governour and Col. Mason refused to be parties to it. Mr. Gerry was the only other member who refused. The objections of the Govr. turn principally on the latitude of the general powers, and on the connection established between the President and the Senate. He wished that the plan should be proposed to the States with liberty to them to suggest alterations which should all be referred to another general Convention to be incorporated into the plan as far as might be judged expedient. He was not inveterate in his opposition, and grounded his refusal to subscribe pretty much on his unwillingness to commit himself so as not to be at liberty to be governed by further lights on the subject. Col. Mason left Philada. in an exceeding ill humour indeed. A number of little circumstances arising in part from the impatience which prevailed towards the close of the business, conspired to whet his acrimony. He returned to Virginia with a fixed disposition to prevent the adoption of the plan if possible. He considers the want of a Bill of Rights as a fatal objection. His other objections are to the substitution of the Senate in place of an Executive Council and to the powers vested in that body—to the powers of the Judiciary—to the vice President being made President of the Senate—to the smallness of the number of Representatives—to the restriction on the States with regard to ex post facto laws—and most of all probably to the power of regulating trade, by a majority only of each House. He has some other lesser objections. Being now under the necessity of justifying his refusal to sign, he will of course, muster every possible one. His conduct has given great umbrage to the County of Fairfax, and particularly to the Town of Alexandria. He is already instructed to promote in the Assembly the calling a Convention, and will probably be either not deputed to the Convention, or be tied up by express instructions. He did not object in general to the powers vested in the National Government, so much as to the modification. In some respects he admitted that some further powers could have improved the system. He acknowledged in particular that a negative on the State laws, and the appointment of the State Executives ought to be ingredients; but supposed that the public mind would not now bear them and that experience would hereafter produce these amendments.

The final reception which will be given by the people at large to this proposed System can not yet be decided. The Legislature of N. Hampshire was sitting when it reached that State and was well pleased with it. As far as the sense of the people there has been expressed, it is equally favorable. Boston is warm and almost unanimous in embracing it. The impression on the country is not yet known. No symptoms of disapprobation have appeared. The Legislature of that State is now sitting, through which the sense of the people at large will soon be promulged with tolerable certainty. The paper money faction in Rh. Island is hostile. The other party zealously attached to it. Its passage through Connecticut is likely to be very smooth and easy. There seems to be less agitation in this[61] state than any where. The discussion of the subject seems confined to the newspapers. The principal characters are known to be friendly. The Governour's party which has hitherto been the popular and most numerous one, is supposed to be on the opposite side; but considerable reserve is practiced, of which he sets the example. N. Jersey takes the affirmative side of course. Meetings of the people are declaring their approbation, and instructing their representatives. Penna. will be divided. The City of Philada., the Republican party, the Quakers, and most of the Germans espouse the Constitution. Some of the Constitutional leaders, backed by the western Country will oppose. An unlucky ferment on the subject in their assembly just before its late adjournment has irritated both sides, particularly the opposition, and by redoubling the exertions of that party may render the event doubtful. The voice of Maryland I understand from pretty good authority, is, as far as it has been declared, strongly in favor of the Constitution. Mr. Chase is an enemy, but the Town of Baltimore which he now represents, is warmly attached to it, and will shackle him as far as they can. Mr. Paca will probably be, as usually, in the politics of Chase. My information from Virginia is as yet extremely imperfect. I have a letter from Genl. Washington which speaks favorably of the impression within a circle of some extent, and another from Chancellor Pendleton which expresses his full acceptance of the plan, and the popularity of it in his district. I am told also that Innis and Marshall are

---

61. JM later inserted an asterisk here and wrote "N. York" as a footnote.

patrons of it. In the opposite scale are Mr. James Mercer, Mr. R. H. Lee, Docr. Lee and their connections of course, Mr. M. Page according to Report, and most of the Judges and Bar of the general Court. The part which Mr. Henry will take is unknown here. Much will depend on it. I had taken it for granted from a variety of circumstances that he would be in the opposition, and still think that will be the case. There are reports however which favor a contrary supposition. From the States South of Virginia nothing has been heard. As the deputation from S. Carolina consisted of some of its weightiest characters, who have returned unanimously zealous in favor of the Constitution, it is probable that State will readily embrace it. It is not less probable, that N. Carolina will follow the example unless that of Virginia should counterbalance it. Upon the whole, although, the public mind will not be fully known, nor finally settled for a considerable time, appearances at present augur a more prompt, and general adoption of the plan than could have been well expected.

When the plan came before Congress for their sanction, a very serious report was made by R. H. Lee and Mr. Dane from Masts. to embarrass it. It was first contended that Congress could not properly give any positive countenance to a measure which had for its object the subversion of the Constitution under which they acted. This ground of attack failing, the former gentleman urged the expediency of sending out the plan with amendments, and proposed a number of them corresponding with the objections of Col. Mason. This experiment had still less effect. In order however to obtain unanimity it was necessary to couch the resolution in very moderate terms.

Mr. Adams has received permission to return with thanks for his services. No provision is made for supplying his place, or keeping up any representation there. Your reappointment for three years will be notified from the office of F. Affairs.[62] It was *made without a negative, eight states* being *present.*[63] *Connecticut however put in a blank ticket,* the *sense of* that *state having been declared against embassies. Massachusetts betrayed some scruple* on *like ground.* Every *personal consideration* was *avowed* and *I believe with sincerity* to have *militated against these scruples.* It seems to be understood that letters to and from the foreign Ministers of the U.S. are not free of postage: but that the charge is to be allowed in their accounts.

The exchange of our French for Dutch Creditors has not been countenanced either by Congress or the Treasury Board. The paragraph in your last letter to Mr. Jay, on the subject of applying a loan in Holland to the discharge of the pay due to the foreign officers has been referred to the Board since my arrival here. No report has yet been made. But I have little idea that the proposition will be adopted. Such is the state and prospect of our fiscal department that any new loan however small that should now be made, would

---

62. TJ had been reappointed minister to France on Oct. 12; see *PJM,* X, p. 220.
63. The italicized words in this sentence and those in the rest of the letter were written in code.

probably subject us to the reproach of premeditated deception. The balance of Mr. Adams' last loan will be wanted for the interest due in Holland, and with all the income here, will, it is feared, not save our credit in Europe from further wounds. It may well be doubted whether the present Government can be kept alive thro' the ensuing year, or untill the new one may take its place.

Upwards of 100,000 Acres of the surveyed lands of the U.S. have been disposed of in open market. Five million of unsurveyed have been sold by private contract to a N. England Company, at ⅔ of a dollar per acre, payment to be made in the principal of the public securities. A negociation is nearly closed with a N. Jersey Company for two million more on like terms, and another commenced with a Company of this City for four million. Col. Carrington writes more fully on this subject.

You will receive herewith the desired information from Alderman Broome in the case of Mr. Burke. Also the Virga. Bill on crimes and punishments. Sundry alterations having been made in conformity to the sense of the House in its latter stages, it is less accurate and methodical than it ought to have been. To these papers I add a speech of Mr. C. P. on the Mississippi business. It is printed under precautions of secrecy, but surely could not have been properly exposed to so much risk of publication. You will find also among the pamplets and papers I send by Commodore Jones, another printed speech of the same Gentleman. The Musæum[,] Magazine,[64] and Philada. Gazettes, will give you a tolerable idea of the objects of present attention.

The summer crops in the Eastern and Middle States have been extremely plentiful. Southward of Virga. They differ in different places. On the whole I do not know that they are bad in that region. In Virginia the drought has been unprecedented, particularly between the falls of the Rivers and the Mountains. The Crops of Corn are in general alarmingly short. In Orange I find there will be scarcely subsistence for the inhabitants. I have not heard from Albemarle. The crops of Tobacco are every where said to be pretty good in point of quantity, and the quality unusually fine. The crops of wheat were also in general excellent in quality and tolerable in quantity.

Novr. 1.

Commodore[65] Jones having preferred another vessel to the packet, has remained here till this time. The interval has produced little necessary to be added to the above. The Legislature of Massts. has it seems taken up the Act of the Convention and have appointed or probably will appoint an early day for

---

64. "Mr. C. P." was Charles Pinckney of South Carolina. His speech of August 16, 1786, dealt with negotiations of a treaty with Spain by John Jay, secretary of foreign affairs. Pinckney urged Congress not to change Jay's instructions which prohibited him from ceding the right of the United States to free navigation of the Mississippi. Although the speech was delivered in 1786, it seems not to have been published until 1787; see *PJM*, X, p. 195. The *American Museum* and the *Columbian Magazine* were both published in Philadelphia.

65. JM later inserted an asterisk here and wrote "Paul" in the margin.

its State Convention. There are letters also from Georgia which denote a favorable disposition. I am informed from Richmond that the new Election-law from the Revised Code produced a pretty full House of Delegates, as well as a Senate, on the first day. It had previously had equal effect in producing full meetings of the freeholders for the County elections. A very decided majority of the Assembly is said to be zealous in favor of the New Constitution. The same is said of the Country at large. It appears however that individuals of great weight both within and without the Legislature are opposed to it. A letter I just have from Mr. A. Stuart names Mr. Henry, Genl. Nelson, W. Nelson, the family of Cabels, St. George Tucker, John Taylor and the Judges of the General Court except P. Carrington. The other opponents he described as of too little note to be mentioned, which gives a negative information of the Characters on the other side. All are agreed that the plan must be submitted to a Convention.

We hear from Georgia that that State is threatened with a dangerous war with the Creek Indians. The alarm is of so serious a nature, that law-martial has been proclaimed, and they are proceeding to fortify even the Town of Savannah. The idea there is that the Indians derive their motives as well as their means from their Spanish neighbours. Individuals complain also that their fugitive slaves are encouraged by East Florida. The policy of this is explained by supposing that it is considered as a discouragement to the Georgians to form settlements near the Spanish boundaries.

There are but few States on the spot here which will survive the expiration of the federal year; and it is extremely uncertain when a Congress will again be formed. We have not yet heard who are to be in the appointment of Virginia for the next year. With the most affectionate attachment I remain Dear Sr. Your obed friend and servant,

Js. Madison Jr.


## Madison to Jefferson

New York Dec. 9, 1787

Dear Sir

Your favour of the 17th. of Sepr. with sundry other letters and packets, came duly by the last packet. Such of them as were addressed to others, were duly forwarded. The three Boxes, marked J. M., G.W. and A D, it appears were never shipped from Havre.[66] Whenever they arrive your commands with regard to the two last shall be attended to, as well as those relating to some of the contents of the first. I have not been able to get any satisfactory account of Willm. S. Browne. Alderman Broom tells me that he professed to receive the

---

66. "G.W." was George Wythe, and "A D" Alexander Donald, a Richmond merchant.

money from him, for the use of Mr. Burke. I shall not lose sight of the subject, and will give you the earliest information of the result of my enquiries. The annexed list of trees will shew you that I have ventured to substitute half a dozen sorts of apples in place of the pippins alone, and to add 8 other sorts of American trees, including 20 of the Sugar Maple. They were obtained from a Mr. Prince in the neighbourhood of this City, who deals largely in this way, and is considered as a man of worth. I learn from him that he has executed various commissions from Europe and the West Indies, as well as places less distant; and that he has been generally very successful in preserving the trees from perishing by such distant transplantations. He does not use moss as you prescribe but incloses the roots in a bag of earth. As moss is not be got, as he says, it is uncertain whether necessity or choice gives the preference to the latter. I inclose a Catalogue of his nursery and annex the price of the sample I send you, that you may, if you incline, give orders for any other supply. I doubt whether the Virga. Red Birds are found in this part of America. Opossums are not rare in the milder parts of New Jersey, but are very rare thus far Northward. I shall nevertheless avail myself of any opportunities which may happen for procuring and forwarding both. Along with the Box of trees, I send by the Packet to the care of Mr. Limozin 2 Barrels of New Town pippins, and 2 of Cranberrys. In one of the latter the Cranberries are put up dry, in the other in water; the opinions and accounts differing as to the best mode. You will note the event of the experiment.

The Constitution proposed by the late Convention engrosses almost the whole political attention of America. All the Legislatures except that of R. Island, which have been assembled, have agreed in submitting it to State Conventions. Virginia has set the example of opening a door for amendments, if the Convention there should chuse to propose them. Maryland has copied it. The States which preceded, referred the Constitution as recommended by the General Convention, to be ratified or rejected as it stands. The Convention of Pennsylvania, is now sitting. There are about 44 or 45, on the affirmative and about half that number on the opposite side; A considerable number of the Constitutional party as it was called, having joined the other party in espousing the federal Constitution. The returns of deputies for the Convention of Connecticut are known, and prove, as is said by those who know the men that a very great majority will adopt it in that State. The event in Massachusetts lies in greater uncertainty. The friends of the New Government continue to be sanguine. N. Hampshire from every account, as well as from some general inducements felt there, will pretty certainly be on the affirmative side. So will New Jersey and Delaware. N. York is much divided. She will hardly dissent from N. England, particularly if the conduct of the latter should coincide with that of N. Jersey and Pennsylva. A more formidable opposition is likely to be made in Maryland than was at first conjectured. Mr. Mercer, it seems, who was a member of the Convention, though his attendance was but for a short time, is become an auxiliary to Chace. Johnson the Carrolls, Govr.

Lee, and most of the other characters of weight are on the other side. Mr. T. Stone died a little before the Government was promulged. The body of the people in Virginia. particularly in the upper and lower Country, and in the Northern Neck, are as far as I can gather, much disposed to adopt the new Constitution. The middle Country, and the South side of James River are principally in the opposition to it. As yet a large majority of the people are under the first description. As yet also are a majority of the Assembly. What change may be produced by the united influence of exertions of Mr. Henry, Mr. Mason, and the Governor with some pretty able auxiliaries, is uncertain. My information leads me to suppose there must be three parties in Virginia. The first for adopting without attempting amendments. This includes Genl. W and the other deputies who signed the Constitution, Mr. Pendleton (Mr. Marshal I believe), Mr. Nicholas, Mr. Corbin, Mr. Zachy. Johnson, Col. Innis, (Mr. B. Randolph as I understand) Mr. Harvey, Mr. Gabl. Jones, Docr. Jones, etc. etc. At the head of the 2d. party which urges amendments are the Governor and Mr. Mason. These do not object to the substance of the Government but contend for a few additional guards in favor of the Rights of the States and of the people. I am not able to enumerate the characters which fall in with their ideas, as distinguished from those of a third Class, at the head of which is Mr. Henry. This class concurs at present with the patrons of amendments, but will probably contend for such as strike as the essence of the System, and must lead to an adherence to the principle of the existing Confederation, which most thinking men are convinced is a visionary one, or to a partition of the Union into several Confederacies. Mr. Harrison the late Governor is with Mr. Henry. So are a number of others. The General and Admiralty Courts with most of the Bar, oppose the Constitution, but on what particular grounds I am unable to say. Genl. Nelson, Mr. Jno. Page, Col. Bland, etc. are also opponents, but on what principle and to what extent, I am equally at a loss to say. In general I must note, that I speak with respect to many of these names, from information that may not be accurate, and merely as I should do in a free and confidential conversation with you. I have not yet heard Mr. Wythe's sentiments on the subject. Docr. McClurg the other absent deputy, is a very strenuous defender of the new Government. Mr. Henry is the great adversary who will render the event precarious. He is I find with his usual address, working up every possible interest, into a spirit of opposition. It is worthy of remark that whilst in Virga. and some of the other States in the middle and Southern Districts of the Union, the men of intelligence, patriotism, property, and independent circumstances, are thus divided; all of this description, with a few exceptions, in the Eastern States, and most of the middle States, are zealously attached to the proposed Constitution. In N. England, the men of letters, the principal officers of Government, the Judges and Lawyers, the Clergy, and men of property, furnish only here and there an adversary. It is not less worthy of remark that in Virginia where the mass of the people have been so much accustomed to be guided by their rulers on all new and intricate questions, they should on the present which certainly surpasses the judgment of the greater part of them, not only go before, but contrary to, their most popular leaders. And the phenomenon is the more wonderful, as a popular ground is taken by all the adversaries to the new Constitution. Perhaps the solution in both these cases, would not be very difficult; but it would lead to observations too diffusive; and to you unnecessary. I will barely observe that the case in Virga. seems to prove that the body of sober and steady people, even of the lower order, are tired of the vicisitudes, injustice and follies which have so much characterised public measures, and are impatient for some change which promises stability and repose. The proceedings of the present assembly are more likely to cherish than remove this disposition. I find Mr. Henry has carried a Resolution for *prohibiting*[67] the importation of Rum, brandy, and other ardent spirits; and if I am not misinformed all manufactured leather, hats and sundry other articles are included in the *prohibition*.[68] Enormous duties at least are likely to take place on the last and many other articles. A project of this sort without the concurrence of the other States, is little short of madness. With such concurrence, it is not practicable without resorting to expedients equally noxious to liberty and œconomy. The consequences of the experiment in a single State, as unprepared for manufactures as Virginia may easily be preconceived. The Revised Code will not be resumed. Mr. Henry is an inveterate adversary to it. Col. Mason made a regular and powerful attack on the port Bill; but was left in a very small minority. I found at the last Session that that regulation was not to be shaken; though it certainly owes its success less to its principal merits, than to collateral and casual considerations. The popular ideas are that by favoring the collection of duties on imports it saves the solid property from direct taxes; and that it injures G. Britain by lessening the advantage she has over other Nations, in the trade of Virginia.

We have no certain information from the three Southern States concerning the temper relative to the New Government. It is in general favorable according to the vague accounts we have. Opposition however will be made in each. Mr. Wiley Jones, and Governour Caswell have been named as opponents in N. Carolina.

So few particulars have come to hand concerning the State of things in Georgia that I have nothing to add on that subject, to the contents of my last by Commodore Jones.

We have two or three States only yet met for Congress. As many more can be called in when their attendance will make a quorum. It continues to be problematical, whether the interregnum will not be spun out through the winter.

We remain in great uncertainty here with regard to a war in Europe. Reports and suspicions are strongly on the side of one. Such an event may be considered in various relations to this Country. It is pretty certain I think that

---

67. JM's italics.          68. JM's italics.

if the present lax State of our General Government should continue, we shall not only lose certain capital advantages which might be drawn from it; but be in danger of being plunged into difficulties which may have a very serious effect on our future fortunes. I remain Dear Sir with the most sincere esteem and affection, Your Obedt. Servt.

P.S. I have delivered your message to Mr. Thomson and settled the pecuniary matter with him.

The letters which you put under the same cover, with the seals of one joining the superscription of the contiguous letter, come when the weather has been warm, in such a State that it is often difficult to separate them without tearing out the superscription. A bit of paper between the adjoining letters over the seal would prevent this inconveniency.

| No. | | | | | | |
|---|---|---|---|---|---|---|
| 1 | —6. | New Town Spitzenburg apples | | | | |
| 2 | —20. | New Town pippins | do. | | | |
| 3 | —6. | Esopus Spitzenburg | do. | } 50 trees at 2/ | £5. 0. 0 | |
| 4 | —6. | Jersey Greening | do. | | | |
| 5 | —6. | R. Island Greening | do. | | | |
| 6 | —6. | Everlasting | do. | | | |
| 7 | —10. | American Plumbs | | ⅙ | 15. | |
| 8 | —8. | live oaks | | 9d. | 6. | |
| 9 | —20. | Sugar Maples | | 2/ | 2. | |
| 10 | —10. | Candle berry Myrtles | | 9d. | 7. 6 | |
| 11 | —6. | Standing American Honey-Suckles | | ⅙ | 9. | |
| 12 | —6. | Three thorned Accacia | | ⅙ | 9 | |
| 13 | —6. | Rhododendrons | | 2/ | 12 | |
| 14 | —6. | Dogwood Trees | | ⅙ | 9 | |
| | | | Box and Matts | | 5. 6 | |
| | | | Dollar at 8 Shillgs.= | | £10. 13. - | |

## *Jefferson to Madison*

Paris Dec. 20, 1787

DEAR SIR

My last to you was of Oct. 8 by the Count de Moustier. Yours of July 18. Sep. 6 and Oct. 24. have been successively received, yesterday, the day before and three or four days before that. I have only had time to read the letters, the printed papers communicated with them, however interesting, being obliged to lie over till I finish my dispatches for the packet, which dispatches must go from hence the day after tomorrow. I have much to thank you for. First and most for the cyphered paragraph respecting myself. These little informations are very material towards forming my own decisions. I would be glad even to know when any individual member thinks I have gone wrong in any instance. If I know myself it would not excite ill blood in me, while it would assist to guide my conduct, perhaps to justify it, and to keep me to my duty, alert. I must thank you too for the information in Thos. Burke's case, tho' you will have found by a subsequent letter that I have asked of you a further investigation of that matter. It is to gratify the lady who is at the head of the Convent wherein my daughters are, and who, by her attachment and attention to them, lays me under great obligations. I shall hope therefore still to receive from you the result of the further enquiries my second letter had asked.

The parcel of rice which you informed me had miscarried accompanied my letter to the Delegates of S. Carolina. Mr. Bourgoin was to be the bearer of both and both were delivered together into the hands of his relation here who introduced him to me, and who at a subsequent moment undertook to convey them to Mr. Bourgoin. This person was an engraver particularly recommended to Dr. Franklin and Mr. Hopkinson. Perhaps he may have mislaid the little parcel of rice among his baggage.[69]

I am much pleased that the sale of Western lands is so successful. I hope they will absorb all the Certificates of our Domestic debt speedily in the first place, and that then offered for cash they will do the same by our foreign one.

The season admitting only of operations in the Cabinet, and these being in a great measure secret, I have little to fill a letter. I will therefore make up the deficiency by adding a few words on the Constitution proposed by our Convention. I like much the general idea of framing a government which should go on of itself peaceably, without needing continual recurrence to the state legislatures. I like the organization of the government into Legislative, Judiciary and Executive. I like the power given the Legislature to levy taxes; and for that reason solely approve of the greater house being chosen by the people directly. For tho' I think a house chosen by them will be very illy qualified to legislate for the Union, for foreign nations etc. yet this evil does not weigh against the good of preserving inviolate the fundamental principle that the people are not to be taxed but by representatives chosen immediately by themselves. I am captivated by the compromise of the opposite claims of the great and little states, of the latter to equal, and the former to proportional influence. I am much pleased too with the substitution of the method of voting by persons, instead of that of voting by states: and I like the negative given to the Executive with a third of either house, though I should have liked it better had the Judiciary been associated for that purpose, or invested with a similar and separate power. There are other good things of less moment. I will now add what I do not like. First the omission of a bill of rights providing clearly and without the aid of sophisms for freedom of religion, freedom of the press, protection against standing armies, restriction against monopolies, the eternal and unremitting force of the habeas corpus laws, and trials by jury in all

---

69. François-Joseph Bourgain was a French miniaturist who settled in Philadelphia; see *PJM*, X, p. 339.

matters of fact triable by the laws of the land and not by the law of Nations. To say, as Mr. Wilson does that a bill of rights was not necessary because all is reserved in the case of the general government which is not given, while in the particular ones all is given which is not reserved might do for the Audience to whom it was addressed, but is surely gratis dictum, opposed by strong inferences from the body of the instrument, as well as from the omission of the clause of our present confederation which had declared that in express terms. It was a hard conclusion to say because there has been no uniformity among the states as to the cases triable by jury, because some have been so incautious as to abandon this mode of trial, therefore the more prudent states shall be reduced to the same level of calamity. It would have been much more just and wise to have concluded the other way that as most of the states had judiciously preserved this palladium, those who had wandered should be brought back to it, and to have established general right instead of general wrong. Let me add that a bill of rights is what the people are entitled to against every government on earth, general or particular, and what no just government should refuse, or rest on inference. The second feature I dislike, and greatly dislike, is the abandonment in every instance of the necessity of rotation in office, and most particularly in the case of the President. Experience concurs with reason in concluding that the first magistrate will always be re-elected if the constitution permits it. He is then an officer for life. This once observed it becomes of so much consequence to certain nations to have a friend or a foe at the head of our affairs that they will interfere with money and with arms. A Galloman or an Angloman will be supported by the nation he befriends. If once elected, and at a second or third election outvoted by one or two votes, he will pretend false votes, foul play, hold possession of the reins of government, be supported by the states voting for him, especially if they are the central ones lying in a compact body themselves and separating their opponents; and they will be aided by one nation of Europe, while the majority are aided by another. The election of a President of America some years hence will be much more interesting to certain nations of Europe than ever the election of a king of Poland was. Reflect on all the instances in history antient and modern, of elective monarchies, and say if they do not give foundation for my fears, the Roman emperors, the popes, while they were of any importance, the German emperors till they became hereditary in practice, the kings of Poland, the Deys of the Ottoman dependancies. It may be said that if elections are to be attended with these disorders, the seldomer they are renewed the better. But experience shews that the only way to prevent disorder is to render them uninteresting by frequent changes. An incapacity to be elected a second time would have been the only effectual preventative. The power of removing him every fourth year by the vote of the people is a power which will not be exercised. The king of Poland is removeable every day by the Diet, yet he is never removed.

  Smaller objections are the Appeal in fact as well as law, and the binding all persons Legislative, Executive and Judiciary by oath to maintain that constitution. I do not pretend to decide what would be the best method of procuring the establishment of the manifold good things in this constitution, and of getting rid of the bad. Whether by adopting it in hopes of future amendment, or, after it has been duly weighed and canvassed by the people, after seeing the parts they generally dislike, and those they generally approve, to say to them 'We see now what you wish. Send together your deputies again, let them frame a constitution for you omitting what you have condemned, and establishing the powers you approve. Even these will be a great addition to the energy of your government.'

At all events I hope you will not be discouraged from other trials, if the present one should fail of it's full effect.

I have thus told you freely what I like and dislike: merely as a matter of curiosity for I know your own judgment has been formed on all these points after having heard every thing which could be urged on them. I own I am not a friend to a very energetic government. It is always oppressive. The late rebellion in Massachusets has given more alarm than I think it should have done. Calculate that one rebellion in 13 states in the course of 11 years, is but one for each state in a century and a half. No country should be so long without one. Nor will any degree of power in the hands of government prevent insurrections. France with all it's despotism, and two or three hundred thousand men always in arms has had three insurrections in the three years I have been here in every one of which greater numbers were engaged than in Massachusets and a great deal more blood was spilt. In Turkey, which Montesquieu supposes more despotic, insurrections are the events of every day. In England, where the hand of power is lighter than here, but heavier than with us they happen every half dozen years. Compare again the ferocious depredations of their insurgents with the order, the moderation and the almost self extinguishment of ours.

After all, it is my principle that the will of the Majority should always prevail. If they approve the proposed Convention in all it's parts, I shall concur in it chearfully, in hopes that they will amend it whenever they shall find it work wrong. I think our governments will remain virtuous for many centuries; as long as they are chiefly agricultural; and this will be as long as there shall be vacant lands in any part of America. When they get piled upon one another in large cities, as in Europe, they will become corrupt as in Europe. Above all things I hope the education of the common people will be attended to; convinced that on their good sense we may rely with the most security for the preservation of a due degree of liberty. I have tired you by this time with my disquisitions and will therefore only add assurances of the sincerity of those sentiments of esteem and attachment with which I am Dear Sir your affectionate friend and servant,

TH: JEFFERSON

P.S. The instability of our laws is really an immense evil. I think it would be well to provide in our constitutions that there shall always be a twelvemonth between the ingrossing a bill and passing it: that it should then be offered to it's passage without changing a word: and that if circumstances should be thought to require a speedier passage, it should take two thirds of both houses instead of a bare majority.

*Madison to Jefferson*

New York Dec. 20, 1787

DEAR SIR

The packet has been detained here since the date of the letter which you will receive along with this, by some preparations suggested by an apprehension of war. The delay is very unfavorable to the trees on board for you.

Mr. *De la Forest* the *Consul here called on me a* few days ago and *told me he had information* that the *farmers general and Mr. Morris* having found their *contract mutually advantageous* are *evading* the *resolutions of the committee* by *tacit arrangements for it's continuance.*[70] He observed that the object of the *farmers was singly profit* that of the *government twofold revenue and commerce.* It was consequently the wish of the *latter* to render the *monopoly as little hurtful* to the *trade with America as possible.* He suggested as an *expedient that farmers should be* required *to divide* the *contract among six or seven houses French and American* who should be *required to ship annually* to *America a* reasonable proportion *of goods.* This he supposed would produce some *competition* in the *purchases here* and would introduce a *competition also* with *British goods here.* The latter *condition he said* could not be well required of, or executed by a *single contractor* and the *government could not abolish the farm.* These ideas were *meant for you.*

Since the date of my other letter, The Convention of Delaware have unanimously adopted the new Constitution. That of Pennsylvania has adopted it by a Majority of 46 against 23. That of New Jersey is sitting and will adopt pretty unanimously. These are all the Conventions that have met. I hear from North Carolina that the Assembly there is well disposed. Mr. Henry, Mr. Mason, R. H. Lee, and the Governour, continue by their influence to strengthen the opposition in Virginia. The Assembly there is engaged in several mad freaks. Among others a bill has been agreed to in the House of Delegates *prohibiting* the importation of Rum, *brandy,*[71] and all other spirits not distilled from some American production. All brewed liquors under the same description, with Beef, Tallow-Candles, cheese etc. are included in the prohibition. In order to enforce this despotic measure the most despotic means are resorted to. If any person be found after the commencement of the

---

70. These italicized words and those in the rest of the letter were written in code, unless otherwise indicated. "The committee" was a group of French officials investigating the monopoly tobacco contract between the Farmers General and Robert Morris; see Jacob Price, *France and the Chesapeake: A History of the French Tobacco Monopoly, 1644–1791 . . . ,* 2 vols. (Ann Arbor, 1973), II, pp. 761–69.

71. JM's italics.

Act, in the use or *possession*⁷² of any of the prohibited articles, tho' acquired previous to the law, he is to lose them, and pay a heavy fine. This is the form in which the bill was agreed to by a large majority in the House of Delegates. It is a child of Mr. Henry, and said to be his favorite one. They first voted by a *majority of 30*.⁷³ that all legal obstruction to the Treaty of peace, should cease in Virginia as soon as laws complying with it should have passed in all the other States. This was the result of four days debate with the most violent opposition from Mr. Henry. A few days afterwards He renewed his efforts, and got a vote, *by a majority of 50*,⁷⁴ that Virginia would not comply until G.B. shall have complied.

The States seem to be either wholly omitting to provide for the federal Treasury, or to be withdrawing the scanty appropriations made to it. The latter course has been taken by Massachusetts, Virginia and Delaware. The Treasury Board seem to be in despair of maintaining the shadow of Government much longer. Without money, the offices must be shut up, and the handful of troops on the frontier disbanded, which will probably bring on an Indian war, and make an impression to our disadvantage on the British Garrisons within our limits.

A letter from Mr. Archd. Stuart dated Richd. Decr. 2d. has the following paragraph "Yesterday a Boat with sixteen men, was brought down the Canal from Westham to its termination which is within one mile and an half of Richmond."

I subjoin an extract from a letter from Genl. Washington dated Decr. 7th. which contains the best information I can give you as to the progress of the works on the Potowmack.

"The survey of the Country between the Eastern and Western waters is not yet reported by the Commissioners, though promised to be made very shortly, the survey being compleated. No draught that can convey an adequate idea of the work on this river has been yet taken. Much of the labour, except at the great falls, has been bestowed in the bed of the river, in a removal of rocks, and deepening the water. At the great falls the labour has indeed been great. The water there (a sufficiency I mean) is taken into a Canal about two hundred yards above the Cateract, and conveyed by a level cut (through a solid rock in some places, and much stone every where) more than a mile to the lock Seats, five in number by means of which when compleated, the craft will be let into the River below the falls (which together amounts to seventy six feet). At the Seneca falls, six miles above the great falls, a channel which has been formed by the river when inundated is under improvement for navigation. The same, *in part*,⁷⁵ at Shannandoah. At the lower falls, where nothing has yet been done, a level cut and locks are proposed. These constitute the principal difficulties and will be the great expence of this undertaking. The parts of the river between

72. JM's italics.
73. JM's italics.
74. JM's italics.
75. JM's italics.

requiring loose stones only to be removed in order to deepen the water where it is too shallow in dry seasons."

The triennial purge administered to the Council in Virga. has removed from their seats Samson Matthews and Mr. Selden. Col. Wm. Heth and Majr. Jos: Egglestone supply their places. I remain Dr. Sir Yrs. Affectly.,

Js. MADISON JR.

*Madison to Jefferson*

[1787?]

[Notes on Impost Duties, Navigation Acts, etc., with Jefferson's Annotations]

10

To abolish the drawbacks of the foreign or impost duty upon all manufactures from grain, upon butter, cheese, wet provisions, oil, whalebone, fish—(Quere [by TJ], also the manufactures from wood)—

11

To abolish the drawbacks of the foreign or imposts Duty upon all manufactures necessary in the building, equipping, or repairing of merchant Vessels and Ships of war (or at least certain of them) such as Sail-cloth Cordage, anchors, sheathing paper, gun powder, cartridge paper—[TJ] The objects of the 10th. and 11th. as also the duty on fish will be covered by the insertion Pa. 17. line 3. of the words 'such articles as we produce ourselves' for in proceeding to lay duties on manufactures from grain, etc. sail cloth etc. drawbacks will naturally be first withdrawn.

12

To prohibit foreign ships from carrying from hence to foreign ports, other than their own, any foreign goods wares or merchandize

[TJ] qu? we cannot expect to force them out of that principle of their navigation act which prohibits all nations from carryg prodns not their own. Consequently the only effect of this measure wd be to deprive ourselves of the transportation from the place of produce to this country.

# 12

# THE CONSTITUTION AND THE MOVEMENT FOR A BILL OF RIGHTS, 1788–1789

*L*ATE IN LIFE, Madison denied that he was "the father of the Constitution." "You give me a credit to which I have no claim," he demurred, " 'in calling me *the* writer of the Constitution of the United States.' This was not, like the fabled Goddess of Wisdom, the offspring of a single brain. It ought to be regarded as the work of many heads and many hands."[1] Nonetheless, Max Farrand, editor of *The Records of the Federal Convention of 1787,* called him "unquestionably the leading spirit" of the Constitution and concluded that "Madison stands preeminent" among the Founders.[2] And, more recently, leading historians such as Clinton Rossiter, Jack Rakove, Michael Kammen, Edmund S. Morgan, Lance Banning, and Robert A. Rutland have given Madison high marks, Rutland labeling him "*the* Founding Father."[3]

1. JM to William Cogswell, Mar. 10, 1834, in Hunt, IX, p. 553.
2. Max Farrand, *The Framing of the Constitution of the United States* (New Haven, Conn., 1913), pp. 196–97.
3. Robert A. Rutland, *James Madison: The Founding Father* (New York, 1987), p. 253. Clinton Rossiter, editor of *The Federalist Papers* (New York, 1961), p. x, says, "Few historians begrudge Madison the title 'Father of the Constitution.' " Also see Rossiter's *1787: The Grand Convention* (New York, 1966; rpt. New York, 1987), pp. 247, 150, in which he concludes that JM was, "beyond a doubt, the leading spirit and . . . 'most efficient member' in this conclave," "a combination of learning, experience, purpose, and imagination that not even Adams or Jefferson could have equalled." Jack Rakove, *The Beginnings of National Politics: An Interpretive History of the Continental Congress* (Cambridge, Mass., 1979), pp. 368, 468, believes that "had Madison never lived, the Constitution would probably not have been written." Michael Kammen, *A Machine That Would Go of Itself: The Constitution in American Culture* (New York, 1986), p. 58, agrees that "James Madison richly deserves his sobriquet as father of the constitution." Edmund S. Morgan, *Inventing the People: The Rise of Popular Sovereignty in England and America* (New York, 1988; rpt. New York, 1989), pp. 267–77, credits Madison with coming up with the Constitution as a solution to the problems of the Confederation period. Lance Banning, " 'To Secure These

THE CONSTITUTION AND A BILL OF RIGHTS, 1788–1789      519

The modest Madison made no such claim.[4] Instead, he concentrated on writing twenty-nine of the eighty-five *Federalist* papers and monitoring the state ratification conventions chosen by the people. From the beginning, Madison kept his friend in France in the dark about *The Federalist,* but he kept him posted on the ratification process, observing in February 1788 that the public "continues to be much agitated by the proposed fœderal Constitution and to be attentive to little else." Delaware, Georgia, and New Jersey had ratified it unanimously, and Pennsylvania had adopted it by a 2-to-1 vote, Connecticut by a 3-to-1 margin.[5]

In Massachusetts, leading Federalists had adopted a conciliatory approach to their opponents, coupling unconditional ratification of the Constitution with a series of amendments to be recommended for adoption by the new Congress.[6] According to Madison, the recommended amendments were "not so much calculated for the [Antifederalist] minority in the Convention, on whom they had little effect, as for the people of the State."[7]

After his first critical reaction to the Constitution, Jefferson gradually warmed to the pragmatic document, viewing the "great mass" of it as good but confessing to one of Madison's colleagues in Congress that "there is also to me a bitter pill, or two." On balance, though, he found himself "nearly a Neutral."[8] But six weeks later, he told Madison that he was "glad to hear that the new constitution is received with favor." He now supported ratification, but

---

Rights': Patrick Henry, James Madison, and the Revolutionary Legitimacy of the Constitution," in *To Secure the Blessings of Liberty: First Principles of the Constitution,* ed. Sarah Baumgartner Thurow (Lanham, Md., 1988), p. 291, refers to JM's "enduring reputation as the Father of the Constitution." For a powerful dissenting opinion—which I find unconvincing—see Forrest McDonald, *Novus Ordo Seclorum: The Intellectual Origins of the Constitution* (Lawrence, Kans., 1985), p. 205, who vigorously attacks "the myth" that JM was the father of the Constitution.

4. Harold S. Schultz, *James Madison* (New York, 1970), p. 77, says that JM's disclaimer "was good history not false modesty." But in Schultz's reconsideration, entitled "James Madison: Father of the Constitution?" *Quarterly Journal of the Library of Congress* (1980): 215–22, he concludes: "However, if to his role at Philadelphia are added his contributions to ratification, to adoption of the first ten amendments, to passage of basic legislation in the first Congress, and to the historiography of the convention, Madison's place among the Fathers of the Constitution is singularly preeminent."

5. The best account of the state ratification conventions is Michael Allen Gillespie and Michael Lienesch, eds., *Ratifying the Constitution* (Lawrence, Kans., 1989), which reviews the fourteen conventions (North Carolina first rejected, then accepted the Constitution) in chronological order from 1787 to 1790.

6. Samuel B. Harding, *The Contest over the Ratification of the Federal Constitution in the State of Massachusetts* (Cambridge, Mass., 1896), pp. 83–104. For a more recent appraisal, see Richard D. Brown, "Shays's Rebellion and the Ratification of the Federal Constitution in Massachusetts," in *Beyond Confederation: Origins of the Constitution and American National Identity,* ed. Richard Beeman, Stephen Botein, and Edward C. Carter II (Chapel Hill, 1987), pp. 113–27.

7. JM to TJ, Feb. 19, 1788, below. See Richard E. Ellis, "The Persistence of Antifederalism after 1789," in *Beyond Confederation,* pp. 295–314, for a fascinating essay.

8. TJ to Edward Carrington, Dec. 21, 1787, in *PTJ,* XII, p. 446. For a provocative article, see Lawrence S. Kaplan, "Jefferson and the Constitution: The View from Paris, 1786–98," *Diplomatic History* 11 (1987): 321–36.

he also wanted amendments in the form of a bill of rights. Not having heard of the Massachusetts approach, he suggested that the first nine conventions ratify the Constitution, thus putting it into operation, but that the last four reject it, obliging Congress "to offer a declaration of rights in order to complete the union. We shall thus have all it's good, and cure it's principal defect."[9]

As the Constitution gained additional ratifications, Jefferson viewed it more and more favorably, ultimately calling it "the wisest ever yet presented to men."[10] Writing to Edward Carrington, Madison's colleague in Congress, he said "I have presumed it would gain on the public mind, as I confess it has on my own. At first, though I saw that the great mass and groundwork was good, I disliked many appendages. Reflection and discussion have cleared off most of these." Indeed, he had quickly abandoned his earlier proposal that nine states ratify and four reject the Constitution in order to obtain amendments. "The plan of Massachusetts is far preferable," he thought, "and will I hope be followed by those [states] who are yet to decide."[11]

Shortly thereafter, Madison spearheaded the ratification campaign in Virginia and followed the Massachusetts example of promising to add amendments subsequent to ratification. Thus, he rejected the proposal of Patrick Henry and the Antifederalists to postpone ratification until a second convention could be called to add "a declaration of rights asserting and securing from encroachment the great principles of civil and religious liberty." Instead, he pledged that once the new Constitution was ratified and operating, "we shall freely, fairly and dispassionately consider and investigate your propositions, and endeavour to gratify your wishes."[12]

Even so, Jefferson's earlier views soon put Madison in an embarrassing position at the Virginia ratification convention. Patrick Henry, the leading opponent of the Constitution, cited Jefferson's view on the need for a bill of rights in his attempt to persuade the convention to reject the Constitution: "This illustrious citizen advises you to reject this government till it be amended. . . . At a great distance from us he remembers and studies our happiness. Living in splendor and dissipation" (Henry could not resist the temptation to take a jab at Jefferson while invoking his name), "he thinks yet of bills of rights—thinks of those little, despised things called maxims."[13] Madison told Jefferson afterward that both Henry and George Mason had "endeavored to turn the influence of your *name even against parts, of which I*

9. TJ to JM, Feb. 6, 1788, below.

10. TJ to David Humphreys, Mar. 18, 1789, in *PTJ,* XIV, p. 678.

11. TJ to Edward Carrington, May 27, 1788, *ibid.,* XIII, pp. 208-9.

12. JM, speech of June 25, 1788, in *PJM,* XI, p. 177. For a perceptive analysis of the Virginia ratifying convention, see Jon Kukla, "A Spectrum of Sentiments: Virginia's Federalists, Antifederalists, and 'Federalists Who Are For Amendments,' 1787-1788," *VMHB* 96 (1988): 277-96. For JM's preconvention views on the "three parties in Virginia," see his letter to TJ, Dec. 9, 1787, above.

13. Malone, II, pp. 172-73.

*knew you approved.* In this *situation I thought it due to truth* as well as that it would be most agreeable to *yourself* and *accordingly took the liberty to state some of your opinions on the favorable side.*"[14]

With ratification by New Hampshire, the ninth state, and Virginia, the tenth, the new federal government would go into effect in 1789. Madison carried Virginia's instrument of ratification to New York and laid it before Congress in July, when he resumed his seat as a Virginia delegate. The New York convention had been in session in Poughkeepsie for two weeks when he wrote Jefferson: "Two thirds of the members assembled with a determination to reject the Constitution, and are still opposed to it in their hearts." But the hope of retaining the federal government in New York was a powerful attraction and might help overcome the opposition.[15] When Alexander Hamilton asked Madison about an Antifederalist proposal for conditional ratification, reserving the right to withdraw from the Union if its amendments were not accepted, Madison firmly rejected the offer. Conditional approval would "not make N. York a member of the Union.... The Constitution requires an adoption *in toto,* and *for ever.* It has been so adopted by the other States," including Virginia, where conditional ratification had been "considered as worse than a rejection."[16]

Although New York dropped its conditions, Madison was worried by its form of adoption. "It is remarkable," he told his friend in France. The unconditional ratification was prefaced by an explanatory bill of rights, containing twenty-three proposed amendments, and followed by thirty-two "recommendatory" amendments.[17] It was also accompanied by a Circular Letter "to the other States on the subject of amendments," urging a second convention, a move that Madison opposed. "The great danger in the present crisis," he wrote Jefferson, "is that if another Convention should soon be assembled, it will terminate in discord, or in alterations to the federal system which would throw back *essential* powers into the State Legislatures. The delay of a few years will assuage the jealousies which have been artificially created by designing men and will at the same time point out the faults which really call for amendment."[18]

Watching the ratification process from Mt. Vernon, George Washington took a generous view of the arguments pro and con. "Upon the whole," he wrote, "I doubt whether the opposition to the Constitution will not ultimately be productive of more good than evil; it has called forth, in its defence, abilities which would not perhaps have been otherwise exerted, that have

14. JM to TJ, July 24, 1788, below. The italicized words were written in code.
15. *Ibid.*
16. JM to Alexander Hamilton, July 20, 1788, in *PJM,* XI, p. 189.
17. For the ratification process in New York, see Linda Grant DePauw, *The Eleventh Pillar: New York State and the Federal Constitution* (Ithaca, 1966), pp. 241–79.
18. JM to TJ, Aug. 10, 1788, below.

thrown new light upon the science of Government: they have given the rights of man a full and fair discussion, and explained them in so clear and forcible a manner as cannot fail to make a lasting impression."[19]

When Jefferson learned that the new government was to go into effect, he sent a congratulatory letter to Madison. "I sincerely rejoice at the acceptance of our new constitution by nine states. It is a good canvas, on which some strokes only want retouching." He made a graceful retreat from his insistence on rotation in office, readily supposing his opinion wrong since the reeligibility of the president for office had aroused no fears in America. But he continued to press for a bill of rights: trial by jury, the right of habeas corpus, freedom of the press, freedom of religion, the abolition of standing armies in peacetime, and restrictions on monopolies. "I hope," he added, ". . . a bill of rights will be formed to guard the people against the federal government, as they are already guarded against their state governments in most instances."[20]

Long before he received Jefferson's letter, Madison had decided that "supplemental safeguards to liberty" should be added to the Constitution after the new government had begun.[21] When he received Jefferson's letter, Madison, who was no enemy to bills of rights—he had approved the Virginia Declaration of Rights in 1776 and, indeed, had improved it by rewriting the clause on freedom of religion—penned one of the most penetrating analyses of liberty and power ever written. "My own opinion," he declared, "has always been in favor of a bill of rights; provided it be so framed as not to imply powers not meant to be included in the enumeration. At the same time," he emphasized, "I have never thought the omission a material defect, nor been anxious to supply it even by *subsequent* amendment, for any other reason than that it is anxiously desired by others. I have favored it because I supposed it might be of use, and if properly executed could not be of disservice."

He had not argued for a bill of rights chiefly because he feared "that a positive declaration of some of the most essential rights could not be obtained in the requisite latitude." The very effort to define them might even limit their scope: "I am sure that the rights of conscience in particular, if submitted to public definition would be narrowed much more than they are likely ever to be by an assumed power." Even when they were protected by "parchment barriers," overbearing majorities had repeatedly violated them. He pointedly reminded Jefferson of the Virginia Declaration of Rights and the enactment of Jefferson's Bill for Establishing Religious Freedom, noting that "a religious establishment would have taken place in that State, if the legislative majority had found as they expected, a majority of the people in favor of the measure."

19. George Washington to John Armstrong, Apr. 25, 1788, in Fitzpatrick, XXIX, pp. 464–67.
20. TJ to JM, July 31, 1788, below.
21. JM to TJ, Sept. 21, 1788, below. See also Jack N. Rakove, "James Madison and the Bill of Rights: A Broader Context," *Presidential Studies Quarterly* 22 (1992): 667–77.

He was convinced "that if a majority of the people were now of one sect, the measure would still take place and on narrower ground than was then proposed," notwithstanding the additional obstacle created by the enactment of Jefferson's landmark bill. "Wherever the real power in a government lies," he concluded in a brilliant attack on formal guarantees, "there is the danger of oppression." Majoritarian democracy could pose formidable threats to individual rights and the liberties of the people:

In our Governments the real power lies in the majority of the Community, and the invasion of private rights is *chiefly* to be apprehended, not from acts of Government contrary to the sense of its constituents, but from acts in which the Government is the mere instrument of the major number of constituents.

Madison pulled no punches in pressing his point, noting that he founded his views on "facts, and reflections suggested by them," whereas Jefferson, perched in Paris, "contemplated abuses of power issuing from a very different quarter."[22] He was, however, more gentle with Jefferson than with another friend in Paris who was also critical of the Constitution: "Had you been a member of that assembly [the Constitutional Convention], and been impressed with the truths that our situation discloses, you would have concurred in the necessity which was felt by the other members. In your closet in Paris and with the evils resulting from too much Government all over Europe fully in your view, it is natural for you to run into criticisms dictated by an extreme on that side. Perhaps in your situation I should think and feel as you do. In mine," he concluded sharply, "I am sure you would think and feel as I do."[23]

In a pessimistic but realistic moment, Madison laid down a general political rule. "Wherever there is an interest and power to do wrong," he told Jefferson, "wrong will generally be done, and not less readily by a powerful and interested party [in a republic] than by a powerful and interested prince [in a monarchy]." Since that was true, he had concluded that parchment barriers—a bill of rights—would serve two useful purposes in both monarchies and republics:

1. The political truths declared in that solemn manner acquire by degrees the character of fundamental maxims of free Government, and as they become incorporated with the national sentiment, counteract the impulses of interest and passion. 2. Altho' it be generally true as above stated that the danger of oppression lies in the interested majorities of the people rather than in usurped acts of the Government, yet there may be occasions on which the evil may spring from the latter sources; and on such, a bill of rights will be a good ground for an appeal to the sense of the community.

Madison concluded his discussion of liberty and power in a popularly elected government with a final observation: "It has been remarked that there

22. JM to TJ, Oct. 17, 1788, below.
23. JM to Philip Mazzei, Oct. 8, 1788, in *PJM,* XI, pp. 278-79.

is a tendency in all Governments to an augmentation of power at the expence of liberty. But the remark as usually understood does not appear to me well founded. Power when it has attained a certain degree of energy and independence goes on generally to further degrees. But when below that degree, the direct tendency is to further degrees of relaxation, until the abuses of liberty beget a sudden transition to an undue degree of power. With this explanation the remark may be true; and in the latter sense only is it in my opinion applicable to the Governments in America. It is a melancholy reflection that liberty should be equally exposed to danger whether the Government have too much or too little power; and that the line which divides these extremes should be so inaccurately defined by experience."[24]

In the middle of their exchange on liberty and power, Madison sent Jefferson a copy of *The Federalist*. "I believe," he added with diffidence, "I never have yet *mentioned to you that publication. It was undertaken last fall by Jay, Hamilton and myself. The proposal came from the two former.* The *execution was thrown by the sickness of Jay mostly on the two others.* Though *carried on in concert the writers are not mutually answerable* for *all the ideas of each other*, there being *seldom time for even a perusal* of the *pieces by any but the writer before they were wanted at the press* and *some times hardly by the writer himself*."[25]

Jefferson happily acknowledged the complete set of essays in *The Federalist*. He had already received the first installment from Edward Carrington, Madison's colleague in Congress, who had named the three authors. After receiving the complete set from Madison, he read it "with care, pleasure and improvement, and was satisfied there was nothing in it by one of those hands, and not a great deal by a second." As for Madison's contributions, which he mistakenly judged to be the most numerous, "It does the highest honor . . . , as being, in my opinion, the best commentary on the principles of government which ever was written," firmly establishing "the plan of government" under the Constitution. "I confess," he concluded "it has rectified me in several points."

But Jefferson still held out for a bill of rights, although he preferred subsequent amendments by Congress rather than by a second convention, "in which case I should not fear any dangerous innovation in the plan." The size of the Antifederalist minorities, he observed, "are too respectable not to be entitled to some sacrifice of opinion in the majority. Especially when a great proportion of them would be contented with a bill of rights."[26]

Long before Madison received this letter, he had concluded that a bill of rights would be useful in laying down "fundamental maxims of free Govern-

24. JM to TJ, Oct. 17, 1788, below.

25. JM to TJ, Aug. 10, 1788, below. The italicized words were written in code. Adrienne Koch interprets JM's delay in mentioning his co-authorship of the *Federalist* essays as "evidence of an unusual strain" in their friendship; see Adrienne Koch, *Jefferson and Madison: The Great Collaboration* (New York, 1950), pp. 46–55.

26. TJ to JM, Nov. 18, 1788, below.

ment" and setting up defenses against "usurped acts of the Government." These views gave Jefferson great satisfaction, but to Madison's arguments in favor of a bill of rights, he added a third: "the legal check which it puts into the hands of the judiciary. This is a body, which if rendered independent, and kept strictly to their department merits great confidence for their learning and integrity." To Madison's objections to the inefficacy of parchment barriers, he ticked off a series of short answers. Parchment barriers are better than no barriers; they are "of great potency always, and rarely inefficacious." Even if a positive declaration of some essential rights were not of the requisite latitude, "half a loaf is better than no bread." The presumption that undelegated powers are reserved might be enough protection of rights if the Constitution covered all material points, "but in a constitutive act which leaves some precious articles unnoticed, and raises implications against others, a declaration of rights becomes necessary by way of supplement." The limited powers of the federal government and the jealousy of the subordinate governments were both useful protections, but a declaration of rights would be a text by which the states could measure the acts of the federal government and the latter could measure the acts of the states. Madison had persuaded him that "the executive in our governments is not the sole, it is scarcely the principal object of my jealousy." Indeed, he agreed that "the tyranny of the legislatures is the most formidable dread at present, and will be for long years." For all these reasons, he was "much pleased that a declaration of rights will be added" to the Constitution by Congress. Moreover, he hoped that it would be done "in that way which will not endanger the whole frame of government or any essential part of it."[27]

While Jefferson warmed to the Constitution and Madison's role in the convention—he later called Madison's notes on the debates "the ablest work of this kind ever executed," done with "a labor and exactness beyond comprehension"[28]—he knew that France, with growing fiscal problems of her own, had cooled to further financial aid for the United States. When he learned that Adams planned to visit the Netherlands before returning to America, Jefferson met him at The Hague, and together they went on to Amsterdam to negotiate yet another loan, "the fourth and final transfusion received from the Netherlands by the American body politic through the agency of John Adams."[29] Adams and Jefferson not only persuaded the Dutch bankers to complete the funding of an earlier loan, they also anticipated the needs for 1789 and 1790, when the new taxing power under the Constitution would first become effective, negotiating an additional loan, subject to congressional approval, to

27. TJ to JM, Mar. 15, 1789, below.
28. TJ to John Adams, Aug. 10, 1815, in Cappon, II, p. 453.
29. Lyman Butterfield, *John Adams and the Beginnings of Netherlands-American Friendship, 1780–1788* (Boston, 1959), p. 29. For the negotiation by Adams and TJ, see Pieter J. Van Winter, *American Finance and Dutch Investment, 1780–1805,* 2 vols. (New York, 1977), I, pp. 294–305.

launch the new government. Jefferson informed Madison that the moneylenders in Amsterdam "look forward to our new government"—and its power to tax—"with a great deal of partiality and interest. They are disposed to have much confidence in it, and it was the prospect of it's establishment which enabled us to set the loan of last year into motion again."[30]

For that reason, Jefferson thought that the first act of the new government should be adequate provision for the foreign debt. "Digest the whole [of the European debts]," he urged Madison, "into a table, shewing the sum of interest due every year, and the portions of principal paiable the same years. Take the most certain branch of revenue, and one which shall suffice to pay the interest and leave such a surplus as may accomplish all the paiments of the capital at terms somewhat short of those at which they will become due." Surpluses could be used to purchase "our paper on the exchange of Amsterdam," keeping it at par and thus enabling the United States to command there at any time "as many millions as that capital can produce."[31]

If speedier action were necessary—if France, for example, called for payment of interest before the new government was established—Jefferson suggested that the Confederation Congress "take on itself to borrow in Amsterdam what may be necessary for them. The new government," he continued, "should by no means be left by the old to the necessity of borrowing a stiver before it can tax for it's interest." What he thought necessary was approval by the Confederation Congress of "the loan of a million (which Mr. Adams and myself have proposed this year)," plus "what may be necessary for the French calls to the year 1790."[32]

Several months later, Jefferson did what he had suggested Madison might do—he prepared a digest of the European debt and worked out a timetable for funding it. And he enclosed another proposal "by a gentleman infinitely better acquainted with the subject," probably a Dutch banker then in Paris.[33] Perhaps Madison, by adding his own ideas to these proposals, could "devise something better than either." Of one thing Jefferson was sure: "Something must be done."[34]

For the political news of Europe, Jefferson often referred Madison to his dispatches to John Jay, secretary of foreign affairs. To Jay and others, Jefferson portrayed himself as a spectator of events that made it appear as if "all the world is run politically mad." By the spring of 1788, he reported that "the gay and thoughtless Paris is now become a furnace of Politics. . . . Men, women,

30. For an account of TJ's trip to Holland, see Edward Dumbauld, *Thomas Jefferson, American Tourist* (Norman, Okla., 1946), pp. 110–16.
31. TJ to JM, May 3, 1788, below.
32. *Ibid.*
33. Julian P. Boyd identifies the author as Jacob van Staphorst; see *PTJ,* XIV, pp. 190–209.
34. TJ to JM, Nov. 18, 1788, below, includes both TJ's and van Staphorst's proposals for funding the foreign debt.

and children talk nothing else; and you know that naturally they talk much, loud and warm. Society is spoilt by it, at least for those who, like myself, are but lookers on."[35]

Lafayette played a prominent role in the French reform movement, and Jefferson's views often reflected his friend's opinion, just as Lafayette was influenced by Jefferson. Both believed that France's centralized government was striving for more popular support at the same time that America's popular leaders were working for more centralized government. And both were advocates of a new constitution and a bill of rights in both countries.[36]

By the middle of 1788, Jefferson was of two minds about royal reforms. On the one hand, the Crown had yielded "one right after the other to the nation." "They have reformed the criminal law," he told Monroe, "acknoleged the king cannot lay a new tax without the consent of the states general, and they will call the states general next year," the first time it had been convened since 1614. "The object of this body when met," he predicted, "will be a bill of rights, a civil list, a national assembly meeting at certain epochs, and some other matters of that kind."[37]

On the other hand, the king had abrogated the power of the provincial parlements by reducing them from representative bodies to mere judicial organizations, substituting for these regional bodies a Plenary Court, a newly created body that was to sit in Paris and serve the whole country.[38] Jefferson quickly condemned "the abolishing, in so great a degree, of the parliaments, and the substitution of so ill composed a body" as the Plenary Court.[39] If the king could remodel the constitution at will, Jefferson told Madison, "this government is a pure despotism: the question then arising is whether a pure despotism, in a single head, or one which is divided among a king, nobles, priesthood, and numerous magistracy is the least bad. I should be puzzled to decide: but I hope they [the French people] will have neither, and that they are advancing to a limited, moderate government, in which the people will have a good share."[40]

When Lafayette joined a group of nobles from Brittany in a petition critical of the king's encroachment on local parlements, he fell into disfavor at

---

35. TJ to Anne Willing Bingham, May 11, 1788, in *PTJ,* XIII, p. 151. For an astute and independent appraisal of the French Revolution, see J. F. Bosher, *The French Revolution* (New York, 1988).

36. See Louis Gottschalk, *Lafayette between the American and the French Revolution, 1783–1789* (Chicago, 1950), and Robert R. Palmer, "The Dubious Democrat: Thomas Jefferson in Bourbon France," *Political Science Quarterly* 72 (1957): 388–404.

37. TJ to James Monroe, Aug. 9, 1788, in *PTJ,* XIII, p. 489.

38. R. R. Palmer, *The Age of the Democratic Revolution: A Political History of Europe and America, 1760–1800,* 2 vols. (Princeton, 1959–64), I, 457–58.

39. TJ to John Brown Cutting, July 24, 1788, in *PTJ,* XIII, pp. 405–6.

40. TJ to JM, July 31, 1788, below.

court and was deprived of his army command—"disgraced," according to Jefferson, "in the ancient language of the court."[41] The twelve Breton deputies who carried the petition to the king were arrested and sent to the Bastille, and Madison feared that Lafayette had also been confined. But Jefferson assured him that royal disfavor would instead make Lafayette a popular hero:[42]

> He has from the beginning taken openly part with those who demand a constitution: and there was a moment that we apprehended the Bastille: but they ventured on nothing more than to take from him a temporary service on which he had been ordered; and this more to save appearances for their own authority than any thing else; for at the very time they pretended that they had put him into disgrace, they were constantly conferring and communicating with him. Since this he has stood on safe ground, and is viewed as among the foremost of the patriots.[43]

Although Jefferson predicted that the Estates General would adopt "a tolerably free constitution, perhaps as free a one as the nation is as yet prepared to bear,"[44] he was not sure that the people were ready "for receiving the blessings to which they are entitled. I doubt, for instance, whether the body of the nation, if they could be consulted, would accept of a Habeas corpus law," he told Madison, "if offered them by the king." If the meeting of the Estates General did not aim at too much or move too fast, he thought that "they may begin a good constitution." Three things seemed easily attainable: "1. their own meeting periodically. 2. the exclusive right of taxation. 3. the right of registering laws and proposing amendments to them as exercised now by the [regional] parliaments."

As the French Revolution heated up, Jefferson was also sure that the French would adopt a bill of rights.[45] "Every body here is trying their hands at forming declarations of rights," he assured Madison. In an attempt to buttress his campaign for an American bill of rights, he added: "As something is going on with you also, I send you two specimens from hence," one by Lafayette "adapted to existing abuses" and another by one of the philosophes, Dr. Richard Gem, that "goes to those possible as well as those existing" abuses. These early drafts of what later became the French Declaration of the Rights of Man and the Citizen were modeled on the Virginia Declaration of Rights of 1776, Jefferson observed, containing "the essential principles of ours accomodated as much as could be to the actual state of things here."[46]

41. TJ to John Jay, Aug. 3, 1788, in *PTJ*, XIII, p. 464.
42. TJ to JM, July 31, 1788, below.
43. TJ to JM, Jan. 12, 1789, below.
44. TJ to JM, Mar. 15, 1789, below.
45. TJ to JM, Nov. 18, 1788, below, and Jan. 12, 1789, below.
46. TJ to JM, Jan. 12, 1789, below. Dr. Gem, a "pure theorist," was an English physician living in France who became TJ's personal physician; see Gilbert Chinard, ed., *The Letters of Lafayette and Jefferson* (Baltimore, 1929), p. 80; Koch, pp. 78–88; and *PTJ*, XIV, pp. 438–40, XV, pp. 384–86.

# THE LETTERS

## *Jefferson to Madison*

Paris Feb. 6, 1788

DEAR SIR

I wrote you last on the 20th. of December since which your's of the same day and of the 9th. have come to hand. The apples and cranberries you were so kind as to send at the same time were all spoiled when they arrived at Havre, so that probably those articles will not keep during the passage. The box of plants is arrived at the Custom house here, but I shall probably not receive them till after I shall have sealed my letter. They are well chosen, as to the species, for this country. I wish there had been some willow oaks (Quercus Phellos Linnaei) among them, either the plants or acorns, as that tree is much desired here, and absolutely unknown. As the red-birds and opossums are not to be had at New York, I will release you from the trouble of procuring them elsewhere. This trouble, with the incertainty of their coming safe, is more than the importance of the object will justify. You omitted to inclose Prince's catalogue of plants which your letter mentions to have been inclosed. I send herewith two small boxes, one addressed to Mr. Drayton to the care of the S. Carola. delegates, with a letter. Will you be so good as to ask those gentlemen to forward the letter and box without delay. The box contains cork acorns, and Sulla, which should arrive at their destination as quick as possible. The other box is addressed to you, and contains, cork acorns, Sulla, and peas. The two first articles are to be forwarded to Monticello to Colo. Nicholas Lewis, taking thereout what proportion of them you please for yourself. The peas are brought me from the South of France and are said to be valuable. Considering the season of the year I think it would be best to sow them at New York, and to send the produce on next winter to such persons as you please in Virginia, in order to try whether they are any of them better than what we already have. The Sulla is a species of St. foin which comes from Malta, and is proof against any degree of drought. I have raised it in my garden here, and find it a luxuriant and precious plant. I inclose you the bills of lading for the three boxes of books which ought to have gone last fall, but are only lately gone by the Juno Capt. Jenkins. Your pedometer is done, and I now wait only for some trusty passenger to take charge of it. I hope there will be one in the March packet. It cost 300. livres. Your watch you will have received by the Ct. de Moustier. With respect to the Mercures de France always forwarded to you for Bannister, I must beg you never to let them go so as to subject him to postage for them.

I am glad to hear that the new constitution is received with favor. I sincerely wish that the 9 first conventions may receive, and the 4. last reject it.

The former will secure it finally, while the latter will oblige them to offer a declaration of rights in order to complete the union. We shall thus have all it's good, and cure it's principal defect. You will of course be so good as to continue to mark to me it's progress. I will thank you also for as exact a state as you can procure me of the impression made on the sum of our domestic debt by the sale of lands, and by federal and state exertions in any other manner. I have not yet heard whether the law passed in Virginia for *prohibiting the importation of brandies.*[1] *If it did, the late arret here for encouraging our commerce will be repealed. The minister will be glad of such a pretext to pacify the opposition.* I do not see that there are at present any strong symptoms of rupture among the Western powers of Europe. Domestic effervescence and the want of money shackle all the movements of this court. Their prevailing sentiments are total distrust of England, disgust towards the k. of Prussia, jealousy of the two empires, and I presume I may add a willingness to restore the affairs of the Dutch patriots, if it can be done without war.

I will beg the favor of you to send me a copy of the American philosophical transactions, both the 1st. and 2d. volumes, by the first packet and to accept assurances of the sincere esteem with which I am dear Sir your affectionate friend and servant,

TH: JEFFERSON

P.S. Among the copies of my Notes to be sent to S. Carolina, be so good as to forward one for Mr. Kinlock whom I think I omitted to name in the list.


*Madison to Jefferson*

New York Feb. 19, 1788

DEAR SIR

By the Count de Moustier I received your favour of the 8th. of October. I received by his hands also the watch which you have been so good as to provide for me, and for which I beg you to accept my particular thanks. During the short trial I have made she goes with great exactness. Since the arrival of the Count de Moustier, I have received also by the Packet Mr. Calonne's publication[2] for myself, and a number of the Mercure's for Mr. Banister. The Bearer was a Mr. Stuart. I had a conveyance to Mr. Banister a few days after the Mercure's came to hand.

The public here continues to be much agitated by the proposed fœderal Constitution and to be attentive to little else. At the date of my last Delaware Pennsylvania and New Jersey had adopted it. It has been since adopted by

1. The italicized words and those in the rest of the letter were written in code.
2. Charles Alexandre de Calonne had been dismissed as comptroller general of finance in Apr. 1787; see John F. Bosher, *French Finances, 1770–1795: From Business to Bureaucracy* (Cambridge, Eng., 1970), pp. 178–82.

Connecticut, Georgia, and Massachusetts. In the first the minority consisted of 40 against 127. In Georgia the adoption was unanimous. In Massachusetts the conflict was tedious and the event extremely doubtful. On the final question the vote stood 187 against 168; a majority of 19 only being in favor of the Constitution. The prevailing party comprized however all the men of abilities, of property, and of influence. In the opposite multitude there was not a single character capable of uniting their wills or directing their measures. It was made up partly of deputies from the province of Maine who apprehended difficulties from the New Government to their scheme of separation, partly of men who had espoused the disaffection of Shay's; and partly of ignorant and jealous men, who had been taught or had fancied that the Convention at Philada. had entered into a conspiracy against the liberties of the people at large, in order to erect an aristocracy for the rich the *well-born*,[3] and the men of Education. They had no plan whatever. They looked no farther than to put a negative on the Constitution and return home. The amendments as recommended by the Convention were as I am well informed not so much calculated for the minority in the Convention, on whom they had little effect, as for the people of the State. You will find the amendments in the Newspapers which are sent from the office of foreign affairs. It appears from a variety of circumstances that disappointment had produced no asperity in the minority, and that they will probably not only acquiesce in the event, but endeavour to reconcile their constituents to it. This was the public declaration of several who were called the leaders of the party. The minority of Connecticut behaved with equal moderation. That of Pennsylvania has been extremely intemperate and continues to use a very bold and menacing language. Had the decision in Massachusetts been adverse to the Constitution, it is not improbable that some very violent measures would have followed in that State. The cause of the inflamation however is much more in their State factions, than in the system proposed by the Convention. New Hampshire is now deliberating on the Constitution. It is generally understood that an adoption is a matter of certainty. South Carolina and Maryland have fixed on April or May for their Conventions. The former it is currently said will be one of the ratifying States. Mr. Chace and a few others will raise a considerable opposition in the latter. But the weight of personal influence is on the side of the Constitution, and the present expectation is that the opposition will be outnumbered by a great majority. This State is much divided in its sentiment. Its Convention is to be held in June. The decision of Massts. will give the turn in favor of the Constitution unless an idea should prevail or the fact should appear, that the voice of the State is opposed to the result of its Convention. North Carolina has put off her Convention till July.[4] The State is much divided it is said. The temper of Virginia,

---

3. JM's italics.
4. JM later placed an asterisk here and added a footnote: "see letter from Col. [William R.] Davie to J.M." Dated June 10, 1789, it is in *PJM,* XII, pp. 210–11.

as far as I can learn, has undergone but little change of late. At first there was an enthusiasm for the Constitution. The tide next took a sudden and strong turn in the opposite direction. The influence and exertions of Mr. Henry, and Col. Mason and some others will account for this. Subsequent information again represented the Constitution as regaining in some degree its lost ground. The people at large have been uniformly said to be more friendly to the Constitution than the Assembly. But it is probable that the dispersion of the latter will have a considerable influence on the opinions of the former. The previous adoption of nine States must have a very persuasive effect on the minds of the opposition, though I am told that a very bold language is held by Mr. H[enr]y and some of his partisans. Great stress is laid on the self-sufficiency of that State, and the prospect of external props are alluded to.

Congress have done no business of consequence yet, nor is it probable that much more of any sort will precede the event of the great question before the public.

The Assembly of Virginia have passed the district Bill of which I formerly gave you an account. There are 18 districts, with 4 new Judges, Mr. Gabl. Jones, Richd. Parker, St. George Tucker and Jos. Prentis. They have reduced much the taxes, and provided some indulgences for debtors. The question of British debts underwent great vicicitudes. It was after long discussion resolved by a majority of 30 against the utmost exertions of Mr. Henry that they should be paid as soon as the other States should have complied with the treaty. A few days afterwards he carried his point by a majority of 50 that G. B. should first comply. Adieu Yrs. Affecty.,

JS. MADISON JR.

P.S. Mr. St. John[5] has given me a very interesting description of a System of Nature lately published at Paris. Will you add it for me. The Boxes which were to have come for myself G.W. and A. D. etc. have not yet arrived.

*Madison to Jefferson*

New York Feb. 20, 1788

DEAR SIR

I have this moment received an answer to a letter written to Mr. W. S. Browne on the subject of Mr. Burke's affairs. The answer is written by direction of Mrs. Brown and informs me that her husband is absent on a voyage to the West Indies and is not expected back till April; that when "he arrives he no doubt will be ready to deliver the effects on proper application. The amount of

---

5. Mr. St. John was Michel-Guillaume St. Jean de Crèvecoeur, author of *Letters from an American Farmer* (London, 1782).

effects I can say nothing to, but they have been stored ever since with care. The cash I believe is the same as you mention—as to tendering any thing but the hard cash you need be under no apprehension. His character is well established in this town (Providence R. Island) and he despises the man that would offer paper when he had received cash." This is all the information I have to give on the subject.

By letters just received from Virginia I find that I shall be under the necessity of setting out in 8 or 10 days for Virginia. I mention this circumstance that it may explain the cause if I should not write by the next conveyance. Yrs. affty.,

Js. MADISON JR.


*Jefferson to Madison*

[Paris] Mar. 8, 1788

DEAR SIR

The bearer of this letter is Mr. Francis Adrian Van der Kemp one of the late victims of patriotism in Holland.[6] Having determined to remove himself and his family to America, his friend the Baron de Capellen,[7] another of those expatriated worthies, has asked of me to give letters of introduction to Mr. Van der Kemp, recommending him for his extraordinary zeal in the cause of liberty, his talents, and his sufferings. These motives, together with a respect for the very estimable person who recommends him, induce me to ask for him your civilities and your services. Uninformed of the part of our country in which he may chuse to settle, I am unable to address him to the particular persons into whose society he may wish to enter. But when he shall have decided on the place of his settlement, you will be able to give, or to procure for him, such letters as may be accomodated to his views. In doing this you will add to the many motives of obligation and esteem with which I am, Dear Sir, Your affectionate friend and humble servt,

TH: JEFFERSON

---

6. See Helen L. Fairchild, *Francis Adrian van der Kemp, 1752–1829: An Autobiography Together with Extracts from His Correspondence* (New York, 1903).

7. For J. D. van der Capellen, see *ibid.*, pp. 103–7, and Palmer, *The Age of the Democratic Revolution*, I, pp. 251, 324–40. Simon Schama, "The Patriot Revolt, 1781–1787," in his *Patriots and Liberators: Revolution in the Netherlands, 1780–1813* (New York, 1977), pp. 64–135, gives a detailed account of the revolution there.

## Madison to Jefferson

Virginia Orange Apr. 22, 1788

DEAR SIR

Being just acquainted by a letter from President Griffin that Mr. Paridise is in N. York and proposes to sail in the first packet for France I drop you a few lines which will go by that conveyance if they arrive in N. York in time; which however I do not much expect.

The proposed Constitution still engrosses the public attention. The elections for the Convention here are but just over and promulged. From the returns (excluding those from Kentucky which are not yet known) it seems probable, though not absolutely certain that a majority of the members elect are friends to the Constitution. The superiority of abilities at least seems to lie on that side. The characters of most note which occur to me, are marshalled thus. For the Constitution, Pendleton, Wythe, Blair, Innis, Marshal, Doctr. W. Jones, G. Nicholas, Wilson Nicholas, Gabl. Jones, Thos. Lewis, F. Corbin, Ralph Wormley Jr. White of Frederik, Genl. Gates, Genl. A. Stephens, Archd. Stuart, Zachy. Johnson, Docr. Stuart, Parson Andrews, H. Lee Jr. Bushrod Washington considered as a young Gentleman of talents: against the Constitution, Mr. Henry, Mason, Harrison, Grayson, Tyler, M. Smith, W. Ronald, Lawson, Bland, Wm. Cabell, Dawson.

The Governor[8] is so temperate in his opposition and goes so far with the friends of the Constitution that he cannot properly be classed with its enemies. Monroe is considered by some as an enemy, but I believe him to be a friend though a cool one. There are other individuals of weight whose opinions are unknown to me. R. H. Lee is not elected. His brother F. L. Lee is a warm friend to the Constitution, as I am told, but also is not elected. So are Jno. and Man Page.

The adversaries take very different grounds of opposition. Some are opposed to the substance of the plan; others to particular modifications only. Mr. H[enr]y is supposed to aim at disunion. Col. M[aso]n is growing every day more bitter, and outrageous in his efforts to carry his point; and will probably in the end be thrown by the violence of his passions into the politics of Mr. H[enr]y. The preliminary question will be whether previous alterations shall be insisted on or not? Should this be carried in the affirmative, either a conditional ratification, or a proposal for a new Convention will ensue. In either event, I think the Constitution and the Union will be both endangered. It is not to be expected that the States which have ratified will reconsider their determinations, and submit to the alterations prescribed by Virga. and if a second Convention should be formed, it is as little to be expected that the same spirit of compromise will prevail in it as produced an amicable result to the first. It will be easy also for those who have latent views of disunion, to

---

8. Edmund Randolph.

carry them on under the mask of contending for alterations popular in some but inadmissible in other parts of the U. States.

The real sense of the people of this State cannot be easily ascertained. They are certainly attached and with warmth to a continuance of the Union; and I believe a large majority of the most intelligent and independent are equally so to the plan under consideration. On a geographical view of them, almost all the counties in the N. Neck have elected fœderal deputies. The Counties on the South side of James River have pretty generally elected adversaries to the Constitution. The intermediate district is much chequered in this respect. The Counties between the blue ridge and the Alleghany have chosen friends to the Constitution without a single exception. Those Westward of the latter, have as I am informed, generally though not universally pursued the same rule. Kentucky it is supposed will be divided.

Having been in Virga. but a few weeks, I can give you little account of other matters, and none of your private affairs or connections, particularly of your two nephews. The Winter here as every where else in the U.S. was very severe, which added to short crops of corn, threatened a great scarcity and high price. It is found however that neither of these evils has taken place. Corn may be purchased for 2 dollars, and even 10s. per barrel. Tobacco is as low at Fredb. as 18/ per Ct. and not higher at Richmond than 22 or 23/. There is at present a very promising spring, especially in the article of fruit. The night before last was so cold as to produce an alarm for the vegetation of all sorts; but it does not appear that any thing less vulnerable than young cucumbers has been injured.

I shall ask the favor of Mr. Griffin to send you by Mr. Paridise, or if he should be gone by some other hand, the debates of the Conventions in Penna. and Massachussetts, and any other publications worth your reading. I am Dear Sir your affect. friend and Servt.,

Js. MADISON JR.

## *Jefferson to Madison*

Paris May 1, 1788

DEAR SIR

The bearer hereof, Monsieur de Warville, is already known to you by his writings, some of which I have heretofore sent you, and particularly his work sur la France et les etats unis.[9] I am happy to be able to present him to you in person, assured that you will find him in all his dispositions equally estimable as for his genius. I need only to ask your acquaintance for him. That will dispose you to shew him all the civilities and attentions which may render his

---

9. For Jacques-Pierre Brissot de Warville, see his *New Travels in the United States of America, 1788*, ed. Durand Echeverria (Cambridge, 1964).

time agreeable in America, and put him into the way of obtaining any information he may want. I am gratified, while rendering him this service, to procure to myself the occasion of repeating to you those sentiments of esteem and attachment with which I am Dear Sir Your sincere friend and humble servant,

TH: JEFFERSON

## Jefferson to Madison

Paris May 3, 1788

DEAR SIR

Mine of Feb. 6. acknoleged the receipt of yours of Dec. 9. and 20. Since that, those of Feb. 19. and 20. are come to hand. The present will be delivered you by Mr. Warville, whom you will find truly estimable, and a great enthusiast for liberty. His writings will have shewn you this.

For public news I must refer you to my letter to Mr. Jay. Those I wrote to him from Amsterdam will have informed you of my journey thither.[10] While there, I endeavored to get as well as I could into the state of national credit there: for tho' I am an enemy to the using our credit but under absolute necessity, yet the possessing a good credit I consider as indispensible in the present system of carrying on war. The existence of a nation, having no credit, is always precarious. The credit of England is the best. Their paper sells at par on the exchange of Amsterdam the moment any of it is offered, and they can command there any sum they please. The reason is that they never borrow without establishing taxes for the paiment of the interest, and they never yet failed one day in that paiment. The Emperor and Empress have good credit enough. They use it little, and have been ever punctual. This country cannot borrow at all there. For tho' they always pay their interest within the year, yet it is often some months behind. It is difficult to assign to our credit it's exact station in this scale. They consider us as the most certain nation on earth for the principal; but they see that we borrow of themselves to pay the interest, so that this is only a conversion of their interest into principal. Our paper for this reason sells for from 4. to 8. per cent below par on the exchange. And our loans are negotiated with the patriots only. But the whole body of money dealers, patriot and Stadholderian, look forward to our new government with a great degree of partiality and interest. They are disposed to have much confidence in it, and it was the prospect of it's establishment which enabled us to set the loan of last year into motion again. They will attend stedfastly to it's first money operations. If these are injudiciously begun, correction, whenever they shall be corrected, will come too late. Our borrowings will always be

---

10. For TJ's collaboration with John Adams in floating a Dutch loan, see Cappon, I, pp. 205–7, 215–25, and Dumbauld, pp. 110–19. The standard account is Van Winter's *American Finance and Dutch Investment,* but see also Schama, pp. 58–63.

difficult and disadvantageous. If they begin well, our credit will immediately take the first station. Equal provision for the interest, adding to it a certain prospect for the principal, will give us a preference to all nations, the English not excepted. The first act of the new government should be some operation whereby they may assume to themselves this station. Their European debts form a proper subject for this. Digest the whole, public and private, Dutch, French and Spanish into a table, shewing the sum of interest due every year, and the portions of principal paiable the same years. Take the most certain branch of revenue, and one which shall suffice to pay the interest and leave such a surplus as may accomplish all the paiments of the capital at terms somewhat short of those at which they will become due. Let the surpluses of those years in which no reimbursement of principal falls, be applied to buy up our paper on the exchange of Amsterdam, and thus anticipate the demands of principal. In this way our paper will be kept up at par, and this alone will enable us to command in four and twenty hours at any time on the exchange of Amsterdam as many millions as that capital can produce. The same act which makes this provision for the existing debts, should go on to open a loan to their whole amount, the produce of that loan to be applied as fast as received to the paiment of such parts of the existing debts as admit of paiment. The rate of interest to be as the government should privately instruct their agent, because it must depend on the effect these measures would have on the exchange. Probably it could be lowered from time to time. Honest and annual publications of the paiments made will inspire confidence, while silence would conceal nothing from those interested to know.

You will perceive by the Comte rendue which I send you, that this country now calls seriously for it's interest at least.[11] The nonpaiment of this hitherto has done our credit little injury, because the government here saying nothing about it, the public have supposed they wished to leave us at our ease as to the paiment. It is now seen that they call for it, and they will publish annually the effect of that call. A failure here therefore will have the same effect on our credit hereafter as a failure at Amsterdam. I consider it then as of a necessity not to be dispensed with that these calls be effectually provided for. If it shall be seen that the general provision before hinted at cannot be in time to comply with the first calls of this country; then it is the present government which should take on itself to borrow in Amsterdam what may be necessary for them. The new government should by no means be left by the old to the necessity of borrowing a stiver before it can tax for it's interest. This will be to destroy the credit of the new government in it's birth. And I am of opinion that if the present Congress will add to the loan of a million (which Mr. Adams and myself have proposed this year) what may be necessary for the

11. The *Comptes rendus au Roi* were reports from the comptroller general to the king; see *PTJ*, XIII, pp. 136–37. For this one, the "very first attempt at a French budget," see Bosher's excellent summary in his chapter entitled "The Founding of the Modern Treasury," in *French Finances*, pp. 197–214.

French calls to the year 1790. the money can be obtained at the usual disadvantage. Tho' I have not at this moment received such authentic information from our bankers as I may communicate to Congress, yet I know privately from one of them (Mr. Jacob Van Staphorst who is here) that they had on hand a fortnight ago near 400,000 florins, and the sale of bonds going on well. So that the June interest which had been in so critical a predicament was already secured. If the loan of a million on Mr. Adams's bonds of this year be ratified by Congress, the applications of the money on hand may go on immediately according to the statement I sent to Mr. Jay. One article in this I must beg you to press on the Treasury board. That is an immediate order for the paiment of the three years arrearages to the French officers. They were about holding a meeting to take desperate measures on this subject when I was called to Holland. I desired them to be quiet till my return, and since my return I have pressed a further tranquillity till July by which time I have given them reason to hope I may have an answer from the Treasury board to my letters of March. Their ill humour can be contained no longer, and as I know no reason why they may not be paid at that time, I shall have nothing to urge in our defence after that.

I do not know *Warville's business in America.*[12] *I suspect him* to be *agent* of a *company* on some *speculation of lands. Perhaps you might connect him usefully* in what *yourself and Monroe* had *proposed.*

You remember the Report drawn by Governor Randolph on the navigation of the Missisipi. When I came to Europe, Mr. Thomson was so kind as to have me a copy of it made out. I lent it to Dr. Franklin and he mislaid it so that it could never be found. Could you make interest with him to have me another copy made and send it to me?[13]

By Mr. Warville I send your pedometer. To the loop at bottom of it you must sew a tape, and, at the other end of the tape, a small hook (such as we use under the name of hooks and eyes.) Cut a little hole in the bottom of your left watch pocket. Pass the hook and tape through it, and down between the breeches and drawers, and fix the hook on the edge of your knee band, an inch from the knee buckle. Then hook the instrument itself by it's swivel-hook on the upper edge of the watch-pocket. Your tape being well adjusted in length, your double steps will be exactly counted by the instrument, the shortest hand pointing out the thousands, the flat hand the hundreds, and the long hand the tens and units. Never turn the hands backward. Indeed it is best not to set them to any given place, but to note the number they stand at when you begin to walk. The adjusting the tape to it's exact length is a critical business, and will cost you many trials. But, once done, it is done for ever. The best way is to have a small buckle fixed on the middle of the tape, by which you can take it up

12. These italicized words and those in the rest of the letter were written in code.
13. JM, not Edmund Randolph, had written the report on the navigation of the Mississippi. See JM to John Jay, Oct. 1780, in *PJM,* II, pp. 127–35; Brant, II, pp. 77–83; and TJ to JM, Nov. 18, 1788, below.

and let it out at pleasure. When you chuse it should cease to count, unhook it from the top of the watch pocket and let it fall down to the bottom of the pocket.

I am to pay to Dr. Ramsay (if he requires it) 936 livres Tournois for a bookseller here. I take the liberty of writing to him that you will answer his draught to that amount. I communicate to him at the same time a proposition from the bookseller to furnish it in books. If he accedes to this, no draught will be made on you. Otherwise I must beg the favor of you to honour his bill and charge it to me. I send you the captain's receipt for the boxes of books forwarded some time ago. My absence prevented the receipt's going to you sooner. I am with sentiments of the most sincere esteem and attachment Dr. Sir your affectionate friend and servt,

TH: JEFFERSON

Neckar des opinions religieuses
Mirabeau aux Bataves
Volney sur la guerre des Turcs } now sent you by Mr. Warville.
Meilhan sur l'esprit et les moeurs


## *Jefferson to Madison*

Paris May 25, 1788

DEAR SIR

The inclosed letter for Mr. Jay being of a private nature, I have thought it better to put it under your cover lest it might be opened by some of his clerks in the case of his absence. But I inclose a press copy of it for yourself, as you will perceive the subject of it referred to you as well as to him. I ask your aid in it so far as you think right, and to have done what you think right. If you will now be so good as to cast your eye over the copy inclosed, what follows the present sentence will be some details, supplementory to that only, necessary for your information, but not proper for me to state to Mr. Jay.[14]

*Mr. Jay.*[15] Tho appointed a minister resident at the court of *Madrid* he never was *received* in that character. He was continually passing from *Paris* to *Madrid* and *Madrid* to *Paris* so that he had no occasion to establish a household at either. Accordingly he staid principally in furnished lodgings. Of all our ministers he had the least occasion for an outfit, and I suppose spent almost nothing on that article. He was of a disposition too to restrain himself within any limits of expence whatever, and it suited his recluse turn. Should he

---

14. TJ suggested that the Confederation Congress settle his accounts as minister to France before the new government under the Constitution began. He asked Jay to consult with JM; see TJ to John Jay, May 15, 1788, in *PTJ,* XIII, pp. 161–64. The account was not settled until 1792; see Malone, II, pp. 204–5.

15. These italicized words and those in the rest of the letter were written in code.

judge of what others should do, by what he did, it would be an improper criterion. He was in Europe as a voyageur only, and it was while the salary was 500 guineas more that at present.

*J. Adams.* He came over when, instead of outfit and salary, all expences were paid. Of rigorous honesty, and careless of appearances he lived for a considerable time as an oeconomical private individual. After he was fixed at *the Hague* and the salary at a sum certain, he continued his oeconomical stile till out of the difference between his expences and his salary, he could purchase furniture for his house. This was the easier as the salary was at 2500 guineas then. He was obliged too to be passing between *Paris* and *the Hague* so as to avoid any regular current of expence. When he established himself, his pecuniary affairs were under the direction of *Mrs. Adams,* one of the most estimable characters on earth, and the most attentive and honourable oeconomists. Neither had a wish to lay up a copper, but both wished to make both ends meet. I suspect however, from an expression dropped in conversation, that they were not able to do this, and that a deficit in their accounts appeared in their winding up. If this conjecture be true, it is a proof that the salary, so far from admitting savings, is inequal to a very plain stile of life, for such was theirs. I presume Congress will be asked to allow it, and it is evident to me, from what I saw while in *London* that it ought to be done, as they did not expend a shilling which should have been avoided. Would it be more eligible to set the example of making good a deficit, or to give him an Outfit, which will cover it? The impossibility of living on the sum allowed, reputably, was the true cause of his insisting on his recall.

*Doctor Franklin.* He came over while all expences were paid. He rented a house with standing furniture, such as tables, chairs, presses etc. and bought all other necessaries. The latter were charged in his account, the former was included in the article of houserent and paid during the whole time of his stay here; and as the established rate of hire for furniture is from 30. to 40. per cent. per annum, the standing furniture must have been paid for three times over during the 8. years he staid here. His salary too was 2500 guineas. When Congress reduced it to less than 2000, he refused to accede to it, asked his recall, and insisted that whenever they chose to alter the conditions on which he came out, if he did not approve of it, they ought to replace him in America on the old conditions. He lived plain, but as decently as his salary would allow. He saved nothing, but avoided debt. He knew he could not do this on the reduced salary and therefore asked his recall with decision.

To *him I* succeeded. He had established a certain stile of living. The same was expected from *me* and there were 500 guineas a year less to do it on. It has been aimed at however as far as was practicable. This rendered it constantly necessary to step neither to the right nor to the left to incur any expence which could possibly be avoided and it called for an almost womanly attention to the details of the houshold, equally perplexing, disgusting, and inconsistent with business. You will be sensible that in this situation no savings could be made for reimbursing the half year's salary ordered to be advanced under the former commission and more than as much again which was unavoidably so applied, without order, for the purchase of the Outfit. The reason of the thing, the usage of all nations, the usage of our own by paying all expences of preceding ministers, which gave them the outfit as far as their circumstances appeared to them to render it necessary, have made me take for granted all along that it would not be refused to me; nor should I have mentioned it now but that the administration is passing into other hands, and more complicated forms. It would be disagreeable to me to be presented to them in the first instance as a suitor. Men come into business at first with visionary principles. It is practice alone which can correct and conform them to the actual current of affairs. In the mean time those to whom their errors were first applied have been their victims. The government may take up the project of appointing foreign ministers without outfits and they may ruin two or three individuals before they find that that article is just as indispensable as the salary. They must then fall into the current of general usage, which has become general only because experience has established it's necessity.

Upon the whole, be so good as to reflect on it, and to do, not what your friendship to me, but your opinion of what is right will dictate. Accept, in all cases, assurances of the sincere esteem and respect with which I am Dear Sir Your friend and servant,

TH: JEFFERSON

## *Madison to Jefferson*

New York July 24 and 26, 1788

DEAR SIR

Your two last unacknowledged favors were of Decr. 20. and Feby. 6. They were received in Virginia, and no opportunity till the present precarious one by the way of Holland, has enabled me to thank you for them.

I returned here about ten days ago from Richmond which I left a day or two after the dissolution of the Convention. The final question on the new plan of Government was put on the 25th. of June. It was twofold 1. whether previous amendments should be made a condition of ratification. 2. directly on the Constitution in the form it bore. On the first the decision was in the negative, 88 being no, 80 only ay. On the second and definitive question, the ratification was affirmed by 89 ays against 79. noes. A number of alterations were then recommended to be considered in the mode pointed out in the Constitution itself. The meeting was remarkably full; Two members only being absent and those known to be on the opposite sides of the question. The debates also were conducted on the whole with very laudable moderation and decorum, and continued untill both sides declared themselves ready for the question. And it may be safely concluded that no irregular opposition to the System will follow in that State, at least with the countenance of the leaders on that side. What local eruptions may be occasioned by ill-timed or rigorous executions of the Treaty of peace against British debtors, I will not pretend to say. But altho' the leaders, particularly H[enr]y and M[a]s[o]n, will give no countenance to popular violences it is not to be inferred that they are reconciled to the event, or will give it a positive support. On the contrary both of them declared they could not go that length, and an attempt was made under their auspices to induce the minority to sign an address to the people which if it had not been defeated by the general moderation of the party, would probably have done mischief.

Among a variety of expedients employed by the opponents to gain proselytes, Mr. *Henry first and after him Col. Mason introduced* the *opinions, expressed in a letter from a correspondent* [*Mr. Donald or Skipwith I believe*][16] and endeavored to turn the influence of your *name even against parts, of which I knew you approved.* In this *situation I thought it due to truth* as well as that it would be most agreeable to *yourself* and *accordingly took the liberty to state some of your opinions on the favorable side.* I am informed that copies or extracts of a letter *from you were handed about at the Maryld. Convention with a like view of impeding the ratification.*

N. Hampshire ratified the Constitution on the 21st. Ult: and made the ninth State. The votes stood 57 for and 46. against the measure. S. Carolina had previously ratified by a very great majority. The Convention of N. Carolina is now sitting. At one moment the sense of that State was considered as strongly opposed to the system. It is now said that the tide has been for some time turning, which with the example of other States and particularly of Virginia prognosticates a ratification there also. The Convention of N. York has been in Session ever since the 17th. Ult: without having yet arrived at any final vote. Two thirds of the members assembled with a determination to reject the Constitution, and are still opposed to it in their hearts. The local situation of N. York, the number of ratifying States and the hope of retaining the federal Government in this City afford however powerful arguments to such men as Jay, Hamilton, the Chancellor Duane and several others; and it is not improbable that some form of ratification will yet be devised by which the dislike of the opposition may be gratified, and the State notwithstanding made a member of the new Union.

At Fredericksburg on my way hither I found the box with Cork Acorns Sulla and peas, addressed to me. I immediately had it forwarded to Orange from whence the Contents will be disposed of according to your order. I fear the advanced season will defeat the experiments. The few seeds taken out here by the President at my request and sown in his garden have not come up. I left directions in Virginia for obtaining acorns of the Willow Oak this fall, which shall be sent you as soon as possible. Col. Carrington tells me your request as

---

16. JM's brackets. These italicized words and those in the rest of the letter were written in code.

to the Philosophical Transactions was complied with in part only, the 1st. volume, being not to be had. I have enquired of a Delegate here from Rhode Island for further information concerning W. S. Brown, but can learn nothing precise. I shall continue my enquiries, and let you know hereafter the result.

July. 26.

We just hear that the Convention of this State have determined by a small majority to exclude from the ratification every thing involving a condition and to content themselves with recommending the alterations wished for.

As this will go by way of Holland I consider its reaching you as extremely uncertain. I forbear therefore to enter further into our public affairs at this time. If the packets should not be discontinued, which is surmised by some, I shall soon have an opportunity of writing again. In the mean time I remain with the sincerest affection Your friend and Servt.,

Js. MADISON JR.

P.S. Crops in Virginia of all sorts were very promising when I left the State. This was the case also generally throughout the States I passed thro' with local exceptions produced in the Wheat fields by a destructive insect which goes under the name of the Hessian fly. It made its first appearance several years ago on Long Island, from which it has spread over half this State, and a great part of New Jersey; and seems to be making an annual progress in every direction.

## *Jefferson to Madison*

Paris July 31, 1788

DEAR SIR

My last letters to you were of the 3d and 25. of May. Yours from Orange of Apr. 22. came to hand on the 10th. inst.

My letter to Mr. Jay containing all the public news that is well authenticated, I will not repeat it here, but add some details in the smaller way which you may be glad to know. The *disgrace of the Marquis de la fayette*[17] which at any other period of their history would have had the worst consequences for *him* will on the contrary mark him favourably to the nation at present. During the present administration he can expect nothing, but perhaps it may serve him with their successors whenever a change shall take place. No change of *the principal* [minister] will probably take place before the meeting of the States general *tho' a change is to be wished, for his operations do not answer the expectations formed of him.*[18] *These had been calculated on his brilliancy in society. He is very feebly aided too. Montmorin is weak tho a most worthy character. He is indolent and*

---

17. The italicized words in this sentence and those in the rest of the letter were written in code.
18. TJ referred to Étienne-Charles de Loménie de Brienne, archbishop of Toulouse and chief of the Royal Council on Finance; see Bosher, pp. 26–46, 198–200.

*inattentive too in the extreme. Luzerne is considerably inferior in abilities to his brother whom you know. He is a good man too, but so much out of his element that he has the air of one huskanoyed.* [19] *The garde des sceaux* [20] *is considered as the principal's bull dog, braving danger like that animal. His talents do not pass mediocrity. The archbishop's brother and the new minister Vildeuil and Lambert have no will of their own.* [21] *They cannot raise money for the peace establishment the next year without the states general much less if there be war, and their administration will probably end with the states general. Littlepage* who was here as a *secret agent for the King of Poland* rather *overreached himself.* He wanted more money. *The King* furnished it more than once. Still he wanted more, and thought to obtain a high bid by saying he was called for *in America* and asking leave to go there. Contrary to his expectation he received leave: but he went to *Warsaw* instead of *America* and from thence to join the *Russian army.* I do not know these facts certainly, but collect them by putting several things together. *The King* then sent an *antient secretary* here, in whom he had much confidence, to look out for a *correspondent, a mere letter writer* for him. A happy hazard threw *Mazzei* in his way. He recommended him, and he is appointed. He has no *diplomatic character* whatever, but is to receive *Eight thousand livres a year as an intelligencer.* I hope this *employment* may have some permanence. The danger is that he will over-act his part.

The *Marquis de la Luzerne* had been for many years *married* to his *brother's wife's sister secretly. She* was ugly, and deformed, but sensible, amiable, and rather rich. When he was *named ambassador to London* with 10000 *guineas a year,* the *marriage* was avowed, and he relinquished his *cross of Malta* from which he derived a handsome revenue, for life, and very open to advancement. *She* staid here, and not long after *died.* His real *affection for her* which was great and *unfeigned* and perhaps the loss of his *order* for so short-lived a satisfaction has thrown him almost *into a state of despondency.* He is *now here.*

I send you a book of Dupont's on the subject of the commercial treaty with England. Tho' it's general matter may not be interesting, yet you will pick up in various parts of it such excellent principles and observations as will richly repay the trouble of reading it. [22] I send you also two little pamphlets of the Marquis de Condorcet, wherein is the most judicious statement I have seen of the great questions which agitate this nation at present. [23] The new regulations

---

19. *Huskanoyed* or *huskanaw* refers to the Indian initiation into manhood, which involved solitary confinement and the use of narcotics; see *PTJ,* XIII, p. 444, and *PJM,* XI, p. 214.

20. Keeper of the seals.

21. The three men were the minister of war, the minister of the royal household, and the comptroller general of finances, respectively.

22. For an excellent summary of du Pont's role in the completion of the commercial treaty between France and England in 1786, see Ambrose Saricks, *Pierre Samuel du Pont de Nemours* (Lawrence, Kans., 1965), pp. 91–98.

23. For a brief discussion of Condorcet's views on the applicability of American natural-rights maxims to France, see Palmer, *The Age of the Democratic Revolution,* I, pp. 278–79.

## The Constitution and a Bill of Rights, 1788–1789

present a preponderance of good over their evil. But they suppose that the king can model the constitution at will, or in other words that this government is a pure despotism: the question then arising is whether a pure despotism, in a single head, or one which is divided among a king, nobles, priesthood, and numerous magistracy is the least bad. I should be puzzled to decide: but I hope they will have neither, and that they are advancing to a limited, moderate government, in which the people will have a good share.

I sincerely rejoice at the acceptance of our new constitution by nine states. It is a good canvas, on which some strokes only want retouching. What these are, I think are sufficiently manifested by the general voice from North to South, which calls for a bill of rights. It seems pretty generally understood that this should go to Juries, Habeas corpus, Standing armies, Printing, Religion and Monopolies. I conceive there may be difficulty in finding general modification of these suited to the habits of all the states. But if such cannot be found then it is better to establish trials by jury, the right of Habeas corpus, freedom of the press and freedom of religion in all cases, and to abolish standing armies in time of peace, and Monopolies, in all cases, than not to do it in any. The few cases wherein these things may do evil, cannot be weighed against the multitude wherein the want of them will do evil. In disputes between a foreigner and a native, a trial by jury may be improper. But if this exception cannot be agreed to, the remedy will be to model the jury by giving the medietas linguae in civil as well as criminal cases. Why suspend the Hab. corp. in insurrections and rebellions? The parties who may be arrested may be charged instantly with a well defined crime. Of course the judge will remand them. If the publick safety requires that the government should have a man imprisoned on less probable testimony in those than in other emergencies; let him be taken and tried, retaken and retried, while the necessity continues, only giving him redress against the government for damages. Examine the history of England: see how few of the cases of the suspension of the Habeas corpus law have been worthy of that suspension. They have been either real treasons wherein the parties might as well have been charged at once, or sham-plots where it was shameful they should ever have been suspected. Yet for the few cases wherein the suspension of the hab. corp. has done real good, that operation is now become habitual, and the minds of the nation almost prepared to live under it's constant suspension. A declaration that the federal government will never restrain the presses from printing any thing they please, will not take away the liability of the printers for false facts printed. The declaration that religious faith shall be unpunished, does not give impunity to criminal acts dictated by religious error. The saying there shall be no monopolies lessens the incitements to ingenuity, which is spurred on by the hope of a monopoly for a limited time, as of 14. years; but the benefit even of limited monopolies is too doubtful to be opposed to that of their general suppression. If no check can be found to keep the number of standing troops within safe bounds, while they are tolerated as far as necessary, abandon them altogether, discipline well the militia, and guard the magazines with them. More than magazine-guards will be useless if few, and dangerous if many. No European nation can ever send against us such a regular army as we need fear, and it is hard if our militia are not equal to those of Canada or Florida. My idea then is, that tho' proper exceptions to these general rules are desireable and probably practicable, yet if the exceptions cannot be agreed on, the establishment of the rules in all cases will do ill in very few. I hope therefore a bill of rights will be formed to guard the people against the federal government, as they are already guarded against their state governments in most instances.

The abandoning the principle of necessary rotation in the Senate, has I see been disapproved by many; in the case of the President, by none. I readily therefore suppose my opinion wrong, when opposed by the majority as in the former instance, and the totality as in the latter. In this however I should have done it with more complete satisfaction, had we all judged from the same position.

Sollicitations, which cannot be directly refused, oblige me to trouble you often with letters recommending and introducing to you persons who go from hence to America. I will beg the favour of you to distinguish the letters wherein I appeal to recommendations from other persons, from those which I write on my own knowlege. In the former it is never my intention to compromit myself, nor you. In both instances I must beg you to ascribe the trouble I give you to circumstances which do not leave me at liberty to decline it. I am with very sincere esteem Dear Sir Your affectionate friend and servt.,

TH: JEFFERSON


*Jefferson to Madison*

Paris Aug. 4, 1788

DEAR SIR

The bearer hereof, Mr. Dobbyns, a native of Ireland, having it in contemplation to dispose of his estate in that country, and to remove with his tenants to America, I have advised him, before he carries the measure into entire execution, to go thither himself, to fix on the part of the country which from climate, soil, and other circumstances would best suit his views, and even to provide a place for the reception of his people on their arrival. His views have at different times, and under different considerations, been attracted by the Chesapeak, the Patowmack, the Ohio, and the Mohocks river. As there is always a possibility that a stranger may fall into the hands of land-jobbers and other sharpers, I take the liberty of asking for him your friendly counsel, and your recommendations of him to good men in whatever quarter he may chuse to visit for the purpose of purchasing, as well as your notice and civilities on every occasion. He comes well recommended to me from a friend in London, and the short acquaintance I have had the honour of having with him here has justified that recommendation.[24] I am with sentiments of the most perfect esteem Dear Sir your affectionate friend and servant,

TH: JEFFERSON

## *Madison to Jefferson*

New York Aug. 10, 1788

DEAR SIR

Mr. Warville has just arrived here, and I sieze an opportunity suddenly brought to my knowledge to thank you for your several favors, and particularly for the pedometer. Answers to the letters must be put off for the next opportunity.

My last went off just as a vote was taken in the Convention of this State which foretold the ratification of the new Government. The later act soon followed and is enclosed. The form of it is remarkable. I enclose also a circular address to the other States on the subject of amendments, from which mischiefs are apprehended.[25] The great danger in the present crisis is that if another Convention should be soon assembled, it would terminate in discord, or in alterations of the federal system which would throw back *essential*[26] powers into the State Legislatures. The delay of a few years will assuage the jealousies which have been artificially created by designing men and will at the same time point out the faults which really call for amendment. At present the public mind is neither sufficiently cool nor sufficiently informed for so delicate an operation.

The Convention of North Carolina met on the 21st Ult: Not a word has yet been heard from its deliberations. Rhode Island has not resumed the subject since it was referred to and rejected by the people in their several Towns.

Congress have been employed for several weeks on the arrangements of times and place for bringing the new Government into agency. The first have been agreed on though not definitively, and make it pretty certain that the first meeting will be held in the third week in March. The place has been a subject of much discussion: and continues to be uncertain. Philada. as least excentric of any place capable of affording due accomodations and a respectable outset to the Government was the first proposed. The affirmative votes were N. Hampshire, Connecticut, Pena. Maryd. Virga. and N. Carolina. Delaware was present and in favor of that place, but one of its delegates wishing to have a

---

24. Mr. Dobbyns (Dobyn) decided to move to the United States; see *PTJ*, XIII, p. 285, XIV, p. 360.
25. For the enclosure, see Governor George Clinton's Circular Letter, July 28, 1788, below.
26. JM's italics.

question on Wilmington previous to a final determination, divided that State and negatived the motion. N. York came next in view, to which was opposed first Lancaster which failed and then Baltimore which to the surprise of every body was carried by seven States, S. Carolina which had preferred N. York to the two other more Southern positions, unexpectedly concurring in this. The vote however was soon rescinded, the State of S. Carolina receding from, the Eastern States remonstrating against, and few seriously arguing the eligibility of Baltimore. At present the question lies as it was originally supposed to do between N. York and Philada. and nothing can be more uncertain than the event of it. Rhode Island which alone was disposed to give the casting vote to N. York has refused to give any final vote for arranging and carrying into effect a system to which that State is opposed, and both the Delegates have returned home.

Col. Carrington tells me he has sent you the first volume of the federalist, and adds the 2d. by this conveyance. I believe I never have yet *mentioned to you that publication.*[27] It *was undertaken last fall by Jay, Hamilton and myself.* The *proposal came from the two former.* The *execution was thrown by the sickness of Jay mostly on the two others.* Though *carried on in concert the writers are not mutually answerable* for *all the ideas of each other,* there being *seldom time for even a perusal* of the *pieces by any but the writer before they were wanted at the press* and *some times hardly by the writer himself.*

I have not a moment for a line to Mazzei. Tell him I have received his books and shall attempt to get them disposed of. I fear his calculations will not be fulfilled by the demand for them here in the French language. His affair with Dorhman stands as it did. Of his affair with Foster Webb I can say nothing. I suspect it will turn out badly. Yrs. affecy.,

Js. MADISON JR.

ENCLOSURE

*The Circular Letter, from the Ratification Convention of the State of New York to the governors of the several states in the Union*[28]

SIR: Poughkeepsie July 28, 1788

We, the members of the Convention of this state, have deliberately and maturely considered the Constitution proposed for the United States. Several articles in it appear so exceptionable to a majority of us, that nothing but the fullest confidence of obtaining a revision of them by a general convention, and an invincible reluctance to separating from our sister states, could have prevailed upon a sufficient number to ratify it, without stipulating for previous amendments. We all unite in opinion, that such a revision will be necessary to recommend it to the approbation and support of a numerous body of our constituents.

We observe that amendments have been proposed, and are anxiously desired, by

---

27. The italicized words in this sentence and those in the rest of the letter were written in code.

28. The Circular Letter is taken from Jonathan Elliot, *Debates in the Several State Conventions on the Adoption of the Federal Constitution* . . . , 5 vols. (Philadelphia, 1859), II, pp. 413-14.

several of the states, as well as by this; and we think it of great importance that effectual measures be immediately taken for calling a convention, to meet at a period not far remote; for we are convinced that the apprehensions and discontents, which those articles occasion, cannot be removed or allayed, unless an act to provide for it be among the first that shall be passed by the new Congress.

As it is essential that an application for the purpose should be made to them by two thirds of the states, we earnestly exhort and request the legislature of your state to take the earliest opportunity of making it. We are persuaded that a similar one will be made by our legislature, at their next session; and we ardently wish and desire that the other states may concur in adopting and promoting the measure.

It cannot be necessary to observe, that no government, however constructed, can operate well, unless it possesses the confidence and good-will of the body of the people; and as we desire nothing more than that the amendments proposed by this or other states be submitted to the consideration and decision of a general convention, we flatter ourselves that motives of mutual affection and conciliation will conspire with the obvious dictates of sound policy to induce even such of the states as may be content with every article in the Constitution to gratify the reasonable desires of that numerous class of American citizens who are anxious to obtain amendments of some of them.

Our amendments will manifest that none of them originated in local views, as they are such as, if acceded to, must equally affect every state in the Union. Our attachment to our sister states, and the confidence we repose in them, cannot be more forcibly demonstrated than by acceding to a government which many of us think very imperfect, and devolving the power of determining whether that government shall be rendered perpetual in its present form, or altered agreeably to our wishes, and a minority of the states with whom we unite.

We request the favor of your excellency to lay this letter before the legislature of your state; and we are persuaded that your regard for our national harmony and good government will induce you to promote a measure which we are unanimous in thinking very conducive to those interesting objects.

We have the honor to be, with the highest respect, your excellency's most obedient servants.

By the unanimous order of the Convention,

George Clinton, *President*

## *Madison to Jefferson*

New York Aug. 23, 1788

Dear Sir

My last went vià England in the hands of a Swiss gentleman who had married an American lady, and was returning with her to his own country. He proposed to take Paris in his way. By that opportunity I inclosed copies of the proceedings of this State on the subject of the Constitution. North Carolina was then in Convention, and it was generally expected would in some form or other have fallen into the general stream. The event has disappointed us. It appears that a large majority has decided against the Constitution as it stands, and according to the information here received has made the alterations proposed by Virginia the conditions on which alone that State will unite with the others. Whether this be the precise State of the case I cannot say. It seems at least certain that she has either rejected the Constitution, or annexed conditions precedent to her ratification.[29] It cannot be doubted that this bold step is to be ascribed in part to the influence of the minority in Virginia which lies mostly in the Southern part of the State, and to the management of its leader.[30] It is in part ascribed also by some to assurances transmitted from leading individuals here, that New York would set the example of rejection. The event, whatever may have been its cause, with the tendency of the circular letter from the Convention of N. York, has somewhat changed the aspect of things and has given fresh hopes and exertions to those who opposed the Constitution. The object with them now will be to effect an early Convention composed of men who will essentially mutilate the system, particularly in the article of taxation, without which in my opinion the system cannot answer the purposes for which it was intended. An early Convention is in every view to be dreaded in the present temper of America. A very short period of delay would produce the double advantage of diminishing the heat and increasing the light of all parties. A trial for one year will probably suggest more real amendments than all the antecedent speculations of our most sagacious politicians.

Congress have not yet decided on the arrangements for inaugurating the new Government. The place of its first meeting continues to divide the Northern and Southern members, though with a few exceptions to this general description of the parties. The departure of Rho. Island, and the refusal of N. Carolina in consequence of the late event there to vote in the question, threatens a disagreeable issue to the business, there being now an apparent impossibility of obtaining seven States for any one place. The three Eastern States and N. York, reinforced by S. Carolina, and as yet by N. Jersey, give a plurality of votes in favor of this City. The advocates for a more central position however though less numerous, seemed very determined not to yeild to what they call a shameful partiality to one extremity of the Continent. It will be certainly of far more importance under the proposed than the present system that regard should be had to centrality whether we consider the number of members belonging to the government, the diffusive manner in which they will be appointed, or the increased resort of individuals having business with the Legislative, Executive and Judiciary departments. If the Western Country be taken into view, as it certainly ought, the reasoning is still further corroborated. There is good ground to believe that a very *jealous eye will be* kept in that *quarter on in*attention *to it and particularly when* involving a *seeming advantage to the eastern states* which have been *rendered extremely suspicious* and *obnox-*

---

29. For North Carolina's rejection of the Constitution, see Louise I. Trenholme, *The Ratification of the Federal Constitution in North Carolina* (New York, 1932).

30. JM meant Patrick Henry.

*ious by the Missisipi project.*³¹ There is *even good ground to believe that Spain is taking* advantage of *this disgust in Kentuckey* and is *actually endeavoring* to *seduce them from the union holding out a darling object which will never be obtained by them as part of the union.* This is a *fact as certain as it is important but which I hint in strict confidence* and with *a request* that no suspicion may be excited of its being known particularly thro the channel of me.³²

I have this moment notice that I must send off my letter instantly, or lose the conveyance. I must consequently defer further communications till another opportunity. In the meantime I am Yrs. affely.,

Js. MADISON JR.

Along with this you will receive a copy of the report you desired from Mr. Thomson, and a copy of the Federalist, a publication mentioned in my last.

*Madison to Jefferson*

New York Sept. 21, 1788

DEAR SIR

Being informed of a circuitous opportunity to France I make use of it to forward the inclosures. By one of them you will find that Congress have been at length brought into the true policy which is demanded by the situation of the Western Country. An additional resolution on the *secret journal* puts an *end to all negotiation with Spain,* referring the subject of a *treaty after this* assertion *of right to the Missisipi to the new government.*³³ The communication in my last will have shewn you the *crisis of things* in that *quarter; a crisis* however not particularly *known to Congress* and will be a *key to* some of the *Kentucky toasts in the Virga. gazette.*³⁴

The Circular letter from the New York Convention has rekindled an ardor among the opponents of the federal Constitution for an *immediate* revi-

---

31. The italicized words in this sentence and those in the rest of the letter were written in code.

32. Patricia Watlington, *The Partisan Spirit: Kentucky Politics* (New York, 1972), pp. 160–65. The Spanish minister Gardoqui talked with John Brown, JM's colleague in the Virginia delegation from the District of Kentucky, about negotiating a commercial treaty if Kentucky became an independent state.

33. The italicized words in this sentence and those in the rest of the letter were written in code. JM used code for the secret resolution, which reads: "*Resolved* That no further progress be made in the negotiations with Spain by the Secretary for foreign affairs, but that the subject to which they relate be referred to the federal government which is to assemble in March next"; see *PTJ*, XIII, p. 626. The enclosures dealt with the two public resolutions concerning the western country, the first denying that Jay had authority to treat with Spain for the surrender of Congress's claim to the navigation of the Mississippi and the second specifically stating that "the free navigation of the river . . . is a clear and essential right of the United States," see *ibid*.

34. For the toasts, see the enclosure from the *Virginia Independent Chronicle* (Sept. 3, 1788), below.

sion of it by another General Convention. You will find in one of the papers inclosed the result of the consultations in Pensylvania on that subject. Mr. Henry and his friends in Virginia enter with great zeal into the scheme. Governour Randolph also espouses it; but with a wish to prevent if possible danger to the article which extends the power of the Government to internal as well as external taxation. It is observable that the views of the Pennsylva. meeting do not rhyme very well with those of the Southern advocates for a Convention; the objects most eagerly pursued by the latter being unnoticed in the Harrisburg proceedings. The effect of the Circular letter on other States is less known. I conclude that it will be the same every where among those who opposed the Constitution, or contended for a conditional ratification of it. Whether an early Convention will be the result of this united effort is more than can at this moment be foretold. The measure will certainly be industriously opposed in some parts of the Union, not only by those who wish for no alterations, but by others who would prefer the other mode provided in the Constitution, as most expedient at present for introducing those supplemental safeguards to liberty against which no objections can be raised; and who would moreover approve of a Convention for amending the frame of the Government itself, as soon as time shall have somewhat corrected the feverish state of the public mind and trial have pointed its attention to the true defects of the system.

You will find also by one of the papers enclosed that the arrangements have been compleated for bringing the new Government into action. The dispute concerning the place of its meeting was the principal cause of delay, the Eastern States with N. Jersey and S. Carolina being attached to N. York, and the others strenuous for a more central position. Philadelphia, Wilmington, Lancaster and Baltimore were successively tendered without effect by the latter, before they finally yielded to the superiority of members in favor of this City. I am afraid the decision will give a great handle to the Southern Antifederalists who have inculcated a jealousy of this end of the Continent. It is to be regretted also as entailing this pernicious question on the new Congress who will have enough to do in adjusting the other delicate matters submitted to them. Another consideration of great weight with me is that the temporary residence here will probably end in a permanent one at Trenton, or at the farthest on the Susquehannah. A removal in the first instance beyond the Delaware would have removed the alternative to the Susquehannah and the Potowmac. The best chance of the latter depends on a delay of the permanent establishment for a few years, untill the Western and South Western population comes more into view. This delay can not take place if so excentric a place as N. York is to be the intermediate seat of business.

To the other papers is added a little pamphlet on the Mohegan language.[35] The observations deserve the more attention as they are made by a

---

35. Jonathan Edwards, *Observations on the Language of the Muhhekaneew Indians . . . and some instances of analogy between that and the Hebrew are pointed out* . . . (New Haven, 1788). On TJ's

man of known learning and character, and may aid reserches into the primitive structure of language as well as those on foot for comparing the American tribes with those on the Eastern Frontier of the other Continent.

In consequence of your letter to Mr. Jay on the subject of "outfit" etc. I had a conference with him, and he agreed to suggest the matter to Congress. This was done and his letter referred back to be reported on. The idea between us was that the reference should be *to a committee but his letter* coming *in at a moment* when *I happened to be out* it was as in *course referred to his department.* His *answer suggested* that as *he might be thought eventually concerned* in *the question* it was most *proper for the consideration of a committee.* I had *discovered that he was not struck* with the *peculiarities of your case even when insinuated to him.* How far the *committee will be so* is more *than I can yet say.* In general I have no doubt that both *it and Congress are well disposed.* But it is probable that the idea of a *precedent will beget much caution* and what *is worse there is little probability of* again having a *quorum of states for the business.*

I learn from Virginia that our Crops both of Corn and Tobacco, (except in the lower Country where a storm has been hurtful) are likely to be very good. The latter has suffered in some degree from superfluous rains, but the former has been proportionally benefitted. Accept my most fervent wishes for your happiness. Yrs affecty.,

Js. MADISON JR.

ENCLOSURE
*Fourth of July Toasts and Sentiments for the Day,
Fayette County, Kentucky*[36]

1st. The United States of America. 2d. The Western World,—perpetual union, on principles of equality, or amicable separation. 3d. The Illustrious GEORGE WASHINGTON, Esq.—may his services be remembered. 4th. The Navigation of the Mississippi, at any price but that of liberty. 5th. Harmony with Spain and a reciprocity of good offices. 6th. Our brethren at the Muskingum, and prosperity to their establishments. 7th. May the savage enemies of America be chastised by arms, and the *jobbing* system of treaties be exploded. 8th. The Convention of Virginia; may wisdom, firmness, and a sacred regard to the fundamental principles of the revolution guide her councils. 9th. Energetic government, on foederal principles. 10th. Trial by jury, liberty of the press, and no standing army. 11th. May the Atlantic be just, the Western States be free, and both be happy. 12th. The memory of departed heroes and patriots. 13th. No paper money; no tender laws, and no legislative interference in private contracts. 14th. The Commonwealth of Kentucke, the Fourteenth luminary in the American constellation, may she reflect upon the original States the wisdom she has borrowed from them.

---

linguistic research, see Clark Wissler, "The American Indian and the American Philosophical Society," *Proceedings* (American Philosophical Society) 86 (1942): 189–204.

36. This enclosure is printed from Edmund C. Burnett, ed., *Letters of Members of the Continental Congress,* 8 vols. (Washington, 1921–38), VIII, p. 934.

## Madison to Jefferson

New York Oct. 8, 1788

DEAR SIR

Herewith inclosed are a letter for yourself forwarded to my hands from General Washington, and two others for the Marquis, one from the same quarter, the other from myself. I put both the last under cover to you, not knowing what regard may be due to newspaper authority, that the Marquis is under the open displeasure of the Court, and may therefore be the less likely to receive letters thro' any other channel. Sometimes the report runs that he is in the Bastile; at another that he is at the head of a revolt in some one of the Provinces.

My last letters have followed each other so quickly and the last of all is of such recent date that this opportunity by a gentleman going to France, enables me to add little to what has been already communicated. The result of the meeting at Harrisburg was the latest event worthy of notice at the date of my last. Nothing has since taken place in relation to the new Government, but the appointment of Mr. Robt. Morris, and a Mr. McClay, to represent Pennsylvania in the Senate. A law has also passed in that State providing for the election of members for the House of Representatives and electors of the President. The act proposes that every Citizen throughout the State shall vote for the whole number of members allotted to the State. This mode of election will confine the choice to characters of general notoriety, and so far be favorable to merit. It is however liable to some popular objections urged against the tendency of the new system. In Virginia, I am inclined to think the State will be divided into as many districts, as there are to be members. In other States, as in Connecticut the Pena. example will probably be followed. And in others again a middle course be taken. It is perhaps to be desired that various modes should be tried, as by that means only the best mode can be ascertained. There is no doubt that Genl. Washington will be called to the Presidency. For the vice Presidency, are talked of principally Mr. Hancock and Mr. Adams. Mr. Jay or Genl. Knox would I believe be preferred to either, but both of them will probably chuse to remain where they are. It is impossible to say which of the former would be preferred, or what other Candidates may be brought forward.

I have a letter from Mr. George Lee Turberville of Virginia requesting me to mention to you a report proceeding from Greenwich that a Docr. Spence and his lady, (the former a Virginian of respectable family in the lower End of the Northern Neck, and whose mother is still living, in a second marriage with a Docr. Thomson of Westmoreland County) were captured on their way to Virginia and carried into Algiers. This event is said to have happened seven or eight years ago, though discovered but lately, it having been taken for granted that the vessel and all on board had perished at sea. I am much inclined to believe that this supposition is the true one, and that the Greenwich story has no foundation. I communicate it nevertheless as requested by Mr. Turberville, that you may have an opportunity of collecting for the friends of Docr. Spence any information which may be interesting to them, and of taking any steps that such information may suggest in behalf of the distressed.

I have already acquainted you with the result of my enquiries in the case of Mrs. Burke. The effects in the hands of Wm. S. Brown had been delivered over to a Mr. Kemble a respectable merchant here, who is administrator to the deceased Burke and who tells me that the whole Estate of the latter does not pay his debts.

I shall send along with this a few seed of the sugar maple, the first and the whole that I have been able to obtain. I wish you all happiness and remain Dr. Sir Yrs. most affecly.,

Js. MADISON JR.

## [Madison's Observations on Jefferson's Draft of a Constitution for Virginia]

[New York ca. Oct. 15, 1788][37]

### Senate.

The term of two years is too short. Six years are not more than sufficient. A Senate is to withstand the occasional impetuosities of the more numerous branch. The members ought therefore to derive a firmness from the tenure of their places. It ought to supply the defect of knowledge and experience incident to the other branch. There ought to be time given therefore for attaining the qualifications necessary for that purpose. It ought finally to maintain that system and steadiness in public affairs without which no Government can prosper or be respectable. This cannot be done by a body undergoing a frequent change of its members. A Senate for six years will not be dangerous to liberty. On the contrary it will be one of its best guardians. By correcting the infirmities of popular Government, it will prevent that disgust against that form which may otherwise produce a sudden transition to some very different

37. In 1783, TJ had sent JM a copy of his draft of a constitution for Virginia to replace the constitution of 1776; see [Jefferson's Draft of a Constitution for Virginia, Monticello, May–June 1783], above. TJ later published his draft in his *Notes on the State of Virginia*, and JM based his "observations" on this draft; see *PTJ*, VI, p. 316, and *PJM*, XI, p. 281. For an analysis of "the sharp differences" between JM and TJ on this subject, see Merrill D. Peterson, *Jefferson and Madison and the Making of Constitutions* (Charlottesville, 1987), pp. 4–6. JM sent his "observations" to John Brown, who had requested "some remarks upon Jeffersons plan of Govt. denoting such alterations as would render it more applicable to the District of Kentucky"; see John Brown to JM, May 12, 1788, and Aug. 26, 1788, in *PJM*, XI, pp. 42–43 and 242–43, and JM to John Brown, Oct. 12, 1788, *ibid.*, p. 280. Although Brown planned to use JM's views in 1788, statehood for Kentucky was delayed until 1792. All italicized words in this letter are JM's.

one. It is no secret to any attentive and dispassionate observer of the political situation of the U.S. that the real danger to republican liberty has lurked in that cause.

The appointment of Senators by districts seems to be objectionable. A spirit of *locality* is inseparable from that mode. The evil is fully displayed in the County representations, the members of which are everywhere observed to lose sight of the aggregate interests of the Community, and even to sacrifice them to the interests or prejudices of their respective constituents. In general these local interests are miscalculated. But it is not impossible for a measure to be accomodated to the particular interests of every county or district, when considered by itself, and not so, when considered in relation to each other and to the whole State; in the same manner as the interests of individuals may be very different in a State of nature and in a Political Union. The most effectual remedy for the local biass is to impress on the minds of the Senators an attention to the interest of the whole Society by making them the choice of the whole Society, each citizen voting for every Senator. The objection here is that the fittest characters would not be sufficiently known to the people at large. But in free Governments, merit and notoriety of character are rarely separated, and such a regulation would connect them more and more together. Should this mode of election be on the whole not approved, that established in Maryland presents a valuable alternative. The latter affords perhaps a greater security for the selection of merit. The inconveniences chargeable on it are two: first that the Council of electors favors cabal. Against this the shortness of its existence is a good antidote. Secondly that in a large State the meeting of the Electors must be expensive if they be paid or badly attended if the service be onerous. To this it may be answered that in a case of such vast importance, the expence which could not be great ought to be disregarded. Whichever of these modes may be preferred, it cannot be amiss so far to admit the plan of districts as to restrain the choice to persons residing in different parts of the State. Such a regulation will produce a diffusive confidence in the Body, which is not less necessary than the other means of rendering it useful. In a State having large towns which can easily unite their votes the precaution would be essential to an immediate choice by the people at large. In Maryland no regard is paid to residence. And what is remarkable vacancies are filled by the Senate itself. This last is an obnoxious expedient and cannot in any point of view have much effect. It was probably meant to obviate the trouble of occasional meetings of the Electors. But the purpose might have been otherwise answered by allowing the unsuccessful candidates to supply vacancies according to the order of their standing on the list of votes, or by requiring provisional appointments to be made along with the positive ones. If an election by districts be unavoidable and the ideas here suggested be sound, the evil will be diminished in proportion to the extent given to the districts, taking two or more Senators from each district.

Electors.

The first question arising here is how far property ought to be made a qualification. There is a middle way to be taken which corresponds at once with the Theory of free Government and the lessons of experience. A freehold or equivalent of a certain value may be annexed to the right of voting for Senators, and the right left more at large in the election of the other House. Examples of this distinction may be found in the Constitutions of several States, particularly if I mistake not, of North Carolina and N. York. This middle mode reconciles and secures the two cardinal objects of Government, the rights of persons, and the rights of property. The former will be sufficiently guarded by one branch, the latter more particularly by the other. Give all power to property, and the indigent will be oppressed. Give it to the latter and the effect may be transposed. Give a defensive share to each and each will be secure. The necessity of thus guarding the rights of property was for obvious reasons unattended to in the commencement of the Revolution. In all the Governments which were considered as beacons to republican patriots and lawgivers, the rights of persons were subjected to those of property. The poor were sacrificed to the rich. In the existing state of American population and American property, the two classes of rights were so little discriminated that a provision for the rights of persons was supposed to include of itself those of property, and it was natural to infer from the tendency of republican laws that these different interests would be more and more identified. Experience and investigation have however produced more correct ideas on this subject. It is now observed that in all populous countries, the smaller part only can be interested in preserving the rights of property. It must be foreseen that America and Kentucky itself will by degrees arrive at this State of Society; that in some parts of the Union a very great advance is already made towards it. It is well understood that interest leads to injustice as well when the opportunity is presented to bodies of men as to individuals; to an interested majority in a republic, as to the interested minority in any other form of Government. The time to guard against this danger is at the first forming of the Constitution and in the present State of population when the bulk of the people have a sufficient interest in possession or in prospect to be attached to the rights of property, without being insufficiently attached to the rights of persons.

Liberty not less than justice pleads for the policy here recommended. If *all* power be suffered to slide into hands not interested in the rights of property which must be the case whenever a majority fall under that description, one of two things cannot fail to happen; either they will unite against the other description and become the dupes and instruments of ambition, or their poverty and dependence will render them the mercenary instruments of wealth. In either case liberty will be subverted; in the first by a despotism growing out of anarchy, in the second, by an oligarchy founded on corruption.

The Second question under this head is whether the ballot be not a better mode than that of voting viva voce. The comparative experience of the States pursuing the different modes is in favor of the first. It is found less difficult to guard against fraud in that than against bribery in the other.

### Exclusions.

Does not the exclusion of Ministers of the Gospel as such violate a fundamental principle of liberty by punishing a religious profession with the privation of a civil right? Does it not violate another article of the plan itself which exempts religion from the cognizance of Civil power? Does it not violate justice by at once taking away a right and prohibiting a compensation for it? And does it not in fine violate impartiality by shutting the door against the Ministers of one religion and leaving it open for those of every other?

The re-elegibility of members after accepting offices of profit is so much opposed to the present way of thinking in America that any discussion of the subject would probably be a waste of time.

### Limits of power.

It is at least questionable whether death ought to be confined to "Treason and murder." It would not therefore be prudent to tie the hands of Government in the manner here proposed. The prohibition of pardon, however specious in theory would have practical consequences which render it inadmissible. A single instance is a sufficient proof. The crime of treason is generally shared by a number and often a very great number. It would be politically if not morally wrong to take away the lives of all, even if every individual were equally guilty. What name would be given to a severity which made no distinction between the legal and the moral offence, between the deluded multitude, and their wicked leaders. A second trial would not avoid the difficulty because the oaths of the jury would not permit them to hearken to any voice but the inexorable voice of the law.

The power of the Legislature to appoint any other than their own officers departs too far from the Theory which requires a separation of the great Departments of Government. One of the best securities against the creation of unnecessary offices or tyrannical powers is an exclusion of the authors from all share in filling the one, or influence in the execution of the other. The proper mode of appointing to offices will fall under another head.

### Executive Governour.

An election by the Legislature is liable to insuperable objections. It not only tends to faction intrigue and corruption, but leaves the Executive under the influence of an improper obligation to that department. An election by the people at large, as in this and several other States, or by Electors as in the appointment of the Senate in Maryland or indeed by the people through any other channel than their legislative representatives, seems to be far preferable.

The ineligibility a second time, though not perhaps without advantages, is also liable to a variety of strong objections. It takes away one powerful motive to a faithful and useful administration, the desire of acquiring that title to a re-appointment. By rendering a periodical change of men necessary, it discourages beneficial undertakings which require perseverence and system, or, as frequently happened in the Roman Consulate, either precipitates or prevents the execution of them. It may inspire desperate enterprises for the attainment of what is not attainable by legitimate means. It fetters the judgment and inclination of the Community; and in critical moments would either produce a violation of the Constitution, or exclude a choice which might be essential to the public Safety. Add to the whole, that by putting the Executive Magistrate in the situation of the tenant of an unrenewable lease, it would tempt him to neglect the constitutional rights of his department, and to connive at usurpations by the Legislative department, with which he may connect his future ambition or interest.

The clause restraining the first magistrate from the immediate command of the military forces would be made better by excepting cases in which he should receive the sanction of the two branches of the Legislature.

### Council of State.

The following variations are suggested: 1. The election to be made by the people immediately, or thro' some other medium than the Legislature. 2. A distributive choice should perhaps be secured as in the case of the Senate. 3. Instead of an ineligibility a second time, a rotation as in the federal Senate, with an abridgement of the term to be substituted.

The appointment to offices is, of all the functions of Republican and perhaps every other form of Government, the most difficult to guard against abuse. Give it to a numerous body, and you at once destroy all responsibility, and create a perpetual source of faction and corruption. Give it to the Executive wholly, and it may be made an engine of improper influence and favoritism. Suppose the power were divided thus: let the Executive alone make all the subordinate appointments; and the Governor and Senate, as in the Federal Constitution, those of the superior order. It seems particularly fit that the Judges, who are to form a distinct department, should owe their offices partly to each of the other departments rather than wholly to either.

### Judiciary.

Much detail ought to [be] avoided in the constitutional regulation of this department that there may be room for changes which may be demanded by the progressive changes in the State of our population. It is at least doubtful whether the number of courts, the number of Judges, or even the boundaries of Jurisdiction ought to be made unalterable but by a revisal of the Constitution. The precaution seems no otherwise necessary than as it may prevent sudden modification of the establishment, or addition of obsequious Judges, for the purpose of evading the checks of the Constitution and giving effect to some sinister policy of the Legislature. But might not the same object be otherwise attained? By prohibiting, for example, any innovations in those particulars without the consent of that department; or without the annual sanction of two or three successive assemblies, over and above the other prerequisites to the passage of a law.

The model here proposed for a Court of appeals is not recommended by experience. It is found as might well be presumed that the members are always warped in their appellate decisions by an attachment to the principles and jurisdiction of their respective Courts and still more so by the previous decision on the case removed by appeal. The only effectual cure for the evil, is to form a Court of Appeals, of distinct and select Judges. The expence ought not be admitted as an objection. 1. Because the proper administration of Justice is of too essential a nature to be sacrificed to that consideration. 2. The number of inferior Judges might in that case be lessened. 3. The whole department may be made to support itself by a judicious tax on law proceedings.

The excuse for non-attendance would be a more proper subject of enquiry some where else than in the Court to which the party belonged. Delicacy, mutual convenience &c. would soon reduce the regulation to mere form; or if not, it might become a disagreeable source of little irritations among the members. A certificate from the local Court or some other local authority where the party might reside or happen to be detained from his duty, expressing the cause of absence as well as that it was judged to be satisfactory, might be safely substituted. Few Judges would improperly claim their wages, if such a formality stood in the way. These observations are applicable to the Council of State.

A Court of Impeachments is among the most puzzling articles of a republican Constitution, and it is far more easy to point out defects in any plan, than to supply a cure for them. The diversified expedients adopted in the Constitutions of the several States prove how much the compilers were embarrassed on this subject. The plan here proposed varies from all of them; and is perhaps not less than any a proof of the difficulties which pressed the ingenuity of its author. The remarks arising on it are 1. That it seems not to square with reason that the right to impeach should be united to that of trying the impeachment, and consequently in a proportional degree, to that of sharing in the appointment of, or influence on the Tribunal to which the trial may belong. 2. As the Executive and Judiciary would form a majority of the Court, and either have a right to impeach, too much might depend on a combination of these departments. This objection would be still stronger, if the members of the Assembly were capable as proposed of holding offices, and were amenable in that capacity to the Court. 3. The House of Delegates and either of those departments could appoint a majority of the Court. Here is another danger of combination, and the more to be apprehended as that branch of the Legislature would also have the right to impeach, a right in their hands of itself sufficiently weighty; and as the power of the Court would extend to the head of the Executive by whose independence the constitutional rights of that department are to be secured against Legislative usurpations. 4. The dangers in the two last cases would be still more formidable; as the power extends not only to deprivation, but to future incapacity of office. In the case of all officers of sufficient importance to be objects of factious persecution, the latter branch of power is in every view of a delicate nature. In that of the Chief Magistrate it seems inadmissible, if he be chosen by the Legislature; and much more so, if immediately by the people themselves. A temporary incapacitation is the most that could be properly authorised.

The 2 great desiderata in a Court of impeachments are 1. impartiality. 2. respectability. The first in order to a right, the second in order to a satisfactory decision. These characteristics are aimed at in the following modification. Let the Senate be denied the right to impeach. Let ⅓ of the members be struck out, by alternate nominations of the prosecutors and party impeached; the remaining ⅔ to be the *Stamen* of the Court. When the House of Delegates impeach let the Judges or a certain proportion of them and the Council of State be associated in the trial. When the Governor or Council impeaches, let the Judges only be associated: When the Judges impeach let the Council only be associated. But if the party impeached by the House of Delegates be a member of the Executive or Judiciary let that of which he is a member not be associated. If the party impeached belong to one and be impeached by the other of these branches, let neither of them be associated, the decision being in this case left with the Senate alone or if that be thought exceptionable, a few members might be added by the House of Delegates. ⅔ of the Court should in all cases be necessary to a conviction and the chief Magistrate *at least* should be exempt from a sentence of perpetual if not of temporary incapacity. It is extremely probable that a critical discussion of this outline may discover objections which do not occur. Some do occur; but appear not to be greater than are incident to any different modification of the Tribunal.

The establishment of trials by Jury and viva voce testimony in *all* cases and in *all* Courts, is to say the least a delicate experiment; and would most probably be either violated, or be found inconvenient.[38]

## Council of Revision.

A revisionary power is meant as a check to precipitate, to unjust, and to unconstitutional laws. These important ends would it is conceded be more effectually secured, without disarming the Legislature of its requisite authority, by requiring bills to be separately communicated to the Executive and Judiciary departments. If either of these object, let ⅔, if both ¾ of each House be necessary to overrule the objection; and if either or both protest

38. JM made a mistake in saying that TJ's draft constitution of 1783 provided for jury trial of the facts in all cases since TJ exempted trials in courts of "Impeachments, of Appeals and Military courts."

against a bill as violating the Constitution, let it moreover be suspended notwithstanding the overruling proportion of the Assembly, until there shall have been a subsequent election of the House of Delegates and a repassage of the bill by ⅔ or ¾ of both Houses, as the case may be. It should not be allowed the Judges or the Executive to pronounce a law thus enacted unconstitutional and invalid.

In the State Constitutions and indeed in the Federal one also, no provision is made for the case of a disagreement in expounding them; and as the Courts are generally the last in making their decisions, it results to them by refusing or not refusing to execute a law, to stamp it with its final character. This makes the Judiciary Department paramount in fact to the Legislature, which was never intended and can never be proper.

The extension of the Habeas Corpus to the cases in which it has been usually suspended, merits consideration at least. If there be emergencies which call for such a suspension, it can have no effect to prohibit it, because the prohibition will assuredly give way to the impulse of the moment; or rather it will have the bad effect of facilitating other violations that may be less necessary. The Exemption of the press from liability in every case for *true facts* is also an innovation and as such ought to be well considered. This essential branch of liberty is perhaps in more danger of being interrupted by local tumults, or the silent awe of a predominant party, than by any direct attacks of Power.


## *Madison to Jefferson*

New York Oct. 17, 1788

DEAR SIR

I have written a number of letters to you since my return here, and shall add this by another casual opportunity just notified to me by Mr. St. John. Your favor of July 31. came to hand the day before yesterday. The pamphlets of the Marquis Condorcet and Mr. Dupont referred to in it have also been received. Your other letters inclosed to the Delegation have been and will be disposed of as you wish; particularly those to Mr. Eppes and Col. Lewis.

Nothing has been done on the subject of the *outfit*,[39] there not having been a Congress of nine States for some time, nor even of seven for the last week. It is pretty certain that there will not again be a quorum of either number within the present year; and by no means certain that there will be one at all under the old Confederation. The Committee finding that nothing could be done have neglected to make a report as yet. I have spoken with a member of it in order to get one made, that the case may fall of course and in a favorable shape within the attention of the new Government. The fear of a precedent will probably lead to an allowance for a limited time of the *salary as*

39. This italicized word and those in the rest of the letter were written in code.

*enjoied originally* by *foreign ministers* in *preference to a separate allowance for outfit.* One of the *members of the treasury board* who ought, if certain facts have *not escaped his memory to witness the reasonableness of your* calculations, *takes occasion I find to impress a contrary idea.* Fortunately *his influence will* not *be a very formidable obstacle to right.*[40]

The States which have adopted the new Constitution are all proceeding to the arrangements for putting it into action in March next. Pennsylva. alone has as yet actually appointed deputies; and that only for the Senate. My last mentioned that these were Mr. R. Morris and a Mr. McClay. How the other elections there and elsewhere will run is matter of uncertainty. The Presidency alone unites the conjectures of the public. The vice president is not at all marked out by the general voice. As the President will be from a Southern State, it falls almost of course for the other part of the Continent to supply the next in rank. South Carolina may however think of Mr. Rutledge unless it should be previously discovered that votes will be wasted on him. The only candidates in the Northern States brought forward with their known consent are *Hancock and Adams* and *between these it seems probable the question will lie.* Both of them *are objectionable and would I think be postponed* by the *general suffrage to several others* if they *would accept the place. Hancock is weak, ambitious, a courtier of popularity given to low intrigue* and *lately reunited by a factious friendship with S. Adams.*

*J. Adams* has made *himself obnoxious to many* particularly in the *Southern states by the political principles avowed in his book.* Others *recolecting his cabal during the war against General Washington,* knowing *his extravagant self importance* and *considering his preference of an unprofitable dignity to* some *place of emolument* better *adapted to private fortune as a proof of his* having *an eye to the presidency conclude* that *he would not be a very cordial second to the General* and that *an impatient ambition* might *even intrigue for a premature advancement.* The *danger would be the greater if* particular *factious characters,* as may be the case, *should get into the public councils. Adams* it appears, is *not unaware of* some *of the obstacles to his wish* and *thro a letter to Smith* has *thrown out popular sentiments as to the proposed president.*

The little pamphlet herewith inclosed will give you a collective view of the alterations which have been proposed for the new Constitution.[41] Various and numerous as they appear they certainly omit many of the true grounds of opposition. The articles relating to Treaties, to paper money, and to contracts, created more enemies than all the errors in the System positive and negative put together. It is true nevertheless that not a few, particularly in Virginia have contended for the proposed alterations from the most honorable and patriotic motives; and that among the advocates for the Constitution there are some

40. JM referred to Arthur Lee.
41. *The Ratifications of the New Federal Constitution, Together with the Amendments, Proposed by the Several States* (Richmond, 1788) omitted the ratifications by states that did not propose amendments (Connecticut, New Jersey, Delaware, Pennsylvania, and Georgia).

who wish for further guards to public liberty and individual rights. As far as these may consist of a constitutional declaration of the most essential rights, it is probable they will be added; though there are many who think such addition unnecessary, and not a few who think it misplaced in such a Constitution. There is scarce any point on which the party in opposition is so much divided as to its importance and its propriety. My own opinion has always been in favor of a bill of rights; provided it be so framed as not to imply powers not meant to be included in the enumeration. At the same time I have never thought the omission a material defect, nor been anxious to supply it even by *subsequent*[42] amendment, for any other reason than that it is anxiously desired by others. I have favored it because I supposed it might be of use, and if properly executed could not be of disservice. I have not viewed it in an important light 1. Because I conceive that in a certain degree, though not in the extent argued by Mr. Wilson, the rights in question are reserved by the manner in which the federal powers are granted. 2. Because there is great reason to fear that a positive declaration of some of the most essential rights could not be obtained in the requisite latitude. I am sure that the rights of conscience in particular, if submitted to public definition would be narrowed much more than they are likely ever to be by an assumed power. One of the objections in New England was that the Constitution by prohibiting religious tests opened a door for Jews Turks and infidels. 3. Because the limited powers of the federal Government and the jealousy of the subordinate Governments, afford a security which has not existed in the case of the State Governments, and exists in no other. 4. Because experience proves the inefficacy of a bill of rights on those occasions when its controul is most needed. Repeated violations of these parchment barriers have been committed by overbearing majorities in every State. In Virginia I have seen the bill of rights violated in every instance where it has been opposed to a popular current. Notwithstanding the explicit provision contained in that instrument for the rights of Conscience it is well known that a religious establishment would have taken place in that State, if the legislative majority had found as they expected, a majority of the people in favor of the measure; and I am persuaded that if a majority of the people were now of one sect, the measure would still take place and on narrower ground than was then proposed, notwithstanding the additional obstacle which the law has since created. Wherever the real power in a Government lies, there is the danger of oppression. In our Governments the real power lies in the majority of the Community, and the invasion of private rights is *chiefly* to be apprehended, not from acts of Government contrary to the sense of its constituents, but from acts in which the Government is the mere instrument of the major number of the constituents. This is a truth of great importance, but not yet sufficiently attended to: and is probably more strongly impressed on my mind by facts, and reflections suggested by them, than on yours which has

42. All italicized words in this letter are JM's.

contemplated abuses of power issuing from a very different quarter. Wherever there is an interest and power to do wrong, wrong will generally be done, and not less readily by a powerful and interested party than by a powerful and interested prince. The difference, so far as it relates to the superiority of republics over monarchies, lies in the less degree of probability that interest may prompt abuses of power in the former than in the latter; and in the security in the former against oppression of more than the smaller part of the Society, whereas in the former [latter] it may be extended in a manner to the whole. The difference so far as it relates to the point in question—the efficacy of a bill of rights in controuling abuses of power—lies in this: that in a monarchy the latent force of the nation is superior to that of the Sovereign, and a solemn charter of popular rights must have a great effect, as a standard for trying the validity of public acts, and a signal for rousing and uniting the superior force of the community; whereas in a popular Government, the political and physical power may be considered as vested in the same hands, that is in a majority of the people, and consequently the tyrannical will of the sovereign is not to be controuled by the dread of an appeal to any other force within the community. What use then it may be asked can a bill of rights serve in popular Governments? I answer the two following which though less essential than in other Governments, sufficiently recommend the precaution. 1. The political truths declared in that solemn manner acquire by degrees the character of fundamental maxims of free Government, and as they become incorporated with the national sentiment, counteract the impulses of interest and passion. 2. Altho' it be generally true as above stated that the danger of oppression lies in the interested majorities of the people rather than in usurped acts of the Government, yet there may be occasions on which the evil may spring from the latter sources; and on such, a bill of rights will be a good ground for an appeal to the sense of the community. Perhaps too there may be a certain degree of danger, that a succession of artful and ambitious rulers, may by gradual and well-timed advances, finally erect an independent Government on the subversion of liberty. Should this danger exist at all, it is prudent to guard against it, especially when the precaution can do no injury. At the same time I must own that I see no tendency in our governments to danger on that side. It has been remarked that there is a tendency in all Governments to an augmentation of power at the expence of liberty. But the remark as usually understood does not appear to me well founded. Power when it has attained a certain degree of energy and independence goes on generally to further degrees. But when below that degree, the direct tendency is to further degrees of relaxation, until the abuses of liberty beget a sudden transition to an undue degree of power. With this explanation the remark may be true; and in the latter sense only is it in my opinion applicable to the Governments in America. It is a melancholy reflection that liberty should be equally exposed to danger whether the Government have too much or too little power; and that the line which divides these extremes should be so inaccurately defined by experience.

Supposing a bill of rights to be proper the articles which ought to compose it, admit of much discussion. I am inclined to think that *absolute* restrictions in cases that are doubtful, or where emergencies may overrule them, ought to be avoided. The restrictions however strongly marked on paper will never be regarded when opposed to the decided sense of the public; and after repeated violations in extraordinary cases, they will lose even their ordinary efficacy. Should a Rebellion or insurrection alarm the people as well as the Government, and a suspension of the Hab. Corp. be dictated by the alarm, no written prohibitions on earth would prevent the measure. Should an army in time of peace be gradually established in our neighbourhood by Britn: or Spain, declarations on paper would have as little effect in preventing a standing force for the public safety. The best security against these evils is to remove the pretext for them. With regard to Monopolies they are justly classed among the greatest nusances in Government. But is it clear that as encouragements to literary works and ingenious discoveries, they are not too valuable to be wholly renounced? Would it not suffice to reserve in all cases a right to the public to abolish the privilege at a price to be specified in the grant of it? Is there not also infinitely less danger of this abuse in our Governments than in most others? Monopolies are sacrifices of the many to the few. Where the power is in the few it is natural for them to sacrifice the many to their own partialities and corruptions. Where the power, as with us, is in the many not in the few, the danger can not be very great that the few will be thus favored. It is much more to be dreaded that the few will be unnecessarily sacrificed to the many.

I inclose a paper containing the late proceedings in Kentucky. I wish the ensuing Convention may take no step injurious to the character of the district, and favorable to the views of those who wish ill to the U. States.[43] One of my late letters communicated some circumstances which will not fail to occur on perusing the objects of the proposed Convention in next month. Perhaps however there may be less connection between the two cases than at first one is ready to conjecture. I am Dr. Sir with the sincerest esteem and affectn. Yours,

Js. MADISON JR

## *Jefferson to Madison*

Paris Nov. 18, 1788

DEAR SIR

My last to you was of the 31st. of July: since which I have received yours of July 24. Aug. 10. and 23. The first part of this long silence in me was occasioned by a knoledge that you were absent from N. York; the latter part,

---

43. The resolves of the Danville convention of July 1788, called for another convention in November to consider the adoption of a state constitution for Kentucky and admission into the Union; see *PJM, XI*, pp. 280, 300.

by a want of opportunity, which has been longer than usual: Mr. Shippen being just arrived here, and to set out tomorrow for London, I avail myself of that channel of conveiance. Mr. Carrington was so kind as to send me the 2d. vol. of the Amer. phil. transactions, the federalist, and some other interesting pamphlets; and I am to thank you for another copy of the federalist and the report of the instructions to the ministers for negotiating peace. The latter unluckily omitted exactly the passage I wanted, which was what related to the navigation of the Missisipi.[44] With respect to the Federalist, the three authors had been named to me. I read it with care, pleasure and improvement, and was satisfied there was nothing in it by one of those hands, and not a great deal by a second. It does the highest honor to the third, as being, in my opinion, the best commentary on the principles of government which ever was written. In some parts it is discoverable that the author means only to say what may be best said in defence of opinions in which he did not concur. But in general it establishes firmly the plan of government. I confess it has rectified me in several points. As to the bill of rights however I still think it should be added, and I am glad to see that three states have at length considered the perpetual re-eligibility of the president as an article which should be amended. I should deprecate with you indeed the meeting of a new convention. I hope they will adopt the mode of amendment by Congress and the Assemblies, in which case I should not fear any dangerous innovation in the plan. But the minorities are too respectable not to be entitled to some sacrifice of opinion in the majority. Especially when a great proportion of them would be contented with a bill of rights.

Here things internally are going on well. The Notables, now in session, have indeed past one vote which augurs ill to the rights of the people. But if they do not obtain now so much as they have a right to, they will in the long run. The misfortune is that they are not yet ripe for receiving the blessings to which they are entitled. I doubt, for instance, whether the body of the nation, if they could be consulted, would accept of a Habeas corpus law, if offered them by the king. If the Etats generaux, when they assemble, do not aim at too much, they may begin a good constitution. There are three articles which they may easily obtain. 1. their own meeting periodically. 2. the exclusive right of taxation. 3. the right of registering laws and proposing amendments to them as exercised now by the parliaments. This last would be readily approved by the court on account of their hostility against the parliaments, and would lead immediately to the origination of laws. The 2d. has been already solemnly avowed by the king: and it is well understood there would be no opposition to the first. If they push at much more, all may fail. I shall not enter further into public details, because my letter to Mr. Jay will give them. That contains a request of permission to return to America the next spring, for the summer

---

44. Edmund Randolph in 1782 had written a report containing additional instructions to the American peace negotiators, which TJ confused with JM's report of 1780 on navigation of the Mississippi; see TJ to JM, May 3, 1788, above.

only. The reasons therein urged, drawn from my private affairs are very cogent. But there is another more cogent on my mind, tho' of a nature not to be explained in a public letter. It is the necessity of attending my daughters myself to their own country, and depositing them safely in the hands of those with whom I can safely leave them. I have deferred this request as long as circumstances would permit, and am in hopes it will meet with no difficulty. I have had too many proofs of your friendship not to rely on your patronage of it, as, in all probability, nothing can suffer by a short absence. But the *immediate* permission is what I am anxious about; as by going in April and returning in October I shall be sure of pleasant and short passages out and in. I must intreat your attention, my friend, to this matter, and that the answers may be sent me thro' several channels.

Mr. Limozin at Havre, sent you by mistake a package belonging to somebody else. I do not know what it contained, but he has written to you on the subject, and prayed me to do the same. He is likely to suffer if it be not returned.

Supposing that the funding their foreign debt will be among the first operations of the new government, I send you two estimates, the one by myself, the other by a gentleman infinitely better acquainted with the subject, shewing what fund will suffice to discharge the principal and interest as it shall become due, aided by occasional loans, which the same fund will repay.[45] I inclose them to you, because collating them together, and with your own ideas, you will be able to devise something better than either. But something must be done. This government will expect, I fancy, a very satisfactory provision for the paiment of their debt, from the first session of the new Congress. Perhaps in this matter, as well as the arrangement of your foreign affairs, I may be able, when on the spot with you, to give some information and suggest some hints, which may render my visit to my native country not altogether useless. I consider as no small advantage the resuming the tone of mind of my constituents, which is lost by long absence, and can only be recovered by mixing with them: and shall particularly hope for much profit and pleasure, by contriving to pass as much time as possible with you. Should you have a trip to Virginia in contemplation for that year, I hope you will time it so as that we may be there together. I will camp you at Monticello where, if illy entertained otherwise, you shall not want that of books. In firm hope of a happy meeting with you in the spring or early in summer I conclude with assurances of the sincere esteem and attachment with which I am, Dear sir, Your affectionate friend and servt,

TH: JEFFERSON

P.S. The inclosed letters are extremely interesting to me, and recommended to your friendly and particular care.

---

45. Dutch banker Jacob van Staphorst was probably the "gentleman infinitely better acquainted with the subject"; see *PTJ*, XIV, p. 195. Both estimates are printed below as Enclosures.

ENCLOSURE
*[Jefferson's Plan for Funding the Foreign Debt]*

[Oct. 1788][46]

A state of the debt due from the U.S. of America
to France, and of the sums of Principal and
Interest paiable each year

| | Capital Livres | Interest Livres | Total Livres | Total Dollars | |
|---|---|---|---|---|---|
| 1787. | 2,500,000 | 1,600,000 | 4,100,000 | 755,083 | The livres are converted into Dollars on the following principles. |
| 1788. | 2,500,000 | 1,485,000 | 3,985,000 | 733,904 | 1. The Spanish Dollar of exchange is equal to 50. sous Courant of Holland, when at par, that is, according to the pure metal they contain. |
| 1789. | 2,500,000 | 1,370,000 | 3,870,000 | 712,725 | |
| 1790. | 2,500,000 | 1,255,000 | 3,755,000 | 691,546 | |
| 1791. | 2,500,000 | 1,140,000 | 3,640,000 | 670,367 | 2. The French sou (of three Livres) *of exchange* is equal to 27⅝ sous Courant of Holland, when at par, that is to say intrinsically. |
| | | | | 3,563,625 | |
| 1792. | 2,500,000 | 1,025,000 | 3,525,000 | 649,187 | Then As 50. Sous Court : |
| 1793. | 2,500,000 | 910,000 | 3,410,000 | 628,008 | 1 Dollar :: 27⅝ Sous Court. : 0.5525 of a Dollar. |
| 1794. | 2,500,000 | 795,000 | 3,295,000 | 606,829 | Consequently 27⅝ S.ct. ÷ 3 = 1 livre = $\frac{5}{3}$ Doll. = 0.1841⅔ Dol. |
| 1795. | 2,500,000 | 680,000 | 3,180,000 | 585,650 | |
| 1796. | 2,500,000 | 565,000 | 3,065,000 | 564,471 | |
| 1797. | 2,500,000 | 450,000 | 2,950,000 | 543,292 | That is to say A livre is 1 Disme-8 cents- 41⅔ mills exactly |
| 1798. | 2,500,000 | 325,000 | 2,825,000 | 520,271 | |
| 1799. | 1,000,000 | 200,000 | 1,200,000 | 221,000 | A dollar is 5.ᵗᵗ43 or 5ᵗᵗ· 8s.-7⅕d. exactly |
| 1800. | 1,000,000 | 150,000 | 1,150,000 | 211,792 | |
| 1801. | 1,000,000 | 100,000 | 1,100,000 | 202,583 | |
| 1802. | 1,000,000 | 50,000 | 1,050,000 | 193,375 | |
| | 34,000,000 | 12,100,000 | 46,100,000 | 8,490,083 | |

The Impost of 5. per cent on European articles was estimated at 777,773 Dollars annually.[47] Suppose then this European impost appropriated sacredly to the paiment of the French debt. Some years there will be Deficiencies which must be made up by borrowing. Other years there will be a Surplus to repay or counterbalance these loans.

The following operation will shew that the annual sum of 777.773 Dollars will, by the year 1803, pay off the French debt principal and interest punctually at the epochs they become due, with the aid of occasional loans; which occasional loans with their interest, however, it will also repay within the same time, and leave a surplus of 310,422 Dollars to be carried to the fund for paying off the Dutch debt.

But note, the expences of making the occasional loans, not being known, are not taken into this account; nor are the expences of collecting the impost.

---

46. In a brilliant piece of detective work, Boyd first published TJ's calculations in *PTJ*, XIV, pp. 190-205, pulling together material from 1788 as well as items that had been mistakenly filed under dates spread between 1790 and 1805.

47. TJ relied upon JM's 1783 estimates of revenue to be yielded by an impost of 5 percent; see W. C. Ford *et al.*, eds., *The Journals of the Continental Congress, 1774-1789*, 34 vols. (Washington, 1904-37), XXIV, pp. 285-87, and Brant, II, pp. 209-36. JM estimated total imports at £3,500,000 or $15,555,554; an impost of 5 percent would yield $777,773.

|       |                                                                 |           | *Dollars*  | *Dollars*  |
|-------|-----------------------------------------------------------------|-----------|-----------|-----------|
| 1791. | Impost of 5. per cent on all European commodities               |           | 777,773   |           |
|       | Deficit to be supplied by New loan ..... 2,785,852              |           | 2,785,852 |           |
|       | Arrearages of Interest & principal to be paid this year         |           |           | 3,563,625 |
|       |                                                                 |           | 3,563,625 | 3,563,625 |
| 1792. | European impost                                                 |           | 777,773   |           |
|       | Deficit to be borrowed                                          | 10,711    | 10,711    |           |
|       | Demand of 1792                                                  | 2,796,563 |           | 649,187   |
|       | Interest of New loan of last year                               |           |           | 139,297   |
|       |                                                                 |           | 788,484   | 788,484   |
| 1793. | European impost                                                 |           | 777,773   |           |
|       | Interest of New loans                                           |           |           | 139,828   |
|       | Demand of 1793                                                  |           |           | 628,008   |
|       | Surplus (to be employed immediately so as to save, or beget, a year's interest) |           |           | 9,937     |
|       |                                                                 |           | 777,773   | 777,773   |
| 1794. | Surplus of 1793                                                 |           | 9,937     |           |
|       | Interest, saved or begotton, on that                            |           | 496       |           |
|       | European impost                                                 |           | 777,773   |           |
|       | Interest on New loans                                           |           |           | 139,828   |
|       | Demand of 1794                                                  |           |           | 606,829   |
|       | Surplus                                                         |           |           | 41,549    |
|       |                                                                 |           | 788,206   | 788,206   |
| 1795. | Surplus of 1794                                                 |           | 41,549    |           |
|       | Interest on that                                                |           | 2,077     |           |
|       | European impost                                                 |           | 777,773   |           |
|       | Interest on New loans                                           |           |           | 139,828   |
|       | Demand of 1795                                                  |           |           | 585,650   |
|       | Surplus                                                         |           |           | 95,921    |
|       |                                                                 |           | 821,399   | 821,399   |
| 1796. | Surplus of 1795                                                 |           | 95,921    |           |
|       | Interest on that                                                |           | 4,796     |           |
|       | European Impost                                                 |           | 777,773   |           |
|       | Interest on New loans                                           |           |           | 139,828   |
|       | Demand of 1796                                                  |           |           | 564,471   |
|       | Surplus                                                         |           |           | 174,191   |
|       |                                                                 |           | 878,490   | 878,490   |

# The Constitution and a Bill of Rights, 1788–1789

|  |  | Dollars | Dollars |
|---|---|---:|---:|
| 1797. | Surplus of 1796 | 174,191 | |
| | Interest on that | 8,709 | |
| | European impost | 777,773 | |
| | Interest on New loans | | 139,828 |
| | Demand of 1797 | | 543,292 |
| | Surplus | | 277,553 |
| | | 960,673 | 960,673 |
| 1798. | Surplus of 1797 | 277,553 | |
| | Interest on that | 13,877 | |
| | European impost | 777,773 | |
| | Interest on New loan | | 139,828 |
| | Demand of 1798 | | 520,271 |
| | Surplus | | 409,104 |
| | | 1,069,203 | 1,069,203 |
| 1799. | Surplus of 1798 | 409,104 | |
| | Interest on that | 20,455 | |
| | European impost | 777,773 | |
| | Interest on New loans | | 139,828 |
| | Demand of 1799 | | 221,000 |
| | Surplus | | 846,504 |
| | | 1,207,332 | 1,207,332 |
| 1800. | Surplus of 1799 | 846,504 | |
| | Interest on that | 42,325 | |
| | European impost | 777,773 | |
| | Interest on New loans | | 139,828 |
| | Demand of 1800 | | 211,792 |
| | Surplus | | 1,314,982 |
| | | 1,666,602 | 1,666,602 |
| 1801. | Surplus of 1800 | 1,314,982 | |
| | Interest on that | 65,749 | |
| | European impost | 777,773 | |
| | Interest on New loans | | 139,828 |
| | Demand of 1801 | | 202,583 |
| | Surplus | | 1,816,093 |
| | | 2,158,504 | 2,158,504 |
| 1802. | Surplus of 1801 | 1,816,093 | |
| | Interest on that | 90,804 | |
| | European impost | 777,773 | |
| | Interest on New loans | | 139,828 |

|  |  | Dollars | Dollars |
|---|---|---:|---:|
|  | Demand of 1802 |  | 193,375 |
|  | Surplus |  | 2,351,467 |
|  |  | 2,684,670 | 2,684,670 |
| 1803. | Surplus of 1802 | 2,351,467 |  |
|  | Interest on that | 117,573 |  |
|  | European impost | 777,773 |  |
|  | Interest on New loans |  | 139,828 |
|  | Principal of New loans |  | 2,796,563 |
|  | Surplus to be transferred in aid of Dutch funds |  | 310,422 |
|  |  | 3,246,813 | 3,246,813 |

State of the Debt of the U.S. in Holland, and of the epochs at which it is paiable, principal and interest

|  | 5 Milln. Flor. 1782. Jun. 11. | Int. 5 p Ct. paiab. Jun. 1 | 1. Milln. Flor. 1787 Jun. 1 | Int. 5 p Ct. paiab. Jun. 1 | 1. Mill. Flor. 1788 Mar. 13. | Int. 5p. Ct. paiab. Jun. 1 | 2 Mill. Flo. 1784. Mar. 9. | Int. 4p. Ct. paiab. Feb. 1. | Total Florins | Total Dollars |
|---|---|---|---|---|---|---|---|---|---|---|
| 1791. |  | 250,000 |  | 50,000 |  | 50,000 |  | 80,000 | 430,000 | 172,000 |
| 1792. |  | 250,000 |  | 50,000 |  | 50,000 |  | 80,000 | 430,000 | 172,000 |
| 1793. | 1,000,000 | 250,000 |  | 50,000 |  | 50,000 |  | 80,000 | 1,430,000 | 572,000 |
| 1794. | 1,000,000 | 200,000 |  | 50,000 |  | 50,000 |  | 80,000 | 1,380,000 | 552,000 |
| 1795. | 1,000,000 | 150,000 |  | 50,000 |  | 50,000 |  | 80,000 | 1,330,000 | 532,000 |
| 1796. | 1,000,000 | 100,000 |  | 50,000 |  | 50,000 |  | 80,000 | 1,280,000 | 512,000 |
| 1797. | 1,000,000 | 50,000 |  | 50,000 |  | 50,000 |  | 80,000 | 1,230,000 | 492,000 |
| 1798. |  |  | 200,000 | 50,000 |  | 50,000 |  | 80,000 | 380,000 | 152,000 |
| 1799. |  |  | 200,000 | 40,000 | 200,000 | 50,000 |  | 80,000 | 570,000 | 228,000 |
| 1800. |  |  | 200,000 | 30,000 | 200,000 | 40,000 |  | 80,000 | 550,000 | 220,000 |
| 1801. |  |  | 200,000 | 20,000 | 200,000 | 30,000 | 312,000 | 80,000 | 842,000 | 336,800 |
| 1802. |  |  | 200,000 | 10,000 | 200,000 | 20,000 | 325,500 | 70,000 | 825,500 | 330,200 |
| 1803. |  |  |  |  | 200,000 | 10,000 | 339,200 | 60,000 | 609,200 | 243,680 |
| 1804. |  |  |  |  |  |  | 363,800 | 50,000 | 413,800 | 165,520 |
| 1805. |  |  |  |  |  |  | 378,000 | 40,000 | 418,000 | 167,200 |
| 1806. |  |  |  |  |  |  | 403,300 | 30,000 | 433,300 | 173,320 |
| 1807. |  |  |  |  |  |  | 770,000 | 20,000 | 790,000 | 316,000 |
|  | 5,000,000 | 1,250,000 | 1,000,000 | 500,000 | 1,000,000 | 550,000 | 2,891,800 | 1,150,000 | 13,341,800 | 5,336,720 |

The European impost of 777.773 Dollars being supposed to be appropriated to the French debt, there will be a residuum of 217.777 arising on the other articles, according to the calculation of 1783. Suppose this raised to 300,000 Dollars, and appropriated to the Dutch debt; and to be reinforced by the European impost as soon as that shall be liberated from the French debt. The following operation shows the effect.

|  |  | Dollars | Dollars |
|---|---|---:|---:|
| 1791. | Residuary impost (that on European articles excluded) supposed raised to | 300,000 | |
|  | Demand of 1791 | | 172,000 |
|  | Surplus (to be so employed immediately as to save or beget a year's interest) | | 128,000 |
|  |  | 300,000 | 300,000 |
| 1792. | Surplus of 1791 | 128,000 | |
|  | Interest (saved or begotten) on that | 6,400 | |
|  | Residuary impost | 300,000 | |
|  | Demand of 1792 | | 172,000 |
|  | Surplus | | 262,000 |
|  |  | | [i.e., 262,400] |
|  |  | 434,000 | 434,000 |
|  |  | [i.e., 434,400] | [i.e., 434,400] |
| 1793. | Surplus of 1792 | 262,000 | |
|  |  | [i.e, 262,400] | |
|  | Interest on that | 13,100 | |
|  | Residuary impost | 300,000 | |
|  | Demand of 1793 | | 572,000 |
|  | Surplus | | 3,100 |
|  |  | 575,100 | 575,100 |
| 1794. | Surplus of 1793 | | 3,100 | |
|  | Interest on that | | 155 | |
|  | Residuary impost | | 300,000 | |
|  | Deficit to be borrowed 248,745 | | 248,745 | |
|  | Demand of 1794 | | | 552,000 |
|  |  | | 552,000 | 552,000 |
| 1795. | Residuary impost | | 300,000 | |
|  | Deficit to be borrowed 244,437 | 493,182 | 244,437 | |
|  | Interest on New loan of 248,745 | | | 12,437 |
|  | Demand of 1795 | | | 532,000 |
|  |  | | 544,437 | 544,437 |
| 1796. | Residuary impost | | 300,000 | |
|  | Deficit to be borrowed 236,659 | 729,841 | 236,659 | |
|  | Interest on New loan of 493,182 | | | 24,659 |
|  | Demand of 1796 | | | 512,000 |
|  |  | | 536,659 | 536,659 |

|       |                                      |         | Dollars | Dollars |
|-------|--------------------------------------|---------|---------|---------|
| 1797. | Residuary impost                     |         | 300,000 |         |
|       | Deficit to be borrowed   228,492     | 958,333 | 228,492 |         |
|       | Interest on New loan of 729,841      |         |         | 36,492  |
|       | Demand of 1797                       |         |         | 492,000 |
|       |                                      |         | 528,492 | 528,492 |
| 1798. | Residuary impost                     |         | 300,000 |         |
|       | Interest on New loan of 958,333      |         |         | 47,916  |
|       | Demand of 1798                       |         |         | 152,000 |
|       | Surplus                              |         |         | 100,084 |
|       |                                      |         | 300,000 | 300,000 |
| 1799. | Surplus of 1798                      |         | 100,084 |         |
|       | Interest on that                     |         | 5,004   |         |
|       | Residuary impost                     |         | 300,000 |         |
|       | Interest on New loan                 |         |         | 47,916  |
|       | Demand of 1799                       |         |         | 228,000 |
|       | Surplus                              |         |         | 129,172 |
|       |                                      |         | 405,088 | 405,088 |
| 1800. | Surplus of 1799                      |         | 129,172 |         |
|       | Interest on that                     |         | 6,458   |         |
|       | Residuary impost                     |         | 300,000 |         |
|       | Interest on New loan                 |         |         | 47,916  |
|       | Demand of 1800                       |         |         | 220,000 |
|       | Surplus                              |         |         | 167,714 |
|       |                                      |         | 435,630 | 435,630 |
| 1801. | Surplus of 1800                      |         | 167,714 |         |
|       | Interest on that                     |         | 8,385   |         |
|       | Residuary impost                     |         | 300,000 |         |
|       | Interest on New loan                 |         |         | 47,916  |
|       | Demand of 1801                       |         |         | 336,800 |
|       | Surplus                              |         |         | 92,183  |
|       |                                      |         |         | [i.e., 91,383] |
|       |                                      |         | 476,099 | 476,099 |
| 1802. | Surplus of 1801                      |         | 92,183  |         |
|       |                                      |         | [i.e., 91,383] |  |
|       | Interest on that                     |         | 4,609   |         |
|       | Residuary impost                     |         | 300,000 |         |
|       | Interest on New loan                 |         |         | 47,916  |
|       | Demand of 1802                       |         |         | 330,200 |
|       | Surplus                              |         |         | 18,676  |
|       |                                      |         | 396,792 | 396,792 |

|       |                                                                 | Dollars   | Dollars   |
|-------|-----------------------------------------------------------------|-----------|-----------|
| 1803. | Surplus of 1802                                                 | 18,676    |           |
|       | Interest on that                                                | 933       |           |
|       | Residuary impost                                                | 300,000   |           |
|       | Surplus of European impost (now liberated from French debt)     | 310,422   |           |
|       | Interest on New loan                                            |           | 47,916    |
|       | Demand of 1803                                                  |           | 243,680   |
|       | Surplus                                                         |           | 338,435   |
|       |                                                                 | 630,031   | 630,031   |
| 1804. | Surplus of 1803                                                 | 338,435   |           |
|       | Interest on that                                                | 16,921    |           |
|       | Joint impost                                                    | 1,077,773 |           |
|       | Interest on New loan                                            |           | 47,916    |
|       | Principal of New loan                                           |           | 958,333   |
|       | Demand of 1804                                                  |           | 165,520   |
|       | Demand of 1805. with a year's interest subtracted for the anticipation |    | 159,239   |
|       | Surplus                                                         |           | 102,121   |
|       |                                                                 | 1,433,129 | 1,433,129 |
| 1805. | Surplus of 1804                                                 | 102,121   |           |
|       | Interest on that                                                | 5,106     |           |
|       | Joint impost                                                    | 1,077,773 |           |
|       | Demand of 1806, with a year's interest subtracted               |           | 164,734   |
|       | Demand of 1807, with two years interest subtracted              |           | 287,273   |
|       | Surplus                                                         |           | 732,993   |
|       |                                                                 | 1,885,000 | 1,885,000 |
|       |                                                                 | [i.e., 1,185,000] | [i.e., 1,185,000] |

Recapitulation of the sums necessary to be borrowed, for the preceding plan, in order that the interest, and instalments of principal both in France and Holland may be paid punctually when due.

|       | France    | Holland |
|-------|-----------|---------|
| 1791. | 2,785,852 |         |
| 1792. | 10,711    |         |
| 1793. |           |         |
| 1794. |           | 248,745 |
| 1795. |           | 244,437 |
| 1796. |           | 236,659 |
| 1797. |           | 228,492 |
|       | 2,796,563 | 958,333 |
|       | 3,754,896 |         |

Note, that in this estimate for sinking the Dutch debt, the expences of the loans are not included, nor the expence of collecting the impost.

ENCLOSURE
*[Jacob van Staphorst's (?) Plan for Funding the Foreign Debt]*

[Oct. 1788][48]

In Order to consolidate the whole Foreign Debt of the United States, and to place it on a regular and simple plan of reimbursement, it will perhaps be the best mode to borrow in Holland 21.000.000 Florins for the payment of the following sums viz.

| | |
|---|---|
| Capital due to France | 34.000.000 Livres |
| interest thereon to Jany. 1792 | 6.850.000 |
| Sundry demands in Europe, say | 4.150.000 |
| | 45.000.000 Livres Tournois |

45. Million livres at the exchange of 54st. per ecû is equal to 21 Million Florins.

When this Loan is accomplished the whole Foreign Debt of the United States will be in Holland, and will consist of the Loans heretofore made in Amsterdam, and the present Loan of 21. millions bearing interest at 5 per Cent per annum, with the condition that the United States shall have a right to pay annually any part of the Capital of this Loan, not exceeding 2.500.000 florins in any one year.

To insure the completion of this Loan, the U. States must levy an impost of 5 per C. ad valorem on all goods imported into the U. States and, if necessary such other additional Duties as will annually produce one Million of Dollars, such Duties to be *sacredly* appropriated first to the payment of the interest and reimbursements of the Loans heretofore made in Holland, and the residue to the payment of the interest and reimbursements of the New Loan. This mode will instantly raise the value of the Old Loans, and so enhance the Credit of the U. States as to secure the success of the New Loan.

The following Calculation will shew that the appropriation of this revenue will sink the whole Foreign Debt of the U. States at the close of the year 1810. excepting only 146.814 florins.

| | | | |
|---|---|---|---|
| 1791. | Old Loans | 430.000 | |
| | New Loan | 1.050.000 | 2.500.000 |
| | for expences of the N loan | 1.020.000 | |
| 1792. | O.L. | 430.000 | |
| | N.Do. | 1.050.000 | |
| | sink of Capital | 1.020.000 | |
| 1793. | O.L. | 1.430.000 | |
| | N.Do. | 999.000 | |
| | sink | 71.000 | |
| 1794. | O.L. | 1.380.000 | |
| | N.Do. | 995.450 | |
| | sink | 124.550 | |

48. Boyd identifies the author as Jacob van Staphorst, a Dutch banker in exile in Paris because of his activities with the patriot party in Holland; see *PTJ*, XIV, p. 195; also see Schama, pp. 110–32.

| Year | Type | Amount |
|---|---|---|
| 1795. | O.L. | 1.330.000 |
| | N.Do. | 989.222 |
| | sink | 180.778 |
| 1796. | O.L. | 1.280.000 |
| | N.Do. | 980.184 |
| | Sink | 239.816 |
| 1797. | Old Loans | 1.230.000 |
| | New Loan | 968.193 |
| | sink | 301.807 |
| 1798. | O.L. | 380.000 |
| | N.Do. | 953.102 |
| | sink | 1.166.898 |
| 1799. | O.L. | 570.000 |
| | N.Do. | 894.757 |
| | Sink | 1.035.243 |
| 1800. | O.L. | 550.000 |
| | N.Do. | 842.995 |
| | sink | 1.107.005 |
| 1801. | O.L. | 842.000 |
| | N.Do. | 787.645 |
| | sink | 870.355 |
| 1802. | Old Loans | 842.000 [i.e., 825.500] |
| | New Loan | 744.117 |
| | sink | 913.883 |
| 1803. | O.Loans | 609.200 |
| | N.Do. | 698.433 |
| | sink | 1.192.367 |
| 1804. | O.L. | 413.800 |
| | N.Do. | 638.814 |
| | sink | 1.447.386 |
| 1805. | O.L. | 418.000 |
| | N.Do. | 466.445 |
| | Sink | 1.515.555 |
| 1806. | O.L. | 433.300 |
| | N.Do. | 490.667 |
| | sink | 1.298.335[49] |
| 1807. | Old Loans | 790.000 |
| | New Loan | 411.665 |
| | sink | 1.298.335 |
| 1808. | O.L. sunk wholly | |
| | N.Loan | 346.750 |
| | sink | 2.153.250 |

49. Boyd notes that this figure should be 1,576,033; see *PTJ*, XIV, p. 201.

|       |            |       |            |       |            |
|-------|------------|-------|------------|-------|------------|
| 1809. | N.L.       |       |            |       | 239.085    |
|       | sink       |       |            |       | 2.260.915  |
| 1810. | N.L.       |       |            |       | 126.000    |
|       | sink       |       |            |       | 2.374.000  |

remains 146.814 Florins on last of Decemr. 1810—as below.

The following calculation will shew the effect of the reimbursement on the loan of 21. million.

|       |            |       |            |       |              |
|-------|------------|-------|------------|-------|--------------|
| 1792. | 21.000.000 |       | 19.062.049 |       | 12.776.288   |
|       | 1.020.000  | 1798. | 1.166.898  | 1804. | 1.447.386    |
|       | 19.980.000 |       | 17.895.141 [50] |       | 11.328.902 |
| 1793. | 71.000     |       | 1.035.243  | 1805. | 1.515.555    |
|       | 19.909.000 |       | 16.859.898 |       | 9.813.347    |
| 1794. | 124.550    | 1800. | 1.107.005  | 1806. | 1.576.033    |
|       | 19.784.450 |       | 15.752.893 |       | 8.233.314 [51] |
|       | 180.778    | 1801. | 870.355    | 1807. | 1.298.335    |
|       | 19.603.672 |       | 14.882.538 |       | 6.934.979    |
| 1796. | 239.816    | 1802. | 913.883    | 1808. | 2.153.250    |
|       | 19.363.856 |       | 13.968.655 |       | 4.781.729    |
|       | 301.807    | 1803. | 1.192.367  | 1809. | 2.260.915    |
|       | 19.062.049 |       | 12.776.288 |       | 2.520.814    |
|       |            |       |            | 1810. | 2.374.000    |
|       |            |       |            |       | 146.814 florins |

## Madison to Jefferson

Philadelphia Dec. 8, 1788

DEAR SIR

This will be handed to you by Mr. Governeur Morris who will embark in a few days for Havre, from whence he will proceed immediately to Paris. He is already well known to you by character; and as far as there may be a defect of personal acquaintance I beg leave to supply it by this introduction.

My two last were of Ocr. 8 and 17th. They furnished a State of our affairs as they then stood. I shall here add the particulars of most consequence, which have since taken place, remembering however that many details will be most conveniently gathered from the conversation of Mr. Morris who is thoroughly possessed of American transactions.

Notwithstanding the formidable opposition made to the new federal gov-

---

50. Boyd notes that this figure should be 17,895,151; *ibid*.
51. Boyd notes that this figure should be 8,237,314; *ibid*.

ernment, first in order to prevent its adoption, and since in order to place its administration in the hands of disaffected men, there is now both a certainty of its peaceable commencement in March next, and a flattering prospect that it will be administred by men who will give it a fair trial. General Washington will certainly be called to the Executive department. Mr. Adams who is *pledged to support him*[52] will probably be the vice president. The enemies to the Government, at the head and the most inveterate of whom, is Mr. Henry are laying a train for the election of Governour Clinton, but it cannot succeed unless the federal votes be more dispersed than can well happen. Of the seven States which have appointed their Senators, Virginia alone will have antifederal members in that branch. Those of N. Hampshire are President Langdon and Judge Bartlett, of Massachusetts Mr. Strong and Mr. Dalton, of Connecticut Docr. Johnson and Mr. Elseworth, of N. Jersey Mr. Patterson and Mr. Elmer, of Penna. Mr. R. Morris and Mr. McClay, of Delaware Mr. Geo: Reed and Mr. Bassett, of Virginia Mr. R. H. Lee and Col. Grayson. Here is already a majority of the ratifying States on the side of the Constitution. And it is not doubted that it will be reinforced by the appointments of Maryland, S. Carolina and Georgia. As one branch of the Legislature of N. York is attached to the Constitution, it is not improbable that one of the Senators from that State also will be added to the majority.

In the House of Representatives the proportion of antifederal members will of course be greater, but can not if present appearances are to be trusted amount to a majority or even a very formidable minority. The election for this branch has taken place as yet no where except in Penna. and here the returns are not yet come in from all the Counties. It is certain however that seven out of the eight, and probable that the whole eight representatives will bear the federal stamp. Even in Virginia where the enemies to the Government form ⅔ of the *legislature*[53] it is computed that more than half the number of Representatives, who will be elected by the *people*,[54] formed into districts for the purpose, will be of the same stamp. By some it is computed that 7 out of the 10 allotted to that State will be opposed to the politics of the present Legislature.

The questions which divide the public at present relate 1. to the extent of the amendments that ought to be made to the Constitution, 2. to the mode in which they ought to be made. The friends of the Constitution, some from an approbation of particular amendments, others from a spirit of conciliation, are generally agreed that the System should be revised. But they wish the revisal to be carried no farther than to supply additional guards for liberty, without abridging the sum of power transferred from the States to the general Government, or altering previous to trial, the particular structure of the latter and are fixed in opposition to the risk of another Convention, whilst the purpose can be as well answered, by the other mode provided for introducing amendments.

52. These italicized words and those in the rest of the letter were written in code.
53. JM's italics.
54. JM's italics.

Those who have opposed the Constitution, are on the other hand, zealous for a second Convention, and for a revisal which may either not be restrained at all, or extend at least as far as alterations have been proposed by any State. Some of this class are, no doubt, friends to an effective Government, and even to the substance of the particular Government in question. It is equally certain that there are others who urge a second Convention with the insidious hope of throwing all things into Confusion, and of subverting the fabric just established, if not the Union itself. If the first Congress embrace the policy which circumstances mark out, they will not fail to propose of themselves, every desireable safeguard for popular rights; and by thus separating the well meaning from the designing opponents fix on the latter their true character, and give to the Government its due popularity and stability.

*Moutier proves a most unlucky appointment.* He is *unsocial, proud* and *niggardly and betrays a sort of fastidiousness toward this country.* He *suffers also from his illicit connection with Madame de Brehan* which is *universally known* and *offensive to American manners. She* is *perfectly soured toward this country.* The *ladies of New York (a few within the official circle excepted)* have for some *time withdrawn their attentions from her. She knows the cause,* is *deeply stung by it, views every thing thro the medium of rancor* and *conveys her impressions to her paramour over whom she exercises despotic sway.* Latterly *their time has* [been] chiefly *spent* in [travelling].[55] The first *vis*[it] *was to an Indian treaty at Fort Schuyler* and *thence to the Oneida town.* The *next to Boston* and *thence to N. Hampshire.* The *last to Mount Vernon from which* they but *lately returned.* On *their journeys* it is *said they often neglect the* most obvious *precautions for veiling their intimacy.* At *Boston he im*prudently *suffered etiquette to prevent even* an *interview with governor Hancock.* The *inhabitants taking part with the governor* neither *visited nor invited the count.* They were the less apprehensive of a misinter*pretation of the neglect*[56] *as the* most *cordial intercourse* had *just preceded between the town* and *the French squadron.* Both the *count and the marchioness are particularly unpopular among their countrymen here.* Such of them as are not under *restraint make very free remarks* and are *anxious for a new diplomatic arrangement.*

It is but right to add to these *particulars that there is reason to believe* that unlucky *impressions were made on the count at his first*[57] probably *by de la Forest, the Consul, a cunning disciple I* take it *of Marbois' politics* and by something in *his communications with Jay* which *he considered as the effect of coldness* and *sourness toward France.*

I am a stranger to the *errand on which G. Morris goes to Europe.* It *relates I presume to the affairs of R. Morris* which *are still much deranged.*

55. TJ furnished the bracketed words, which had been encoded erroneously by JM.

56. JM made an error in encoding *"the neglect"* but corrected it when his letters to TJ were returned to him after 1826.

57. JM omitted a word or phrase here, probably "meeting after his arrival"; see *PJM,* XI, p. 385.

I have received and paid the draught in favor of Docr. Ramsay; I had before paid the order in favor of Mr. Thomson, immediately on the receipt of your letter. About 220 dollars of the balance due on the last state of our account, were left in Virginia for the use of your Nephews. There are a few lesser sums which stand on my side of the account which I shall take credit for, when you can find leisure to forward another statement of your friendly advances for me.

I shall leave this place in a day or two for Virga. where my friends who wish me to co-operate in putting our political machine into activity as a member of the House of Representatives, press me to attend. They made me a candidate for the Senate, for which I had not allotted my pretensions. The attempt was defeated by Mr. Henry who is omnipotent in the present legislature and who added to the expedients common on such occasions, a public philippic against my federal principles. He has taken equal pains in forming the Counties into districts for the election of Representatives to associate with Orange such as are most devoted to his politics, and most likely to be swayed by the prejudices excited against me. From the best information I have of the prevailing temper of the district, I conclude that my going to Virga. will answer no other purpose than to satisfy the Opinions and intreaties of my friends. The trip is in itself very disagreeable both on account of its electioneering appearance, and the sacrifice of the winter for which I had assigned a task which the intermission of Congressional business would have made convenient at New York. With the sincerest affection and the highest esteem I am Dear Sir yrs.

Js. Madison Jr.

The letter herewith inclosed for Mr. Gordon is from Mr. Cyrus Griffin.[58] The other from Mr. Macarty an American Citizen settled in France, but at present here on business.[59] He appears to be a very worthy man and I have promised to recommend his letter to your care, as a certain channel of conveyance.

## *Madison to Jefferson*

Philadelphia Dec. 12, 1788

Dear Sir

The inclosed letter has been just sent me by Miss Rittenhouse and I avail myself of the delay of Mr. Morris to give it a conveyance. Since mine

58. William Gordon, an English clergyman, emigrated to America in 1770 and returned to England in 1786, where he published *The History of the Rise, Progress, and Establishment of the Independence of the United States* in 1788; see *PJM*, XI, p. 385. Cyrus Griffin was a member of the Virginia congressional delegation who was then serving as president of Congress; *ibid.*, p. 346.

59. William Macarty had settled in L'Orient in 1781. He returned to New York to settle his business accounts; see *PTJ*, XII, pp. 604–5.

already in the hands of Mr. Morris further returns have been received from the Western Counties of this State, which tho' not the entire residue, reduces the final result to certainty. There will be seven representatives of the federal party, and one a moderate antifederalist. I consider this choice as ensuring a majority of friends to the federal Constitution, in both branches of the Congress; as securing the Constitution against the hazardous experiment of a Second Convention; and if prudence should be the character of the first Congress, as leading to measures which will conciliate the well-meaning of all parties, and put our affairs into an auspicious train.

I am charged by Monsr. St. Trise, who is here, with his compliments to you. He is an officer in the French Cavalry, and appears to be an agreeable worthy man.[60] With every sentiment of esteem and attachment I am Dear Yr. friend and Servt.,

JS. MADISON JR.

## Jefferson to Madison

Paris Jan. 12, 1789

DEAR SIR

My last to you was of the 18th. of Nov. since which I have received yours of Sep. 21. and Oct. 8. with the pamphlet on the Mohiccon language, for which receive my thanks. I endeavor to collect all the vocabularies I can of the American Indians, as of those of Asia, persuaded that if they ever had a common parentage it will appear in their language.

I was pleased to see the vote of Congress of Sep. 16. on the subject of the Missisipi, as I had before seen with great uneasiness the pursuit of other principles which I could never reconcile to my own ideas of probity or wisdom, and from which, and my knolege of the character of our Western settlers, I saw that the loss of that country was a necessary consequence. I wish this return to true policy may be in time to prevent evil. There has been little foundation for the reports and fears relative to the M. de la Fayette. He has from the beginning taken openly part with those who demand a constitution: and there was a moment that we apprehended the Bastille: but they ventured on nothing more than to take from him a temporary service on which he had been ordered; and this more to save appearances for their own authority than any thing else; for at the very time they pretended that they had put him into disgrace, they were constantly conferring and com-

---

60. For TJ's recommendations of the Chevalier de St. Trise, see *ibid.*, XIII, pp. 122–23

municating with him. Since this he has stood on safe ground, and is viewed as among the foremost of the patriots. Every body here is trying their hands at forming declarations of rights. As something of that kind is going on with you also, I send you two specimens from hence. The one is by our friend of whom I have just spoken. You will see that it contains the essential principles of ours accomodated as much as could be to the actual state of things here. The other is from a very sensible man, a pure theorist,[61] of the sect called the oeconomists, of which Turgot was considered as the head. The former is adapted to the existing abuses; the latter goes to those possible as well as to those existing.

With respect to Doctr. Spence, supposed to have been taken by the Algerines, I think it extremely probable.[62] Obrian, one of our captives there, has constantly written to me, and given me information on every subject he thought interesting. He could not have failed to know if such a capture had been made, tho' before his time, nor to inform me of it. I am under perpetual anxiety for our captives there.[63] The money indeed is not yet ready at Amsterdam; but when it shall be, there are no orders from the board of Treasury to the bankers to furnish what may be necessary for the redemption of the captives: and it is so long since Congress approved the loan, that the orders of the Treasury for the application of the money would have come if they had intended to send any. I wrote to them early on the subject and pointedly. I mentioned it to Mr. Jay also merely that he might suggest it to them. The paiments to the foreign officers will await the same formality.

I thank you for your attention to the case of Mrs. Burke.

We have no news of Dr. Franklin since July last when he was very ill. Tho' the silence of our letters on that subject is a proof that he is well, yet there is an anxiety here among his friends. We have lately had three books published which are of great merit in different lines. The one is in 7. vols. 8vo. by an Abbé Barthelemy, wherein he has collected every subject of Graecian literature, after a labour of 30. years. It is called les voiages d'Anacharsis. I have taken a copy for you, because the whole impression was likely to be run off at once. The second is a work on government by the Marquis de Condorcet, 2.v. 8vo. I shall secure you a copy.[64] The 3d. are the works of the K. of Prussia, in 16 vols. 8vo.[65] These were a little garbled at Berlin before printed. The government lais it's hands on all which come here, and change some leaves. There is a genuine edition published at Basle, where even the garblings of Berlin are

---

61. The "pure theorist" was Dr. Richard Gem, TJ's physician in Paris; see *ibid.*, XIV, pp. 438-40. See also Koch, pp. 78, 84-85.

62. See TJ's correction in TJ to JM, Mar. 15, 1789, below, which substitutes "improbable."

63. See H. G. Barnby, *The Prisoners of Algiers: An Account of the Forgotten American-Algerian War, 1785-1797* (London, 1966).

64. Marquis de Condorcet, *Essai sur la constitution et les fonctions des assemblées provinciales* (Paris, 1788); see *PJM*, XI, p. 414.

65. The works of Frederick the Great were published in 1788; see *ibid.*

reestablished. I doubt the possibility of getting a copy, so vigilant is the government as to this work. I shall obtain you one if it be possible. As I write all the public news to Mr. Jay, I will not repeat it to you.

I have just received the Flora Caroliniana of Walter; a very learned and good work. I am with very sincere esteem and respect Dear Sir, Your friend and servt,

TH: JEFFERSON

P.S. I beg you to find sure occasions for the inclosed which are interesting to me.

ENCLOSURE
*[Proposed Declaration of the Rights of Man Drawn Up by the Marquis de Lafayette]*

La nature a fait les hommes egaux, et les distinctions entre eux necessitées par la monarchie, ont pour base, et doivent avoir pour mesure l'utilité generale.

Les droits de l'homme assurent sa proprieté, sa liberté, son honneur, sa vie; nulle atteinte ne peut y etre portée qu'en vertu de loix consenties par lui, ou ses representans, anterieurement promulguées, et appliquées par un tribunal egal.[66]

Toute souveraineté reside essentiellement dans la nation. Le gouvernement se divise en trois pouvoirs, le Legislatif qui doit etre principalement exercé par une assemblée representative nombreuse, librement et frequemment eluë; l'Executif, qui appartient uniquement au roi, dont la personne est sacrée et les ministres responsables; le Judiciaire qui doit etre confié à des tribunaux dont la seule fonction soit de garder le depot des loix, et de les appliquer literalement aux causes qui leur sont soumises, et dont l'organisation et le regime assurent aux juges leur independance, au public leur impartialite, aux parties les moyens de justification, et une distribution facile de la justice.

L'impot doit etre consenti pour un terme court, et proportionne aux vrais besoins dans l'octroi, et aux vraïes facultés dans la repartition.

Le commandement des troupes appartient au roi seul, et leur obeissance n'a de bornes que celles qui garantissent la liberté publique.

L'homme doué de la voix et de la pensée ne peut etre molesté ni pour ses opinions, ni pour la communication de ses idées, à moins qu'il n'ait violé l'ordre social ou l'honneur particulier, auquel cas il est soumis à la loi.

Et comme le progrès des lumieres et l'introduction des abus necessitent de tems en tems une revision de la constitution, il doit etre indiqué pour des epoques eloignées mais fixes, une convocation de deputés dont le seul objet soit de reintegrer la nation dans tous ses droits en la metant à meme de reformer son gouvernement.

Translation[67]

Nature has made men equal, and distinctions between them necessitated by the monarchy are founded upon and must be measured by the general good.

The rights of man assure his property, liberty, honor, and his life. No limitation to these rights can be introduced except by due process of laws accepted either

---

66. Chinard reads this as "un tribunal Legal," and Boyd notes that the Lafayette manuscript also reads the same way; see Chinard, p. 136, and *PTJ*, XIV, p. 440.
67. The translation is from Chinard, pp. 137–38.

by him or his representatives and previously promulgated and enforced through a regular tribunal.

All sovereignty rests essentially in the Nation.

Government is divided into three powers : Legislative which is exercised by a representative assembly numerous, freely and frequently elected; Executive which belongs solely to the King whose person is sacred and to his responsible ministers; Judiciary, which must be entrusted to tribunals whose only function is to preserve the body of laws and to apply them literally to cases submitted to them, with such an organisation and regime as to insure to the judges their independence, and to the public their impartiality, and to the interested parties means of justification and an easy distribution of justice.

Taxes must be consented upon for a short term and must be proportioned to true needs when established and to true (paying) capacity when assessed.

The command of the army is in the hands of the King alone, their obedience has no limits except those which guarantee public liberty.

Man endowed with voice and thought cannot be molested either for his opinions or for communicating his ideas, unless he violates social order or personal honour, in which case he is responsible before the law.

And whereas, the progress of enlightenment and the introduction or abuses necessitate from time to time a revision of the constitution, distant but fixed dates must be determined for a convocation of the deputies with the sole object to reinstate the nation in all its rights by enabling it to reform its governement.[68]

ENCLOSURE

*[Proposed Declaration of the Rights of Man Drawn Up by Dr. Richard Gem]*

Principes generaux relatifs à un etat politique.

1°. Point de distinction arbitraire entre les citoyens, ni noblesse, ni pouvoir, ni charge hereditaire.

2°. Le droit d'elire le corps des representants doit resider dans les proprietaires du territoire: ainsi les citoyens qui possedent un certain revenu en fonds de terre jouiroient exclusivement du droit de cité.

3°. L'etat doit etre homogene, avoir une unité parfaite dans toutes ses parties, meme constitution, et meme legislation, et ne doit point avoir des sujets.

4°. L'etat ne doit point avoir d'alliance avec des nations etrangeres, excepté en tems de guerre.

5°. Le code civil, criminel, ainsi que toutes les institutions quelconques doivent etre conformes à la justice universelle.

6°. Tout le corps des citoyens doit etre formé en milice.
7°. La liberté religieuse en entier.
8°. La liberté entière de l'industrie et du comerce.
9°. La liberté de la presse.
10°. La loi de habeas corpus.

---

68. For a brief discussion of this statement, that one generation has no right to bind succeeding generations, and TJ's view that "the earth belongs always to the living generation," see *ibid.*, pp. 80–82. See also TJ to JM, Sept. 6, 1789, below.

11°. Les jugemens par jurés
12°. L'impot territorial unique.
13°. Les biens des parens doivent se partager egalement entre les enfans.
14°. Point de substitutions.
15°. Le divorce, ou dissolution du contrat de mariage.

### Translation[69]

General principles relative to a political state.

1. No arbitrary distinction among citizens, neither nobility, nor power, nor hereditary office.

2. The right to elect the body of representatives must reside in the proprietors of territory; thus, citizens who possess a certain income from land will exclusively enjoy full political rights.

3. The state must be homogeneous, must have a perfect unity in all its parts, even in its constitution and its legislation, and must not have subjects.

4. The state must not have any alliance with foreign nations, except in time of war.

5. The civil and criminal codes, as well as all institutions whatsoever, must be consistent with universal justice.

6. The whole body of citizens must be formed as a militia.

7. Religious liberty must be complete.

8. Complete liberty of industry and commerce.

9. Liberty of the press.

10. The law of habeas corpus.

11. Judgments by juries.

12. The land tax only.

13. The property of parents must be inherited equally by the children.

14. No substitutions [a legal term used in wills and testaments to favor one potential heir over another].

15. Divorce, or dissolution of the marriage contract.

## *Jefferson to Madison*

Paris Mar. 15, 1789

DEAR SIR

I wrote you last on the 12th. of Jan. since which I have received yours of Octob. 17. Dec. 8. and 12. That of Oct. 17. came to hand only Feb. 23. How it happened to be four months on the way, I cannot tell, as I never knew by what hand it came. Looking over my letter of Jan. 12th. I remark an error of the word 'probable' instead of 'improbable,' which doubtless however you

---

69. I am indebted to Dr. John Hurt for preparing this translation.

had been able to correct. Your thoughts on the subject of the Declaration of rights in the letter of Oct. 17. I have weighed with great satisfaction. Some of them had not occurred to me before, but were acknoleged just in the moment they were presented to my mind. In the arguments in favor of a declaration of rights, you omit one which has great weight with me, the legal check which it puts into the hands of the judiciary. This is a body, which if rendered independent, and kept strictly to their own department merits great confidence for their learning and integrity. In fact what degree of confidence would be too much for a body composed of such men as Wythe, Blair, and Pendleton? On characters like these the 'civium ardor prava jubentium'[70] would make no impression. I am happy to find that on the whole you are a friend to this amendment. The Declaration of rights is like all other human blessings alloyed with some inconveniences, and not accomplishing fully it's object. But the good in this instance vastly overweighs the evil. I cannot refrain from making short answers to the objections which your letter states to have been raised. 1. That the rights in question are reserved by the manner in which the federal powers are granted. Answer. A constitutive act may certainly be so formed as to need no declaration of rights. The act itself has the force of a declaration as far as it goes: and if it goes to all material points nothing more is wanting. In the draught of a constitution which I had once a thought of proposing in Virginia, and printed afterwards, I endeavored to reach all the great objects of public liberty, and did not mean to add a declaration of rights.[71] Probably the object was imperfectly executed: but the deficiencies would have been supplied by others in the course of discussion. But in a constitutive act which leaves some precious articles unnoticed, and raises implications against others, a declaration of rights becomes necessary by way of supplement. This is the case of our new federal constitution. This instrument forms us into one state as to certain objects, and gives us a legislative and executive body for these objects. It should therefore guard us against their abuses of power within the feild submitted to them. 2. A positive declaration of some essential rights could not be obtained in the requisite latitude. Answer. Half a loaf is better than no bread. If we cannot secure all our rights, let us secure what we can. 3. The limited powers of the federal government and jealousy of the subordinate governments afford a security which exists in no other instance. Answer. The first member of this seems resolvable into the 1st. objection before stated. The jealousy of the subordinate governments is a precious reliance. But observe that those governments are only agents. They must have principles furnished them whereon to found their opposition. The declaration of rights will be the text whereby they will try all the acts of the federal government. In this view it

---

70. Part of a longer quotation from Horace's *Odes*, which may be translated as follows: "The man tenacious of his purpose in a righteous cause is not shaken from his firm resolve by the frenzy of his fellow-citizens bidding what is wrong"; see *PJM,* XII, pp. 16–17.

71. William Peden, ed., *Notes on the State of Virginia, by Thomas Jefferson* (Chapel Hill, 1955; rpt. New York, 1982), pp. 209–22, prints TJ's draft constitution for Virginia.

is necessary to the federal government also: as by the same text they may try the opposition of the subordinate governments. 4. Experience proves the inefficacy of a bill of rights. True. But tho it is not absolutely efficacious under all circumstances, it is of great potency always, and rarely inefficacious. A brace the more will often keep up the building which would have fallen with that brace the less.

There is a remarkeable difference between the characters of the Inconveniencies which attend a Declaration of rights, and those which attend the want of it. The inconveniences of the Declaration are that it may cramp government in it's useful exertions. But the evil of this is shortlived, moderate, and reparable. The inconveniencies of the want of a Declaration are permanent, afflicting and irreparable: they are in constant progression from bad to worse. The executive in our governments is not the sole, it is scarcely the principal object of my jealousy. The tyranny of the legislatures is the most formidable dread at present, and will be for long years. That of the executive will come in it's turn, but it will be at a remote period. I know there are some among us who would now establish a monarchy. But they are inconsiderable in number and weight of character. The rising race are all republicans. We were educated in royalism: no wonder if some of us retain that idolatry still. Our young people are educated in republicanism. An apostacy from that to royalism is unprecedented and impossible.

I am much pleased with the prospect that a declaration of rights will be added: and hope it will be done in that way which will not endanger the whole frame of the government, or any essential part of it.

I have hitherto avoided public news in my letters to you, because your situation ensured you a communication of my letters to Mr. Jay. This circumstance being changed, I shall in future indulge myself in these details to you. There had been some slight hopes that an accomodation might be effected between the Turks and two empires. But these hopes do not strengthen, and the season is approaching which will put an end to them for another campaign at least. The accident to the king of England has had great influence on the affairs of Europe. His mediation joined with that of Prussia would certainly have kept Denmark quiet, and so have left the two empires in the hands of the Turks and Swedes. But the inactivity to which England is reduced, leaves Denmark more free, and she will probably go on in opposition to Sweden. The K. of Prussia too had advanced so far that he can scarcely retire. This is rendered the more difficult by the troubles he has excited in Poland. He cannot well abandon the party he had brought forward there. So that it is very possible he may be engaged in the ensuing campaign. France will be quiet this year, because this year at least is necessary for settling her future constitution. The States will meet the 27th. of April: and the public mind will I think by that time be ripe for a just decision of the Question whether they shall vote by orders or persons. I think there is a majority of the nobles already for the latter. If so, their affairs cannot but go on well. Besides settling for themselves a tolerably free constitution, perhaps as free a one as the nation is as yet prepared to bear, they will fund their public debts. This will give them such a credit as will enable them to borrow any money they may want, and of course to take the feild again when they think proper. And I believe they mean to take the feild as soon as they can. The pride of every individual in the nation suffers under the ignominies they have lately been exposed to: and I think the states general will give money for a war to wipe off the reproach. There have arisen new bickerings between this court and that of the Hague, and the papers which have passed shew the most bitter acrimony rankling at the heart of this ministry. They have recalled their Ambassador from the Hague without appointing a successor. They have given a note to the Diet of Poland which shews a disapprobation of their measures. The insanity of the King of England has been fortunate for them as it gives them time to put their house in order. The English papers tell you the king is well: and even the English ministry say so. They will naturally set the best foot foremost: and they guard his person so well that it is difficult for the public to contradict them. The king is probably better, but not well by a great deal. 1. He has been bled, and judicious physicians say that in his exhausted state nothing could have induced a recurrence to bleeding but symptoms of relapse. 2. The Prince of Wales tells the Irish deputation he will give them a definitive answer in some days: but if the king had been well he could have given it at once. 3. They talk of passing a standing law for providing a regency in similar cases. They apprehend then they are not yet clear of the danger of wanting a regency. 4. They have carried the king to church: but it was his private chapel. If he be well, why do not they shew him publicly to the nation, and raise them from that consternation into which they have been thrown by the prospect of being delivered over to the profligate hands of the prince of Wales. In short, judging from little facts which escape in spite of their teeth, we may say the king is better, but not well. Possibly he is getting well; but still, time will be wanting to satisfy even the ministry that it is not merely a lucid interval. Consequently they cannot interrupt France this year in the settlement of her affairs, and after this year it will be too late.

As you will be in a situation to know when the leave of absence will be granted me which I have asked, will you be so good as to communicate it by a line to Mr. Lewis and Mr. Eppes? I hope to see you in the summer, and that if you are not otherwise engaged, you will encamp with me at Monticello for a while. I am with great and sincere attachment Dear sir Your affectionate friend and servt,

TH: JEFFERSON

# 13

# "THE GREAT RIGHTS OF MANKIND": THE ADOPTION OF THE BILL OF RIGHTS, 1789

LONG BEFORE the new national government was organized under the Constitution in 1789, the Confederation expired ignobly. After October 10, 1788, Congress failed even to convene since a quorum could not be mustered for ordinary business. Indeed, throughout the year, Congress simply marked time when it was in session. "To your demand to know what we are doing in Congress," a Massachusetts delegate wrote in the spring, "I answer—almost nothing. . . . The states have been in such a flutter about the new, that they haved hardly paid attention to the old government."[1]

The final act of the Confederation Congress was the passage of an election ordinance on September 13, 1788, setting the date for the first presidential election under the new Constitution and establishing March 4, 1789, as "the birthday of the new Government."[2] It was a foregone conclusion, Madison informed his friend in Paris, that "General Washington will be the first by a unanimous suffrage. It is held to be certain that Mr. Adams . . . will have the second appointment," although some votes would be "thrown away in order to prevent a possible competition for the Presidency." In Virginia, he added, "federalism was also proved to be the prevailing sentiment of the people," with seven of its ten new congressmen on the side of the Constitution. Patrick Henry still dominated the Virginia legislature, however, and had blocked Madison's election as a senator. Instead, Richard Henry Lee and

---

1. Samuel A. Otis to James Warren, Apr. 26, 1788, in Merrill Jensen and Robert A. Becker, eds., *The Documentary History of the First Federal Elections, 1788–1790,* I (Madison, 1976), p. 11.
2. *Ibid.*, pp. 132–33. JM uses this phrase in his letter to TJ, Mar. 29, 1789, below.

William Grayson, ardent Antifederalists—members of "the disaffected party," as Madison termed them—were chosen by the legislature. Henry also tried to prevent Madison's election to the new House of Representatives, carving out an election district by a method later called "gerrymandering" and persuading James Monroe to run against him. Madison and Monroe met in debates throughout the district, often traveling together. In one amusing incident, Madison's partisans carried a sick voter to the polls, where he promptly voted for Monroe! Madison won easily—1,308 to 972—and he assured Jefferson, Monroe's mentor, that he and Monroe had preserved their friendship "from the smallest diminution" by keeping in mind the distinction "between political and personal views."[3]

During his campaign for Congress, Madison promised to work for a bill of rights as amendments to the Constitution. Although he had opposed previous alterations prior to ratification, circumstances had now changed and so had he. With the Constitution ratified by "a very great majority of the people of America" and the new government ready to begin, he agreed that proper amendments "may serve the double purpose of satisfying the minds of well meaning opponents, and of providing additional guards in favour of liberty. . . . It is my sincere desire," he told George Eve, a Baptist minister near his home, "that the Constitution ought to be revised, and that the first Congress meeting under it, ought to prepare and recommend to the States for ratification, the most satisfactory provisions for all essential rights, particularly the rights of conscience in the fullest latitude, the freedom of the press, trials by jury, security against general warrants, etc."[4]

Once in office, he conjectured that the new government would be much more democratic in practice than its critics had predicted. He informed Jefferson that the Federalist majority would make some conciliatory sacrifices to the Antifederalist minority "in order to extinguish opposition to the system, or at least break the force of it, by detaching the deluded opponents from their designing leaders." In short, he viewed the movement for amendments as the final step in the ratification process.[5]

Madison was aware of the awesome responsibility that the American people had shouldered when they ratified the Constitution. For the first time in history, an entire people had ordained, established, and ratified an organic law, creating a new federal government for a new nation. In this vast, uncharted field, he quickly noted the "want of precedents": "we are in a wilderness without a single footstep to guide us," he told Jefferson. But he was also

---

3. JM to TJ, Mar. 29, 1789, below. The anecdote is reported in Gordon DenBoer, "The First Federal Elections: A Bridge from the Ratification Conventions to the First Federal Congress," *Manuscripts* 39 (1987): 293–300.

4. JM to George Eve, Jan. 2, 1789, in *PJM,* XI, pp. 404–5.

5. JM to TJ, Mar. 29, 1789, below. See also Charlene Bickford and Kenneth Bowling, "The First Federal Congress: A Second Sitting of the Federal Convention," *Manuscripts* 39 (1987): 301–8.

optimistic: "Our successors will have an easier task, and by degrees the way will become smooth short and certain."[6]

Congress met even before Washington was inaugurated as president, and Madison was quickly recognized as the "first man" in the House of Representatives. Fisher Ames of Massachusetts, who soon won a reputation as an orator and an opponent of Madison, credited the Virginian's role as a leader in the new Congress to his "excellent understanding" and his "quality of judgment."

> He is possessed of a sound judgment, which perceives truth with great clearness, and can trace it through the mazes of debate, without losing it. . . . As a reasoner, he is remarkably perspicuous and methodical. He is a studious man, devoted to public business, and a thorough master of almost every public question that can arise, or he will spare no pains to become so, if he happens to be in want of information. What a man understands clearly, and has viewed in every different point of light, he will explain to the admiration of others, who have not thought of it at all, or but little, and who will pay in praise for the pains he saves them.[7]

In his effort to maintain a republican simplicity for the new government, Madison fought attempts by the Senate to confer princely or exalted titles on the president and vice president. In Great Britain, the Houses of Commons and Lords always responded to speeches by the king, a precedent that Congress followed; but the Senate sought to bolster the dignity of the executive branch with high-toned titles reminiscent of aristocracy or monarchy. In the House of Representatives, according to Ames, "not a soul said a word *for* titles." Indeed, the House unanimously condemned the use of any titles, preferring the "naked dignity" of *President* and *Vice President* to such "degrading appendages" as "Excellency, Esqr. etc.," Madison happily informed Jefferson. But the Senate, led by Jefferson's friend, Vice President John Adams, proposed to address Washington as "*His Highness the President of the U.S. and protector of their liberties,*" Madison wrote, and "*J. Adams espoused the cause of titles* with great *earnestness*." The issue became "*a serious one between the two houses*," with Madison and "the friends of Republicanism" arguing that "our new Government was not meant to substitute either Monarchy or Aristocracy, and that the genius of the people is as yet adverse to both."[8]

A flabbergasted Jefferson condemned the Senate's campaign for titles as "*the most superlatively ridiculous thing I ever heard of.*" The House had shown "genuine dignity in exploding adulatory titles; they are the offerings of abject baseness, and nourish that degrading vice in the people." As for Adams, a perplexed Jefferson could think of only one explantion: "It is a proof the more

---

6. JM to TJ, June 13, 1789, below, and June 30, 1789, below.

7. Fisher Ames to George Minot, May 29 and 31, 1789, in Fisher Ames, *Works of Fisher Ames,* ed. Seth Ames, 2 vols. (Boston, 1854), I, pp. 35, 49. For a solid biography of Ames, see Winfred E. A. Bernhard, *Fisher Ames: Federalist and Statesman* (Chapel Hill, 1965).

8. JM to TJ, May 9, 1789, below, and May 23, 1789, below. The italicized words were written in code. The Senate finally decided to follow the practice adopted by the House.

of the justice of the *character given by Doctr. Franklin of my friend: 'Always an honest man, often a great one, but sometimes absolutely mad.'* "⁹

The creation of the new federal government, Madison thought, offered an opportunity to solve some of the political, economic, and social problems that had bedeviled the Confederation in the 1780s. Taking the lead in the House debates, he set the agenda with three basic proposals: the creation of an adequate revenue system to establish public credit, the development of shipping and navigation legislation to free the new nation from its old dependency on Britain, and the formulation of a commercial system of reciprocity that discriminated in favor of nations that had signed treaties of commerce and amity with the United States.

Madison, like Jefferson, favored commercial discrimination as a means of breaking Britain's hold on American trade. But he knew that old habits die hard and that his task was made more difficult because the intellectual climate in New York, the new nation's temporary capital, was "steeped in Anglicism." Nonetheless, he saw no reason "to *give* away every thing that could *purchase*" concessions, such as admission of American vessels to the West Indies trade. He contended that "our trade at present entirely contradicted the advantages expected from the Revolution, no new channels being opened with other European nations, and the British channels being narrowed by a refusal of the most natural and valuable one to the U.S."¹⁰

Madison also wished to promote trade with France, with whom Jefferson had negotiated a commercial treaty. And he was convinced that America could force Great Britain to reconsider her restrictive policy, "her dependence on us being greater than ours on her. The supplies of the United States," he told Jefferson, in summarizing his argument in Congress, "are necessary to the existence, and their market to the value, of her islands." For these necessities, Britain traded "either superfluities or poisons," unnecessary or luxurious items, which Americans "could do almost wholly without . . . and better without than with many of them."¹¹ Although Madison persuaded the House to incorporate discrimination in its commercial legislation, the Senate opposed "any discrimination whatsoever, contending that even G. Britain should stand on the same footing with the most favored nations." The Senate majority argued that the United States was "too dependent on her [Britain's] trade to risk her displeasure by irritating measures which might induce her to put us on a worse footing than at present."¹² When the Senate eliminated discrimination, the House accepted the decision, although Madison viewed it as only a

---

9. TJ to JM, July 29, 1789, below, and Aug. 28, 1789, below. The italicized words were written in code. See James H. Hutson, "John Adams' Title Campaign," *New England Quarterly* 41 (1968): 30–39. Adams thought that "Highness was not high enough," personally preferring "the title of Majesty."

10. JM to TJ, May 9, 1789, below, and June 30, 1789, below.

11. JM to TJ, June 30, 1789, below.

12. *Ibid.*

temporary defeat, one which he and Jefferson tried on several occasions to reverse.[13]

Jefferson was appalled that Madison's plan for commercial retaliation had failed. Placing France "on a mere footing with the English" was reverse discrimination, he thought, giving a great deal more to the former enemy than to the ally, "if the maxim be true that to make unequal quantities equal you must add more to the one than the other." But that was his only disappointment with the new federal government. "In every other instance," he told Madison, "the new government has ushered itself to the world as honest, masculine and dignified."[14]

Madison also took the lead in creating the executive departments, introducing resolutions to establish foreign affairs, war, and finance as "auxiliary offices to the President." Jay would probably head the first and Knox the second, as they had under the Confederation, Madison predicted, although Jay was also mentioned for the Treasury Department along with Alexander Hamilton. "The *latter is perhaps best qualified* for that *species of business*," Madison said, "and *on that account would be prefered* by those *who know him personally*." And Madison added to his friend in Paris, "I have been asked whether *any appointment at home would be agreeable to you*."[15]

Although Madison gave priority to organizing and funding the new government, he also took seriously his campaign pledge to work for a bill of rights and other constitutional amendments. Just five days after Washington's inaugural, Madison announced that he would introduce the subject of amendments later in the month. He had two reasons for his timing. The president's only specific recommendation for legislative action in his inaugural address, which Madison had drafted, suggested the need for amendments to protect "the characteristic rights of freemen." But he also cautioned against "every alteration that might endanger the benefits of an United and effective Government." Madison moved promptly for another reason. His colleague, Theodorick Bland, who had been elected as an Antifederalist, presented the next day the Virginia legislature's proposal for a second Constitutional Convention, which Madison consistently opposed as an attempt to make "alterations of the federal system" that would weaken the new government by returning essential powers to the states.[16]

---

13. See Drew R. McCoy, "Republicanism and American Foreign Policy: James Madison and the Political Economy of Commercial Discrimination, 1789 to 1794," *WMQ* 31 (1974): 633–46, and Drew R. McCoy, *The Elusive Republic: Political Economy in Jeffersonian America* (Chapel Hill, 1980; rpt. New York, 1982), pp. 136–65.

14. TJ to JM, Aug. 28, 1789, below.

15. JM to TJ, May 27, 1789, below. The italicized words were written in code.

16. See JM to TJ, Aug. 10, 1788, above. Also see Brant, II, p. 264, and John C. Miller, *The Federalist Era: 1789–1801* (New York, 1960), p. 22. During the eight days of debate on the bill-of-rights amendments in August 1789, JM described the discussions as "difficult and fatiguing" and "exceedingly wearisome," calling them in one instance the "nauseous project of amendments." He was referring here not to the substance of the amendments, but to the process of getting them through Congress; see Paul Finkelman, "James Madison and the Bill of Rights," in

On June 8, 1789, Madison introduced his set of amendments that ultimately became the federal Bill of Rights, a move designed to demonstrate "that those who have been friendly to the adoption of the constitution . . . were as sincerely devoted to liberty and a republican government, as those who charged them with wishing the adoption of the constitution in order to lay the foundation of an aristocracy or despotism."

Madison made four basic points in his effort to reconcile liberty with authority. First, the Constitution was meant to implement the principles of the American Revolution and to secure the rights announced in the Declaration of Independence by protecting the liberty for which men had "valiantly fought and honorably died."[17]

Second, there was no inherent tension between the Constitution and the Bill of Rights. Instead, Madison viewed the amending process as "a revisal of the constitution" and proposed that his "declaration of the rights of the people" should be "incorporated into [the text of] the constitution," not added to it at the end as a codicil. The Bill of Rights would not only be supplementary to the Constitution; it would be complementary, not antithetical. "There is a neatness and propriety in incorporating the amendments into the constitution," he argued. "In that case the system will remain uniform and entire; it will certainly be more simple, when the amendments are interwove into those parts to which they naturally belong." He wanted them to "stand upon as good foundation as the original work" and not "create unfavorable comparisons."[18]

Third, the ratification of the Bill of Rights would, thus, be the final step in the ratification of the Constitution, one meant to render the Constitution "as acceptable to the whole people of the United States, as it has been found acceptable to a majority of them." Although the Constitution had been ratified by eleven of the thirteen states, he said, "in some cases unanimously, in others by large majorities," North Carolina and Rhode Island were still outside the Union, having refused to ratify the Constitution until it had been amended. If a bill of rights was added, he predicted that "a re-union" of the original thirteen states would take place quickly and that "we should see that disposition prevailing in those states that are not [yet] come in, that we have seen prevailing [in] those states which are."

Finally, in a spirit of "amity and moderation," he wished to reassure

---

*Supreme Court Review for 1990,* ed. Gerhard Casper, Dennis J. Hutchinson, and David A. Strauss (Chicago, 1991), pp. 301–47.

17. JM's speech of June 8, 1789, is in *PJM,* XII, pp. 197–209. For a cogent analysis of the linkage between the Declaration of Independence and the Constitution, see Lance Banning, " 'To Secure These Rights': Patrick Henry, James Madison, and the Revolutionary Legitimacy of the Constitution," in *To Secure the Blessings of Liberty: First Principles of the Constitution,* ed. Sarah Baumgartner Thurow (Lanham, Md., 1988), pp. 280–304.

18. JM, speech of Aug. 13, 1789, in *PJM,* XII, p. 333. See Alfred F. Young, "Conservatives, the Constitution, and the 'Spirit of Accomodation,' " in *How Democratic Is the Constitution?,* ed. Robert A. Goldwin and William A. Schambra (Washington, 1980), pp. 117–47, for a thoughtful analysis.

"the great body of the people" who had opposed the Constitution because they thought "it did not contain effectual provisions against encroachments" upon their liberties. A bill of rights would "provide those securities for liberty which are required by a part of the community." Even though such guarantees might be depicted as "paper barriers," they would "establish the public opinion in their favor, and rouse the attention of the whole community." And it was to that wider public—the whole community—that he wanted to reach. His goal, he insisted, was "to satisfy the public mind that their liberties will be perpetual."

Personally, Madison denied that the unamended Constitution had placed basic rights in jeopardy. He had argued in the Virginia ratification convention that adoption of the unamended Constitution would "increase the security of liberty more than any government that ever was," and he never retreated from his position that the Constitution was a functional bill of rights.[19] Even as he outlined his declaration of the rights of the people, he observed that those who were dissatisfied with the Constitution because it lacked a bill of rights had been "mistaken." But he would "conform to their wishes" because "a great number of our fellow citizens think these securities necessary."

At the beginning of his speech, he had said that his amendments would "expressly declare the great rights of mankind secured under the constitution," a flat statement that the rights of the people were not only secure under the Constitution, but were already secured. But even though he cited the "We the people" prologue to the Constitution, which announced that "they ordained and established a new system, for the express purpose of securing to themselves and posterity the liberties they had gained by arduous conflict," he quickly conceded that if "the public in general, as well as those in particular who opposed the adoption of this constitution," wanted additional safeguards "for effectual provision against encroachments on particular rights," these should be "expressly stipulated for in the constitution by the declaration of rights."[20]

"If all power is subject to abuse," he argued, ". . . then it is possible the abuse of the powers of the general government may be guarded against in a more secure manner than is now done, while no one advantage, arising from the exercise of that power, shall be damaged or endangered by it. We have in this way something to gain, and, if we proceed with caution, nothing to lose." He observed that "the people of many states, have thought it necessary to raise barriers against power in all forms and departments of government, and I am inclined to believe, if once bills of rights are established in all the states as well as the federal constitution, we shall find that although some of them

---

19. Jonathan Elliot, ed., *The Debates in the Several State Conventions on the Adoption of the Federal Constitution* . . . , 5 vols. (Washington, 1888), III, pp. 96, 408–9. See Robert Rossum, "*The Federalist*'s Understanding of the Constitution As a Bill of Rights," in *Saving the Revolution: The Federalist Papers and the American Founding*, ed. Charles R. Kesler (New York, 1987), pp. 219–33, for a careful analysis.

20. JM, speech of June 8, 1789, in *PJM,* XII, pp. 197–99.

are rather unimportant, yet, upon the whole, they will have a salutary tendency."

Madison's amendments were modeled on the Virginia Declaration of Rights of 1776 as well as proposals made by seven state ratifying conventions.[21] As a preface to the "We the people" clause, he proposed a statement that "all power is originally vested in, and consequently derived from the people":

> That government is instituted, and ought to be exercised for the benefit of the people; which consists in the enjoyment of life and liberty, with the right of acquiring and using property, and generally of pursuing and obtaining happiness and safety.
>
> That the people have an indubitable, unalienable, and indefeasible right to reform or change their government, whenever it be found adverse or inadequate to the purposes of its institution.[22]

Then followed a series of civil-liberty guarantees to be corkscrewed into the text of the Constitution: freedom of religion, speech, press, assembly, and petition; the right to bear arms; protection against the quartering of troops in homes in peacetime; protection against double jeopardy; prohibition of unreasonable searches and seizures, excessive bail, and cruel and unusual punishments; a guarantee against deprivation of life, liberty, or property without due process of law; and the right to a speedy, public, and fair trial. This enumeration of rights did not exhaust or diminish "the just importance of other rights retained by the people," nor did it "enlarge the powers delegated by the constitution." Instead, the guarantees were meant as "actual limitations of such powers, or . . . [were] inserted merely for greater caution." To make this point crystal clear, Madison proposed that "the powers not delegated by this constitution, nor prohibited by it to the states, are reserved to the States respectively"; this was amended later by adding to the final phrase "or to the people."

In addition to the Bill of Rights' limitations on federal power, Madison proposed an amendment of his own, one found nowhere in the extensive debates in the ratification conventions or in the pamphlets of the period: "No *State* shall violate the equal rights of conscience, or the freedom of the press, or the trial by jury in criminal cases." This was Madison's final attempt to write the federal veto of state laws into the Constitution and underscored his view that the principal threat to individual rights came from unjust majority factions in the states "operating . . . against the minority." "I think there is more danger of those powers being abused by the state governments than by the government of the United States. The same may be said," he added for emphasis, "of other powers which they possess, if not controuled by the general principle, that laws are unconstitutional which infringe the rights of the community."

---

21. Edward Dumbauld, *The Bill of Rights and What It Means Today* (Norman, Okla., 1957), pp. 173–205, gives an abbreviated list of the proposed amendments. See also Randy E. Barnett, ed., *The Rights Retained by the People: The History and Meaning of the Ninth Amendment* (Fairfax, Va., 1989), pp. 353–85.
22. Congress rejected the idea of a prefix when it decided to add the Bill of Rights at the end of the Constitution.

"It is proper," he added, "that every government should be disarmed of powers which trench upon those particular rights." He acknowledged that "the equal rights of conscience, freedom of the press"—he had already designated these two as "those choicest privileges of the people"—"or trial by jury in criminal cases" were protected in some states by a bill of rights, but he saw no reason "against obtaining even a double security on those points." Moreover, some states had no bill of rights and others had "very defective ones." Although Madison persuaded the House to accept this restriction on state majorities "in favor of the minority" and individual rights—he called it "the most valuable amendment in the whole list"—the Senate failed to approve it.[23]

Madison promptly notified Jefferson about his proposed amendments, which protected fundamental liberties while carefully avoiding "every thing of a controvertible nature that might endanger the concurrence of two-thirds of each House and three-fourths of the States." That explained, he added, "the omission of several amendments which occur as proper," a polite way of saying that he had had to reject Jefferson's suggestions for greater restrictions on monopolies, standing armies, and habeas corpus. Even though Jefferson argued that stronger barriers should be erected against government power in these areas, Madison flatly opposed such amendments as impediments to effective government, believing that there were sufficient safeguards already incorporated in the Constitution on each of these subjects.[24]

Jefferson was pleased that a bill of rights was to be added to the Constitution. "I like it as far as it goes," he remarked coolly. But he added captiously, "I should have been for going further," and he listed five technical suggestions, all of them viewed by Madison as substantial restrictions on the power of the government to act—indeed, one of them would have narrowed the definition of freedom of the press.[25]

As a veteran of congressional proceedings, however, Jefferson knew that there was no chance, at this late date, of getting his proposals accepted, for he added: "If we do not have them now, I have so much confidence in my

23. See JM's draft of the Bill of Rights, June 8, 1789, enclosed in JM to TJ, June 30, 1789, below. For JM's discussion, see *PJM*, XII, pp. 206–8.

24. JM to TJ, June 30, 1789, below. The basic study is Robert A. Rutland, *The Birth of the Bill of Rights* (Chapel Hill, 1955). For a review of recent writings on the subject, see James H. Hutson, "The Birth of the Bill of Rights: The State of Current Scholarship," *Prologue* 20 (1988): 143–61. For a detailed legislative history, see Kenneth R. Bowling, "'A Tub to the Whale': The Founding Fathers and Adoption of the Federal Bill of Rights," *JER* 8 (1988): 223–51, and Helen E. Veit, Kenneth Bowling, and Charlene Bickford, eds., *Creating the Bill of Rights: The Documentary Record from the First Federal Congress* (Baltimore, 1991).

25. TJ to JM, Aug. 28, 1789, below. For a critique of TJ's suggestion on the press, see Leonard W. Levy, *Jefferson and Civil Liberties: The Darker Side* (Cambridge, Mass., 1963), pp. 48–49. Also see Herbert Storing, "The Constitution and the Bill of Rights," in *The American Founding: Politics, Statesmanship, and the Constitution*, ed. Ralph A. Rossum and Gary L. McDowell (Port Washington, N.Y., 1981), pp. 41–45.

countrymen as to be satisifed that we shall have them as soon as the degeneracy of our government shall render them necessary."[26]

Long before Jefferson wrote this letter late in August 1789, Madison had prodded the House into action on his proposed amendments.[27] A Committee of Eleven (North Carolina and Rhode Island had not yet ratified the Constitution) reviewed and rewrote the amendments, altering the style but not the substance of Madison's original draft. The committee reported on July 28, and Congress, moved to action by Madison's persistence, debated the amendments from August 13 until August 24.

During these debates, Roger Sherman of Connecticut suggested that the amendments should not be woven into the text of the Constitution but should be kept separate and added as a Bill of Rights at the end of the Constitution. The House list had included seventeen amendments, but the Senate combined these into what Madison labeled twelve "simple, acknowledged principles."[28] The first two, which dealt with the maximum number of congressmen and their pay, were rejected, but the remaining ten became the Bill of Rights when Virginia became the eleventh state to ratify them on December 15, 1791. By that time, Jefferson was secretary of state, and it was this champion of a declaration of rights, appropriately enough, who announced that Madison's Bill of Rights had been officially added to the Constitution.[29]

Jefferson's cool critique and philosophical rationale did not convert Madison to the cause of a bill of rights; Madison gave as good as he got in that classic exchange. Instead, it was his reaction to the constant pressure from the state ratification conventions, whose delegates had been chosen by the people, his experience in the Virginia ratification convention, and his campaign for a seat in the new Congress that convinced him that guarantees of individual rights should be added to the Constitution after it had been ratified uncondi-

26. TJ to JM, Aug. 28, 1789, below. For a detailed analysis of JM's and TJ's debate about the Bill of Rights, see James Morton Smith, " 'The Great Rights of Mankind': Thomas Jefferson, James Madison, and the Bill of Rights," *Colonial Williamsburg Journal* 12 (1989): 19-28.

27. For succinct summaries on framing and ratifying the Bill of Rights, see Robert A. Rutland, "Framing and Ratifying the First Ten Amendments," in *The Framing and Ratification of the Constitution,* ed. Leonard W. Levy and Dennis J. Mahoney (New York, 1987), pp. 305-16, and Leonard W. Levy's essay "Bill of Rights," in *Encyclopedia of American Political History: Studies of the Principal Movements and Ideas,* ed. Jack P. Greene, 3 vols. (New York, 1984), I, pp. 104-25. See also Patrick T. Conley and John P. Kaminski, eds., *The Bill of Rights and the States: The Colonial and Revolutionary Origins of American Liberties* (Madison, 1990).

28. Rutland, "Framing and Ratifying the First Ten Amendments," p. 313.

29. TJ to the governors of the several states, Philadelphia, Mar. 1, 1792, printed in *Harper's Magazine* 226 (1963): 43, under the heading "First Things First," cited in Bernard Schwartz, *The Great Rights of Mankind: A History of the American Bill of Rights* (New York, 1977), pp. 186-87. The notification was buried as the third item in a form letter that sent authenticated copies of "an Act concerning certain fisheries of the United States" and "an Act to establish post roads and post offices within the United States." One of the two amendments that was not ratified between 1789 and 1791, the one barring Congress from voting itself instant pay raises, was ratified 203 years later, on May 7, 1992, as the Twenty-seventh Amendment when Michigan became the thirty-eighth state to ratify it.

tionally. His decision was based on his pragmatic appraisal of national politics and the need to conciliate the Antifederalist minority. But it involved more than concessions to the Antifederalists. Just as he had viewed the amendments first recommended by Massachusetts as "not so much calculated for the minority in the Convention, on whom they had little effect, as for the people of the State,"[30] so, too, was his move at the federal level designed to assure the people of the United States that "the preservation of the sacred fire of liberty, and the destiny of the Republican model of Government" were, as President Washington said in his inaugural address, "justly considered as *deeply*, perhaps as *finally* staked, on the experiment entrusted to the American people."[31]

Nonetheless, Jefferson's arguments confirmed Madison in his judgment and spurred him forward in his efforts to redeem his pledge to work for amendments. His sponsorship of these amendments makes him indisputably "the Father of the Bill of Rights." His initiative in the first federal Congress allowed the Federalists to complete the ratification process by meeting public demands to better secure individual liberties without altering the powers of the new government.

If the preamble to the Constitution states that "We the People of the United States" established the Constitution "in Order to form a more perfect Union, establish Justice, insure domestic Tranquility, provide for the common defence, promote the general Welfare, and secure the Blessings of Liberty to ourselves and our Posterity," it seems altogether fitting and proper that the Bill of Rights appears as an epilogue to assure the American people "that their liberties will be perpetual," as Madison told Congress. The Constitution and the Bill of Rights were the supreme culmination of the American Revolution. Together they established a democratic form of republican rule that placed limitations on simple majoritarianism in order to preserve individual liberty; at the same time, they created a more powerful general government and a more perfect Union than existed under the Confederation.

Although Jefferson followed the progress of the new government in America with continuing interest, his attention was diverted by the explosion of 1789 that ushered in the French Revolution, an event that would be "for ever memorable in history," as this eyewitness told Madison.[32] When the Estates General assembled at Versailles early in May, Jefferson observed that "the revolution of France has gone on with the most unexampled success hitherto." Although there had been some bread riots, this mob violence, he concluded wrongly, was not related to the constitutional revolution. But the quick flow of events soon persuaded him that "the revolution of France" was no longer an orderly political and constitutional debate among reasonable men that could be mediated by the king. As soon as the Estates General met,

30. See JM to TJ, Feb. 19, 1788, above.
31. For JM's role in drafting Washington's address, see *PJM,* XII, pp. 120-24.
32. TJ to JM, July 22, 1789, below.

he told Madison that it faced "serious difficulties which it had been hoped the progress of reason would have enabled them to get over." What he meant was that he had expected that the three ancient orders would merge as one, with the nobles and clergy agreeing to come over "to the side of the people in the great question of voting by persons or orders." When the two privileged orders refused to sit with the commons as a single house and vote as individuals, the Third Estate stood firm, deciding "to vote by persons or to go home."[33]

For six weeks, the three estates engaged in parliamentary maneuvering, with Jefferson a daily witness to the debates. He usually attended the commons, which was pushing for the elimination of "all distinction of orders." "The Commons have in their chamber almost all the talents of the nation," he told Madison; "they are firm and bold, yet moderate." He thought "the Noblesse on the contrary are absolutely out of their senses." His assessment of the clergy was almost as caustic: "[they] are waiting to profit of every incident to secure themselves and have no other object in view."

By the middle of June, the commons refused to consider itself as an estate at all and invited "the other two orders to come and verify their powers in common." Whether they joined or not, the commons would "do the business of the nation. This was on the 10th," Jefferson continued in his play-by-play account to his friend: "On the 15th. they moved to declare themselves the national assembly," the only true representatives of the French people. Moreover, the Assembly authorized the collection of existing taxes, a bold move that implied that the Assembly might prohibit collection if its revolutionary will should be resisted.[34]

One month later, Jefferson traced the upheaval in July that transformed the constitutional movement in France into a popular revolution. Until that time, the reform movement had been a relatively orderly process taking place in meetings authorized by the king. In their Tennis Court Oath, however, the National Assembly announced their determination to establish a constitution for the kingdom on secure foundations and never to separate until they had achieved that goal. Pressed by the privileged orders, the king "took on himself to decide the great question of voting by persons or by orders," as Jefferson reported. In a royal session with the three orders, the king tried to straddle the issue, allowing joint meetings and vote by head in affairs of general interest "for the present session of the estates only" but preserving "the ancient and constitutional rights of the three orders, the form and constitution of future Estates-General, feudal and manorial property, and honorific privileges and useful rights of the first two orders."[35] In the showdown, the king had sided with the aristocracy, although he ordered nobles and clergy to join with the

33. TJ to JM, May 11, 1789, below.
34. TJ enclosed "the proposition relative to taxes" in his letter to JM, June 18, 1789, below.
35. Georges Lefebvre, *The Coming of the French Revolution* (Princeton, 1947), p. 86; R. R. Palmer, *The Age of the Democratic Revolution: A Political History of Europe and America, 1760–1800*, 2 vols. (Princeton, 1959–64), I, p. 481.

commons for current sessions. With that decision, Jefferson wrote, "it was imagined all was now settled."

But the king had also ordered troop concentrations near Paris and Versailles, presumably with the intention of dissolving the National Assembly, although he claimed, as Jefferson noted, that they were meant "only to preserve the tranquillity of Paris and Versailles." He also dismissed his chief minister, who had supported the commons, and reorganized his whole ministry for the use of force. Jefferson linked the troop movements with the reorganization of the ministry: "On the 11th. [of July] there being now 30,000 foreign troops in and between Paris and Versailles Mr. Necker was dismissed and ordered to retire privately." On the twelfth, Paris learned of Necker's abrupt dismissal; and when indignant crowds assembled, "a body of cavalry were advanced into Paris to awe them. The people," supported by French guards who sided with them, "attacked and routed them," Jefferson reported, "killing one of the cavalry and losing a French guard."

"The insurrection became now universal," and Jefferson gave a detailed account of the revolutionary eruption that he witnessed over the next ten days: the seizure of arms at the Invalides; the fall of the Bastille and the decapitation of its commanders; the organization of a committee of safety in Paris that named Lafayette as commander of a city militia; the resignation of the new ministry and the recall of Necker; the flight of the king's brother and other courtiers in search of foreign aid; and the king's capitulation. All these things Jefferson described for Madison in a hasty letter of July 22.

When the king agreed to the removal of troops and then accompanied deputies from the Estates General on a conciliatory trip to Paris, Jefferson gave Madison an eyewitness account of the monarch's reception:

All the streets thro which he passed were lined with Bourgeois armed with guns, pistols, swords, pikes, pruning hooks, scythes, and whatever they could lay hold of, about 60,000. The States general on foot on each side of his coach, the M. de la Fayette at their head on horseback. He returned to Versailles in the same order to the great joy of the remaining courtiers who feared he would have been detained in Paris.[36]

In the same letter, Jefferson reported the decapitation of an aristocrat by the mob and the dragging of his body "by the enraged populace thro' the principal streets of Paris." To Maria Cosway, he wrote with macabre humor: "The cutting off of heads is become so much a la mode that one is apt to feel of a morning whether their own is on their shoulders."[37]

By the end of August, he told Madison that "the tranquillity of the city has not been distrubed since my last." He was sure that the aristocrats had brought on their own downfall: "Never was there a country where the practice of governing too much had taken deeper root and done more mischeif." To

---

36. TJ to JM, July 22, 1789, below.
37. TJ to Maria Cosway, July 25, 1789, in *PTJ,* XV, p. 305.

another correspondent, he observed that "the nation has made a total resumption of rights" and now had "as clean a canvas to work on here as we had in America."[38] "Their declaration of rights is finished," he told Madison, and the Assembly was ready to work on a constitution.[39]

Although no plan had yet been presented, Jefferson knew what was going on behind the scenes, hosting a dinner at Lafayette's request for eight members of the National Assembly who were debating constitutional provisions. He sketched the outlines of a constitution, with a government headed by a hereditary king, an all-powerful house of representatives, perhaps a senate or council of revision with "no other power as to laws but to remonstrate against them to the representatives," and a judiciary system, "with trial by jury in criminal cases certainly, perhaps also in civil." "In short," he concluded, "ours has been professedly their model," although he expected changes as circumstances dictated. Indeed, the American experience "has been treated like that of the bible, open to explanation but not to question."[40]

Jefferson wrote only two more letters to Madison from France. In one, he announced that his request for a six-month leave, which he had initiated in 1788, had finally been granted.[41] His penultimate letter, which became famous for his argument that *"the earth belongs . . . to the living,"* was dated September 6, 1789, but he confessed to Madison that he did not know when he would mail it. Instead, he carried it to America two months later and held it for another two months before mailing it to Madison on January 7, 1790. But as soon as he had written the letter, he gave a copy to Dr. Richard Gem, a friend of Lafayette, and three days later he sent a correction to Gem, apologizing for "the hurry in which I wrote my letter to Mr. Madison, which is in your hands."[42]

If he wrote the letter to Madison in a hurry but was in no rush to mail it, why was it written when it was? Why not wait and write the letter aboard ship on his way home and hand it to Madison at their reunion meeting? In the letter, he confessed that it contained no news. He also observed that the essay "at first blush . . . may be rallied, as a theoretical speculation," but he suggested

---

38. TJ to comte de Diodati-Tronchin, Aug. 3, 1789, *ibid.*, p. 326.

39. For the remarkable parallelism between the French Declaration of the Rights of Man and the Citizen and the Virginia Declaration of Rights of 1776, see Palmer, I, pp. 518–21, which presents a chart showing which portions of the French Declaration were modeled on the Virginia Declaration. Chinard states that the French Declaration "was essentially American in its inspiration, that Jefferson had a hand in it," collaborating with Lafayette, who introduced it in the National Assembly on July 11; see Gilbert Chinard, ed., *The Letters of Lafayette and Jefferson* (Baltimore, 1929), p. 82. Lefebvre, p. 214, agrees that "the influence of America is beyond question," noting that "the inspiration and content of the American and French declarations were the same." For Lafayette's early draft, see TJ to JM, Jan. 12, 1789, above. See also Joyce Appleby, "America As a Model for the Radical French Reformers," *WMQ* 28 (1971): 267–86.

40. TJ to JM, Aug. 28, 1789, below.

41. TJ to JM, Sept. 17, 1789, below.

42. TJ to Richard Gem, Sept. 9, 1789, in *PTJ*, XV, pp. 398–99. For Gem's draft of a Declaration of the Rights of Man, see TJ to JM, Jan. 12, 1789, above.

that it was "solid and salutary" and would "furnish matter for a fine preamble to our first law for appropriating the public revenue." Yet he had known for ten days, because Madison had told him so triumphantly, that the first revenue law under the new Constitution had already passed both houses "and will be forthwith made a law by the concurrence of the President."[43]

Julian P. Boyd, the distinguished editor of *The Papers of Thomas Jefferson*, has suggested that, "far from being an authentic letter to Madison"—he also calls it an "ostensible letter to Madison"—it was an analysis of constitutional issues in France converted "into the form of a letter to Madison primarily as a protective device,"[44] a prudent move to avoid any possibility of a charge of undiplomatic interference in the internal affairs of the nation to which he was accredited.[45]

The subject, Jefferson wrote, "comes into my head" at a time when "we are immersed here on the elementary principles of society." Although he argued that "this principle that the earth belongs to the living" was applicable in every country, it was most especially applicable to France. And all of his examples, except for his final paragraph about the first American revenue law, were taken from French history. His basic argument was boldly stated. Starting with the self-evident proposition *"that the earth belongs in usufruct to the living,"* he formulated the principle that generations, like individuals, have natural rights. His mathematical calculations demonstrated that a generation during its majority spanned nineteen years. Since "the dead have neither powers nor rights" over the living, he concluded that every debt, every constitution, every law "naturally expires at the end of 19 years. If it be enforced longer, it is an act of force, and not of right."

Although the proposition was formulated for France, Jefferson thought the concept so important that it should be placed "among the fundamental principles of every government." Indeed, he reiterated his allegiance to the idea throughout his life, but he softened it when Madison's criticism persuaded him to incorporate the principle of tacit assent.[46]

---

43. See JM to TJ, June 30, 1789, below. TJ received this letter on Aug. 27, 1789; see *PTJ*, XV, p. 229.

44. Concerned about overstepping the line of diplomatic propriety, TJ visited the French foreign minister the day after hosting Lafayette's constitutional discussion and explained his actions; see Noble E. Cunningham, Jr., *In Pursuit of Reason: The Life of Thomas Jefferson* (Baton Rouge, 1987), p. 127.

45. *PTJ*, XV, pp. 384–91.

46. The fullest discussion of TJ's concept is in Adrienne Koch, *Jefferson and Madison: The Great Collaboration* (New York, 1950), pp. 62–96. For JM's critical appraisal of it, see JM to TJ, Feb. 4, 1790, below.

---————————— THE LETTERS ————————————

## Madison to Jefferson

New York Mar. 29, 1789

DEAR SIR

My last was committed in December to Mr. Gouverneur Morris. I was then on my way to Virginia. The elections for the new government commenced shortly after my arrival. The first was of Electors, to Ballot for a President and Vice President. The successful candidates were General Wood, Mr. Zachy. Johnson, Genl. Edward Stephens, Doctor David Stuart, Mr. W. Fitzhugh of Chatham, Mr. Warner Lewis of Gloucester, Mr. Jno. Harvey, Mr. Walk, of or near Norfolk, Mr. Kello of Southampton. These nine were federalists. The remaining three, Mr. Patrick Henry, Mr. Roane of King and Queen, and Mr. Pride of Amelia, were of the adverse party. Two of the former party did not attend. The votes were unanimous with respect to General Washington, as appears to have been the case in each of the States. The secondary votes were given, among the federal members, chiefly to Mr. J. Adams, one or two being thrown away in order to prevent a possible competition for the Presidency. Governor Clinton was the secondary choice of the anti-federal members. In the succeeding election of Representatives, federalism was also proved to be the prevailing sentiment of the people. The successful candidates on this list are Mr. Moore, late of the Executive Council (from Rockingham,) Mr. Alexander White, Mr. Richard Bland Lee, Mr. John Page, (Rosewell,) Mr. Samuel Griffin, Mr. Brown, member of the old Congress, (from Kentucky,) J. Madison, Col. Parker, (late nav. officer at Norfolk,) Col. Isaac Coles, (of Halifax,) and Col. Bland. Of these, the seven first have been on the side of the Constitution; the three last in the opposition. Col. Parker appears to be very temperate, and it is not probable that both the others will be very inveterate. It was my misfortune to be thrown into a contest with our friend, Col. Monroe. The occasion produced considerable efforts among our respective friends. Between ourselves, I have no reason to doubt that the distinction was duly kept in mind between political and personal views, and that it has saved our friendship from the smallest diminution. On one side I am sure it is the case.

Notwithstanding the lapse of time since the birthday of the new Government, (the 4th of March,) I am under the necessity of informing you that a quorum is not yet formed, either in the Senate or House of Representatives. The season of the year, the peculiar badness of the weather, and the short interval between the epoch of election and that of meeting, form a better apology for the delay than will probably occur on your side of the Atlantic.

The deficiency at present in the House of Representatives requires two members only for a Quorum, and in the Senate one only. A few days will, therefore, fit the Body for the first step, to wit, opening the Ballots for the President and Vice President. I have already said that General Washington will be the first by a unanimous suffrage. It is held to be certain that Mr. Adams, though refused a great many votes from different motives, will have the second appointment. A considerable delay will be unavoidable, after the ballots are counted, before the President can be on the spot, and, consequently, before any Legislative act can take place. Such a protraction of the inactivity of the Government is to be regretted on many accounts, but most on account of the loss of revenue. A prospect of the Spring importations led to the appointment of the first meeting at a time which, in other respects, was unseasonable.

It is not yet possible to ascertain precisely the complexion of the new Congress. A little time will be necessary to unveil it, and a little will probably suffice. With regard to the Constitution, it is pretty well decided that the disaffected party in the Senate amounts to two or three members only; and that in the other House it does not exceed a very small minority, some of which will also be restrained by the federalism of the States from which they come. Notwithstanding this character of the Body, I hope and expect that some conciliatory sacrifices will be made, in order to extinguish opposition to the system, or at least break the force of it, by detaching the deluded opponents from their designing leaders. With regard to the system of policy to which the Government is capable of rising, and by which its genius will be appreciated, I wait for some experimental instruction. Were I to advance a conjecture, it would be, that the predictions of an anti-democratic operation will be confronted with at least a sufficient number of the features which have marked the State Governments.

Since my arrival here I have received your favor of November 18th. It had been sent on to Virginia; but not reaching Fredericksburg before I passed that place, it followed me back hither. I am much concerned that your scheme of passing the ensuing summer in your native country has been defeated. Mr. Jay, with whom I have conversed on the subject, tells me that his answer to your public letter has explained the impossibility of giving effect to your wishes, no Congress having been formed under the old Confederation since the receipt of your letter, or, indeed, since the expiration of the last federal year.[1] The most that can now be done will be to obtain from the new authority, as early as possible, some act which may leave the matter to your own discretion. Perhaps it may be neither more inconvenient to your private nor to the public affairs to make your visit in the fall instead of the Spring, and to pass the Winter instead of the Summer in America. The same cause on which you are to charge your disappointment in this instance prevented a decision on the question of outfit, stated in one of your former communications.

With some printed papers containing interesting articles, I inclose a man-

1. Under the Articles of Confederation, the "federal year" began on the first Monday in November; see Jensen and Becker, I, p. 11.

uscript copy of Col. Morgan's invitation to persons disposed to seek their fortunes on the Spanish side of the Mississippi.[2] There is no doubt that the project has the sanction of Gardoqui. It is a silly one on the part of Spain, and will probably end like the settlements on the Roman side of the Danube, with the concurrence of the declining empire. But it clearly betrays the plan suggested to you in a former letter, of making the Mississippi the bait for a defection of the Western people. Some of the leaders in Kentucky are known to favor the idea of connection with Spain. The people are as yet inimical to it. Their future disposition will depend on the measures of the new Government.

I omitted to mention that a dispute between the Senate of this State, which was federal, and the other branch, which was otherwise, concerning the manner of appointing Senators for the Congress, was so inflexibly persisted in that no appointment was made during the late session, and must be delayed for a considerable time longer, even if the dispute should on a second trial be accommodated. It is supposed by some that the superintending power of Congress will be rendered necessary by the temper of the parties. The provision for the choice of electors was also delayed until the opportunity was lost; and that for the election of Representatives so long delayed that the result will not be decided till tuesday next. It is supposed that at least three out of the six will be of the federal party. In New Jersey, the inaccuracy of the law providing for the choice of Representatives has produced an almost equal delay, and left room for contests, which, if brought by the disappointed candidates into the House, will add a disagreeable article to the list of its business.

I am much obliged for the two estimates on the subject of our foreign debt, and shall turn your ideas to the account which they deserve.


*Madison to Jefferson*

New York May 9, 1789

DEAR SIR

My last was of the 29th. March. A few days ago I had the pleasure of yours of the 12. Jany. I thank you for your attention to the works of the Abbè Barthelemy and the Marquis Condorcet, and wish much that your attempts to procure me a genuine copy of the King of Prussia's [writings] may succeed.

I send you herewith the first No. of the Congressional Register, which will give you *some idea*[3] of the discussions in the new Legislative. You will see at once the strongest evidences of mutilation and perversion, and of the illiteracy of the Editor. The following Nos. shall go after it, as conveyances occur, unless they should be found wholly unworthy of it. The deliberations of the H. of Representatives have been cheifly employed on the subject of an Impost.

2. See Max Savelle, *George Morgan: Colony Builder* (New York, 1932).
3. JM's italics. See Marion Tinling's "Thomas Lloyd's Reports of the First Federal Congress," *WMQ* 18 (1961): 519-45, for an excellent account.

Opinions have been considerably divided on the quantum of duties that would be practicable, and in some instances on the ratio of different duties likely to operate differently in different States that would be just. In general the interests and ideas of the Northern and Southern States have been less adverse than was predicted by the opponents or hoped by the friends of the new Government. Members from the same State, or the same part of the Union are as often separated on questions from each other, as they are united in opposition to other States or other quarters of the Continent. This is a favorable symtom. The points on which most controversy has been raised are 1st. The duty on molasses. 2. The discrimination between nations in, and those not in treaty. The arguments against what appears a proportionate duty on molasses to that on rum, turned on its disproportion to the value of the article—the effect on the trade in it which yields the only market for certain exports from the Eastern States—the effect on the fisherys in which both rum and molasses are consumed, and finally the effect on the poor in that part of the Union where the latter enters into their ordinary diet. The opposite arguments have been that a proportion to the duty on rum was essential to the productiveness of the fund as well as to the rules of justice as applied to different States some of which consume foreign and some country rum, that if the proportion was not violated the trade in molasses could not be affected, nor the distilleries injured, that the effect on the fisheries would be too small to be felt, and that the poor who consume molasses would escape the burden falling on the poor who consume sugar. By the inclosed printed resolutions you will see the rates on these articles as they yet stand.[4] It is not improbable that further efforts will be made to reduce that on Molasses. Some of the other rates have been altered since they were printed! I do not note them because they are not yet in their final State. It will become a serious question whether a general reduction of the rates shall be made or not, on the idea of the danger of smuggling. The discrimination between Nations in and not in Treaty, has given birth to three distinct and urgent debates. On the last the minority was very small for putting G. B. at once on the same footing with the most favored nation. This policy tho' patronized by some respectable names is cheifly abetted by the spirit of this City, which is steeped in Anglicism. It is not improbable from the urgency of its representative that a further effort may be yet made.

Not knowing how far the present conveyance may be a certain one I decline on reflection inclosing the Register untill a more direct opportunity offers when I will add sundry matters which I have not time now to put in Cypher.

Inclosed is the speech of the President with the address of the House of Representatives and his reply. You will see in the caption of the address that we have pruned the ordinary stile of the degrading appendages of Excellency, Esqr. etc. and restored it to its naked dignity. *Titles*[5] to both the President and vice President were formally and unanimously condemned by a vote of the

---

4. Enclosure not found.      5. JM's italics.

House of Representatives. This I hope will shew to the friends of Republicanism that our new Government was not meant to substitute either Monarchy or Aristocracy, and that the genius of the people is as yet adverse to both. Accept my ardent wishes for your happiness. Yrs. affectly.,

Js. MADISON JR.

*Jefferson to Madison*

Paris May 11, 1789

DEAR SIR

My last to you was of the 15th. of March. I am now in hourly expectation of recieving my leave of absence. The delay of it a little longer will endanger the throwing my return into the winter, the very idea of which is horror itself to me. I am in hopes this is the last letter I shall have the pleasure of writing you before my departure.

The madness of the king of England has gone off, but left him in a state of imbecillity and melancholy. They talk of carrying him to Hanover. If they do, it will be a proof he does not mend, and that they take that measure to authorize them to establish a regency. But if he grows better they will perhaps keep him at home to avoid the question Who shall be regent? As that country cannot be relied on in the present state of it's executive, the King of Prussia is become more moderate: he throws cold water on the fermentation he had excited in Poland. The K. of Sweden will act as nobody not even himself can foresee: because he acts from the caprice of the moment, and because the discontents of his army and nobles may throw him under internal difficulties while struggling with external ones. Denmark will probably only furnish it's stipulated aid to Russia. France is fully occupied with internal arrangement. So that on the whole the prospect of this summer is that the war will continue between the powers actually engaged in the close of the last campaign, and extend to no others. Certainly it will not extend this year to the Southern states of Europe.

The revolution of France has gone on with the most unexampled success hitherto. There have been some mobs occasioned by the want of bread in different parts of the kingdom, in which there may have been some lives lost, perhaps a dozen or twenty. These had no professed connection *generally*[6] with the constitutional revolution. A more serious riot happened lately in Paris in which about 100 of the mob were killed. This execution has been universally approved, as they seemed to have no view but mischief and plunder. But the meeting of the states general presents serious difficulties which it had been hoped the progress of reason would have enabled them to get over. The

6. TJ's italics.

nobility of and about Paris have come over as was expected to the side of the people in the great question of voting by persons or orders. This had induced a presumption that those of the country were making the same progress, and these form the great mass of the deputies of that order. But they are found to be where they were centuries ago as to their disposition to keep distinct from the people, and even to tyrannise over them. They agree indeed to abandon their pecuniary privileges. The clergy seem at present much divided. Five sixths of that representation consists of the lower clergy, who being the sons of the peasantry are very well with the tiers etat. But the bishops are intrigueing and drawing them over daily. The tiers etat is so firm to vote by persons or to go home, that it is impossible to conjecture what will be the result. This is the state of parties, as well as we can conjecture from the conversation of the members, for as yet no vote has been given which will enable us to calculate on certain ground. Having formerly written to you on the subject of our finances I inclose you now an Abstract of a paper on that subject which Gouverneur Morris communicated to me. You will be a better judge of it's merit than I am. It seems to me worthy [of] good attention.

I have a box of books packed for you which I shall carry to Havre and send by any ship bound to N. York or Philadelphia. I have been so inexact as to take no list of them before nailing up the box. Be so good as to do this, and I will take with me my bookseller's account, which will enable us to make a statement of them. They are chiefly Encyclopedies from the 23d. to the 30th. livraison. Paul Jones has desired me to send to yourself and Colo. Carrington each his bust. They are packed together in the same box. There are 3. other boxes with 2 in each for other gentlemen. I shall send them all together and take the liberty of addressing them to you.

I rejoice extremely to hear you are elected in spite of all cabals. I fear your post will not permit me to see you but in New York, and consequently for a short time only. I shall much regret this. I am with sentiments of sincere attachment and respect dear Sir Your friend and servt.,

TH: JEFFERSON

ENCLOSURE

*Abstract of Mr. G. Morris's plan of American finances*[7]

Preliminary operation

Consider all requisitions from Congress on the states as *non-avenues.*[8] This gets rid of the adjustment of Quotas for the past.

Settle the sum due from the Union to each state for it's contributions in money, provisions, etc. and after taking credit for money etc. furnished to such state, let the balance be constituted a debt from the Union to the respective states bearing an interest of 6. per cent.

---

7. The plan is printed in full in Jared Sparks, *The Life of Gouverneur Morris, with Selections from His Correspondence and Miscellaneous Papers,* 3 vols. (Boston, 1832), III, pp. 469–78.

8. TJ's italics. TJ used "*non-avenues*" to mean canceled; see *PTJ,* XV, p. 124.

With the principal of this debt each state may, in the first place take up their own public paper (by commuting with the holders) or with the interest of it they may in the first place pay the interest of their own paper to the holders. The interest on the balance will support the state government.

The states may therefore abandon to the Union all the subjects of taxation.

### I.

Let the Union lay an Impost of 5. per cent on importations. This will bring in from 1½ to 2. millions of Dollars.

Open a loan in Europe sufficient to pay the foreign debts and somewhat more in *surplus*. This would be (suppose) about 12. millions of Dollars, which at an interest of 5. percent, would require 600,000 Dollars, and would leave about 1. million a year of the impost.

However instead of appropriating a specific part of this impost to the loans
1. Appropriate the whole to pay this interest in the first place.
2. To support government for a year or two till our other taxes become productive.
3. The surplus to form an Aggregate fund.

### II.

Lay a direct tax of ¹⁄₂₀ of all produce, paiable in kind (in the nature of a tythe) but commutable for half it's value in money. Should this produce more than the state's quota, let the surplus go to the state. The state legislature may then be entrusted with fixing the objects on which it falls, their value, the places of delivery, sale of the produce, conduct of the receivers etc.

This tax of ¹⁄₄₀ should be appropriated.
1. To the military and naval establishments.
2. To pay the interest of the debts of the Union to the respective states.
3. The surplus into the aggregate fund.

### III.

Postages and a tax on civil process form a 3d. fund. Appropriate it
1. To the Civil list.
2. The surplus into the Aggregate fund.

The Aggregate fund thus formed of the residuary parts of all the taxes, must
1. pay the interest of the domestic debt.
2. contingencies.
3. form a sinking fund to pay the capital of the general debts of the union. In the administration of this Sinking fund fix a certain order of paiment so as to ensure paiment to the holders; but at the same time leave a portion of it free to be employed by the executive according to their discretion in buying up the general debts. They might begin (if they saw it expedient) with buying the debts, to be constituted from the Union to the separate states, according to the above preliminary proposition.

## Madison to Jefferson

New York May 23, 1789

DEAR SIR

This will I expect be handed you by a young gentleman, Mr. Colden, the son of an amiable lady of that name within the circle of my acquaintance in this place.[9] I need not apprize you that the family, of which Governour Colden is the ancestor, is a respectable one. The young gentleman has been in Scotland for some years, pursuing his education, and with the approbation of his friends proposes to visit France before he returns to his native country. Such countenance and attentions as it may be convenient for you to shew him, will I have reason to believe be well placed, and will add to the many obligations under which I lie.

My last inclosed copies of the President's inauguration Speech and the answer of the House of Representatives. I now add the answer of the Senate. It will not have escaped you that the former was addressed with a truly republican simplicity to G. W. Presidt. of the U.S. The latter follows the example, with the omission of the personal name, but without any other than the constitutional title. The proceeding on this point was in the House of Representatives spontaneous. The imitation by the Senate was *extorted*.[10] The question *became a serious one*[11] *between the two houses. J. Adams espoused the cause of titles* with great *earnestness.* His *friend R. H. Lee altho elected as a republican enemy* to *an aristocratic constitution* was *a most zealous second.* The *projected title was—His Highness the President of the U.S. and protector of their liberties.* Had the *project succeeded it would have* subjected the *President to a severe dilemma* and given *a deep wound to our infant government.*

It is with much pleasure I inform you that *Moustier begins to make himself acceptable* and *with still more* that *Madam Brehan begins to* be *viewed in the light* which *I hope she merits* and which was so little *the case when I wrote by Mr. Morris.*

The collection bill is not yet passed. The duties have been settled in the House of Representatives and are before the Senate. They produced a good deal of discussion and called forth in some degree our local feelings. But the experiment has been favorable to our character for moderation, and in general the temper of the Congress seems to be propitious. I do not enter farther at present into the account of their proceedings, because I expect this will go by the way of Scotland, and be long on the way, being intended principally as a letter of introduction, and because I have received notice of a conveyance in a few days, which will be more direct and convenient. With my best wishes I am Dear Sir Yrs. affectly.,

Js. MADISON JR

9. Alexander Colden was the son of Henrietta Bethune Colden; see *ibid.*, pp. 148–49.
10. This italicized word and those in the rest of the letter were written in code.
11. TJ supplied this word, which JM omitted when he encoded this sentence.

## Madison to Jefferson

New York May 27, 1789

DEAR SIR

Since my last which was written on Sunday last and included an introduction of young Mr. Colden who is to be the bearer of it from Scotland where he now resides, I have had the pleasure of yours of March 15. My former letters will have made known to you the obstacles to a licence for your visit to America. The new authority has not yet taken up your application. As soon as the auxiliary offices to the President shall be established and filled which will probably not be long delayed, I hope the subject will be decided on, and in the manner you wish. It is already agreed in the form of resolutions that there shall be three departments one for finance, another for foreign affairs, and the third for war. The last will be continued in the hands of General Knox. The second will remain with Mr. Jay if he chooses to keep it. The first is also to be under one head, though to be branched out in such a manner as will check the administration. *Chancellor*[12] *wishes this department* but will *not succeed.* It will be *given I think to Jay or Hamilton.* The *latter is perhaps best qualified* for that *species of business* and *on that account would be prefered* by those *who know him personally.* The *former*[13] is *more known by character throughout the U.S.*

I have been asked whether *any appointment at home would be agreeable to you.* Being *unacquainted with your mind I* have not *ventured on an answer.*

The Bill of rates which passed the House of Representatives a few days ago is not yet come down from the Senate. The duties will it is said be pretty much reduced. In a few instances perhaps the reductions may not be improper. If they are not generally left as high as will admit of collection, the dilemma will be unavoidable, of either maiming our public credit in its birth, or resorting to other kinds of taxation for which our constituents are not yet prepared. The Senate is also *abolishing the discriminations in favor of nations in treaty* whereby *Britain will be quieted in the enjoyment of our trade as she may please to regulate it* and *France discouraged from her efforts at a competition* which it is not *less our interest than hers to promote.* The *question was agitated* repeatedly *in the house of representatives* and *decided at last almost unanimously in favor of some monitory proof* that *our new government* is[14] *able and not afraid to encounter the restrictions of Britain.* Both *the senators from Virginia particularly Lee go with the majority of the senate.* In this *I suspect the temper of the party which sent them* is as little *consulted as in the conduct of Lee in the affair of titles* and *his opinion in relation to the western country.*

---

12. At a later time, JM added "Livingston." This word and the other italicized words in this letter were written in code.
13. JM encoded *"latter"* instead of *"former,"* and late in life he corrected his error; see *PJM,* XII, pp. 185–86.
14. At a later time, JM supplied this word, which he had omitted when he encoded the sentence.

I have already informed you that *Madam Brehan is every day* recovering *from the disesteem and neglect into which reports had thrown her* and that *Moustier is also becoming more and more acceptable* or at least *less and less otherwise*. His *commercial ideas are* probably neither *illiberal nor unfriendly to this country*. The contrary has been *supposed*. When *the truth is ascertained and known*, unfavorable *impressions will be* still *more removed*.

The subject of amendments was to have been introduced on Monday last; but is postponed in order that more urgent business may not be delayed. On Monday sevennight it will certainly come forward. A Bill of rights, incorporated perhaps into the Constitution will be proposed, with a few other alterations most called for by the opponents of the Government and least objectionable to its friends.

As soon as Mr. Brown arrives who is the Representative of Kentucky, the admission of that district to the character of a State and a member of the union, will claim attention. I foresee no difficulty, unless local jealousy should couple the pretensions of Vermont with those of Kentucky: and even then no other delay than what may be necessary to open the way for the former through the forms and perhaps the objections of this State,[15] which must not be altogether disregarded.

The proceedings of the new Congress are so far marked with great moderation and liberality; and will disappoint the wishes and predictions of many who have opposed the Government. The spirit which characterises the House of Representatives in particular is already extinguishing the honest fears which considered the system as dangerous to republicanism. For myself I am persuaded that the biass of the federal is on the same side with that of the State Governments tho' in a much less degree. Yrs. truly,

Js. MADISON JR.


## Madison to Jefferson

New York June 13, 1789

DEAR SIR

The letter herewith enclosed from Col. H. Lee with the papers accompanying it fully explain themselves.[16] Inclosed also is a letter from Mr. P. Carr, who has been here several weeks.[17] One of his inducements to visit N. York during the present vacation, was a hope of falling in with you on your visit to America. I regret much both your disappointments. It is not yet in my power

15. At a later time, JM added "N. York."

16. Henry Lee's letter dealt with the Potomac canal and land speculation at the Great Falls of that river; see Henry Lee to TJ, Mar. 6, 1789, in *PTJ,* XIV, pp. 619-20, and Henry Lee to JM, Mar. 8, 1789, in *PJM,* XII, p. 7, and Mar. 14, 1789, *ibid.,* pp. 12-13.

17. See Peter Carr to TJ, May 29, 1789, in *PTJ,* XV, pp. 155-57.

to say when the cause of yours will be removed. Every step taken under the new System is marked with tardiness; the effect of that want of precedents which give a mechanical motion to business under old establishments.

To the above inclosures is added a chart of the Great falls copied from a draught sent me by Col. Lee. I should have observed that all the papers from him, except this are duplicates, the originals having been consigned by a conveyance from Alexanda. to the care of Mr. Mason who resides at Bourdeaux, to be forwarded to Paris.

This will go by a Gentleman, Mr. Joy, who is returning to London, and will be forwarded by such opportunity as he may judge sufficiently certain.[18] Considering it as likely to be long on the way, and having written pretty lately to you, I shall suspend further communications till a more direct and convenient channel presents itself. The Newspaper inclosed will shew you the form and extent of the amendments which I thought it adviseable to introduce to the H. of Representatives as most likely to pass thro' ⅔ of that House and of the Senate and ¾ of the States.[19] If I am not mistaken they will if passed, be satisfactory to majority of those who have opposed the Constitution. I am persuaded they will be so to a majority of that Description in Virginia. I wish you all happiness and am Dear Sir Yrs most affectly.,

Js. MADISON JR

Note—Let the amendments follow—


*Jefferson to Madison*

Paris June 18, 1789

DEAR SIR

My last to you was of May 11. Yours of Mar. 29. came to hand ten days ago: and about two days ago I received a cover of your hand writing, under which was a N. York paper of May 4. and a letter from Mr. Page to Mazzei. There being no letter from you makes me hope there is one on the way which will inform me of my Congé. I have never received Mr. Jay's answer to my public letter of Nov. 19. which you mention him to have written, and which I fear has been intercepted.[20] I know only from you that my letter got safe to hand. My baggage has been made up more than a month, so that I shall leave Paris almost in the instant of receiving the permission.

The campaign begins under unfavorable auspices for Russia. The death of the grand Seignior, who was personally disposed for peace, has brought a

18. For Mr. Joy, see Bradford Perkins, "George Joy, American Propagandist at London, 1805–1815," *New England Quarterly* 34 (1961): 191–210.

19. At the bottom of the letter, JM added: "Note—Let the amendments follow." They were enclosed in JM to TJ, June 30, 1789, below.

20. TJ received Jay's letter of Mar. 9, 1789, on July 28, 1789; see *PTJ,* XIV, pp. 628–29.

young and ardent successor to the throne, determined to push the war to extremity. Her only ally, the emperor, is in articulo mortis, and the grand Duke of Tuscany, should he succeed, loves peace and money. Denmark is forbidden by England and Prussia to furnish even it's stipulated maritime aid. There is no appearance of any other power's engaging in the war. As far as I can discover, the king of England is somewhat better in his head, but under such a complete depression of spirits, that he does not care how the world goes, and leaves his ministers to do as they please. It is impossible for you to conceive how difficult it is to know the truth relative to him, he is environed in such an atmosphere of lies. Men who would not speak a falsehood on any other subject, lie on this from a principle of duty: so that even eye witnesses cannot be believed without scanning their principles and connections; and few will stand this of the very few permitted to see him.

Committees of conciliation having failed in their endeavors to bring together the three chambers of the States general, the king proposed a specific mode of verifying their powers; for that having been the first question which presented itself to them, was the one on which the question of voting by persons or orders was first brought on. The Clergy accepted unconditionally. The Noblesse accepted on conditions which reduced the acceptance to nothing at all. The Commons considered this as a refusal on the part of the nobles, and thereupon took their definitive resolution, to invite the other two orders to come and verify their powers in common, and to notify them they should proceed with or without them to verify, and to do the business of the nation. This was on the 10th.

On the 15th. they moved to declare themselves the national assembly. The debates on this were finished yesterday when the proposition was agreed to by 400 and odd against 80 odd. The minority agreed in substance but wished some particular amendment. They then immediately made the proposition relative to taxes which I inclose you, as this moment stated to me by memory by a member who left the assembly a little before the question, because there was no opposition to the matter but only to the form. He assures me, on the information of another member who was present, that Target's motion passed.[21] We shall know I think within a day or two whether the government will risk a bankruptcy and civil war rather than see all distinction of orders done away, which is what the commons will push for. If the fear of the former alternative prevails, they will spin the matter into negociation. The Commons have in their chamber almost all the talents of the nation; they are firm and bold, yet moderate. There is indeed among them a number of very hot headed members; but those of most influence are cool, temperate, and sagacious. Every step of this house has been marked with caution and wisdom. The Noblesse on the contrary are absolutely out of their senses. They are so furious they can seldom debate at all. They have few men of moderate talents,

---

21. Guy-Jean-Baptiste Target, a leading lawyer of the Third Estate, proposed that existing taxes were illegal but should be collected provisionally until replaced by the Estates General.

and not one of great in the majority. Their proceedings have been very injudicious. The clergy are waiting to profit of every incident to secure themselves and have no other object in view. Among the commons there is an entire unanimity on the great question of voting by persons. Among the noblesse there are about 60. for the commons and about three times that number against them. Among the clergy about 20 have already come over and joined the commons, and in the course of a few days they will be joined by many more, not indeed making the majority of that house, but very near it. The bishops and archbishops have been very successful by bribes and intrigues in detaching the Curés from the Commons to whom they were at first attached to a man. The Commons are about 554. in number, of whom 344 are of the law. These do not possess an influence founded in property: but in their habits of business and acquaintance with the people, and in their means of exciting them as they please. The Curés thro' the kingdom form the mass of the clergy, they are the only part favorably known to the people, because solely charged with the duties of baptism, burial, confession, visitation of the sick, instruction of the children and aiding the poor, they are themselves of the people and united with them. The carriages and equipage only of the higher clergy, not their persons, are known to the people and are in detestation with them. The souldiers will follow their officers, that is to say their captains, lieutenants, and ensigns. These are of the lower nobility, and therefore much divided. The Colonels and higher officers are of the higher nobility, are seldom with the souldiers, little known to them, not possessing their attachment. These circumstances give them little weight in the partition of the army.

I give you these miscellaneous observations that knowing somewhat the dispositions of the parties you may be able to judge of the future for yourself, as I shall not be here to continue it's communication to you. In hopes to see you soon I conclude with assurances of the perfect esteem and respect with which I am Dear Sir Your friend and servant,

TH: JEFFERSON

ENCLOSURE

*[Extract of Proceedings of the National Assembly]*

le 17. Juin 1789.

La Chambre, assemblée vers les 10. heures du matin, lecture faite de l'arrêté de la veille, on a passé aux voix la motion suivante:

Arrêté que la Chambre des communes seroit constituée sous la dénomination d'assemblée nationale.

Que les deux chambres privilegiées n'ayant point fait vérifier leurs pouvoirs, pouroient et seroient admises à la dite vérification, soit ensemble ou individuelement.

M. Bailly, nommé Président provisoire, a prêtté serment à la chambre, ainsi que les deux sécrétaires. La chambre a fait le sien aussi.

M. Target a proposé la motion suivante comme nécessitée par la premiere:

Arrêté par la chambre que toutes les impositions actuelles n'ayant point eté sanctionnées sont toutes illégalles. Que cette illégalité a été reconnue par le Roi et les Cours

Souveraines, que cependant la chambre nationalle considerant les inconveniens qui resulteroient de la suppression des impots, elle ordonne que ceux qui se perçoivent continueront à l'etre jusqu'au dernier Jour de la tenue des Etats généraux actuels.

Translation[22]

June 17, 1789

The Chamber, assembled about 10 o'clock in the morning, reading of the decree of yesterday having been done, passed by voice vote the following motion:

Decreed that the Chamber of Commons would be constituted under the denomination of National Assembly.

That the two privileged chambers[,] not having had their credentials verified, would be and should be admitted to the said verification, either in groups or individually.

M. Bailly, named temporary President, took his oath to the Chamber, as did the two secretaries. The Chamber took its oath also.

M. Target proposed the following motion as having been made necessary by the first:

Decreed by the Chamber that all existing taxes not yet having been sanctioned are all illegal. That this illegality has been recognized by the King and the Sovereign Courts, that, however, the National Chamber considering the inconvenience which would result from the suppression of taxes, orders that those that are being collected will continue to be collected down to the last day of the session of the actual Estates General.


## Madison to Jefferson

New York June 30, 1789

DEAR SIR

By this conveyance you will receive permission through Mr. Jay to make your proposed visit to America. I fear it will not reach you in time for your arrival here before the commencement of the windy season; yet I hope the delay will not oblige you to postpone your voyage till the Spring.

The federal business has proceeded with a mortifying tardiness, chargeable in part on the incorrect draughts of Committees, and the prolixity of discussion incident to a public body, every member of which almost takes a positive agency, but principally resulting from the novelty and complexity of the subjects of Legislation. We are in a wilderness without a single footstep to guide us. Our successors will have an easier task, and by degrees the way will become smooth short and certain.

My last informed you of some of the difficulties attending a regulation of the duties. The bill on that subject has at length received the fiat of both Houses and will be forthwith made a law by the concurrence of the

---

22. I am indebted to Dr. John Hurt for this translation.

President. The rates are not precisely on the scale first settled by the House of Reps. The most material change is in the articles of rum and molasses. The necessity of preserving a certain ratio between them is obvious. The ratio sent to the Senate was that of 12 cents on the former and 5 do. on the latter. The Senate returned them in the ratio of 8 and 2½. which has, after a conference, prevailed.

The Senate has prevailed on another point in the bill which had undergone more discussion and produced more difficulty. It had been proposed by the H. of Reps. that, besides a discrimination in the tonnage, a small reduction should be made in the duty on distilled spirits imported from countries in treaty with the U. States. The Senate were opposed to any discrimination whatsoever, contending that even G. Britain should stand on the same footing with the most favored nations. The arguments on that side of the question were that the U.S. were not bound by treaty to give any commercial preferences to particular nations—that they were not bound by gratitude, since our allies had been actuated by their own interest and had obtained their compensation in the dismemberment of a rival empire—that in national and particularly in commercial measures, gratitude was moreover, no proper motive, interest alone being the Statesman's guide—that G.B. made no discrimination against the U.S. compared with other nations; but on the contrary distinguished them by a number of advantages—that if G.B. possessed almost the whole of our trade it proceeded from causes which proved that she could carry it on for us on better terms than the other nations of Europe—that we were too dependent on her trade to risk her displeasure by irritating measures which might induce her to put us on a worse footing than at present—that a small discrimination could only irritate without operating on her interests or fears—that if any thing were done it would be best to make a bolder stroke at once, and that in fact the Senate had appointed a committee to consider the subject in that point of view.

On the other side it was contended that it would be absurd to *give*[23] away every thing that could *purchase* the stipulations wanted by us, that the motives in which the new Government originated, the known sentiments of the people at large, and the laws of most of the States subsequent to the peace shewed clearly that a distinction between nations in Treaty and nations not in Treaty would coincide with the public opinion, and that it would be offensive to a great number of citizens to see G.B. in particular put on the footing of the most favored nations, by the first act of a Government instituted for the purpose of uniting the States in the vindication of their commercial interests against her monopolizing regulations—that this respect to the sentiments of the people was the more necessary in the present critical state of the Government—that our trade at present entirely contradicted the advantages expected from the Revolution, no new channels being opened with other European

---

23. JM's italics, as are the rest of the italicized words in this letter.

nations, and the British channels being narrowed by a refusal of the most natural and valuable one to the U.S.[24]—that this evil proceeded from the deep hold the British monopoly had taken of our Country, and the difficulty experienced by France Holland, etc. in entering into competition with her—that in order to break this monopoly, those nations ought to be aided till they could contend on equal terms—that the market of France was particularly desireable to us—that her disposition to open it would depend on the disposition manifested on our part, etc. etc.—that our trade would not be in its proper channels untill it should flow *directly* to the countries making the exchange, in which case too american vessels would have a due share in the transaction, whereas at present the whole carriage of our bulky produce is confined to British Bottoms—that with respect to G.B. we had good reason to suppose that her conduct would be regulated by the apparent temper of the new Government—that a passiveness under her restrictions would confirm her in them, whilst an evidence of intention as well as ability to face them would ensure a reconsideration of her policy—that it would be sufficient to begin with a moderate discrimination, exhibiting a readiness to invigorate our measures as circumstances might require—that we had no reason to apprehend a disposition in G.B. to resort to a commercial contest, or the consequences of such an experiment, her dependence on us being greater than ours on her. The supplies of the United States are necessary to the existence, and their market to the value, of her islands. The returns are either superfluities or poisons. In time of famine, the cry of which is heard every three or four years, the bread of the United States is essential. In time of war, which is generally decided in the West Indies, friendly offices, not violating the duties of neutrality, might effectually turn the scale in favor of an adversary. In the direct trade with Great Britain, the consequences ought to be equally dreaded by her. The raw and bulky exports of the United States employ her shipping, contribute to her revenue, enter into her manufactures, and enrich her merchants, who stand between the United States and the consuming nations of Europe. A suspension of the intercourse would suspend all these advantages, force the trade into rival channels from which it might not return, and besides a temporary loss of a market for ¼ of her exports, hasten the establishment of manufactures here, which would so far cut off the market forever. On the other side, the United States would suffer but little. The manufactures of Great Britain, as far as desirable, would find their way through other channels, and if the price were a little augmented it would only diminish an excessive consumption. They could do almost wholly without such supplies, and better without than with many of them. In one important view the contest would be particularly in their favor. The articles of luxury, a privation of which would be salutary to them, being the work of the indigent, may be regarded as necessaries to the manufacturing party: that it was probable nothing would be done at this session, if at all, in the way projected in the Senate; and in case a discord of opinion as to the

---

24. At a later time, JM added the footnote "with the West Indies."

mode, the degree, and the time of our regulations should become apparent, an argument would be drawn from it in favor of the very policy hitherto pursued by Great Britain. The event of the tonnage bill, in which the discrimination was meant to be most insisted on by the House of Representatives, is not yet finally decided. But here, also, the Senate will prevail. It was determined yesterday in that House to *adhere* to their amendment for striking out the clause, and there is no reason to suppose that the other House will let the Bill be lost.[25] I mentioned in my last that both the Senators of Virginia were for admitting Britain to an equality with the most favored nation. This was a mistake as to Grayson.

The other bills depending relate to the collection of the Impost, and the establishment of a war, foreign, and Treasury Department. The bills on the two first of these departments have passed the House of Representatives, and are before the Senate. They gave birth to a very interesting constitutional question—by what authority removals from office were to be made. The Constitution being silent on the point, it was left to construction. Four opinions were advanced: 1. That no removal could be made but by way of impeachment. To this it was objected that it gave to every officer, down to tide waiters and tax gatherers, the tenure of good behavior. 2. That it devolved on the Legislature, to be disposed of as might be proper. To this it was objected that the Legislature might then dispose of it to be exercised by themselves, or even by the House of Representatives. 3. That it was incident to the power of appointment, and therefore belonged to the President and Senate. To this it was said that the Senate, being a *Legislative* body, could not be considered in an *Executive* light farther than was expressly declared; that such a construction would transfer the trust of seeing the laws duly executed from the President, the most responsible, to the Senate, the least responsible branch of the Government; that officers would intrench themselves behind a party in the Senate, bid defiance to the President, and introduce anarchy and discord into the Executive Department; that the Senate were to be Judges in case of impeachment, and ought not, therefore, to be previously called on for a summary opinion on questions of removal; that in their Legislative character they ought to be kept as cool and unbiased as possible, as the constitutional check on the passions and parties of the other House, and should, for that reason also, be as little concerned as possible in those *personal* matters, which are the great source of factious animosities. 4. That the Executive power being generally vested in the President, and the Executive function of removal not expressly taken away, it remained with the President. To this was objected the rule of construction on which the third opinion rested, and the danger of creating too much weight in the Executive scale. After very long debates the 4th opinion prevailed, as most consonant to the text of the Constitution, to the policy of mixing the Legislative and Executive Departments as little as possible, and

---

25. JM's prediction was confirmed on July 1, 1789, when the House agreed to the Senate's amendment to strike out the discrimination clause.

to the requisite responsibility and harmony in the Executive Department. What the decision of the Senate will be cannot yet be even conjectured. As soon as the bills are passed, Mr. Jay and General Knox will of course have their commissions renewed.

The bill relating to the Treasury Department is still before the House of Representatives. The Board will be discontinued, but the business will be so arranged as to make the comptroller and other officers checks on the Head of the Department. It is not clear who this will be. The members of Congress are disqualified. Hamilton is most talked of.

The Senate have in hand a bill for the Judiciary Department. It is found a pretty arduous task, and will probably be long on its way through the two Houses.

Inclosed is a copy of sundry amendments to the Constitution lately proposed in the House of Representatives. Every thing of a controvertible nature that might endanger the concurrence of two-thirds of each House and three-fourths of the States was studiously avoided. This will account for the omission of several amendments which occur as proper.[26] The subject will not be taken up till the revenue and Department bills are passed.

The President has been *ill.* His fever terminated in a large anthrax on the upper end of his thigh, which is likely to confine him for some time. Wishing you an expeditious and safe passage across the Atlantic, I am, my dear Sir, yours, etc.

ENCLOSURE
*[Madison's Draft of the Bill of Rights, June 8, 1789]*[27]

The amendments which have occurred to me, proper to be recommended by congress to the state legislatures, are these:

First. That there be prefixed to the constitution a declaration—That all power is originally vested in, and consequently derived from the people.

That government is instituted, and ought to be exercised for the benefit of the people; which consists in the enjoyment of life and liberty, with the right of acquiring and using property, and generally of pursuing and obtaining happiness and safety.

That the people have an indubitable, unalienable, and indefeasible right to reform or change their government, whenever it be found adverse or inadequate to the purposes of its institution.

Secondly. That in article 1st. section 2, clause 3, these words be struck out, to wit, "The number of representatives shall not exceed one for every thirty thousand, but each state shall have at least one representative, and until such enumeration shall be made." And that in place thereof be inserted these words, to wit, "After the first actual enumeration, there shall be one representative for every thirty thousand, until the

26. JM enclosed unbound sheets from the printed *Journals of the House of Representatives* for June 8, 1789, the day when he proposed his Bill of Rights amendments; see JM to TJ, June 30, 1789, below. These sheets were issued as separate weekly numbers of Lloyd's *Congressional Register* of debates, the second number of volume I appearing on June 23, 1789; see Tinling, 543. JM's amendments are printed from this source in *PJM*, XII, pp. 197–209, and as "Enclosure: [Madison's Draft of the Bill of Rights, June 8, 1789]," below.

27. *PJM*, XII, pp. 200–3. See n. 26, above.

number amount to     after which the proportion shall be so regulated by congress, that the number shall never be less than     nor more than     but each state shall after the first enumeration, have at least two representatives; and prior thereto."

Thirdly. That in article 1st, section 6, clause 1, there be added to the end of the first sentence, these words, to wit, "But no law varying the compensation last ascertained shall operate before the next ensuing election of representatives."

Fourthly. That in article 1st, section 9, between clauses 3 and 4, be inserted these clauses, to wit, The civil rights of none shall be abridged on account of religious belief or worship, nor shall any national religion be established, nor shall the full and equal rights of conscience be in any manner, or on any pretext infringed.

The people shall not be deprived or abridged of their right to speak, to write, or to publish their sentiments; and the freedom of the press, as one of the great bulwarks of liberty, shall be inviolable.

The people shall not be restrained from peaceably assembling and consulting for their common good; nor from applying to the legislature by petitions, or remonstrances for redress of their grievances.

The right of the people to keep and bear arms shall not be infringed; a well armed, and well regulated militia being the best security of a free country: but no person religiously scrupulous of bearing arms, shall be compelled to render military service in person.

No soldier shall in time of peace be quartered in any house without the consent of the owner; nor at any time, but in a manner warranted by law.

No person shall be subject, except in cases of impeachment, to more than one punishment, or one trial for the same offence; nor shall be compelled to be a witness against himself; nor be deprived of life, liberty, or property without due process of law; nor be obliged to relinquish his property, where it may be necessary for public use, without a just compensation.

Excessive bail shall not be required, nor excessive fines imposed, nor cruel and unusual punishments inflicted.

The rights of the people to be secured in their persons, their houses, their papers, and their other property from all unreasonable searches and seizures, shall not be violated by warrants issued without probable cause, supported by oath or affirmation, or not particularly describing the places to be searched, or the persons or things to be seized.

In all criminal prosecutions, the accused shall enjoy the right to a speedy and public trial, to be informed of the cause and nature of the accusation, to be confronted with his accusers, and the witnesses against him; to have a compulsory process for obtaining witnesses in his favor; and to have the assistance of counsel for his defence.

The exceptions here or elsewhere in the constitution, made in favor of particular rights, shall not be so construed as to diminish the just importance of other rights retained by the people; or as to enlarge the powers delegated by the constitution; but either as actual limitations of such powers, or as inserted merely for greater caution.

Fifthly. That in article 1st, section 10, between clauses 1 and 2, be inserted this clause, to wit:

No state shall violate the equal rights of conscience, or the freedom of the press, or the trial by jury in criminal cases.

Sixthly. That article 3d, section 2, be annexed to the end of clause 2d, these words to wit: but no appeal to such court shall be allowed where the value in controversy shall not amount to     dollars: nor shall any fact triable by jury, according to the course of common law, be otherwise re-examinable than may consist with the principles of common law.

Seventhly. That in article 3d, section 2, the third clause be struck out, and in its place be inserted the clauses following, to wit:

The trial of all crimes (except in cases of impeachments, and cases arising in the land or naval forces, or the militia when on actual service in time of war or public danger) shall be by an impartial jury of freeholders of the vicinage, with the requisite of unanimity for conviction, of the right of challenge, and other accustomed requisites; and in all crimes punishable with loss of life or member, presentment or indictment by a grand jury, shall be an essential preliminary, provided that in cases of crimes committed within any county which may be in possession of an enemy, or in which a general insurrection may prevail, the trial may by law be authorised in some other county of the same state, as near as may be to the seat of the offence.

In cases of crimes committed not within any county, the trial may by law be in such county as the laws shall have prescribed. In suits at common law, between man and man, the trial by jury, as one of the best securities to the rights of the people, ought to remain inviolate.

Eighthly. That immediately after article 6th, be inserted, as article 7th, the clauses following, to wit:

The powers delegated by this constitution, are appropriated to the departments to which they are respectively distributed: so that the legislative department shall never exercise the powers vested in the executive or judicial; nor the executive exercise the powers vested in the legislative or judicial; nor the judicial exercise the powers vested in the legislative or executive departments.

The powers not delegated by this constitution, nor prohibited by it to the states, are reserved to the States respectively.

Ninthly. That article 7th, be numbered as article 8th.

## Jefferson to Madison

Paris July 22 and 23, 1789

DEAR SIR

My last to you was of the 18th. of June. Within a day or two after yours of May 9. came to hand. In the rest of Europe nothing remarkeable has happened; but in France such events as will be for ever memorable in history. To begin where my last left them, the king took on himself to decide the great question of voting by persons or by orders, by a declaration made at a Seance royale on the 23d. of June. In the same declaration he inserted many other things, some good some bad. The Tiers undismayed resolved that the whole was a mere nullity, and proceeded as if nothing had happened. The majority of the clergy joined them, and a small part of the Nobles. The uneasiness produced by the king's declaration occasioned the people to collect about the palace in the evening of the same day. The king and queen were alarmed and sent for Mr. Necker. He was conducted to and from the palace amidst the acclamations of the people. The French guards were observed to be mixed in

"THE GREAT RIGHTS OF MANKIND," 1789        625

great numbers with the people and to participate of their passions. This made so decisive an impression that the king on the 27th. wrote to the Clergy and Nobles who had not yet joined the Tiers, recommending to them to go and join them. They did so, and it was imagined all was now settled. It was soon observed however that troops, and those the foreign troops, were marching towards Paris from different quarters. The States addressed the king to forbid their approach. He declared it was only to preserve the tranquillity of Paris and Versailles; and I beleive he thought so. The command of those troops was given to the Marshal Broglio, and it was observed that the Baron de Breteuil was going daily to Versailles. On the 11th. there being now 30,000 foreign troops in and between Paris and Versailles Mr. Necker was dismissed and ordered to retire privately. The next day the whole ministry was changed except Villedeuil and Barentin. Breteuil, Broglio, and Vauguyon were the principal persons named in the new. A body of cavalry were advanced into Paris to awe them. The people attacked and routed them, killing one of the cavalry and losing a French guard. The corps of French guards gathered stronger, followed the cavalry, attacked them in the street (the rue basse du rempart) and killed four. (I did not know this last fact with certainty when I wrote to Mr. Jay. It is therefore not in my letter. I since have it from an eye witness.) The insurrection became now universal. The next day (the 13th.) the people forced a prison and took some arms. On the 14th. a committee was named by the city, with powers corresponding to our committees of safety. They resolve to raise a city militia of 48,000 men. The people attack the invalids and get a great store of arms. They then attack and carry the Bastille, cut off the Governor's and Lieutenant governors heads, and that also of the Prevost des marchands discovered in a treacherous correspondence. While these things were doing here, the council is said to have been agitating at Versailles a proposition to arrest a number of the members of the States, to march all the foreign troops against Paris and suppress the tumults by the sword. But the decapitations being once known there and that there were 50, or 60,000 men in arms, the king went to the States, referred every thing to them, and ordered away the troops. The city committee named the Marquis de la Fayette commander in chief, they went on organizing their militia, the tumults continued, and a noise spread about Versailles that they were coming there to massacre the court, the ministry etc. Every minister hereupon resigned and fled, the Count d'Artois Prince of Condé, Duke de Bourbon, the family of Polignacs, the Ct. de Vaudreuil, Abbé Vermont confessor of the queen and keystone of all the intrigues, all fled out of the kingdom. The king wrote to recall Mr. Necker, reappointed Monmorin and St. Priest, friends of Necker, and came with the States general to Paris to satisfy the city of his dispositions. All the streets thro which he passed were lined with Bourgeois armed with guns, pistols, swords, pikes, pruning hooks, scythes, and whatever they could lay hold of, about 60,000. The States general on foot on each side of his coach, the M. de la Fayette at their head on horseback. He returned to Versailles in the same order to the great joy of the remaining courtiers who feared he would have been detained in Paris. The tumults of the city had pretty well subsided, but to-day they have been revived by a new incident. Foulon, one of the fugitive ministers was taken in the country, (it is said by his own tenants) and brought to Paris. Every possible effort of persuasion was exerted in vain to save him. He was forced from the hands of the gardes Bourgeoises by the mob, was hung, and after severing his head, the body was dragged by the enraged populace thro' the principal streets of Paris. The Intendant of Paris (de Chauvigny) accused of having been in the riots with the late ministry and who had fled, was taken at Compiegne, and a party of 200 militia horse are now gone for him. If they bring him to Paris it will be impossible to save him. Monsieur de la Luzerne was reappointed minister of marine yesterday.

Your last letter sais nothing of my leave of absence. The season is now so advanced towards the Equinox, that if it comes to hand I shall not leave Europe till that be over. Indeed this scene is too interesting to be left at present. But if the permission does not come in time for my passage in the fall, the necessity of my going is so imperious, that I shall be in a most distressing dilemma. I am with sincere esteem and respect Dear Sir Your affectionate friend and servt.,

TH: JEFFERSON

P.S. July 23. I just learn that Bertier de Chauvigny was brought to town in the night last night and massacred immediately.

## *Jefferson to Madison*

Paris July 29, 1789

DEAR SIR

I wrote you on the 22d. Since that I have received yours of the 23d. of May. The *president's title as proposed by the senate was the most superlatively ridiculous thing I ever heard of.*[28] It is a proof the more of the justice of the *character given by Doctr. Franklin of my friend: 'Always an honest man, often a great one, but sometimes absolutely mad.'*[29] I wish *he* could have been here during the late scenes. If he could then have had one fibre of *aristocracy* left in his frame he would have been a proper subject for *bedlam.* The tranquility of this place has not been disturbed since the death of Foulon and Bertier. Supplies of bread are precarious, but there has not as yet been such a want as to produce disorder, and we may expect the new wheat harvest to begin now in ten or twelve days. You will wonder to find the harvest here so late: but from my observations (I guess, because I have not calculated their result carefully) the sun does

---

28. The italicized words in this sentence and in the rest of the letter were written in code.

29. For Franklin's description of Adams, see his letter to Robert R. Livingston, July 23, 1783, in Benjamin Franklin, *The Writings of Benjamin Franklin,* ed. Albert Henry Smyth, 10 vols. (New York, 1907), IX, p. 62.

not shine here more than 5. hours of the 24. through the whole year. I inclose you some papers worth notice, which indeed have principally induced me to address you so soon after my last. I am with perfect esteem and attachment Dear Sir Your friend and servt,

TH: JEFFERSON


*Jefferson to Madison*

Paris Aug. 28, 1789

DEAR SIR

My last to you was of July 29. Since that I have received yours of May 27. June 13. and 30. The tranquillity of the city has not been disturbed since my last. Dissensions between the French and Swiss guards occasioned some private combats in which five or six were killed. These dissensions are made up. The want of bread for some days past has greatly endangered the peace of the city. Some get a little bread, some none at all. The poor are the best served because they besiege perpetually the doors of the bakers. Notwithstanding this distress, and the palpable impotence of the city administration to furnish bread to the city, it was not till yesterday that general leave was given to the bakers to go into the country and buy flour for themselves as they can. This will soon relieve us, because the wheat harvest is well advanced. Never was there a country where the practice of governing too much had taken deeper root and done more mischeif. Their declaration of rights is finished. If printed in time I will inclose a copy with this. It is doubtful whether they will now take up the finance or the constitution first. The distress for money endangers every thing. No taxes are paid, and no money can be borrowed. Mr. Necker was yesterday to give in a memoir to the Assembly on this subject. I think they will give him leave to put into execution any plan he pleases, so as to debarrass themselves of this and take up that of the constitution. No plan is yet reported; but the leading members (with some small differences of opinion) have in contemplation the following. The Executive power in a hereditary king, with a negative on laws and power to dissolve the legislature, to be considerably restrained in the making of treaties, and limited in his expences. The legislative in a house of representatives. They propose a senate also, chosen on the plan of our federal senate by the provincial assemblies, but to be for life, of a certain age (they talk of 40. years) and certain wealth (4 or 500 guineas a year) but to have no other power as to laws but to remonstrate against them to the representatives, who will then determine their fate by a simple majority. This you will readily perceive is a mere council of revision like that of New York, which, in order to be something, must form an alliance with the king, to avail themselves of his veto. The alliance will be useful to both and to the nation. The representatives to be chosen every two or three years. The judiciary system is less prepared than any other part of their plan. However they will abolish the parliaments, and establish an order of judges and justices, general and provincial, a good deal like ours, with trial by jury in criminal cases certainly, perhaps also in civil. The provinces will have assemblies for their provincial government, and the cities a municipal body for municipal government, all founded on the basis of popular election. These subordinate governments, tho completely dependant on the general one, will be entrusted with almost the whole of the details which our state governments exercise. They will have their own judiciary, final in all but great cases, the Executive business will principally pass through their hands, and a certain local legislation will be allowed them. In short ours has been professedly their model, in which such changes are made as a difference of circumstance rendered necessary and some others neither necessary nor advantageous, but into which men will ever run when versed in theory and new in the practice of government, when acquainted with man only as they see him in their books and not in the world. This plan will undoubtedly undergo changes in the assembly, and the longer it is delayed the greater will be the changes: for that assembly, or rather the patriotic part of it, hooped together heretofore by a common enemy, are less compact since their victory. That enemy (the civil and ecclesiastical aristocracy) begins to raise it's head. The lees too of the patriotic party, of wicked principles and desperate fortunes, hoping to pillage something in the wreck of their country, are attaching themselves to the faction of the Duke of Orleans, that faction is caballing with the populace, and intriguing at London, the Hague and Berlin and have evidently in view the transfer of the crown to the D. of Orleans. He is a man of moderate understanding, of no principle, absorbed in low vice, and incapable of abstracting himself from the filth of that to direct any thing else. His name and his money therefore are mere tools in the hands of those who are duping him. *Mirabeau is their chief.*[30] They may produce a temporary confusion, and even a temporary civil war, supported as they will be by the money of England; but they cannot have success ultimately. The king, the mass of the substantial people of the whole country, the army, and the influential part of the clergy, form a firm phalanx which must prevail. Should those delays which necessarily attend the deliberations of a body of 1200 men give time to this plot to ripen and burst so as to break up the assembly before any thing definitive is done, a constitution, the principles of which are pretty well settled in the minds of the assembly, will be proposed by the national militia (*that is by*[31] *their commander*) urged by the individual members of the assembly, signed by the king, and supported by the nation, to prevail till circumstances shall permit it's revision and more regular sanction. This I suppose the pis-aller[32] of their affairs, while their probable event is a peaceable settlement of them. They fear a war from England Holland and Prussia. I think England will give money, but not make war. Holland

---

30. The italicized words in this sentence and in the rest of the letter were written in code.
31. JM supplied this word, which was not encoded by TJ.
32. JM added a marginal note: "the worst event."

would soon be afire internally were she to be embroiled in external difficulties. Prussia must know this and act accordingly.

It is impossible to desire better dispositions towards us, than prevail in this assembly. Our proceedings have been viewed as a model for them on every occasion; and tho in the heat of debate men are generally disposed to contradict every authority urged by their opponents, ours has been treated like that of the bible, open to explanation but not to question. I am sorry that in the moment of such a disposition any thing should come from us to check it. The placing them on a mere footing with the English will have this effect. When of two nations, the one has engaged herself in a ruinous war for us, has spent her blood and money to save us, has opened her bosom to us in peace, and receive us almost on the footing of her own citizens, while the other has moved heaven, earth and hell to exterminate us in war, has insulted us in all her councils in peace, shut her doors to us in every part where her interests would admit it, libelled us in foreign nations, endeavored to poison them against the reception of our most precious commodities, to place these two nations on a footing, is to give a great deal more to one than to the other if the maxim be true that to make unequal quantities equal you must add more to the one than the other. To say in excuse that gratitude is never to enter into the motives of national conduct, is to revive a principle which has been buried for centuries with it's kindred principles of the lawfulness of assassination, poison, perjury etc. All of these were legitimate principles in the dark ages which intervened between antient and modern civilisation, but exploded and held in just horror in the 18th century. I know but one code of morality for man whether acting singly or collectively. He who says I will be a rogue when I act in company with a hundred others but an honest man when I act alone, will be believed in the former assertion, but not in the latter. I would say with the poet 'hic niger est, hunc tu Romane caveto.'[33] If the morality of one man produces a just line of conduct in him, acting individually, why should not the morality of 100 men produce a just line of conduct in them acting together? But I indulge myself in these reflections because my own feelings run me into them: with you they were always acknoleged. Let us hope that our new government will take some other occasion to shew that they mean to proscribe no virtue from the canons of their conduct with other nations. In every other instance the new government has ushered itself to the world as honest, masculine and dignified. It has shewn genuine dignity in my opinion in exploding adulatory titles; they are the offerings of abject baseness, and nourish that degrading vice in the people.

I must now say a word on the declaration of rights you have been so good as to send me. I like it as far as it goes; but I should have been for going further. For instance the following alterations and additions would have pleased me. Art. 4. 'The people shall not be deprived or abridged of their right

---

33. The translation of the quotation, from Horace's *Satires,* reads: "That man is black of heart; of him beware, good Roman"; see *PJM,* XII, p. 365.

to speak to write or *otherwise*[34] to publish any thing but false facts affecting injuriously the life, liberty, property, or reputation of others or affecting the peace of the confederacy with foreign nations. Art. 7. All facts put in issue before any judicature shall be tried by jury except 1. in cases of admiralty jurisdiction wherein a foreigner shall be interested, 2. in cases cognisable before a court martial concerning only the regular officers and souldiers of the U.S. or members of the militia in actual service in time of war or insurrection, and 3. in impeachments allowed by the constitution.—Art. 8. No person shall be held in confinement more than —— days after they shall have demanded and been refused a writ of Hab. corp. by the judge appointed by law nor more than —— days after such writ shall have been served on the person holding him in confinement and no order given on due examination for his remandment or discharge, nor more than —— hours in any place at a greater distance than —— miles from the usual residence of some judge authorised to issue the writ of Hab. corp. nor shall that writ be suspended for any term exceeding one year nor in any place more than —— miles distant from the station or encampment of enemies or of insurgents.—Art. 9. Monopolies may be allowed to persons for their own productions in literature and their own inventions in the arts for a term not exceeding —— years but for no longer term and no other purpose.—Art. 10. All troops of the U.S. shall stand ipso facto disbanded at the expiration of the term for which their pay and subsistence shall have been last voted by Congress, and all officers and souldiers not natives of the U.S. shall be incapable of serving in their armies by land except during a foreign war.' These restrictions I think are so guarded as to hinder evil only. However if we do not have them now, I have so much confidence in my countrymen as to be satisfied that we shall have them as soon as the degeneracy of our government shall render them necessary.

I have no certain news of P. Jones. I understand only in a general way that some persecution on the part of his officers occasioned his being called to Petersburgh, and that tho protected against them by the empress, he is not yet restored to his station. Silas Deane is coming over to finish his days in America, not having one sou to subsist on elsewhere. He is a wretched monument of the consequences of a departure from right.

I will before my departure write Colo. Lee fully the measures I pursued to procure success in his business, and which as yet offer little hope, and I shall leave it in the hands of Mr. Short to be pursued if any prospect opens on him.

I propose to sail from Havre as soon after the 1st. of October as I can get a vessel: and shall consequently leave this place a week earlier than that. As my daughters will be with me, and their baggage somewhat more than that of mere voyageures, I shall endeavor if possible to obtain a passage for Virginia directly. Probably I shall be there by the last of November. If my immediate attendance at New York should be requisite for any purpose, I will leave them with a relation near Richmond and proceed immediately to New York. But as I

---

34. JM's italics.

do not foresee any pressing purpose for that journey immediately on my arrival, and as it will be a great saving of time to finish at once in Virginia so as to have no occasion to return there after having once gone on to the Northward, I expect to proceed to my own house directly. Staying there two months (which I believe will be necessary) and allowing for the time I am on the road, I may expect to be at New York in February, and to embark from thence, or some eastern port.

You ask me if I would accept any appointment on that side the water? You know the circumstances which led me from retirement, step by step and from one nomination to another, up to the present. My object is a return to the same retirement. Whenever therefore I quit the present, it will not be to engage in any other office, and most especially any one which would require a constant residence from home.

The books I have collected for you will go off for Havre in three or four days with my baggage. From that port I shall try to send them by a direct occasion to New York. I am with great and sincere esteem Dr. Sir your affectionate friend and servant,

TH: JEFFERSON

P.S. I just now learn that Mr. Necker proposed yesterday to the National assembly a loan of 80. millions, on terms more tempting to the lender than the former, and that they approve it, leaving him to arrange the details in order that they might occupy themselves at once about the constitution.


*Jefferson to Madison*

Paris Sept. 6, 1789

DEAR SIR

I sit down to write to you without knowing by what occasion I shall send my letter. I do it because a subject comes into my head which I would wish to develope a little more than is practicable in the hurry of the moment of making up general dispatches.

The question Whether one generation of men has a right to bind another, seems never to have been started [stated?] either on this or our side of the water.[35] Yet it is a question of such consequences as not only to merit

35. Despite this statement, TJ had, at an earlier date, tried to persuade Lafayette to include the principle about the "rights of succeeding generations" in his draft of the Declaration of the Rights of Man. Georges Lefebvre, a leading historian of the French Revolution, wrote that "it was in fact with Jefferson, as early as January 1789, that LaFayette discussed his project 'for a Declaration;' the text that he presented to the Assembly on July 11, with the accompanying letter, has been found in the papers of the ambassador of the United States, annotated by his hand"; see Lefebvre, p. 214. Gilbert Chinard made the same point in 1929, noting that "the second text of Lafayette's declaration was annotated by Jefferson in pencil"; see Chinard, pp. 80-82, 140. For full discussions of this famous letter, see *PTJ*, XV, pp. 384-91, and Koch, pp. 62-96. For variations between the recipient's copy presented here and the file copy, see *PTJ*, XV, pp. 392-98, and *PJM*, XII, pp. 382-88.

decision, but place also, among the fundamental principles of every government. The course of reflection in which we are immersed here on the elementary principles of society has presented this question to my mind; and that no such obligation can be so transmitted I think very capable of proof.

I set out on this ground, which I suppose to be self evident, *'that the earth belongs in usufruct to the living'*:[36] that the dead have neither powers nor rights over it. The portion occupied by any individual ceases to be his when himself ceases to be, and reverts to the society. If the society has formed no rules for the appropriation of it's lands in severalty, it will be taken by the first occupants. These will generally be the wife and children of the decedent. If they have formed rules of appropriation, those rules may give it to the wife and children, or to some one of them, or to the legatee of the deceased. So they may give it to his creditor. But the child, the legatee, or creditor takes it, not by any natural right, but by a law of the society of which they are members, and to which they are subject. Then no man can, by *natural right*,[37] oblige the lands he occupied, or the persons who succeed him in that occupation, to the paiment of debts contracted by him. For if he could, he might, during his own life, eat up the usufruct of the lands for several generations to come, and then the lands would belong to the dead, and not to the living, which would be the reverse of our principle.

What is true of every member of the society individually, is true of them all collectively, since the rights of the whole can be no more than the sum of the rights of the individuals.

To keep our ideas clear when applying them to a multitude, let us suppose a whole generation of men to be born on the same day, to attain mature age on the same day, and to die on the same day, leaving a succeeding generation in the moment of attaining their mature age all together. Let the ripe age be supposed of 21. years, and their period of life 34. years more, that being the average term given by the bills of mortality to persons who have already attained 21. years of age. Each successive generation would, in this way, come on, and go off the stage at a fixed moment, as individuals do now. Then I say the earth belongs to each of these generations, during it's course, fully, and in their own right. The 2d. generation receives it clear of the debts and incumberances of the 1st. the 3d of the 2d. and so on. For if the 1st. could charge it with a debt, then the earth would belong to the dead and not the living generation. Then no generation can contract debts greater than may be paid during the course of it's own existence. At 21. years of age they may bind themselves and their lands for 34. years to come: at 22. for 33: at 23. for 32. and at 54. for one year only; because these are the terms of life which remain to them at those respective epochs.

But a material difference must be noted between the succession of an

---

36. TJ's italics.
37. TJ's italics.

individual, and that of a whole generation. Individuals are parts only of a society, subject to the laws of the whole. These laws may appropriate the portion of land occupied by a decedent to his creditor rather than to any other, or to his child on condition he satisfies the creditor. But when a whole generation, that is, the whole society dies, as in the case we have supposed, and another generation or society succeeds, this forms a whole, and there is no superior who can give their territory to a third society, who may have lent money to their predecessors beyond their faculties of paying.

What is true of a generation all arriving to self-government on the same day, and dying all on the same day, is true of those in a constant course of decay and renewal, with this only difference. A generation coming in and going out entire, as in the first case, would have a right in the 1st. year of their self-dominion to contract a debt for 33. years, in the 10th. for 24. in the 20th. for 14. in the 30th. for 4. whereas generations, changing daily by daily deaths and births, have one constant term, beginning at the date of their contract, and ending when a majority of those of full age at that date shall be dead. The length of that term may be estimated from the tables of mortality, corrected by the circumstances of climate, occupation etc. peculiar to the country of the contractors. Take, for instance, the table of M. de Buffon wherein he states 23,994 deaths, and the ages at which they happened. Suppose a society in which 23,994 persons are born every year, and live to the ages stated in this table. The conditions of that society will be as follows. 1st. It will consist constantly of 617,703. persons of all ages. 2ly. Of those living at any one instant of time, one half will be dead in 24. years 8. months. 3dly. 10,675 will arrive every year at the age of 21. years complete. 4ly. It will constantly have 348,417 persons of all ages above 21. years. 5ly. And the half of those of 21. years and upwards living at any one instant of time will be dead in 18. years 8. months, or say 19. years as the nearest integral number. Then 19. years is the term beyond which neither the representatives of a nation, nor even the whole nation itself assembled, can validly extend a debt.

To render this conclusion palpable by example, suppose that Louis XIV. and XV. had contracted debts in the name of the French nation to the amount of 10,000 milliards of livres, and that the whole had been contracted in Genoa. The interest of this sum would be 500. milliards, which is said to be the whole rent roll or nett proceeds of the territory of France. Must the present generation of men have retired from the territory in which nature produced them, and ceded it to the Genoese creditors? No. They have the same rights over the soil on which they were produced, as the preceding generations had. They derive these rights not from their predecessors, but from nature. They then and their soil are by nature clear of the debts of their predecessors.

Again suppose Louis XV. and his cotemporary generation had said to the money-lenders of Genoa, give us money that we may eat, drink, and be merry in our day; and on condition you will demand no interest till the end of 19. years you shall then for ever after receive an annual interest of *12⅝ per cent.[38] The money is lent on these conditions, is divided among the living, eaten, drank, and squandered. Would the present generation be obliged to apply the produce of the earth and of their labour to replace their dissipations? Not at all.

I suppose that the recieved opinion, that the public debts of one generation devolve on the next, has been suggested by our seeing habitually in private life that he who succeeds to lands is required to pay the debts of his ancestor or testator: without considering that this requisition is municipal only, not moral; flowing from the will of the society, which has found it convenient to appropriate lands, become vacant by the death of their occupant, on the condition of a paiment of his debts: but that between society and society, or generation and generation, there is no municipal obligation, no umpire but the law of nature. We seem not to have percieved that, by the law of nature, one generation is to another as one independant nation to another.

The interest of the national debt of France being in fact but a two thousandth part of it's rent roll, the paiment of it is practicable enough: and so becomes a question merely of honor, or of expediency. But with respect to future debts, would it not be wise and just for that nation to declare, in the constitution they are forming, that neither the legislature, nor the nation itself, can validly contract more debt than they may pay within their own age, or within the term of 19. years? And that all future contracts will be deemed void as to what shall remain unpaid at the end of 19. years from their date? This would put the lenders, and the borrowers also, on their guard. By reducing too the faculty of borrowing within it's natural limits, it would bridle the spirit of war, to which too free a course has been procured by the inattention of money-lenders to this law of nature, that succeeding generations are not responsible for the preceding.

On similar ground it may be proved that no society can make a perpetual constitution, or even a perpetual law. The earth belongs always to the living generation. They may manage it then, and what proceeds from it, as they please, during their usufruct. They are masters too of their own persons, and consequently may govern them as they please. But persons and property make the sum of the objects of government. The constitution and the laws of their predecessors extinguished then in their natural course with those who gave them being. This could preserve that being till it ceased to be itself, and no longer. Every constitution then, and every law, naturally expires at the end of 19 years. If it be enforced longer, it is an act of force, and not of right.

It may be said that the succeeding generation exercising in fact the power of repeal, this leaves them as free as if the constitution or law had been expressly limited to 19 years only. In the first place, this objection admits the right, in proposing an equivalent. But the power of repeal is not an equivalent. It might be indeed if every form of government were so perfectly contrived

38. TJ used the asterisk to add this footnote: "100£, at a compound interest of 5. percent, makes, at the end of 19. years, an aggregate of principal and interest of £252-14, the interest of which is 12£-12s-7d which is nearly 12⅝ per cent on the first capital of 100.£."

that the will of the majority could always be obtained fairly and without impediment. But this is true of no form. The people cannot assemble themselves. Their representation is unequal and vicious. Various checks are opposed to every legislative proposition. Factions get possession of the public councils. Bribery corrupts them. Personal interests lead them astray from the general interests of their constituents: and other impediments arise so as to prove to every practical man that a law of limited duration is much more manageable than one which needs a repeal.

This principle that the earth belongs to the living, and not to the dead, is of very extensive application and consequences, in every country, and most especially in France. It enters into the resolution of the questions Whether the nation may change the descent of lands holden in tail? Whether they may change the appropriation of lands given antiently to the church, to hospitals, colleges, orders of chivalry, and otherwise in perpetuity? Whether they may abolish the charges and privileges attached on lands, including the whole catalogue ecclesiastical and feudal? It goes to hereditary offices, authorities and jurisdictions; to hereditary orders, distinctions and appellations; to perpetual monopolies in commerce, the arts and sciences; with a long train of et ceteras: and it renders the question of reimbursement a question of generosity and not of right. In all these cases, the legislature of the day could authorize such appropriations and establishments for their own time, but no longer; and the present holders, even where they, or their ancestors, have purchased, are in the case of bonâ fide purchasers of what the seller had no right to convey.

Turn this subject in your mind, my dear Sir, and particularly as to the power of contracting debts; and develope it with that perspicuity and cogent logic so peculiarly yours. Your station in the councils of our country gives you an opportunity of producing it to public consideration, of forcing it into discussion. At first blush it may be rallied, as a theoretical speculation: but examination will prove it to be solid and salutary. It would furnish matter for a fine preamble to our first law for appropriating the public revenue; and it will exclude at the threshold of our new government the contagious and ruinous errors of this quarter of the globe, which have armed despots with means, not sanctioned by nature, for binding in chains their fellow men. We have already given in example one effectual check to the Dog of war by transferring the power of letting him loose from the Executive to the Legislative body, from those who are to spend to those who are to pay. I should be pleased to see this second obstacle held out by us also in the first instance. No nation can make a declaration against the validity of long-contracted debts so disinterestedly as we, since we do not owe a shilling which may not be paid with ease, principal and interest, within the time of our own lives.

Establish the principle also in the new law to be passed for protecting copyrights and new inventions, by securing the exclusive right for 19. instead of 14. years. Besides familiarising us to this term, it will be an instance the more of our taking reason for our guide, instead of English precedent, the habit of which fetters us with all the political heresies of a nation equally remarkeable for it's early excitement from some errors, and long slumbering under others.

I write you no news, because, when an occasion occurs, I shall write a separate letter for that. I am always with great and sincere esteem, dear Sir Your affectionate friend and servt,

TH: JEFFERSON

## *Jefferson to Madison*

Paris Sept. 17, 1789

DEAR SIR

I have sent to Havre the following packages, with directions to send them by the first vessel to New York to your address. TI. No. 29. a box of books. These were packed before I took a list of them, therefore I cannot inform you of it's contents. I believe the whole are for you; tho' should it be otherwise the person's name will always be found written on or in the book.

TI. No. 33. T.I. No. 34. T.I. No. 35. Three boxes containing each of them two busts in plaister of Admiral P. Jones which he destines for yourself, Genl. St. Clair, Mr. Ross of Philadelphia, Mr. Charles Thomson, Colo. Wadsworth and Colo. Carrington, and of which he asks your and their acceptance. I trouble you with the consignment to avoid the confusion and errors that might have taken place if consigned severally. In the box No. 29. I have put a collection of the proofs in tin of the medals voted by the U.S. (except two, of which the dies are in America) the medals themselves not being allowed to be taken, I desired the workmen to let me have two sets of their last proofs; for their manner is, as their work proceeds, to make impressions of it in pure tin, in order to correct etc. These proofs are in fact more delicate than the medals themselves, and the last of them shew the impressions complete. I have had them arranged in a frame, under glass etc. and beg your acceptance of them.[39] This letter will go with the boxes. I am with sincere esteem, Dear Sir, Your affectionate friend and servt,

TH: JEFFERSON

## *Madison to Jefferson*

New York Oct. 8, 1787 [i.e., 1789]

DEAR SIR

A concurrence of motives has detained me here since the adjournment of Congress. One of them has been a hope of your arrival within the time. I set off tomorrow for Philada. where I shall remain some days, and not without a continuance of the same hope. I need not tell you how much pleasure I should

---

39. The medals are illustrated in *PTJ,* XVI, pp. 53–66.

feel in making my journey to Virginia coincide with yours, nor with how much patience I should on that account alone await your arrival were it certainly to be at a short date. But I wish on a public account to see you as soon as possible after you become informed of the new destination provided for you.[40] It is of infinite importance that you should not disappoint the public wish on this subject. Be persuaded of this truth, with proper opportunity it can be demonstrated to you. Let me particularly intreat you not to yield hastily to objections. The President is anxious for your acceptance of the trust. The Southern and Western Country have it particularly at heart. To every other part of the Union it will be sincerely acceptable. Drop me a line the moment you get on shore. If I receive it in Philada. I will if possible wait for you. Your appointment will not interfere with your intended trip to Virginia. *I know*[41] that the President does not mean that it shall. If I should be gone from Philada. your letter will follow me. Directions will be given for that purpose. I shall leave this in the hands of Mr. St. Trise, who will watch the first moment of putting it into yours. He is I believe already known to you. If he is not, his worth recommends him to this opportunity of being so. Yours mo: affectly.

Js. MADISON JR

*Madison to Jefferson*

Fredericksburg Nov. 1, [1789]

DEAR SIR

In the letter left for you in N. York on my leaving that place I omitted to mention to you three names which solicit a Clerkship in the office which will be under your direction. They are Mr. Fisher, Mr. Smith, and Mr. Orr. The first has vouchers of his pretensions which will enable you to decide readily on them. The second is a son of Merriwether Smith. I am not personally acquainted with him but am told he is a youth of real merit. The third is a nephew of Colo. Grayson. I have never seen him but understand that he is a youth of parts, and if put into a proper line might rise into consequence. My information however comes thro' a channel that may be partial. In mentioning these names I fulfil an expectation which circumstances have produced. You will understand at the same time that nothing more is meant than merely to lead you into proper inquiries, and enable you to form proper comparisons.

I am this far on my way to Orange. I was detained in Philada. a fortnight after I determined to await no longer your arrival, by an indisposition, which is still troublesome to me, but not worse than when I left Philada. I am Dr. Sir yr. mo: affectly.

Js. MADISON JR

40. Washington's appointment of TJ as secretary of state had been confirmed on Sept. 26, 1789.
41. JM's italics.

# 14

# THE CONGRESSMAN AND THE SECRETARY OF STATE, 1790

*L*ESS THAN A MONTH after he became president, George Washington asked Madison if Jefferson would serve in his administration. "Being *unacquainted with your mind*," Madison told his friend, "*I* have not *ventured on an answer*."¹ Caught up in the midst of the French Revolution, Jefferson promptly decided that he did not want an appointment at home, but instead preferred to retain his post in France or to retire from public life: "Whenever therefore I quit the present, it will not be to engage in any other office, and most especially any one which would require a constant residence from home."²

While Jefferson's letter was in transit, Washington decided to offer the veteran diplomat the post of secretary of state, basing his decision on "the talents and disposition which I knew you to possess and entertain for the Service of your Country."³ When Jefferson landed at Norfolk in November 1789, he learned from news accounts of his nomination; Washington's letter caught up with him two weeks later. On his leisurely progress westward to Monticello, he postponed a decision, even after the Virginia legislature—both the House and the Senate—congratulated him on being called "to fill a Post in which you may be engaged in a manner suitable to your talents."⁴

From Richmond, he made the "plunge into the Forests of Albemarle," arriving at Monticello just before Christmas.⁵ A day or two after Christmas,

1. JM to TJ, May 27, 1789, above.
2. TJ to JM, Aug. 28, 1789, above. Because the ship carrying this letter had to put in to port for repairs, JM did not receive it until late in January, after TJ's return to the United States; see JM to TJ, Jan. 24, 1790, below.
3. George Washington to TJ, Oct. 13, 1789, in *PTJ*, XV, p. 519.
4. *PTJ*, XVI, pp. 11–12.
5. TJ to William Short, Dec. 14, 1789, *ibid.*, p. 28.

Madison "took a ride to Monticello," his first visit to Jefferson's home, where the two friends had a warm reunion after a separation of five and a half years.[6] They talked of many things, Jefferson recalled, while "I had the happiness of possessing you at Monticello": the Mississippi question, American captives held in Algeria, the effort to introduce American salt provisions into France, and Jefferson's letter about the earth belonging to the living.[7] But Madison's chief reason for his hasty visit was to consult with Jefferson about "the new destination provided for you. It is of infinite importance that you should not disappoint the public wish on this subject." As President Washington's emissary, Madison assured his friend that "the President is anxious for your acceptance of the trust. The Southern and Western Country have it particularly at heart. To every other part of the Union it will be sincerely acceptable."[8]

Madison failed to persuade Jefferson, but he reported optimistically to the president: "All whom I have heard speak on the subject are remarkably solicitous for his acceptance, and I flatter myself that they will not in the final event be disappointed."[9] As soon as he returned to Congress, Madison orchestrated a campaign of persuasion, beginning with the president, who wrote Jefferson immediately "after the arrival of Mr. Madison, who I understood had been with you." The secretary of state would play a "*very* important" role in "the successful Administration of the general Government," an object that Washington considered "of almost infinite consequence to the present and future happiness of the Citizens of the United States."[10]

Three days later, Madison followed up the president's letter to assure his friend that "a universal anxiety is expressed for your acceptance; and to repeat my declarations that such an event will be more conducive to the general good, and perhaps to the very objects you have in view in Europe, than your return to your former station."[11] Nor did Madison overlook local pressure. He seems to have collaborated with an Albemarle County committee headed by James Monroe, which prepared an address of welcome for their distinguished neighbor. Declaring that it was they who first "elected you our representative," the committee argued that "America has still occasion for your services."[12]

In his response to his neighbors, Jefferson foreshadowed his decision. Acknowledging that his neighbors' suffrage had ushered him onto the stage of

6. JM to George Washington, Jan. 4, 1790, in *PJM,* XII, p. 467.
7. TJ to JM, Jan. 9, 1790, below. See also *PTJ,* XVI, p. 126n.
8. JM to TJ, Oct. 8, 1789, above.
9. JM to George Washington, Jan. 4, 1790, in *PJM,* XII, p. 467.
10. George Washington to TJ, Jan. 21, 1790, in *PTJ,* XVI, pp. 116-18.
11. JM to TJ, Jan. 24, 1790, below.
12. *PTJ,* XVI, pp. 170-78. Boyd argues that "the timing, the matter, and the tone of the address" suggest that JM had discussed the address with Monroe and the other signers. Also see Peterson, p. 393, and Malone, II, pp. 246-48.

public life "in the holy cause of freedom," he pledged to serve "wherever I may be stationed," bowing to "the will of my country."[13] Two days after his response to his neighbors, Jefferson notified the president and Madison of his acceptance and asked Madison to find him "a temporary and decent" lodging in New York.[14]

While the friends were together at Monticello, Jefferson had mentioned his Paris letter about the earth belonging to the living, but he had absentmindedly forgotten to hand it to Madison after carrying it from France. Since he wanted Madison's opinion on his generational theory, he carefully reviewed the four-month-old letter, found no reason to alter it, and finally mailed it to New York for Madison's consideration.[15]

Madison's response must have been a severe test of their friendship. Although he praised Jefferson's idea as "a great one" and confessed that many of his first thoughts coincided with those of his friend, he was skeptical of the doctrine, observing that it was not "in *all* respects compatible with the course of human affairs." As he understood Jefferson's argument, it involved four propositions: since the earth belongs to the living, not the dead, the living generation can only bind itself; by Jefferson's calculations, a generation spans nineteen years, and the validity of every act of society is limited to that term; every declaration of public will to be valid must be expressly enacted; and in every society, the will of the majority binds the minority.

Madison then methodically demolished each of these propositions, usually on practical grounds although in one case he listed objections "both in Theory and practice." For purposes of his rebuttal, he divided the political acts of a society into three categories: a fundamental constitution, laws containing some provisions making them irrevocable at the will of the legislature, and ordinary laws involving no such irrevocable quality. Having just been through an extraordinarily difficult campaign to frame and implement a fundamental constitution, Madison strongly opposed the idea of each generation having to go through that ordeal at predictably fixed dates. He ticked off three objections: a government so often revised would lose "those prejudices in its favor which antiquity inspires, . . . a salutary aid to the most rational Government in the most enlightened age"; total revision periodically would engender pernicious factions that might not otherwise come into existence; and a government that ended with a fixed date would almost certainly end in an interregnum.

As for laws containing elements irrevocable by the legislature, Madison thought that Jefferson's doctrine should not apply in at least three categories: land, debts, and other obligations. If the earth were the gift of nature to the

13. See TJ's response to the Albemarle welcome, Feb. 12, 1790, in *PTJ*, XVI, pp. 178–79.
14. TJ to JM, Feb. 14, 1790, below.
15. TJ to JM, Jan. 9, 1790, below.

living, the title extended to the earth "in its natural State only," he argued. "The *improvements* made by the dead form a charge against the living who take the benefit of them." As for debts, they could be incurred for purposes that benefited posterity as well as the present generation; "such perhaps is the present debt of the U. States," which might take longer than nineteen years to discharge. As for other kinds of obligations, Madison was convinced that there was "a foundation in the nature of things, in the relation which one generation bears to another, for the *descent* of obligations from one to another. Equity requires it. Mutual good is promoted by it."

Finally, even ordinary laws probably did not need or require express reaffirmation every nineteen years. Under Jefferson's doctrine, however, unless they were kept in force by new acts "regularly anticipating the end of the term, all the rights depending on positive laws, that is, most of the rights of property would become absolutely defunct." There would be violent struggles periodically between "those interested in reviving and those interested in new-modelling the former state of property." Land values would depreciate, the reverence for contractual obligations would weaken, and "the steady exertions of industry produced by permanent laws" would decline.

After this barrage of criticism of "the difficulties inseparable" from Jefferson's unworkable scheme, Madison could find no relief except "in the received doctrine that a tacit assent may be given to established Constitutions and laws, and that this assent may be inferred, where no positive dissent appears." Without tacit assent, there would be no civil society. Madison flatly rejected Jefferson's idea that the right of the majority to bind the minority was founded on the law of nature. Majority rule was not decreed by the law of nature, where "*unanimity* was necessary." It flowed, instead, "from compact founded on conveniency" for civil society. If neither tacit nor implied assent could be assumed, "where no positive evidence forbids, persons born in Society would not on attaining ripe age be bound by acts of the Majority; and either a *unanimous* repetition of every law would be necessary on the accession of new members, or an express assent must be obtained from these to the rule by which the voice of the Majority is made the voice of the whole."

After rejecting all of the examples that Jefferson had used to validate his generational theory, Madison concluded that "a limitation of the validity of national acts to the computed life of a nation, is in some instances not required by Theory, and in others cannot be accomodated to practice." But he then softened his critical remarks, observing that it is always easy "to espy the little difficulties immediately incident to every great plan." His remarks, he concluded, were not meant "to impeach either the utility of the principle in some particular cases; or the general importance of it in the eye of the philosophical Legislator." Indeed, it would give him pleasure to see the principle announced in federal legislation to prevent the living generation from imposing "unjust or unnecessary burdens" on their successors. "But," he added, "this is a pleasure which I have little hope of enjoying." As a veteran legislative leader, he noted that the spirit of philosophical legislation "is by no means the fashion here, either within or without Congress." It would be years before "many of the sublime truths which are seen thro' the medium of Philosophy, become visible to the naked eye of the ordinary Politician."[16]

Jefferson's theory, with its argument against public debts binding the next generation, reached Madison at the moment Congress was debating Alexander Hamilton's "Report on Public Credit," the proposal for funding the national debt. It recommended pledging a portion of the government's revenue to the payment of principal and accumulated interest on the Revolutionary war debt, which totaled more than $52 million. The foreign debt, including the $1.5 million of interest in arrears on the French debt, amounted to $11.7 million; and the domestic debt, including $13 million in overdue interest, had reached $40.4 million. In addition, the war debts of the states were estimated at $25 million. Hamilton proposed that the federal government assume the state debts and that the total obligation of $77 million be paid at face value in specie.

"On the foreign debt," Madison informed Jefferson, "the vote has been unanimous." He reported that efforts had been made to scale down the domestic debt, a move that he opposed. He accepted the necessity of funding that debt in full, but he broke with Hamilton by proposing to discriminate between the original holders of government securities—soldiers, farmers, and merchants—and subsequent purchasers, often speculators who had paid only a fraction of the nominal value.[17] "My idea," he wrote, "is . . . that the highest market price only should be allowed to the purchasers, and the balance be applied to solace the original sufferers, whose claims were not in conscience extinguished by a *forced* payment in *depreciated* certificates. The equity of this proposition is not contested."[18]

Madison thought that discrimination in favor of the original holders was based on both justice and morality, arguing that America should erect monuments of her gratitude to those who saved her liberties, not "to those who had enriched themselves in her funds" by speculating in the national debt. Hamilton agreed that the plight of those who had sold for a fraction of the face value of their certificates was "a hard one," but he rejected discrimination between groups of creditors as "equally unjust and impolitic" and as ruinous to the

---

16. JM to TJ, Feb. 4, 1790, below. TJ, who always adhered to his doctrine, never commented on JM's philosophical chiding, but late in life he did incorporate the idea of tacit assent into his theory; see TJ to Thomas Earle, Sept. 24, 1823, in L. and B., XV, pp. 470–71. Adrienne Koch, *Jefferson and Madison: The Great Collaboration* (New York, 1950), pp. 62–96, has the fullest discussion of the exchange between the two friends, but she relies on a version of JM's letter that he revised after TJ's death. *PJM,* XIII, pp. 18–26, and *PTJ,* XVI, pp. 146–54, print both versions of JM's letter.

17. On speculation in the public debt, see E. James Ferguson, *The Power of the Purse: A History of American Public Finance, 1776–1790* (Chapel Hill, 1961), pp. 281–86.

18. JM to TJ, Feb. 14, 1790, below.

public credit. Congress agreed with Hamilton by a 3-to-1 margin and sent the funding bill to the Senate.[19]

Jefferson arrived in the nation's capital after "this game was over, and another was on the carpet," the assumption by the federal government of the Revolutionary war debts of the states. As Jefferson later recalled, he was "a stranger to the ground, a stranger to the actors on it, so long absent as to have lost all familiarity with the subject, and as yet unsure of its object"; accordingly, he "took no concern in it." But he observed that "this measure produced the most bitter and angry contests ever known in Congress, before or since the union of the states." In 1783, Madison had proposed assumption in order to win support for the federal impost; at that time, Virginia's war debt exceeded her prorated portion of the state requisition to pay all state debts. By 1790, however, the Old Dominion had retired half of its war debt, and Hamilton's proposal, as he told Jefferson, "would be peculiarly hard on Virginia." Madison, therefore, proposed to link assumption with "a final settlement and *payment* of balances among the States," but he added that "an assumption even under such circumstances is liable to powerful objections. In the form proposed that object would be impeded . . . , because it interests South Carolina and Massachusetts, who are to be chiefly relieved, against such a settlement and payment."[20]

Conflicting state interests led to a deadlock in Congress, with the Madisonian bloc trying to separate funding from assumption, and the Hamiltonian bloc arguing "no assumption, no funding." Several New England congressmen agreed with a Connecticut colleague who argued that if assumption failed, "I shall despair of the National Government."[21] Others talked of secession, and Senator Richard Henry Lee of Virginia joined them, saying he would prefer dissolution of the Union "to the rule of a fixed insolent northern majority."[22]

Just as the House was deadlocked over assumption, the Senate was deadlocked over the permanent location of the nation's capital. Hamilton found a way out of the double deadlock by proposing a bargain to Jefferson, his colleague in Washington's cabinet: the national capital on the Potomac in exchange for funding with assumption. Jefferson later recalled the encounter:

Hamilton was in despair. As I was going to the President's one day, I met him in the street. He walked me backwards and forwards before the President's door for half an hour. He painted pathetically the temper into which the legislature had been wrought,

19. Brant, III, pp. 290–305, and John C. Miller, *The Federalist Era, 1789–1801* (New York, 1960), pp. 33–45.

20. JM to TJ, Mar. 8, 1790, below. For TJ's description of his role in the battle over assumption, see his "Anas," in *Thomas Jefferson: Writings,* ed. Merrill D. Peterson (New York, 1984), pp. 667–68.

21. Ferguson, pp. 306–25, discusses fully the fight over assumption, as does John C. Miller, *Alexander Hamilton: Portrait in Paradox* (New York, 1959), pp. 229–54.

22. Miller, *Federalist Era,* p. 47.

the disgust of those who were called the Creditor states, the danger of the secession of their members, and the separation of the states.

As members of the Washington administration, Hamilton argued, they should act in concert. "I told him I was really a stranger to the whole subject," Jefferson recalled, ". . . that undoubtedly if it's rejection endangered a dissolution of our union at this incipient stage, I should deem that the most unfortunate of all consequences, to avert which all partial and temporary evils should be yielded."

Accordingly, Jefferson invited Hamilton to dine the next day with him and another friend or two to discuss "a compromise which was to save the union." Madison joined them at that time. After "some mutual sacrifices of opinion," it was agreed that "whatever importance had been attached to the rejection of this proposition [of assumption], the preservation of the union, and of concord among the states was more important" than assumption. If the House vote, which rejected assumption, was to be rescinded, however, some members would have to change their votes. "But it was observed that this pill would be peculiarly bitter to the Southern States, and that some concomitant measure should be adopted to sweeten it a little for them."

The "concomitant measure" was the capital. Hamilton, a New Yorker, agreed to work to move the capital from New York to Philadelphia for ten years, before it moved permanently to Georgetown. Jefferson and Madison agreed to get at least two "Potomac members" in Virginia or Maryland to change their votes on assumption.[23] The diners succeeded, and both the residence bill for the nation's capital and the funding bill with assumption passed.[24]

Madison voted against assumption, but he accepted it "as an unavoidable evil, and *possibly* not the worst side of the dilemma."[25] He also upheld the constitutionality of the residence bill.[26] With the compromise enacted, he thought that it was "now incumbent on us all to make the best of what is done. The truth is," he added, "that in a pecuniary light, the assumption is no longer

---

23. See TJ's "Anas," pp. 668–69. TJ does not mention JM in this memorandum, but in another memorandum he does discuss bringing "Mr. Madison and Colo. Hamilton to a friendly discussion of the subject"; see "Jefferson's Account of the Bargain on the Assumption and Residence Bills," [1792?], in *PTJ*, XVII, pp. 205–8. Jacob E. Cooke, "The Compromise of 1790," *WMQ* 27 (1970): 523–45, denies that the dinner-table agreement had any effect on the enactment of the compromise, but Kenneth R. Bowling, "Dinner at Jefferson's: A Note on Jacob E. Cooke's 'The Compromise of 1790,'" *WMQ* 28 (1971): 629–48, confirms the connection. Norman K. Risjord, "The Compromise of 1790: New Evidence on the Dinner Table Bargain," *WMQ* 33 (1976): 309–14, also confirms the negotiations over the compromise but suggests they were more complicated than TJ's version.

24. As a part of the Compromise of 1790, Congress also passed a bill to settle state wartime accounts, as JM had earlier proposed; see Ferguson, pp. 322–43.

25. JM to James Monroe, July 24, [25?], 1790, in *PJM*, XIII, p. 283.

26. See JM's memorandum to TJ, [ca. July 14, 1790], below.

of much consequence to Virginia. . . . She will consequently pay no more to the general Treasury than she now pays to the State Treasy."²⁷

Although Jefferson later called his role in the sectional bargain the worst error of his political life, he accepted the compromise at the time as containing "something to displease and something to soothe every part of the Union, but New York, which must be contented with what she has had." In the negotiations, he told Monroe, he saw "the necessity of yielding for this time to the cries of the creditors in certain parts of the union, for the sake of the union, and to save us from the greatest of all calamities, the total extinction of our credit in Europe."²⁸

Credit was an essential element in the conduct of foreign policy, Jefferson argued. "Our business is to have great credit and to use it little. Whatever enables us to go to war, secures our peace."²⁹ If war broke out in Europe, he hoped that the United States could remain neutral, becoming "the carriers for all parties as far as we can raise vessels."³⁰ "Our object is to feed, and theirs to fight," he wrote one friend; "I hope the new world will fatten on the follies of the old," he told another.³¹

Jefferson's thoughts on public credit, war, peace, and neutrality were formulated when war threatened to erupt between Great Britain and Spain, whose territories bordered the United States. The Nootka Sound incident began when the Spanish seized a British expedition attempting to establish a fur-trading base on a remote harbor on Vancouver Island, over which Spain claimed jurisdiction. In the event of war, Spain was sure to call on its ally, France, which might force the United States into the conflict either from its commitments to France or in defense of its territory.

In response to President Washington's request for policy recommendations, Jefferson conferred with Madison, who concurred in his outline of policy contingent on war between Spain and Great Britain. Their greatest fear was that the latter might strike at Spanish Louisiana and the Floridas. If Britain succeeded in conquering these territories, the secretary and the congressman observed, "she will encircle us compleatly" by land and by sea. "Instead of two neighbors balancing each other, we shall have one, with more than the strength of both."

To avoid the danger of "so overgrown a neighbor," they were willing to go to war, if necessary; "our resources of taxation and credit [are] equal to

---

27. JM to James Madison, Sr., July 31, 1790, in *PJM*, XIII, p. 285. Congress lowered Hamilton's estimates by several million dollars so that the sum allotted to Virginia, according to Madison, represented "about her proportion of the whole, and rather exceeding her present debt."
28. TJ to James Monroe, June 20, 1790, in *PTJ*, XVI, p. 537.
29. TJ to James Monroe, July 11, 1790, *ibid.*, XVII, p. 25.
30. TJ to Edward Rutledge, July 4, 1790, *ibid.*, XVI, p. 600.
31. TJ to James Monroe, July 11, 1790, *ibid.*, XVII, p. 25, and TJ to Edward Rutledge, July 4, 1790, *ibid.*, XVI, p. 601.

this." But war might not be necessary. "Delay gives us many chances to avoid it altogether." Indeed, in the event of war between Great Britain and Spain, "we are disposed to be strictly neutral," prepared to extract "a price for our assistance" from one side or the other.[32]

Jefferson followed up this advice with letters to diplomatic representatives of the United States in Great Britain and Spain, indicating his willingness to bargain either way for American advantage. France, if drawn in on Spain's side, would want to reduce the number of her ally's enemies: "She cannot doubt that we will be of that number," Jefferson wrote William Short in Paris, "if she does not yield our right to the common use of the Missisipi, and the means of using and securing it."[33] If the British wanted the United States to be neutral, they should realize "that we should contemplate a change of neighbours with extreme uneasiness; and that a due balance on our borders is not less desirable to us, than a balance of power in Europe has always appeared to them." The United States would be neutral "*if they will execute the treaty fairly,* and *attempt no conquests adjoining us.*"[34]

In order to ascertain the reaction of the United States to a war between Spain and Great Britain, the British ministry, which had no official diplomatic representative in America, directed Lord Dorchester, governor-general of Canada, to send an intelligence officer to New York to collect information. Major George Beckwith, Dorchester's aide, who had visited the United States on earlier missions, reestablished contact with Hamilton, who had neglected to report his earlier clandestine conversations with the Canadian operative. However, the secretary of the treasury in the summer of 1790 informed both the president and the secretary of state in general terms of his new conversations with Beckwith but without detailing the full extent of the discussions. In his dispatches reporting on American opinion, Beckwith, who served as Dorchester's secret agent, referred to Hamilton as "Number 7" and gave full reports to his superiors of his meetings with the secretary of the treasury. In one such communiqué, he noted that Hamilton differed from Jefferson on the conduct of foreign policy, and he summarized Hamilton's position by quoting him:

If it shall be judged proper to proceed in this business by the sending or appointing a proper person to come to this country to negotiate on the spot, whoever shall then be Our Secretary of State, will be the person in whose department such negotiation must originate, and he will be the channel of communication with the President; in the turn of such affairs the most minute circumstances, mere trifles, give a favorable bias or otherwise to the whole. The President's mind I can declare to be perfectly dispassionate on this subject. Mr. Jefferson our present Secretary of State is I am persuaded a gentle-

---

32. TJ and JM to George Washington, July 12, 1790, below.
33. TJ to William Short, Aug. 10, 1790, in *PTJ,* XVII, p. 121.
34. TJ's italics; TJ to Gouverneur Morris, Aug. 12, 1790, *ibid.,* p. 127.

man of honor, and zealously desirous of promoting those objects, which the nature of his duty calls for, and the interests of his country may require, but from some opinions which he has given respecting Your government, and possible predilections elsewhere, there may be difficulties which may possibly frustrate the whole, and which might be readily explained away. I shall certainly know the progress of negotiation from the president from day to day, but what I come to the present explanation for is this, that in any case any such difficulties should occur, I should wish to know them, in order that I may be sure they are clearly understood, and candidly examined.[35]

The threat of war between Great Britain and Spain ended quickly in 1790, when Spain, lacking the firm support of France, capitulated to a British ultimatum. But the imbroglio yielded two benefits for the United States. The early discussion of American neutrality in case of a European war helped chart the foreign-policy course later followed by the United States in the wars of the French Revolution. And the British, who had refused to exchange ministers with the United States, decided that the new nation, under the new Constitution, was powerful enough to rate a properly accredited minister plenipotentiary. Unfortunately, it also revealed a growing rift in President Washington's cabinet between his two chief advisers, Secretary of the Treasury Alexander Hamilton and Secretary of State Thomas Jefferson.

After Jefferson joined Madison in New York, they no longer exchanged letters, preferring instead to discuss matters face-to-face. Besides their joint memorandum to President Washington on neutrality, they consulted, again at the president's request, on the proper method of conveying official communications from the states through the channel of the president to the House of Representatives and the Senate.[36] The only other evidence of their official collaboration is in Madison's queries concerning Jefferson's "Report on Weights and Measures," a proposed decimal system for establishing national— even international—uniformity in weights, measures, and currency.[37]

During the same period, when Jefferson was suffering from a protracted migraine, he asked Madison as a personal favor to copy a passage from a French biographical dictionary so that he could give George Wythe an answer to a question he had raised, and Madison quickly complied.[38]

35. Report of conversation, July 15, 1790, in Syrett, VI, p. 497. Such meddling by the secretary of the treasury led Julian P. Boyd to entitle his study of TJ and Hamilton's relationship at this time *Number 7: Alexander Hamilton's Secret Attempts to Control American Foreign Policy* . . . (Princeton, 1964). The fullest exploration of Beckwith's role is in Frank T. Reuter, " 'Petty Spy' or Effective Diplomat: The Role of George Beckwith," *JER* 10 (1990): 471–92.

36. TJ to JM, [ca. Mar. 30, 1790,], below, and TJ and JM to George Washington, [Apr. 1, 1790], below, conveying JM's recommendations.

37. JM to TJ, [ca. May 20, 1790], below. For a brief discussion, see Malone, II, pp. 276–81; for a fuller analysis, see *PTJ,* XVI, pp. 602–75.

38. JM copied a passage on Phlegon from Ladvocat's *Dictionnaire historique et bibliographie portatif* (Paris, 1777), which TJ then translated in his letter to George Wythe, June 13, 1790, in *PTJ,* XVI, p. 495.

Although there are few personal letters to document their friendship during this period, Jefferson had watched from Paris the meteoric rise of Madison's reputation in the Virginia legislature, the Confederation Congress, the Constitutional Convention, the campaign for ratification, and the brilliant push in the new Congress for a bill of rights. On the way to New York to become secretary of state, Jefferson confided to Benjamin Rush, during a stopover in Philadelphia, that he considered his friend to be "the greatest man in the world,"[39] and he quickly obtained a portrait of him by Robert Edge Pine to add to those of other "principal American characters" that he possessed or proposed to acquire.[40]

---

## THE LETTERS

### Jefferson to Madison

Monticello Jan. 9, 1790

Dr. Sir

I wrote the inclosed letter to you a little before I left Paris, and having no occasion to send it, I brought it with me. I mentioned it to you when I had the happiness of possessing you at Monticello, but still forgot to give it to you. After so long lying by me, and further turning the subject in my mind, I find no occasion to alter my mind. I hazard it therefore to your consideration.[1]

I expect with anxiety the President's ultimate determination as to what is to be done with me. I cannot bring myself to be indifferent to the change of destination, tho' I will be passive under it. I am with great esteem your sincere friend and servt,

Th: Jefferson

---

39. Rush recorded TJ's remarks on Mar. 17, 1790, when the statesman stopped in Philadelphia; see Benjamin Rush, *The Autobiography of Benjamin Rush: His Travels through Life together with his Commonplace Book for 1789–1813,* ed. George W. Corner (Princeton, 1948), p. 181.

40. TJ used these words in requesting John Adams's portrait in 1786, the first painting in his collection of American characters; see Cappon, I, p. xxiii. For the statement that "Jefferson came to own a portrait of James Madison painted in 1790," see Harold E. Dickson, "'TH. J.' Art Collector," in *Jefferson and the Arts: An Extended View,* ed. William Howard Adams (Washington, 1976), p. 120. Late in life, he acquired a bust of Madison; see *ibid.,* p. 126. JM acquired a copy of Gilbert Stuart's 1805 portrait of TJ in 1806; see Noble E. Cunningham, Jr., *The Image of Thomas Jefferson in the Public Eye: Portraits for the People, 1800–1809* (Charlottesville, 1981), pp. 1–2. It is now owned by the Colonial Williamsburg Foundation and hangs in the reconstructed colonial Capitol of Virginia.

1. The enclosed was TJ to JM, Sept. 6, 1789, above, written in Paris, about "the earth belonging to the living."

## Madison to Jefferson

New York Jan. 24, 1790

DEAR SIR

A dysenteric attack at Georgetown with its effects retarded my journey so much that I did not arrive here till a few days ago. I am free at present from the original complaint, but a little out of order with the piles generated by that or the medicine it required.

The Cato in which were the busts of P. Jones and the box of books for myself never arrived till the day before yesterday, having sprung a leak which obliged her to put into an English Port. Every thing consigned to me appears as far as the parcels are yet opened to have escaped injury. I beg you to accept my unfeigned thanks for the proof medals, of which the value is much enhanced in my estimation by the circumstance which demands that tribute. I have supposed that I could not better dispose of the letters to Mr. Eppes as well as that to Col: Lewis than by inclosing them to yourself.

The business of Congs. is as yet merely in embryo. The principal subjects before them are the plans of revenue and the militia, reported by Hamilton and Knox. That of the latter is not yet printed, and being long is very imperfectly understood. The other has scarcely been long enough from the press to be looked over. It is too voluminous to be sent entire by the mail. I will by the next mail commence a transmission in fractions. Being in possession at present of a single copy only I can not avail myself of this opportunity for the purpose. You will find a sketch of the plan in one of the newspapers herewith inclosed. Nothing has passed either in Congs. or in conversation from which a conjecture can be formed of the fate of the Report. Previous to its being made, the avidity for stock had raised it from a few shillings to 8/ or 10/. in the pound, and emissaries are still exploring the interior and distant parts of the Union in order to take advantage of the ignorance of holders. Of late the price is stationary, at or fluctuating between the sums last mentioned. From this suspence it would seem as if doubts were entertained concerning the success of the plan in all its parts.

I take for granted that you will, before the receipt of this, have known the ultimate determination of the President on your appointment. All that I am able to say on the subject is that a universal anxiety is expressed for your acceptance; and to repeat my declarations that such an event will be more conducive to the general good, and perhaps to the very objects you have in view in Europe, than your return to your former station.

I do not find that any late information has been received with regard to the Revolution in France. It seems to be still unhappily forced to struggle with the adventitious evils of public scarcity, in addition to those naturally thrown in its way by antient prejudices and hostile interests. I have a letter from Havr. of the 13th. Novr. which says that wheat was then selling at 10 livrs. per

Bushel, and flour at 50 livs per 100 ℔. and the demand pressing for all kinds of materials for bread. The letter adds that a bounty of 2 livs per 100 ℔. marc on wheat and on flour in proportion etc. etc. was to commence the 1st. Decr. last and continue till the 1st. of July next, in favor of imports from any quarter of the globe. With the sincerest affection I am Dr. Sir your Obedt. friend and Servt.,

Js. Madison

Previous to the arrival of the Cato I was favored with your letter of [28] of Augst. and several pamphlets.

## Madison to Jefferson

New York Feb. 4 1790

Dear Sir

Your favor of the 9th. of Jany. inclosing one of Sepr. last did not get to hand till a few days ago. The idea which the latter evolves is a great one, and suggests many interesting reflections to legislators; particularly when contracting and providing for public debts. Whether it can be received in the extent your reasonings give it, is a question which I ought to turn more in my thoughts than I have yet been able to do, before I should be justified in making up a full opinion on it. My first thoughts though coinciding with many of yours, lead me to view the doctrine as not in *all* respects compatible with the course of human affairs. I will endeavor to sketch the grounds of my skepticism.

"As the earth belongs to the living, not to the dead, a living generation can bind itself only: In every society the will of the majority binds the whole: According to the laws of mortality, a majority of those ripe at any moment for the exercise of their will do not live beyond nineteen years: To that term then is limited the validity of *every* act of the Society; Nor within that limitation, can any declaration of the public will be valid which is not *express*." This I understand to be the outline of the argument.[2]

The acts of a political Society may be divided into three classes.
1. The fundamental Constitution of the Government.
2. Laws involving stipulations which render them irrevocable at the will of the Legislature.
3. Laws involving no such irrevocable quality.

However applicable in Theory the doctrine may be to a Constitution, it seems liable in practice to some very powerful objections. Would not a Government so often revised become too mutable to retain those prejudices in its favor which antiquity inspires, and which are perhaps a salutary aid to the most

---

2. This is JM's paraphrase. The italics in this paragraph and throughout the letter are his also.

rational Government in the most enlightened age? Would not such a periodical revision engender pernicious factions that might not otherwise come into existence? Would not, in fine, a Government depending for its existence beyond a fixed date, on some positive and authentic intervention of the Society itself, be too subject to the casualty and consequences of an actual interregnum?

In the 2d. class, exceptions at least to the doctrine seem to be *requisite* both in Theory and practice:

If the earth be the gift of nature to the living their title can extend to the earth in its natural State only. The *improvements* made by the dead form a charge against the living who take the benefit of them. This charge can no otherwise be satisfyed than by executing the will of the dead accompanying the improvements.

Debts may be incurred for purposes which interest the unborn, as well as the living: such are debts for repelling a conquest, the evils of which descend through many generations. Debts may even be incurred principally for the benefit of posterity: such perhaps is the present debt of the U. States, which far exceeds any burdens which the present generation could well apprehend for itself. The term of 19 years might not be sufficient for discharging the debts in either of these cases.

There seems then to be a foundation in the nature of things, in the relation which one generation bears to another, for the *descent* of obligations from one to another. Equity requires it. Mutual good is promoted by it. All that is indispensable in adjusting the account between the dead and the living is to see that the debits against the latter do not exceed the advances made by the former. Few of the incumbrances entailed on nations would bear a liquidation even on this principle.

The objections to the doctrine as applied to the 3d. class of acts may perhaps be merely practical. But in that view they appear to be of great force.

Unless such laws should be kept in force by new acts regularly anticipating the end of the term, all the rights depending on positive laws, that is, most of the rights of property would become absolutely defunct; and the most violent struggles be generated between those interested in reviving and those interested in new-modelling the former state of property. Nor would events of this kind be improbable. The obstacles to the passage of laws which render a power to repeal inferior to an opportunity of rejecting, as a security against oppression, would here render an opportunity of rejecting an insecure provision against anarchy. Add, that the possibility of an event so hazardous to the rights of property could not fail to depreciate its value; that the approach of the crisis would increase this effect; that the frequent return of periods superseding all the obligations depending on antecedent laws and usages, must be weak[en]ing the reverence for those obligations, co-operate with motives to licentiousness already too powerful; and that the uncertainty incident to such a state of things would on one side discourage the steady exertions of industry produced by permanent laws, and on the other, give a disproportionate advantage to the more, over the less, sagacious and interprizing part of the Society.[3]

I find no releif from these consequences, but in the received doctrine that a tacit assent may be given to established Constitutions and laws, and that this assent may be inferred, where no positive dissent appears. It seems less impracticable to remedy, by wise plans of Government, the dangerous operation of this doctrine, than to find a remedy for the difficulties inseparable from the other.

May it not be questioned whether it be possible to exclude wholly the idea of tacit assent, without subverting the foundation of civil Society?

On what principle does the voice of the majority bind the minority? It does not result I conceive from the law of nature, but from compact founded on conveniency. A greater proportion might be required by the fundamental constitution of a Society if it were judged eligible. Prior then to the establishment of this principle, *unanimity* was necessary; and strict Theory at all times presupposes the assent of every member to the establishment of the rule itself. If this assent can not be given tacitly, or be not implied where no positive evidence forbids, persons born in Society would not on attaining ripe age be bound by acts of the Majority; and either a *unanimous* repetition of every law would be necessary on the accession of new members, or an express assent must be obtained from these to the rule by which the voice of the Majority is made the voice of the whole.

If the observations I have hazarded be not misapplied, it follows that a limitation of the validity of national acts to the computed life of a nation, is in some instances not required by Theory, and in others cannot be accomodated to practice. The observations are not meant however to impeach either the utility of the principle in some particular cases; or the general importance of it in the eye of the philosophical Legislator. On the contrary it would give me singular pleasure to see it first announced in the proceedings of the U. States, and always kept in their view, as a salutary curb on the living generation from imposing unjust or unnecessary burdens on their successors. But this is a pleasure which I have little hope of enjoying. The spirit of philosophical legislation has never reached some parts of the Union, and is by no means the fashion here, either within or without Congress. The evils suffered and feared from weakness in Government, and licentiousness in the people, have turned the attention more towards the means of strengthening the former than of narrowing its extent in the minds of the latter. Besides this, it is so much easier to espy the little difficulties immediately incident to every great plan, than to comprehend its general and remote benefits, that our hemisphere must be still more enlightened before many of the sublime truths which are seen thro' the medium of Philosophy, become visible to the naked eye of the ordinary Politi-

---

3. JM had made the same point in *The Federalist* Number 62.

cian. I have nothing to add at present but that I remain always and most affectly. Yours,

     Js. MADISON JR.


## Madison to Jefferson

[New York, ca. Feb. 11, 1790]

DEAR SIR

By the last mail I acknowledged the receipt of your favor of the 9th. Ult: and hazarded a few remarks on the subject of that of Sepr. last from Paris.

The newspapers forwarded by me from time to time will have exhibited something of the complexion of the politics here, particularly as they relate to the public debt. On this subject the H. of Reps. is at this moment deliberating. All that can be gathered from the sentiments disclosed, is that a great variety will be found in them.

Mrs. Greene has become disappointed in receiving no late accounts from her son in Paris, and I have been requested in her behalf, to enquire whether you can in any manner relieve her anxieties.[4] If this should get to hand time eno' before you mean to set out for this place, I will thank you for an answer to the enquiry.

Every one who mentions the subject of your appointment to me, seems to have much solicitude for your undertaking it, as well as that the benefit of your services may be enjoyed as soon as possible. Yrs. mo: affectly,

     Js. MADISON JR.


## Madison to Jefferson

New York Feb. 14, 1790

DEAR SIR

We proceed slowly in business. The Report of Mr. Hamilton has been, of late, the principal subject of debate. On the foreign debt the vote has been unanimous. On the domestic, a reduction of the transferred principal has been brought into view by several arguments and propositions. My idea is that there should be no interference of the public in favour of the public either as to principal or interest, but that the highest market price only should be allowed to the purchasers, and the balance be applied to solace the original sufferers, whose claims were not in conscience extinguished by a *forced* payment in *de-*

---

4. Catherine Greene was the widow of General Nathanael Greene. Their son, George Washington Greene, had been sent to France in 1788, where Lafayette guided his studies; see *PTJ,* XIII, pp. 156–57.

*preciated* certificates.⁵ The equity of this proposition is not contested. Its impracticability will be urged as an insuperable objection. I am aware of the difficulties of the plan, but believe they might be removed by one-half the exertion that will be used to collect and colour them.

A Bill for taking a census has passed the House of Representatives, and is with the Senate. It contained a schedule for ascertaining the component classes of the Society, a kind of information extremely requisite to the Legislator, and much wanted for the science of Political Economy. A repetition of it every ten years would hereafter afford a most curious and instructive assemblage of facts. It was thrown out by the Senate as a waste of trouble and supplying materials for idle people to make a book. Judge by this little experiment of the reception likely to be given to so great an idea as that explained in your letter of September.⁶

## Jefferson to Madison

Monticello Feb. 14, 1790

DEAR SIR

I received your favor of Jan. 24. the day before yesterday; the President's of the 21st. was 16 days getting to my hands. I write him by this occasion my acceptance, and shall endeavor to subdue the reluctance I have to that office which has increased so as to oppress me extremely. The President pressed my coming on immediately, and I have only said to him in general that circumstances, uncontroulable by me, will not let me set out till the last of next week, say the last day of the month. I meant to ask you to explain to him the particular reason. My daughter is to be married on the 25th. to the Mr. Randolph whom you saw here. His father will come only a day or two before that to arrange the provision we mean to make for the young couple, and that this may be perfectly valid it's execution must take place before the marriage. Thus you see that the happiness of a child, for life, would be hazarded were I to go away before this arrangement is made.⁷

We were greatly alarmed by the report of the attack on your health at Georgetown. The return of your brother from that place first quieted our apprehensions. I hope this will find you perfectly reestablished. All is quiet here. Our countrymen are thrown into a wheat-fever by the price of wheat now 10/3 the bushel. We are offered a dollar at our barns here for the growing crop.

Where in N. York will you advise me to go in the first instance on my

---

5. JM's italics.

6. JM was reenforcing his argument against TJ's generational theory "that the earth belongs in usufruct to the living," suggesting that if the Senate rejected such a useful proposal as the taking of a census, it would give even shorter shrift to TJ's theory.

7. Martha "Patsy" Jefferson married Thomas Mann Randolph on Feb. 23, 1790.

arrival? Be so good as to think and even provide for me if you can a temporary and decent birth, and lodge a line at Mrs. House's in Philadelphia where I shall be about the 13th. and at New York the 15th. of March. I shall see you so soon that I need only add here assurances always true of the sincere esteem and respect of Dear Sir your affectionate friend and servt,

TH: JEFFERSON

## Madison to Jefferson

New York Mar. 8, 1790

DEAR SIR

The newspapers will have shewn you the late proceedings of the House of Representatives. The present subject of deliberation is the proposed assumption of the State debts. Opinions are nearly balanced on it. My own is no otherwise favorable to the measure than as it may tend to secure a final settlement and *payment*[8] of balances among the States. An assumption even under such circumstances is liable to powerful objections. In the form proposed that object would be impeded by the measure, because it interests South Carolina and Massachusetts, who are to be chiefly relieved, against such a settlement and payment. The immediate operation of the plan would be peculiarly hard on Virginia. I think, also, that an increase of the federal debt will not only prolong the evil, but be further objectionable as augmenting a trust already sufficiently great for the virtue and number of the federal Legislature.

## Jefferson to Madison

[New York ca. Mar. 30, 1790]

TH: J. TO MR. MADISON

I forgot to take your final opinion last night as to the mode of conveying *official communications from the states through the channel of the President to the two federal houses.*[9] Whether it will be best to do it

1. By message from the president through Mr. Lear?
2. By d[itt]o through Th:J. appearing personally?
3. By do. through do. by way of letter?

Be so good as to say what you think. I must be troublesome to you till I know better the ground on which I am placed. Indeed this consultation is by the desire of the president.
R.S.V.P.

8. JM's italics.
9. TJ's italics.

## Jefferson and Madison to George Washington

[New York Apr. 1, 1790]

Th: Jefferson has the honor to inform the President that Mr. Madison has just delivered to him the result of his reflections on the question *How shall communications from the several states to Congress through the channel of the President be made?*

'He thinks that in no case would it be proper to go by way of *letter from the Secretary of state:* that they should be delivered to the houses either by the Secretary of state in person or by Mr. Leir.[10] He supposes a useful division of the office might be made between these two, by employing the one where a matter of fact alone is to be communicated, or a paper delivered etc. in the ordinary course of things and where nothing is required by the President; and using the agency of the other where the President chuses to recommend any measure to the legislature and to attract their attention to it.'

The President will be pleased to order in this what he thinks best. T. Jefferson supposes that whatever may be done for the present, the final arrangement of business should be considered as open to alteration hereafter. The government is as yet so young, that cases enough have not occurred to enable a division of them into classes, and the distribution of these classes to the persons whose agency would be the properest.

He sends some letters for the President's perusal praying him to alter freely any thing in them which he thinks may need it.


## Madison to Jefferson, Commenting on His "Report on Weights and Measures"[11]

[New York ca. May 20, 1790]

Quer. if a fixed temperature might not be got by referring to a thermometer, the freezing point being the natural standard.

Quer. as to the inaccuracy of English calculations of London Pendulum?

Quer. if a mode of distributing actual standards thro' the states should not be suggested at the close of the report.

Quer. would not *uniform* cylinders be as easily measured and judged of, as squares.

Quer. if the *Quarter* and Chauldron should not be measures.

---

10. Tobias Lear was President Washington's secretary.
11. For JM's collaboration with TJ on the preparation of TJ's "Report on Weights and Measures," see *PTJ,* XVI, pp. 607–8, 612, 614.

p. 14/15 Quer. as to the inference from the coinciding circumstances relative to the Avoird. and Troy. Specific weight of wheat and Rain water to[o] accurate and philosoph[ical] for antient times, and allso a cubic foot.

pa. 3 *bottom.* quer. if lower extremity not a better expression and if *defined at both extremities*—quer. as the measurement must be not from the upper extremity but the center of suspension.

Is the difficulty of obtaining a rod perfectly uniform in size etc. not worth noting as an *uncertainty,* tho' too inconsiderable to form an objection?

p. 13. Would not the pottle be better defined by diminishing its depth. 15 I. exceeds a convenient proportion to 3 I. square.

p. 23. Easy of comparison.


*Jefferson and Madison to George Washington*
[New York] July 12, 1790

Th: Jefferson had a conference yesterday with Mr. Madison on the subject recommended by the President. He has the honor of inclosing him some considerations thereon, in all of which he believes Mr. Madison concurred. He has sketched the heads only, as the President's mind will readily furnish the developement of each. He will wait on the president at one aclock on some other business, and then and at all other times be ready to enter more into the details of any part of the subject the president may chuse.

ENCLOSURE
*[Jefferson and Madison's Outline of Policy Contingent on War between England and Spain]*[12]

Heads of consideration on the conduct we are to observe in the war between Spain and Gr. Britain and particularly should the latter attempt the conquest of Louisiana and the Floridas.

The dangers to us should Great Britain possess herself of those countries.

She will possess a territory equal to half ours, beyond the Missisipi

She will seduce that half of ours which is on this side the Missisipi

  by her language, laws, religion, manners, government, commerce, capital.

  by the possession of N. Orleans, which draws to it the dependance of all the waters of Misspi

  by the markets she can offer them in the gulph of Mexico and elsewhere.

She will take from the remaining part of our States the markets they now have for their produce by furnishing those markets cheaper with the same articles. Tobacco, rice, indigo, bread, lumber, naval stores, furs.

---

12. For the war crisis of 1790, see *ibid.,* XVII, pp. 35–108.

> She will have then possessions double the size of ours, as good in soil and climate.
> She will encircle us compleatly, by these possessions on our land-board, and her fleets on our sea-board.
> Instead of two neighbors balancing each other, we shall have one, with more than the strength of both.

Would the prevention of this be worth a war?
> Consider our abilities to take part in a war.
>> Our operations would be by land only.
>> How many men should we need to employ?—Their cost?
>> Our resources of taxation and credit equal to this.
> Weigh the evil of this new accumulation of debt
>> Against the loss of markets, and eternal expence and danger from so overgrown a neighbor.
> But this is on supposition that France as well as Spain shall be engaged in the war. For with Spain alone, the war would be unsuccessful, and our situation rendered worse.

No need to take a part in the war as yet. We may chuse our own time.
> Delay gives us many chances to avoid it altogether.
>> In such a choice of objects, Gr. Britain may not single out Louisiana and the Floridas.
>> She may fail in her attempt on them.
>> France and Spain may recover them.

If all these chances fail, we should have to re-take them.
> The difference between retaking, and preventing, overbalanced by the benefits of delay.

Delay enables us to be better prepared:

To obtain from the allies a price for our assistance.

Suppose these our ultimate views. What is to be done at this time?

1. As to Spain?
> If she be as sensible as we are that she cannot save Louisiana and the Floridas,
>> Might she not prefer their Independance to their Subjection to Grt. Britain?
>> Does not the proposition of the Ct. d'Estaing furnish us an opening to communicate our ideas on this subject to the court of France, and thro them to that of Madrid? And our readiness to join them in guaranteeing the independance of those countries?
> This might save us from a war, if Gr. Britain respects our weight in a war.
> And if she does not, the object would place the war on popular ground with us.

2. As to England? Say to Beckwith
> 'that as to a Treaty of commerce, we would prefer amicable, to adversary arrangements, tho the latter would be infallible, and in our own power:
> That our ideas are that such a treaty should be founded in perfect reciprocity; and would therefore be it's own price:
> That as to an Alliance, we can say nothing till it's object be shewn, and that it is not to be inconsistent with existing engagements:
> That in the event of war between Gr. Brit. and Spain we are disposed to be strictly neutral:
> That however, we should view with extreme uneasiness any attempts of either power to seize the possessions of the other on our frontier, as we consider our

own safety interested in a due balance between our neighbors.' [It might be advantageous to express this latter sentiment, because if there be any difference of opinion in their councils, whether to bend their force against North or South America, or the islands, (and certainly there is room for difference) and if these opinions be nearly balanced, that balance might be determined by the prospect of having an enemy the more or less, according to the object they should select.][13]

TH: JEFFERSON
July. 12. 1790.

*Madison to Jefferson*

[New York ca. July 14, 1790][14]

... this reasoning is inforced by the clause (Art. 2. Sect 1.) which says the list of votes of the electors shall be transmitted to the seat of Govt. directed to the President of the Senate, who in presence of the Senate and H. of Reps. shall open the certificate etc. The seat of *Congs.* then must be at the seat of Govt. It is admitted that the seat of Govt. can not be where the *Ex: part* of the Govt. does not sit. The 3 branches then must sit together and each having a will independent of the other, all must concur in saying where the common seat shall be, that is, a law ought to pass for the purpose.

*Madison to Jefferson*

[New York ca. Aug. 29, 1790][15]

"The act for establishing the temporary and permanent seats of the Government of the U. States" requires the following steps for carrying the latter into effect.

13. The brackets are in the manuscript.
14. This incomplete memorandum is the only record of JM's opinion on the constitutionality of the bill fixing the nation's capital at Philadelphia for ten years prior to its removal to a district on the Potomac. He sent it to TJ, who, at the request of President Washington, prepared an opinion supporting the constitutionality of the residence bill; see *PJM,* XIII, pp. 278–79, and *PTJ,* XVII, pp. 163–208.
15. JM's "Memorandum on Executing the Residence Act" is analyzed in *PTJ,* XIX, pp. 3–73, in an exhaustive editorial note entitled "Locating the Federal District." For a readable account, see Kenneth R. Bowling, *Creating the Federal City, 1774–1800: Potomac Fever* (Washington, 1988).

1. The appointment of three Commissioners
    of sufficient respectability
        having good will to the general object without any particular bias of private interest. Quer. If local situation or interest be an objection outweighing the advantage of proximity and zeal for the object, as the President is to prescribe the place, and the Commissioners only to define the district, and as the subsequent discretion in the Commissioners will give no opportunity of sacrificing their trust to local considerations. The essential point seems to be that the Commission should be filled by men who prefer any place on the Potowmac to any place elsewhere. On this supposition, it may be easy to find men who would suit.
        residing (a majority at least) so conveniently to the scene of business as to be able to attend readily and gratis
    Should it be adviseable after securing a majority near at hand to make an appointment with a view to attach particular parts of the Union to the object, N. England, particularly Massachusetts, first occurs—and next, S. Carolina and Georgia.

| | | |
|---|---|---|
| Mr. Ellicott | Mr. Gorum | |
| Mr. Fitzhugh (of Chatham) | [Gorham] | Mr. Bull |
| Mr. Loyd (of Annapolis) | Mr. O. Wolcott | Mr. Tucker |
| Revd. Mr. Lee Massey | Mr. of R.Isd. | Mr. Baldwin[16] |

2. That the President inform himself of the several rival positions; leaving among them inducements to bid against each other in offers of land or money. As the location when compleated by the survey will not be mutable by the President, it may be well to have the offers so framed as to become ipso facto absolute in favor of the U. S. on the event which they solicit.
3. That the President direct the survey of the District which he shall ultimately elect. It seems essential that the District should comprehend the water adjoining the establishment, and eligible that it should comprehend the opposite shore. The legality of this seems to be decided by the clause confining the purchase or acceptance of land for the use of U. S. "to the East side of the river within the said district" which imply that the *whole* district was not *necessarily* to be on *that*

---

16. JM grouped his suggestions geographically. "Near at hand" included Andrew Ellicott from Maryland, who was appointed surveyor of the federal district in February 1791; William Fitzhugh of Chatham, a planter from Stafford County, Virginia; Edward Lloyd IV from Maryland; and Lee Massey, a lawyer and former rector of Truro Parish in Fairfax County, Virginia. New England included Nathaniel Gorham, a merchant and land speculator from Charlestown, Massachusetts, and Oliver Wolcott from Connecticut. South Carolina included John Bull, who had served as a delegate to the Confederation Congress, and Thomas Tudor Tucker, a representative in Congress from 1789 to 1793; TJ appointed him as treasurer of the United States in 1801.

side.—Quer: whether it will not be convenient to accept in the first instance so much less than 10 miles square as will allow places to be afterwards taken in, which may not now be attainable, or it may not be prudent now to accept.
4. The district being defined and the requisite quantity of ground secured, the next step must be to fix the site for the public buildings—and provide for the establishment or enlargement of a town within the district. As no special authority is given for the latter purposes the consent of proprietors will be necessary: but as they will have a common interest with the public, voluntary arrangements between them and the Commissioners may be readily procured in favor of any plan which the President may patronize. Should any difficulties be apprehended on this point they can be guarded against in the negociations preliminary to the actual location of the district.
5. The plan for the public buildings is to be approved by the President. The Commissioners will no doubt submit different ones formed by themselves, or obtained from ingenious Architects. Should it be thought proper to excite emulation by a premium for the best, the expence is authorized, as an incident to that of the buildings.
6. The completion of the work will depend on a supply of the means. These must consist either of future grants of money by Congress, which it would not be prudent to count upon, of State Grants, of private grants, or the conversion into money of lands ceded for public use which it is conceived the latitude of the term "use" and the spirit and scope of the act will justify.